THE JEWS OF BYZANTIUM

D1238969

JUDAIC STUDIES SERIES

Leon J. Weinberger, General Editor

The Jews of Byzantium

1204–1453

STEVEN B. BOWMAN

FOREWORD BY ZVI ANKORI

THE UNIVERSITY OF ALABAMA PRESS

WITHDRAWN

Highland Park Public Library

949.500492
B788

DS
135
.M43
B68
1985

Copyright © 1985 by
The University of Alabama Press
University, Alabama 35486
All rights reserved
Manufactured in the United States of America

Publication of this book has been assisted
by a grant from the Publications Program
of the National Endowment for the Humanities.

Library of Congress Cataloging in Publication Data

Bowman, Steven.
The Jews of Byzantium (1204–1453)

(Judaic studies series)
Bibliography: p.
Includes index.
1. Jews—Byzantine Empire—History. 2. Byzantine Empire—History—1081–1453. 3. Byzantine Empire—Ethnic relations. I. Title. II. Series.
DS135.M43B68 1985 949.5′004924 83-17230
ISBN 0-8173-0198-4

JESUIT - KRAUSS - McCORMICK - LIBRARY
1100 EAST 55th STREET
CHICAGO, ILLINOIS 60615

לזכר נשמותיהם של הורי
הנאהבים
בחייהם ובמותם לא נפרדו

To the Memory of My Parents,
Who Provided First Lessons

CONTENTS

PART II: Documents and Excursuses

MAPS

FOREWORD

THE STUDY of Byzantine Jewry—of its political and social history no less than its cultural institutions and achievements—has long been the stepchild of Jewish scholarship. Having inherited from their West European mentors a disdain for the supposedly decadent Greekdom of the Middle Ages as against the glory that was classical Greece, the nineteenth-century Founding Fathers of modern Jewish historiography tended to discount the millennium of Jewish experience in the climate of the Byzantine Empire. Consciously or not, they dismissed its import for Jewish studies, viewing it as both intrinsically irrelevant and of no consequence for the understanding of subsequent developments in other parts of the Jewish world.

Objective circumstances, too, which in the course of the fifteenth and sixteenth centuries had irrevocably transformed Greek Jewish society in its ancient native setting, did not make the conscientious historian's exploratory forays into the earlier centuries any easier. In a matter of a few generations the demographic composition and the very character of the Jewish population in what by then became Ottoman Greece had changed beyond recognition. Inundated by successive waves of Spanish-speaking Jewish immigrants, fleeing the excesses of Inquisition, and joined in the early sixteenth century by the Arabic-speaking ancient Jewries of the Middle East, which were incorporated into the Sultanate by Ottoman expansionism, the native Greek-speaking Jewish communities found themselves gradually eclipsed by the newcomers' economic and intellectual superiority, by their language, way of life, and sheer numbers. Thus it happened that, while Greek Jewry of classical times had evoked the interest of several researchers, the eventual "sephardization" of Mediterranean Jewish communities had caused the indigenous Greek Jewish stratum to be lost in the process and disappear from the accounts of historians, though of course not from the territory itself.

Rediscovering this "lost" Greek-speaking segment of Mediterranean Jewry and presenting it in its medieval and early modern milieu is indeed the contribution of a handful of Jewish byzantinists of the twentieth century. In fact, it was only on the very eve of World War II that the first English treatment of the theme—Joshua Starr's *The Jews in the Byzantine Empire*—has made its appearance in print. While several new chapters within the small overall chronological bracket have been added since by subsequent researchers, Starr remains to this day the best authority on the subject.

Starr's book, however, does not cover the whole range of Byzantine Jewish history. Offering both a monographic survey (as Part One) and a chronologically arranged anthology of texts and *regesta* (in Part Two), it deals only with the period preceding the partition of the Empire in the Fourth Crusade, i.e., until 1204 A.D. The difficult, and to a large extent confused period from the Fourth Crusade until the final takeover by the Turks in 1453 has only partially and very fragmentarily been reconstructed from the then known printed sources by Starr in his subsequent summary, *Romania*. A comprehensive treatment of that later period, one that would include also the manuscript materials that have come to light in the past three decades, remained so far a desideratum.

Dr. Bowman's present book comes to fill the gap. As such it truly is a pioneering venture, long overdue, and a notable contribution to general and Jewish historical scholarship. As a matter of fact, it is the logical sequel of Starr, both chronologically and by way of its format, offering as it does, too, a monographic analysis in Part One and a collection of texts and *regesta* in Part Two. It certainly is bound to become as Starr's book is the indispensable tool for the use of the general byzantinist and the student of Jewish history alike.

Bowman has marshaled the full range of the multilingual material—alas, that material is not very rich and entails many a problem of methodology and interpretation—and has arrived at some novel conclusions that may change many of the conventional opinions regarding the period and its history. Moreover, there are Greek sources that, even though available in print, have never before been drafted in the service of Jewish historiography; in Bowman's presentation they now help draw new perspectives on Jewish life in the late Middle Ages. Also, Bowman has used to good advantage the latest achievements of Hebrew codicology, such as dating manuscripts by watermarks, thus correcting many an error in the identification and chronology of Byzantine Hebrew literary works (still unpublished) and of their authors.

Is this the definitive study on the subject? It surely will be so for many years. Still, I trust that Dr. Bowman will be the first to join me in the hope that his book, besides fulfilling the needs of the *present,* will, more than anything else, stimulate further research in the *future* in this all-too-neglected area of Jewish studies. This work, eventually, will help fill the gaps that still mar our knowledge of the Byzantine Jewish experience of the Late Middle Ages.

ZVI ANKORI

PREFACE

A MONOGRAPH ON the history of the Jews in the Byzantine Empire and its former territories from the Fourth Crusade to the Ottoman conquest of Constantinople needs no justification. In the forty-five years since Joshua Starr offered the still basic work on the period before 1204, only a brief survey, by the same author, has appeared to whet our appetites for the material still buried in the sources. The present monograph is therefore a preliminary attempt to present these sources for the later period. Due to the state of the field and to the nature of the material, it was decided to employ the same framework used by Starr for the period 641–1204. The present monograph, then, is divided into two parts. The first (which may be read independently) constitutes an essay which places the documents in part II within a chronological and topical framework; the second contains all the relevant texts in an English translation, with notes and bibliographical references appended to each. In the first part, the sources are designated by parentheses and boldface type.

The present study should be considered as an introduction to the Jewish experience after the Fourth Crusade. Further research is necessary before the ramifications of the material introduced and summarized here can be fully integrated into Late Byzantine history. Still, the pace of research into the general Byzantine story has so increased in recent years that it seems justifiable to gather all of the available information in one study. In this way, an overall picture can be presented, as well as delineation of a number of areas of future research.

A work of this nature is, perforce, dependent upon the findings of many scholars in different areas of research. Moreover, its interdisciplinary nature oversteps the bounds of two seemingly independent fields: Byzantine and Jewish studies. Yet it is difficult to understand the one without the other. The interdependence of both fields is readily acknowledged throughout the present work.

The following study has been a constant companion for the past decade and a half. In sending it forth to a life of its own, the author remembers with gratitude those institutions and individuals who freely offered their assistance and encouragement over the years of research and writing: the indefatigable library staffs of Ohio State University, the Klau Library of Hebrew Union College, the Classics Library and the Modern Greek Collection at the University of Cincinnati, Dumbarton Oaks, the Gennadeion Library in Athens, and the Hebrew University of Jerusalem, including the Hebrew Palaeography Project located there.

To my teachers I owe everything, except the errors that have slipped into my text: to Schafer Williams, who introduced me to medieval history and provided encouragement through the years; to Zvi Ankori, whose advice and scholarship have contributed greatly to the present study; and to readers and colleagues for their comments: Peter Topping, David Jacoby, Martin Arbagi, and Benny Kraut. Other colleagues who discussed specific questions are acknowledged in the notes to parts I and II.

Several institutions have succored me over the years, and it is a singular pleasure to take this opportunity to render my appreciation. The Center for Medieval and Renaissance Studies at Ohio State University supported me during my graduate career, when the bulk of the present work took shape as a dissertation; the memory of Francis Lee Utley will forever honor that institute. My thanks to the Gennadeion and Fulbright Committees for the opportunity to spend two delightful and rewarding years in Athens and to the American School of Classical Studies for hosting me. The Memorial Foundation for Jewish Culture has kindly supported my researches in the history of Greek Jewry in recent years. Finally, I am grateful to the Hebrew University of Jerusalem for the hospitality offered me through a postgraduate fellowship, which allowed for the completion of the present manuscript in a unique city, and to the University of Cincinnati for its unstinting support in the final stages of its revision.

S. B.

ABBREVIATIONS

AHR *American Historical Review*

Ankori, *Karaites* Zvi Ankori, *Karaites in Byzantium: The Formative Years, 970–1100* (New York and Jerusalem, 1959)

b. ben (son of)

Baron, *SRHJ* S. W. Baron, *A Social and Religious History of the Jews*. 2d ed., vols. I–XVIII (New York, 1958–83)

Beck, *Kirche* Hans-Georg Beck, *Kirche und Theologische Literatur im Byzantinischen Reich* (Munich, 1959)

BNJ *Byzantinisch-neugriechische Jahrbücher*

Braude-Lewis, *Christians and Jews* B. Braude and B. Lewis, eds., *Christians and Jews in the Ottoman Empire*, vols. I–II (New York and London, 1982)

BSOAS *Bulletin of the School of Oriental and African Studies*

BZ *Byzantinische Zeitschrift*

Cassuto, *Vatican* U. Cassuto, *Bibliothecae Apostolicae Vaticanae . . . Codices Vaticani Hebraici* (Vatican City, 1956)

CMH *Cambridge Mediaeval History*

Cp. Constantinople

CSHB *Corpus Scriptorum Historiae Byzantinorum*

Dölger, *Regesten* Fr. Dölger, ed., *Regesten der Kaiserurkunden des oströmischen Reiches von 565–1453*, vols. III, IV, V (Munich, 1932–65)

DOP *Dumbarton Oaks Papers*

DVL *Diplomatarium Veneto-Levantinum,* G. M. Thomas, ed., vols. I–II (Venice, 1880–99)

EEBS Ἐπετηρὶς Ἑταιρείας Βυζαντινῶν Σπουδῶν

EI *Encyclopaedia of Islam,* vols. I–IV (Leiden, 1913–34)

EI² *Encyclopaedia of Islam,* new ed. (Leiden, 1960–)

EIV *Enẓiklopedyah Ivrit* (Encyclopaedia Hebraica)

EJ *Encyclopaedia Judaica*

EL Ἐγκυκλοπαιδικὸν Λεξικὸν Ἐλευθερουδάκη

ERE *Encyclopaedia of Religion and Ethics*

gr. graecus (a)

GOTR *Greek Orthodox Theological Review*

Heb. Hebrew

HPP Hebrew Palaeography Project of the Israel Academy of Sciences and Humanities (Jewish National and University Library)

HUCA *Hebrew Union College Annual*

Iorga, "Notes" N. Iorga, "Notes et extraits pour servir à l'histoire des Croisades aux XVᵉ siècle," *Revue de l'orient latin,* vols. 4–8 (reprinted in 3 vols.) (Paris, 1899–1902)

JA *Journal asiatique*

Jacoby, "Quartiers juifs" D. Jacoby, "Les quartiers juifs de Constantinople à l'époque byzantine," *Byzantion,* 37 (1967), 167–227

Jacoby, "Status of Jews" D. Jacoby, "On the Status of Jews in the Venetian Colonies in the Middle Ages," (Hebrew) *Zion,* XXVIII (1963), 57–69

JE *Jewish Encyclopedia*

JESHO *Journal of the Economic and Social History of the Orient*

JHS *Journal of Hellenic Studies*

JJS *Journal of Jewish Studies*

JQR *Jewish Quarterly Review*

JRAS *Journal of the Royal Asiatic Society*

Krauss, *Studien* S. Krauss, *Studien zur byzantinisch-jüdischen Geschichte* (Vienna, 1914)

KS *Kirjath Sepher*

Laurent, *Actes des Patriarches* V. Laurent, *Les régestes des actes du Patriarcat de Constantinople,* vol. I, *Les actes des patriarches.* Fasc. IV, *Les régestes de 1208 à 1309,* "Le Patriarcat byzantin," serie I (Paris, 1971)

Maltezou, *Venetian Bailo* X. A. Maltezou, Ὁ Θεσμὸς τοῦ ἐν Κωνσταντινουπόλει Βενέτου βαΐλου (1282–1453) (Athens, 1970)

Mann, *Texts* J. Mann, *Texts and Studies in Jewish History and Literature,* vol. I (Cincinnati, 1931), vol. II (Philadelphia, 1935)

MGWJ *Monatsschrift für Geschichte und Wissenschaft des Judenthums*

MHE Μεγάλη Ἑλληνικὴ Ἐγκυκλοπαιδεία

MM F. Miklosich and J. Müller, eds., *Acta et Diplomata graeca medii aevi sacra et profana,* vols. I–VI (Vienna, 1860–90)

MPG Migne, *Patrologia Graeca* (cited by vol. and column)

ms., mss. manuscript(s)

Munk, "Oratoire" S. Munk, "Manuscrits hébreux de l'Oratoire à la Bibliothèque Nationale de Paris, notes inédits," *ZHB,* XIII (1909), 24–31, 58–63, 92–94, 123–27, 153–58, 181–87

MWJ *Magazin für die Wissenschaft des Judentums*

Neubauer, *Bodleian* A. Neubauer, *Catalogue of the Hebrew Manuscripts in the Bodleian Library,* vols. I–II (Oxford, 1886–1906)

n.s. new series

o.s. old series

PAAJR *Proceedings of the American Academy for Jewish Research*

Paraspora Fr. Dölger, *ΠΑΡΑΣΠΟΡΑ: 30 Aufsätze zur Geschichte, Kultur und Sprache des Byzantinischen Reiches* (Ettal, 1961)

Polychordia Festschrift Fr. Dölger (Amsterdam, 1966)

Polychronion Festschrift Fr. Dölger (Heidelberg, 1966)

R. rabbi, rav

REB *Revue des études byzantines*

REG *Revue des études grecques*

REJ *Revue des études juives*

Rosanes, *Israel be-Togarmah* S. A. Rosanes, *Divrei Yemei Yisrael be-Togarmah,* vol. I (Tel Aviv, 1930); *Histoire des Israélites de Turquie et de l'Orient,* vols. II–VI (1938–45)

Sathas, *MB* K. Sathas, Μεσαιωνικὴ Βιβλιοθήκη, vols. I–VI (Venice, 1872–94)

Sathas, *Mnemeia* K. Sathas, Μνημεῖα Ἑλληνικῆς Ἱστορίας, *Documents inédits relatifs à l'histoire de la Grèce au moyen age,* vols. I–IX (Paris, 1880–90)

Soloviev-Mošin, *Grčke* A. Soloviev and V. Mošin, *Grčke Povelje Srpskih Vladara* (Belgrade, 1936)

Starr, *JBE* Joshua Starr, *The Jews in the Byzantine Empire, 641–1204* (Athens, 1939)

Starr, *Romania* Joshua Starr, *Romania, the Jewries of the Levant after the Fourth Crusade* (Paris, 1949)

Steinschneider, *Bodleian* M. Steinschneider, *Catalogus Librorum Hebraeorum in Bibliotheca Bodleiana,* vols. I–III (reprint; Berlin, 1931)

Steinschneider, *Leiden* M. Steinschneider, *Catalogus Codicum Hebraeorum Bibliothecae Academiae Lugduno-Batavae* (Leiden, 1858)

Steinschneider, *Muenchen* M. Steinschneider, *Die hebräischen Handschriften der K. Hof- und Staatsbibliothek in Muenchen* (Zweite Auflage, Munich, 1895)

Tafel-Thomas, *Urkunden* G. L. Tafel et G. M. Thomas, eds., *Urkunden zur ältern Handels- und Staatsgeschichte der Republik Venedig,* vols. I–III (Vienna, 1856–57)

Teshuvoth HaRID Isaiah ben Mali di Trani, *Responsa,* ed. A. Y. Wertheimer (2d ed.; Jerusalem, 1975)

Thiriet, *Régestes* F. Thiriet, *Régestes des déliberations du Sénat de Venise concernant la Romanie,* vols. I–III (Paris, 1958–61)

Vat. Vatican

von Thalloczy, *Acta Albaniae* L. von Thalloczy et al., *Acta et Diplomata res Albaniae mediae aetatis illustrantis* (Vienna, 1918)

VV *Vizantiiski Vremmenik*

Weinberger, *Anthology* Leon Weinberger, *Anthology of Hebrew Poetry in Greece, Anatolia and the Balkans* (Cincinnati, 1975)

ZHB *Zeitschrift für hebräische Bibliographie*

I

POLITICAL, SOCIAL, ECONOMIC, AND INTELLECTUAL LIFE

INTRODUCTION

THE STORY of the Jews in Greece is a long and fascinating venture in the interaction of two peoples and the respective cultures that they developed. It is a story that spans some three and a half millennia and one that, in all of its complexity, has yet to be properly surveyed. It entails, in effect, an examination of the twin bases of Western civilization, which intertwine throughout its continuum like a double helix. The present work intends to examine only part of this interaction, namely, those 300 years which represent the last chapter in the medieval Greek civilization of the Byzantine Empire.

By the year 1200 the Greek–Jewish encounter was already some 2,500 years old, and Jews had been living in Greece for nearly 2,000 years. Most scholarship has been concerned with the Hellenistic period of this encounter primarily as a prolegomenon to the rise and subsequent victory of Christianity in the Aegean area. More recently—that is, within the last two generations—students of the Byzantine period (330–1453) have been interested in what may be termed the continuing story of the Jews in Greece. Thus a number of separate studies have examined the period from the foundation of Constantinople as the capital of the (Christian) Roman Empire until the Fourth Crusade, when that empire received a near-mortal blow at the hands of Western Christians. The last dynasty of that empire, the Palaiologoi (1258–1453), and its relations with the Jews have not yet been properly examined, especially in light of its value for the subsequent history of the Jews in Greece during the Ottoman period of the mid-fifteenth through the early nineteenth centuries in southern Greece and into the twentieth century for the northern areas.

Before we turn to some aspects of the Palaeologan period, then, some background in the first millennium of Christian Greek (henceforth "Byzantine") and Jewish encounter may be of value. Research into the history of the Jews in the first century has indicated that fully half of the known Jewish settlements outside Palestine were flourishing in the Greek-speaking cities of Greece and Asia Minor. Moreover, the general level of cultural and intellectual integration of these communities was quite high: Philo of Alexandria's description (*Legatio ad Gaium*) of the Greek-speaking diaspora provides a valuable background to the intellectual career of Saul/Paul of Tarsus, a Hellenized Jew who was the prime factor in the spread of Christianity in that area, and the ultimate success of Christianity in the city-states of the Aegean world.

But not all Jews accepted the new salvation, so well fitted to the Hellenistic environment of the region, enunciated by Paul in the first century—nor even in the fourth century, when this religion was fostered as the new political ideology of a Roman Empire which would govern from Constantinople for the next 1,100 years. True, many Jews accepted the new religion, especially in the wake of governmental legislation that intended to make their adherence to Judaism a distinct disadvantage to their participation in the affairs of the empire. At the same time, the twin principles of Roman tolerance and Christian theology allowed the more staunchly committed Jews to survive the vicissitudes of the religious persecutions of pagans and religious heretics in the fourth and fifth centuries and remain a severely depleted, yet still intact, Jewish community. Not even the outright persecution of the Jewish communities by the Byzantine emperors from the seventh through the tenth centuries could stamp out a Jewish presence in the empire. In fact, as first shown by Zvi Ankori, the victories of the Byzantine crusades in the second half of the tenth century brought impetus to the expansion of the Jewish communities through a renewed toleration by the government, which in turn led to absorption of the Jewish communities in the reconquered eastern provinces and fostered an immigration that the reinvigorated empire was able to attract to its midst.

This new immigration allowed the opportunity for a hitherto unavailable diversity to emerge which was to quicken the social and religious traditions of Byzantine Jewry. New settlements appeared which followed the economic developments of an expanding Byzantine society. Newcomers from the East brought a new set of traditions, in particular those which 300 years' experience with the talmudically oriented academies of an

Islamic Babylonia had made paramount among the Jewries of that far-flung civilization. Moreover, it also brought the challenge of a young and vigorous sect of nontalmudically oriented Jews, the Karaites, who had successfully challenged the Jewish authorities of Babylonia for two centuries. To all of these challenges, the older, crippled communities of native Greek-speaking Jews, whose traditions harked back to equally old Palestinian traditions, with their autochthonous customs and intellectual outlook, had to compete. The ensuing competition was to give rise to lively confrontation and adaptation throughout the eleventh and twelfth centuries.

During the period before 1204, the Byzantine Empire was the most powerful economic and cultural factor in the Mediterranean world. During this and the subsequent Palaeologan period, religious, social, financial, political, and artistic influences radiated beyond its borders. Many of these influences still survive, as a witness to the role that this empire played in stimulating the expansion of Mediterranean civilization. And despite the political decline of this empire during the tenure of its last dynasty, the religious, cultural, and artistic influence continued, primarily in the developing Renaissance West and the emerging Orthodox North.

A factor that should not be minimized in any assessment of this empire is the existence of numerous ethnic groups that shared in the dominant Greco-Roman-Christian culture. One of these groups that played a constructive role in this empire was the Jews. Though never more than a small numerical minority in the multinational and multilingual realm, their story is important for a number of reasons. Throughout the history of the empire their settlement was almost entirely urban and was located in the important trade centers of the empire. Their role in the prestigious imperial monopoly of the silk industry was not insignificant, and harked back to an autonomous and competitive tradition. Their physicians and interpreters supplied both the imperial and private sectors with much-needed services. At the same time, their life and literature represented for their contemporary environment a physical continuity with that biblical world of which Christian Byzantium considered itself the direct descendant. Their presence, in effect, added one more dilemma to the Byzantine attempt to harmonize the conflicting traditions of Roman tolerance and Christian truth.

The difficulties that confront the student of Byzantine Jewry for the period before 1204 are compounded by the complexities that permeated the empire until the Ottoman conquests in the mid-fifteenth century. Despite the plethora of sources in a multitude of languages, they are strangely silent about the Jews, and too there is a lack of Jewish source material. Therefore each fragment has to be carefully assessed against the fullest background of its contemporary environment—whenever it can be dated. In contradistinction to the Latin Christian and Islamic orbits, where enough material is extant to study internal developments within the Jewish communities, the story of Byzantine Jewry must be studied primarily through the general historical framework, into which each fragment must be pieced as into a disjointed puzzle.

A further difficulty is the complexity resulting from the continually shifting borders of the Byzantine world. Byzantine political control ebbed and flowed as a consequence of the vicissitudes of its history. In a nonsyncopated way, the Orthodox civilization of Byzantium maintained its own, independent rhythms. Moreover, the invasions of new ethnic elements continually affected the status of the Jews in the areas that the new conquerors came to control. Occasionally these invaders were absorbed into the Byzantine tradition. By the later centuries, only the heavy hand of the Ottoman Turks was able to impose uniformity over the myriad of independent rulers astride the carcass of the truncated empire.

The period of the Palaiologoi introduced a new set of complex factors to the relations of Byzantine Jews with their environment. While the influence of the Orthodox church remained strong throughout the areas which the empire had once controlled, the last three centuries of Byzantium present the picture of an empire collapsing into itself, until at the end only the capital and a few appendages were left. How Greek Christians and Jews related to each other in this state of flux, and how each related to the myriad of new conquerors who superimposed their civilizations and attendant norms, whether Western Christian or Eastern Muslim, is a fascinating chapter in the sociology of majority-minority relations.

At the same time, then, that the basic parameters of the internal Jewish story have to be delineated—that is, the nature and the patterns of settlement by Jews in the Balkans and Anatolia, their economic endeavors, the question of Jewish messianic thought and expectations and intellectual pursuits, and the sectarian rivalries within the Jewish communities, including the possible influence of contemporary non-Jewish movements—the rapidly changing nature of the outside environment must not be lost sight of. In a bewildering variety of ways, the various Jewish communities were to come to grips with rule by Greek overlords, Bulgarians and Serbs, Western Crusaders known as Franks, Venetians, and Genoese, and finally Muslim Turks.

The complex political history of the area created a problem of identity and status for the inhabitants of the various political units within it. Given the mobility of certain elements of the population, in particular Jews, it became necessary for these different rulers to negotiate a recognized identity and legitimate status for these individuals, especially those who took the opportunity to change their residence. In the case of Jews, the problem arose of defining their proper relationship to the veteran Jewish community of the new locale, among which they took up residence in order to enjoy the social and religious opportunities available through established communal institutions. At the same time, their economic responsibilities to their former overlords had to be clarified.

Nor in the discussion of the status of individual Jews or their communities should one be tempted to draw parallels with the much-discussed question of Jewish status or Jewish serfdom in the Latin West. In fact, the Byzantine sources are too sparse for anyone even to attempt to define the parameters of the problem within the orbit of that culture. Any attempt to introduce the question, if based upon comparison with a preconceived Western situation, will only compound the confusion inherent in the problem.

These peculiarities, however, should not obscure the traditional themes of the Byzantine Christian and Jewish encounter. Once the Palaiologoi had become the legitimate heirs to the Byzantine throne through their reconquest of the capital in Constantinople (1261), they became heirs also to the problem of a Jewish minority in an Orthodox Christian society. The Jews, for their part, were citizens (albeit second class) of the Byzantine Empire from its inception and thus were entitled to the rights and privileges of Rhomaioi (Romans), even though they were subject to various restrictions as Jews. How the emperors handled this inheritance, in a way that was beneficial to both parties, represents one of the more fascinating facets of this period.

Another reversal of traditional roles by the other fundamental institution of the empire is evident in the attitude of the church from 1204 to 1453. The church, after all, was an integral part of the government of the empire. As such, it was subject to the emperor's direction; yet, at the same time, it exerted its own influence on Byzantine law and society in general.

The church in the thirteenth century was different from the church in the fourteenth and fifteenth centuries as a result of the new intellectual and mystical currents that swept through the Byzantine world, a world that during the fourteenth and fifteenth centuries far exceeded the physical limits of the political empire. These influences upon the church affected the traditional relationships between a triumphant Christianity and a ubiquitous Judaism whose very existence presented a recurrent challenge to the former's claim as the true interpretation of the divine will as revealed through the lessons of history. So much was this the case that the victorious advance of Islam and the ethno-theological challenges of Roman (Western) Catholic and Armenian Christianity did not suffice to oust Judaism from its inherited role as the *bête-noir* of Orthodox Christianity.

We shall begin our survey of the source material for the period after 1204 with a general review of Byzantine imperial and ecclesiastical attitudes and actions toward the Jews, and include a discussion of the problem of a Jewish tax in latter-day Byzantium. Next will follow a chapter on the material for a map of Jewish settlement during the Palaeologan period. The next two chapters will deal, respectively, with the social and communal life of Byzantine Jewry and with the intellectual story, as these can be reconstructed from the few extant sources. The end of the Byzantine Empire and the effect this period had upon the Jews will complete our survey of the last three centuries of Byzantium.

The translated sources in part II are arranged chronologically for the convenience of the reader, and constitute the majority of notices that have been unearthed for the period from the beginning of the thirteenth century to the end of the fifteenth.

ONE

BYZANTIUM AND THE JEWS

Though fully integrated within the Greco-Roman culture of Byzantine civilization, the Jews maintained a separate identity. More than many another ethnic group in the empire, the Jews embraced Hellenic culture and the Greek language. Alongside other groups (including Armenians), they were an organized urban minority with a long tradition of autonomous communal rule. At the same time, the citizenship that they had enjoyed under pagan Rome had been steadily eroded to second class under her Christian successors. By the time paganism was outlawed and the major heresies suppressed, the Jews and their religion remained the only non-Christian minority that was tolerated within the empire. The emergent Christian civilization found itself confronted with the problem of reconciling its victory to the stubborn survival of its maternal rival.

The two power structures of the empire reacted to the presence of the Jews in different ways. As head of the state and the church, the emperor felt entitled to take direct action to influence, or even eradicate, Judaism. Justinian (527–65) was the first emperor to set a precedent for interference with the social and religious practices of Judaism. Heraklios (610–41) was the first emperor to convert the Jews by force to Christianity, and was followed throughout the Middle Byzantine period by Leo III (717–41), Basil I (867–86), and Romanos I Lekapenos (919–44). As we shall see, John Vatatzes (1222–54) was to make a similar attempt during the mid-thirteenth century.

The church, on the other hand, saw itself as the legitimate defender of the Jews when they were faced with an edict of forced conversion. Under normal conditions, however, the church put constant pressure on Jews to see the "error of their ways" and convert to the "true faith." Sermons harped on the theme; dialogues, whether actual or literary exercises, reinforced it. The various Orthodox liturgies, too, constantly denigrated Judaism as an ungrateful mother and the Jews as deicides. Judaism, in fact, was the perfect foil for teaching Christianity to the masses. Christians were seen as the True Israel and therefore the recipients of biblical blessings, while Jews were shown to be rebels or sinners and thus deserving of the biblical curses against Edom, etc. Was not their degraded status in Byzantium a reflection of the church's teachings on the Jews? Unquestionably, this constant pressure affected popular attitudes toward the Jews, especially in the tension-filled period preceding Easter.

There is, then, an apparent paradox in the conflicting imperial and ecclesiastical attitudes toward the Jews. The former tried to outlaw Judaism, during periods of tension, as a means of establishing a religious unity within the embattled empire. At other times the emperors maintained pressure on the Jews through secular law, which restricted their social and economic activities within the Byzantine world. This official denigration as much reflected as set the tone for the ecclesiastical and popular attitudes toward Jews. The ecclesiastics saw themselves as foes of Judaism but defenders of individual Jews. The constant pressure on Jews to convert voluntarily was aimed at proving the truth of Christianity; *forced* baptism, however, would negate the messianic import of their conversion. Therefore the church stood against the emperor during attempts to achieve unity through forced baptisms of Jews.

During the Palaeologan period, we shall find a shift in the attitudes of emperor and church toward the Jews. For reasons of state, the emperors emerge as defenders of the Jews, at least while in office. The church, on the other hand, once in the hands of monks, increased its attacks on the "dark forces" that threatened their Orthodox civilization.

The tension that these rival policies engendered within the Byzantine world is an unexamined chapter in the complicated story of Byzantine politics. Actually, it represents only part of a larger question, namely, the attitude of the secular and religious authorities toward the absorption and assimilation of the ethnic minorities with whom they came into contact.

Imperial Policy

There is no official or unofficial statement by a Byzantine emperor, during the Palaeologan period, regarding the status of Jews, *de jure* or *de facto,* that compares with the clear-cut claims of the Holy Roman emperor toward his

Jewish subjects.[1] Still, inasmuch as the older laws were still applicable, the inferior status of the Jews within Byzantine society was enforced.[2] As with any other Byzantine subjects, the emperor could dictate their legal, social, and economic fate. The emperor, too, could occasionally revive his prerogative to persecute the Jews.

By the sixth century, Jews had been denied the right to teach in state universities, to serve in the army, to work in government service, or to hold public office, with the occasional exception of the burdensome decurionate.[3] Moreover, legislation was enacted that struck at their economic status by placing severe restrictions on their right to own or trade in slaves.[4] Justinian, in the mid-sixth century, went even further and interfered with their practice of Judaism. He legislated against their calendar, the study of religious texts, social practices, and even religious beliefs.[5] Later emperors went so far as to proscribe Judaism.[6]

While there was precedent in Roman law and Christian theology for many of these actions, their purpose was to harass the Jewish population and encourage it to join the Christian community.[7] Many undoubtedly did, over the course of centuries. Yet, despite even the proscription of Judaism, Jews survived—in part due to the efforts of the church, which refused to accept forced converts, and in part due to changed circumstances which necessitated changes in imperial policy.[8] This pattern of occasional persecution is evident in the thirteenth century and is best understood against the background of historical developments in the rump states of Epiros and Nicaea.

1. The two codes of the Palaeologan period were the secular work of George Armenopoulos and the ecclesiastic collection of Matthew Blastares (see below, this chapter). Neither the *Hexabiblos* nor the *Syntagma* contains any statement to this effect, nor does there exist in Byzantium anything resembling the Jewish charters which were issued to Jews by pope and emperor in Roman Catholic areas. Cf. Baron, *SRHJ,* XVII, 11ff and notes.

2. Cf. Ph. Argenti, *Religious Minorities of Chios: Jews and Roman Catholics* (Cambridge, 1970), chap. II; Starr, *JBE,* part I; J. Parkes, *The Conflict of the Church and the Synagogue. A Study in the Origins of Anti-Semitism* (London, 1934), chap. 6.

3. *Codex Theodosianus* 16.8.16; 16.8.24; and the Const. Sirm. 6 of Valentinian III; on the Decurionate, cf. 16.8.2–3; 12.1.99; 12.1.157; 12.1.165 and passim; also *Codex Iustinianus* 1.5.12. (Hereafter *C. Th.* and *C. J.*)

4. *C. Th.* 16.9.1–2 and 3.1.5; 16.9.4–5; C. J. 1.3.54 and 1.10.2; and passim.

5. *C. J.* Novella 146.

6. Starr, *JBE,* chap. I; Z. Ankori's remarks in his "Greek Orthodox Jewish Relations in Historical Perspective—The Jewish View," *GOTR,* XXII (1977), 43–47.

7. *Inter alia,* cf. remarks by Demetrios Khomatianos in document 18.

8. Cf. remarks by D. Constantelos, "Greek Orthodox Jewish Relations in Historical Perspective," *GOTR,* XXII (1977), 12, and Ankori, ibid., p. 46.

The political and geographical fragmentation of Byzantium, which began in 1204, resulted in a struggle among five powers for a share in the spoils. These included the Byzantine states in Nicaea, Epiros, and Trebizond, each claiming the legitimacy of imperial succession; the Western Catholics, known locally as Phrangoi (i.e., Franks), of various origin, in central Greece and Morea; the Slavs in the North; the Venetian colonies on the islands and coasts of Greece; and various Turkic powers that were pressing from the East. Four independent Greek areas arose within the former boundaries of the Empire of the Komnenoi to vie with the Franks, Slavs, Venetians, and Turks. The Empire of Nicaea, in northwest Anatolia, constituted the main strength of the exiled Byzantine court and church hierarchy that, ultimately, restored the imperial tradition to Constantinople.

In Trebizond, a scion of the Komnenoi laid claim to the imperial title and persevered in this claim until the heavy hand of Mehmet II absorbed this last vestige of Byzantine power and ended the history of this romantic kingdom in 1461. By 1214 Trebizond was cut off from the west by the Seljuk occupation of Sinope and restricted to the southeast littoral of the Black Sea, supported by a tiny hinterland. In the Peloponnesos, or Morea, a semi-independent Greek state, allied to the capital, arose after 1261 to contend with Frankish Morea and the Venetian seaports. Initially, it was restricted to the fortresses of Mistra, Maina, and Monemvasia and their hinterlands. However, by 1430, save for the Venetian outposts of Coron and Modon in the south and Argos and Nauplia in the east, the Greeks controlled all of the Peloponnesos. Of all the Byzantine areas during the Palaeologan period, it proved to be the strongest ally of the capital and the bastion of Byzantine civilization in Greece.

To the west, the Despotate of Epiros controlled the western mountains and coastal region of Epirote Greece until the first quarter of the fourteenth century. For nearly a century it competed with Serbia and the capital for the privilege of defending Orthodoxy in this area. The Despotate of Epiros finally disappeared before the advances of Stephan Dušan, whose sweep to the south conquered many Byzantine towns during his long reign (1331–55). These areas were henceforth cut off from Byzantine rule, for the Ottomans were the ultimate heirs of Stephan's conquests.

By the end of the first quarter of the thirteenth century, the Greeks, having recovered from the shock of 1204, began to expand beyond the borders of their refuges. Michael Doukas Angelos Komnenos secured a hold over the region, stretching from Dyrrachium to the Gulf of Corinth, and left it to his brother Theodore in 1214. By 1222 Theodore had advanced east through Thessaly and Macedonia, as far as Serres. In 1224 Thessalonica surrendered, after a long siege, and became his capital. With most of Macedonia and Thessaly as far south as the Spercheus River now under his control, Theodore was crowned as emperor in the spring of 1224 by Demetrios Khomatianos, the archbishop of Ochrida. Fired with a vision of regaining Constantinople, Theodore turned against his nearest rival, the powerful Bulgarian Czar John Asen II (1218–41), with whom he had an alliance against John Vatatzes, his distant rival emperor in Nicaea.[9] In the spring of 1230 the gamble failed, and Theodore was defeated and blinded at Klokotnica on the Marica.[10] His brother continued to rule in Thessalonica, Thessaly, and Epiros, but the territory from Dyrrachium to Adrianople was now under the aegis of the Bulgars. As the most powerful Christian ruler in Macedonia, it was Asen's turn, with the help of John Vatatzes, to besiege Constantinople. Though he tried in 1235 and 1236, he was not able to take the capital. With his death in 1241, the Bulgarian threat disappeared.[11]

In 1229,[12] the year before his attack on John Asen, Theodore persecuted the Jews under his control. What areas of his empire were affected

9. See A. Vacalopoulos, *Origins of the Greek Nation: The Byzantine Period, 1204–1461* (New Brunswick, 1970), pp. 31–34, for a sympathetic survey of Theodore's reign.

10. A. A. Vasiliev considers "the battle of Klokotinitza one of the turning points in the history of the Christian east in the thirteenth century." His analysis of the sequence of events goes one step beyond the letter of Jacob ben Elia (to be discussed presently), which makes no mention of Theodore's plotting (*History of the Byzantine Empire*, II [Madison, 1961], 524).

11. *CMH*, IV, part I, pp. 310–15; G. Ostrogorsky, *History of the Byzantine State* (New Brunswick, 1969), pp. 387–89.

12. The letter of Jacob ben Elia places the event after Theodore's imperial coronation (1224): וכאשר יבוא היהודי לפניו היה עלם עיניו וישחק עליו יושב בשמים ויתן לו כסות עינים. The phrase "sitting on high" may refer to the imperial throne, which was raised and lowered to impress visitors; cf. *Megillath Ahimaʿaṣ* (ed. A. Neubauer, *Medieval Jewish Chronicles* [Oxford, 1895], II, 116f) for a description of the impression that such imperial tricks made on visitors. The passage refers to the ninth century; the chronicle was written in the eleventh century. For a tenth-century description, cf. Liutprand of Cremona, *Antapodesis,* chap. V (trans. F. A. Wright, *The Works of Liutprand of Cremona* [London, 1930]). Moreover, Jacob ben Elia emphatically places the events just before Theodore's attack on Asen (1230); cf. document 30 in part II for a weak assist to this date. In his treatment of Theodore's reign, Nicol makes no reference to this action (*The Despotate of Epirus* [Oxford, 1957], chaps. 3–5).

cannot be fully ascertained;[13] it is clear from our Hebrew source, however, that he initiated some kind of anti-Jewish action or policy, and that the reason for it was connected with his need for money.[14] That Theodore, as a Greek and a Christian, hated Jews can be seen from our main source, the letter of Jacob ben Elia to Pablo Christiani. That the Jews may have irked the local Greek leaders during the period of Latin rule by accommodating the anti-Orthodox establishment can be surmised; after all, they owed little to the previous Byzantine authority. Still, any argument that the primary reason for this action was the result of a heightened Greek nationalism (*pace*, Starr) must supply an explanation for the delay between 1224 (the capture of Thessalonica) and 1229.[15] It should also be noted that no Byzantine source alludes to Theodore's actions or attitudes toward the Jews.

The suggestion, therefore, that the prospect of confiscating the wealth and possessions of the Jews prompted Theodore to initiate his policy against them should not be dismissed (**24**). If the date 1229 can be accepted, then Theodore's actions should be seen as part of his preparations for war; they were an attempt to supplement his meager resources, which were insufficient to outfit the forces necessary for his anticipated campaigns. Jacob ben Elia's letter indeed emphasizes the violent expropriation of Jewish liquid capital. It does not hint at any proscription of Judaism, save for the remark that he "profaned our faith," which may in this case be rhetorical. Also, the added mention of Theodore's imperial disrespect to the Jews who approached him suggests that his actions were an *ad hoc* measure, rather than a determined effort to proscribe Judaism, as John Vatatzes later attempted. Since the battle of Klokotnica took place within a year of these actions, their effect upon the Jews was only temporary and, in all probability, limited to the general area of Thessalonica and its environs, where the main force of the emperor was located. After his victory, John Asen, who had Jews in his entourage, no doubt ordered Manuel, Theodore's younger brother and successor, to mitigate this policy, if indeed it had continued. The loss of much of Macedonia and Thrace, in any event, would

13. The responsum of Demetrios Khomatianos, archbishop of Ochrida, to Konstantine Kabasilas, metropolitan of Durazzo, assumes no persecution of the Jews in either area. The document (18) may therefore predate Theodore's action; cf. Starr, *Romania*, p. 81.

14. The letter of Jacob ben Elia states: ויהי לשטן לבני עמנו וחלל דתנו שלל ממונם ובזז הונם.

15. Starr, *Romania*, p. 81. See below, note 23 and text. The thesis seems anachronistic in this context.

have brought any affected Jewish communities in these regions under the control of the Bulgarian czar.

The Jews who are mentioned in Asen's entourage may have been refugees from Theodore's persecution, since the czar reminded them of the suffering that Theodore had inflicted on their coreligionists. More likely, they were part of the czar's medical staff, since their reluctance to blind Theodore, the unfortunate prisoner, seems more in line with their medical ethics than any fear for repercussions on their brethren still under Byzantine control. That they finally submitted to the czar's threats and gouged out Theodore's eyes is only to be expected. Still, their skill spared his life, since the punishment of blinding was sometimes followed by the death of the victim.

This incident marks one of the two recorded occasions in the thirteenth century when Jews were used to carry out a sentence of blinding (**24**, **29**). If we take into account the number of times that this punishment was meted out to Byzantine nobles in the twelfth and thirteenth centuries alone, the use of Jews on these two occasions seems accidental, a case of being in the right place at the wrong time, rather than an established tradition (exc. C).

After his escape from the Bulgarian camp, Theodore, though barred from the purple by his condition, remained a powerful behind-the-scenes influence in the politics of Macedonia and Epiros. Nor did he take revenge on either the Jews or on John Asen. The first were to be the victims of John Vatatzes, twenty-five years later; the second became his son-in-law.

The continued shifts in policy of John Asen had thrown every power in the region off balance: Theodore had met his match. Manuel weakly held on to Thessalonica; the Latin emperors, either too young or too old, were merely pawns in the game; the distant Vatatzes could only bide his time.

In 1242, the year after Asen's death, the Nicaean forces, under John Vatatzes, marched against Thessalonica, only to be halted by the Mongol threat on the eastern marches of their homeland.[16] The warning was sufficient. The ruler of Thessalonica acknowledged John Vatatzes as his em-

16. Ostrogorsky, *History*, p. 397; A. Heisenberg, "Kaiser Johannes Batatzes der Barmherzige. Eine mittelgriechische Legende," *BZ*, XIV (1905), 160; Vacalopoulos, *Origins* (pp. 35–40), is the most recent panegyric on Vatatzes. For his career, cf. Alice Gardner, *The Lascarids of Nicaea. The Story of an Empire in Exile* (London, 1912), chaps. 7–10. A more recent study is Michael Angold, *A Byzantine Government in Exile: Government and Society under the Laskarids of Nicaea (1204–1261)* (Oxford, 1975).

peror and contented himself with the title of Despot. In 1246 the Nicaean emperor attacked the weakened Bulgarians and reconquered for the Byzantines those areas which Theodore had lost. Surrounded by Vatatzes' forces, Thessalonica opened her gates at the end of 1246. Only Constantinople remained beyond his control. His death on November 3, 1254 (he had suffered during his last years from an undetermined disease), signaled the end of Nicaean ascendance.

John Doukas Vatatzes (1222–54) has been recognized as one of the most important rulers to emerge in the Byzantine period. His victorious career buttressed the Empire of Nicaea against the Turkic powers that threatened its eastern flank and sufficiently weakened his rivals to prepare for the restoration of the capital by one of his successors. At the height of his career, he had greatly enlarged his empire, an indication of the recuperative power and continued strength of the Byzantines in Asia Minor in the thirteenth century.[17] Most of the Balkans, too, save for Frankish Morea, was under his control. Internally, he had reorganized the administration of the state and of justice, while Byzantine churches and Christian society in general benefited from his pious bounty. His frugality was legendary, as was his promotion of agriculture, viniculture, and stock breeding.[18] In 1243 he promulgated a sumptuary decree in an attempt to control excesses among his nobility and to restrain the export of gold to the Italians and Turks.[19] As a result of his policies, the hyperper may have risen in value nearly 75 percent over its value under the Komnenoi.[20]

This reorganization of the Empire of Nicaea has to be seen in the context of the economic situation that was to plague the successor Palaeologan state until its fall to the Ottomans. The Palaiologoi lost the trade to the East, never regained mastery of the sea, and had no effective hinterland to exploit; in addition, they had to support the burden of an increased bureaucracy and the expense (at least initially) of a worldwide diplomacy. On the other hand, the Empire of Nicaea was essentially a land-

17. Cf. G. Arnakis, *Hoi protoi Othomani. Symbole eis to problema tes ptoseos tou Hellenismou tes Mikras Asias (1282–1337)* (The First Ottomans: A Contribution to the Problem of the Decline of Hellenism in Asia Minor [1282–1337]) (Athens, 1947), prologue.

18. Ostrogorsky, *History*, p. 394.

19. G. I. Bratianu, *Recherches sur le commerce génois dans la Mer Noire au XIIIe siècle* (Paris, 1929), p. 81, citing Nikephoras Gregoras, *Historia Byzantina* (ed. L. Schoper, *CSHB*), I, 43; cf. Vasiliev, *History*, II, 547–48.

20. So argues R. Guilland, *La politique intérieure de l'empire de Byzance de 1204 à 1341* (Paris, 1959), p. 23; cf. Angold, *Byzantine Government*, chap. VI and esp. pp. 117f.

based and land-oriented empire. Whereas, previous to 1204, Byzantium's power and wealth derived in large part from her control of the sea and maritime revenues, the overseas trade of Nicaea was completely controlled by the Italian merchants and her land trade was based on agricultural products and oriented eastward into Turkic Anatolia. Thus demoted from the status of a great power, with its concomitant burden of an international diplomacy (which a location at Constantinople would have demanded), the Empire of Nicaea was able to strengthen itself internally in preparation for the return to Constantinople.[21] Indeed, it was the full treasury that Michael Palaiologos inherited that supported his far-flung policies and intrigues.

It is also against the above developments that one must view the events of 1254, when the ailing Vatatzes ordered the Jews throughout the Empire of Nicaea to convert to Christianity. (Our source, unfortunately, does not list specifics [**24**].) That this act was different from that of Theodore's is evident from the comments of Jacob ben Elia, who is our unique source for both the Jewish policies of Theodore in Thessalonica and John Vatatzes in Nicaea. The reliability of his remarks on the Byzantine scene may be tested against Jacob's list of the persecutions of Jews in other areas of the Mediterranean and several places in the Muslim world, each of which is verifiable from other sources. His description, too, of Vatatzes' disease, while it parallels the account of Nikephoros Gregoras, also brings to mind Josephus' description of Herod's sufferings, which were interpreted as a divine punishment for his sins against the Jews (**24**).

As we have seen, Theodore's actions, a quarter of a century earlier, were most likely connected with his war preparations against John Asen; our source especially emphasizes his financial motives. The record of Vatatzes' order, on the other hand, is quite different. It clearly states that the emperor ordered the Jews residing within the Empire of Nicaea to convert to Christianity and enter the Byzantine church. No mention is made of confiscation and expropriation of wealth; indeed, the state of the treasury obviated the necessity for this type of revenue raising.

No satisfactory answer has yet been offered for Vatatzes' forced baptism of the Jews. One opinion has it that ultra Greek nationalism was the reason, while another proposes that it was the emperor's contribution to

21. D. A. Zakythinos, *Crise monétaire et crise économique à Byzance du XIIIe au XVe siècle* (Athens, 1948), pp. 7f.

the war being waged against the Manichaeans and other heretics.[22] Both these suggestions are based on the assumption that Vatatzes was conducting affairs rationally and that his actions toward the Jews were part of a coherent policy. This, however, was not necessarily the case, and the chronology of events points to another possibility.

For the last six months of his life, Vatatzes suffered greatly from a disease that ravaged his mind and his body.[23] It was during this period, in 1254, that the order went out for the conversion of the Jews (**24**). It is likely that this order was the result of the aberrations that the emperor suffered in his last days. Notwithstanding the lack of Byzantine corroboration of this forced conversion, it is not improbable that the policy and decree remained in effect through the brief reign of his son and successor, Theodore II Laskaris. Our source suggests no official change in policy until the reign of Michael VIII Palaiologos.[24]

The supplanting of the Laskarid dynasty by Michael Palaiologos in 1259 brought a positive change for the Jews—although the reign of the first Palaiologos is nearly a total blank insofar as the Jewish story is concerned. The only piece of information, aside from occasional hints of settlements, that pertains to his attitude toward the Jews is the remark of Jacob ben Elia that Michael VIII summoned the Jewish leaders in his realm and invited them to support him as emperor. Thus Michael's first act toward the Jews, according to our source, was the revocation of John Vatatzes' order of forced baptism. At the same time, however, he made it clear to the Jews that he expected them to show their appreciation for his assistance (**24**). This is the first indication we have of a specific Palaeologan attitude toward the Jews—an attitude, it should be emphasized, that was a positive reversal of

22. Starr (*Romania,* pp. 20–21) ascribes this action to an "upsurge of nationalism"; see above, note 15 and text. R. Guilland (*La politique religieuse de l'empire byzantin de 1204 à 1341* [Paris, 1959], p. 64) couples this anti-Jewish action of Vatatzes with the latter's previously declared war against the Manicheans. Both motives would complement each other if we were dealing with a young and healthy Vatatzes; however, his debilitated condition suggests another reason.

23. Ostrogorsky (*History,* p. 394) places his death on November 2, 1254, and ascribes these sufferings to severe epileptic fits; cf. Gardiner, *Lascarids of Nicaea,* pp. 192 and 204f.

24. The letter of Jacob ben Elia is the only source that might place Jews in Constantinople during the reign of Michael VIII; they may have followed him back soon after the conquest, although there is no direct evidence to support such a supposition. Jacoby surmises the presence of Venetian Jews in Constantinople not before 1277; cf. his "Quartiers juifs," pp. 189–94, and, most recently, "Les Vénitiens naturalisés dans l'empire byzantin," *Travaux et Mémoires,* 8 (1981), 227 and passim.

the former hostility of the state toward its Jewish subjects. In contradistinction to all previous imperial policy toward the Jews, this attitude, for whatever self-serving purposes, marks the Palaeologan period as a prolegomenon to the better-known Ottoman treatment of the Jews. In the generations that separate Michael VIII from Mehmet II, we shall find several instances of imperial protection of and assistance to their Jewish subjects.

Whether this was an officially declared new policy on the part of Michael VIII is unclear; at the very least, it was a pragmatic action to further the limited resources of the government. Michael's rather unorthodox manner of acquiring the imperial title had made him many enemies at Nicaea. The church, for one, could always wield the club of illegality over his head. True, Michael could appoint the reigning patriarch; but he could never be absolutely certain of his loyalty. The noble families, for their part, considered themselves just as worthy of the throne as the Laskarids or the Palaiologoi. Moreover, Michael's attempts at reunion with Rome offended the religious sentiments of all but his closest adherents, while his naval and economic dependence on the Republics of Venice and Genoa irked the pride of the rival nobility. Also, his insatiable need for gold to finance his military campaigns and more important diplomatic intrigues bore heavily on the already oppressed masses.

In the face of grudging support and underlying opposition among his Orthodox subjects, Michael looked for other sources of support. He seems to have found part of this support among the minority ethnic groups in the empire. His predecessor, John Vatatzes, had reinvigorated the native Byzantine population and sought to strengthen his independence by a conservative rusticity. Michael, however, looked to the Armenians and Jews for some of the financial resources he needed. Welcoming them back to the city, he allowed them religious and economic liberties, for which his newfound supporters were not ungrateful. We have to wait thirty years before there are sources for the presence of Jews in the city itself, and another ten before the specific attacks of an irate clergy came to bear upon the problem; however, the emergence of a strong Jewish and Armenian influence in the city in the reign of Andronikos II lends weight to the suggestion that their settlements there date from early in the reign of the first Palaiologos.

This attitude of Michael VIII cannot, of course, be considered official or binding on his successors. Indeed, our suggestion may be an overinterpretation of an admittedly limited reference. Even so, it should not be considered too suspect. As we shall see, sources from the reign of Michael's son and successor suggest a continuation of Michael's attitude toward the Jews. This nonharassment of Jews and Armenians very likely continued, to the mutual benefit of both sides, until the destruction of the empire in the mid-fifteenth century.

This attitude is seen most clearly within the context of the chaotic economic situation that plagued the empire throughout the Palaeologan period. A number of Venetian documents outline a series of controversial practices that strained the relations between Andronikos II and the Venetian Doge in 1319 and 1320.[25] In the main, these concerned the rights and privileges of Venetian merchants to deal in corn, wine, and skins in the capital. Though the latter was the least serious of the disputed subjects, this question of who was to prepare the skins is important for the light it sheds upon the imperial attitude toward the Jews. The documents show that two groups of Jews were living in Constantinople, in a number of areas. One group, of course, consisted of Byzantine subjects who lived in the Vlanka Quarter; the other of Venetian Jews who lived not only in the Venetian Quarter and elsewhere in the city, but also in the Vlanka Quarter alongside the Byzantine Jews (see chapter 2). Wherever their location within the city, the Venetian Jews were under the protection of the Venetian Bailo.

The controversy arose when some Venetian Jews who lived outside the Venetian Quarter came into conflict with imperial agents.[26] The former invoked the rights of a Venetian merchant; the latter recognized no difference between Venetian and other Jews. Such an oversight, whether deliberate or accidental, was common among Byzantine officials. Of course, we do not know whether all of the Jews concerned were entitled to Venetian protection. The fact that Venetian and Byzantine Jews lived together may have clouded the distinction between them, to the point where each group claimed the status of the other whenever it was to its advantage. In other areas of the city, Byzantine subjects also claimed a Venetian status in order to enjoy the latter's preferred tax status.[27] In this case, however,

25. Cf. Starr, *Romania,* pp. 28ff, and Jacoby, "Quartiers juifs," pp. 196ff.

26. The affair has been pieced together by Starr (*Romania,* pp. 28–31), based on documents (37, 38, 39), as well as the account in D. Minotto, *Chronik der Familie Minotto* (Berlin, 1901), I, 195, 218, 234–35.

27. Cf. J. Chrysostomides, "Venetian Commercial Privileges under the Palaeologi," *Studi Veneziani,* 12 (1970), 267–356, for a summary of the general problem with more recent comments by Jacoby, "Les Vénitiens naturalisés," passim.

the question of status was not as important as the division of labor. Byzantine Jews had a monopoly on tanning hides while Venetian Jews were allowed to prepare furs. The controversy flared when the latter, for some unknown reason, began to prepare skins, which was the province of the Byzantine Jews. The emperor protested this violation of his monopoly; Venice, of course, ignored his protest. The emperor then confiscated the skins of the Venetian Jews, who in turn protested to the Republic. The diplomats took over from the bureaucrats at this point, and thus began the bitter exchange outlined in the documents.

Against this background of commercial rivalry and confused identities, the emperor was forced to define the legal and economic status of the Venetian Jews vis-à-vis the other Venetians residing in Constantinople. From an official and legal perspective, anyone who identified himself as a Venetian, and was so recognized by the Venetian Bailo, was entitled to the privileges of a Venetian as allowed in the treaties.[28] With respect to their economic prerogatives, Venetian Jews were permitted freedom of movement and settlement throughout the empire and, further, were accorded the right to live *anywhere* in the capital. They were also allowed to buy, sell, or rent real estate anywhere in the city in return for an annual payment.[29] These last provisions implemented the recognition of the Venetian status of these Jews and ensured their right to enjoy the benefits of the treaties between Venice and Byzantium.

This problem of the Venetian Jews had not, of course, been anticipated by the framers of the earlier Veneto-Byzantine treaties. During the twelfth century, Venice had been concerned with securing from the still strong empire a foothold in the capital, while in the thirteenth century she had to offset the influence of the Genoese. By the fourteenth century her major goals were achieved, and she enjoyed a preeminent position in the empire. The empire, on the other hand, having lost control of the foreign trade, was forced to affirm its control over the domestic economy. For this reason, the emperor tried, at first verbally and then by force, to restrict the Venetians

28. To be sure, this article shows up only in later documents; cf. Maltezou, *Venetian Bailo,* p. 135, rubric 33: "concerning what one must pay in order to receive a *privilegium* that he is a Venetian." This feature, however, was probably written into the statutes of the baili of Constantinople; there is no doubt that it was an old stipulation. See Jacoby, "Les Vénitiens naturalisés," pp. 217ff.

29. In no way can this be construed as a special Jewish tax; rather, this right suggests that Jews could and did settle in many parts of the city.

from processing hides. This restriction implies an attempt to protect his own tanners and fur dealers (who happened to be Jews in this case) and the various revenues that accrued from their trade.[30]

Not even direct imperial interference with local administration was sufficient to settle the problem of imperial taxation of Venetian Jews, a taxation considered illegal by Venice, and of treating them in general as subjects of the empire (**134**). The Venetian Jews apparently never received compensation for the loss of their goods. By leaving the matter unresolved, the emperor and his men were on record that any attempt by Venetian Jews to infringe upon the market of Byzantine Jewish fur and hide traders would invoke bureaucratic repercussions, and perhaps even physical danger.

If the emperor found it difficult to support his subjects in a strictly economic controversy that was part of his general problems with the Venetian stranglehold over the Byzantine economy, he was at least able to control the areas within which his Jews could reside. Throughout the medieval world, Jews tended to establish communities in urban areas centered around their synagogues. This natural tendency of a well-organized diasporic group to occupy specific quarters was not, of course, restricted to Jews. With respect to the Byzantine scene, however, the question is whether this practice was voluntary or reflected an imperial policy which forced them to live in certain quarters.

From the small amount of material at our disposal, it seems that such a policy existed. Demetrios Khomatianos, in his well-known responsum, states quite clearly that certain areas were put aside for minority groups who were allowed to live in an Orthodox society (**18**). Ethnicity was usually defined by religious affiliation in Byzantium. The appearance, then, of a special quarter, designated *ʿebraike,* in various cities of the empire is a reflection of this official policy, which controlled a natural process through a set location for the Jewish quarter. Venetian Jews, outside Constantinople, were no doubt accustomed to live among their coreligionists, just as many did in the capital.

Andronikos II asserted this control over settlement during his dispute with Venice. In the extant Latin translation of a lost Greek letter to the Venetian Doge (**37**), his prerogative is thus defended: "*nostri Iudei quedem*

30. A question worth investigating is the presence of non-Jewish tanners and fur dealers in the capital who were subject to the emperor. We have not found any sources to indicate that they existed. Ankori has argued the exclusivity of tanning as a Jewish profession; cf. *Karaites,* p. 176n, and below (exc. B).

appropriata possessio sunt Imperii et ideo datus eis locus deputatus habitationi in quo habitantes exercent proprias artes, reddentes Imperio illud quod ordinatum est eis."[31] Clearly, these Byzantine Jewish subjects (did the statement include *all* Jewish subjects?) were settled by imperial order in a specific place. At the same time, local Jews who managed to acquire Venetian status, whether by coming from areas subject to the Republic or by purchasing naturalization, were entitled to live anywhere in the city. Most of them no doubt chose to live either within the Venetian Quarter or with their Byzantine coreligionists.

Just as the emperor could control their residence, he may have been able to control their economic pursuits. One of the Jewish areas of settlement in Constantinople was the Vlanka Quarter, where, as Maximus Planudes relates, the emperor had established a colony of Jewish tanners (**21**).[32] These Jews, in fact, constituted a distinct trade corporation under imperial control. It has been argued (from indirect evidence) that tanning became an exclusively Jewish vocation during the Macedonian period as a result of an official policy of degradation.[33] The social disdain for this profession was shared by Jews in other economic pursuits, in particular the prestigious silk manufacturers, as well as Christians.[34] Even so, these remarks of Planudes are the first direct evidence that some (if not all) of the tanners were Jews under the immediate control of the imperial government.

Yet it is not impossible that this situation reflects an administrative structure which had its origins in the pre-1204 empire. Jews, after all, had been engaged in tanning since the Roman period. The question is whether the vocation was exclusively Jewish in the Palaeologan period. While there are no indications to support or deny such a theory,[35] it is as likely as not

31. Starr, *Romania,* p. 112; *DVL,* p. 142. If this passage is to be accepted as a special tax, then it was a tax on imperial tanners who happened to be Jews, and not vice versa. Dölger himself, while recognizing this as a special tax ("Es ergibt sich daraus das Fortbestehen einer Judensondersteuer im 14. Jahrhundert"), understood that "proprias artes" referred to the "Lederindustrie"; cf. "Die Frage," pp. 23–24 (= *Paraspora,* p. 376), and below, note 71.

32. For a discussion of this source in connection with imperial factories and revenues, see section below, "Taxation."

33. See below, part II, exc. B, and cited bibliography.

34. Cf. Benjamin of Tudela's comments on Pera (exc. A) and commentary by Ankori, *Karaites,* p. 141.

35. See above, note 30. Ankori's argument was not directed at the Palaeologan period. Still, see his quotations from Foscarini, regarding Crete, as late as the sixteenth century, in *Michael,* vol. VII (1981), passim.

that references to tanning in a given area might be an indication that Jewish tanners were also to be found. Such centers, then, might include Philadelphia,[36] Trebizond,[37] and possibly Amphissa (Salona).[38]

In addition to their concern with the economic activities of Byzantine Jews who were resident in the capital, the Palaiologoi occasionally made

36. Theodore Laskaris once quipped that Nikaea was famous for philosophy, Corinth for music, Thessaly for weaving, and Philadelphia for tanning (*De naturale communione, MPG,* vol. CXL, col. 1354); J. Dräseke, "Theodore Laskaris," *BZ,* 3 (1894), 500; Vasiliev, *History,* II, 549; Vacalopoulos, *Origins,* p. 39.

37. The Trebizond data come from a legend incorporated in Evliya Çelebi's *Seyāhatnāme* (in the translation of Joseph von Hammer prepared for the Oriental Translation Fund, *Narrative of the Travels in Europe, Asia, and Africa in the Seventeenth Century, by Evliya Efendi* [London, 1834], II, 49–50): "There have been no Jews at Trebizonde since the time of Sultán Sélim, who was governor of the town, the following circumstance was the cause; a Dervish discovered on a piece of leather (*saffian*), that was handed about for sale, an inscription, written in a way not to be observed by everybody, which implored the assistance of all religious Moslems, to deliver two innocent Moslem youths tyrranically shut up in the Jewish tanneries. The Dervish having explained the inscription to Prince Sélim, a general search of all the Jewish tanneries took place by an armed force, when not only the two brothers, lost many years before, but many other Moslem boys were found, on whose backs the Jewish tanners had worked in tanning their skins. This discovery occasioned a general slaughter and banishment of the Jews, none of whom have since dared to show their faces at Trebisonde, the inhabitants of which town are a religious and devout people."

These tanneries were located by Evliya Çelebi outside one of the east gates that led from the town to the inner fortifications (ibid., pp. 44–45) called the Tanner's Gate (the other was the New Friday's Gate). The remarks of Evliya Çelebi (like those of most travelers) should be taken with caution, especially those not based on personal observation. Still, the existence of Jewish tanneries in the fifteenth century is not a historical impossibility. See below, chap. 2 ("Anatolia") for the material on Jews in Trebizond in the Byzantine period.

38. One of the victims of the Kalomiti persecutions in Negroponte (= Egripon, the modern Chalkide in Euboea) took refuge in Salona (= Amphissa) at the beginning of the fourteenth century (see document 30). We may well ask why Salona, unless there was a Jewish settlement there; his brothers had fled to communities where we know Jews lived. Benjamin of Tudela, of course, had found a colony of Jews in nearby Krissa, but he does not mention Amphissa. In the medieval section of Amphissa, high above the present-day town, is an impressive number of tanneries which supply much of the finished leather to the factories of Athens. I have not been able to discover when these tanneries were established, but their location suggests medieval origins. Mertzios (*Mnemeia Makedonikas Historias* [Thessaloniki, 1947], p. 199) notes the production of silk in Salona in 1470. If it could be shown that silk production was a feature of the economy in the fourteenth century, then another incentive for a Jewish presence in Salona would be established.

For the Jewish tanners of Modon and Coron, cf. Starr, *Romania,* chap. IV, and for those of Crete, the studies of Ankori, "Jews and the Jewish Community in the History of Mediaeval Crete," *Proceedings of the 2nd International Congress of Cretological Studies* (Athens, 1968), III, passim; "The Living and the Dead," *PAAJR,* XXXIX–XL (1970–71), passim, and "Giacomo Foscarini and the Jews of Crete," *Michael* (1981), VII, 79–87.

use of their professional services in the imperial bureaucracy. Only a few instances of Jews in imperial service have been recorded for posterity. Andronikos III, for example, made use of a recent immigrant from Syria as an interpreter (**51**). The chief physicians of both Manuel I (in the twelfth century) and the last Komnenos of Trebizond (in the fifteenth) were also Jews (exc. A, 144). Although such use of Jews was contrary to Byzantine laws of earlier periods,[39] there is no indication that government officials or the clergy took offense at the practice, save for occasional tirades against Jewish doctors.[40]

One might add that a converted Jew was not barred from government service. Indeed, conversion was the ultimate show of loyalty to the regime and was accordingly rewarded. Still, only a few instances have been recorded. Manuel II's confessor, a convert named Makarios, occasionally served as his ambassador (**123**), while Philotheos Kokkinos, to whom tradition has ascribed Jewish ancestry, eventually became Patriarch (**93**).

In one other area the emperor could control the fate of his Jewish subjects. He could downgrade their status to some sort of dependency, whether fiscal or physical, or upgrade it, depending on the circumstances. Several texts from the reign of Andronikos II illuminate this control.

Toward the end of his reign, Andronikos II issued two chrysobulls to the Church of Ioannina, both of which contain brief references to Jews. The information from these two chrysobulls, which, incidentally, is the first documentary data we have on the existence of Jews in Ioannina, concerns Jews who were resident in the city and several others who owed obligations to the church. The chrysobull of February 1319, in confirming the previous charter of the governor Syrgiannes Palaiologos Philanthropenos, states that the Jews of Ioannina are to live in a free and undisturbed state, just as the other settlers (**36**). Modern-day scholars have recognized in this text a new policy of toleration toward the Jews on the part of the Palaiologoi, and suggested that it was applicable not only to the Jews of Ioannina alone but to all the Jews of the empire.[41]

39. Cf. Starr, *JBE,* pp. 144ff, no. 83, and passim.

40. See following section.

41. Starr, *Romania,* p. 113; N. Bees, "Übersicht über die Geschichte des Judenthums von Janina (Epirus)," *BNJ,* II (1921), 163–65; P. Charanis, "The Jews in the Byzantine Empire under the First Palaeologi," *Speculum,* XXII (1947), 76–77; and most recently Baron, *SRHJ,* XVII, 10f.

The actual situation may have been somewhat more restricted. It seems that, to date, the commentators on this passage have ignored the implications of the last phrase of the text, "κατὰ τοὺς λοιποὺς ἐποίκους." All apparently understood *epikous* as "inhabitants." The word, however, means "immigrant," "settler," or "colonist," and may be considered as synonymous, for our purposes at least, with the ancient term *metoikos*.[42] Thus it would refer to a resident of a city who is not the holder of the ancient civic rights and privileges, but settles in the city under special dispensation. Thus, it seems to me, this passage may be an indirect witness to the immigration of Jews into Ioannina in recent years, for security or economic reasons, who managed to effect their inclusion in a general statement supporting the privileges of other new settlers in the city.

The fortress of Ioannina, at this time, was the bastion of the Byzantine presence in Epiros.[43] With the loss of much of the surrounding area to the Serbians and Catalans, it is only natural to expect large numbers of rural inhabitants to have sought the protection of the strong walls of the seat of the governor. The Jews of Ioannina, whether of long standing or recent arrival, were accorded by statute the protection of the city, along with the new arrivals; however, they were not admitted to the local privileges of the veteran Greek community. In addition to the new arrivals during the Palaeologan period, there was already another group of "immigrants," in this case Christian, from the period when Ioannina was under the control of the Despotate of Epiros. The latters' continued presence and privileges were resented by the local Ioanninites for several generations after their initial arrival (**36n**).

The chrysobull of June 1321, in confirming all the possessions of the Church of Ioannina, mentions, *inter alia,* three Jews, the children of Namer, David, and Shemarya (**43**). From the context, it seems that these Jews (or more) in some way constituted the "possessions" of the church and that they owed it certain unspecified obligations.[44] How they arrived at that condition is unknown. Clearly, however, their status antedated the

42. Cf. Sophocles, *Greek Lexicon,* s.v. ἐποικίζω, and Liddel and Scott, *Greek Dictionary,* s.v. ἔποικος and μέτοικος. Sophocles defines μετοικίστης as an immigrant, indicating a shift in meaning by the medieval period, most likely as a result of the Jewish exile after 70 C.E.

43. On the status of Ioannina, cf. study by Bees (cited in note 41); Ostrogorsky, *History,* pp. 443–44. On the Serbian advances under Uroš II Milutin (1282–1321), cf. *CMH,* IV, part I, 533–34; and for the Catalans. ibid., pp. 348–49.

44. Starr, *Romania,* p. 61, note 44.

promulgation of this chrysobull and, perhaps, stems even from the last days of the Despotate of Epiros. Moreover, it seems unlikely that these Jews were included in the rather sweeping statement of the chrysobull of 1319. Rather, it seems that at some point in the early fourteenth century, or even earlier, the descendants of the three Jews, if not their fathers, prior to the issuance of this chrysobull, were assigned as property to the Church of Ioannina.[45] Hence these two chrysobulls suggest at least two, if not three, different statuses among the Jews of Ioannina in the first quarter of the fourteenth century: (1) that of three Jewish families as "possessions" of the Church of Ioannina; (2) a group of recent immigrants to the city who enjoyed some special prerogatives; and (3) the veteran Jewish community who may not have been included in the definition *epoikoi*. The last group would have included the contemporaries of Namer, David, and Shemarya. Since this information is found in two imperial chrysobulls, it is apparent that the imperial government was the arbiter of their different statuses.

Ecclesiastical Attitudes

By the second half of the thirteenth century, Christian attitudes toward the Jews and their religion had undergone nearly 1,200 years of development. The postures that would appear during the last centuries of Byzantium reflect more the political vicissitudes of the church than any adjustment of this longstanding theological position. A few summary remarks may serve to point out its effect upon the Christian society of Byzantium.[46]

45. For a recent discussion of rural *paroikoi* in the fourteenth century, cf. A. Laiou-Thomadakis, *Peasant Society in the Late Byzantine Period* (Princeton, 1977), pp. 142–58. Her survey shows that the term was extremely fluid and that each case has to be studied against the local background. Does their status, then, conform to the conditions of urban *paroikoi*? The answer would seem to be in the affirmative if they lived in the city. See below, note 78.

46. The attitude of the church toward the Jews in its theological and social context has been the subject of scholarly investigation for over a century. The following works all contain references to the older literature: J. Parkes, *Conflict of the Church and the Synagogue* (London, 1934), with select bibliography and commentary on the sources. His thesis is valuable but somewhat overstated: while religious traditions contain the seeds of theological disdain, it is the political use to which these teachings are put that determines their historical impact; A. Lukyn Williams, *Adversus Judaeos. A Bird's-Eye View of Christian Apologiae until the Renaissance* (Cambridge, 1935); J. Juster, *Les Juifs dans l'empire romain: leur condition juridique, économique et sociale,* 2 vols (Paris, 1914); S. L. Guterman, *Religious Toleration and Persecution in Ancient Rome* (London, 1951), offers an interesting perspective on the legal position of Jews in the eastern Mediterranean as opposed to the status of their coreligionists in the western

The New Testament is the font of Christianity. Its ambivalent traditions toward the rival synagogue provided the justification for attacks against Judaism, as well as the theological underpinnings for the church's later defense of the Jews. Paul, of course, is the source for both. For him the new covenant (cf. Jeremiah 31) of faith in the Christ had replaced the old covenant with Abraham: circumcision of the heart for that of the flesh, love instead of the law. At the same time, he emphasized that a remnant would be saved through grace (Romans 9–11). Still, it was not difficult, during succeeding generations, for adherents of the New Israel to use the same biblical texts to strengthen their identity as the Jews had done to re-create theirs after the destruction of the Second Temple. Even after the final break between the two groups over the question of the Messiah (was it Jesus who would come again, or Bar Kokhba, who liberated Jerusalem from 132–35 ?), Christians continued to enjoy the veneration derived from the renowned antiquity of the Jews. The crisis engendered by the sack of Rome in 410 prompted Augustine's apologetic historico-theological book, *Civitas Dei,* to strengthen this connection, as a response to the pagan charge that the Christians had betrayed the gods.

With the victory of Christianity as, first, the preferred and then the official religion of the Roman Empire, the question of truth became an academic exercise to be refined by subsequent generations of theologians. Eusebius' two tracts, *Praeperatio Evangelica* (Judaism) and *Demonstratio Evangelica* (Christianity), served as the official statement of the new political theology of the Christian Roman Empire. Judaism was declared defeat-

---

Mediterranean under the republic and early empire; M. Simon, *Verus Israel: étude sur les relations entre Chrétiens et Juifs dans l'empire romain* (135–425) (Paris, 1948; 2d ed., 1964); H. Idris Bell, *Jews and Christians in Egypt* (London, 1924); A. Harnack, *The Mission and Expansion of Christianity in the First Three Centuries,* tr. James Moffatt (rev. ed.; New York, 1962); R. Wilde, *The Treatment of the Jews in the Greek Christian Writers of the First Three Centuries* (Washington, D.C., 1949).

Cf. Greek Orthodox–Jewish consultation in *GOTR,* vol. XXII, no. 4 (Spring 1977), especially essays by S. Siegel, "Judaism and Eastern Orthodoxy: Theological Reflections," pp. 63–69, T. Stylianopoulos, "New Testament Issues in Jewish-Christian Relations," pp. 70–79, and J. Agus, "Judaism and the New Testament, pp. 80–87. The development of Eastern Orthodoxy in its Byzantine and Greek phases, especially with reference to the Jews, has been examined in the same symposium by D. Constantelos, "Greek Orthodox Jewish Relations in Historical Perspective," pp. 6–16, and Zvi Ankori, "Greek Orthodox Jewish Relations in Historical Perspective—The Jewish View," pp. 17–57 (passim). Also cf. earlier surveys in Starr, *JBE,* and A. Sharf, *Byzantine Jewry from Justinian to the Fourth Crusade* (New York, 1971), and in general Baron, *SRHJ,* vols. II and III, passim, and notes.

ed, as were the other rivals of Christianity. Judaism alone, however, was never banned during those early centuries of struggle, and not until the changed circumstances of the seventh century would such an option be pursued by the state. Throughout the nine centuries preceding the Palaeologan era, church councils attempted to erect social barriers between Christians and Jews at the same time that they taught the victory of the true faith (Orthodoxy) over its errant and rejected mother. The efficacy of these traditions for subsequent ecclesiastical nomographers is shown by their appearance in later Byzantine codes (*infra*). Yet when an emperor (Leo III) went beyond persecuting the Jews and actually banned their faith, it was a church council (Nicaea II in 787) that called for the right of the crypto Jews to practice their ancestral religion as allowed by traditional Roman law.

Theology thus dictated that Judaism was an error and Judaizing a heresy, but Jews, though persecuted and second-class citizens, had to survive because their voluntary conversion to Christianity would presage the imminent arrival of the Messiah. It was a thin line to argue and an even harder one to practice. Still, throughout the history of the empire there are many recorded instances of individuals, both within the church and among the laity, who maintained tolerant attitudes toward Jews. Despite these singular cases, which perhaps were more common than historical sources record, an underlying social animosity toward Jews existed in the Byzantine world and was capable of bursting into open persecution when enflamed by internal stress or external pressures.

This theological tradition and concomitant social attitude toward the Jews and Judaism continued throughout the Palaeologan period. Yet it was modified by the physical and socio-economic fragmentation of the empire, as well as by the protection some Jews derived from their connections with either Latin or Muslim powers in the area. Not that such connection was any guarantee, as events in far-off Kaffa would show. Clearly, the hands of the emperor were tied under these circumstances. At the same time, there were other, more positive reasons for his nonpersecution of the Jews.

The Palaeologan church underwent several important changes, to the detriment of the Jewish position, when it came under the control of monks, whose world reflected a nonrational battle between Christ and the Devil—with the Jews as visible allies of the latter. In its attempt to establish both a dogma and a way of life, the church had seen any deviation from its orthodoxy as heresy, with the latter most effectively defined as "Judaizing." True, many of the condemned practices were derived from biblical prece-

Highland Park Public Library

dent, through study or through contact or exposure to the contemporary Jewish population. Also, newer heresies, such as Bogomil, based on dualistic influences, were best combated through the traditional arguments, forged over generations, against Jews. Thus heretics were called "Jews," whether or not Judaizing tendencies were present in their ideology or practice.

Also, the fourteenth century witnessed the victory of mystical tendencies in Orthodox Christianity through the absorption of Hesychasm into the church. Such a redirection of the organized religion of the empire—similar phenomena can be seen in the Roman Catholic, Muslim, and Jewish worlds—left no room for a dialogue with its perceived hereditary adversary. With the decline of empire, Orthodoxy turned inward to explore new spiritual avenues. In the worsening conditions of the age, polemics against the Jews were revived and sharpened as one means of coping with the rise of the new religious threat from a strong Roman Catholicism and a victorious Islam, which, between them, occupied ever more areas of the former Byzantine world.

In terms of an official statement of church policy toward the Jews, the responsum of Demetrios Khomatianos, the archbishop of Ochrida (1217–35), is perhaps the best introduction for the period after 1204. His remarks represent the attitude of the upper clergy, in its capacity as upholder of the imperial law, when the latter conformed to the proper interpretation of church traditions. When the archbishop (and later patriarch of the Epirote Empire) was asked about the proper status of Armenians in a Christian empire, he broadened his reply to present his interpretation of the official imperial policy toward the three *bêtes-noires* of the Orthodox world: Jews, Armenians, and Muslims. They were permitted to live in Christian lands; however, their quarters were to be segregated to prevent contamination of the Orthodox population through exposure to their heretical practices. Moreover, they should not be allowed more freedom than was necessary for their existence, so that they might be enticed to convert to the majority religion (**18**).

About a century later, Matthew Blastares prepared his *Syntagma,* an encyclopedia of earlier secular and ecclesiastical rulings which the monk considered applicable to fourteenth-century Byzantine society. The references to the Jews in the *Syntagma* are therefore reflective of the contemporary attitude of the church toward Jews and the problem of Judaizing heresies.

The *Syntagma* is arranged alphabetically (57). Such an arrangement, not uncommon to the area, has the advantage of combining in one section the essential rulings of both church and state on a given subject.[47] Chapter IV of the letter *I,* for "Ioudaios," contains the basic material referring to Jews that Matthew Blastares considered particularly relevant for his contemporaries. In it, Christians are warned to avoid social and religious contact with Jews; they may not celebrate festivals with them or even inadvertently show respect to their traditions by, for example, avoiding work on the Sabbath. Prohibited, too, are communal bathing, intermarriage, and the exchange of gifts (the latter probably a reference to the Jewish custom of exchanging gifts during Purim). In compliance with secular law, the church is forbidden to convert a fugitive Jew who seeks the protection of the church to escape punishment or, even, his responsibilities. The converse, however, was for obviously different reasons: Jews are forbidden to circumcise a Christian catechumen.

So far, Blastares was repeating Orthodox traditions. In the middle of this chapter, interestingly enough, appears a long excursus on the Orthodox attitude toward the unleavened bread (*azyma*), which was a major area of disagreement with the Latin church. To Blastares, the Latin use of unleavened bread reflected Judaizing tendencies. Judaizing heresies are also mentioned in the *Syntagma* (all connected with the Passover and Easter celebrations), but it is not known if these heresies still existed in the fourteenth century. Byzantine religious texts continually recite the litany of contemporary and historical heresies.[48] This excursus however, is a warning to the Orthodox population: Just as you are to avoid Jews, you must also avoid cultural influences that may subtly challenge your faith.

Both Khomatianos and Blastares subsume the theological position to the more obvious problem of social contact, which posed the immediate danger of personal and intellectual influence. Behind these attempts to erect barriers between the Jewish and Christian subjects of the empire was a

47. Compare the treatise of the twelfth-century Byzantine Karaite sage Judah Hadassi, *Eshkol ha-Kofer* (Gozlow, 1836), which contains a summary of the biblical laws with a Karaite interpretation, arranged alphabetically within a framework of ten chapters, one for each commandment.

48. Bearing in mind the caveat voiced by students of Byzantine law that the law need not reflect the contemporary situation, we should remember that the *Syntagma* was widely used by the Orthodox in the Balkans during the succeeding centuries (57n). Therefore its attitude toward the Jews forms one element of the later religious and social attitude of East European Christian society toward the Jews in its midst.

fear that the presence of a well-organized Jewish community, flourishing despite restrictions, would present a viable alternative to the claims of the Orthodox church. Moreover, the samé community argued its position from the very font of Scriptures, which made it a much greater intellectual danger than even the religious success of Islam, which had attracted many converts from the defeated Christian population.[49] It may even be that the church projected its fears vis-à-vis Islam against the background of its traditional polemic with the Jews (*infra*), especially in later periods when it was clearly on the defensive. Clearly, social barriers, as well as visible signs of degradation, were regarded as the best protection for the unsophisticated masses.

Another facet of the paternalistic attitude of the higher clergy can be seen in the tradition of literary debate with Judaism. Reflecting a variety of purposes, this activity continued throughout the Palaeologan period—indeed, well into the Ottoman period and even beyond.[50]

The thirteenth-century example of a literary polemic, couched in terms of a dialogue, comes from the pen of Nikolaos of Otranto. Born in Otranto in the middle of the twelfth century, Nikolaos became a monk at Casole, where he took the name of Nektarios, and remained its abbot until his death in 1235. The role of Nikolaos in the early thirteenth-century Latin–Orthodox debate is still not fixed. Further study of his *Discourse against the Jews* and his treatises against the Latins is a *desideratum*.[51] It is of particular interest to note, especially in the context of the present discussion, that Nikolaos' *Discourse against the Jews* is his longest work. Such a phenomenon is not unique in the ecclesiastical literature of the thirteenth through the fifteenth century. While the text, unfortunately, still remains in manuscript, a recent description of its seven arguments enables us to gain some insight into its contents (17).

The *Discourse* seems to have been a result of confrontations Nikolaos had with Jews of his home town (Otranto) in the aftermath of his first trip to Greece. The subjects they discussed pertained to the perennially debated problems of Trinity, Christology, Messianism, the two natures of Christ,

49. Cf. Sp. Vryonis, *The Decline of Medieval Hellenism in Asia Minor and the Process of Islamization from the Eleventh through the Fifteenth Century* (Berkeley, 1971), passim.

50. Cf. Bowman, "Two Late Byzantine Dialogues with the Jews," *GOTR*, XXV (1980), 83–93.

51. Cf. comments by M. Hoeck and R. T. Loenertz, *Nikolaos-Nektarios von Otranto Abt. von Casole* (Rome, 1965), pp. 66–68.

the Virginity of Mary, and Resurrection. While the arguments of Nikolaos add nothing new to the standard subjects of the Jewish–Christian debate, the *Discourse* possibly sheds a little light on Orthodox–Jewish relations during the early thirteenth century. The author traveled to a number of Byzantine centers, including Constantinople, Thessalonica, and Thebes, two of which (at least) harbored large and influential Jewish communities.[52] Though Nikolaos may have been concerned at the outset of his journey with the problems of Latin influence on the Byzantine church, he found it necessary to devote great efforts to refute the arguments so ably presented by the Jews in Otranto after his return from Greece.[53]

Why, we may ask, did Nikolaos engage in such debate, which necessitated his *Discourse?* It may be that only a literary format was chosen and that no actual debate took place; this style, after all, is well known in fourteenth- and fifteenth-century Byzantium. Be that as it may, there seems to be little doubt that the dialogues he penned reflected others that had been repeated many times during his travels in Byzantium. Thus, we may suggest, his contacts with Byzantine Jews necessitated a formal summary and refutation of Jewish arguments against the Orthodox position. His debating "opponent," however, was the Jewish community of Otranto, represented by a certain Jacob.[54] Despite the proximity of Latins and Orthodox in southern Italy, the Jews were seen by Nikolaos as a more immediate challenge, if not merely a more convenient foil.

Later generations of Byzantine ecclesiastics continued to sharpen their pens and their arguments with polemics against Judaism. Through a misidentification, scholars for some time thought there was a Patriarch of Jerusalem, named Thaddeus Pelusiotes, who wrote a tract against the Jews at the end of the thirteenth century.[55] It appears, however, that the tract

52. According to Beck (*Kirche,* pp. 669–70), he accompanied Cardinal Benedict. For the comments of Benjamin of Tudela on these cities, see below, part II, exc. A.

53. Cf. Hoeck and Leonertz, *Nikolaos-Nektarios von Otranto,* pp. 82–88, suggesting that he apparently knew enough Hebrew to support some of his arguments.

54. "Here [Otranto] are about 500 Jews at the head of them being R. Menahem, R. Caleb, R. Meir, and R. Mali," in Adler's edition, pp. 9–10.

55. Gesner-Simler (*Bibliotheca* [Tiguri, 1574], p. 644) was the first to suggest this, based on the citation in *Bibliotheca universalis* (1545): "Thaddaei Pelusiensis libra contra Iudaeos; manusc. in biblioth. Henrici Memmii." S. G. Mercati ("Il trattato contro i Giudei di Taddeo Pelusiota e una falsificazione di Constantino Paleocappa," *Bessarion,* 39 [1923], 8–14) lists several modern scholars who repeated the error. G. Bardy ("Thadée de Péluse adversus Iudaeos," *Revue dell'Orient Chrétien,* series 3, II [1920–21], 280–87) argued that the tract in question was plagiarized from the chronicle of George the Monk.

was written by Matthew Blastares (**54**) and ascribed to the fictional Thaddeus by the well-known scribe and forger Constantine Paleocappa in the sixteenth century.[56] Matthew Blastares is better known as the author of the *Syntagma,* written about 1335.

The fourteenth century produced a number of other tracts against the Jews. These were followed in the fifteenth century by several "debates." Though these treatises continue the tradition of Nikolaos of Otranto and others, most of them appear to be literary theological exercises rather than records of actual confrontations. The *Dialogue against the Jews* (**46**), for example, of Andronikos Palaiologos, the nephew of the emperor Andronikos II, may be an indirect result of the letter that had been sent by Patriarch Athanasios to the emperor, instructing him to provide a Christian education for his nephews (**34a**). Andronikos was not the only noble to pen such essays. Toward the middle of the fourteenth century, John VI Kantakouzenos, having retired to a monastery after his stormy political career, wrote a treatise against Judaism, in nine chapters, under his monastic name John Christodoulos (**78**). A decade or so later, the Metropolitan of Nicaea, Theophanes III, produced his *magnum opus,* an "apology against the Jews" (**97**). One of his major arguments, following a long Christian tradition, was that modern Judaism (i.e., of the fourteenth century) was no longer related to ancient Judaism.[57] As early as the fourth century, Eusebius of Caesarea had argued that the Old Testament was the *praeperatio* while the New Testament was the *demonstratio evangelica,* and that Christians had inherited the spiritual legacy of Ancient Israel in the flesh and had become the New Israel in spirit.[58] Theophanes, incidentally, had been a supporter of John Kantakuzenos in the Palamite controversy, and this may well have been one reason for his tract.[59]

56. Mercati, "Il trattato," pp. 12f: "Nè questa è la falsificazione che grava sulla coscienza de Constantino Paleocappa . . . . E propriamente fittizo è *Thaddaîos Pēlusiótēs,* scrittore, che non è mai esistito, mentre invece è estitito un *Matthaios hieromónachos*. . . . Il falsario ha dunque camminato sulla falsariga dell' inizio del trattato di Matteo Blastares. . . . L'appelativo *hieromónachos* gli sembrò forse troppo meschino per eccitare l'appetitio dei bibliofili!" Summary in Beck, *Kirche,* pp. 688–89.

57. Beck, *Kirche,* p. 746.

58. In a sermon given at the beginning of the fourteenth century, the patriarch Athanasios repeated the idea that God had substituted the Christian people for old Israel; cf. Laurent, *Actes des patriarches,* no. 1692, pp. 479–82. The theme, of course, is embedded in Christian thought; cf. Simon, *Verus Israel,* chap. III.

59. Beck, *Kirche,* p. 746.

Gennadios Scholarios, writing nearly a century later, knew the works of Theophanes.[60] Since one of Gennadios' well-known passages examines the question of nationality, one may wonder whether his casuistic attempts to distinguish between a Jew by religion and a Judean—that is, an individual's accidental birth in Judea—were a reflection of the ideas he received from Eusebius via Theophanes or whether they were aimed at his own flock, still shaken by the loss of independence and prestige after 1453 (**145**). More likely, the patriarch's insistence on a clear distinction between a *Ioudaios* born in Judea and a *Ioudaios* by religion is a reflection of both his own and his flock's disoriented state. Before 1453, Gennadios would not have hesitated to identify himself as a *Romaios,* an Orthodox Christian citizen of the Roman Empire whose capital was Constantinople. After 1453, however, Gennadios was a Christian subject of an Ottoman sultanate and was permitted only those privileges accorded a *zimmi,* a member of a protected religion. Therefore he had to redefine his identity both for himself and for the Christians he led, and for this reason he wavered between the designation "Hellene," one who was non-Turkish speaking, and "Christian," that is, a non-Muslim.

A similar case may be made for another tract, which ostensibly stems from the eve of the conquest of Constantinople, that purports to record the debate between a Jew and the emperor John VIII (**133**). Overcome by the theological prowess of his adversaries, the Jew converted, thus providing this sad reign with its only "momentous conquest."[61] Such debates were not uncommon, especially in a society as theologically oriented as that of the Palaiologoi. Yet, though not implausible, it is questionable whether this debate took place. The text is found in the *Chronicon Maius* of Makarios Melissenos, a lengthy work which was produced in 1573–75. Though based upon the shorter *Chronicon Minus* of George Sphrantzes, modern scholars have ascribed the additional material to Makarios himself. Since the debate between Xenos and John VIII occurs only in the *Maius,* it belongs more to the history of the sixteenth century (with the valuable light it sheds on Greek attitudes and life during this period) than to the last decade of Byzantium (**133n**).

60. Ibid.; compare Theophanes' argument with that presented earlier by Nikephoras Blemmydes (*Epitome Logica, MPG,* 142, col. 753). It would be interesting to know if the philosopher included contemporary Jewry in his definition of τὸ γένος τῶν Ἰουδαίων.

61. The phrase is Edward Gibbon's, from *The Decline and Fall of the Roman Empire,* ed. J. B. Bury (London, 1902), VII, 99; cited by Starr, *Romania,* p. 28.

Thus the two tractates that we possess from the early years of Ottoman rule, though cast in the form of dialogues, are more representative of a literary genre whose goal was to provide answers or polemical frameworks for the faithful against inner doubts or the arguments of Jews.[62] The lower clergy, on the other hand, was not marked by such intellectual tolerance, based as it was upon a longstanding legal and theological tradition. Its world was peopled by demons and heretics; its orthodoxy had to be defended at all costs and in all ways against the inroads of the heterodox. To it, the Jews were still deicides, as defined by church traditions. At the beginning of the fourteenth century, the Patriarch Athanasios recalled his monastic training by referring to the Jews as "τὴν θεοκτόνον συναγώγην" (**33**).

Though Jews were liable to salvation through conversion, they were suspected of potential acts of blasphemy. Such, at least, is the impression one gets from the continued popularity of stories of icon desecration in the pilgrim literature of the period, some of which included the theme of the bleeding icon of Christ, victim of a Jew's knife (**1**). This theme was considerably embellished during succeeding generations (**101**), with one version identifying the culprit as a chess-playing Jew (**103**). The legend of the Jewish moneylender, which in its seventh-century form praised the Jew's actions, in this period took on the negative dimensions of the later Shylock tradition.[63] Its Eastern version, moreover, still appeared within the framework of the older accusation (**102**). On the other hand, the eschatological expectations of the masses continued to assume a mass conversion of Jews to Christianity as a prelude to salvation. Though Jews are referred to in a recorded church service in the traditional way, "accursed," they could benefit from divine guidance to baptism, as opposed to other non-Christians who would be converted by the sword (**3**). One wonders to what extent these monastic traditions and folklore accounts, circulating primarily in Constantinople, influenced visiting ecclesiastics and their coreligionists at home, as well as the Orthodox urban neighbors of Jews.[64] Unfortunately,

62. Cf. comments in author's "Two Late Byzantine Dialogues with the Jews."

63. Cf. comments by B. N. Nelson and J. Starr, "The Legend of the Divine Surety and the Jewish Moneylender," *Annuaire du l'Institut de Philologie et d'Histoire Orientales,* 1 (1932–33), 289–338.

64. In 1480 a story similar to that in documents 1 and 91 was told to an anonymous pilgrim in Venice; cf. *Le voyage de la Saincte Cyté de Hierusalem,* ed. Ch. Scheffer (*Recueil de voyages et de documents pour servir à l'histoire de la géographie depuis le XIIIe jusqu'à la fin du XVIe siècle* [Paris, 1882], 2: 17). See below (note 70), studies of Halperin and Ettinger on the Byzantine anti-Jewish heritage in Russia.

our information on popular attitudes toward Jews is extremely limited. The Corfu custom of stoning Jews during Easter may have been only local.[65] Clearly, however, it was part of a general tradition of degradation, as was the text of the Cyprus passion play.[66]

All Byzantine territories, no matter how fragmented politically and administratively, spoke in one voice insofar as ecclesiastical attitudes toward the Jews were concerned. The nonpolemical tone which was found among the higher clergy in the thirteenth century became decidedly antagonistic in the fourteenth. Whereas previously it was in the main the voice of the intellectual that commented on Jews and Judaism, during the reign of Andronikos II the monks, representing the lower clergy and more popular traditions, gained control of the offices of the church, and especially the patriarchate. Considering themselves officially, and not only morally, the guardians of Orthodoxy, their attacks on Jews appeared in their correspondence, tractates, and sermons. Thus in his letter to the emperor Andronikos II, Maximus Planudes castigated him on several grounds. (The monk's animosity toward the Jewish tanners was based not only on the general medieval dislike for their malodorous and polluting occupation, but also their "unpleasantness of belief" [**31**].) What really annoyed Planudes was the location of the synagogue on former church grounds and assignment of the whole area to Jews as their living and working quarter. In the absence of other information pertaining to this particular church, we can only assume that it had been abandoned, along with most of the quarter. Perhaps this church formed part of a small monastic or imperial complex which, though in ruins, provided a clearly delineated area within which to house the tanners.[67]

The Patriarch Athanasios gives us, from his perspective, an economic and religious picture of heretics at the beginning of the fourteenth century. In his letter to the basileus, Athanasios, while hinting at the increased economic role of Jews, Armenians, and Muslims in Constantinople, is more concerned with the religious aspects of their presence (**33**). Thus he castigates Andronikos for allowing the Armenians to bribe their way through the higher levels of the Byzantine bureaucracy, for allowing the

65. Cecil Roth, "The Eastertide Stoning of the Jews and Its Liturgical Echoes," *JQR*, ns, XXXV (1945), 361–70.

66. *The Cyprus Passion Cycle*, ed. A. C. Mahr (Notre Dame, Ind., 1947), and comments by Starr, *Romania*, p. 45 and note 27.

67. See below, chap. 2, note 10 and text.

Muslims their own mosques in the capital, and for permitting "the deicidal synagogue" to wield great influence through the services of one Kokalas.[68] The zeal of this monk-turned-patriarch is further evidenced in two other letters written about the same time: the aforementioned letter to the emperor, instructing him on providing a Christian education for his nephews, the other to the monastery of Chora (**34a, 34b**).

Athanasios took other opportunities to convey his displeasure at the overt presence of Jews in the capital. His remark that even a Jew could feel pity at witnessing the persecution of Byzantines is, to be sure, not very flattering but not particularly damning; the same imagery is used by a middle-class intellectual in Thessalonica in the following generation (**34c, 64**). However, his invective against Jewish doctors is matched only by that of Joseph Bryennios several generations later (**35, 79**).

The attacks of Athanasios, then, reflect his religious background and an economic reality, the latter perhaps not as accurate as it could have been since he ignores the role of the Venetians in this context. Still, a religion-oriented attack is to be expected from a zealous monk of any period. At the same time, his socio-economic comments allow us an insight into the impact of the Jewish presence in the capital during the second generation of Palaeologan rule. In sum, the observations of our witness, albeit hostile, show that there was some Jewish influence at the court of Andronikos, especially through the emperor's official, Kokalas; that enough Christians were indebted to Jews to raise the ire of the patriarch; that the Jews openly expressed their religious views; and that Jewish doctors also served the Christian community. Even if we allow for exaggeration in the patriarch's rhetoric, we have evidence of a well-established Jewish community.

This continued antagonism toward Jews and Judaism is but one indication that in the Nicaean and Palaeologan periods the *new* archenemy and heretic, the Latin church, had not entirely displaced the old sense of hostility toward Jews, Armenians, and Muslims. It is probably not coincidental that, a generation after the patriarch Athanasios voiced his doubts about

68. See *The Correspondence of Athanasius I Patriarch of Constantinople,* ed. and tr. Alice-Mary Talbot ([Washington, D.C., 1975], p. 349), for a possible identification of this individual as the father-in-law of the *protovestarius* Andronikos Palaiologos, nephew of Andronikos II; his first name may have been George (*pace,* Hopf; *Chroniques Gréco-romaines,* p. 529). If he is the same one mentioned in the letter, we have a situation whereby the bride's father and the groom's uncle are both pro-Jewish (in terms of their policy) while the groom and his patriarch resort to polemics against the Jews—surely not a situation conducive to household peace. In the heresy trial of Chionios in 1336 (*MM,* I, 177), we find a Γεωργίος Κωκαλᾶ Κρίτος τοῦ Θεοφρουρήτου Φωσάτου τοῦ Σεναχήρειμ.

exposing the Orthodox to Jewish influence, the capital found itself judging a Thessalonican scandal involving a certain Chionios and his brothers who were accused of Judaizing. Though the charge was quickly proved spurious and the defendants were acquitted, it is important to note the nature of the charge: Judaizing. From the account, it is clear that the accusation was made in order to bring Chionios before an imperial court because of his actions and statements in behalf of the harassed Jews of Thessalonica. By coming to their aid, he was seen by his detractors to be sympathetic to Judaism. Therefore, their personal animosity was best expressed in theological terms, which guaranteed that the subsequent charge would be sufficient to warrant a full trial in the capital rather than a local disciplinary action.[69] The suspicions raised during this trial were perhaps more applicable to other areas of the Orthodox world, namely, those no longer subject to the secular arm of the emperor.

The Chionios affair was only one aspect of the situation brought about by the shifting political constellations in the fourteenth century, in which the condition of the Jew was constantly improving. In Byzantium proper, the economic position of Jews changed markedly for the better under the sponsorship of the imperial government; their influence perhaps reached the high levels of government circles, and various officials were accused of succumbing to their power. In the Bulgarian state, a welcome was about to be extended to Jewish immigrants, possibly through the influence of Theodora, the Jewish wife of John Alexander (1331–65) (**76**). The subsequent impact of Jews upon that society was so suspect that they were accused of fostering the revival of heresy there and in the neighboring Serbian territories. This charge eventually led to the condemnation of converts to Judaism by the Council of Trnovo in 1360. Other ecclesiastical pressure there seems to have resulted in the execution of several Jewish leaders.[70]

69. See below, chap. 2, "Thessalonica."

70. On Theodora, see Romanes, *Israel be-Togarmah,* p. 6; C. Jirecek, *Geschichte der Bulgaren* (Prague, 1876), p. 312; Krauss, *Studien,* p. 68; H. Kechales, *Koroth Yehudei Bulgaria* (Tel Aviv, 1971), I: 78ff; on the Serbian Judaizers, see J. Meyendorff, "Grecs, Turcs et Juifs en Asie Mineure au XIVe siècle," *Polychordia,* pp. 211–17. The daughter of Theodora and John Alexander was Tamar, later married to Murat I, and the historical tradition of a Jewess (according to Jewish law, she would be considered such) in the sultan's harem may be a source for the legend that Mehmet II, son of Murat II, was born of a Jewish mother. Cf. F. Babinger, *Mehmed the Conqueror and His Time* (Princeton, 1978), pp. 11f, where he mentions a Stella (Estella = Esther), who was possibly an Italian Jewess.

B. Krekić ("The Role of the Jews in Dubrovnik," *Viator,* 4 [1973], 266f) suggests that three leaders of the Jews were executed through these actions of the church. However, it seems that one was saved by converting, the second was killed by a mob, and only the third was

The widespread toleration for Jews in the fourteenth century by the secular rulers of the Balkans, whether Byzantine, Bulgarian, or Ottoman, can be seen through the spread of Jewish settlements (*infra*) and, as well, by the influence of Jews in the economic and religious spheres. The extent of this toleration is further evidenced by the futile attempts of the various Orthodox churches to curb the settlements themselves or the spread of various Judaizing heresies. The church, to be sure, was more concerned during this period by the potential threat of Roman Catholics, Armenians, and the continuing heresy of the Bogomils, rather than by Jews. That this attitude toward Jews was partly due to the self-interest of the rulers is evident from the practices of Andronikos II (*supra*) and the marital relations of John Alexander. It may also, in part, have been due to the well-known toleration of Jews in the powerful neighboring Ottoman state.

---

executed; see discussion of the Bulgarian sources in D. Obolensky, *The Bogomils* (Middlesex, 1948; reprint, 1972), pp. 262ff and 258f; cf. also Kechales, ibid., pp. 84ff.

A similar situation occurred at the end of the next century in Russia, where Judaizing tendencies had become so widespread that many of the nobility, as well as some members of the royal family, were counted among its adherents. Novgorod was "cleansed" and the sect extirpated in a Russian bloodbath. Soon afterward, the rulers enacted that henceforth no Jews were permitted to set foot in Russia upon penalty of death. On the Russian Judaizers, see G. Vernadsky, *Russia at the Dawn of the Modern Age* (New Haven and London, 1959), index s.v. "Heresy of the Judaizers"; for a sixteenth-century note of the ban of Jews in Russia, see "Le Pélerinage du Marchand Basile Posniakov aux saints lieux de l'orient (1558–1561)" in Khitrowo, *Itinéraires russes en Orient* (Geneva, 1889), p. 290, where Poliakov informs the patriarch of Alexandria that "n'ont pas de demeure dans le royaume de notre souverain; il a même defendu le commerce aux Juifs & leur a fermé l'entrée de son territoire." By comparison, Poland was a major center of Jewish settlement, undergoing a golden age of its own. For a vivid look at Russian society in this period, see L. E. Berry and R. O. Crummey, eds., *Rude & Barbarous Kingdom: Russia in the Accounts of Sixteenth-Century English Voyagers* (Madison, 1968).

The whole question has been reviewed (with extensive bibliography) by Charles Halperin in "Judaizers and the Image of the Jew in Medieval Russia: A Polemic Revisited and a Question Posed," *Canadian-American Slavic Studies,* 9:2 (Summer 1975), 141–55. A fundamental study (unknown to Halperin) is S. Ettinger, "The Muskovite State and Its Attitude towards the Jews," (Hebrew) *Zion,* XVIII (1953), 138–66; pages 159–68 deal with the Judaizing heresy against the background of political, social, and economic tensions within Muscovite society at the end of the fifteenth century. See also Ettinger's further study, "Jewish Influence on the Religious Ferment in Eastern Europe at the End of the Fifteenth Century," (Hebrew) *Y. F. Baer Jubilee Volume* (Jerusalem, 1960), pp. 228–47.

Kaleb Afendopoulo, the late fifteenth- and early sixteenth-century Karaite savant, wrote two contemporary elegies on the expulsion of Jews from various countries, including Russia: ארצות לועזים וארצות רוסיא וליטבא; cf. *Catalogue of the Hebrew MSS. in the Collection of Elkan Nathan Adler* (Cambridge, 1921), p. 74, #911; colophon published by Neubauer, *Bodleian,* II, #2751, dated 1494.

Taxation

A question that has been asked by historians of Byzantine Jewry for the past fifty years is whether they were subjected to a special taxation.[71] The documents that support an argument for or against such taxation for the period prior to 1204 are too sparse for a definite conclusion.[72] The only unequivocally Jewish tax was the *aurum coronarium*. This tax was imposed in the second quarter of the fifth century and was derived from the annual shekel that Jews of the Roman Empire sent to support the Patriarch *tōn Iudaiōn* in Palestine. In 425 the incumbent, Gamliel VI, died without a direct heir; four years later, Theodosius II recognized the vacancy as permanent, thus effectively abolishing the office. The shekel payment was diverted to the imperial treasury and became a regular tax. There is no indication, from any source, how long this payment continued.

On the basis of a handful of fragmentary references and allusions from the Middle Byzantine period, three theories have been advanced: (1) that the Jews paid one special tax, in lieu of the regular taxes that were levied upon the Christian population; (2) that they paid a derogatory "nuisance" tax in addition to the regular taxes that were levied upon the Christian population; and (3) that the Jews paid no special tax.[73] For the Paleologan

71. The extent of the bibliography is only one indication of the lack of agreement: F. Dölger, *Beiträge zur Geschichte der byzantinischer Finanzverwaltung besonders des 10. und 11. Jahrhunderts* (Leipzig and Berlin, 1927); A. Andreades, "Deux livres récents sur les finances byzantines," *BZ,* XXXVIII (1929), 287–333 (reprinted in his *Oeuvres,* I, 587–90); idem, "Les Juifs et le fisc dans l'empire byzantine," *Mélanges Charles Diehl* (Paris, 1930), I, 7–29 (= *Oeuvres,* I, 629–59); Dölger, in *BZ,* XXXIII (1931), 453–54; G. Ostrogorsky, in *Seminarium Kondakovianum,* V (1932), 319–21; Dölger, "Die Frage der Judensteuer in Byzance," *Viertel-jahrschrift für Sozial- und Wirtschaftsgeschichte,* XXVI (1933), 1–24 (reprinted in *Paraspora,* pp. 358–83); Andreades, "The Jews in the Byzantine Empire," *Economic History,* III (1934), 1–23; Starr, *JBE;* Dölger, in *BZ,* XL (1941), 291ff; P. Charanis, "The Jews in the Byzantine Empire under the first Palaeologi," *Speculum,* XXII (1947), 75–77; Starr, *Romania*; idem, "The Status of the Jewries of the Levant after the Fourth Crusade," *Actes VI*ᵉ *Cong. Intern. Etudes Byzantines* (Paris, 1950), I, 199–204; Ankori, *Karaites,* pp. 81–84; Sima Ćirković, "The Jewish Tribute in Byzantine Regions," (Serbian) *Zbornik Radova,* 4 (1957), 141–47 (my thanks to Mrs. Mateja Matejic for her translation of this article for me); Ph. Argenti, "The Jewish Community in Chios during the Eleventh Century," *Polychronion,* pp. 39–68 (= *The Religious Minorities of Chios,* pp. 63–92); A. Sharf, *Byzantine Jewry,* chap. XI.

72. Ankori, *Karaites,* pp. 182–84; Baron, *SRHJ,* III, 190–92 and 321f (notes).

73. Starr (*Romania,* pp. 111f) argues that it was a local and occasional imposition: Sharf follows this suggestion (*Byzantine Jewry,* p. 198); Dölger and Andreades accept a derogatory additional tax; Charanis and Cirkovic accept a special Jewish tax, the latter widespread (see his list, p. 145); Ostrogorsky denied a special tax, as did Starr originally. See also document 55n. Cf. Sharf, *Byzantine Jewry,* chap. 11, especially note 7 and references cited.

period, the documentation is somewhat more extensive, but it is doubtful whether it is more conclusive.[74]

Several imperial texts from the fourteenth century cast light upon the problem of Jewish taxation during the Palaeologan period. At the same time, they raise more questions than they answer. A case in point is the chrysobull of 1333, in which Andronikos III Palaiologos awarded a certain monk the custody of the monastery of Ostrine near Serres in Macedonia (**55**). Revenues to support the monastery were allocated from neighboring areas and also from imperial properties within the *kastro* of Zichna. Among the latter was a sum due the imperial fisc from Jews who resided *within* the fort.

This document has a bearing on the debate over the existence of a special Jewish tax during the Palaeologan period. All scholars concerned with the problem of a Jewish tax *before* 1204 cite this text as proof of a Jewish tax under the Palaiologoi and, by extension, of such a tax before 1204 as well (**55n**). The phrase τὰ ἀπαιτούμενα χάριν τέλους ἐτησίως shows that the 20 hyperpera were the total (?) funds which had earlier been paid by the Jews of Zichna to the imperial fisc and were later awarded to the monastery of Ostrine. Were these 20 hyperpera indeed a tax, as has been the accepted view? Perhaps they constituted the annual rent paid by Jews for the houses they occupied within the fort?

Much depends on our interpretation of the term *telos*. It has been pointed out that *telos* includes several types of payments, *viz.*, annual rent for a house and also the annual tax of a monastery to its diocese.[75] The ambiguity inherent in the term, apparent in the variety of definitions that can be attributed to *telos,* makes it difficult to stress, as did Andreades and other scholars, that this document represents the strongest argument for the existence of a Jewish tax in the Palaeologan period (**55n**). It was normal for the Byzantine government to allocate its income from individuals, villages, and direct and indirect taxation to various ecclesiastical institutions, public officials, and private individuals.[76] Therefore, before we can assess the meaning of this document within the present discussion, we

74. Starr claimed that Jews paid a special tax before 641 and after 1204 (*JBE,* pp. 11–17). The first part is accepted by all scholars, based on the *aurum coronarium* (but how late was that continued?); the second is more debatable.

75. Ćirković, "Jewish Tribute," p. 144. For another instance of *telos* as rent, see below, document 130.

76. Laiou, *Peasant Society,* p. 143 and passim.

must know whether there were other Jews in Zichna, besides the unknown number who resided in the *kastro,* who owned the property on which they lived, and their status prior to the issuance of this chrysobull. (Parenthetically, we should note that their settlement within the *kastro* most likely reflected imperial policy [*supra*].) Since this is the only document we possess on the Jews of Byzantine Zichna, we have to admit the equal likelihood that the imperial government assigned to the monastery of Ostrine the income it derived from a special tax upon the Jews of the *kastro*—or, more simply, that this money represented rents from imperial properties occupied by (some of ?) the Jewish community.[77]

The problem is complicated by the mention of these Jews during the subsequent Serbian period. In 1345, Stephan Dušan, having occupied Serres, was requested by the monks of Saint John Prodromos at Menoikeion to renew their privileges and possessions (**68**). Among these possessions were the Jews of Zichna. The annual payment of 20 hyperpera, assessed in 1333, is not mentioned in Dušan's chrysobull; however, the Jews who resided within Zichna are enumerated as "possessions" of the monastery. Were these the same Jews who were mentioned in 1333? If so, we might further inquire whether this "possession" by the monks of St. John Prodromos entailed the same obligations as those of the descendants of Namer, David, and Shemarya, who were listed as possessions of the Church of Ioannina. The earlier chrysobull to the monk Jacob is clear in assigning some sort of income from the Jews to the monastery. May we assume that, in the eyes of the monastery, this annual (= perpetual?) income constituted "possession" and that the succeeding chrysobulls, issued by the Serbian rulers, reflected the monastery's claims, based on this interpretation?

No further clarification of this problem can be found in Dušan's chrysobull of 1348 to the monastery of Likousada in Thessaly (**75**). There a Jew, called Namer, successfully petitioned for his release from a dependent status vis-à-vis the monastery. The nature of the relationship, however, is not defined. In another chrysobull, issued by Dušan's successor, the emperor Stephan Uroš, to the Lavra of St. Athanasios on Mount Athos, the *telos* of the Jews near St. Constantine was awarded as revenue to the

77. Zakythinos (*Crise monétaire,* p. 87) does not discuss the implications of this text: "en 1333, Andronic céde au moine Jacques la somme de vingt hyperperes perçus annuellement sur les Juifs de Zichna."

monastery (**88**). Here, too, the rendering of the term *telos* as "rent" may be an alternative interpretation to a special tax on these Jews.

Such are the imperial texts from the fourteenth century that provide information on the problem of a Jewish tax in the Palaeologan empire. In the absence of additional material, the investigator must base his position on an interpretation of the term *telos* insofar as the question of taxation is concerned. Since the texts also speak of some kind of possession, as claimed by the ecclesiastical institutions and ratified by the imperial authority, it may be possible to speak of a "fiscal possession" wherein the ecclesiastical institution was guaranteed certain revenues from a Jewish community or individual Jew. In imperial charters to these churches and monasteries we *do* find Jews enumerated among their "possessions." This occurred in both the Byzantine chrysobulls and in the revised Serbian reissues of these charters (an indication of the well-known Byzantinization of the Serbian bureaucracy in the so-called Roman, i.e., Byzantine, part of that empire). But the term "possession" must be carefully defined. The phenomenon of church ownership, while rare with respect to Jews, was common with respect to the general Christian population. Individuals, as well as whole villages, were assigned to monasteries and churches for the upkeep of these institutions. But does the term, when applied to Jews, mean physical possession or only fiscal possession? And what restrictions, if any, did this status place upon the mobility of the Jews affected by it?

Clearly, the question of a special Jewish tax cannot be resolved from the imperial documents preserved in church archives, at least insofar as the Palaeologan period is concerned.[78] Unfortunately, because of the disap-

78. Ph. Argenti has analyzed the three chrysobulls, dated 1049, 1062, and 1079 (to the monastery of Nea Moni on Chios), which mention the *kephaleteíon* paid by 15 Jewish families ("The Jewish Community in Chios"). He argues that these Jews paid no taxes other than the *kephaleteíon* and, in addition, they were required to live on monastic property. The question is whether the *kephaleteíon* was "a Jewry tax." Argenti answers in the affirmative, "because a special Jewry-tax appears under different appelation throughout the mid and late Byzantine period" (p. 68). (Argenti's treatment of this material has been criticized by Jacoby in his extensive review of the latter's book [*BZ*, LXVI (1973), 108–11].) As we have seen, the latter supposition rests upon a false premise; there is no indisputable proof for a special tax during the Palaeologan period.

We may conclude from the Chios chrysobulls that the Jews of Chios were treated as a collective unit by the Byzantine government and that their resources, along with other fiscal units (viz., *paroikoi*, etc.), were assigned to the monastery as revenue sources for its support. Such a view sidesteps the question of a special Jewry tax which has dominated the histo-

pearance of the imperial archives we are forced to deal with such fragmentary and insufficient material.

Some further information is available from the aforementioned Latin translation of Andronikos' letter to Venice. In that letter occurs the phrase "*reddentes Imperio illud quod ordinatum est eis.*" Does this indicate that the Jews, *qua* Jews, paid a special tax to the empire? Within the context of the entire section (**37**), it appears that the phrase refers to a general tax (possibly in kind) on artisans who worked under imperial sponsorship (in this instance, the Jewish tanners of the Vlanka Quarter).[79]

Venetian texts, insofar as they deal with the situation within the empire, are apposite and perhaps shed some light on the general problem of taxation. A text from the early fifteenth century lists "the sums which the Venetian Jews pay annually to the Lord Bailo and to the Officials in the Curia" (**116**). During the two years that each Venetian Bailo held office, the Jews had to pay him certain sums in the form of gifts.[80] These sums included payments on the arrival of the new Bailo (every two years), on the election of the Jewish leaders (elected biannually), payments on various feast days, and certain other gifts. The importance of this document cannot be overestimated; it is the *only* detailed list of special taxes that Jews paid. True, these sums were applicable to Jews who lived in the capital and held a Venetian identity. No source indicates whether these taxes were a Venetian innovation or whether they paralleled a Byzantine situation for which no

riography of Byzantine Jewry for more than a generation (1930–70). Such a concern, it seems to me, was dictated as much by overreliance on earlier Roman and Western medieval Catholic parallels as by the apologetic trends of the historiography of the 1930s. Clearly, Jews were treated as a distinctive group for political, religious, and fiscal reasons, as were other groups within the empire. Some of the taxes they paid (all only ephemerally mentioned!) may have been assessed precisely because they were Jewish; some might have been punitive, as in Thessalonica; some may even have been discriminatory (although we have no unequivocal knowledge of any as such). A more proper approach to such questions would treat each occurrence within its local context and not extrapolate such data as a blanket indicator of the status of Jews in the empire. The situation in the Palaeologan empire, if not in earlier periods as well, was too complex for such a view to be valid, at least in light of the extant source material.

79. See above, note 31, and below, chap. 2, note 15.

80. In this case boots and brooms; in Dyrrachium, Jews had to supply a bolt of cloth. It would seem that these gifts were a tax in kind, assessed by the Venetian authorities over and above any other taxes the Jews had to pay them. They thus provide information on the economic pursuits of the Jews in these cities; however, they do not provide any information on the Byzantine situation, whether previous or contemporary. See following note.

confirmation is available.[81] It should be noted that the amount was minimal, less than 100 hyperpera a year. At the same time, it should be emphasized that the tax revenues raised from the Venetian Jews were used mainly for the support of ecclesiastical processions.

An important document from the last days of Byzantine rule in Constantinople, a Venetian complaint against Byzantine exactions from Venetian Jews, sheds further light on the taxation of Venetian Jews and Byzantine Jews. Evidently the imperial authorities, hard pressed for revenues, were not too careful to define the fiscal authorities under which the inhabitants of Constantinople lived, and thus aliens who had commercial immunity were occasionally harassed by officials. As a result of this infringement of Venetian commercial privileges, we have some indication of the indirect taxes to which Jews in Constantinople were subject, for example, providing certain undefined services (*angaria*), and various port duties (**134**). While the Venetian Jews had to pay more or less direct taxes to the Bailo (different from the exactions their coreligionists were assessed in Negroponte and other Venetian colonies), the imperial Jews were subject, as were the other citizens of Byzantium, to a series of indirect taxes. Indirect revenues to the imperial fisc had long before replaced direct taxation as the major source of the empire's income.[82] The Jews contributed their share of the imperial revenue, not only *qua* Jews but also as taxpaying subjects of the Byzantine Empire.

Though no record exists of a special Jewish tax in the capital under the Palaiologoi, as opposed to a regular set of payments by the Jews in the Venetian Quarter there, there is evidence that Jews paid a special tax in

81. Many students of Byzantine-Jewish history have been forced, by lack of contemporary sources, to use data from a later period or from areas no longer under Byzantine control. In this way, evidence from Venetian colonies has been interpreted as inheritance from the Byzantine period, the continuity of legal traditions under changing masters. We too have made use of this argument in some cases, but there is always the possibility that this has been overdone. One caveat to be emphasized from such an *argumentum ex traditione* is that after 1204 many Latin traditions were superimposed over Byzantine custom and law, producing a new mixture peculiar to thirteenth- and fourteenth-century Balkan history. Also, Latin animosity to the Jews was imported. Still, Andreades' argument ("The Jews," pp. 21–23) that Latin innovations created the hostility between Jews and Christians in the period after the Latin conquest notwithstanding, there was a long history in Byzantium of animosity, both literary and legal, toward Jews throughout the period before 1204.

82. A. Andreades, "Public Finances; Currency, Public Expenditures, Budget, Public Revenues," in Baynes and Moss, eds., *Byzantium: An Introduction to East Roman Civilization* (Oxford, 1948), pp. 81–82.

Thessalonica (**122**). The sum of 1,000 hyperpera that the Venetian Republic claimed from Jews after the purchase of the city bore more heavily on the Jews as the situation in the city deteriorated and the population decreased. Continued petitions to Venice reduced the sum to 800 hyperpera, but only in the event the city were besieged by the Ottomans. It is doubtful whether the Jews of Thessalonica could raise even that much under the circumstances. Was there a pre-Venetian precedent for such a tax? If so, it might answer the question of a Byzantine antecedent to the taxes leveled elsewhere upon Jews by the succeeding Venetian authorities.

It has long been known that in the eleventh century the Rabbanite Jews of Thessalonica were fined 1,000 hyperpera by the Byzantine authorities for their part in a local Rabbanite–Karaite feud.[83] It has been suggested that this assessment may be the basis for the fifteenth-century claim of the Venetians.[84] If this suggestion is correct, then we have evidence that a fine evolved into a local tax.[85] On the other hand, given the paucity of material pertaining to the Jews of Thessalonica from the eleventh to the fifteenth century, we would be on safer grounds were we to table the above suggestion. More likely, this fifteenth-century assessment had nothing to do with the earlier amount, and was only a coincidence. The amount parallels those that Jews were assessed in other Venetian colonies.

Thus the question of a uniform Jewish tax in the Palaeologan period may be answered in the negative. None of the later texts at our disposal mentions a specific Jewish tax.[86] Where the text is ambiguous, the translation of *telos* as "rent," instead of "tax," with the assignation of these rents for the support of the church, as some indirect taxes went for the support of officials, is equally possible. The Venetian document from 1411 shows that

83. Mann, *Texts and Studies,* I, 48–51; translated by Starr (*JBE,* no. 125, p. 183) as follows: "A violent enmity developed between us, and many disputes took place. They slandered the Rabbanites, and the congregation was fined almost a thousand IPRNIIR." Mann suggested reading the last term as *hyperperi*; cf. Ankori, *Karaites,* p. 330, note 77.

84. Ankori, *Karaites,* pp. 329–30.

85. Beginning in 1061 (Ankori, pp. 331–34), with repercussions later in the century (Sharf, *Byzantine Jewry,* pp. 196f). Ankori argues further (p. 335) that the incident is indicative of the "religious autonomy" of the Karaites "within the framework of the Jewish community," an autonomy which "was officially recognized by government and safeguarded by law."

86. The only tax which has been convincingly argued to be a "Jewish tax" is the *kephaleteíon* mentioned in the three chrysobulls to the monastery of Nea Moni on Chios; see above, note 78. This term appears in no other document, however, not even in pre-1204 texts, let alone any from the Palaeologan period. Cf. Argenti, *Religious Minorities of Chios,* pp. 63–92.

Jews contributed to the costs of the Venetian feast days (along with the rest of the colony?). On the other hand, Constantinopolitan Jewry was subject to a variety of indirect taxes or payments for the privilege of maintaining an autonomous communal organization. By the end of the period, some of these taxes were also assigned to individuals in lieu of salary. Because of the insufficient material at our disposal, more may not be said than that Jews, during the Late Byzantine period, appear not to have occupied a unique fiscal position within the empire. This supposition is supported, albeit in a negative way, by the lack of any statement on the subject in the *Hexabiblos* and the *Syntagma*.

TWO

JEWISH SETTLEMENTS

THE CONQUEST of Constantinople by the soldiers of the Fourth Crusade shattered the unity of the region for the next two and a half centuries. All Byzantine subjects, both Christian and Jewish, found themselves subject to different masters and different social systems. While some of the Byzantine subjects were incorporated into the small Greek states that succeeded in establishing themselves on the perimeters of the former empire, the continual warfare of the period threw their allegiances and identities into a constant state of flux. For the Jews, conditions were even more complicated since their position in Byzantine-held territories was subject to the restrictions that had been inherited from earlier centuries, while among the various Latin powers their situation reflected both local Christian animosity and attitudes imported from Western Europe. However, the status of Jews, relative to Christians, improved considerably in those areas conquered by the Turks. The general instability of the area during the period from the Fourth Crusade through the reign of Mehmet the Conqueror contributed to the state of flux that characterized Jewish settlement during this period. A considerable number of Jews were constantly on the move, ever seeking new areas of social and economic opportunity. Many Jews, however, remained in their ancestral community.

The relationship between continuity of settlement and the new areas which appear on a map of Jewish settlements from the twelfth century through the fourteenth is made difficult by the paucity of sources that bear upon this question. The major source for the twelfth century is, of course, the itinerary of Benjamin of Tudela (exc. A). In his travels, Benjamin visited some twenty-five cities in the empire, and in most of these he found Jews.

His journey was selective since he followed the principal sea route (with a few minor excursions). It is therefore necessary to supplement his list of communities with occasional reference to other areas of the empire, e.g., Macedonia. However, difficulties arise because we do not have a full list of communities in the empire, especially for periods prior to the second third of the twelfth century. Only a few of the sites identified in the sources contained Jews prior to 1204. The other locales, preserved in bills of sale appended to manuscripts or identified in rabbinic responsa, were areas perhaps new to Jewish settlement. Nevertheless, the fact that they were inhabited by Jews of Byzantine origin suggests that, depending on local circumstances, their settlement in those places may have antedated the Fourth Crusade. A review of the material on the areas of Jewish settlement will perhaps shed some light on their continuity.

Constantinople

The center of Byzantine Jewry before the Fourth Crusade was the capital of the empire. In terms of numbers, location, and influence, this Jewry made the greatest impression on Jewish travelers to the empire. Other cities, such as Thebes, also harbored large communities, but that of Constantinople benefited most because the city was the capital of the empire, the leading commercial center of the Mediterranean. Benjamin of Tudela relates that he found 2,000 Rabbanite and 500 Karaite Jews in Pera, the suburb just "across" the Golden Horn. This was the largest community that he found in the empire (exc. A)—indeed, the largest Jewish concentration outside Baghdad. His numbers, whatever their exact meaning—whether the entire body of Jewish inhabitants, or household heads, taxpayers, or guild members—suggest the existence of a large and wealthy community in twelfth-century Constantinople.[1] Through 1204, the continuity of this Jewish

1. M. N. Adler, *The Itinerary of Benjamin of Tudela* (London, 1907), pp. 14 (English text) and 16–17 (Hebrew text); Starr, *JBE*, p. 231; below, part II, exc. A. Ankori (*Karaites*, pp. 140–48) argues that Benjamin's description refers to only part of the Jewish population of Constantinople, i.e., the silk manufacturers' guild and the tanners. In general, he argues, Benjamin's figures should be multiplied by a factor of five to give the number of individuals. For Constantinople, this would give a population of at least 10,000 Rabbanite and 2,500 Karaite Jews in Pera, plus an undetermined number elsewhere in Pera and Constantinople. Jacoby ("Quartiers juifs," pp. 185f) argues that the size of the Jewish Quarter in Pera was too small to embrace such a large number of Jews; he therefore reads Benjamin's figures for Constantinople as reflecting the total number of Jews in the capital. See also Baron, *SRHJ*, XVII, 300ff, note 4, and below, chap. 3, "Estimates of Romaniote Population."

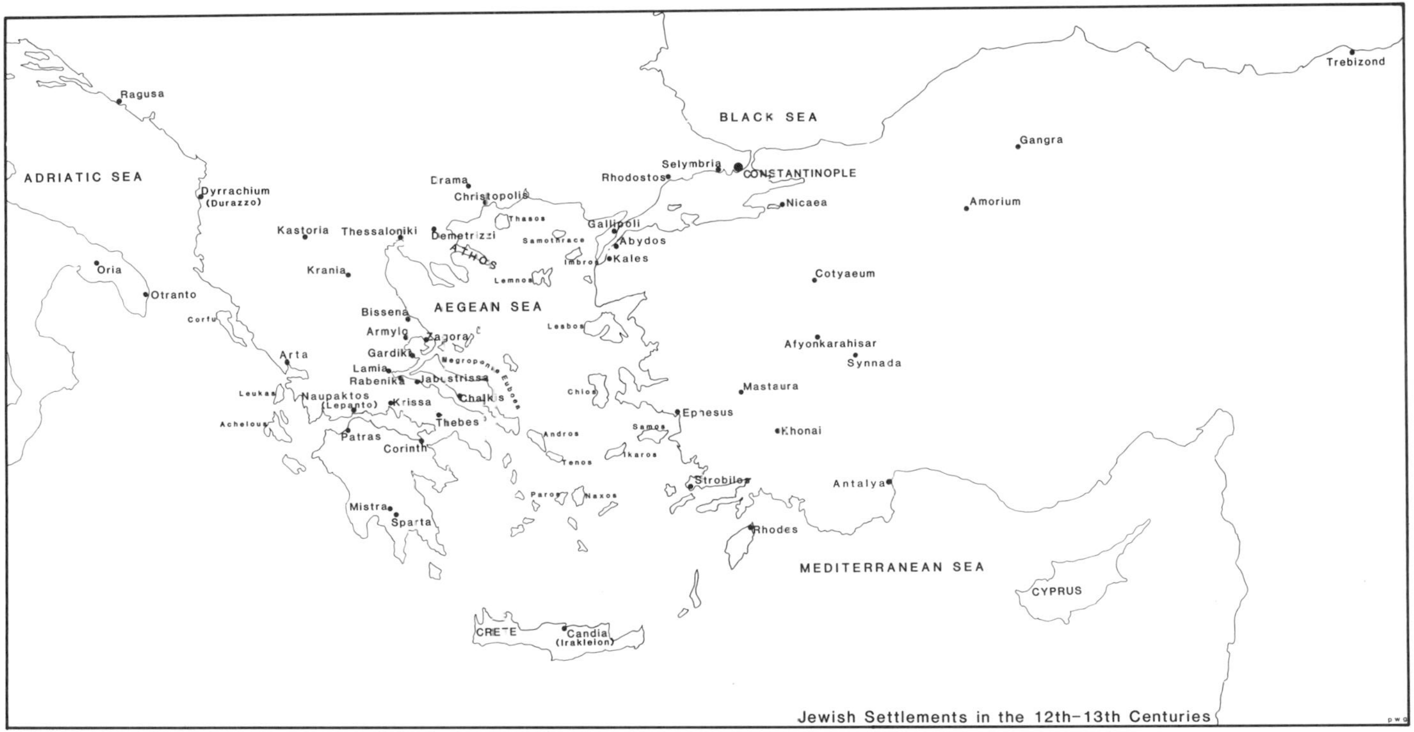

Jewish Settlements in the 12th–13th Centuries

community, physically located in Pera, is borne out by subsequent Crusader sources (**12**).

From the period of the Fourth Crusade to the reign of Michael VIII Palaiologos in Constantinople (1204–61), we have no further information on the Jewish community in Pera. This lack of documentation poses the most serious of the problems surrounding the question of continuity of a Jewish settlement in Constantinople or its suburbs during the period from the Crusader conquest to the reign of Andronikos II (1282–1328). But we have several Crusader reports from the period of the Latin conquest of 1204 which clearly confirm the continued prosperity of the community that Benjamin visited and described so admirably (**12**). Moreover, they indicate that the armies of the Fourth Crusade laid waste to whole areas of the city through wanton destruction and looting, which precipitated the subsequent decline of the city. The Jewish Quarter, too, was put to the torch, and no doubt was sacked previously. This suggestion is supported by the Crusader historian who noted the wealth of this area, the wealth of a sophisticated city that awed the semibarbarian soldiers from the West.

Thus at the beginning of the Latin Empire, Pera, the wealthy quarter that housed Genoese and other Italian merchants, as well as Jewish merchants, craftsmen, and tradesmen in the area around the Tower of Galata, called Stenon, was burned during the Crusader attack on that citadel. But Pera was not destroyed completely, nor was it abandoned; in fact, the area was rebuilt soon after the halt in hostilities. The question remains, however, whether Jews moved back into the rebuilt quarter or took up new residence elsewhere. The total lack of sources precludes any definite statement as to where the Jewish community was located during the Latin period.

Individual Jews, however, may have been located in the Venetian areas of Constantinople during the Republic's era of hegemony in the capital. As a result of the partition of the Byzantine Empire, Venice controlled the Patriarchate of Constantinople and possessed three-eighths of the capital itself. In addition, the Republic of St. Mark, which received the lion's share of the partition in terms of ports of call and economic privileges, became the unchallenged mistress of the Adriatic and Aegean trade until the Byzantine reconquest in 1261. It is not implausible, therefore, that among the Venetian subjects who came to the capital from her new colonies were some local Jewish merchants. While we do not hear of such Jews until the early fourteenth century, it would not have been necessary, in the early thirteenth century, for these Jews to have sought a Venetian status since they were totally within the free-trade market that was operated by Venice.[2]

Could there have been Jews in other parts of Constantinople proper? As early as the twelfth century, there are indications that individual Jews, at least, may have lived in the city. Solomon the Egyptian, the esteemed physician of Manuel I Komnenos, in whom Benjamin of Tudela took such great interest, is one such example. Interpreters, too, may have lived in or near the palace complex. There are also traditions, current during the Ottoman period, that some synagogues dated from Byzantine times.[3] It is as likely, however, that these date from the Palaeologan period.[4]

On the other hand, several sources point to the exclusion of Jews from Constantinople before 1204, and possibly until 1261. To begin with, there is the express statement of Benjamin of Tudela that "the Jews do not live among them [i.e., Greek Christians] inside the city, for they have transferred them across the strait . . . the place in which the Jews live is called Pera." Until further evidence is available or stronger arguments to the contrary are presented, this source must remain the most weighty argument for the absence of Byzantine Jews from the capital a generation before 1204.[5] Benjamin, after all, after visiting both the capital and Pera, states that there were no Jews in Constantinople proper; and there are no sources available to prove him in error.

Less helpful toward a solution of this problem is the rumor concerning a ban on settlement in the capital reported by the sixteenth-century historian Solomon ibn Verga (exc. B). Neither he nor his sources had any idea regarding the period of the purported ban. However, his report may be an echo of Benjamin's earlier remarks. At best, Ibn Verga's text is a mixture of several overlapping traditions, one of which contains the story of an attempted forced conversion under an unknown Byzantine emperor, while another refers to a subsequent change of policy, followed by a series of harsh decrees which, coincidentally, summarize many of the restrictions of pre-Palaeologan Jewish life. Although this source cannot apply to the period after 1204, it may be a dim memory of the persecution under Ro-

2. On the Venetian Jews, see above (chap. 1) and below (chap. 3).
3. Ankori, *Karaites,* p. 142 and notes 210, 212, and above, note 1.
4. Ankori, *Karaites,* note 212, and p. 140, note 198.
5. For a different interpretation of this text, see ibid., p. 143, note 214, and his text.

manos Lekapenos (914–44).[6] The evidence for the period immediately preceding 1204, then, points to the absence of Jews (save perhaps for occasional individuals) from Constantinople.

The period of the Latin Empire poses different problems. Any argument for the presence of Jews in the city is necessarily restricted by the total absence of sources. Even the letter of Jacob ben Elia to his apostate relative, Pablo Christiani (ca. 1270), ignores the Latin Empire, although he *does* mention persecution at that time in nearby Epiros and Nicaea.[7] All that can be deduced from his silence is that perhaps no persecution of Jews in the Latin areas was known to him. Actually, the later appearance of Jews in Constantinople, during the reign of Andronikos II (1282–1328), is the first evidence that Jews lived within the city. Both the location of the Jewish Quarter and the provenance of these Jews, first mentioned in passing in the report of a Muslim merchant dated 1293, constitute interesting problems. This reference increases in importance, especially in light of the possibility that the data he supplies may be applicable to the last years of the reign of Michael VIII.

Be that as it may, he informs us that Jews and Muslims occupied separate quarters *in* the city, each surrounded by a wall, the gates of which were closed in the evening at the same time as those of the city. The location of neither quarter, however, can be identified with certainty.[8] Moreover, it is not clear whether actual quarters are referred to or areas within the bazaar, so vague is his description—especially when compared with that of Ibn Battuta, who visited the city a generation later (**52**).

A quarter inside Constantinople is unambiguously located by the monk Maximus Planudes in his letter to Andronikos II, written circa 1300. In this letter he castigates the emperor for establishing a colony of Jewish tanners in the Vlanka Quarter (**31**).[9] From his remarks, it appears that this

6. A discussion of the problems of this tradition follows the text in part II, exc. B (below).

7. Discussed above in chap. 1, "Imperial Policy."

8. Cf. Jacoby ("Quartiers juifs," pp. 190 and 192), who suggests that this source refers to the Vlanka Quarter. Coincidentally, in the same year, Aaron ben Joseph, the leader of the Karaite community in Byzantium, completed his commentary on the Bible; see below, chap. 4, "Karaite Scholarship." His reference to the "Rabbanites who are *there* in that place called Solchat" shows that he wrote his commentary after leaving there, and finished it in 1293–94. Tradition does not identify where in Byzantium he lived and taught. Most likely it was Constantinople or Pera (but see below this chapter, "Thessaly and Macedonia").

9. For a discussion of this source in connection with imperial factories and revenues, see above, chap. 1, "Taxation."

group of Jews, constituting a distinct trade corporation of tanners, had been recently resettled under imperial auspices and, presumably, under imperial protection. Their location was the immediate vicinity of the Church of Saint John Prodromos.[10] (Why they were resettled and where they came from is not known.) The only other tanners we hear of are those whom Benjamin had found so distasteful in Pera. If these two groups were in any way related, we wonder why it was necessary to move them from an area where they were settled, over a century before, to one in which no Jews (so far as we know) had ever been located. It may well be that as his influence in Genoese Pera decreased, the Basileus decided to remove his tanners (i.e., Byzantine citizens) to an area over which he had more direct control, that is, within the city.[11] It was in the Vlanka Quarter that Andronikos I Komnenos had his palace; therefore, it may have been in or near that area that Andronikos II Palaiologos had his tanners settled.

The Vlanka was ideal for a tannery. Formerly known as the Eleutherios Quarter, it was large, sparsely inhabited, and full of gardens, though its harbor had long been replaced by the neighboring harbor of Theodosios, which was smaller and more easily accessible to shipping. Thus the harbor of Eleutherios could have been turned into a sewer by the tanners with less complaint than when they spilled their dirty liquids into the streets of Pera.[12] The fact that these tanners happened to be Jews seemed of importance only to the abovementioned monk.[13]

Zvi Ankori has theorized that the profession of tanning, a basic process in the fur and skin trade, in which the Jews of Constantinople played a significant role, was forced upon the Jews by the imperial government during the Macedonian period in the wake of the persecution of Romanos Lekapenos.[14] The lack of reference to non-Jews as tanners during the

10. Maximus Planudes is the only source to mention this church. The only (other?) church known from this quarter is that of Theoktonos; cf. R. Janin, *Constantinople Byzantine, développement urbain et repertoire topographique* (Paris, 1950; revised and augmented, Paris, 1964), p. 325. We cite only the revised edition; the first does not mention the Planudes text.

11. *Infra.*

12. Cf. Janin, *Cp. Byz.*, and R. Guilland, "Les ports de Byzance sur la Propontide," *Byzantion,* 23 (1953), 181–238 (reprinted in his *Etudes de topographie de Constantinople byzantine* [Amsterdam, 1969], II, 95).

13. What relation did this colony of tanners in the Vlanka Quarter have with the area which the wife of Andronikos II gave to the Venetian hide workers in document 38? Could these two sources refer to the same colony of tanners?

14. See below, part II, exc. B, and cited bibliography.

subsequent Byzantine period would seem to support this view of an official degradation. Also, he argues, as a corollary to the social disdain for the profession, the tanners were demoted institutionally. The profession was listed as a subsection of the softeners' guild rather than as an independent guild, like the other professions.[15]

Ankori's thesis emerged from an analysis of the social situation in the tenth, eleventh, and twelfth centuries, coupled with the relevant sections of the Book of the Eparch.[16] Still, it is only in the Palaeologan period, beginning with the remarks of Planudes, that direct evidence is available to show that some, if not all, of the tanners were under the immediate control of the imperial government. Though it is tempting to see this state of affairs as based upon an earlier precedent, which the Palaeologan emperors exploited to their own advantage, there is no documentary evidence to this effect.[17]

The thesis poses two problems which are of importance in determining the areas of settlement of Jews after the Fourth Crusade. If the profession of tanning was exclusively practiced by Jews, then any area within the former empire where tanning traditions survived would be an area of Jewish settlement or, at the very least, an area where Jewish tanners could be found. Such sites might include the cities of Philadelphia, Trebizond, and possibly Amphissa (medieval Salona).[18] The second problem concerns the location of the main Jewish Quarter in Constantinople during the Palaeologan period.

Several sources mention or suggest areas where Jews lived in Constantinople during the Palaeologan period. The unidentified Jewish Quarter, mentioned by the Muslim merchant, and the Vlanka Quarter, where the Jewish tanners lived, have already been noted. In the mid-fourteenth century, Stephan of Novgorod located some Jews as living near the "Jewish Gates"; these have been alternately placed on the Golden Horn

15. Ankori (*Karaites*, p. 176, note 28) argues for evidence of a Jewish tanning guild in the Book of Prefect and, even further, "the exclusively Jewish membership of the tanning profession." On Jewish tanners, cf. Andreades, "The Jews," p. 8, note 1; Dölger, "*Die Frage,*" pp. 10, 23–24; Starr, *JBE*, pp. 29, 136, 225; Vacalopoulos, *Origins of the Greek Nation: The Byzantine Period, 1204–1461* (New Brunswick, 1970), p. 39, citing a thirteenth-century aside to tanning in Philadelphia; and below, part II, exc. B.

16. Ankori, *Karaites*, pp. 176ff.

17. Cf. review of A. Sharf's *Byzantine Jewry from Justinian to the Fourth Crusade* (New York, 1971) by D. Jacoby in *BZ*, LXVI (1973), 403–6.

18. See above, chapter 1, notes 35ff.

and on the Marmara coast (77). A map in a fifteenth-century copy of Christopher Buondelmonti's *Liber Insularum Archipelagi* designates a Porta Judeca, leading to the Golden Horn from the northeast section of the city.[19] Finally, there is the observation, recorded by Nicolo Barbaro, that the Ottoman fleet during the final stage in 1453 disembarked at the Giudecca (Hebraike), located on the other side of the city from the harbor, that is, in the south (**138**).

With the exception of the map of Buondelmonti, all of the above references could be applied to the Vlanka Quarter. For this reason, David Jacoby has proposed that the main Judaica was located in the Vlanka Quarter.[20] The reference to a Jewish Gate in the north of the city would therefore have no bearing on the actual presence of Jews there; rather, it would be a toponymic anachronism dating back to the eleventh and early twelfth century, when the Jewish Quarter actually was located there, somewhere to the east of the Porta Perama (also known as the Porta Hebraica).[21]

19. Gennadeion Manuscript 71, fol. 36v. The map indicates seven gates leading to the Golden Horn; two in the west lead from the Blachernae Palace; the remaining five branch off from a road parallel to the Golden Horn (the Via Drungarius?) which ends at the Serail. The middle gate of these five is designated Porta Judeca. Jacoby ("Quartiers juifs," pp. 172–73) relies on the plans of Buondelmonti reproduced by G. Gerola ("La vedute di Constantinopoli di Christoforo Buondelmonti," *Studi Bizantini e neoellenici,* 3 [1931], 247–49) and a photo of the Paris manuscript (Bibl. Nat., lat. 4825, reproduced in Ph. Sherrard, *Constantinople, Iconography of a Sacred City* [London, 1965], facing p. 18). The Gennadeion manuscript appears to have one of the better maps; however, it, also, is too roughly drawn to make an exact identification.

20. "Quartiers juifs," p. 193.

21. The precise boundaries of the Judaica during the period of the Komnenoi have yet to be established. Scholarly consensus accepts the general location for the eleventh and the first half of the twelfth century (cf. exc. A) along the southern shore of the Golden Horn. Cf. Starr, *Romania,* pp. 27 and 32; Jacoby, "Quartiers juifs," pp. 193ff; Janin, *Cp. Byz.,* p. 260; Guilland, "La chaine de la Corne d'Or," in his *Etudes byzantines,* pp. 293–97 (reprinted from *EEBS,* 25 [1955], 88–120, and included in his *Etudes,* II, 121–46).

The problem is whether the Jewish Quarter formed the border of the Venetian Quarter, in which case it would be located at the Porta Perama (alternately known as the Porta Hebraica), or whether it lay farther to the east, behind the Porta Neorion, or even east of the Porta Piscaria. Cf. discussion in Alexander Van Millingen, *Byzantine Constantinople, the Walls of the City and Adjoining Historical Sites* (London, 1899), pp. 218–19, and Janin, *Cp. Byz,* p. 260. Guilland ("La chaine," p. 281) states: "La porte [du Perama] fut appelée par les Latines Porta Hebraica ou Porte juive, du nom de la colonie juive karaite etablié dans la voisonage." He is quite singular in placing a colony of Karaites there in the Latin period. The document cited by the Karaites is from the seventeenth century; cf. Van Millingen, *Byz. Cp.,* p. 221, note 8. The Porta Neorion was called, after 1453, the Porta Hebraica, a misinterpretation for Porta Horaia, which in turn was derived from the word Neorion; cf. Guilland, "La chaine," pp.

Jacoby's thesis tallies well with the information supplied by Benjamin of Tudela. According to Benjamin, the Jewish Quarter, originally located on the Golden Horn, somewhere between the Porta Perama and the Porta Eugenius, was removed to Pera, where Benjamin found it in the late 1160s. This quarter was sacked by the Crusaders in 1204. Between the end of the reign of Michael Palaiologos and the early years of his successor, Andronikos II, Byzantine Jewish subjects were established in the Vlanka Quarter, which remained the site of the main Judaica until the Ottoman period.

The thesis thus accounts for all the sources that mention a Judaica in the city. In the absence of any reference to an area of special concentration of Byzantine Jews in Constantinople during the Palaeologan period, Jacoby's thesis that the Judaica (or, more properly, the Hebraike, i.e., the area designated for Jews by official imperial policy) was located in the Vlanka will have to stand.

If the location of the Byzantine Judaica has been identified, this is not to say that all Jews were restricted to it. On the contrary. Whereas former

---

280, 293–95; Van Millingen, *Byz. Cp.*, p. 221; and M. Franco, *Essai sur l'histoire des Israélites de l'empire ottoman* (Paris, 1897), pp. 20–21. Byron Tsangadas has suggested (in a private discussion) that the Judaica extended from inside the Petri Gate to the Yahudi Kapîsî (i.e., the Porta Hebraica of the Ottoman period; see his *Fortifications and Defense of Constantinople* [New York, 1980], chap. V). Jacoby ("Quartiers juifs," pp. 173f) suggests a location in the vicinity of the Porta Piscaria.

The boundaries of the Judaica are referred to only in relation to the Venetian Quarter. Cf. quotes from Anna Komnena on the Jewish wharf and the Byzantine-Venetian treaties (*apud* Tafel-Thomas, *Urkunden*), cited by Van Millingen (*Byz. Cp.*, pp. 217–18) and discussed by Jacoby ("Quartiers juifs," pp. 169–70); texts and commentary by Starr (*JBE*, p. 203, #152). The references are insufficient for a definite statement. At present, one can only say that the Judaica under the Komnenoi lay in the northeast corner of the city, somewhere between the Porta Perama to the west and the Porta Eugenius to the east.

It was precisely in this area, however, that the foreign merchants were assigned quarters according to their city of origin. Janin (*Cp. Byz.*, chap. XV, pp. 245–60) lists them as follows from west to east: Venetians, from the Porta Drungarius to the Porta Perama; Amalfitans, between the Venetians and the Pisans; Pisans, midway between the Porta Neorion and the Porta Hikanitissa to the Porta Veteris Rectoris; Genoese, from the Porta Veteris Rectoris (today's Sirkeci) to the Porta Eugenius (today's Yaliköşkkapi). Therefore we may ask why the Jewish Quarter was located in this area prior to 1204. Ankori (*Karaites*, p. 138 and note 191) has pointed out that even Byzantine provincials were considered "aliens" in Constantinople, and for this reason the quarter of the Jews would have been placed among those of the foreign merchants. See, further, his argument that this location reflected an "interplay of ethno-religious and occupational factors" (ibid., pp. 140–41).

imperial policy had been to restrict Jews to a specific quarter as a reflection of their religious peculiarity as well as their occupational proclivity, the Palaeologan period witnessed the spread of Jews throughout the city and its environs. While not all Jews who exercised such mobility were subject to the empire, those with a Venetian or a Genoese identity can be found in the areas set aside for these republics. Nevertheless, there were Romaniote or local Jews whose new status was disputed by the imperial officials.

To begin with areas of known settlement, a document from the middle of the fourteenth century locates a neighborhood of Venetian Jews inside the Venetian Quarter (**63**). The area referred to in the will of Isaac Catalanus as "Cafacalea where the Venetian Jews dwell" has been identified with the area known as Tahtakale during the Ottoman period and located near the main bazaar.[22] Jews with Venetian status were entitled by treaty to live, rent, or even buy *anywhere* in the city. Thus we find them sharing housing with Byzantine Jewish subjects in the Vlanka Quarter. No doubt the superior privileges accorded the former induced many of the wealthier Byzantine Jews in that quarter to apply for (and attain) Venetian status. During the fourteenth century, as Venice tried to increase her physical presence in the city as a support for her attempts to control the economy of the capital, such new identities were easily obtained for both Christian and Jewish subjects of the empire.[23] The other areas in the city where Venetian Jews chose to live are not identified. Given the necessary gregariousness of any medieval socio-religious community, such individuals, who chose to live in areas outside the concentrated community, would not have made an impact on their environment *qua* Jews but as privileged Venetians.

In addition to the Vlanka Quarter, the Cafacalea district of the Venetian Quarter, and other scattered locales within the city, Jews were to be found across the Golden Horn. A number of Jews, both former Byzantine subjects and those from the Genoese colonies in the Black Sea, succeeded in attaining Genoese identity and moving to its major entrepôt in Pera.[24] Jacoby suggests that the area which Andronikos II gave to the Genoese in Pera included the former Judaica. Be that as it may, documents from the

22. Jacoby ("Quartiers juifs," pp. 205–8) suggests that they lived in the shadow of the bailo's house.

23. Cf. J. Chrysostomides, "Venetian Commercial Privileges under the Palaeologi," *Studi Veneziani*, 12 (1970), 267–356.

24. Jacoby, "Quartiers juifs," pp. 207 and 215f.

fourteenth and fifteenth centuries show the presence of Jews within the Genoese quarter. No connection, however, has as yet been established between these Jews and the ones who inhabited the area in 1204.

Farther west, the area of Hasköy has been the site of a Karaite community, as well as the Jewish graveyard, since the Ottoman period.[25] The location of the Karaite community during the Palaeologan period, however, has not been definitely established.[26] Benjamin of Tudela, we recall, found them sharing the Jewish Quarter in Pera during the late twelfth century. Did the Karaites seize the opportunity, occasioned by the disruption of the Jewish Quarter in 1204, and establish a separate quarter during the thirteenth century? It may be that several Karaite quarters were established during the period, since we find the tradition—albeit from the late fifteenth century—that Karaites were to be found on the Asian side of the Bosporos in Keramia, a suburb of Chalcedon (**149n**).

Thus the problem that vexes the student of Constantinopolitan Jewry—Were there any Jews in Constantinople in the early thirteenth century?—is replaced, so far as the fourteenth and fifteenth centuries are concerned, by the question: In what areas of the capital proper and in Pera did the Jews reside? Before the Ottoman conquest, then, Jews were present in several areas of Constantinople and Pera.[27] The majority of these Jews were Romaniote; however, among them were Jews from the various colonies of Venice and Genoa, the beginnings of a Spanish (Sephardi) migration to the new opportunities opened by the Eastern entrepôt (from the developing and expanding Spanish kingdoms), and occasional immigrants from Egypt and Syria.[28] As early as the fourteenth century, then, the Jewish population of Constantinople anticipated that variety of congregations, based on the *Landsmannschaft* principle, that was to be the basic feature of Jewish life under the Ottomans.

25. Van Millingen, *Byz. Cp.*, p. 223, note 8.

26. Jacoby (ibid., pp. 175–77) argues that there were Jews in Hasköy (Picridion) since the eleventh century.

27. Starr argued that there were Jews in Is Pegas, based upon the report of Anthony of Novgorod (documents 2, 4). The usefulness of that detail from Anthony's text was held doubtful by Ankori on methodological grounds (*Karaites*, pp. 145–46); cf. Jacoby, "Quartiers juifs," for a different view. Ankori has emphasized that "Cassim Pasha, Pera and Galata form, strictly speaking, three contiguous boroughs" and that foreign travelers "were apt to confuse the two names (Pera and Galata) or use them in their diaries and itineraries interchangeably or in a perplexingly vague manner." See below, chap. 5, "Areas of Settlement," and part II document 134.

28. See below, chap. 3, "Social Structure, Mobility, Tensions."

Thrace and Macedonia

Information on Jewish settlements in Thrace and Macedonia during the thirteenth century is sparse indeed. While we have some indication of the areas of settlement during the Macedonian and Komnenian periods, data become sufficiently available for these areas only in the fourteenth and fifteenth centuries. This hiatus of over a century, coupled with the disparity in actual sites inhabited, makes it difficult to correlate the information from the twelfth and the fourteenth century in order to argue for a continuity of settlement. At the same time, however, several sites suggest a continuity of settlement from the earlier period through the end of the empire. Therefore the question of continuity should not be argued in the negative; at the very least, it should be left open until such time as new sources are discovered which bear upon the problem.

Benjamin of Tudela's route in the twelfth century brought him through the following cities of Thrace and Macedonia which contained a Jewish settlement: Constantinople (*supra*), Gallipoli, Abydos, Christopolis, Drama, Demetrizi, and Thessalonica (*infra*). To this list must be added the western emporium of Kastoria.[29] All of these communities are either well-known seaports or way stations on the Via Egnatia.

Information for the early thirteenth century allows us to add the western terminus of that major southern Balkan trade route to our list. The city of Dyrrachium is expressly identified as the site of a Jewish community in the responsa of Isaiah ben Mali of Trani, the well-known early thirteenth-century Tosaphist from southern Italy. Dyrrachium became one of the important cities of the Despotate of Epiros—no doubt a continuation of the role it had played during the Middle Byzantine period as the terminus of overland trade through the Balkans and as a major western window of the empire on the Adriatic. There is little reason to doubt that its Jewish community participated actively in the commercial life of this city. The continuity of the Jewish community in Dyrrachium, through changes in regimes and economic vicissitudes, is amply borne out by documents from the fourteenth and fifteenth centuries. Only one other city is identified as possessing a Jewish community in the otherwise anonymous responsa of Isaiah of Trani.[30] It is Gortzanos, which has been identified as part of the

29. Cf. Starr, *JBE,* and Ankori, *Karaites,* index, s.v.

30. S. Schechter, "Notes on Hebrew MSS. in the University Library at Cambridge," *JQR,* os, IV (1892), 94–96. He cites there several Byzantine authors whose works Isaiah had used, viz., R. Isaac ben Malki-Zedek of Siponto, R. Baruch from Greece, R. Hillel from

hinterland of Dyrrachium (**13**). It may be that other of his unidentified correspondents lived in the western Balkans. (Another responsum is interesting for the information it provides on a Greek-speaking Jewish convert who moved to Gallipoli [**5***].)

Unquestionably, the thirteenth century saw the continued settlement of Jews along the Via Egnatia, even though information is extremely scarce. There are indications of such settlement only in Dyrrachium, Thessalonica (*infra*), and an unidentified community in Thrace. A bill of sale, dated 1288, indicates the presence of a Karaite community somewhere in Thrace (**26***). Earlier Karaite settlements in Macedonia and Thrace can only be inferred from the polemical remarks of Tobias ben Eliezer of Kastoria, in the eleventh century, and from Karaite settlement patterns during the period of the Komnenoi.[31] While no continuity can be inferred on the basis of such disparate sources, the bill of sale marks the beginning of a documented Karaite presence in Thrace, and particularly in Adrianople, from the late thirteenth century until the Ottoman conquest of that city.

Sources pertaining to the fourteenth and fifteenth centuries permit us to expand this list considerably. Indeed, new areas of Jewish settlement appear in the sources of the fourteenth century. In Serres, a Jewish scribe was busy copying grammatical treatises at the beginning of the century (**32**). Three decades later, a Jewish settlement is noted nearby, *inside* Fort Zichna (**55**). (That the revenues of these Jews were assigned to the monastery of Saint John Prodromos is a special problem that has been dealt with elsewhere.)[32] Other Jews were located near the monastery of Likousada in Thessaly and "the place" (?) neighboring on Saint Constantine (**75, 88**). Elsewhere in Macedonia and Thrace, Jews lived in the cities of Ochrida, Kastoria, and Silivri (Selymbria). Ochrida was the birthplace of the Romaniote bibliophile Judah ibn Moskoni in 1328 (**87**), and Kastoria was the

---

Greece (probably Hillel ben Eliakim), and R. Abraham from Thebes. Of Isaiah's contemporary correspondents (i.e., the thirteenth century), he mentions an R. Simḥa, some unnamed Kohanim, R. Leon, and an R. Isaac of Romania. The last-named is referred to occasionally as *he-ḥaḇer* and *rabbana*. Schechter accounts for the anonymity of the correspondents by intentional omission of the titles of the responsa on the part of later copyists due to the severity of Isaiah's language toward them. For a different analysis, cf. introduction to the recent edition of *Teshuvoth HaRID* by Rabbi Abraham Wertheimer. See below, chap. 4, "Rabbinic Scholarship."

31. Cf. Ankori, *Karaites*, passim.

32. See above, chap. 1, "Taxation."

home of at least four *paytanim* (liturgical poets) in the second half of the century and another in the fifteenth.[33] As for Silivri, Rabbanite tradition locates the home of the twelfth-century scholar Hillel ben Eliakim there, and a late Karaite tradition places a community there during the last generation of the Byzantine period. On the other hand, direct reference to a fourteenth-century settlement in Silivri is presently unavailable, although it is not an unlikely possibility.

To date, although there has been sound scholarly speculation on the subject, no information has appeared for the existence of either a Rabbanite or a Karaite community in Byzantine Adrianople. However, new techniques in the study of Hebrew manuscripts have allowed for a more accurate dating of colophons. One text, in particular, which has been traditionally dated to the late fifteenth century, has been correctly redated to the early fourteenth.[34] On the basis of this manuscript, we can identify four Karaite scribes in the city of Adrianople in 1335–36 (**56**). The presence, then, of a Karaite community in Adrianople in the second quarter of the fourteenth century signals the parallel existence there of a Rabbanite community.[35] This text is the first documentary evidence for a Jewish community in Adrianople during the Byzantine period, and provides a basis for the later presence of Greek-speaking Jews in the city when it served as the second Ottoman capital a generation later.[36]

Other areas may have harbored Jews during this period. The suggestion was made by George Ostrogorsky that Jews were on the island of

33. See below, chap. 4, "Romaniote Poetry and Liturgy."

34. The watermarks in the manuscript date from the 1330s and 1340s; one, in fact, has been dated to 1329. Therefore the date in the colophon (1335–36) must be accepted as contemporary unless we wish to assume two difficult possibilities: (1) our scribe made a mistake in the date and (2) a scholar, 150 years after the manufacture of this paper, made use of it for his scribal work. See below, part II document 56n, for further discussion.

35. Cf. the two general rules of Rabbanite and Karaite settlement formulated by Ankori (*Karaites*, pp. 118–19). Still, all the evidence on the Jews in Byzantine Adrianople comes from the Karaite community. We have no direct evidence for a Rabbanite community there. See following note.

36. The son of an Adrianopolitan scribe was plying his trade in Solchat in 1363 and 1389–90 (presumably, he lived there during the intervening period). Since he completed a Bible manuscript in the former year, he very likely could not have been in Adrianople after the Ottoman conquest. His name was Judah ben Eliahu, the Adrianopolitan. Thus Eliahu becomes the fifth Karaite scribe known to us in the last generation of Byzantine Adrianople—surely an indication of a fair-sized Karaite community there! For Judah's colophons, cf. HPP files Y299 and D193; also E. Deinard, *Massa Krim* (Warsaw, 1878), pp. 66f, and below, part II document 26*.

Thasos in the late fourteenth century (based on the occurrence of the toponym ʿEbraiokastro in a chrysobull dated 1394 [**104n**]). This may not have been the case, however. The plethora of sites in Greece with the name ʿEbraiokastro ("Rhamnous" is the *locus classicus* in Attika) is based on folk traditions which, in most cases, cannot be substantiated by other sources. On the other hand, Jewish quarters in Crete have been identified through the survival of the toponym Ioudaia or Ioudaike, and ʿEbraïke or Obrake within the urban area.[37] The difference, however, between a long-settled quarter referred to in documents over many centuries, which survives in the folk memory of a given area, as opposed to a single occurrence of the term ʿEbraiokastro in reference to an uninhabited ruin on a fortified hill, is not insignificant.

While onomastic traditions, such as the continued use of Slavic place names in Epiros and other parts of Greece, can be used to identify locales in an area that was inundated by Slavic tribes, the apparently random assigning of various names to a fortified hill by local peasants does not necessarily reflect ethnographic history. The caveat voiced by William Leake and others, after they had been frustrated by many such folk traditions, should not go unheeded.[38] Therefore we must approach each occurrence of the term ʿEbraiokastro and its derivatives (e.g., ʿEbraionisi off the Argolid coast) with caution and not identify it, at first glance, with a former settlement of Jews. Moreover, the fact that Jews lived inside fortified areas during the Ottoman period, which may account for the general designation ʿEbraiokastro, whether or not Jews lived there, clouds any possibility of discovering the origins of the settlement in Byzantine times unless there is a clear indication, as in the case of Zichna.

One seventeenth-century example may suffice to clarify the above statement.[39] During his visit to Corinth, Evliya Çelebi did not note any

37. Ankori, "Jews and the Jewish Community in the History of Mediaeval Crete," *Proceedings of the 2nd International Congress of Cretological Studies* (Athens, 1968), III, 313–14 and passim.

38. Patrick Leigh Fermor (*Roumeli, Travels in Northern Greece* [London, 1966], p. 203) makes the following observation: "Villagers . . . are not accurate . . . : sometimes 'Evraioi' or 'Ovraioi' means little more than 'foreign' and sometimes it merely designates a Greek speaking a different dialect, such as Tzakonian."

39. Cf. John H. Finley Jr., "Corinth in the Middle Ages," *Speculum*, VII (1933), 477–98, for history. In 1676 Spon and Wheler visited the Akrokorinth and described an area on the eastern side of the fortress called Ovraiokastro. Their respective descriptions (conveniently reproduced by R. Carpenter and A. Bon in *The Defenses of Acrocorinth and the Lower Town*

Jews on the Akrocorinth among the 1,500 Muslims and Christians there. Yet the eastern side of the fortress was known to contemporaries as the Obraiokastro. The last recorded presence of Jews in the city of Corinth was in the mid-fifteenth century (*infra*); they can be placed in the surrounding area, however, in the seventeenth century.[40] While it is quite possible that Jews may have moved up to the Akrocorinth, along with the rest of the population, during the continual periods of insecurity in the area, we have no source that mentions them in the city prior to Evliya's visit.[41]

To sum up, the occurrence of the toponym ʿEbraiokastro (as the occurrence of its parallel term Gyphtokastro) should be used, if at all, only with great caution to indicate the previous presence of a Jewish settlement on that site, unless there is a physical or literary hint to support such an assumption.[42]

Ottoman cadastral registers from the seventeenth century are valuable for the light they shed on Jewish settlements in the area during the fourteenth century.[43] These registers list, *inter alia,* the communities that were uprooted by Mehmet II and resettled in Constantinople as part of his

[Corinth III, part II; Cambridge, Mass., 1936], pp. 147–48) are as confusing geographically as they are historically. Pierre MacKay has translated Evliya Çelebi's account of his visit in 1668 in his article "Acrocorinth in 1668, a Turkish Account," *Hesperia,* XXXVII (1968), 386–97. Though Evliya does not refer to the eastern side of the Akrokorinth as Ovraiokastro, he does call it the "new Castle." In neither the European nor the Turkish accounts do we find reference to Jews living on the Akrokorinth in the seventeenth century.

Rabbinic sources, on the other hand, not unexpectedly refer to the presence of Jews in the vicinity of Corinth. In a study in preparation ("Corintho-Judaica: A Review of the Literary and Archaeological Evidence"), we hope to show the extent of Jewish settlement in Corinth and environs in the seventeenth century.

40. See below ("Peloponnesos" and part II document 136) for the visit of a Jewish scribe in 1456 which suggests the likelihood of a community, although the colophon does not, as is customary, indicate this. An Abraham of Corinth is identified as a sixteenth-century scribe, although the date mentioned in that manuscript is nearly a century earlier; cf. S. Poznanski, *Beitrage zur Karäischen Handschriften-und Bücherkunde* (Frankfurt a.M., 1918), p. 4, no. 9.

41. An anonymous Venetian visitor to Corinth on the eve of the Ottoman conquest of Morea indicated that all the inhabitants had taken refuge on the Akrokorinth at this time. Cf. Ziebarth, "Ein griechischen Reisenbericht des fünfzehnten Jahrhunderts," *Mittheilungen des deutschen archaeologischen Instituts in Athen,* XXIV (1899), 72–88 (esp. p. 78).

42. No one, to my knowledge, has raised the problem of the small island off the coast of Epidauros called Ebraionisi.

43. See below, chap. 5.

policy of rebuilding the depopulated capital. A parallel list to this Ottoman cadastral data is contained in an undated Hebrew source found in a nineteenth-century publication of a midrashic text (**154**). Both of these sources complement the material that has survived in contemporary Byzantine and Serbian sources. They indicate that in almost all the heavily populated and well-fortified areas of Thrace and Macedonia on the old Roman road from Dyrrachium to Constantinople, the Via Egnatia, there were Jewish settlements. These communities include Adrianople, Didymotikon, Serres, Thessalonica, Monastir, Štip, Kastoria, Ochrida, and Dyrrachium. Only three of the above cities appear here for the first time; however, the likelihood that contemporary data for an earlier Jewish presence on the site have disappeared should not be ignored (*infra*).

To the north, several Bulgarian settlements are mentioned by our sources. To the extent that they indicate the dispersion of Romaniote Jews, this information should not be ignored. The Ottoman cadastral registers (noted above) show the existence of communities in Nicopolis and Yambol, while Judah ibn Moskoni's discovery of a commentary by the late twelfth-century scholar R. Abishai of Zagora suggests that Jews may have continued to live in Zagora in the thirteenth and fourteenth centuries. In the middle of the fourteenth century, Elnatan ben Moses Kalkes visited Zagora during his peregrinations.[44] The name of this traveler, Kalkes, may be a Hebraic mispronunciation of Kilkes, a small center to the north of Thessalonica, and thus reflect the location of a Jewish community there during the Late Byzantine period.

Finally, we should note the presence of small Karaite communities in the hinterland of Constantinople. This datum dates from the late fifteenth century; however, the traditions may well go back to the fourteenth century. In his discussion of the Karaite ritual for Torah readings, Kaleb Afendopolo mentions, in passing, the communities of Selembrya and Burgaz (= Sozopolis) (**150**). Such incidental information leads us to suspect that small Jewish communities could be found in other outlying territories of the constricted empire during its denouement, for example, Rhodosto and Heraclea (*infra*).

44. The incipit of Vat. ms. 284 (including the *Eben Saphir*) of Elnatan ben Moses Kalkes (see below, chap. 5, "Rabbinic Scholarship" and "Mystical Tradition") cites this city: שר בן איש אמר נתן בן משה בהיות משותת [משוטט] ונע ונד במקום זגורא רוח אל הציקתני in Assemani. *Bibliothecae Apostolicae Vaticanae Codicum Manuscriptorum catalogus* . . . (Paris, 1926), I, 253; cf. *MWJ*, III (1976), 45.

Thessalonica

The Jewish communities of Ottoman Thessalonica are justly famous; their presence during the antecedent Byzantine period is less well known. Still, there is no reason to doubt their presence in Thessalonica from the late twelfth through the early years of the fifteenth century.[45] The 500 Jews whom Benjamin of Tudela found there were engaged in the manufacture of silk; and it may not be only a historical coincidence that the major economic occupation of Thessalonican Jewry during the Ottoman period was the textile industry. We should assume, then, as a framework for our discussion, that unless there is evidence to the contrary, the settlements noted by Benjamin continued through the first part of the thirteenth century. Moreover, the persecution of Jews by Theodore Angelos, on the eve of his anti-Bulgarian campaign, was shown to be an indication that a well-established Jewish community in the city was necessary to attract his avarice on that occasion.[46] Such a community would not have disappeared in the ensuing changed political circumstances, which should have favored continued settlement.

The available evidence from the fourteenth century is somewhat more substantial. To begin with, there is direct evidence for the presence of Jews in Thessalonica. The information comes from a colophon to a commentary on Maimonides' *Guide to the Perplexed* that was copied in Thessalonica in 1329 (47). The presence of a Jewish scribe in the city in 1329 is the only documentary evidence for the existence of a community there in the early fourteenth century. The contents of this colophon throw incidental light on the intellectual interests of that community.

This direct evidence for the presence of Jews in Thessalonica in the fourteenth century is supported by occasional hints in the contemporary literature. The Patriarch Philotheos Kokkinos (1352–54, 1364–76), it has been suggested, traced his origins to the Jewish community of that city.[47] The patriarch, however, merely indicates his Thessalonican origins in his

45. As does Starr (*Romania,* p. 77).

46. See above, chap. 1, "Imperial Policy." Franz Dölger ("Zur Frage des jüdischen Anteils"; reprinted in his *Paraspora,* pp. 378–83) provided the first attempt at balancing Starr's negative view.

47. V. Laurent, in his article "Philothée Kokkinos" in *Dictionaire de théologie catholique* (XII, 1498), was the first to cite this, relying on the patriarch's autobiographical statements in his prologue to the life of his friend Saint Germanos. The name Kokkinos ("red faced") was derived from the continual embarrassments that the young convert was subjected to at the school of Thomas Magister. Both these statements were repeated by P. Joannou in his article

prologue to the life of Saint Germanos. The source for his Jewish background is the barb that Demetrios Kydones included in his letter defending his brother Prokoros Kydones during the latter's dispute with the patriarch (**93**). This dispute had become a *cause celèbre,* and thus the insulting reference to Philotheos' Jewish origin was used by at least one of the patriarch's antagonists. Still, this tradition about Philotheos' background, albeit hostile and reminiscent of older Christian libels, if accepted as factual, supports our other evidence for a Jewish presence in Thessalonica in the early fourteenth century.[48]

To some extent, other ecclesiastical sources support this contention. In 1336 an official, named Chionios, was brought before an ecclesiastical court. The record of the trial shows, *inter alia,* that there were Jews in the city and that their settlement there preceded the more recent arrival of those Greek Christians (whether refugees or immigrants) who began to insult them. It was, in fact, Chionios' support of the Jews that precipitated his problems.[49] Now the trial was not concerned with the attitudes of the Christians toward the Jews in Thessalonica, but rather with the possibility that Chionios may have secretly converted to Judaism or, at best, was a Judaizer. The latter accusation, of course, was made against anyone whose conduct deviated from normative Orthodox practice.[50] The accusation had been

---

"Vie de S. Germain l'Hagiorite par son contemporain le patriarche Philothée de Constantinople" (*Analecta Bollandiana,* LXX [1952], 35–114). Beck (*Kirche,* pp. 723–24) merely states: "er wurde etwa 1300 von einer jüdischen Mutter in Thessalonike geboren." Also repeated by S. I. Kourouses in his article on Philotheos in *Threskeutike kai Ethike Enkyklopaideia* (Athens, 1967), II, 1119.

Modern Greek Orthodoxy has chosen to ignore Philotheos' alleged Jewish origins. There is no mention of the tradition in either the scholarly apparatus or the text of the two recently printed nineteenth-century lives of the patriarch edited by Basil I. Dentake (*Bios kai Akolouthia tou hagiou Philotheou [Kokkinou] Patriarchou Konstantinoupoleos [1353–1354 kai 1364–1376] tou theologou* [Athens, 1971]).

48. Cf. Parkes, *Conflict of the Church and Synagogue,* for examples.

49. Dölger, "Zur Frage des jüdischen Anteils," pp. 379–80. For the date, cf. Jean Meyendorff, "Grecs, Turcs et Juifs en Asie Mineure au XIV siècle," *Polychordia,* p. 214, note 6. The affair is summarized by Joseph Nehama in *Histoire des Israélites de Salonique* (Saloniki, 1935), I, 103–7. I. S. Emmanuel (*Histoire des Israélites de Salonique* [Paris, 1936], I, 42) says that this affair proves that the Jews of Thessalonica enjoyed "une certain tolerance." Starr, who used Nehama's book on other occasions, does not mention this affair.

Dölger (note 7) suggested that Chionios fulfilled a "quasiampliche Funktion." We have no indication that such a position existed in the official bureaucracy of the Palaeologan period. It may well have been a local position with jurisdiction in civil actions between Jews and Christians, or in cases involving Jews alone that were not adjudicated in rabbinic courts. Compare the position of the *strategos,* mentioned in Starr (*JBE,* p. 222, no. 172).

50. Cf. Parkes, *Conflict of the Church and Synagogue,* passim.

leveled after he had run into certain jurisdictional conflicts with the archbishop of Thessalonica and his relatives. Whether the charges were true or whether they had been fabricated to turn the case into a religious trial is not clear. It is quite possible that, in an age of bureaucratic corruption and weakened imperial authority, a contrary ruling, based upon religious grounds and coupled with a hint of heresy, would have more effect than an imperial dictum supporting either party's jurisdiction (**58**).

The affair, involving the question of the popular strength of Orthodox Christianity in the fourteenth century, has been linked with an interesting group of apostates in Ottoman-controlled Anatolia due to a similarity of the names Chionios and Chiones. In the mid-fourteenth century, Gregory Palamas, while a prisoner at the court of the Ottoman Sultan Orkhan, came into contact with a group that he called Chiones. The origin of this name is obscure and has been sought against both an Ottoman and a Christian background.[51] While the former suggestions have not been accepted, it has been argued that the Chiones were apostate Christians who chose conversion to Judaism as their way of accommodation to the new Muslim regime.[52] This suggestion seems too unlikely: no Jewish or Muslim source acknowledges such a possibility. Classical Islam did not permit transfer from one protected religious group to another, either from Christianity to Judaism or vice versa, and encouraged only conversion from these two religions to the ruling religion. Still, it is not impossible that, in the syncretistic atmosphere of the Ottoman court, some individuals may

51. The Christian background was suggested by Meyendorff ("Grecs, Turcs, et Juifs," p. 214). On the other hand, we may note the name of Gregory Chioniadis of Trebizond to show the diffusion of the name in the Byzantine world.

George Arnakis suggested that Chiones represented a corruption of the Arabic al-Akhiyan in his article "Gregory Palamas among the Turks and Documents of His Captivity as Historical Sources" (*Speculum,* XXVI [1951], 113–14. Paul Wittek disagreed in his review of Arnakis' article "Chiones" (*Byzantion,* XXVI [1959], 421–23) and traced the name back to the Turkish *hoca*. Arnakis reaffirmed his original position in "Gregory Palamas, the Chiones and the Fall of Gallipoli" (*Byzantion,* XXII [1952], 305–12).

52. Meyendorff, "Grecs, Turcs et Juifs," pp. 213–14: "l'identité des *Chiónes*: apostate Chrétiens, ils ont adopté le Judaïsme pour se 'rapprocher' des Turcs et pour d'assimiler aux occupants . . . il existait donc, en Asie Mineure ce groupe des *Chiónes* qui préférait trouver refuge dans le Judaïsme, dont les livres saints étaient vénéres à la fois par les Chrétiens et les Musulmans. Leur attitude s'explique peut-être par les faveurs que les Ottomans accordaient aux communautés juives des pays conquis." Speros Vryonis, in *The Decline of Medieval Hellenism in Asia Minor* ([Berkeley, 1971], pp. 426–27), sees the Chiones as "a group of Jews . . . who had apostacized to Islam." See survey of the problem by A. Phillippides-Braat, "La Captivité de Palamas chez les Turcs," *Travaux et Mémoires* (1979), VII, 214–18.

have converted to Judaism or to a Judaizing sect.[53] In the light of the available evidence, however, identification of the Chiones as Christian converts to Judaism cannot be accepted.

Rather, a different interpretation may be suggested, one that would fit the reality of Muslim civilization. The Chiones were indeed converts to Islam, as they themselves admitted to Palamas: "We heard of the Ten Commandments that Moses brought down (from the mountain) which were engraved on stone tablets, and we know that the Turks observe them; therefore we have abandoned our former convictions, and we came to them, and we have ourselves become Turks."[54] The question is from what did they convert?

It is extremely unlikely that they had been Jews. Byzantine sources call them Jews only *after* their conversion; their ethnic and religious origin is not discussed and therefore is unclear.[55] Perhaps they were Christian or semipagan mountain folk who, having survived in the hinterland between Byzantine and Muslim civilizations, were influenced (by unknown circumstances) to "come down" to Bithynia and join the Ottomans, who settled them in the environs of Brusa. Clearly, their conversion to a new identity followed upon their resettlement. To a Byzantine ecclesiastic who challenged this identity, they replied that the Muslims, like the Jews, recognized the universality of the Decalogue of Moses. But whereas their action was defensible in their own eyes, to Palamas they were manifestly Jews (in the derogatory meaning of the term). Thus Palamas, along with the other sources cited by scholars, preferred to disguise this apostasy by referring to the Chiones as Judaizers, for the same reasons that Chionios, because of the peculiar circumstances surrounding that affair, was branded a Judaizer. Whatever the reality behind the Chiones, it has not been established that the name Chionios is connected to it.

By midcentury, Thessalonica began to recover from the disastrous effects of the Zealot experiment in "democracy." The overthrow of the traditional

53. We may cite as one example from a neighboring area the father of Gregory Abu'l-Faraj (Bar Hebraeus), the thirteenth-century Syriac scholar, who was a Jewish physician named Aaron.

54. Ἡμεῖς ἠκούσαμεν δέκα λόγους οὓς γεγραμμένους κατήγαγεν Ὁ Μωϋσῆς ἐν πλαξὶ λισίναις καὶ ὄιδαμεν ὅτι ἐκείνους κρατôυσιν οἱ Τοῦρκοι, καὶ ἀφήκαμεν ἅπερ ἐφρονοῦμεν πρότερον, καὶ ἤλθομεν πρὸς αὐτούς, καὶ ἐγενόμεθα καὶ ἡμεῖς Τοῦρκοι. Cited by Meyendorff, p. 213n.

55. Ἀφ' ὧν ἤκουσα πρότερον περὶ αὐτῶν καὶ αφ' ὧν λέγουσιν ἀρτίως Ἑβραῖοι ὄντες ἀναφαίνονται, ἀλλ'οὐ Τοῦρκοι· ἐμοὶ δὲ νῦν οὐ πρὸς Ἑβραίους ὁ λόγος. Ibid.

ruling class in favor of the people was marked by bitter internecine warfare. Nothing, unfortunately, is known of the presence or condition of the Jews during this turbulent period.[56] There is some indication, however, that the middle-class intelligentsia at this time harbored no great animosity toward the Jews (**64**). Alexios Makrembolites, of course, mentions the Jews (and the Muslims) only in a general way, and his *Dialogue* does not suggest that these remarks were based on direct observations from daily Thessalonican life. The paucity of laws regarding Jews in the *Hexabiblos* of George Armenopoulos, who was Nomophylax of Thessalonica during this period, also seems to suggest that their presence in that city was inconspicuous (**67**).

The lack of literary material is paralleled by the lack of physical evidence, although this should come as no surprise. The epitaphs of the famous Jewish graveyard of Thessalonica do not predate 1500, the period when the newly settled Sephardi Jewry entered a period of uninterrupted growth and development that continued well into the twentieth century.[57]

The vast ecclesiastical literature of the period sheds even less light on the question of a Jewish presence in Thessalonica. The sermons of Gregory Palamas, the defender of the fourteenth-century Orthodox mystical movement known as Hesychasm, contain some references to Jewish customs and beliefs. These may have been derived, however, from anti-Jewish or even Jewish tracts.[58] The sermon, too, of the Patriarch Philotheos Kokkinos, on the falseness of the Jewish Sabbath, may perhaps reflect a contemporary observation (and if so, in Constantinople). It is also possible that such a sermon may be an *apologia* for his alleged Jewish origins.[59]

In 1387 Thessalonica fell to the Ottomans for the first time; it was not regained by the Byzantines until 1403. During this sixteen-year period, there may have been an immigration of Jews into Thessalonica. Elsewhere,

56. Emmanuel (*Israélites de Salonique,* p. 43) gives no sources for his statement that the Jews were caught between the Zealots and the nobles: "sous l'un et l'autre régime, les Juifs durent beaucoup souffrir." The situation, though, may have been exactly that.

57. The published epitaphs from that graveyard (collected in I. S. Emmanuel, *Gedole Saloniki le-Dorotam* [Tel Aviv, 1936]) are all dated between 1500 and 1661.

58. Cf. J. Meyendorff, *Introduction à l'étude de Grégoire Palamas* (Paris, 1959), p. 396.

59. Cf. Constantine Tryantaphyllos, ed., *Sylloge Hellenikon Anekdoton* (Venice, 1874), pp. 88–90. Such attacks by converts are common in religious tradition. Rarely, however, are they as influential as those of Saint Romanos Θεοϱϱήτωϱ, whose cantica, written in the sixth century, remained popular throughout the Byzantine period. Cf. *Sancti Romani Melodi Cantica,* I, *Cantica Genuina,* ed. Paul Maas and C. A. Trypanis (Oxford, 1963), XVf. Cf., in general, Paul E. Kahle, *The Cairo Genizah* (2d ed.; Oxford, 1959), pp. 34–48.

the Ottomans made use of the Jews as general merchants, army contractors, physicians, and advisors. The Jews, after all, could be trusted to serve Ottoman interests, whereas the hostile Christian population could not. Therefore any evidence for the presence of Jews in Thessalonica after 1387 has to take into account the possibility that these Jews came in the wake of the Ottoman conquest.[60] Thus our one possible reference to Jews there in the late fourteenth century is derived from the epithet of the father of Shlomo Sharbit ha-Zahav, who was known as Eliahu mi-Salonikiyo—that is, from Thessalonica. However, neither his dates nor those of his son are beyond dispute, although the late fourteenth century is not unlikely.[61] After their recovery of the city in 1403, the Byzantines tried to govern it for twenty years.[62] In 1423 Thessalonica was sold to Venice. After seven disastrous years, the city fell again to the Ottomans, at the end of March 1430.

An incident in 1429 sheds further light on the presence of Jews in Thessalonica. Just six months before the capture of the city, its beloved Archbishop Simon died. In medieval fashion, the citizens interpreted his sudden death as an omen of imminent divine punishment to the city. The departed ecclesiastic, therefore, was lamented by the whole populace, and among his mourners were the Jews of the city. We might well wonder whether the attitude of the Jews toward the archbishop, reflected in their grief at his death, antedated the Venetian purchase of the city. At any rate, it is an indication that Byzantine Jews did not consider all ecclesiastics antagonistic toward them (**124**).

Whatever the Jewish population may have been during the first Ottoman occupation of Thessalonica or the subsequent Byzantine interim, it declined after the Venetian purchase of the city. For example, the total popu-

60. This caveat concerning the Ottoman interlude was ignored by Dölger ("Zur Frage," p. 133) (= *Paraspora,* pp. 382–83) in his citing of the otherwise dubious material from the monk Nathaniel Argernes (in *MM,* II, 515, line 30, and 251, line 15): οἱ τῆς ἡμετέρας πίστεως and ἀλλότριοι τῆς ἡμετέρας πίστεως which "können wohl kaum etwas anderes sein als Angehörige der jüdischen Religion." While this may very well be the interpretation of the *allótrioi,* it does not necessarily follow that it refers to a colony of Jews in Thessalonica.
There are no sources for the statements by Emmanuel (*Israélites de Salonique,* p. 46) and Nehama (*Histoire des Israélites,* pp. 107–8) that Spanish and French refugees settled in Thessalonica, although it is not unlikely. Chances are they would have gone to Adrianople first.

61. See below, chap. 4, "Intellectual Trends."

62. In that very year we find a Sephardi scribe working in Thessalonica (108).

lation in 1423 has been estimated at perhaps 40,000; by 1430 only some 7,000 were left to suffer the Ottoman sack of the city. During their occupation, the Venetians had allowed the citizens of Thessalonica to sell their property and emigrate. In view of the favorable conditions afforded the Jews in neighboring Ottoman Adrianople, it is unlikely that many Jews would have chosen to live in the inhospitable atmosphere of the Venetian-ruled city.[63]

The information on the problem of the Jewish tax in Thessalonica supports this view.[64] In 1425 the Jews petitioned Venice to release them from the annual tax of 1,000 hyperpera. They claimed that the wealthier Jews had left the city, and that the few Jews who remained were too poor to raise such a large amount. That such was the case, only two years after Venice assumed control over the city, shows the extent of the plight of the local Jewry. The petition had to be repeated in 1429. Also, the annual tax may reflect the tax status prior to 1423 (**122**).[65]

Epiros and the Western Provinces

The story of the Jewish settlement in western Greece is shrouded in darkness. Chance notices occasionally appear, however, which suggest a pattern of settlement that can be paralleled from other areas which are better documented. The persecution by Theodore Angelos, whose territorial heartland included the western mountains of Epiros, was probably restricted to Thessalonica. If our suggested dating of the events is correct, there was little time for his short-term policy to affect any Jews in Epiros. In any event, the area shifted first to Bulgarian rule and back to Byzantine, a generation later to the Serbians, and finally to the Ottomans.

The city of Ioannina remained a bastion for the population of the surrounding area and the seat of government throughout the period. Aside from local Jewish traditions, which place a community there during the Macedonian period, our first documentary evidence for such a community comes from imperial documents of the early fourteenth century.[66] While

63. Cf. Emmanuel, *Israélites de Salonique,* p. 50, note 124; Nehama (*Histoire des Israélites,* pp. 109–10) places the Venetians in particularly bad light.

64. See above, chap. 1, "Taxation," and part II document 122.

65. Ibid.

66. Starr (*JBE*) cites the legends for an earlier settlement; see above (chap. 1, notes 41ff and text) for fourteenth-century texts and their interpretation.

there are a number of problems in interpreting these texts, they indicate the existence of at least two distinct groups of Jews in the capital of Byzantine Epiros (*supra*). One group, mentioned in a chrysobull of 1319, consisted of recent immigrants to the city, most likely as a result of the general land flight that swelled the city's population (**36**). The second, named in a chrysobull of 1321, were already residents of longer duration, since they are designated as "possessions" of the Metropolitan Church of Ioannina (**43**). Despite these two separate and contemporary pieces of information about the Jews in Ioannina, we have no information about the normative community there. A bill of sale, dating from the 1430s, indicates the survival of its Romaniote community[67] and, moreover, suggests the continued influence of the halakhic teachings of the south Italian sage, Isaiah ben Mali of Trani, in western Greece.

Many areas of the western Balkans were lost to Greek rule during the fourteenth century, in particular the port of Dyrrachium, whose importance as the western terminus of the Via Egnatia was noted above. Still, we may note, as supporting evidence for the likelihood of a continuity of settlement by Romaniote Jews throughout the period, the few data that have survived concerning the Jewish community of that city. In 1323 an Irish pilgrim passed through the city and noted a small Jewish presence among the humble and mixed population of that port, which had not yet completely recovered from the devastating effects of the great earthquake nearly half a century prior to his visit (**45**). Three documents from the Venetian period illuminate the vicissitudes of the Dyrrachium community from the late fourteenth century through the dire economic situation that plagued the Jewish community at the beginning of the fifteenth (**94, 95, 106**).[68]

In the fourteenth and fifteenth centuries, the Adriatic port of Parga, in Epiros, was a flourishing entrepôt for Venetian and local merchants. The chance inclusion of this city by Kaleb Afendopoulo in his discussion of the Karaite ritual for the reading of the Torah is our sole indication for the

67. See below, chap. 3, note 64.

68. Cf. B. Krekić, "The Role of the Jews in Dubrovnik (Thirteenth–Sixteenth Centuries)," *Viator*, 4 (1973), 260f. Based on Ragusan archival sources, the author notes the first appearance of a Jew in the city in 1324, if not 1281. The necessity to supplement the archival material by other sources, especially with respect to the problem of settlement, is emphasized by the material assembled here. Where only archival material is available, on the other hand, one should not necessarily assume that it reflects the entire situation. Krekić's article contains information on Jewish settlements in other areas of the Balkans.

existence of a Karaite community in Parga and, *ipso facto,* a Rabbanite one as well (150).

The commercial and administrative center of Epiros was Arta. It was the natural crossroads for the east–west and north–south trade routes, and it maintained its own riverport. Because it maintained connections with Ioannina to the north and Naupaktos (= Lepanto) to the south (*infra*), both of which sustained Jewish communities in the fourteenth and fifteenth centuries, it seems unlikely that Jews would have neglected the opportunity to settle there also. Still, the unequivocal existence of a Romaniote community in Arta is noted only in the sixteenth-century collection of responsa of Benjamin Ze'eb b. Mattathiah of Venice.[69] The only possible reference to a Jewish community there during the Byzantine period, that of Benjamin of Tudela, poses a number of problems.[70]

Corfu also maintained a Jewish population throughout the fourteenth and fifteenth centuries. Since Benjamin of Tudela had found only one Jew (a dyer) there, its history for the twelfth and thirteenth centuries is nearly a complete blank.[71]

Thessaly and Central Greece

Benjamin of Tudela's route in the 1160s took him through a number of cities in Central Greece and Thessaly, in most of which he found a Jewish community. These include Krissa, midway between the rich olive plain and Delphi; Thebes, still today the industrial center of Boeotia; Egripon (= medieval Negroponte = contemporary Chalkis); Jabustrissa (unidentified); Rabenika; Zeitun-Lamia; Gardiki; Armylo, on the Gulf of Volos; and Bissena. Of these locales, only Thebes, Egripon, Zeitun-Lamia, and Armylo maintained their importance during subsequent vicissitudes, and of the latter, only Zeitun-Lamia remained in the hands of the Palaiologoi until the twilight of the empire. Information about these cities and others in the region, dating from the post-Byzantine period, is of value for recon-

69. Republished in two volumes (Tel Aviv, 1958).

70. On the problem of Larta-Arta, cf. Starr, *JBE,* p. 233, and part II, below, exc. A. The names Artanusi in document 83 and Artachino (63) may reflect onomastic evidence. The community of Arta is often cited in the responsa of Benjamin Ze'eb (see above, note 69). During the thirteenth and fourteenth centuries, Arta was a capital and thus fits one criterion for Jewish settlement. See below, "Lessons of Settlement."

71. See below, chap. 3, note 13.

structing the parameters of Romaniote history and for establishing a basis for the story of the later Sephardi communities there. Moreover, connections were never lost between the Jews of Byzantine and non-Byzantine areas during the Palaeologan period.

We hear little more of the 2,000 Jews of Thebes, whom Benjamin noted, save an occasional hint regarding scholars in the city. In 1218, Judah al-Ḥarizi visited Thebes during his peregrinations through the East (Thebes, incidentally, is the only Balkan city that he mentions by name). He too was impressed by the wine and the conversation, which reflected the level of scholarship among Byzantine Jewry. At the same time, he shows a Spaniard's bias by harshly criticizing the quality of the local poetry, with the exception of the renditions of Michael bar Kaleb, who had studied in Spain (**16**). In addition to al-Ḥarizi's other remarks, the scope of scholarly achievement may suggest continuation of the strong economic base that was noted a generation earlier by Benjamin of Tudela.[72]

The only other thirteenth-century reference to Jews in this region is a near contemporary notice concerning Halmyros. An unpublished letter of John Apokaukos, dating from the first decade of the thirteenth century, mentions Greeks, Westerners, and Jews in the trade and manufacture of cloth in Halmyros.[73] It is worthwhile to emphasize that Armylo (= Halmyros) was a major commercial port in the twelfth century, with Venetian, Genoese, and Pisan merchants frequenting this natural outlet for the goods of Thessaly. Benjamin noted some 400 Jews there, one of whose leaders may have come—at some time—from Italy. In the wake of the Fourth Crusade, the city came even more under the control of Venice.

72. On the other hand, the earliest epitaph to survive from Thebes is dated in the 1330s; cf. below, part II document 60. The vicissitudes of the Catalan period lie at the base of the decline of Theban economy; we do not know where the large Jewish population mentioned by Benjamin of Tudela relocated (cf. below, exc. A, note to "Thebes"); for general background, cf. K. Setton, *Catalan Domination of Athens, 1311–1388* (London, 1975).

In the second half of the thirteenth century, Moses Galimidi fled from Thebes, and his son sought refuge there in the early fourteenth.

73. The letter is cited by N. Bees in "Leon-Manuel Makros, Bishop of Bella, Kalospites, Metropolitan of Larissa, Chrysoberges, Metropolitan of Corinth," (Greek) *EEBS,* II (1924), 134; and in Nicol, *The Despotate of Epirus,* p. 15, note 27. The importance of the Jews in the cloth trade should not be underestimated; see below, chap. 4, "Economic Pursuits." It is not clear whether the incident described by Isaiah of Trani (document 5*) indicates a community in Gallipoli.

Apokaukos' observation suggests that the Jewish community there continued to flourish.

It is not until the end of the thirteenth century that further information appears for the presence of Jews in the area. Though our source, an anonymous letter from Negroponte, dates most likely from the early fourteenth century, it suggests that some of the locales mentioned as areas of Jewish residence contained Jews in the thirteenth century. The latter, which relates the story of the Kalomiti–Galimidi feud, mentions seven cities where Jews could be found: Negroponte (= Egripon), Thebes, Corinth, Adro, Salona, Constantinople, and Khrimini (30). (Constantinople has already been dealt with, and the settlements at Corinth and Khrimini will be discussed below, with the other settlements of the Peloponnesos.) There is sufficient material in the Venetian archives for a separate study of the Jews of Negroponte during the Venetian period of that island's history.[74] It will suffice here to note that both the Kalomitis and the Galimidis were Romaniote Jews and that, despite the vicissitudes of their relationship, connections continued during the late thirteenth and early fourteenth centuries between the Jews of Thebes and the neighboring port of that island.

The city of Salona (modern Amphissa) lies above the Gulf of Itea and represents the terminus of the route through the mountains on the north shore of the Gulf of Corinth. Salona is, moreover, on the opposite side of the Itean Gulf from Delphi and Krissa. Unfortunately, we have no further information on the Jews of this area until the Ottoman period. Nor, beyond this one reference to a Jew in Salona during the Frankish period, can we extrapolate information on the presence or nature of a Jewish community there or the reasons for his choice of that city.[75]

Adro represents a problem in that no such toponym has been identified in the area. Adro, however, may very possibly refer to the island of Andros. Loss of the sibilant from the nominative suffix (*os* → *o*) is common in medieval and modern spoken Greek, which drop such endings, while the *n* could be assimilated to the following letter (**30n**).[76] The anonymous letter

74. Cf. Starr, *Romania,* chap. III, with supplementary material by David Jacoby in his "Status of Jews," pp. 59–64; cf. also Jacoby's "Inquisition and Converts in Crete and Negroponte in the 14th and 15th Centuries," (Hebrew) *Sefunoth,* 8 (1964), pp. 301–18.

75. See above, chap. 1, note 38.

76. We are, it should be remembered, dealing with a Hebrew rendering of an oral Greek name. Cf. Ercule for Hercules *apud* Benjamin of Tudela. Also see below (this chapter), "Anatolia," for the problem of Kal'a'sher = Kara Hisar (?).

from Negroponte indicates some areas of Jewish settlement which are new to any map. At the same time, it shows a continuity of settlement in such centers as Thebes and Negroponte.

Also at the beginning of the fifteenth century, a Jewish scribe was active on the island of Naxos (**110**), and the community long maintained connections with Crete.

Despite the large corpus of documentary and literary material that has survived from the period of the Catalan domination of Thebes, no reference to any Jewish presence there during the fourteenth century has yet appeared.[77] Jewish sources, scarce though they are, parallel this silence.[78] It is doubtful, however, that the large community that Benjamin noted would have totally disappeared, even though it no doubt constricted during the economic decline suffered by Boeotia during the period of the Catalans. The only other references to a Jewish community in Thebes, aside from Benjamin's comments, date from the fourteenth century. Of the once large community that flourished there in the twelfth century, not one trace remains, and from this community, which we can follow for over five centuries, only a few gravestones have survived.[79] Two of them date from the middle of the Catalan period, an indisputable proof that there was an organized community of Jews in Thebes at the time (**60**). Toward the end of the Catalan period, a Jewish scribe was at work there through the spring of 1367 (**92**).

One other city appears as a site of a Jewish community during the fourteenth century. Judah ibn Moskoni visited the city of Verroia and found a Jewish library there, which suggests the presence of a congregation, however small (**87**). Also, the Ottoman cadastral registers report that a Romaniote community was transferred from Verroia to Constantinople in the wake of the conquest of the former.

Such information, it has been successfully argued, shows that these communities should be dated from at least the fourteenth century, even if no corroborating material were available. In the case of Verroia, of course, we have the independent and contemporary observation of Judah ibn Moskoni.

77. Cf. K. Setton, *Catalan Domination of Athens,* for a survey of sources.
78. Cf. author's "Jews in Fourteenth-Century Thebes," *Byzantium,* L (1980), 403f.
79. Cf. author's "Jewish Epitaphs from Thebes," *REJ,* CLXI (1982), 317ff.

The Peloponnesos

During his journey, Benjamin visited two ports in the Peloponnesos, Patras and Corinth, where he noted Jewish communities. The only other Byzantine reference to Jews in the Peloponnesos is the tenth-century story of Saint Nikon in Sparta. Information from the thirteenth century, though sparse indeed, supplies valuable information. The few fragments that have been discovered allow us to reconstruct a pattern that is not too different from what we should expect to find elsewhere in the late thirteenth and the fourteenth centuries, namely, one that reflects the new insecurities in the wake of the fragmentation of the Byzantine Empire and the later attempts to reunite it. Under these conditions, Jewish settlements tended to gravitate to coastal entrepôts or to appear in the new administrative centers of the period. Yet, we should emphasize, our information is based upon chance survivals of fragmentary allusions that may not reflect the actual situation. The question of continuity of settlement between the late twelfth and the thirteenth century must remain open insofar as other areas of Greece are concerned. For the Peloponnesos, we have little information on pre-1204 settlements, other than the abovementioned references to Patras, Corinth, and, much earlier, Sparta.

After the Fourth Crusade the Peloponnesos was more commonly referred to as the Morea.[80] During the thirteenth century, there were two important centers of Jewish settlement: the coastal entrepôt of Patras, at the entrance to the Gulf of Corinth, and the inland capital of the Principality of Achaea, Andravida. During the 1260s and 1270s, the wandering mystic, Abraham Abulafia, set down twice in Greece, and all that we know of Patras during this century is contained in his autobiographical remarks. There we learn that during his first visit, in 1261, he remained long enough in the area to find himself a wife, one of the local Greek Jewesses (**22**). During his second recorded trip to Greece, eighteen years later when he was in his late thirties, he visited Patras, possibly to enjoy the hospitality of his wife's family while writing the first of his books on prophecy (**26**).

The information on Andravida antedates Abulafia's first visit and may have assisted in his decision to visit Greece for a period of time.[81] The

80. Cf. A. Bon, *La Morée franque,* passim.

81. Cf. author's "Messianic Excitement in the Peloponnesos," *HUCA,* LII (1981), 195–202.

reference is contained in the fragment of a letter outlining messianic excitement in Sicily and Morea (**21**), and may be dated to 1257. In any case, it should be read against the background of the messianic excitement engendered among Jews through their error in identifying the Mongols with the Lost Tribes of Israel, to whom tradition ascribed the role of redeemers of the persecuted Jews.[82] Abulafia, we should note, set out from Spain to reach the Ten Tribes, hidden beyond the fabled River Sambatyon. Failure to pass beyond Acre resulted in his return home, with a perhaps not coincidental stopover in Greece.

Contained within the story of the *loʿez min Morea,* an unknown Peloponnesian "xenophone," is a reference to the three communal leaders of Andravida: R. Elia ha-Parnas, Mar Leon, and R. David ha-Melammed. This mention of three communal leaders suggests a community of no mean size, at least 50 families. If we recall that Benjamin of Tudela had found 50 Jews in Patras a century earlier, under the leadership of three communal officials, we may derive a similar figure for Andravida.[83] What is important here is that Andravida does not appear in any source before the Crusaders' conquest of Morea in 1205.[84] Their choice of the conveniently located village of Andravida (in the center of the Plain of Elis) for the capital of the Principality of Achaea must have turned it into a major commercial center

82. The whole question of messianic expectations among Byzantine Jewry in the thirteenth century should be reexamined. While our text indicates that the Jews of Andravida were affected by reports, and Abulafia's connection with Patras is suggestive, we may note here that rumors of this excitement evidently reached the West. An overlooked passage in the chronicle of Matthew of Paris supports this possibility: "Multi Judaeorum de partibus transmarinis [i.e., Outremère or Syria-Palestine], praecipue autem de imperio [i.e., the Byzantine Empire], credentes, quod plebs Tartarorum et Cumanorum essent de genere eorum, quos dominus in montibus Caspiis precibus magni Alexandri quondam inclusit, convenerunt, etc.: "nunc venit tempus, quo libra mur, etc. Exierunt namque fratres nostri, tribus scilicet Israel quondam incluse, ut subdant sibi et nobis mundum universum sub anno 1241." This passage was printed by J. Aronius, *Regesten zur Geschichte der Juden im fränkischen und deutschen Reiche bis zum Jahre 1273* (Berlin, 1882–1902), pp. 228ff. Aronius, however, understood *imperio* as the Holy Roman Empire, as did subsequent commentators on the passage. Cf. Y. Epstein in *Tarbiz* (1940), II, 219, and A. Z. Eshkoli, *Tenuoth Meshiḥiyoth be-Yisrael* (Jerusalem, 1957), I, 191f. The context is clear, however; he is referring to the Eastern Empire, *praecipue autem de imperio,* or Byzantium. Therefore we have to take into consideration the possibility that the Jews of Morea in particular, and Greek Jewry in general, were in a state of messianic agitation from 1241 to 1260, and perhaps beyond. See previous note.

83. See below, chap. 3, "Organization of the Community."

84. Cf. Bon. *La Morée franque,* p. 318.

for the western Morea.[85] Jews from Patras and other areas of Morea would have been attracted to this center, so that after nearly two generations of Frankish rule we find a new community in Andravida that rivaled in size the older community in Patras.

Another locale in Morea may have harbored a Jewish population in the thirteenth century.[86] Sparta, which had a Jewish population of unknown size in the tenth century, declined rapidly during the early thirteenth century. By the late 1240s, a new location was sought to defend the populace from the incursions of the Slavs. A few kilometers to the west of the ancient city stood a cheese-shaped hill (μιζήθρα), strategically located to seal the passes by which Slav marauders descended to the undefended plain. It was in 1249 that William Villehardouin built a fortress atop the hill referred to as Mizithra or Mistra. The question is, When did Jews begin to inhabit the town that developed in the shadow of the Frankish fortress? Did they join the founding generation during the exodus from Sparta, in the wake of the war unleashed by William from 1262 to 1264? (The war was part of his attempt to regain control of Mistra and other centers that had been surrendered to the Byzantines by the "Ladies' Parliament" in return for his release from a Constantinopolitan prison.)

Unfortunately, we have no documentary or literary evidence for a Jewish community there before the second half of the fourteenth century.[87] We may argue that the chance survival of a colophon (*infra*), mentioning a Jewish community there at that time, is only added proof for a situation that we should have expected, namely, that a Jewish community could not have been absent from the capital of the Byzantine Despotate of Morea. However, such a surmise only reaches back to the first half (if not the beginning) of the fourteenth century.[88] There is just no proof, then, for or against a Jewish presence in Mistra in the second half of the thirteenth century. And though we may strongly suspect their presence in such cen-

85. Cf. Jean Longnon, "The Frankish States in Greece, 1204–1311," in Setton, *Crusades,* vol. II, chap. V, with bibliography.

86. Bees, "Jews of Mistra." Andreades ("The Jews in the Byzantine Empire," pp. 13–14, note 2) follows Bees's proposals. See author's "Jewish Settlement in Sparta and Mistra," *BNJ,* XXII (1979), 131ff.

87. Bees ("Jews of Mistra") would have Jews in Mistra as early as the Frankish occupation of the hill (1249–62). See my study, cited in previous note. The existence of a separate Jewish quarter is indicated in a fifteenth-century source (*infra*).

88. See below, "Lessons of Settlement," and note 91.

ters as Modon, Corinth, and other such locales in Morea, no sources have yet been uncovered to support such a contention.

One of the places of refuge selected by the Galimidi sons in their escape from the clutches of the Kalomitis of Negroponte was an unidentified locale written as KhRMINI. Since it may be argued that all the other places they chose were within a certain radius of Negroponte, such a site should also be near. In Latin sources, the medieval name for Sparta is occasionally rendered as La Cremonie (**30n**). Therefore, the anonymous letter of Negroponte may imply the likelihood of an unsuspected Jewish community in the environs of Sparta at the turn of the fourteenth century.

Neighboring Mistra had attracted a Jewish community by the fourteenth century. To be sure, our first dated evidence for its presence is from a colophon dated 1387 (**100**), but it is clear that a community existed in Mistra before the activity of the scribe Shlomo ben Moshe Pangelo. Indeed, it is doubtful whether Jews could have been absent from the political, economic, and cultural center of the Byzantine Peloponnesos. Moreover, their presence would have followed soon after establishment of effective and safe Byzantine control of the area—certainly by the beginning of the fourteenth century, if not earlier. The first Greek evidence for a Jewish presence in Mistra appears only in the fifteenth century, in the chronicle of George Sphrantzes and the satire "The Descent of Mazaris into Hades."[89] From then until the nineteenth century, a number of Hebrew, Greek, Italian, and Turkish sources record their continuous settlement there.[90]

By the beginning of the fifteenth century, the center of Byzantine civilization had shifted from the beleaguered capital to the newly established court of the Despots of Morea in Mistra, where arts and letters flourished in an atmosphere far more conducive to productivity than in besieged Constantinople. In succeeding years, the Despots gradually reconquered much of the Morea, until, near the midpoint of the fifteenth century, the whole peninsula was under their control or influence. Throughout this new center of Hellenism were a number of well-established Jewish communities, many of which can be documented from the fourteenth century. We have noted the late fourteenth-century community

89. *Infra* and part II documents 119, 122.

90. Cf. author's "Jewish Settlement in Sparta and Mistra," and "Jewish Epitaphs from Mistra" (in *Michael*, vol VII), edited with Daniel Spiegel. These epitaphs date primarily from the sixteenth and seventeenth centuries.

in Mistra, and scholarly traditions attribute to Trype, one of the suburbs of Mistra, an interesting Jewish past.

The origin of the legends ascribing Jewish traditions to Trype can be explained by modern historiography. The legends arose through a misreading of a passage in the chronicle of George Sphrantzes that pertains to the capital and its environs: "Mistra and all the towns around it, namely Koula, 'Evraike Trype, Tzeramios, Pankota, Sklavochorion" (**132**). Naturally, such a phrase as "'Evraike Trype" was bound to raise interesting questions by researchers into the history and ethnography of the area. The whole problem, however, can be easily resolved. By placing a comma between 'Evraike and Trype, we remove from the latter its Jewish reputation and restore to history the fifteenth-century record of the existence of a Jewish Quarter called "'Evraike outside of Mistra."[91] Further support for the presence of Jews in Mistra is found in the satire "The Descent of Mazaris into Hades," written circa 1415 at the court of the Despots. The mention of seven nations in the environs of the capital—Lacedaemonians, Italians, Peloponnesians, Slavs, Illyrians, Egyptians, and Jews—parallels Sphrantzes' list of seven towns, as restored above. The number seven, of course, harks back to Herodotos' description of Lakonia (**119, 132n**).[92]

The last notice of Jews in Mistra during the Byzantine period comes from the eve of the Ottoman conquest of Morea. In 1460 a Jew from Mistra, who had been studying astronomy in Constantinople, was returning to his home as part of the rearguard of the Ottoman army. While the army was encamped near Kalavryta, the author, Samuel Poto, witnessed an eclipse of the sun, which he then explained to the superstitious Turks. He also informs us that Jews, by specific order, were exempted from forced labor by the Ottoman army (**143**).[93] Presumably, Samuel Poto remained in

91. A Jewish quarter, in all probability dating from their original settlement in Mistra, was located on the northwest slope of the hill, outside the postern gates that led from the upper city. This area is outside the walls of the upper town, which was built during the first half of the reign of Andronikos II. Cf. Kevin Andrews, *Castles of the Morea* (Princeton, 1953), p. 169, for a description of Levasseur's eighteenth-century drawing of the town; also author's "Jewish Settlement in Sparta and Mistra," pp. 133ff, and (in general) S. Runciman, *Mistra* (London, 1980).

92. See above, notes 37f and text, and below, part II document 104, for Ebraiokastron; cf. author's "Jewish Settlement" (pp. 134–37) with parallels in Crete cited there.

93. The source is not entirely clear regarding the possibility of a Jewish community in Kalavryta. The Jews who are mentioned may be merely part of the baggage train that brought up the rear of the army. The evidence for a Jewish community in Kalavryta during the Ottoman period will be discussed in my "Corintho-Judaica" (forthcoming).

Mistra after its surrender, and taught astronomy there, since we find his student copying his works at the end of the century.[94]

Jews were to be found in other Peloponnesian centers during the fourteenth and fifteenth centuries. Three sources, for example, document the presence of Jews in Corinth during the fourteenth century. We recall that one of the Galimidi sons fled to Corinth, then moved on to Thebes after an earthquake. More substantial material is available for the second half of the century. During the mid-1360s, a consortium of Jews is recorded in control of the "grand commercium" of the port (**89**). A clue to the identity of these Jews may be found in a document dealing with the suit of Giovanni Cremolini against the daughter of Nerio Acciaiuoli.[95] *Inter alia,* it is related that during the defense of Corinth against the Despot Theodore's attack, Carlo Tocco found it necessary to sell some of Nerio's jewels in order to finance a mission to Bayezid Yilderim, then on campaign in Wallachia.[96] These jewels were "sold or pawned in Negropont through Abraham Calomiti, a Jew from Corinth, who handed the money to Leonardo, Carlo's brother, at Bodonitsa."[97]

Now the Kalomiti family was already established in Negroponte at the beginning of the century.[98] This influential family, with its extensive resources in Negroponte and solid reputation with the Venetian administration there, was the most likely agency to supply the necessary funds in return for the jewels. The whole transaction was conveniently handled by Abraham, head of their branch office in Corinth. If this supposition is valid, we may further suggest that it is not improbable to identify the consortium of Jews who bought the "grand commercium" as representing the same interests, namely, the Kalomitis of Negroponte.[99] Should this prove to be the case, we have little evidence for the size of the Jewish community in Corinth, beyond the supposition that a branch of the Kalomiti family had

94. The student's name was Joseph Kavilan. See chap. 4, "Intellectual Trends"; the colophon, however, does not mention the place of copy.

95. The affair has been summarized by J. Chrysostomides in "Corinth 1394–1397: Some New Facts," *Byzantina,* 7 (1975), 91ff.

96. Archivo di Stato di Venezia, Lettere di Rettori (Busta unica), no. 76, f. 8; cited by Chrysostomides (above).

97. Chrysostomides, "Corinth 1394–1397," p. 91.

98. Cf. part II document 30; Jacoby ("Status of Jews") traces four generations of the family, until 1373.

99. Since Jacoby carries the Kalomiti geneology only to 1373, there is no indication as yet of Abraham's relationship to David's three great-grandsons.

been established there, along with their employees, to look after the family's interests.

There are no Byzantine sources to illuminate the history of the Jews in Corinth after its reoccupation by the Despots in 1395/96.[100] Through its location at the eastern end of the Gulf of Corinth, the ancient city was well suited to control both the east–west and the north–south trade across the Isthmus. At the time of the Byzantine reconquest, however, Corinth had greatly declined, since the Venetians preferred to bypass it and sail around the Peloponnesos in their heavily protected fleets. The Despots soon realized that they were unable to protect the Isthmus and, accordingly, they very soon sold the city to the Knights Hospitallers. However, the rule of the latter was shortlived. Due to the hatred of the Orthodox population for the Latins, the military order resold the city to the Despot in 1404. The curtain of silence that dropped over the Jewish community is briefly raised, on the eve of the Ottoman conquest of Morea, through the chance survival of a colophon from a wandering scribe, dated 1456 (**136**).

Jews were present in the other major ports of the Peloponnesos during the fourteenth and fifteenth centuries. The "two eyes" of Venice, Modon and Coron, supported communities of Jewish merchants and occasional workers; the former (for a while) officially employed a Jewish doctor.[101] There is also evidence that the Jews of Patras were in communication with their coreligionists in the southern tip of the peninsula, as evidenced by the marriage of Solomon ben Abraham to the daughter of Elijah of Modon (**130**). Along the west coast, Jews are reported to have been in Clarentza, the mainland port for the island of Zakynthos (**127**). The source, more concerned with the Catalan pirate and his captives, does not indicate whether the Jews he mentioned actually lived there or elsewhere. Rather, it seems that these Jews may have been from Zakynthos, which in succeeding centuries harbored prosperous Jewish communities. The presence of other Jewish communities in the area—Coron, Modon, Patras, Lepanto, Corfu,

100. Unfortunately, the surviving epigraphy in Corinth is undatable. The one piece that has been published by Starr ("The Epitaph of a Dyer in Corinth," *BNJ,* XII [1936], 42–49) was assigned by him to the tenth to eleventh centuries. An edition of all the extant Hebrew epigraphy from Corinth is in progress (above, note 39). For the date 1395/96, cf. Chrysostomides, "Corinth 1394–1397," p. 96. A half-century later, in 1456, we find a Jewish scribe there; see below, part II document 136.

101. See Starr, *Romania* (p. 66 and his chap. IV), for a survey of the Jews in these two colonies. See below, part II document 108.

and Parga—suggests that there was a contemporary settlement of Jews on Zakynthos. It is also possible that these Jews, involved in the slave transaction, were merchants who were captured during an all too common pirate action. At the same time, the possibility should not be ignored that Jews were living in Clarentza, a corollary of their settlement (earlier noted) in Andravida.

Patras, however, was the main entrepôt of the Gulf of Corinth and, as such, had sustained a Jewish community that was first noted in the twelfth century. The continuity of a Jewish presence in the city can be surmised from the biographical data of Abraham Abulafia (**22, 26**) and the references that survive from the end of the fourteenth century.[102] Further evidence is supplied from the existence there of a Jewish scribe and his patron in 1410 (**109**). The latter, plainly a Sephardi by his name, indicates the appearance of wealthy Spanish immigrants, even at this early date who were interested in local Romaniote scholarship. An important notice in the chronicle of George Sphrantzes identifies the location of the ʿEbraike of Patras, wherein these Jews lived and worked. The source indicates that during the Byzantine assault on the city in 1429 at least one counterattack was mounted by the defenders from the Porta Hebraicae (**124**).[103] Patras, then is the second Peloponnesian town, along with Mistra, of which we have evidence of a Jewish Quarter called *ʿEbraike*. This evidence may perhaps be sufficient to extend this designation of a Jewish Quarter so-called to each locale in which we have identified the existence of a Jewish community.

During the fourteenth century, Patras was under the rule of the Latin archbishop. It is clear from the surviving records that, during this period, Jews owned property within the city and plots outside the walls, in particular in the neighborhood of Strô (**130**).[104] These records are the first indica-

102. Printed by E. Gerland, *Neue Quellen zur Geschichte des lateinischen Erzbistums Patras* (Leipzig, 1903), and commented on by Starr, *Romania,* chap. V. On the history of Jews in Patras, cf. K. N. Triantaphyllos, *Historikon Lexikon ton Patron* (Patras, 1959), pp. 103–4, and his second edition of S. N. Thomopoulos, *Historia ton Poleon Patron* (Patras, 1950), pp. 432–37. Additional material can be found in this author's "A Corpus of Hebrew Epitaphs in Patras," *Archeologikon Deltion,* 31 (1976; appeared in 1980), 49–75.

103. Sphrantzes notes that the gate was also called Zeugalateion.; cf. Tryantaphyllos, *Lexikon,* s.v. and author's study (to be corrected accordingly) cited previous note. I suspect that it was located in the western part of the city which was the main commercial route to the interior. Cf. Hélène Saranti-Mendelovici, "A propos de la ville de Patras aux 13e–15e siècles," *REB,* 38 (1980), pp. 228ff.

104. Starr, *Romania,* pp. 73–74.

tion, since the twelfth century, that mainland Jews were connected with cultivatable land (**131**).[105] On the other hand, evidence for such a connection is available for fourteenth-century Crete and Euboea. On the mainland, however, such a relationship with the land was not always continuous, especially during the transition from Frankish to Byzantine rule.

A case in point involved a scion of the Leonessa family, one of the large landowning families in the area, and a local Jew with family connections in Modon (**130**). The latter, Solomon ben Abraham, was accused of not paying rent for a plot of land that he had leased from the estate of Giles de Leonessa (possibly prior to the Byzantine conquest of Patras); of having made a garden on this plot, thereby increasing its value; and, by reason of these two acts, usurping title to this property. Solomon's defense, on its surface, seems legitimate. He acknowledged that he had legally occupied the land for some years and had improved it. On the other hand, he denied defaulting on the rent, claiming that it had never been solicited. To support his argument, he presented a document (apparently a deed) that gave him the land. Despite Solomon's spirited defense, the court, consisting of Greek and Latin notables, found for Nikolas de Leonessa, their peer, and condemned Solomon the Jew. That there was something out of the ordinary in their decision is indicated by the remission of part of the normal penalty. Still, Solomon lost the land, its contents, and a sum representing the annual unpaid rent (*telos!*).

Chances are that we may have here an inkling of a systematic reclamation of property on the part of the noble families of Patras, who had either rented out land or, in some way, let its title lapse during the Latin period. With the appearance of a new Byzantine regime, though still bound by the feudal assizes of the previous Latin period, these nobles attempted to regain or reestablish their legitimate possession of their former property. The new Byzantine government, after all, had not changed by much the judicial structure of the city, whose customary law had been based on the *Assizes of Romania*. They merely added to it a representative of the central government in Mistra.[106]

105. The Jews of Byzantine Italy, of course, owned their own land; cf. Starr, *JBE,* pp. 27–28. Benjamin of Tudela recorded a settlement of farmers in continental Greece in the twelfth century: "Thence it is a day and a half's journey [from Naupaktos] to Krissa [below Delphi] where about 200 Jews live apart. They sow and reap on their own land." Cited by Starr, *JBE,* p. 229, and below, exc. A.

106. Cf. Jacoby, *Les Assizes de Romania,* pp. 180–81.

On the northern shore of the Gulf of Corinth, opposite Patras, was the port of Lepanto or Naupaktos, which had been purchased by Venice in 1408. (Though more properly located in Acarnania, and thus part of the hinterland of Epiros, the intimate relations between this port and Patras make it convenient to discuss the material pertaining to the Jews in Naupaktos here, rather than in the section that deals with western Greece.) A record from 1430 preserves information concerning large-scale commercial dealings between the two ports of Naupaktos and Patras, involving several Jewish bankers (**126**). Both Meshullam ben Mordecai and Aaron ben Missael were business associates of the same Leonessa family that had successfully sued Solomon ben Abraham for his land. Still other Jews were partners to the Leonessae (**126**), and one Jew appeared as witness for Katherina de Leonessa (**126n**). The fact of these partnerships, in both neighboring ports, prior to the Byzantine conquest of Patras may well suggest, despite the lack of documentation from the subsequent Byzantine period, that such dealings were continued after the conquest.[107]

Anatolia

The available information on Jewish settlement in Anatolia prior to the Fourth Crusade allows us to place Jews in thirteen or fourteen cities, comprising the major commercial centers on the broad overland road network throughout the western part of the peninsula. Moreover, Benjamin of Tudela, despite the confused recitation of his Aegean section, places Jews on the islands of Lesbos (= Mytilini), Chios, Samos, and Rhodes. Crete, of course, sustained a continuous Jewish presence in many areas of that island from the Hellenistic period until the twentieth century. Crete, however, was lost to the empire after the Fourth Crusade, and the story of its Greek- and Italian-speaking Jewish communities more properly belongs to a survey of the Venetian commercial empire. This section will be concerned with western Anatolia and the islands along its shore, as well as scattered information on settlements around the Black Sea.

Thirteenth-century information is very sparse and each fragment of

107. P. Christopoulos ("The Jewish Community of Naupaktos," [Greek] *Proceedings for the Society of Central Greek Studies* [1968], I, 277–300) has a summary of what is known of this community and its surviving epigraphy. See author's study, cited above (note 102), for additional material.

data poses a number of problems in its interpretation.[108] For example, a hitherto unidentified locale is mentioned in a mid-thirteenth-century record concerning the sale of a biblical scroll (**23**). The city is referred to as KAL'A'ASHET or KAL'A'ASHER. The latter form may very likely indicate a Hebrew transliteration of the Turkic Kara-Hisar.[109] The same biblical scroll, interestingly enough, appears in another document, dated thirteen years earlier, when it was originally sold and the legality of the owner's right to sell was established. Internal evidence—use of a Greek name for the mother (Eudokia) and a Hebrew name for the son (Kaleb), a name rather common in the Byzantine sphere—suggests a Byzantine milieu (**20**). The toponymic data in the records concerning this scroll, if our reading is correct, may be the only indication that the Jews in Asia Minor were not seriously affected by the conversion attempt of John Vatatzes in the Empire of Nicaea in 1254.[110] This suggestion depends, of course, on which of the many Kara-Hisars in Anatolia is meant.

Three Hebrew epitaphs from Nicaea were published by A. M. Schneider.[111] Unfortunately, they are difficult to date and have been tentatively assigned to the twelfth or thirteenth century by their editor.[112] With the appearance of an imperial court at Nicaea in the early thirteenth century, it is difficult to accept that these epitaphs represent the end of a Jewish presence in the city. Indeed, the persecution of Jews, instigated by John Vatatzes (*supra*) later in the century, argues for a Jewry visible to the emperor and his court in Nicaea.

One area in Paphlagonia that remained for a time under the control of the emperors in Nicaea furnishes the only dated documentary evidence for an identifiable Jewish community in Anatolia in the thirteenth century. The

108. For the evidence on Jews in Anatolia prior to 1204, see Ankori, *Karaites,* pp. 113–16. The cities mentioned are Ephesus, Attaleia, Nicaea, Pylae, Nicomedia, and possibly Gangra (*infra,* note 113). Strobilos, on the coast; Khonai; Amorium; Cotyaeum; Mastaura inland. Cf. comments and texts in Starr, *JBE,* index, s.v., and *infra,* exc. A, no. II.

109. For a discussion of this possibility and probable sites, see part II document 23n. It is also possible that these two documents may be of Karaite origin. In this event, they would reflect the presence of both Rabbanite and Karaite Jews there.

110. See above, chap. 1, "Imperial Policy."

111. *Die Römischen und Byzantinischen Denkmäler von Iznik-Nicaea* (Berlin, 1943), pp. 36–37. It may have been in Nicaea that Michael VIII informed the Jewish leaders that their persecution by the Laskarids was at an end. See above, chap. 1, "Imperial Policy."

112. Our examination of one stone *in situ,* i.e., immured in the outer wall of the mosque adjacent to the museum in Nicaea, points up the necessity to reedit these epitaphs. The one we examined may be dated to the late twelfth or early thirteenth century.

city of Gangra (= Germanicopolis) supported a well-established Karaite community and, *ipso facto,* a Rabbanite community alongside it (**14**).[113] Of these three cities—Kara-Hisar (?), Nicaea, and Germanicopolis—only Nicaea is recorded as having a Jewish population prior to the thirteenth century. Moreover, while all three cities contained Greek-speaking or Romaniote Jewish communities and (at least one of them) a Karaite community, only Nicaea and Gangra were indisputably under the control of the Byzantines during the period indicated by the documents.

The fourteenth century witnessed the gradual disappearance of Byzantine rule from western Anatolia. At the same time, evidence of a Jewish community should suggest that such a community was composed of Romaniote Jews, even if no clear evidence to that effect is available. As we shall see, the majority of references to Jews in Anatolia during this century *do* indicate their Romaniote character. A Karaite anecdote, concerning dietary laws in Nicomedia, provides the unique reference to Jews in that city between the end of the sixth century and the end of the sixteenth century.[114] The reference, containing Romaniote names, even though dated two years after the Ottoman conquest of Nicomedia, clearly suggests the survival of a Romaniote community from the Byzantine period (**61**). The only other indication of a Jewish presence in that city is derived from the tradition that the Karaite scholar, Aaron ben Elijah, was born there in the first quarter of the fourteenth century (**61n**). The information thus derived on the Jews of Nicomedia clearly suggests that during the last generation of Byzantine rule in that city, its Jewish population contained both a Rabbanite and a Karaite community.

The remaining information on Jewish settlements in Anatolia during the fourteenth century comes from the period after the Ottoman conquests there. Even so, it provides valuable information for the reconstruction of settlement patterns of Romaniote Jews from the previous Byzantine period (*infra*). Ibn Battuta noted a Jewish quarter in Antalya (**48**) where Jews are known to have been settled since at least the eleventh century. Other contemporary sources indicate their presence in Laodikeia (**87**), Ephesus (**63**), Aydin (**49**), and Nicomedia (*supra*). Ottoman cadastral registers from

113. See above, note 35. Ankori suggests a Karaite settlement there as early as the twelfth century (*Karaites,* p. 126).

114. Cf. also Samuel Poznanski, *Beitrage zur Karäischen Handschriften-und Bücherkunde,* p. 14, no. 79, and Ankori, *Karaites,* pp. 130ff.

the seventeenth century shed further light on areas of Jewish settlement in Anatolia during the fourteenth century. These registers, we recall, list the communities that were uprooted by Mehmet II and resettled in Constantinople as part of his policy of rebuilding the depopulated capital. The communities uprooted from Anatolia include Bursa,[115] Antalya (and one of its hinterland suppliers, Borlu), Sinope (on the Black Sea), and two locales near Aydin, Çine and Tire. The parallel Hebrew list includes one city that does not appear in the Ottoman sources: Palatia, the medieval site of ancient Miletus. Farther to the north, a Romaniote scribe identified his home (in 1387) as Manissa, in the emirate of Saruhan (**99**). To this list we may add a likely Jewish community in both Trebizond and Philadelphia during the thirteenth and fourteenth centuries.[116]

The islands off the western shores of Anatolia apparently were an area of earlier settlement by Greek-speaking Jews. The confusing section of Benjamin of Tudela's itinerary does not allow us to identify more than a few of the major centers that they inhabited. These include Mytiline, Chios, Samos, and Rhodes. At the same time, his text suggests that Jews were present on other islands as well. Evidence from the fourteenth and fifteenth centuries is even more sparse in terms of extent of settlement. Actually, there are references only to Chios and Rhodes.

Chios was subject to Byzantium until the middle of the fourteenth century; in 1346 it passed to the control of the Genoese, who were better able to exploit its commercial value (**87**). Rhodes, on the other hand, was conquered and taken from the Turks by the Knights Hospitallers at the beginning of the fourteenth century. These island Jewish communities may not have been affected by the general turmoil on the mainland, although the state of our sources makes any such statement speculative.

New areas of settlement, as well as the reinvigoration of older sites, around the shores of the Black Sea appear in the sources of the fourteenth and fifteenth centuries. The ports of Solchat, Tana, and Kaffa contained both Rabbanite and Karaite communities. In Solchat, for example, the notice of a Rabbanite–Karaite calendar feud in 1278 informs us of the

115. A fourteenth-century colophon identifies a member of the Jewish community in Bursa as Shlomo ha-Nasi, son of the holy high priest [כג״ק] Jesse ha-Nasi of Trnovo in J.T.S. Micr. 8225 (acc. 01183 Marshal case), f. 316^{v}; cf. description of ms. in *JQR*, LVII (1967), 528–43.

116. See above, chap. 1, notes 61 and 62.

presence of both communities in this important commercial center (**25**). Therefore, there may have been commercial motives for the temporary destruction of this community by the Genoese in 1365 (**90**). By the end of the century, however, scribes were again active in Solchat, which indicates the reestablishment of Jewish communities there.[117] A chance notice, dated 1362, identifies a Jewish merchant as an inhabitant of Tana (**105n**). The existence of Jews in the port of Kaffa is noted only at the end of the fourteenth century, by Johann Schiltberger, an ex-Crusader, who saw the Ottoman realm as a slave of its rulers. In Kaffa, he found both Rabbanite and Karaite Jews (**105**).

As is to be expected, then, the commercial entrepôts of the Crimea attracted Jews and sustained their communities during the period of Genoese exploitation of this area, despite the vicissitudes inherent in the ensuing commercial rivalries. In the Caucasus emporium of al-Macher, the North African globetrotter, Ibn Battuta, encountered a Spanish Jewish merchant who had traveled there via Constantinople. This chance encounter is but one indication of the popularity of this trade route in the fourteenth century (**50**).

Along the western shore of the Black Sea, one of the towns that well into the fifteenth century remained part of the hinterland of Constantinople, and a last vestige of imperial rule, was Sozopolis (= Burgaz). At the end of the fifteenth century, Kaleb Afendopolo cites the presence of a Karaite community there, presumably from the Byzantine period (**150**). On the southern shore of that commercial lake, we have already noted the late reference to a Romaniote community in Sinope.

The only other port that could have sustained a Jewish community was the city of Trebizond, capital of the Empire of the Grand Komnenoi, which remained an outpost of Byzantine civilization until the second half of the fifteenth century. Trebizond most likely contained a Jewish community. Unfortunately, the only possible reference to the existence of Jews there is a twelfth-century colophon, the reading of which poses a number of problems.[118] The only other evidence for the presence of Jews in Trebizond comes from the eve of the fall of that city to the Ottomans (**144**). A general

117. See above, note 36. The continuous traffic between the Karaites of Solchat and Adrianople is becoming very clear; see below, part II document 26*, and the career of Aaron ha-Rophe (*infra,* chap. 4).

118. Ankori, *Karaites,* pp. 122ff. The community is designated as Tirapzin.

argument may be posited that Jews could not have been absent from this important commercial center, given their presence throughout the entrepôts of the Black Sea.

Lessons of Settlement

The question of continuity of settlement among Romaniote communities from the period of the Komnenoi through the gradual reunification of their empire under the aegis of the Ottomans cannot be answered beyond any doubt. However, the information that has survived indicates that in a number of areas where Jews were known to have been settled in the twelfth century, they reappear in the sources of the fourteenth and fifteenth centuries. Moreover, since many of these Jews are Greek speaking, it is possible that Jews were settled in these areas even prior to their first appearance in the sources. Still, we should be cautious and relate such a continuity only in such cases as are historically possible. Thus we should not anticipate a Jewish settlement in Andravida, for example, before its emergence as a major center in the thirteenth century.

Direct evidence for the existence of Jewish settlements in the first two-thirds of the thirteenth century is available for only the following cities: Pera, Halmyros, Thebes, Patras, Andravida, Dyrrachium, Gortzanos, Kara-Hisar (?), and Gangra. Indirect evidence suggests a Jewish presence in Constantinople and Nicaea. On the other hand, there are no sources to suggest a break in the continuity of the (at least) forty-four Jewish communities that were spread throughout the Balkans and Anatolia in the twelfth century (exc. A). Unless such evidence becomes available through the discovery of new sources, there is no reason to assume that an early thirteenth-century map of Jewish settlements would differ much from the map of the twelfth century.

The fourteenth century poses a different set of problems. Aside from the identified areas of settlement, there is a teasing reference to a ubiquity that cannot be clarified with any certainty. During his dispute with Venice from 1319 to 1321, Andronikos II refers to "those same-mentioned Venetian Jews, many of whom are from the towns and rural lands (*castris et terris*) of Our Empire." This reference suggests that Venetian Jews were widely spread throughout imperial lands. It should be emphasized that a corresponding settlement of Byzantine Jews should also be assumed, since our source states clearly that Venetian Jews settled among the already established Byzantine Jewish communities. Even so, we have little information to identify these *castra et terras*.[119] Some of them were unquestionably in areas that were under Venetian control but which the imperial government still considered (at least tacitly) imperial land: "from the towns and rural lands of Our Empire." These unidentified locales, then, may not necessarily be included in the general patterns to be discussed.

Among the cities mentioned throughout this chapter as harboring Jewish populations are the new political centers of the Palaeologan period. Nicomedia, for example, was the last Byzantine stronghold in Bithynia; Ioannina was the seat of the governor of Epiros; Serres later became almost an independent Serbian state because of its location; and Mistra was the seat of the Despotate of Morea. In addition to the political centers, which offered the twin benefits of protection within the walls of a fortified city and the economic opportunities of an administrative hub, Jews were also present, to a smaller degree, in some of the *less* important localities. However, the above list shows that, by and large, Jewish settlement tended to gravitate toward seats of government.

Indeed, it is noteworthy that, to our knowledge, few of the abovementioned cities are among the locales that harbored Jews before the fourteenth century. This is no mere coincidence. Given the great changes in the political map of Greece in the thirteenth century (autonomous kingdoms in Epiros, the Peloponnesos, and Macedonia, and the growing independence of Bulgarians and Serbs), coupled with incessant warfare and the resultant destruction of the countryside, economic activities were no doubt curtailed, and many areas that had flourished in the twelfth century lost their prosperity. Thus, while the initial years of the thirteenth century would not radically change the map of Jewish settlement in Greece, as drawn by Benjamin of Tudela (and his route, we should remember, was selective), a late thirteenth- and fourteenth-century map should reflect only those areas for which we have sources to justify the presence of Jews. On the other hand, the trend toward settlement in some administrative centers suggests, despite the sparsity of source material, that Jews were likely to be found in other major administrative centers as well. Therefore, any area in mainland Greece during the thirteenth, fourteenth, and fifteenth centuries

119. For a list of *castra* in Epiros, Thessaly, Central Greece (Hellas), and the Peloponnesos, cf. V. Hrochova, "Le commerce vénitien et les changements dans l'importance des centres de commerce en Grèce du 13e au 15e siècle," *Studi Veneziani*, IX (1967), 3–34.

that was recognized as an important military and administrative center may well have harbored a Jewish community, whether or not a source to this effect is at hand.

Jewish settlements in Anatolia during the fourteenth century seem to have gravitated toward the coasts. To be sure, we lack any contemporary Turkic sources, and our information for the interior is therefore severely limited. However, Greek, Arabic, Latin, and Hebrew sources indicate a clear trend. Whereas Jewish settlements during the pre-1204 period in Anatolia were along the great network of Roman roads that carried the bulk of the commerce of the area,[120] in the fourteenth century, reflecting the breakdown of control over the road system and the subsequent decline of the internal trade of Anatolia, Jewish settlements disappeared from the interior and were to be found in the capitals of the coastal emirates or in their seaports.

The same trend is evident in those areas of Europe which once formed part of the Byzantine Empire, although the stability of overland trade through the fourteenth century enabled the Jews to maintain settlements in some of that area's larger inland centers. The Jewish communities in Bulgaria, Thrace, and Macedonia especially illustrate this continuity of settlement in inland cities. Bulgarian centers include Nicopolis, Yambol, and Zagora. In almost all the heavily populated and well-fortified areas of Thrace and Macedonia which followed the old Roman road from Dyrrachium to Constantinople, the Via Egnatia, there were Jewish settlements: Adrianople, Didymotikon, Serres, Thessalonica, Monastir, Stip, Kastoria, Ochrida, and Dyrrachium. Central Greece supported communities in Verroia, Lamia-Zeitun, Thebes, and Salona. The Peloponnesos contained Jewish communities in Corinth, Patras, Coron, and Modon. In many of the main commercial centers on the islands surrounding Greece and along the Aegean coast of Anatolia were long-established Jewish communities: Corfu, Negroponte, Rhodes, Chios, and the emporia of Venetian Crete: Candia, Canea, and Rethymno.

Some twenty-seven former Byzantine cities in the Balkans, Greece, and the islands are known to have harbored Jews during the post-Byzantine occupation of these cities in the fourteenth century. The indication from the available evidence is that these Jewish settlements, while widely scattered, were geared to the principal trade routes of the period. Twenty-

120. Cf. Ankori, *Karaites,* chap. III.

two of them, in fact, were located in major inland centers and seaports, while the others represented important island emporia. In many instances a pre-1204 community in these locales can be documented. It was these communities that, in the course of the fourteenth and fifteenth centuries, were to come under the control of the expanding Ottoman state.

THREE

COMMUNAL ORGANIZATION AND SOCIAL LIFE

THE PRIMARY reasons for the general neglect of Romaniote communal life by modern scholarship are not difficult to discern. Byzantine Jewry has always been a historical stepchild to the better-known Sephardi communities of the Ottoman Empire, which have left us a plethora of communal records and responsa, grave inscriptions, travelers' descriptions, and governmental registers to attract the interest of researchers.[1] The lack of source material for the earlier Romaniote communities contributed to this scholarly neglect. Moreover, Byzantine-Jewish scholarship for the past two generations has been concerned primarily with the relations between the Jews and the imperial government and their role in the socio-economic structure of the empire. Only a few studies, therefore, have appeared since Samuel Krauss's pi-

1. On the general neglect of, even bias against, medieval Greek Jewry by Jewish scholarship, see Ankori's sections in "The Strange Ways of Bias" and "Greek Jewry Lost . . . and Rediscovered," in *GOTR,* XXII (1977), 19–22 (also in *Journal of Ecumenical Studies,* XIII [1976], 535–38). The article by S. Assaf, "On the Family Life of Jews in Byzantium," (Hebrew) *Be-Ohale Ya'akov* (Jerusalem, 1943), pp. 99–106, is devoted to the internal life of the Romaniotim. By comparison, studies of the responsa of the sixteenth century have greatly increased our knowledge of the internal life of the Sephardi communities. Cf., *inter alia,* S. Assaf, "The Organization of the [Jewish] Courts in Turkey in the 17th Century," (Hebrew) *ha-Olam,* vol. 7; M. Goodblatt, *Jewish Life in Turkey in the XVIth Century* (New York, 1952); I. M. Goldman, *The Life and Times of Rabbi David Ibn Abi Zimra* (New York, 1970); Leah Bornstein, "The Spiritual Structure and Courts of the Jews in the Ottoman Empire in the 16th and 17th Centuries," (Hebrew) M.A. thesis (Bar Ilan University, 1972). Her recent doctoral thesis also includes the eighteenth-century material. See, as well, a number of doctoral dissertations in Hebrew and English on individual authors of responsa.

oneering *Studien zur byzantinisch-jüdische Geschichte,*[2] and these have been restricted to the period prior to 1204, though later parallels are often cited. The terminus 1204 was borrowed from Byzantine historiography; yet, as we have seen, it is not necessarily pertinent to the Jewish story. A new phase in Byzantine Jewish history began only later in that century, with the advent of the Palaiologoi, who made a conscious and constructive use of Jewish and other ethnic resources in their attempts to balance Venetian and Genoese economic pressures.

The history of the Romaniote communities, it should be emphasized, continued well into the Ottoman period and, indeed, has survived to the present day. The inherent conservatism of Jewish communities thus preserves material on the communal structure, customs, and intellectual life of these communities in the literature that postdates the Ottoman conquest.[3] It would not be outside the limits of the present chapter, therefore, to review the relevant information for the period before 1204; nor, by the same token, should the material from the Ottoman period be excluded.[4] At the same time, we shall be careful to note where changes from the earlier patterns may have occurred during the Palaeologan period or in the subsequent Ottoman period. While the extant material on the structure of the Byzantine Jewish communities in the two and a half centuries following the Fourth Crusade is sparse indeed, what little there is suggests that the communities handled their internal affairs in much the same way from the early years of the empire until the Ottoman conquest. Both sectors of the Jewish population, the normative Rabbanite community and the Karaites, had a parallel communal structure. Although their intercommunal relations were not always peaceful, toward the end of the period a marked rapport between the two groups developed.

Organization of the Community

The Jewish community in the Byzantine Empire was a legally recognized autonomous group according to the pagan Roman tradition, which de-

2. Krauss, *Studien* (1914); Starr, *JBE* (1939); Ankori, *Karaites* (1959); and A. Sharf, *Byzantine Jewry from Justinian to the Fourth Crusade* (1971). The recent doctoral dissertation of Joseph Hacker (Hebrew University of Jerusalem) deals with the Romaniote community.

3. Almost all of the responsa cited in Assaf's article (above, note 1) were written after 1453.

4. Thus, while the internal history of the Jews during these first two centuries is being clarified, no work can yet replace the multivolume study of Solomon Rosanes, *Israel be-*

clared it a *religio licita*. Legislation under the Christian empire restricted Jewish privileges but retained the right of Jews to exist within an autonomous community. Several Christian emperors temporarily revoked this status and persecuted the Jews. When the general situation returned to normal, however, their original status as an autonomous legal entity was always restored. The many advantages available to Jews during periods of legal recognition were sufficient to encourage reestablishment of their communities soon after each persecution.[5]

As an autonomous group, the Jewish community spoke with one voice, through a delegated spokesman, to the government. Whether the spokesman was appointed by the Jews or by the imperial government is a question that cannot be answered with certainty for many of the Jewish communities. On the other hand, there is information to show that the leaders of certain groups—for example, the Jewish guilds—were imperial appointees. The statement of Benjamin of Tudela regarding Thessalonica clearly supports this view: "R. Samuel ha-Rav . . . is appointed by royal authority as head of the Jews."[6] The term *ha-Rav* ("the Rabbi") may also have been the Hebrew designation for the head of the community (as opposed to the head of the guild, called in Greek *exarchos*), who was at the same time the chief Jewish spokesman to the government. In this respect, however, the appearance of the title in only three other Byzantine communities, namely, Armylo, Bissena, and Pera, and not in the other twenty-two cities that Benjamin visited, causes some difficulties. The rabbi of Thebes, on the other hand, has the more exalted title *ha-Rav ha-Gadol,* that is, "the Chief Rabbi."[7]

Other leadership titles were employed as well. In Armylo, where we have noted that one of its leaders was called *ha-Rav,* its other two leaders are referred to as *ha-Parnas* and *ha-Rosh*. In Pera, only two of the four

Togarmah (vol. I) and later titled *Koroth ha-Yehudim be-Turkiah* (vols. II–IV; vols V–VI deal with the 18th and 19th centuries). The researches of Joseph Hacker promise to fill this gap.

5. J. Juster, *Les Juifs dans l'empire romain*, 2 vols. (Paris, 1914); J. Parkes, *The Conflict of the Church and the Synagogue* (London, 1930); S. Baron, *The Jewish Community* (Philadelphia, 1948), I, 111–16; on the four persecutions before 1204, cf. Starr, *JBE*, chap. I; for the two persecutions in the thirteenth century, see above, chap. 1, "Imperial Policy."

6. For the argument that these particular Jews constituted a guild of Jewish silkworkers and that R. Samuel was the government-appointed *exarchos* of the guild, cf. Ankori, *Karaites*, pp. 149–50.

7. The term *archirabbinos* was used in modern Greece before World War II (in Volos).

leaders who are mentioned have communal titles, again *ha-Rav* and *ha-Parnas;* the other two jumbled terms have been interpreted as scholarly epithets (exc. An). The title *parnas* is attested to a number of times in the thirteenth century. One of the communal leaders in Andravida was a *parnas* while the other was apparently a teacher (David ha-Melammed) (**21**). David Kalomiti led the community of Negroponte in the late thirteenth century with the same title. An epitaph from Thebes, dated 1337–38, identifies the grandfather of the deceased as Shlomo ha-Parnas; so he, too, must have functioned in the second half of the thirteenth century.[8] During the same period, the father of the fourteenth-century scholar Shemarya Ikriti was a *parnas* in Crete. Finally, an Eliahu ha-Parnas was attested in 1271 under circumstances suggesting a Greek milieu.[9] These examples are sufficient to show that the term was widespread as a communal title during the second half of the thirteenth century.

Benjamin of Tudela's information on the communal leadership of Byzantine Jewry, despite occasional textual problems, is the most descriptive source we have. It indicates that in almost all the larger communities (over 100) a committee of three, consisting of rabbis and laymen, was in charge, while in smaller communities (up to 50) usually only two leaders are denoted. In some, the title *ha-Rav* or *ha-Rav ha-Gadol* refers to a government-appointed or -sanctioned leader of a specific group; however, this may not necessarily be the case for the general community leadership. To parallel this, a late thirteenth-century source (albeit from Venetian Euboea) provides the information that one man, David ha-Parnas, controlled not only the external relations of the community of Chalkis, with the current overlords, but also had ultimate authority, presumably, over Moses Galimidi, who performed all of its internal functions (**30**). Such a situation suggests a small community in Negroponte at the turn of the fourteenth century.

A generation later, Adoniah Kalomiti, who was active as a scribe in Thessalonica, refers to his father, R. Aba Kalomiti, by a number of honorifics: *ha-nagid, ha-rosh, ha-maskil, kevod mori ve-rabbi* (**47**). Only the first three terms concern us here, and the third would cause little note were it

8. Cf. author's "Jewish Epitaphs in Thebes," *REJ,* vol. CLXI (1982), epitaph 3, and his "Jews in Fourteenth-Century Thebes," *Byzantion,* L (1980), 405. The possibility should not be ignored that the term *parnas,* on occasion, might have evolved into a family name. It is not known where Shlomo ha-Parnas lived.

9. Neubauer, *Bodleian,* I, #296. It is not impossible that he may be the same as Elia ha-Parnas of Andravida, who was functioning in 1257.

not used in a special way by Karaite savants (**14**). Here, however, it means "intellectual" or "scholar." The first two terms, on the other hand, were commonly used in the medieval period to designate communal leaders. Jewish leaders in Islamic areas, particularly Egypt, were known as *negidim* (plural of *ha-nagid*).[10] The term *ha-rosh*, as we have seen, was commonly used to distinguish Jewish leaders in Greek cities. The use of the term *nagid* in a Byzantine milieu, however, is restricted to this one text and thus may reflect the scribe's desire to honor his father with a communal title that had won such renown in Egypt during the previous century. We may further suggest that his father was the same Aba Kalomiti, the son of David ha-Parnas, the lay leader of Negroponte,[11] who had inherited the mantle of leadership of that community. Thus the scribe's description of his father's official position compares with the description of David Kalomiti in the anonymous letter from Negroponte (**30**). We may also note that although David was autonomous in his extensive commercial dealings, his son Aba (if not David himself) was restricted in his judicial prerogatives over the Jewish community of Negroponte (**30**, n. 26).

In the Byzantine sphere, on the other hand, we have only two references to Jewish communal leaders during the entire period of the Palaiologoi. The first concerns the meeting of Michael VIII with the Jewish leaders (no titles are mentioned), where he announced the end of the Laskarid persecution and also his plans (albeit tacitly stated) for rebuilding the empire with their help (**24**). The second is the romantic account of the elevation of Moses Kapsali to the position as "judge and leader of the Jews."[12] The same source suggests that he held an analogous position during the previous Byzantine period (**141**).

Latin sources from the fourteenth century provide some comparative data. The head of the Jewish community of Dyrrachium during the Venetian period is referred to as "*magister Judaye de Durachio*" (**95**). Thus the tradition of one spokesman for the Jewish community continued into post-Byzantine times in one former imperial city. In Corfu, on the other hand, the leadership of the community had been reorganized in the post-Byzan-

10. For a general summary, cf. "Nagid" in *EJ*, XIII, 758–64. A Hebrew translation of the formula of appointment in Mamluk Egypt can be found in A. N. Pollak, "The Jews and the Egyptian Treasury in the Times of the Mamlukes and the Beginnings of the Turkish Regime," (Hebrew) *Zion*, I (1935), 34–36.

11. Cf. document 30, note 26, and text for his prerogatives.

12. See below, chap. 5, note 34.

tine period to include two *memunim,* two supervisors, and two *parnasim.*[13] This arrangement paralleled that later in use among the Venetian Jews in Constantinople at the beginning of the fifteenth century. At that time there were *sex capita* who were organized into a *consilium* and a *maior consilium.*[14]

The Greek titles for the leaders were suggested by M. Romanos.[15] All were attested in the late Roman period. The designation for the president of the synagogue was *archi-synagogus*; a Latin equivalent is found among the Venetian Jews of Constantinople in the fifteenth century, that is, *caput sinagoge.* The term for council paralleled Greek usage, that is, *gerousia*; its Latin equivalent, of course, was *consilium.* The members of the *gerousia* would be known as *archontes,* a term commonly used in Middle Greek society and later adopted by the Frankish rulers of Morea. During the Ottoman period, leaders of the community were collectively referred to as *tobei ha-kahal,* possibly a Hebrew reflection of the Greek term *archontes,* or perhaps *kreittones.*[16]

Such, then, are all occurrences of communal titles on the mainland from Benjamin's visit in the twelfth century to the Ottoman conquest in the fifteenth. This is a far cry from the wealth of information and rich terminology available in Jewish sources from Venetian Crete, in particular the surviving communal statutes of Candia. To what extent the latter represent continuity from Byzantine times remains to be explored.[17] Still, the information is sufficient to provide an outline of the titles of leadership among

13. M. Romanos, "Histoire de la communauté israélite de Corfou," *REJ,* XXIII (1891), 63–74; Krauss, *Studien,* p. 89. One of them may have been included in the delegation to Venice cited in document 98.

14. Cf. D. Jacoby, "Les Juifs vénitiens de Constantinople et leur communauté du XIIIe au milieu du XVe siécle," *REJ,* CXXXI (1972), 397–410.

15. See above, note 13. This was the basis for Abraham Galante's remarks, *Les Juifs de Constantinople sous Byzance* (Istanbul, 1940), pp. 36, 45–46. Sharf (*Byzantine Jewry,* p. 179) invented a twelfth-century date for this list.

16. The titles are listed by Krauss, *Studien,* pp. 86–88, and Galante, *Juifs de Constantinople,* pp. 36, 45–46. Compare Baron, *The Jewish Community,* I, 95–107, for the Greco-Roman period. See below, note 22.

17. Cf. lists in A. S. Artom and M. Cassuto, eds., *Takkanoth Kandia we-Zichronothehah* (Jerusalem, 1943), passim; Starr, "Jewish Life in Crete under the Rule of Venice," *PAAJR* (1942), passim. The government-recognized leader of the Jewish community during the Venetian period was known as *condestabulo,* i.e., "chief constable," while the powerful chairman of the burial society was called *Rosh ha-Kabbarim.* Cf. Z. Ankori, "The Living and the Dead," *PAAJR,* XXXIX–XL (1970–71), 98f. The former title, of course, reflects its Venetian provenance.

Romaniote Jewry, namely, a council of scholars with one, the *primus inter pares,* if not a government appointee, at least ratified as such and supported by a council of elders. The latter were likely drawn from the wealthier members of the community, as was the practice in Romaniote communities during the Ottoman period (*infra*). Also, the size of both councils was apparently determined by that of the local Jewish population. In some smaller communities, such as Negroponte, a secular oligarchic leadership may have emerged to deal with the government.

Because of the complicated religious traditions that governed Jewish society in the Middle Ages, the Jewish community had to regulate many functions which other religious groups usually left to private industry. The dietary laws, for example, are sufficiently complicated to necessitate a man specially trained in the ritual slaughter of animals. Even so authorized, a *shoḥet* could, on occasion, be somewhat lax, at least in the eyes of the neighboring Karaite community, as one Nicomedian sage was quick to point out. Moreover, a *sofer* or professional scribe, corresponding to the Latin *notarius,* was needed to draw up documents in Hebrew and/or the local language. The council, too, had its own scribe, or rather secretary, the *grammateos,* who took care of the community records.

The rabbi usually acted as judge or *shofet* for the community. However, if cases became too burdensome or complicated for one man, he would coopt two (or more) scholars to assist him, especially in serious cases as outlined by traditional Jewish law. Use of these Jewish courts, however, was voluntary; examples are available of occasions when Jews made use of gentile courts where they expected a more favorable ruling or before which their Christian adversaries were entitled to bring them.[18] Wealthy Jewish merchants, therefore, would be more likely to resort to these courts. In the Venetian colony in Constantinople, a surviving will of the fourteenth century, drawn up according to Christian formulae, indicates that the Jews there may have frequented the bailo's court, rather than resort to their own (if they had one) or to local rabbis. The colony, of course, comprised Jewish merchants, and is not remembered for its scholarly achievements. Indications suggest that the Venetian Jews also drew up their documents in both

18. See above, chap. 1, and part II document 134, for the question of taxation. Cf. Starr, *JBE,* p. 222, no. 171. Evidence to this effect comes to us from Crete and is shown to have continued all through Venetian times; cf. Z. Ankori, "From *Zudecha* to *Yahudi Mahallesi,*" in *S. W. Baron Jubilee Volume* (New York, 1974), I, 25–89.

Hebrew and Latin.[19] The average Jew, however, was at considerable disadvantage before such a court, since Byzantine law did not allow him to bear witness against a Christian unless the latter agreed (**67**).

Even so, such restrictions would not necessarily deter a complainant who expected an adverse decision from a Jewish judge—say, for example, in divorce proceedings or family property disputes. In the early thirteenth century, Isaiah of Trani remarks on such use of non-Jewish courts, which undermined the authority of Jewish leaders (**11**). It is not impossible that the Romaniote community paralleled this practice by the use of both Greek and Hebrew. The Jewish court, in general, may have had a government-appointed Christian liaison. Prior to the twelfth century, there apparently had been such an official, for example, the *strategos* of the Stenon (a Christian), to deal with secular law. Manuel Komnenos put the Jews back under the jurisdiction of the general courts, at least those in the capital.[20] Chionios may have filled such a position in fourteenth-century Thessalonica, although any example from that city, which so prided itself on its ancient customs, is not necessarily representative of the normative situation.[21] Not until the recognition of the Jewish community by Mehmet II did the Jewish court become obligatory for all normative Jews.

Other communal posts included that of *darshan,* who delivered the homily (in Greek) during the synagogue service; *shamash* or beadle; *ḥazzan,* the reader in the synagogue; and perhaps a *gabbai* to handle the synagogue finances. Material from the Ottoman period informs us of the *tobei ha-kahal,* or *tubei ha-ʿir,* at one time called *memunim,* who supervised the affairs of the synagogue and administered its tax obligations. These Hebrew terms parallel the above mentioned *archontes,* and both refer to the more respected and well-to-do members of the community. This function, then, may have been included among the activities of the *gerousia.*[22]

One of the most important services that the community provided was the preparation and burial of the deceased. For this purpose, each commu-

19. Cf. Jacoby, "Les Juifs vénitiens de Cp.," and Ankori, "From *Zudecha* to *Yahudi Mahallesi.*"

20. Starr, *JBE,* p. 222, no. 172.

21. See part II document 58 and above, chap. 2, "Thessalonica."

22. Cf. studies by Galante and Baron cited above (note 16). Fourteenth-century Byzantine texts show that the κρείττονες ("best") played a powerful role in village life; cf. A. Laiou-Thomadakis, *Peasant Society in the Late Byzantine Empire* (New Brunswick, 1977), p. 63.

nity possessed a *ḥevra kadisha,* or burial society, whose membership consisted of volunteers (indeed, it was a *miṣvah* to thus respect the dead), although it tended to become hereditary, and was autonomous within the Jewish community.[23] Two other posts which might be found were that of the *mohel,* who circumcised the newborn males, and the *melammed,* who taught them when they were old enough for school. In the larger cities, any number of officials would be appointed by the community and supported by intracommunal taxation. In smaller communities, one man usually combined several functions. In Negroponte, for example, Moses Galimidi acted as judge, scribe, ritual slaughterer, and teacher (30).

The appearance of Romaniote Jews in Venetian colonies, some with the status of a Venetian and others maintaining a Byzantine identity (*infra*), allows us to follow them into the main Venetian entrepôt in the empire, into the heart of Constantinople.[24] Moreover, since precious little information on the structure of the Romaniote community has survived from the Palaeologan period, and data therefore must be sought from the preceding twelfth century and the succeeding Ottoman era, we are most fortunate to have contemporary information on the organization of the Venetian Jews in Constantinople during the fourteenth and fifteenth centuries. It should be remembered, however, that the Venetian Jews adjusted their previous communal experiences to conform to the realities of the Venetian colony and, for this reason, their organization differed sufficiently from that of their coreligionists that analogies to the latter should be held to a minimum.

The independent, autonomous status conferred by Michael VIII on the Venetian colony continued until the conquest of the city by Mehmet II.[25] This colony also contained an autonomous group of Jews who held a Venetian status (*infra*). As part of the larger Venetian colony, its organization was established and supervised by the Bailo who was responsible for all the Venetians in the capital. Even so, within the overall structure of the Venetian colony the Venetian Jews constituted a separate entity and were allowed to govern their own affairs. At the same time, the organization of

23. See sources cited by Ankori in "The Living and the Dead," pp. 38–44 and 95ff, notes 143–44; Baron, *The Jewish Community,* I, 93–94; and above, note 17.

24. See above, chap. 1, note 25 and text.

25. Cf. Jacoby, "Les Juifs vénitiens de Cp."

their community was outlined in the general constitutions promulgated by the various bailos.

The recently published extracts of the constitution of Franciscus Michael, the Venetian Bailo in Constantinople from 1410 to 1412, contain several paragraphs that outline the appointment, qualifications, term of office, and board of review for the heads of the Venetian Jews, no matter where they lived in the city.[26] The rules for selection of these leaders (*capita*) were strict. Paralleling Jewish law, only one member from a family could serve at a time. From the Jewish point of view, this would not impose undue hardship on the family business, while from the Bailo's perspective it discouraged nepotism and the natural tendency toward oligarchy in many a contemporary Jewish (and non-Jewish) community (**115**). At the same time, subject to payment of a small fine, the privilege of being elected one of the communal leaders could be declined. Illness or business trips were deemed sufficient reason to obviate even that minimal payment (**115**).

Once the six leaders were elected,[27] two were to serve successively for a period of four months (**114**). A close check was kept on their activities, with both the successive leaders and the community at large responsible for reviewing their books. At the end of the year, another public examination took place, during which any member of the Venetian community at large could voice a complaint against the Jewish leaders. To ensure maximum efficiency, both the leaders and any new Jews in the colony had to be registered in the official acts of the Bailo. The minor bureaucratic expenses were offset by a small fee charged to the registrant. The Venetian synagogue served not only as the center of their social and religious life; it was there that the elections for the leaders took place, along with public examination of their term of office (**113**).

Social Structure, Mobility, Tensions

The Jewries of Byzantium represent a complex microcosm within the larger Byzantine society. During the centuries Jews from different lands and persuasions had continually added their characteristics to the indigenous Greek-speaking communities. Two major distinctive groups were the

26. By X. A. Maltezou, *Venetian Bailo*. Part II of her study contains the Latin texts.
27. On the problem of the dates mentioned in document 106, i.e., elections in March and September, cf. Jacoby, "Les Juifs vénitiens de Cp."

normative Rabbanite community, which normally followed older Palestinian traditions, and the "sectarian" Karaite community, which followed an independent adjustment of biblical law to Byzantine conditions. Though they rapidly assimilated to the dominant Hellenic culture prior to the Fourth Crusade, tensions continued between the veteran Rabbanite community and the immigrant Karaites.[28] Benjamin of Tudela noted that the two groups in Pera lived in the same area, separated by a fence. Clearly, such a physical structure denoted serious animosities, occasional record of which has survived from the eleventh through the fifteenth century throughout the area from Thessalonica to the Crimea. These tensions between the two contending interpretations of Judaism remained, despite later efforts to accommodate Karaite tradition to the realities of a Byzantine diaspora and continually to adapt them to the vagaries of a Christian society.[29] Nor should it be overlooked that such attempted flexibility caused serious tensions among conservative elements within the Karaite communities, although evidence to this effect does not appear before the fifteenth century.

The areas of contention between the Rabbanites and the Karaites covered nearly the entire range of the socio-religious tenets of Judaism. By this period, Rabbanite Jews had evolved local interpretations of what may be called a talmudic civilization, which provided a common framework of prayer, ritual, and tradition that was familiar to most other Jews. The Karaites rejected this framework and attempted to base their identity on the Bible, the Hebrew language, and a direct connection with the land of Israel. The diasporic experience of Byzantium and elsewhere, however, soon forced them to adjust their traditions in such a way as to develop parallels to the normative Rabbanite culture.[30]

The major frictions were in the areas of calendar, Scripture, and ritual. Since the Karaites followed a different calendar reckoning than the Rabbanites, the most obvious result was that their holidays were usually celebrated on different dates from their coreligionists'. Karaite reliance on visual sighting of the new moon, as opposed to the Rabbanite use of a precalculated calendar, often resulted in a day or two difference in the

28. Cf. Ankori, *Karaites,* passim.

29. Cf. Zvi Ankori, "Bashyachi," (Hebrew) in *EIV,* IX, 960–63, and his Hebrew essay "House of Bashyachi and Its Reform," introduction to Elijah Bashyachi's *Addereth Eliahu* (Ramlah, 1966).

30. Ibid.

beginning of the month and the attendant *rosh ḥodesh* celebration. In a religious community, such a difference could be, and often was, interpreted as desecration of the holy day. This area of contention was gradually eliminated as the Karaites adopted the rabbinic calendar (**28**). At the same time, such reforms were not necessarily welcomed within the Karaite community by conservatives.

Another area of contention was the different tradition of interpretation that each group employed in its reading and commenting on the Scriptures. The problems that emerged from random conversation between a Karaite and a Rabbanite over the portion of the week were sufficient to indicate that some sort of compromise or change be made. Probably in the thirteenth century, the Karaites shifted the beginning of their Torah-reading cycle to the spring month of Nisan, while the Rabbanites continued to begin their cycle in the autumn month of Tishre (**149**). Thus each group read a different portion of the Torah each week, all through the Palaeologan period.

The differing rituals of both communities added to the barriers between them. The Karaites, of course, possessed their own synagogue, with its attendant educational system. Also, they may have had their own graveyard, if the situation during the Ottoman period applies to Palaeologan times. The Karaites, too, were stricter about certain dietary laws while, at the same time, ignoring certain Rabbanite dietary regulations.[31] Thus they would have had to employ their own ritual slaughterer. Their prayerbook, not formally arranged before the end of the thirteenth century, was markedly different from that of the Rabbanite service. The latter was extremely fluid throughout the Palaeologan period and was not codified in print before the sixteenth century.

The independent but parallel communal structure of the Karaite community necessitated a close-knit society. The Karaites, after all, were few in number and were surrounded by their occasionally hostile coreligionists and a wider circle of unfriendly Christians. This compounded isolation was behind an important feature of their life in Byzantium, namely, imperial recognition of their autonomy from the Rabbanite community.[32] While such a situation is not clearly expressed in any source from the Byzantine

31. Cf. *Iggereth Gid ha-Nasheh* of Elijah Bashyachi, preceding the Gozlow edition of *Addereth Eliahu* (1835). See below, chap. 4, note 77.

32. On the nineteenth-century claim of independence for reasons of political expediency, cf. Ankori, *Karaites,* pp. 40 and 59, and literature cited; for an Ottoman notice, cf. part II document 153.

period, the claim was made, and subsequently recognized by the Ottomans, that such had been the case before the conquest. This claim, indeed, became the basis for the communal autonomy of the Karaite community during the Ottoman period (**152, 153**).

To the tension between the Rabbanite Jews of Romaniote origin and the Karaite Jews of Romaniote and other provenance, other groups added their potential for social strife. During the fourteenth and fifteenth centuries there appeared in the empire individuals identified as "Venetian Jews." Occasionally we hear of "white Venetian Jews," although the connection of the latter with the former is unclear, as is the precise meaning of the term. Jews who were entitled to the privileges of a Venetian constituted a special group within the empire in particular and the entire Levant in general. That they did not come from Venice is clear, since the Republic did not allow Jews to settle there during our period. Therefore they had to stem from those local Romaniote Jews who succeeded in purchasing or otherwise obtaining a Venetian identity, or from Jews who immigrated into the region from Spain, Italy, or even the Black Sea settlements (although the latter more likely would have sought, and obtained, a Genoese identity). The parallel phenomenon among Christians who were recruited by the rival Italian city-states of Genoa and Venice, as part of their political and economic maneuverings within Byzantium, is well known. Of interest to us are the social problems that may have arisen between Jews and Christians within the Venetian colony and between Venetian Jews and Byzantine Jews within the empire.

Jews who held Venetian status were to be found living both with the Venetian colony in Constantinople and within the *ʿebraike* of the capital among their coreligionists. The only Jews in the fourteenth century who lived with the Venetian colony and are identified by name are Isaac Catalanus and his relatives. It may well be that those Jews who had immigrated eastward during that period, as Isaac did from Spain, preferred to live within the Venetian Quarter rather than to assimilate to the local Romaniote social and religious life by living among their coreligionists. Such considerations may, on occasion, have influenced the residential preference of some Venetian Jews, even though a document from the fifteenth century shows the existence of Romaniote Jews from Crete, with Venetian status, residing within the Venetian Quarter.[33] In this way, though their daily contact with their coreligionists would have been reduced to a minimum,

33. Jacoby, "Quartiers juifs," document II.

their overall relations were probably more harmonious than those between Venetian Jews and the local, Byzantine Jews among whom they resided.

Since some of the local Romaniote Jews succeeded in obtaining a Venetian status, difficulties were bound to arise between these privileged Jews and their coreligionists who remained Byzantine subjects—and, in addition, between the former and Byzantine officials. The complex affair involving the Jewish tanners of the Vlanka Quarter (*supra,* chapter 1) sheds light on several aspects of the problem. In the first place, it indicates that Venetian Jews *did* live in the Vlanka Quarter, even though the area had originally been set aside for the emperor's Jewish tanners. It also shows that the division of labor between the two groups of Jews, wherein the Byzantines controlled the tanning of hides and the Venetians the preparation of furs, had broken down when the latter infringed upon the Byzantine monopoly and began to tan hides. It was the Byzantine Jews who complained to imperial officials, who then acted to protect a state monopoly.

Clearly, occupational necessity overrode the traditional Jewish hesitance to involve non-Jewish authorities in their local or communal disputes. The Byzantine government, though weakened considerably by the political and economic vicissitudes experienced under Andronikos II, briefly reestablished its authority by severely punishing the Venetian Jews for their infringement of the treaty. The latter protested to their protectors, who in turn brought the matter before the Byzantine authorities. The entire affair became one more source of friction between Venice and Byzantium over the former's highly privileged position within the Byzantine economy.

There were other occasions when the imperial authorities tried to loosen Venetian control over Jews with Venetian status, by their refusal to recognize that identity. Such attempts should be seen in the light of the larger perspective of Christian and Jewish Byzantine subjects' abandoning their Byzantine identity for the more privileged and profitable status of a Venetian or Genoese. The empire tried to regain its subjects more forcefully during those rare periods of imperial self-assurance.[34] In the case of the Jews, matters were aggravated by the fact that some Venetian Jews chose to live in the large Judaica with their Byzantine coreligionists. Apparently, too, some Byzantine Jews succeeded in living outside the Judaica, in areas

34. J. Chrysostomides, "Venetian Commercial Privileges under the Palaeologi," *Studi Veneziani,* 12 (1970), passim.

where Jews with Venetian status were entitled to own or rent houses. The Venetian Bailo therefore took the emperor's intentions into account. Provisions were included in the constitution of the Venetian colony to avoid any pretext for such imperial interference. One clause, of which the rubric only has been published, forbade the sale of houses in the area where Venetian Jews lived to any Byzantine Jews, unless the Venetian Jews were previously consulted and gave their consent (**112, 116**). Thus, it was hoped, one of the causes of the 1319–20 dispute—namely, the difficulty of deciding whether a Jew was entitled to Venetian status or was actually a Byzantine subject—might be eradicated.

Social tensions between the wealthy Jewish merchants who led the community and the Jewish artisans who comprised the bulk of its constituency are a general phenomenon familiar to students of medieval Jewish history. The wealthy enjoyed political and economic prerogatives, and occasionally the learned were to be counted among the ranks of the wealthy. Benjamin of Tudela, for example, notes that the heads of the Jewish guilds during the late twelfth century were rabbis. In normative circumstances, on the other hand, the learned were more likely subject to the whims of the wealthy.

A case in point is that of Moses Galimidi and his relationship with David Kalomiti in Negroponte at the beginning of the fourteenth century (**30**). In the beginning, the relationship between the two men was quite harmonious. Moses Galimidi, who immigrated to Negroponte from Thebes, served as the sole religious functionary in the community, later married into the upper stratum of the community, and also served as the righthand man of David Kalomiti, the leader of the community. At some point he entered into a dependent status with the latter.[35] The Hebrew text is not entirely clear on the legal relationship between the two: the term it used is *ʿebed,* which in its biblical meaning may refer to either a slave or a servant. David apparently possessed many *ʿabadim.* While some of these may have been slaves—although this was forbidden by ecclesiastical and

35. The commentary accompanying the transcription of the letter published by Carlo Bernheimer ("Document relatif aux Juifs de Négropont," *REJ,* LXV [1913], 224–30) can be safely ignored. Starr devoted a major part of his chapter on Negroponte to a commentary on this letter (*Romania,* pp. 48–54). Jacoby has brought supplementary material which both reinforces and supersedes some of Starr's assertions ("Status of Jews"). The documents brought forth in that article treat the status of the family of David Kalomiti from 1268 to 1373 (pp. 59–64).

civil law in both Western and Eastern Christendom—it is not impossible that the Hebrew term may reflect the Greek *paroikoi,*[36] who were peasants tied to the farmlands that David purchased. While the status of Moses was different from that of the household and field dependents of David, it was clearly a dependent status, even though the relationship was symbiotic for a number of years. After the death of David the relationship deteriorated into one that was unbearable to the Galimidi family (or so our source suggests). It would appear that the close proximity of the sons of Moses and David and the perhaps differing intellectual capabilities of each group led to rivalries that could only be resolved by the Kalomiti exerting their prerogatives as leaders of the community and publicly humiliating the Galimidi family.

Such social pressures may have contributed to the social mobility of Romaniote Jewry during this period. Economic incentive no doubt played an even larger part in such mobility; yet social pressures within a small community would facilitate the decision to seek opportunity elsewhere. Moses Galimidi went from Thebes, a center of Jewish scholarship and economic opportunity, to Negroponte, a small but prosperous community. While it would seem that he was welcome as a scholarly resource, a hint at the legal problems surrounding his decision is the unclear phrase "fleeing from his lords." This may suggest that his mobility was restricted and that he was in some sort of dependent status in Thebes. (The situation there, however, is totally obscured by lack of sources.) Later, one of his sons fled to Thebes, after the breakup of the Galimidi family and the dispersal of Moses' sons, who fled to settlements in the general area. Almost a generation later, we find a scion of the Negroponte Kalomitis in Thessalonica, where he was earning his living as a scribe, and by the end of the century a branch of the family was established in Corinth. The spread of the Kalomiti family reflected its economic interests.

Other Jews traveled freely throughout the area and intermarried with the local Jewry. Such contacts were advantageous for economic and social connections. Abraham Abulafia visited his Greek family when he began to do serious writing. A Jew from Patras intermarried with a family from Modon. Jews from Crete emigrated to Constantinople. To be sure, the latter are found in the Venetian colony there; no doubt others joined their

36. The general term for a dependent status during the period was *paroikos*. On its application in Nicaea, see M. Angold, *A Byzantine Government in Exile* (Oxford, 1975), and in Macedonia, Laiou, *Peasant Society*.

Romaniote coreligionists in the Judaica.[37] The congregation in Naxos maintained close ties with Crete. Spanish Jews, filtering eastward as part of a general migration to the eastern Mediterranean basin, would provide a nucleus for the stepped-up migration that began at the end of the fourteenth century as a result of the persecutions in Spain. Italian Jews had already appeared in the area, during the twelfth century, as can be seen from names such as Lombardo (noted by Benjamin of Tudela). Nor were immigrants from the East and North lacking. The Arabic-speaking Syrian Jew at the court of Andronikos is but one example of the former.

At the same time, the link between Thrace and the Crimea, as noted in the development of the Karaite communities in later Palaeologan times, was not restricted to members of that sect. From the 1370s, Byzantine Jews freely traveled from Constantinople to Ottoman Adrianople to take advantage of the economic, social, and intellectual assets of that bustling capital.[38] Also, in the decades prior to the Ottoman conquest of Thessalonica, Jews abandoned that declining city for the lure of Ottoman opportunity. Jews who held Venetian or Genoese status would have traveled freely throughout the areas under the control of their protectors. Within the Balkans, the lures of Constantinople forged contacts between Jews who were resident in the capital and those in neighboring Bulgaria. A look at the traditional trade routes, both overland and by sea, points out that Jews from areas in economic contact would not hesitate to settle in areas of opportunity. The change of status from a Byzantine Jew to a Venetian Jew or to a subject of the Ottomans—or to one of the myriad rulers in the fragmented remains of the former Empire of the Komnenoi—would not have deterred him from seeking a new life among his coreligionists, most of them Romaniotes, who lived throughout this region.

Nor should migration westward be ignored, although it is only hinted at in the sources. During the pre-1204 period, students are noted in Western *yeshivoth*; tradition has ascribed to Moses Kapsali a study tour in Italy during the fifteenth century.[39] The names al-Constantini and Anatoli became prestigious family names among Spanish Jewry at an early period,[40]

37. See above, note 33.

38. A study of the Jews in Ottoman Adrianople during the ninety years that it served as the capital of the young sultanate is a desideratum; cf. Ankori, *Karaites,* indev s.v., and article "Adrianople" (Hebrew) in *EIV.*

39. See below, chap. IV, note 132.

40. Cf. Y. Baer, *The Jews in Christian Spain,* 2 vols. (Philadelphia, 1961–66), index s.v.

and scholars from Crete appeared in Italy and Spain during the fifteenth century.[41] Though sparse indeed, such references suggest that Romaniote migrations were not limited to the Greek-speaking world.

Tensions between the Christian community and the Jewish community were not uncommon (*supra,* chapter 1). While there were economic relations and even partnerships between Jews and Christians, and Jews served in the administrations of various Christian rulers or as their physicians, an underlying social and religious hostility no doubt was exacerbated by the arrival of the more prejudiced Western Christians, in particular the Venetians.[42] The animosity of Catholics toward Jews, when transported to the eastern Mediterranean, was increased when coupled with the fact that Romaniote Jews were viewed as part of the local Greek-speaking population, whom Catholics looked down upon as heretics and as subjects. These complicated animosities further served to isolate the Jew from the mainstream of local life and necessitated development of a parallel and restricted Jewish society. The same held true for other minorities in the region, such as Armenians and Muslims. The Jews, however, had no point of mutual contact with either their compatriots, their rulers, or other minorities, with perhaps the exception of Muslims. The latter would find among the Jews ritually pure foods which were not available in the Christian market. There they would also find merchants with connections in their home cities. Moreover, the Jews, as a religious group, would not be openly hostile to Islam, as were Christians.[43]

Relations between Jews and Christians took a number of other forms, aside from the normal social and economic intercourse alluded to above. Some Jews, as was noted previously (chapter 1), were considered "possessions" of various ecclesiastical institutions. Where this "possession" entailed fiscal responsibilities, these Jews were no doubt afforded considerable autonomy.[44] Depending upon whether these Jews lived in a large city,

41. Cf. M. Steinschneider, "Candia, Cenni di Storia Litteraria . . . ," *Mosé,* Vols. II–VI (1879–83), passim.

42. Much of our source material on this subject comes from Crete and has been discussed in the articles of Starr and Ankori.

43. Thus it is possible that their respective quarters may have been placed adjacent to or near each other.

44. Starr (*Romania,* p. 112) cites the case of Strobilos Jews who owed a tax, wherever they may be. While this case has a bearing on the question of a uniform tax before 1204, it is also important for the suggestion that these Jews, while maintaining their tax responsibility, were allowed some freedom of movement.

where they could be more secure in their restricted quarter, their relations with their Christian neighbors, especially during the tension-filled holiday season from the Jewish Purim through the Christian Easter, would be insecure at best.[45] Moreover, their isolation within a Christian society would become dangerous in the face of increased tensions between the conquering Catholics and the conquered Orthodox. Individual Jews would be even more insecure, especially those whose mobility was totally restricted, as in the case of slaves. (Jews were not usually found as slaves during the medieval period. Those who were captured as war prizes or taken prisoner by pirates were soon ransomed by their coreligionists, according to well-established rules and procedures which had been developed over the centuries. During our period, no Jews are recorded as slaves within the Byzantine orbit. Several are noted, however, in the surrounding regions: a female Jewish slave in Euboea and another Jew in Crete who had been consigned to the galleys.)[46]

General hostility against Jews, coupled with the social advantages of belonging to the majority society, may have induced individuals to abandon the Jewish community and convert to Christianity. The number of cases that have come to light is sufficiently low (a mere handful) to suggest that this means of advancement of personal status and career did not have high

45. For a feeling of the tensions that could build up within the Christian community, cf. N. Kazantzakis, *The Greek Passion* (New York, 1953), and its implications for the Jewish community in C. Roth, "The Eastertide Stoning of the Jews and Its Liturgical Echoes," *JQR*, ns, XXXV (1945), 361–70.

46. A Jewess was claimed as a slave by Bonifacio da Verona, who, after the battle of Kephisos (1311), where the Lombard lords of Euboea and the pride of Frankish Achaea were liquidated by the Catalans, emerged as the strongman of Euboea. Bury thought that she was a subject of Venice; cf. his "The Lombards and the Venetians in Euboea (Part 2: 1303–1340)," *JHS*, 8 (1887), 200–203. Karl Hopf ("Urkundliche Mittheilungen über die Geschichte von Karystos auf Euboea in dem Zeitraume von 1205–1470," in *Sitzungsberichte der philos.-histor. Klasse der Kais. Akademie der Wissenschaften*, bd. XI, Vienna, 1853, s. 555f) relates the incident as follows: "So wiegerte er [Bonifacius] sich 1313 zum Bau der Euböotischer Flotte beizustenern, reclamirte ohne Recht eine Jüdinn als seine angebliche Sclavinn und liess sogar zu, das die Bewohner 'cuiusdam insulae,' die er besass, ohne Zweifels Aegina's, ein mit Gerste beladenes Schiff des Jacopo Buticlaro ausplünderten." That there may have been Jews on medieval Aegina was suggested by B. Mazur, *Studies in Greek Jewry* (Athens, 1935), I, 34–35.

For the case of an unransomed Jewish galley slave on a Venetian vessel, cf. Starr, "Jewish Life in Crete under the Rule of Venice," p. 73. We do not find any Jewish slaves listed in Ch. Verlinden's fairly exhaustive study, *L'esclavage dans l'Europe médiévale*, vol. 2 (Ghent, 1977). Cf. also M. Balard, *La Romanie génoise*, I–II (Rome, 1978), index, s.v.

priority among Romaniote Jews. Only one or two examples of successful converts have survived. An ecclesiastic, by the name of Makarios, served as both confessor and occasional ambassador for Manuel II (**123**). The problem of Philotheos Kokkinos, who was accused by his enemies of being Jewish, has been discussed elsewhere (chapter 2). In lower-strata Byzantine society, other converts may be noted. It was here, perhaps, that a larger number of conversions took place, but because of the loss of Byzantine archives their absolute number must remain a mystery.

Still, only a few examples have survived. Joshua Starr noted the case of a convert, one Israel ben Abraham, baptized as Manuel, who lived near Kastoria in Macedonia in the first half of the thirteenth century.[47] Angeliki Laiou found a John "of the Jews," also a convert, who lived in the village of Gomatou near Mount Athos in Macedonia at the beginning of the fourteenth.[48] Both of these examples survived in ecclesiastical archival material and appear in cases describing the ownership of property. The small plots claimed by these converts suggest that, for whatever purpose they took the fateful step of converting to the majority Orthodox society, their resultant condition was not especially enviable. A third convert is alluded to in Gallipoli; however, neither his former Hebrew name nor his new Christian identity is known (**5***).

While any discussion of the extent of conversion to Christianity in the Late Byzantine period must be restricted because of the paucity of source material, the above examples indicate that a number of factors, known to be prevalent in other societies, were also at work. Conversions took place for any number of reasons: love, money, religious conviction, or psychological need. We have already indicated that the problem of forced conversion was ephemeral in the thirteenth century and did not exist under the Palaeologoi, as opposed to the vicissitudes of the Jewish community during the Middle Byzantine period. The church, too, was willing to accept only serious converts, and ordered its ministers to reject those who wished to convert for other than purely religious motives, especially lawbreakers or those who wished to find release from a dependent or slave status (**57**). All of the converts noted above appear to have lived in non-Jewish areas or, in the case of the Gallipoli convert, been divorced from the Jewish community.

47. *Romania,* p. 21.
48. *Peasant Society,* p. 134.

Only through physical separation could social animosity between a convert and his former coreligionists be avoided. The remarks of Isaiah of Trani are indicative of this animosity: converts to Christianity are to be considered traitors and in no way can their testimony be acceptable to a Jewish court, since they may contravene the spirit and the letter of Jewish law for vindictive reasons. Christians, on the other hand, may testify in behalf of a Jew (**5***). Such a harsh attitude is understandable and reflects the parallel Byzantine judicial system which severely restricted Jewish privileges in cases involving members of the opposite faith (**67**). Further, the total rejection of a convert by his family and community inevitably brought serious repercussions in matters of inheritance and other property rights. As early as the fourth century, Christian Roman law had to deal with protection for those who chose to join the majority society. Despite explicit treatment of the problem in later codes, there is little doubt that their rights were not watched over by the church. After all, a convert to the dominant faith should not be punished for abandoning a despised faith. At the same time, the pressures of such conversions on the stability of family and community must have been immense—even greater when the convert initiated litigation and subjected his relations to the embarrassment of a hostile court.

Economic Pursuits

Inasmuch as the Jews were a predominantly urbanized group, centered in the major cities of the empire, it is apparent that their economic concerns would be trade and manufacture. Still, there are hints that all Jews were not so occupied. The twelfth-century report of Benjamin of Tudela informs us of a rural Jewish community near Krissa, engaged in some sort of agriculture (exc. A). Also, the commentaries on *Sifre* and *Sifra* by Hillel ben Eliakim contain a great deal of material on the care and pruning of orchards, and other agricultural hints, that seem to reflect practical value. During succeeding centuries, records show that Jews owned plots and gardens within cities (**130**). Other Jews were engaged in the age-old urban vocation of buying and renting real estate (**37ff, 106**).[49] There were also professionals, namely, doctors and government interpreters (**35, 79, 51, 129**). Most of our information indicates, however, that most Jews made

49. For real estate transactions during the twelfth century, cf. Ankori, *Karaites,* pp. 178f.

their living as wholesale or retail merchants and as manufacturers or workers in various industries.[50]

The large-scale merchants dealt mostly in cloth, including various kinds of raw and manufactured silk, wool, cotton, etc. The twenty-five or so merchants listed in Giacomo Badoer's *Libro dei Conti* were primarily involved in trading raw materials or manufactured cloth, for example, "*pani, veli, drapieri, pichi, seda, oropele.*" Occasionally, we hear of Jews trading in other commodities. These same Venetian Jews (in Constantinople), in addition to their major concern with textiles, now and then handled such products as *arzenti* and *piper*—in huge amounts that indicate how lucrative was such trade in chemicals and spices. In Dyrrachium, the head of the community contracted for a boatload of salt (**94**); in Lepanto, several Jews were involved in shipping iron to Patras (**126**). The fine kosher wines of Crete, however, were produced by local Christians, under the supervision of Jewish entrepreneurs, and were transshipped to observant homes in Constantinople by Christians (**134**). None of the Jewish merchants listed in the accounts of Giacomo Badoer for the years 1436 to 1440 were involved in shipping this wine.[51] Crete also produced kosher cheeses for export under the same system.[52] The Kalomiti family, based in Negroponte but with connections and branches in surrounding towns, was engaged in a number of economic activities, such as leasing agricultural lands, financial management, and otherwise advising the Lombard lords of the island. While it is uncertain whether it was they who bought the rights to the grand commerchium in Corinth in 1369 (**89**), their resources made them a source for the liquid capital so often needed by the feudal rulers of the area.[53]

By this period, Jews were no longer involved in the slave trade in the

50. For the Byzantine period, we do not have the wealth of data on Jewish vocations available from the Ottoman period; cf. examples in Goodblatt, *Jewish Life in Turkey.* Other responsa collections from the Ottoman period show that in the smaller towns Jews performed a number of economic activities, e.g., entrepreneurs in the manufacture and trade of silk and later of tobacco, small retailers, even a peddler in Acarnania, traveling through villages with his wagon full of ouzo. On the value of rabbinic responsa for Ottoman economic history in general, see H. Gerber, "Enterprise and International Commerce in the Economic Activity of the Jews of the Ottoman Empire in the 16th–17th Centuries," (Hebrew) *Zion,* XLIII (1978), 38–67 and ii–iv (English summary).

51. See below, chap. 5, note 6.

52. Cf. Ankori, "Jews and the Jewish Community in the History of Mediaeval Crete." A number of responsa of Isaiah of Trani deal with the problems arising from wine shipped by non-Jews and its possible contamination. Cf. also *Teshuvoth Ha RID,* #117.

53. See above, chap. 2, "Peloponnesos."

eastern Mediterranean. They were, of course, barred from this activity by ecclesiastical and secular law; more importantly, however, they had long been supplanted in such activity by the greater resources and organization of the Italian city-states. Still, several instances of Venetian Jews' selling slaves are recorded: one Callo Cirnichiote Iudeo in Constantinople in 1394[54] and a Jewish resident of Tana in 1363.[55] While more cases may eventually be found in unpublished notarial registers or account books, the available evidence suggests that the role of Jews in the slave trade during this period was minimal and that Venetian Jews, rather than Imperial Jews, were involved in this activity.

It was the textile industry that was the mainstay of economic life for the Jewish community. We have already discussed the government-controlled guild of tanners which Andronikos II had established in the Vlanka Quarter, and the report of Benjamin of Tudela, albeit a century earlier than our period, corroborates the pervasive role of Jews in the manufacture and dyeing of silk cloth in the Byzantine Empire. The few data that can be added from succeeding centuries indicate continued concentration in this area.

In the second half of the thirteenth century, a well-known halakhic scholar in Italy, R. Ṣidkiyahu ha-Rofe, included in his compendium *Shibbole ha-Lekket* a chapter on *Din Kilayē Begadim* (Regulations regarding hybrid garments).[56] This particular problem, concerning which garments were ritually satisfactory and the correct procedure for their manufacture, was, as the author observes, one of the most complicated problems in talmudic law. Particularly vexing for the scholar was the absence of any talmudic commentary on the mishnaic tractate *Kilaʿim*.[57] This scholarly problem made it even more difficult for the cloth manufacturers to produce

54. They were of course barred from this activity by ecclesiastical and secular law; more importantly, they had already been supplanted by the greater resources and organization of the Italian city-states. The case is cited in *Bernardo de Rodulfis notario in Venezia (1392–1399), a cura di Giorgio Tamba* (Venice, 1974), pp. 109–10. I wish to thank Professor Jacoby for this reference.

55. See below, part II document 105n. After listing pages of Venetian slave dealers, Verlinden finally found one Jew, a resident of Tana, who sold a young Tartar slave. This unique incident is enough for him to extrapolate a number of Jewish dealers who thus contributed to the extraordinary cosmopolitanism of the market in Tartar slaves in Tana. On the Crimean slave market in general, see M. Balard, *La Romanie génoise,* I, 289ff and passim.

56. Part II, edited by Rabbi Menahem Ze'ev Ḥasida (Jerusalem, 1969), pp. 70–78.

57. Ibid., 71: ואני בעצמי יודע כי הלכות כלאים כמה מעורבבין הם,מפני שמסכת כלאים אין לה גמרא.

a product that was ritually acceptable to a Jewish community which continued to observe the biblical commandments regarding *sha'aṭnez,* the prohibition against mixing wool and linen in a garment. Therefore, it is interesting to note that the abovementioned chapter includes an observation by "R. Moses Cohen in the land of Greece" (otherwise unknown), for whom the author evidently had considerable respect.[58] R. Moses had heard that some people (presumably in Greece) had forbidden the use of hemp with wool, evidently under the impression that hemp was in the same category as flax.[59] Since wool cannot be mixed with flax in a ritually pure garment, this opinion obviated the use of hemp in the making of woollen cloth.[60] R. Ṣidkiyahu refuted this view, at least for the Ashkenazi sphere of activity, and supplied evidence that everywhere in the Western diaspora the accepted custom was to wear wool sewn with hemp.[61]

The problems pertaining to the manufacture of nonhybrid garments were particularly vexing for Byzantine Jews, given their role in the textile industry. These difficulties may explain what preoccupied some of the great scholars whom both Benjamin of Tudela and Judah al-Ḥarizi found in the manufacturing centers of Thebes and Constantinople. Surely they came under investigation by Hillel ben Eliakim in his commentaries to *Sifre* and

58. Ibid., p. 76. He was a contemporary of the author, if we can accept the reference (p. 175) as indicating the same individual: גדול דורינו הנמצאים עכשו אדו[ננו] ר׳ מאיר ומו[משה] הכהן הר״ר אביגדור[כהן–צדק].

59. An overlooked passage in Herodotus (IV.74) may shed some light on the origins of this opinion. During his description of the Scythians, Herodotus notes their cultivation of hemp and adds that the Thracians made a cloth from it that so resembled linen that it was difficult even for an expert to tell the difference. Could it be that this literary tradition was still known in Greece? It is not impossible, given the continued study of Greek classics in Byzantium. The traditional use of hemp for garments in Byzantine Greece, on the other hand, suggests that the local Jews would have banned the use of hemp with wool, based on the halakhic principle of "erecting a fence around the Torah," i.e., of avoiding a violation of biblical law by interdicting anything that might lead to a confused interpretation of that tradition. Egyptian Jewry did not know of the problem, while Ashkenazi Jewry was too recent to be familiar with the Thracian tradition and practice. See following note.

60. Ibid., p. 74: תשובה זו השיב הר״ר משה כהן בארץ יון : לשמע אוזן שמענו שבני אז׳ם מהנדסין לענין קנבוס ואוסרין אותו לגבי צמר כדין פשתן. Cf. Ankori (*Karaites,* pp. 174f) for a discussion of the Karaite view of *sha'aṭnez apud* Hadassi; cf. also *Tosaphoth HaRID,* #61.

61. Ibid., pp. 74f: ויבינו מדין קנבוס שלאו בכלל פשתן הוא . . . ומוציאין לעז על הראשונים שנהגו בו היתר מימי אבותיהם בכל ארץ הגולה אשכנז, וצרפת, אנגלאטירא פרובנצא, שכולם לובשין צמר תרופה בקנבוס ואין מהרהר בדבר ושמא יעלה בלב שום אדם מה היא מתני׳.

Sifra (**15n**). Moreover, the technical problems and their continued study may provide some background for the long-known but still undated bilingual commentary on the mishnaic tractates *Kilaʿim* and *Sheviʿith*.[62] The parallel lists, in Hebrew and colloquial Greek, of the technical and botanical terms of these tractates no doubt were of considerable value for the workers, their foremen, and attending rabbis. Whatever the date of the manuscript, surely it remained in use longer than that. An occasional Greek gloss on the subject of textiles in a biblical commentary also points up the practical necessity for close familiarity with the subject.[63]

Romaniote Customs

Life in the Romaniote community, as in other Jewish communities, was based on the customs codified in the late second century in the Mishnah of the Palestinian Academy, under the leadership of Judah ha-Nasi. In the succeeding 300 years, before the codification of the Palestinian and Babylonian Talmuds, Romaniote Jewry developed a communal life that was distinctly peculiar to its Greco-Roman and, later, Byzantine environment. Thus we should expect to find Romaniote life exhibiting a blend of local custom, superimposed on traditional practices, with occasional influence from immigrating groups such as the Karaites and, later, the Sephardim. Some characteristics of Romaniote Jewry can be seen in the few documents we have concerning their social practices.

Material on the social life of Romaniote Jewry during the Palaeologan period is almost totally lacking. Most of our information comes from the early thirteenth century in the comments of R. Isaiah of Trani, the south Italian Tosaphist whose influence was respected even among the Franco-German rabbinic scholars. On a number of occasions his authoritative ruling was sought by communities in western Greece. Some material can

62. Cf. A. Papadopoulou-Kerameos, "Glossarion hebraiokoellenikon," (Greek) *Festschrift zu . . . Dr. A. Harkavy* (St. Petersburg, 1908), pp. 68–90. The editor suggests a connection with the dialect of Cyprus but does not hazard a date; edited by F. Kukules, "A Hebrew-Greek Glossary," (Greek) *BZ*, XIX (1910), 422–29; and J. Starr, "A Fragment of a Greek Mishnaic Glossary" (*PAAJR*, VI [1934–35], 353–67), who dated it tentatively to the tenth or eleventh century.

63. For a Greek gloss of the thirteenth century, cf. Neubauer, *Bodleian*, I, #296, for the commentary on the term המסכת in Judges 14:14: ובלשון יון אָדִי שמקלפין הבגד הארוז בו from the Greek ὑφάδι (= woof).

also be gleaned from the many collections of responsa which appeared during the Ottoman period.[64]

It is in the area of marriage customs that most of the evidence has survived. This is not surprising, given the nature of our major source: the responsa of Isaiah of Trani, which, from a rabbinic perspective, deal with this very important area of religious life. The differences between Romaniote marital customs and those of other Jewries were sufficient to cause considerable confusion regarding the proper understanding of rabbinic tradition. One such difference involved the Romaniote custom pertaining to the "seven blessings" of the marriage ceremony (**5**). According to rabbinic tradition, a marriage ceremony had to take place in two stages, first *kiddushin* (betrothal), followed (usually within a year) by *nissu'in* (marriage). The Romaniote custom, however, was to perform the ceremony of betrothal and recite the seven blessings—even though the latter properly constituted part of the ceremony of marriage—and then, under the impression that the pair was married, allow cohabitation (**9**). The question posed to R. Isaiah was, What constitutes *nissu'in*? In the case where the seven blessings had been recited during the *kiddushin* ceremony but the couple had not yet been under the *ḥuppah* (bridal canopy), nor had the *ketubah* (marriage contract) been read, was the couple legally married? Isaiah answered that their cohabitation was not, according to Jewish law, that of man and wife, but rather that of two engaged people, since without the reading of the *ketubah,* in which the groom acknowledges his responsibilities to the bride, the rabbinic marriage cannot be consummated.[65]

64. On Isaiah of Trani and the Tosaphists, cf. S. Schechter, "Notes on Hebrew Mss. in the University Library at Cambridge," *JQR,* os, IV (1882), 90–100, and E. E. Urbach, *Ba'ale ha-Tosaphot* (Jerusalem, 1968), index s.v. Isaiah of Trani continued to influence Epirote Jewry in later generations. MS Heb 35 in the Houghton Library of Harvard University, which contains his decisions on *Seder Moed* and *Hilkhoth mezuzah tephillin ve-tsitsit,* was owned in 1432 in Ioannina by the brothers Shabbetai and Menahem. The scribe Shem Tob ben Abraham may have been a local Romaniote; cf. folio 250 (actually numbered folio 252). Cf. *Hebrew Manuscripts in the Houghton Library of the Harvard College Library. A Catalogue,* prepared by M. Glatzer, ed. Ch. Berlin and R. G. Dennis (Cambridge, Mass., 1975), MS Heb 35.

For the later responsa, cf. Assaf, "Family Life" (Hebrew). The responsa of Eliahu Mizrahi were reprinted in Jerusalem in 1938; those of Benjamin Ze'eb ben Mattathias were printed in Venice in 1639 and reprinted in Tel Aviv in 1958.

65. The problem, stripped of the legal ramifications of Jewish law, may perhaps be more easily understood within the context of local custom. The phenomenon of peasant marriages in the Balkans is well known. These entail cohabitation prior to formalization or sanctification of marriage vows through the auspices of the church. Apparently the Jews had assimi-

The Romaniote understanding of the formula of *kiddushin* caused a scandal in one unidentified community. The prospective groom, ignorant of Hebrew, asked his friend to repeat the ritual formula (*harei 'ath mekuddesheth li* = behold, you are sanctified unto *me*) at the ceremony. The friend did so and, taking advantage of the situation (and the young lady), claimed the woman as his legal wife. The community was dumbfounded, yet the woman remained his wife for many years and bore him a family (**10**). Another question was asked by a man who, having enjoyed a long married life, wished to celebrate the marriage ceremony again. Isaiah's answer was to the point: Was once not enough? If you wish to celebrate the marriage ceremony again, you will have to divorce the woman first.[66]

Not all Romaniote customs differed from those of other Jewries. Romaniote Jewry paralleled their Ashkenazi coreligionists in sanctifying child marriages.[67] This custom, as elsewhere, led to a number of divorces (**7**). Occasionally it was necessary to resort to the secular courts to implement these divorces, since the latter were not responsible to the social concerns inherent in a Jewish marriage and, therefore, were likely to be more lenient (**11, 96***).

Non-Jewish customs also found their way into the Romaniote wedding ceremony. Romaniote Jews, for example, adopted the local Christian practice of crowning the bridal couple with marriage wreaths (*stefanomata*) during the engagement ceremony (**9**). Apparently, then, recitation of the seven blessings and the laying on of the wreaths constituted one form of the wedding among Romaniote Jewry. Later the couple was left to consummate the "marriage," while the guests moved off to another house to continue the celebration.

Romaniote Jewry differed from their coreligionists in the important ritual requirement of *teḥila*, the postmenstrual bath, regularly required for

lated this custom and legitimized it, to their satisfaction, by emphasizing the nature of the "seven blessings" and including them in the betrothal ceremony. Then, after a year, the match would be formally sanctified by performing the actual marriage ceremony.

66. *Teshuvoth HaRID,* #30.

67. Here again we should note parallels to Byzantine law and custom; cf. E. Patlagean, "L'enfant et son avenir dans la famille byzantine (IVe–XIIe siècles)," *Annales de démographie historiques* (Paris, 1973), pp. 85–93, esp. pp. 86f and 88f for the problem of engagement and cohabitation. S. D. Goitein's researches into the Jewish society of Egypt during the tenth through the thirteenth centuries have indicated that child marriages there were quite rare; cf. his *A Mediterranean Society,* III, *The Family* (Berkeley and Los Angeles, 1978), pp. 76–79.

all married women. The rabbis of Romania apparently based themselves on the decision of the Byzantine sage, Hillel ben Eliakim, whose commentary on *Sifra,* written in the late twelfth century, was widely respected.[68] Isaiah of Trani was a personal witness to an unsuccessful attempt to reintroduce the normative ritual. A Jew from Crete had married into an unidentified mainland community (presumably in the western provinces). When he tried to get his wife to take the ritual bath, the women of the community harassed her for going against the local custom. Even Isaiah was unsuccessful in his attempts to change this practice, until he issued a ban against the offending women (**8**).

The problem may have stemmed from something more than a divergent rabbinic opinion. A tradition, attached to Elazar ben Samuel of Verona (early thirteenth century), relates how he admonished two scholars from Greece because of their makeshift *mikvah.* The latter, not wishing to expose their wives to the stares of the fishermen when they took their ritual bath in the sea, dug a pool and filled it with "drawn water" to the proper volume. Elazar was not willing to accept their sanctioning of this pool for use as a *mikvah.*[69]

It is not entirely clear, but it seems that Romaniote Jews, basing themselves on their millennial-long exposure to the availability of public baths in the Greco-Roman world, interpreted the early rabbinic sources in such a way as to allow their use for the required ritual bath.[70] At the same time, more sensitive to the developing customs of a pietistic Ashkenazi Jewry or the more authoritative older traditions of Islamic Jewry, some Romaniote Jews attempted to follow what was rapidly becoming normative Jewish

68. Cf. Neubauer, *Bodleian,* I, #424, 425, 426, 427, and HPP G187, discussing Frankfurt Universitätsbibliothek MS Heb 4° 2. On the latter, see below part II document 15.

69. מעשה בשני תלמידי חכמים בארץ יון שלא היו רשאין נשותיהן לטבול בים מפני העם שבספינות על איי הים ועשו בור בעיר ושפכו מים שאובין על שפתו מחוצה לו ד׳ אמות והמשיכום לתוך הבור והכשירו .המקוה לטבילה ושלח להם הר׳ אלעזר מוורונא-הוסיפו הכשרות וכו׳. Cited by H. Gross, "Das handschriftliche Werk Assufot Analekten," *MWJ,* X (1881), 71; noted by Starr, *Romania,* p. 22, note. 7.

Compare the tradition recorded in the so-called *Letter of Aristeas* (ed. H. St. J. Thackeray) with translation and commentary by Moses Hadas (Philadelphia, 1951): (305) ὡς δέ ἔθος ἐστὶ πᾶσι τοῖς 'Ιουδάιοις, ⟨ἀπονιψάμενοι⟩ τη θαλάσσῃ τὰς χεῖρας, ὡς ἂν εὔξωνται πρὸς τὸν φεόν . . . Cf. Josephus, *Antiquities,* 14.258; Acts 16:13; and the archeological support, supplied by E. Sukenik (*Ancient Synagogues in Palestine and Greece* [1934], pp. 49f) that the Jews of these areas built their synagogues near water.

70. It seems also that the Romaniote attitude in general toward the ritual bath reflects their Greco-Roman traditions; cf. *Teshuvoth HaRID,* #111.

practice, which demanded a constant flow of water through the *mikvah*. The church, of course, had long tried to restrict social interaction through canons that prohibited attendance at public baths when Jews were there (57). Whether this ever took the form of a legal prohibition is not recorded. At the base of the scholarly disagreement of Isaiah of Trani with Hillel ben Eliakim's opinion lies a social problem that had existed since at least the fourth century, namely, the desirability, on the part of ecclesiastics, of effecting social barriers between Jews and Christians.

Another area where Romaniote custom differed from that of other Jewries was in regulation of the *nedunia* (dowry).[71] The general custom was that the husband took possession of the dowry and, subject to certain conditions, kept it for the duration of the marriage. A Romaniote Jewess, on the other hand, maintained the dowry for her personal use. That such dowries could be considerable can be seen from the items listed in an eleventh-century marriage contract from the empire.[72] Moreover, not only did the wife maintain possession during her life, but even after her death her husband did not inherit the property.[73] In most instances it reverted to her father's family.

This practice remained strongest in the centers of Romaniote life. When the Sephardim came to the Ottoman Empire at the end of the fifteenth century, they were shocked by it. Within a few generations, Romaniote Jewry in general accepted the Toledan custom that the husband share the dowry with the wife's sons or relatives.[74] Some Romaniote communities in outlying areas had modified this practice earlier. The community of Vidin in Bulgaria, for example, adjusted the traditional Romaniote custom, apparently in the face of social pressure from Hungarian and other Ashkenazi immigrants, in the second half of the fourteenth

71. Assaf, "Family Life," pp. 102–4. Cf. Jacoby, "Quartiers juifs" (pp. 223–27, esp. p. 225), for a document describing dowry customs in the Venetian Jewish community in Constantinople in 1424. For the contemporaneous custom among the Jewish communities in the Islamic world, cf. Goitein, *A Mediterranean Society,* III, B, 2–3 and passim.

72. T. Reinach, "Un contrat de marriage du temps de Basile le Bulgaroctone," *Mélanges offerts à M. G. Schlumberger* (Paris, 1924), I, 118–32, and Starr, *JBE,* pp. 187–89, no. 130; originally published by J. Mann. See below, part II document 20, for bibliography.

73. ומאי דכתב מר על מה שנהגו ברומניאה שאין האיש יורש את אשתו *Teshuvoth HaRID,* #65. M. A. Friedman, *Jewish Marriage in Palestine* (Tel Aviv and New York, 1980), I, 402, note 30 and whole section.

74. Cf. Assaf, "Family Life," (Hebrew) p. 104. Interestingly enough, the Sephardim apparently abandoned this custom of Toledo at the very time the Romaniotes adopted it.

century (**96***). Such adjustment is one indication of the more attractive customs that were based upon the more convincing rabbinic scholarship of the Ashkenzim and Sephardim, and helps to explain the rapid acceptance of their influence and the ultimate absorption of the majority of the Romaniotim in the centuries following the conquest of Constantinople.

A further Romaniote custom that differed from normative Jewish practice involved court cases that concerned monetary matters (**11**). Apparently the Byzantine Jewish judge allowed both parties to give testimony against each other. The argument of Isaiah of Trani against this custom was that if their cheating one another brought them both to court, how could their testimony be trusted to clarify the facts of the case? We should expect, had the records survived, that the majority of decisions that emanated from the Romaniote courts were compromises between the two defendants rather than a judgment for the injured side. Perhaps this type of jurisprudence was forced upon the Jewish court by the fact that some Jews were accustomed to resort to the non-Jewish courts.

Regarding these differences from normative Jewish tradition, scholarly opinion has generally agreed in tracing it back to Karaite influence, with its parallels to the Romaniote custom regarding ritual baths,[75] restrictions on the husband's inheriting his wife's property,[76] and influence in calendar matters.[77] While all the sources for similar occurrences of Karaite influence on Rabbanite customs in Byzantium from 1204 until the end of the empire have not been exhausted, the available evidence suggests that

75. Schechter, "Notes on Hebrew Mss.," pp. 99–100.

76. Assaf, "Family Life," (Hebrew) p. 104. We may note here, however, a parallel in Orthodox customary law cited by N. J. Pantazopoulos, *Church and Law in the Balkan Peninsula during the Ottoman Period* (Thessaloniki, 1967), pp. 57ff. During the Ottoman period the Greeks initiated the custom of *trachoma,* i.e., a payment to the prospective groom in addition to the regular dowry. In 1767, the patriarch Samuel I tried to abolish this new payment. His canon VI contains a parallel to the older Romaniote custom and may reflect a late Byzantine practice: "for the reason that in some places, as in Bulgaria and also elsewhere, an old habit has been preserved, according to which the bridegroom does not receive and does not obtain from the bride, not only aspers (i.e., *trachoma*), but neither and utterly no dowry, he moreover is indebted to pay to his father-in-law and his mother-in-law against the maintainance [*sic*] and breeding of their child a small amount determined in order to receive the daughter, this habit is to be preserved, protected and to take place unhindered, as it is one of the good habits of the olden times and not one of the present." One of the reasons for this canon was the custom of parents to endow the daughter with almost all their wealth (cf. p. 58). Also, for the custom of dividing the property into three parts (including the dowry) after death, cf. pp. 66f, esp. note 32.

77. Ankori, *Karaites,* pp. 252, 255–56.

such influence was not insignificant. The stricter dietary laws among the Karaites were the ostensible reason behind the charge of laxity in ritual affairs levied against the Rabbanite *shoḥet* in Nicomedia. Such public charges were apparently one way in which such influence was asserted.

It should not be forgotten, however, that Byzantine Christian custom and law also exerted influence upon the Romaniote community. The abovementioned *stefanomata* in the wedding ceremony is one example, and the code of George Armenopoulos states that while Jews may not testify against Christians, they may bear witness against each other in a Byzantine court (**67**). In the matter of dowry, too, Byzantine custom followed Roman law, to the extent that property remained within the family, with the right of inheritance going first to children or their descendants or, in the absence of issue, to siblings and parents, as well as their collateral relatives.[78] Moreover, listing the contents of the dowry is found among both Christians and Jews.[79] The latter no doubt reflects the same Byzantine law.

In effect, the study of Romaniote customs (and indeed Romaniote society in general) must take into account at least three factors. The first is Byzantine law and custom, which set the framework for the functioning of Jewish society and influenced Romaniote Jews to the varying degrees of their assimilation to the majority society. The second is Jewish law and custom, as developed within the Romaniote community, based upon local adjustment of earlier Palestinian practice with the changing Byzantine environment. The third is the influence of Babylonian Jewish custom, as reflected in its Talmud and reinterpreted by Ashkenazi Jewry on the basis of its peculiar adjustment to Western Christian society. Nor should sectarian influence be discounted, although it too was subject to the processes that acted upon the normative community.

78. Armenopoulos, *Hexabiblos,* pp. 626–32, and Laiou, *Peasant Society,* pp. 104f.
79. Laiou, *Peasant Society,* p. 90, and below, part II document 96*.

FOUR

LANGUAGE AND LITERATURE

THE INTELLECTUAL pursuits of Romaniote Jews reflected their geographical location within the Jewish and gentile world. Direct heir to Palestinian Jewish traditions on the one hand, they were also heir to the teachings of the Greco-Roman world. We find among Romaniote Jewry a rich blend of Hellenistic Jewish and Palestinian rabbinic traditions, and both of these intellectual currents continued through the end of the empire. Also, during the succeeding centuries Romaniote Jewry continued to study and develop the mystical and homiletic traditions that emanated from the Palestinian center. This intellectual base was never wholly superseded by the emphasis on legalistic interpretation introduced by the Babylonian academies in their attempt to establish a centralized bureaucratic control over the far-flung Islamic-Jewish communities which so greatly influenced the later-developing Ashkenazi communities, with their reliance on a talmudic way of life.[1] The study of midrashic and kabbalistic texts, then, constituted one of its major intellectual preoccupations. In the Palaeologan period, we also find emphasis on the study of astronomy and grammar. Further, Romaniote Jewry, throughout its history, expended great effort on religious poetry, which reached its peak during the period 1350–1550. This interest resulted in a fluid prayer service, which was codified in several different traditions only in the sixteenth century—that is, when the creative elements and the energy of the Romaniote com-

1. Cf. Starr, *JBE,* p. 215, no. 164.

munities were being overcome by the increasing influence of the newly arrived Sephardi communities.[2]

Rabbinic Scholarship

The study of classic rabbinic texts, though perhaps not the main source of intellectual stimulus, was not neglected. The late twelfth-century commentaries of Hillel ben Eliakim on *Sifre* and *Sifra* are good examples (**15**), despite an occasional dissent by Isaiah of Trani (**8**).[3] The halakhic works of Isaiah himself were considered authoritative in Epiros at least, as evidenced by their continued use in the fifteenth century.[4] Still, the names of only a few thirteenth-century Romaniote scholars have survived, due in part to an unfortunate anonymity of respondents in the extant responsa of Isaiah of Trani; only an R. Simkha and R. Isaac of Romania are specifically named as his contemporaries.[5] Elsewhere we hear of a nebulous Baruch ha-Yevani who died either in 1200 or circa 1260.[6] David ha-Parnas of Negroponte, too, was deemed learned in traditional lore—the Bible, Mishnah, Talmud, ***dikduk*** (grammar), and ***sebara*** (logical exegesis)—as was Moses Galimidi of Thebes (the latter was apparently a trained Talmudist). Between them they sired and trained a succeeding generation of scholars (**30, 47**). The sons of Moses Galimidi and David Kalomiti are only a few of the scholars known to us by name in the fourteenth century.

2. Cf. studies by S. Bernstein, "The Caffa Maḥzor, Its History and Development," (Hebrew) *Festschrift Shmuel-Kalman Mirsky* (New York, 1958), pp. 451–538, and his "A Selection of Poems from a Ms. of the Corfu Maḥzor," (Hebrew) *Festschrift Abraham Weiss* (New York, 1964), pp. 233–47; Daniel Goldschmidt, "On the Maḥzor Romania," (Hebrew) *Sefunoth*, 8–9 (1964), 207–36; and Weinberger, *Anthology*.

3. Eliahu Mizraḥi, in his late fifteenth- or early sixteenth-century supercommentary to Rashi, mentions him a number of times; also, he cites several Byzantine scholars from the Komnenian period: R. Abraham Zutra, R. Isaac Zutra and Meyuḥas (ben Eliyahu).

4. See above, chap. 3, note 64. Still, he had respect for Byzantine scholarship as evidenced by his remarks: קהילות רומניה הקדושים אשר חכמה ותבונה בהמה ויש שבח לאל כח בידם לישא וליתן בעומקה של הלכה ומשיבי מלחמה שערם, שמהם תצא הוראה לכל ישראל. Translated below, part II document 11.

5. See above, chap. 2, note 30, for a list of the twelfth-century scholars from Byzantium mentioned by R. Isaiah; and Starr, *JBE*, chaps. V–VI, for those in earlier Byzantine history.

6. Rosanes, *Israel be-Togarmah*, p. 206. He is possibly the same R. Baruch mentioned by Isaiah of Trani; see previous note. On the problem of identification, see Y. N. Epstein, "On Rabbenu Barukh of Greece," (Hebrew) *Tarbiz*, XVI (1944–45), 49–53, and his earlier study, "Rabbenu Barukh of Aleppo," (Hebrew) ibid. (1940), pp. 27–62; and also A. Obadiah, "Rabbi Eliahu Mizraḥi," (Hebrew) *Sinai*, 5 (1939–40), 402 note 47.

Two better-known Rabbanite scholars of the fourteenth century are Shemarya of Negroponte, also called Shemarya ha-Ikriti (from his family's connection with Crete), and his pupil Judah ibn Moskoni, from Ochrida. Shemarya b. Elijah was born before the turn of the fourteenth century.[7] His father was a communal official (*parnas*) in Crete, and his ancestors had lived for a while in Rome. Shemarya, too, maintained connections with Rome, although he is usually associated with Negroponte (**51**). Unfortunately, we have very few data to reconstruct his biography. He is mentioned as alive in 1346 by the Karaite scholar Aaron b. Elijah (**69**), and Judah ibn Moskoni suggests that he completed his studies with Shemarya in the previous year (**87**). He was dead by 1358, which, given a normal life span, would place his birth toward the end of the thirteenth century (**84**). His grandson was living in Patras in 1410, by which date his son Ismael had died (**109**). The latter, then, may have been born late in the first quarter of the fourteenth century. Ismael was at least his second son, since Shemarya indicates the death of his firstborn while he was working on his commentary to the Bible. (Portions of the latter were dedicated to Robert, king of Naples, in 1328.) After the death of his firstborn, he taught his younger son Talmud—indeed, prepared a commentary for him on most of the text. It is probably within the context of the above-noted royal patronage that he spent some of his twenty-five years as a translator (**53**). After 1328, he moved to Negroponte, where Judah ibn Moskoni eventually became his student. There, *inter alia,* he prepared his supercommentary on Ibn Ezra and, circa 1346–47, wrote his *Sefer Amasyahu,* a handbook of biblical apologetics. (More exact dates and places are at present unavailable.) He seems to have spent most of his career alternating between Greece and Italy. He died after 1352, the year his detractor suggests his revelation as Messiah. Since his grandson lived in Patras, we may assume that his son Ismael (we know of no other children) remained somewhere in Greece—Crete, Negroponte, or Patras.[8]

In tune with the intellectual currents among Romaniote Jewry,

7. His full name was: שמריה בן החכם הנדיב מרנא ורבנא אליא הפרנס האיקריטי בן יעקב בן דוד בן הרב אליא רומנוס בן הנדיב ובנו דוד הצנוע איש רומי; cited in his *Commentary to Song of Songs* (ms., Paris 897, folio 12a).

8. The latest study of his career is in C. Sirat, "Letter of Shemaryah ben Elijah on Creation," (Hebrew) in *Eshel Beer Sheba,* 2 (1980), 199–227. Dr. Sirat corrects a number of errors in earlier biographies, and shows that it is impossible to prove that Shemaryah was ever in Spain.

Shemarya was trained in philosophy (both Jewish and non-Jewish), medicine, and poetry, as well as traditional rabbinic literature. Moreover, he is the first known Romaniote scholar to translate directly from Greek to Hebrew (**53**). His literary activity included commentaries on the aggadic material in the Talmud and most of the biblical books, philosophical essays, and liturgical poetry.[9] His opinion of his qualifications was apparently unrestrained, and this egocentrism may be behind the later charge that he had messianic pretensions (rather than any intent to fill that role). He did not hesitate to criticize all philosophers when the occasion arose (**73**); yet he deigned to recognize Moses (Maimonides) as an equal in certain respects (**73**) and relied upon him in others (**73n**). It is not surprising, then, to find this self-assured polymath castigating his contemporaries for the intellectual chaos that permeated their scholarship (**51**).

Avoiding a well-rounded approach, some Jews, according to Shemaryah, studied the Bible only and ignored the Talmud, and others vice versa. Of those interested only in the Bible, some were content merely to accept the literal meaning, while others sought in it the solution to all mysteries. Among the latter were those who read the Bible in the light of the rational sciences, and an opposite group that studied it according to kabbalistic traditions. Amid such diversity, only the abilities and comprehensive view of R. Shemaryah could bring forth a true understanding of the Bible which would reunite the efforts of divergent scholars and bring respite to Israel.

We do not know any of Shemaryah's teachers. It has been suggested that he studied with Abraham Abulafia, because of the later charge that he had messianic pretensions. The suggestion is as erroneous as the charge

9. A partial list of these includes: commentaries on Esther, Song of Songs, Genesis and Exodus, Kaddish prayer, and Job; *piyyutim* in the *Maḥzor Romania*; commentaries on talmudic and midrashic Aggadah; *Sefer Eleph ha-Magen*; *Sefer Amasyahu* on the Pentateuch (a philosophical inquiry); *Sefer ha-Mora* on Creation, a study correcting current philosophical opinion (Steinschneider thought these last two works might have been the same treatise under different titles); *Sefer Higgayon* on logic. Cf. Steinschneider, *Leiden* (pp. 212 and 397), for excerpts and also for translations of several philosophical treatises into Hebrew from the Greek. Cf. Steinschneider, "Candia, Cenni di Storia Letteraria, Articolo III. Secolo XIV," *Mosé, Antologia Israelitica* (Corfu, 1879), II, 456–62; A. Geiger, "Notes" (Hebrew) in *he-Halus,* II (Lemberg, 1853), 25–26, and "Addenda on R. Shemaryah ha-Ikriti," (Hebrew) ibid., pp. 158–60 (both reprinted in his *Gesammelte Abhandlungen*); Neubauer, "Documents inédits," *REJ,* X (1885), 86–92.

On the place of Shemaryah in contemporary Jewish philosophy, cf. Shalom Rosenberg, "Logic and Ontology in Jewish Philosophy in the 14th Century" (unpublished dissertation

itself. Abulafia left Greece shortly after 1279—a date too early for Shemaryah, who died between 1352 and 1358.[10] More likely the students who continued Abulafia's traditions could have served as his teachers, although we have seen that the Aegean Jewish communities did not lack their own scholarly infrastructure. In reality, his father would have initiated his schooling, most likely in Crete, where he served as a communal official.

Judah b. Moses or, to give him his Greek name, Leon b. Moskoni—although he mixes the two and calls himself Judah ibn Moskoni (and so shall we)—was born in Ochrida in 1328.[11] By his mid-teens, he had already

---

[in Hebrew], Hebrew University of Jerusalem, 1973), 1:94–100, containing a bibliography of Shemaryah's works. The most recent study is by C. Sirat, cited in previous note. Cf. also Steinschneider, *Die hebräischen Uebersetzungen der Mittelalters* . . . (Berlin, 1893), I, 498f, and for a contemporary parallel in Latin, pp. 489ff.

10. See below, "Mystical Tradition."

11. Of his father, nothing further is known, save that he died sometime after 1363, since the various formulae following his name indicate that he was still alive at that date (see below); for Judah's biography, cf. I. Molho, *Histoire des Israélites de Castoria* (Thessaloniki, 1938), p. 15; for literary works, cf. Steinschneider, "Judah Mosconi," in his *Gesammelte Schriften* (Berlin, 1925), I, 536–74.

We may note here the use of the double name: Greek for the general public and the other Hebrew for use within the Jewish community. This fact has been obscured by the mistaken reading of his name which he signs: אני יהודה המכונה ליאון בה״ר משה המכונה מושקוני (both in his introduction to the commentary on Ibn Ezra [published in *Oṣar Tob,* p. 1] and his introduction to *Sefer Josippon* [*apud* Hominer, p. 36]: "Judah known as Leon son of R. Moses known as Moskoni").

No one has yet taken note of this literal translation of the signature, and for this reason he is always cited—erroneously—as Judah or Leon b. Moses Mosconi. The latter name is somewhat unusual because the last part, Moskoni, derives from the Greek Μοσχάς or Μόσχος, or in Latin "Mosca" and, ultimately, from the Hebrew "Moshe" (Moses); cf. Z. Ankori, "The Living and the Dead," *PAAJR,* vol. XXXIX–XL (1970–71), note 135.

Coincidentally, the first Jew that we meet in Greece is one Μόσχος Μοσχίωνος Ἰουδαῖος, who appears as a manumitted slave in Oropos, Attika, in 129 B.C.E. (cf. B. Petrakou, Ὁ Ὠροπός καὶ τὸ ἱερόν τοῦ Ἀμφιαράου [Athens, 1968], p. 193 and notes 1–2). The suffix *-ni* may represent a term of endearment, a diminutive, some local dialect; or, more simply, the name Moskoni may be the Hebrew form of Μοσχόνιος, which, however, is unattested, just as this appearance of "Moskoni" is our earliest (and unique?) reference to this name. Whatever the case, the name Moskoni cannot be a family name here because in each part of the signature he gives, first, the Hebrew name whereby he was known in the synagogue, followed by its designation in Greek: Judah = Leon and Moshe = Moskoni, both of which are direct equivalents of the Hebrew original. To emphasize our argument, we may note that he calls himself Judah ibn Moskoni (*apud* Hominer, p. 37). This interpretation of the signature suggests quite clearly that in Ochrida, at least Hellenized Jews were accustomed to use Greek equivalents of their Hebrew names in public.

For another occurrence of Μόσχος (מושכו), cf. Cambridge, Geniza fragment, T-S 8.J.19 33.

begun his intellectual peregrinations, which were to last for the better part of his life. In the mid-1340s he was studying with Shemarya ha-Ikriti in Negroponte. There, the beginnings in grammar, logic, mysticism, philosophy, and Talmud that he acquired in his home city (perhaps under the initial tutelage of his father) were developed under the charismatic teaching of the sage of that island. As a youth in his late teens (in 1345), armed with the training he received from Shemarya, he began his wanderings in pursuit of manuscripts on or about Abraham ibn Ezra (**87**).

The impression one gets from his travel notes is that Ibn Ezra was the best-known and most influential of the biblical commentators among Romaniote Jewry (both Rabbanite and Karaite), with copies of and commentaries on his works diffused throughout the Mediterranean.[12] Our bibliophile relates that he saw over thirty manuscripts of his works during his travels. Few were the Eastern scholars discovered by Judah ibn Moskoni who could match Ibn Ezra's encyclopedic knowledge, however; and so they were content, for the most part, to write monographs on various aspects of his commentaries. Such studies included that of R. Kaleb Korsinos of Constantinople (perhaps late twelfth or possibly early thirteenth century) on grammar, R. Eliahu of Serres (probably late thirteenth century) on astronomy (**32n**), and the encyclopedic attempt of R. Shemarya himself (**87**). Needless to say, Judah ibn Moskoni wrote his own supercommentary on Ibn Ezra, on which he was working in 1363.[13]

This errant scholar[14] indulged in other literary research. For example, he collated four or five manuscripts to produce the best extant copy of the

12. On the influence of Abraham ibn Ezra in the Byzantine and Karaite worlds; cf. Ankori, *Karaites,* index s.v., and his "Elijah Bashyachi," (Hebrew) *Tarbiz,* XXV (1955), 60–63, 194–98, and M. Friedlaender, *Essays on the Writings of Abraham ibn Ezra,* vol. IV (London, 1877). In Thebes in 1367, the scribe Shemaryah was copying the major astronomical works of Abraham ibn Ezra: *Sefer Reshith Ḥokhmah, Sefer ha-Ta'amim, Sefer ha-Moladoth, Sefer ha-Me'oroth, Sefer ha-Meḥabrim, Sefer ha-Olam u-Maḥbaroth ha-Meshartim,* and *Sefer Mishpetei ha-Olam.* Cf. list in Neubauer, *Bodleian,* I, #2518; date corrected in author's "Jews in Fourteenth-Century Thebes," *Byzantion,* vol. L (1980). See below, part II document 32.

However, Judah emphasizes that any scholar must begin his study of the Torah with Rashi's commentary: ולכן הראוי לכל משכיל לקרוא פ׳ רבי שלמה בספר התורה טרם קראו פ׳ החכם הנזכ׳; "Introduction to Ibn Ezra," *Oṣar Tob,* p. 9.

13. Already, at the age of 35; in his comments to Ibn Ezra on Exodus 12:1 he mentions the date 2 Shebat 5122, i.e., 1363.

14. ואני יהודה המכונה ליאון בה״ר משה המכונה משקוני יבמ״י ומ״י ברצות ה׳ אלהי ישראל להשימני מהגולים מעיר אל עיר וממלכה אל ממלכה וחסדו ורחמיו לא עזבוני מעודי ועד היום הזה (cf. edition cited in following note, p. 36) and avid book collector (ibid., p. 37): וקניתי לי ספרים רבים בכל חכמה.

Sefer Josippon in the later Middle Ages.[15] Judah ibn Moskoni gives an insight into his reasons for his edition of the *Sefer Josippon* that are of particular interest for the attitude of fourteenth-century Byzantine Jewry to their surroundings.[16] After receiving his initial and formal education with a variety of scholars (whom he does not identify), he relates in his introduction to the text (which he wrote in 1356)[17] his decision to search

15. The whole text, collated from the Vienna (5304), Mantua (5238–40), and Constantinople (5270) editions, has been reprinted by H. Hominer with an introduction by R. Abraham Wertheimer (Jerusalem, 1957; multiple editions) and with the introduction of Judah ibn Moskoni. Both of these editors—of the fourteenth and twentieth century—accept the attribution of *Sefer Josippon* to Joseph ben Gorion ha-Kohen (i.e., Josephus Flavius). Since the sixteenth century, however, it has been recognized that the text is a pseudepigraphon. Steinschneider (*Bodleian,* #6033, col. 1547) suggeted its provenance as north Italy from the ninth to the tenth century. For differing views and résumé of current literature, cf. discussion by Baron, *SRHJ,* VI, 189ff and 417ff.

D. Flusser, of the Hebrew University of Jerusalem, has prepared a scholarly edition of the *Sefer Josippon* (vol. I, *Text and Scholia* [Jerusalem, 1978]; vol. II, 1980); cf. his preliminary studies (all in Hebrew): "The Author of the Book of Josippon: His Personality and His Age," *Zion,* XVIII (1953), 109–26 and English summary; his review in *Kiryath Sefer,* 34 (1959), 458–63; and, more recently, "The Author of *Sefer Josippon* as an Historian," in *Mekomam shel Toldoth 'Am Yisrael bi-Misgereth Toldoth ha-'Amim* (The place of Jewish history within the framework of world history) (Jerusalem, 1973), pp. 203–26. The last article and his study from *Zion* have been reprinted as part of the introduction to a photocopy of the original text: David Flusser, ed., *Josippon, The Original Version, MS Jerusalem 8°41280 and Supplements* (Jerusalem, 1978).

Flusser has shown conclusively that the Hebrew text is based primarily on the medieval Latin Josephus (cf. edition by Franz Blatt, *Acta Jutlandica,* XXX, 1 = *Humanistik serie,* 44, Aarhus, 1958, and Flusser's review cited above), which was translated from the Greek in 576, and that this Latin translation, plus the Apocrypha, were used and occasionally amplified by a Jew in southern Italy to produce the Hebrew Josippon in 953. Flusser's edition thus presents the shorter text available in Italy and northern France, while Judah ibn Moskoni's edition, by far the most popular and influential among later generations of Jewish readers, is about a third longer. Cf. author's "A Tenth-Century Byzantine-Jewish Historian," *Byzantine Studies,* vol. X, 1 (1983).

16. Some attitudes from Romaniote *paytanim* are listed in Weinberger, *Anthology,* pp. 13ff, English section.

17. This date is derived as follows. In an interesting passage in his introduction to *Sefer Josippon,* Judah ibn Moskoni noted that about 780 years had passed since the date he found in the text: "508 years since the destruction of the Second Temple." The medieval date for the latter disaster was 68 C.E.; therefore the date in his manuscript would correspond to 508 plus 68, or 576 C.E. If we add to this date his 780 years, the result is 1356 C.E. (On the Josippon date, cf. Flusser in *Zion,* note 24 and text. [I should like to thank Professor Flusser for discussing with me this unique tenth-century Byzantine-Jewish history and its fourteenth-century Romaniote editor.]) The passage in which Judah ibn Moskoni speaks so highly of Pope Gregory I (594–604) and indicates that he saw some Latin books (suggesting that he pursued his research in some non-Jewish libraries in the West) needs to be investigated in light of Flusser's researches into the Latin sources of *Sefer Josippon.*

out scholarly books that had maintained their reputation to his day. Whereupon he set out to examine and purchase manuscripts throughout the Mediterranean.[18] When he came across a copy of *Sefer Josippon* and read it, he found its words "as sweet as honey in my mouth." For Judah ibn Moskoni there were four main reasons for the importance of the work: (1) scholars should look into it to strengthen their souls against the pressures of conversions, so prominent in every generation; (2) the wise would find in it insights (*sodoth*) and hints concerning the end of days; and (3) the reader would learn from it the deeds of valor of his ancestors, as well as stories about the Temple—in other words, memories of the days when Jews walked with heads high, as opposed to their contemporary status of exile and suffering.[19] The fourth reason is the most important: "For when we see how the sins of our fathers caused the exile, then we shall truly understand that our own sins lengthen the time to the end of our own redemption. Thus we shall better our ways to return to the Lord and to serve Him in a completely true way in order that He will repatriate us."

Further in his introduction, he emphasized the antiquity of the *Sefer Josippon* and, indirectly, its authority for Jewish scholars:[20] "And know too that this book which is known to us as Josippon is the first book written for Jews after the completion of the Prophets and Hagiographa [i.e., the last two divisions of the Hebrew scriptures], and it preceded the composition of the Mishnah and the Talmud. Moreover, it preceded the writing of all the books of our ancestors which they wrote to explain the Pentateuch, the Prophetic writings, and the remaining sacred texts on the basis of midrash." Clearly, Judah is criticizing the prevalence of midrashic commentaries on the Bible so popular among Romaniote Jewry, including his teacher Shemaryah. Clearly, too, he is excited by a text which he feels is a history contemporary to the destruction of the Second Temple.

While he was correct in identifying the *Sefer Josippon* as a reliable history, he dated it too early. Even so, its view of the period about which rabbinic writings describe only the sacrificial cult and their intellectual ancestry must have been refreshing to this overly bright rationalist student.[21] His interest

18. Clearly, his discovery of the *Sefer Josippon* was a by-product of his primary research on Ibn Ezra and, no doubt, occurred during the journeys described in the introduction to the latter's commentary on the Torah. See previous note.

19. Text *apud* Hominer, p. 39.

20. Ibid.

21. On his rationalism, see his commentary to Exodus 33:21 and remarks there on the anthropomorphic midrash *Shi'ur Koma* in Steinschneider, "Judah Moskoni," p. 556.

in history may have been due to the contemporary Byzantine historiographical tradition. More likely it presented a descriptive and logical framework within which to place his rabbinic training. Judah discovered a number of manuscripts of the *Josippon*—some were complete, others lacked pages, and some had been badly edited or copied. So impressed was he with the book that the young scholar deemed it necessary to restore the text in order to make available the deeper insights it offered. The edition he collated was the one chosen by Jacob Tam ibn Yahya for the first printing of the *Sefer Josippon* in Constantinople in 1510. (In retrospect, Judah ibn Moskoni reminds us of the better-known Renaissance Latin scholars who wandered throughout the eastern Mediterranean two generations later in search of manuscripts of ancient Greek authors.)[22]

A handful of other known Rabbanite scholars from the Palaeologan period slightly lift the veil which obscures Byzantine Jewish intellectual life. R. Elnatan b. Moses Kalkes, for example, wrote a lengthy kabbalistic treatise entitled *Eben Saphir*.[23] Apparently the author, who calls himself on occasion Nathan or designates himself by some other mystical name, lived in Constantinople and wrote his book in the last third of the fourteenth century.[24] In several places he kindly remembers his teacher, R. Isaiah b. Immanuel, presumably also from the capital. The work remains in manuscript, yet a synopsis of its twenty-two sections (by Solomon Munk) allows us some insight into the state of kabbalistic (and to some extent philosophical) studies in Palaeologan Byzantium.[25] Nor was pure philosophy ig-

22. On parallel phenomena in late thirteenth- and early fourteenth-century Byzantine scholarship, cf. R. Browning, "Recentiores non deteriores," *Bulletin of the Institute of Classical Studies,* VII (London, 1960), 11–21; reprinted in his *Studies on Byzantine History, Literature and Education* (London: Variorum Reprints, 1977).

23. Cf. Munk, "Oratoire," pp. 24–26, 41–42. The manuscript consists of two volumes containing approximately 350 closely written folios. See below, "Mystical Tradition," for a description of the contents. The name Kalkes is possibly derived from the city of Kilkis, some 40 miles north of Thessalonica.

24. He mentions the dates 1367 and 1370, in addition to a reference to the plague in 1345. Moshe Idel, who has examined the manuscript in greater detail, informs me that it was written closer to the end of the fourteenth century. The author, he suspects, may well have studied in Spain.

25. See above, note 23. In a long digression, the author shows himself a staunch defender of Maimonides against his Spanish detractors. Abraham Abulafia had begun this tradition in Greece in the previous century with his kabbalistic commentary on Maimonides' *Guide for the Perplexed*. Cf. also H. Wirszubski, "Liber Redemptionis: An Early Version of Kabbalistic Commentary on the *Guide for the Perplexed* by Abraham Abulafia in a Latin Translation of Flavius Mithridates," (Hebrew) *Proceedings of the Israel Academy of Sciences and Humanities* (1969), 3, 135–49. See M. Idel, "Abraham Abulafia's Works and Doctrines,"

nored: R. Joseph ha-Yevani authored a Hebrew abridgment of Aristotle's *Logic* (**91**), while the *Guide for the Perplexed* of Moses Maimonides was copied, studied, and defended against its detractors during the fourteenth century. Romaniote *paytanim,* too, were accustomed to use philosophical themes and terminology in their compositions.[26] Also, the copyist of a philosophical work in Naxos at the beginning of the fifteenth century cites with effusive praise his teacher, R. Judah al-Konstantini, who is otherwise unknown (**110**).

Scribal colophons from the fifteenth century indicate continued interest in rabbinical works. In 1424 an Ephraim ben Shabbetai from Romania bought a copy of *Novellae* to Rashi's commentary on the Pentateuch (**121**); two decades later, the scholia of R. Tam to Rashi's commentary were copied by Elkanah b. Elia for Elia b. Judah; and in the same year (1443) the same scribe copied the scholia of Ḥiskiah b. Manoaḥ.[27] Both onomastic and palaeographic evidence indicates Romaniote provenance for the manuscripts. In addition to the influence of these Ashkenazi scholarly works, we find continued study of earlier Byzantine commentaries, in particular the biblical commentary of Meyuḥas b. Eliahu (twelfth century?), recopied in 1469.[28] Also, Gaonic classics were not unknown: a scribe from Mistra, Yeḥiel b. Moses, copied the first post-talmudic halakhic work, *She'iltoth de-Rav Aḥai* in 1481.[29]

The above works constitute only part of the intellectual resources that sustained the cultural framework of Romaniote Jewry.[30] As more Late Byzantine Jewish texts become identified, the resources of this Jewry can be better studied against the background of its period. Also, the very important question of the extent of Sephardi influence on the intellectual world of Romaniote Jewry can be better assessed. On the other hand, as our

---

unpublished dissertation (in Hebrew), Hebrew University of Jerusalem, 1976 (with English summary).

26. Cf. Weinberger, *Anthology,* pp. 7–8 and passim.

27. H. Zotenberg, *Catalogue des manuscrits hébreux et samaritains de la bibliothèque imperiale* (Paris, 1886), #167, nos. 2 and 3; the script is identified as Greek or Karaite.

28. *Catalogue of the Hebrew MSS in the Collection of Elkan Nathan Adler* (Cambridge, 1921), #2366.

29. Ibid.

30. We have not touched upon the wealth of material available for the study of the intellectual history of Cretan Jewry. Cf. bibliography in Steinschneider, "Candia," *Mosé,* II–V, passim, and Cassuto, *Vatican.*

knowledge of the period advances, treatises that formerly were considered Late Byzantine are liable to be reidentified as non-Byzantine.

In dispute today are two works which have been ascribed to our period. The ethical treatise, *Sefer ha-Yashar,* has been traditionally ascribed to Zeraḥiah ha-Yevani, a Balkan scholar of the fourteenth century. Rather detailed arguments against this identification and even against the existence of such a scholar, have been put forth recently.[31] Moreover, none of the extant manuscripts stems from the Balkans, leading a recent editor of the text to doubt its traditional attribution.[32] The second work, the polemical *Sel'a ha-Maḥlokoth* of Abraham Roman, we strongly suspect, was mistakenly identified as an early fifteenth-century text by Steinschneider. It is more likely that this treatise is a product of the seventeenth or early eighteenth century (**111**). Indeed, such polemics must have been rare, as Christianity was the dominant faith and the church served as a department of state within the Byzantine Empire. Still, though such treatises were against the law (**67**), there are to be found anti-Christian chapters among Jewish authors. Judah Hadassi's *Eshkol ha-Kofer* (twelfth century) is perhaps the most noteworthy example. The theme is also found among Romaniote *piyyutim.*

Karaite Scholarship

The Karaites of Byzantium had already developed their strong scholarly traditions in the eleventh century. This scholarship is also evidenced in the fourteenth century. The question is whether a scholarly tradition existed in the thirteenth century among the local Karaites. A bill of sale, dated 1288, is the only clue discovered to date which sheds some light upon this question (**26***). The notice records the sale of a philosophical treatise, titled *Midrash ha-Ḥokhma,* to an unknown scholar, named Joseph b. ha-Kadosh Mordecai, in an unidentified Karaite community in Thrace (**26* n**). This work, composed in the 1240s by the Rabbanite scholar Judah b. Solomon ha-Kohen, represents the first scientific encyclopedia written by a Jewish scholar. The appearance of such a work in Karaite circles in Greece within a generation of its translation into Hebrew by the author (possibly in Italy) is

31. Cf. A. T. Shrock, "The Authorship of the Ethical Treatise Entitled Sefer ha-Yashar," *JQR,* ns, LXI (1971), 175–87, and LXV (1974–75), 18–31.

32. *Sefer hayashar: The Book of the Righteous,* ed. and tr. by Seymour J. Cohen (New York, 1973), p. xi.

evidence that Karaite savants were aware of contemporary philosophical developments. This same tendency is found among the two great scholars who led Byzantine Karaites from the late thirteenth through the first two-thirds of the fourteenth century. Aaron b. Joseph was aware of Maimonides and Abraham ibn Ezra, while Aaron b. Elijah cites his contemporary Shemaryah of Negroponte.

These two Aarons, in particular the latter, became a major influence upon subsequent generations of Byzantine as well as Crimean and Polish Karaites. Due to their near-contemporaneity, later Karaites found it necessary to designate the former "the Elder" and the latter "the Younger" to differentiate between these two like-named scholars. Coinciding with the death of Aaron b. Elijah in 1369, the Karaite center shifted to the recently conquered Ottoman capital of Adrianople, where its development followed a different path than that of either the Karaites or the Rabbanites who remained in Byzantium.

Aaron b. Joseph came from the Crimea, probably from Solchat, the main Karaite center there. His intellectual pursuits included medicine, philosophy, and biblical studies, as well as a fair attempt at liturgical poetry and a codification of the Karaite prayerbook.[33] His knowledge of rabbinics was considered more proficient than that of any previous Karaite scholar, especially in his study and use of the Talmud, the commentaries of Maimonides on the Torah, and the works of Abraham ibn Ezra.[34] With regard to the Talmud, he was one of the first Karaites to argue that, as the Oral Law antedates the Rabbanites, the material in the Mishnah and Gemara was legitimate study for the Karaites.[35] It is not surprising, therefore, that

33. He is identified as a philosopher, and both he and his father are designated as physicians. Indeed, his father was a witness to a multiple birth, which must be regarded as an obstetrical record (nine babies!): וטעם וישרצו שהיו בבטן אחד ב׳ ג׳ד׳ ושמענו מפי אנשים נאמנים כי ראו בעיניהם שאשה אחת ילדה תשעה בבטן אחד. ואדוני אבי יר״א (ירחמהו אלהים) ראה זה בעיניו. Cf. *Mibḥar, Exodus,* p. 1b. The epithet following his father's name suggests that he was deceased.

34. So much so that later Karaite tradition had it that he had studied with Maimonides; cf. H. Graetz, *Divrei Yemei Israel,* tr. by S. P. Rabbinowitz and annotated by A. Harkavy (Warsaw, 1908), 5:264n.

35. The logical continuation was the acceptance of all early rabbinic material in the Talmud and Midrash (which was understood to date from before the rise of Karaism as a separate sect). Such is the tenor of the statement by Aaron b. Joseph, *Mibḥar,* introduction, 9a (cf. Ankori, *Karaites,* p. 232, note 53): ואין לטעון בעדנו שגם אנחנו נשענים על הכתוב ועל הקש ועל ההעתקה. זו ההעתקה אינה הורסת הרשום בכתב אמת ואינה בחלוקה נעתקה. אך היא בפה אחד מכל ישראל סוף דבר אני לא אמנע ברכי המצות שלא אזכיר בתוך הבאור מדברי המשנה וחפצי בהם להיותם בדרך סמך and this principle was attributed by Aaron to his Karaite

Aaron was the first Karaite officially to sanction reliance on the Rabbanite precalculated calendar, instead of the traditional Karaite reliance upon the appearance of the *abib* in the Land of Israel (**28**).

Aaron b. Joseph is best known through his three extant works which reflect the above traditions. His most popular treatise is the *Sefer ha-Mibḥar,* written in 1293/94, a commentary on the Torah in which he relies heavily on Maimonides and Ibn Ezra.[36] Copies of this work were available in the market well into the fourteenth century, as well as in all later periods (**55**).[37] Of the remaining biblical books, only the prophetic portion of his commentary has appeared in print, under the name *Mibḥar Yesharim,*[38] which covers only Joshua-Isaiah. He also wrote a grammatical aid to study the biblical text, titled *Kelil Yofi.*[39]

As the leading Karaite scholar in Byzantium in the late thirteenth century, Aaron b. Joseph attempted to establish regularity in the Karaite synagogue there by contributing to and editing an arrangement of the prayerbook.[40] Not content with the traditional Karaite material, he included in his arrangement *piyyutim* from the Spanish Golden Age—among others, those of the Rabbanites Shlomo ibn Gabirol, Judah ha-Levi, and Abraham ibn Ezra. Nor was he averse to including his own verses, though these tended to be more didactic than lyrical.[41] On the other hand, Aaron

---

predecessors: ורוב משכילי גלותנו עשו ככה עד שהרב נס׳ בן נח חיב לבני עמנו ללמוד המשנה והתלמוד and justified on the basis of its being Jewish and not restrictively rabbinic scholarship: ואין זה תפארת לבעלי הקבלה כי רוב המאמרים אמרי אבותינו הם. Also cf. Z. Ankori, "Elijah Bashyachi," (Hebrew) *Tarbiz,* XXV (1955–56), 189 and 201. This position was reiterated almost two centuries later by Elijah Bashyachi: שרוב המשנה והתלמוד דברי אבותינו הם.

36. *Mibḥar,* preface: שמו מבחר ומחברתו יקרה לכל קורא בו מבחר ישרים ומחשב אהרן הדל נתנו בנו יוסף שנת הנ״ד ספורים. He reiterates the date in his final comments to the Book of Deuteronomy: בשנת הד״ן; cf. וזאת הברכה לז:. See also document 25.

37. Printed in Gozlow, 1835. His full name is cited there: פירוש על התורה להרב אהרון הראשון קדוש ה׳ הפילוסוף האלהי הרופא נ״ע בן הרב רבנו יוסף הרופא זצ״ל.

38. Printed in Gozlow (1833–34) and bound with the commentary of Jacob ben Reuben to Jeremiah through Chronicles, which the latter called *Sefer ha-Osher.* On this earlier Karaite commentator, cf. Ankori, *Karaites,* s.v.

39. Printed in Gozlow in 1847 and based on the edition of Isaac Tishby, printed in Constantinople, 1581, with corrections by Isaac Troki. His commentaries also emphasized his interest in grammar and its importance for understanding the biblical texts; cf. his complaints against earlier commentaries, *Mibḥar,* introduction: שאין פירושיהם על פי הדקדוק.

40. Tradition does not record where he lived. Both Constantinople and Adrianople were major Karaite centers in the fourteenth century. It is likely that he lived in one of these cities. The only reference to a Karaite settlement in the thirteenth century is in Byzantine Thrace.

41. Graetz, *Divrei Yemei Israel,* 5:263; Ankori, *Karaites,* p. 236.

b. Joseph was not free from the general Karaite predilection during the period 1250–1500 for passé intellectual problems, such as anti-Saadyan and anti-Mishawite polemics and the Muslim Kalam.[42]

Little more material is available for Aaron b. Elijah. Following Karaite manuscript tradition, which has attached the epithet "Nicomedian" to his name, modern scholarship, too, accepts his origin from the city of Nicomedia in Asia Minor.[43] The *one* text we have on Jews in Nicomedia in the fourteenth century comes from the period immediately after the Ottoman conquest of the city (**61**); so the tradition of Aaron b. Elijah's birth there becomes our only information on Jews in Nicomedia in Byzantine times.[44] The latest argument for the date of Aaron's birth suggests that it was between 1315 and 1320, and probably close to 1320.[45] There is no dispute about his end: a source records his death, during an epidemic, shortly after Rosh ha-Shanah in 1369 (**96**). It was possibly before the Ottoman conquest of Nicomedia that he moved to Constantinople, first to further his studies, then to assume the leadership of the Karaite community there.[46] It was also in the capital that, sometime after 1354, he completed his code of Karaite law, *Gan ʿEden* (**80–81**).

Though his life was cut short in his prime, Aaron b. Elijah produced three great works which rank him as one of the leading luminaries of Karaite literary history. His *Kether Torah* was a commentary on the Pentateuch; his *Gan ʿEden* became an authoritative code of Karaite law which was cited frequently even in its fifteenth-century successor, the *Addereth Eliahu* of Elijah Bashyachi, and was never fully superseded by the latter; while his *ʿEṣ Ḥayyim* was the last great compendium of Karaite philosophy. Presumably, all three were written in Constantinople, although tradition mentions only the code as having been written there.[47] Aaron also contributed some *piyyutim* to the Karaite liturgy.

42. Ankori, *Karaites,* pp. 364 and 372n. Of course the latter may have been necessitated by his sources, i.e., treatises and commentaries from the period when these problems were actively competing with Karaism; cf. *Mibḥar,* introduction. Karaites, too, were *au courant* with contemporary Jewish philosophy; see below.

43. Ankori, *Karaites,* p. 135, note 183.

44. See above, chap. 2, "Anatolia."

45. Ankori, *Karaites,* p. 134, note 176.

46. We do not know when he left Anatolia, or if he returned there after the Ottoman conquest of Nikomedia. It is more than likely that until his death he remained in the capital, which was the most important Karaite center of the day. Cf. Ankori, *Karaites,* p. 134, note 178.

47. S. Poznanski (*The Karaite Literary Opponents of Saʿadia Gaon* [London, 1908], pp. 80f) dates the three works 1362, 1354, and 1346.

Of the teachers whom Aaron b. Elijah mentions with great respect, it seems probable that R. Yehudah, his maternal uncle, was his early tutor in Nicomedia, while R. Moses, his father-in-law, may have resided either in Nicomedia or Constantinople.[48] That the former city may have been the home of R. Moses is suggested by the pamphlet on dietary laws which the latter wrote between 1339 and 1346, alluding to a local case in Nicomedia (**61**). Both of these teachers died before 1346 (**70, 74**). Another of Aaron b. Elijah's teachers, R. Joseph, died in late spring, 1369 (**96**).

The Karaite communities of Byzantium, though once strong and numerous, declined rapidly after the death of Aaron b. Elijah. This was due as much to the plagues, which depopulated the empire, as to the rise of a new Karaite center in Ottoman Adrianople. As the Byzantine Karaite leadership deteriorated, new pupils were lacking. In fact, so little of Karaite traditions was remembered that the fourteenth-century Shemarya of Negroponte was mistakenly considered a Karaite (due probably to frequent mention of him by Aaron b. Elijah [**69**]), while the great work of Judah Hadassi, *Eshkol ha-Kopher,* had sunk into oblivion.[49] Its fifteenth-century copyist, Shabbetai b. Eliahu, was considered one of the savants for restoring Hadassi's work to the community; yet it had been written only some 300 years before (**148**). Moreover, many Karaite students, deprived of intellectual leadership, forsook their teachers and frequented the Rabbanite places of learning. The acceptance of these pupils in the generation after the Ottoman conquest, however, was dependent upon an oath by Karaite students that none of the teachers of rabbinic tradition would be slandered in public.[50] This Karaite dependence on Rabbanite schools contributed to the intellectual rapprochement between the two groups in the second half of the fifteenth century, a rapprochement that had been initiated by the first Karaite leader during the Palaeologan period, Aaron b. Joseph.

The Byzantine story was not truly reflective of Karaite scholarship in the late fourteenth and the fifteenth centuries. Within a generation after the

48. Ankori, *Karaites,* pp. 136, note 184, and p. 137, note 187.

49. Cf. Graetz, *Divrei Yemei Israel,* 5:262. This was already noted by Kaleb Afendopolo, *Naḥal Eshkol* prefacing the Gozlow edition (1836) of *Eshkol ha-Kofer*; cf. Ankori, in *Tarbiz,* XXV (1955), 59f.

50. Cf. quote from R. David Konforte, *Kore ha-Doroth* (Venice, 1740), p. 31b, and Rosanes, *Israel be-Togarmah,* p. 25n.

conquest of Adrianople,[51] a Karaite school was founded there whose head, Menaḥem Bashyachi, began to enact major changes in the Karaite tradition. These changes were influenced greatly by the first immigration wave of Sephardi (Catalan) Rabbanite teachers (following the 1391 massacre in Spain), who made available to the Karaites the wealth of their intellectual traditions. Menaḥem's grandson, Elijah Bashyachi, succeeded him as head of the Karaite community after its relocation in Constantinople in the wake of the Ottoman conquest of that city in 1453. Elijah's code, the *Addereth Eliahu,* included the reforms of the Bashyachi family and became the normative code for Karaites during the Ottoman period.[52]

Shortly after the arrival in Adrianople of those earliest Spanish refugees, an increased Rabbanite influence appeared among the Karaites. The impoverished refugees, bearers of the Renaissance spirit that was pervading Western intellectual life, found fertile fields among the Karaites, Turks, and Greeks in which to plant both their Jewish and general learning. Arriving at a time when Karaite education was depressed, they reintroduced the Sephardi traditions of teaching the philosophy and poetry of Abraham ibn Ezra, and the *halakha* and thought of Maimonides.[53] Moreover, the anti-Karaite polemics of Judah ha-Levi and Abraham ibn Daud paradoxically became the sources for Elijah Bashyachi's study of Karaite origins.[54] The impact of these Sephardi teachers, in particular R. Ḥanoch Saporta and R. Yabetz, contributed to the pro-Rabbanite reforms of the Bashyachi family and, by extension, to that intellectual rapprochement between the Karaites and Rabbanites which was the hallmark of the first generation of Ottoman Jewry.

After the death of the Byzantine Karaite leader Aaron b. Elijah, the Karaite community in Adrianople slowly inherited the mantle of leadership, which had to be developed under the new conditions created by the Ottoman conquest of that city. At the same time, they benefited from the upgrading

51. On the Karaites in Byzantine Adrianople in the fourteenth century, see above, chap. 2, "Thrace and Macedonia."

52. See section below, "Intellectual Trends."

53. We noted above that these subjects were part of the curriculum of Balkan scholars in the fourteenth century, viz., Judah ibn Moskoni and his Karaite contemporary, Aaron b. Elijah, and the latter's predecessor Aaron b. Joseph.

54. Z. Ankori, "House of Bashyachi and Its Reforms," (Hebrew) introduction to Elijah Bashyachi's *Addereth Eliahu* (Ramlah, 1966), p. 12, and, in more detail, in *Tarbiz,* XXV (1955), 183–91.

of Adrianople as the capital of the empire, which was bound to attract new economic and intellectual resources to the city. They were the first Karaites to receive direct benefits from the influx of Sephardi scholars after 1391. The Karaites in Byzantium, on the other hand, remained without effective leadership in the two generations after the death of Aaron b. Elijah. During this period they were forced to go to Rabbanite teachers for their training.

By 1420, however, the school of Menaḥem Bashyachi, the Karaite leader in Adrianople, was attracting students from Constantinople; the latter, upon their return, would become major figures in the Karaite intellectual story of the late fifteenth century.[55] The best known of these students was Elijah Bashyachi and his disciple Kaleb Afendopolo (the latter also studied with Rabbanite scholars).[56] The school, as well as the center of Karaism, shifted back to Constantinople soon after the Ottoman conquest, though not without opposition from conservative Karaite elements in Adrianople (**148, 149**).[57] Still, the reestablishment of a Jewish center in Constantinople after the conquest was a direct stimulus toward narrowing the gap between the Rabbanites and the Karaites.

Karaite interest in Rabbanite philosophy and poetry was continued, of course; but, more important, the social barriers between the two groups were lowered by Karaite adoption of what were traditionally considered Rabbanite customs. These fundamental changes in Karaite customs were initiated by the Bashyachi school in Adrianople under the guidance of Menaḥem b. Joseph and his son Moses Bashyachi. They were continued by Menaḥem's grandson Elijah Bashyachi, who succeeded to the leadership of the Karaite community in the capital in the latter half of the fifteenth century and codified them in the last major code of Karaite law, his *Addereth Eliahu*.

One of the major differences between Karaites and Rabbanites had involved the calendar. The former's reliance upon visual sighting of the new moon had early marked Karaite independence from the normative Rabbanites, who had long substituted a precalculated calendar. In addition to visual sighting of the moon, the Karaites relied on reports from Israel announcing the ripening of the *abib* there in order to date their celebration of the spring festival of Passover. Of the many instances when Karaites

55. Cf. article "Bashyachi" (Hebrew) by Ankori in *EIV,* IX, 960–63, and essay cited in previous note.

56. Cf. Steinschneider, "Kaleb Afendopolo," in his *Gesammelte Schriften,* I, 184–96.

57. Cf. Mann, *Texts and Studies,* II, 292, and above, "Aftermath."

found it necessary to celebrate their holidays on a different date from Rabbanites, only a few have come down to us from the period under discussion (**25, 59, 147**). On these occasions, feelings ran high, and once (at least) the repercussions of these intracommunal disputes went far beyond the Jewish community.[58] One of the reforms initiated by the House of Bashyachi was to allow communities of Karaites who lived outside of Israel to use a precalculated calendar (**147**).[59]

A second major reform involved the weekly reading of the Torah. At the beginning of the Palaeologan period the Karaites had shifted the beginning of their cycle to Nisan, when they began the new year, as opposed to the traditional Rabbanite date in Tishre.[60]

A third area of contention, though not as volatile as the previous two, was the Karaite prohibition of the use of fire on the Sabbath. The Karaites condemned the Rabbanite use of candles on Friday evenings as a violation of the biblical injunction against work. In 1440 Menaḥem Bashyachi issued a *takkanah* that allowed the Karaites to light Sabbath candles and thereby bring some cheer into their homes. This last reform was condemned by conservatives, in particular the exiles from Parga, who had not been exposed to the Sephardi influence on the Karaites in Adrianople. Under the leadership of Elijah Bashyachi, however, Sabbath candles became the normative practice of Ottoman Karaites.[61]

In this way, the major religious differences between the two groups were glossed over and the previous causes of friction reduced. This reduction in animosity, first on an intellectual level and later on the social level, began early in the Palaeologan period but reached fulfillment in the first generation after the Ottoman conquest of Constantinople. Some differences remained, of course, although for the majority of the Karaites and Rabbanites they were not major issues. Rather, this deemphasis on the social differences between the two groups contributed to that rapprochement which made this generation of Romaniote scholars the most productive in Romaniote history.

58. See above, chap. 2, "Thessalonica."

59. Aaron b. Joseph had already suggested this in his *Mibḥar* at the end of the fifteenth century; see document 28.

60. The reason for this shift is not given, but it was likely connected with the attempt to perpetuate social and religious cleavage with the Rabbanite community. Nisan was also a logical choice, since one of the biblical calendars recognizes it as initiating a new year.

61. Cf. Ankori, "House of Bashyachi," pp. 2f; and *Karaites*, p. 235 and index s.v. "Sabbath."

Intellectual Trends

At the beginning of the last generation of Byzantine rule, Romaniote scholars could be found throughout the Balkans. R. Dosa b. Moses ha-Yevani or Bizanti, for example, was studying at the *yeshivah* of R. Shalom Ashkenazi of Neustadt in Vidin. By 1429 he had already written his super-commentary to Rashi on the Torah.[62] His younger contemporary, R. Shlomo b. Eliahu Sharbit ha-Zahav (ca. 1420–ca. 1501/2), who may have been born in Morea, moved to Ephesus (in 1426) and later taught there. He wrote books on astronomy and grammar, and commentaries on Ibn Ezra, as well as *piyyutim*.[63] His name, Sharbit ha-Zahav, means "golden scepter" and is apparently a translation of the Greek name Chrysokokkos. Interestingly enough, we find several Byzantine Christian scholars with the same name—his contemporaries—who were also physicians, astronomers, teachers, and, by virtue of their travels and scholarship, geographers.[64]

In addition to Romaniote scholars, the first leaders from Ashkenazi and Sephardi backgrounds were beginning to appear. As already noted, the first major attacks against the Jews in Spain began in 1391, and were followed by another major wave in 1415. Continued persecutions and ex-

62. Copied on Tuesday, 18 Kislev 1429, by David b. Samuel for Eliahu b. Joseph Strogilo (שתרוגילו). For the date, see HPP C40, ms. Oxford, Bodleian, MICH 261; cf. Neubauer, *Bodleian,* I, #203.

63. On these scholars, cf. Rosanes, *Israel be-Togarmah,* pp. 14 and 31. We may also note a Dosa b. Joseph who wrote J.T.S. micr. 2469 in 1461 in Constantinople (i.e., Poli; see below, document 154n); cf. HPP D116. Zotenberg (*Catalogue . . . de la bibliothèque imperiale,* #1042) places Shlomo b. Eliahu Sharbit ha-Zahav in the year 1374, but cf. Graetz, *Divrei Yemei Israel,* 6:300f, and articles below (by Meisles) for discussion of his dates; also cf. excerpts from Joseph Beghi's *Iggereth Kiriah Ne'emanah* in Steinschneider, *Leiden,* p. 392, and Mann, *Texts and Studies,* II, 305. Weinberger (*Anthology,* #34) reproduces his playful dialogue between Sabbath and Ḥanukkah, which he wrote for the Sabbath of that holiday; cf. comments in English section, p. 11. The poem is also edited by I. Meisles, "The Song of Rivalry between Sabbath and Chanukah by R. Solomon b. Eliahu Sharvit ha-Zahav," (Hebrew) *Bar-Ilan Annual,* XIII (1976), 224–33, and for a biography of the author, his "Shir ha-Otioth [The song of letters], Rabbi Shlomo ben Eliahu Sharvit Hazahav," (Hebrew) *Tagim, Review of Jewish Bibliography,* 5–6 (1975), 41–69. His collected poems were printed in Warsaw in 1893. His full name is signed Shlomo b. Elia Sharbit ha-Zahav mi-Salonikiyo in his astronomical work *Mahalakh ha-Kokhavim* (Vat. MS 393).

64. *Ha-Mazkir, Hebräische Bibliographie,* VIII (1865), p. 28, note 6, and Steinschneider, *Leiden,* p. 122; cf. Cassuto, *Vatican,* p. 156. On the fourteenth-century Chrysokokkoi, cf. U. Lampsides, "George Chrysococcis, le médecin, et son oeuvre," *BZ,* XXXVIII (1938), 312–22. Lampsides found three men by this name in the late fourteenth and the fifteenth centuries. See also A. Tihon, "L'astronomie byzantine (du Ve au XVe siècles)," *Byzantion,* 51 (1981), 616ff.

pulsions of Jews in Western and Central Europe also set in motion waves of emigrants, some of whom found their way to the southern Balkans. Their solid training in traditional Jewish texts soon made them the dominant factors on the local educational scene. This penetration (which we have noted before) deserves a special study of its own, but it may suffice here to mention only the more famous: Isaac Saporta of Catalonia, who became the teacher of the Ashkenazim in Adrianople and a well-known scholar; Gedalya ibn Yahya of Lisbon; and Isaac Ṣarfati, an Ashkenazi, who also taught in Adrianople during this period.[65]

At the same time, it should not be overlooked that Romaniote Jews assisted the Sephardim in their intellectual adjustment to the new environment. Other translations than Aristotle's *Logic* must have been made for these non-Greek-speaking scholars (**91**). Also, a number of local tracts were copied by Romaniote scribes for wealthy Sephardi patrons (**109**). The appearance of Sephardi scholars in the East, therefore, should be seen as initiating a two-way process wherein they and their Romaniote hosts exchanged their intellectual traditions, with the latter contributing Greek originals in Hebrew garb as well as their local contributions and commentaries on religious and secular subjects.

The leader of Romaniote Jewry in Constantinople on the eve of the Ottoman conquest was possibly Moses Kapsali, who was born in Crete circa 1420 and lived to the end of the century. He was trained in the *yeshivoth* of Italy, where he received a thorough grounding in Ashkenazi disciplines. Tradition has it that his reputation as the "judge and leader of the Jews" advanced his candidacy for appointment as the first leader of Constantinopolitan Jewry after the conquest, a position he maintained until the end of the century.[66]

65. Cf. A. Obadiah, "R. Eliahu Mizraḥi," (Hebrew) *Sinai,* 6 (1940), 75, and ibid., 5 (1939–40), 409f. Isaac Ṣarfati is best known for his circular letter sent (ca. 1430 or 1454) to the Jews in Western and Central Europe extolling the toleration and other benefits of life under the Ottomans. Cf. Graetz, *Divrei Yemei Israel,* 6:300ff and appendix 6, pp. 428–31. There is *no* evidence for the date of the letter; this has been emphasized by Rabinowitz in his appendix to Graetz. Therefore it cannot be used to extol Mehmet II's tolerance (which, however, is attested in other Hebrew sources), as does F. Babinger, *Mehmed the Conqueror and His Times* (Princeton, 1978), p. 412. For a partial translation cf. Franz Kobler, ed., *A Treasury of Jewish Letters* (London, 1952), I, 283–85; a scholarly edition of the letter is a *desideratum.*

66. Ibid., for his vita and influence. See below, chap. 5, note 33, and Graetz, *Divrei Yemei Israel,* 6:302ff and appendix 7, pp. 431–38.

Romaniote Jewry produced two prominent intellects in the second half of the fifteenth century, and each was born at the beginning of the last Byzantine generation in the capital: the Rabbanite Mordecai Komatiano and the Karaite Kaleb Afendopolo. Both studied in Adrianople during their youth, the former unwillingly, the latter perhaps more appreciatively; each, however, returned home soon after the conquest.[67] Mordecai Komatiano has left a legacy of some fifteen works on astronomy, grammar, biblical commentaries, and *piyyutim*; some of the latter have even been included in the Karaite prayerbook. Among his writings is a polemic against Shabbetai b. Malkiel ha-Kohen of Crete.[68]

As the leading intellect in Constantinople in the second half of the fifteenth century (he was the student of Ḥanoch Saporta), Komatiano earned the respect of the Karaites by accepting them as his pupils. Many other rabbis followed his example and thus contributed to the rapprochement between the two groups. Others disagreed. One of the leaders of the opposition was Moses Kapuṣato ha-Yevani (ca. 1457–90 fl.), a biblical

67. Mordekai b. Eliezer Komatiano indicates a forced stay ("a captivity in a foreign land, in Adrianople") during his youth. Vat. MS 105 contains his commentary on Abraham ibn Ezra's *Yesod Mora,* with an introductory poem: אמר מרדכי בן אלעזר כומטיאנו יעֹמֹשׁ הקוסטנטיני היוני. בהיותי בשביה בארץ נכריה. בעיר אנדרינופולי. אשר נטיתי שם אהלי. ראיתי אנשים חכמים ונבונים. and other important allusions to the exciting intellectual world that he found there, as well as his relations with Karaite students, viz., Joseph Reviṣi (רבצי). Cf. Naphtali Ben-Menahem, *Mi-Ginze Yisrael be-Vatikan* (Jerusalem, 1954), pp. 64–65, and Cassuto, *Vatican,* p. 156.

68. Rosanes, *Israel be-Togarmah,* pp. 26–30, and Graetz, *Divrei Yemei Israel,* 6:300ff. His full name was R. Mordecai b. Elazar Komatiano, the Greek of Constantinople. Rosanes claimed that his family came from France, but the name Komatiano is decidedly Greek; cf. Demetrios Khomatiano, archbishop of Ochrida! We also find the name among Jewish merchants in a Venetian commercial register of the 1430s, viz., Saracaia (= Zeraḥia) Comatiano, Salachaia Chomatiano, Signorin de Lazaro Comatiano, in *Il Libro dei Conti di Giacomo Badoer,* ed. U. Dorini and T. Bertelè (Rome, 1956), passim; cf. Cassuto, *Vatican,* p. 156. (Could Lazaro be a reflection of Elazar, the name of Mordecai Komatiano's father? This would help expain where he got the money to study in Adrianople.) An "Anastos Comathianos ebreus" appears in a document edited by Jacoby ("Quartiers juifs," p. 225); on the name Anastas and variants, cf. Ankori, "The Living and the Dead," notes 77, 79, 80, 80a, 82. These references show, if not only the connections with, perhaps even the presence of Romaniote Jews within the Venetian colony in Constantinople. See above, chap. 2, and chap. 3 notes 15ff and text. The Italian form Comatiano, already found in Crete in the thirteenth century (cf. Leonardo Marcello, *Notaio in Candia, 1278–1281, a cura di Mario Chiaudano e Antonio Lombardo* [Fonti per la Storia di Venezia, Sez. III. Archivi Notarili] [Venice, 1960], #570), should be more properly transcribed as Khomatiano (in Hebrew it begins with a *khaf*) in order to reflect its Greek provenance.

commentator and *paytan*.[69] His polemics against the Karaites were so bitter as to call forth counterattacks by Komatiano and by the two leading Karaite scholars of the period, Elijah Bashyachi and Kaleb Afendopolo (**85**). Eventually, the efforts of Moses Kapuṣato supplied the necessary support to the campaign of Isaiah Missini and Shabbetai Malkiel ha-Kohen to bar the Karaites from Rabbanite schools, and a ban to that effect was issued by Moses Kapsali. The failure of this ban was evident from the outset: Rabbanite scholars continued their teaching. The ban was finally negated in the well-known responsum of Elijah Mizraḥi.[70]

Around the time of the conquest of Constantinople, R. Ephraim b. Gershom ha-Rofe made a list of the scholars in the capital with whom he studied or visited.[71] Originally from Verroia, Ephraim wandered via Zeitun to Constantinople, where he made his acquaintances, and eventually settled in Negroponte, where he became head of the community. His list includes Mordecai Komatiano from whom he learned mathematics and astronomy; R. Shabbetai b. Malkiel (ha-Kohen); R. Eliahu (Mizraḥi?); R. Shemaria; R. David Kalomiti; R. Moses (Kapsali?); R. Judah; R. Menaḥem; R. Ḥayyim; R. Shlomo (Sharbit ha-Zahav); R. Isaiah b. Proto; R. Yehonatan; and one upon whom he lavishes considerable praise, R. Shlomo of Mistra, who was evidently a *shoḥet*.[72] Other scholars of the period include R. Menaḥem b. Moses Tamar in Thes-

69. For example, cf. Weinberger, *Anthology*, #35.

70. Cf. excerpts from the Karaite work of Joseph b. Moses Beghi, *Iggereth Kiriah Ne'emanah*, in Mann, *Texts and Studies*, II, 294ff (commentary by Mann) and 302ff (text). For the Rabbanite account, cf. responsum #57 of Eliahu Mizraḥi.

71. *Ha-Mazkir. Hebräische Bibliographie*, XVII (1877), 134–36. The date is either 1450 or 1455, according to Steinschneider (p. 111), based on the reference to הדו״ר. Since he mentions a Byzantine noble, we prefer the date preceding the conquest.

72. Ibid., p. 136:

וברשות כ״ר שלמה מזיתרא, אשר הוא נזר התורה, ושמן מן המנורה הטהורה, ומצות י״י עליו ברה, וחברתו נעימה וישרה, ודיבורו יקרה, ולשכמו יקר ומשרה, ואין בפיהו זרה, ואמרתו לכל לב קשורה, ונעימה והדורה, ועונה לכל איש מהרה, ואם היה יכולת בידו היה מוציא כל אדם מצרה, ואם ישחט בהמה טהורה, או חמור ופרה, ויבוא לבודקה בדין וכשורה, אם היא כשרה, עונה במהרה, ואומר לבעל הפרה, תדליק הכירה, ועשה צלי הירכיים והשדרה, ולך אכול אותה בשמחה ושירה, ואם היא טרפה משיב בנפש מרה, ואומר לבעל הכשבה והשעירה, דבוקה היא וצרורה ואיני יכול להכשירה, ולך בנחוצה בשערה, אולי תמצא שם איש למכור בשרה, ואם לא יכול למוכרה, תנה תשורה, ויהוה לך יוסיף ימים לעזרה, ואם בשתים אלה לא תעשה פשרה, תשליכנה בבור כרה, ולא ירד לקדרה, כי כן גזירת התורה, ואמרת מפרשי הגמרא, וערוכה היא ושמורה, וכל מי שידבר בזו הצווי צרה, יבוא עליו עברה, מאת איום ונורא, והמקיימו מכל רע לא יירא. וברשות כל הקהל כל אחד ואחד בפרט כפי מעלתו וחכמתו ודיעתו אבאר פסוק אחד.

salonica, who was the pupil of R. Shabbetai b. Malkiel ha-Kohen (both mentioned above); and the Peloponnesian R. Isaiah Missini.[73] During this period, several Jews from Mistra can be identified.[74] A Yeḥiel b. Moses, for example, was active as a scribe in 1481, and Joseph Kavilan was copying astronomical texts there in 1495.[75] The latter was a student of Samuel Poto of Mizithra (Mistra), who had studied astronomy with Mordecai Komatiano in Constantinople and who returned to his native city at the time of its conquest by Mehmet II (143).[76]

Karaite scholarship, too, was in full bloom during this period. The head of the community in Constantinople was Elijah Bashyachi (ca. 1420–90), whose *Addereth Eliahu,* the last major code of Karaite law, canonized the reforms that had been initiated earlier in the century in Adrianople.[77]

73. Rosanes, *Israel be-Togarmah,* pp. 30 and 33. Missini is explained by Rosanes as the city of Messina in Sicily (p. 89). More accurately, we should read Mesene in the Peloponnesos. Mann notes (in his *Texts and Studies,* II, 300f, note 13) that "the reading Misene is an easy corruption of Mishetsi as in Joseph Beghi's *Iggereth Kiriah Ne'emanah* (or vice versa)." In responsum #58 of Eliahu Mizraḥi, he is mentioned as "my friend the honorable R. Isaiah Misene" (p. 192, col. 2). The R. Isaiah in Patras, whom Rosanes lists, is most likely the same as R. Isaiah Misene. See J. Hacker, "Some Letters on the Expulsion of the Jews from Spain and Sicily," (Hebrew) in *Studies in the History of Jewish Society . . . Presented to Professor Jacob Katz . . .* (Jerusalem, 1980), pp. 71ff, for the little that we know of this Peloponnesian sage and his academy in Istanbul after the conquest.

74. A correspondent of R. Jacob Kolon, the leading Italian jurist in the second half of the fifteenth century, was mistakenly identified as being from Mistra; cf. David Konforte, *Kore ha-Doroth,* ed. D. Cassel (Berlin, 1846), p. 28b, listing a R. Jacob of Mistra from the responsa of Jacob Kolon (#19, 20, 161). However, he is listed in the source as ר' יעקב מיישטרו and הר' יעקב מיישטרא; i.e., his name was R. Jacob Maestro.

An anonymous letter from the community of Mizithra to Michael ben Kohen Balbo can be found in Vat. MS 105, f. 158b. The question and his answer precede the latter's dirge on the fall of Constantinople (fol. 162a) and thus may possibly be dated to the period immediately before the conquest. Some of the same phrases may be found in both, e.g., בכחו הגדול בין הים ובין מגדול. On the Mistra congregation in Constantinople after the conquest, see M. A. Epstein, *The Ottoman Jewish Communities and Their Role in the Fifteenth and Sixteenth Centuries* (Freiburg, 1980), appendix I.

75. Cf. Zotenberg, *Catalogue . . . de la bibliothèque imperiale,* #309.

76. Cf. J.T.S., micro. 2581; HPP D160. A Shabbetai b. Poto of Ioannina was a scribe in Ioannina in 1458, where he copied Menahem Recanati's commentary on the Torah and added his own glosses. Cf. C. Sirat and M. Beit-Arié, *Manuscrits médiévaux en caractères hébräiques* (Jerusalem–Paris, 1972), I, 112. Two generations later, a Shabbetai b. Abraham Poto copied Hillel b. Eliakim's commentary on Sifra from the manuscript discussed in document 15.

77. Cf. his controversy with Moses Kapsali over the laws concerning the sciatic nerve and its definition in Romaniote *kashruth* in his *Iggereth Gid ha-Nasheh* (Epistle concerning the sciatic nerve), printed in the Gozlow edition of *Addereth Eliahu* (1835). Elijah Mizraḥi begins his commentary on the Torah with an excursus on the sciatic nerve, obviously in response to the Karaite position.

Elijah's death, in 1490, prevented him from completing his work; his pupil and brother-in-law, Kaleb Afendopolo, added several sections, but he too died before completing it. Kaleb also contributed studies in astronomy and mathematics.[78] Other Karaite scholars of the period included Abraham b. Jacob Bali and Joseph Revişi. The latter, along with Elijah Bashyachi, had studied with Mordecai Komatiano.[79]

The story of the intra-Karaite feuds over the social and intellectual rapprochement with the Rabbanites comes into focus at the end of the period under discussion and so lies beyond the immediate scope of the present work. Rather, it is sufficient to note that strong opposition existed among the Karaites as well as among the Rabbanites. The level of polemic evident in the dispute is but one more indication of the depth of scholarship attained by the intellects of the period.[80]

Romaniote Poetry and Liturgy

Nearly all the Jewish scholars of the Palaeologan period, both Rabbanite and Karaite, wrote secular and religious poems. Many of their productions, moreover, were singled out for inclusion within the local *maḥzorim* (prayerbooks) that were arranged in the early Ottoman period. It is these *paytanim* who are the best known of the period 1350–1550. More poets and their poems undoubtably lie hidden in the manuscripts of the period.[81]

Our earliest source on Romaniote poetry after 1204 is the Spanish poet and traveler Judah al-Ḥarizi. His acerbic comments reflect his Spanish background, where Hebrew poetry, in tandem with developments in Arabic poetry there, reached heights that are reflected in history's perception of that period as a Golden Age. What is overlooked by modern assessments that rely upon Spanish standards is that Byzantine poetry, the direct heir of Palestinian traditions, was rarely influenced by the Arabizing style of the

78. Nor did he ignore the lighter side of life, as can be seen in the study by Michal Saraf, "The 'Discussion between Wine and the Poet' by Kaleb Afendopolo the Karaite," (Hebrew) in *Papers on Medieval Hebrew Literature Presented to A. M. Haberman . . .*, ed. Zvi Malachi (Jerusalem, 1971), pp. 343–61.

79. Rosanes, *Israel be-Togarmah,* p. 47; Mann, *Texts and Studies,* II, 298.

80. Cf. extracts from Joseph Beghi in Mann, ibid., pp. 302–15, with his introductory comments, pp. 294–302.

81. See examples from 61 *paytanim* in Weinberger, *Anthology,* and comments in English section, as well as his *Romaniote Penitential Poetry* (New York, 1980).

Spanish contemporaries.[82] Rather, it reflected the same inspiration and tradition that produced the poetry from Byzantine southern Italy which is preserved in most Ashkenazi *maḥzorim*.[83] Even so, the younger style was not unappetizing, as evidenced by the later inclusion of Sephardi classics in the Rabbanite and Karaite services of Byzantium. Nevertheless, Judah's impressions of Byzantine scholarship, along with the observations of earlier visitors to the empire, such as Benjamin of Tudela and Petaḥiah of Regensburg, are valuable. His comment that poetry was considered by many Romaniotes to be their preeminent art, surpassing even their mastery of other branches of knowledge, is especially revealing (**16**). Byzantine Jews, as we shall see, continued to experiment with the *piyyut* throughout their history.

Despite the lack of biographical data for these *paytanim*, we may list a number of them (perhaps 60 are known by name, and a number of anonymous pieces) to emphasize their ubiquity among Romaniote Jewry. Judah al-Ḥarizi praised three of the Byzantine poets: Michael bar Kaleb of Thebes, Joseph b. Abtalyon, and Moses bar Ḥiyya. Some twenty of the latter's poems were included in the *Maḥzor Romania*, the *Maḥzor Bene Roma*, and the Karaite *Maḥzor* (**16n**). A number of other thirteenth-century poets are known, for example, Abraham Ḥazzan b. Isaac b. Moses, David Peppi, Mordecai of Nicaea, and Kaleb Nenni b. Shabbetai. The Crimea is represented by the prolific *paytan* Joseph b. Jacob Kala'i, known as Karafan, from Chufut-Kale, the well-known Karaite center there (with Solchat and Kaffa). His Crimean origin may explain why some of his poems were included in the Karaite prayer service, although we have seen that Aaron b. Joseph was not averse to including Rabbanite compositions in his arrangement of the prayerbook. On the other hand, it has been suggested that Joseph was a Karaite.[84]

Over a dozen poets are known from the fourteenth century. Several of them are scholars who made their mark in other areas as well, namely,

82. Weinberger, *Anthology*, p. 12.

83. Cf. Hebrew studies by Yonah David, *Shirei Zebadiah* (Jerusalem, 1972), *Shirei Amitai* (Jerusalem, 1975), and *Shirei Elya bar Schemaya* (New York and Jerusalem, 1977); and the material in *The Chronicle of Ahima'aṣ*.

84. Cf. examples in Weinberger, *Anthology*. One of Joseph's poems was edited by Weinberger in *HUCA*, XXXIX (Cincinnati, 1968), 11 (Hebrew section). For Karafan, Krauss (*Studien*, p. 83) suggested "from Corfu"; Weinberger suggests χορυφαιος. Cf. Zunz, *Literaturgeschichte der Synagogalen Poesie* (Berlin, 1865), p. 339n, and below, part II document 14.

Shlomo b. Eliahu Sharbit ha-Zahav, Shemarya ha-Ikriti, and the Karaite savant Aaron b. Elijah.[85] Other *paytanim* include Rabbana Mordecai b. Shabbetai he-'Arokh, Elnatan ha-Kohen, Leon b. Michael ha-Parnas (5 poems), Moses Ḥazzan b. Abraham (33 poems), Shabbetai b. Joseph (3 poems), Samuel Kyr b. Shabbetai ha-Rophe (5 poems), Shabbetai b. Mordecai (2 poems), Shabbetai Ḥabib b. Abishai (12 poems). Kastoria was the center of a paytanic tradition that dates back to Tobias b. Eliezer. Later poets there include David b. Eliezer, known as Rabbana David (12 poems); David b. Jacob (?); Eliezer b. Abraham; and Menaḥem b. Eliezer (5 poems). A generation later, Elia b. Abraham followed; three of his poems survive in the *Maḥzor Romania*.[86]

The fifteenth century produced even more: Shemarya ha-Kohen (1 poem), Rabbana Samuel b. Natan ha-Parnas (3 poems), Moses ha-Kohen b. Mamal ha-Vardi (2 poems), Menaḥem Tamar b. Moses (25–26 poems), Mordecai Komatiano, and Moses Kapsali; another *paytan* from Constantinople was Moses Kapuzato.[87] Other *paytanim* were to be found throughout the area: Moses Kilki of Chios (1 poem), Shabbetai b. Kaleb of Arta, Elijah ha-Kohen Çelebi of Anatolia. Crete, too, is well represented: Elkanah b. Shemarya (1 poem) and his father Shemarya b. Elkanah (4 poems), Jacob b. Eliezer (2 poems), Shalom b. Joseph 'Anabi (12 poems), and later Moses b. Elijah del Medigo (1 poem).[88]

A number of other poets are known, and examples of their work have been published.[89] It should also be noted that the tradition of composition continued well into the Ottoman and even modern Greek periods, although many of the later *piyyutim* appear only on epitaphs.[90] The paucity of material from the earlier periods restricts present-day study to those

85. See chapter sections above, "Rabbinic Scholarship," "Karaite Scholarship," and "Intellectual Trends."

86. Sh. Bernstein, *Piyyutim ve-Paytanim Ḥaddashim mi-ha-Tekuphah ha-Byzantinith* (Jerusalem, 1941), p. 1 (the first 80 pages of this collection were reprinted from *Ḥoreb*, 5 [1939], 43–122). Cf. Zunz, *Literaturgeschichte*, passim; also see studies in *HUCA* by Weinberger, with further examples in his *Anthology*. For Kastoria, the older survey by Molho, *Histoire des Israélites de Castoria* (p. 15), is still useful although based on Zunz (pp. 383–84 and 386). Also cf. H. Schirmann, "A Collection of Hebrew Poetry from Turkey in the National Library," (Hebrew) *KS*, XII (1935–36), 394; also cf. Weinberger, *Bulgaria's Synagogue Poets: The Kastoreans* (Cincinnati, 1983).

87. See above, "Intellectual Trends," and part II document 85.

88. Cf. examples in Weinberger, *Anthology*.

89. Cf. studies by Zunz, Bernstein, and Weinberger.

90. Cf. examples in my editions of the epitaphs of Patras and Mistra.

formalized and religious pieces that were preserved in the Romaniote synagogue services. Historically, however, these should be seen as but one aspect of a pervasive cultural phenomenon among Jews that paralleled the predilection of their Christian compatriots for poetry and song.

The special rite of Romaniote Jews followed the earlier Palestinian tradition, especially its *piyyut* style, and remained fluid throughout the Byzantine period. A noteworthy feature in the service is the large number of *piyyutim,* some of whose composers are noted above. The *Maḥzor Romania,* which is one crystallization of this rite, is also the parent of the *maḥzorim* of Corfu, Kaffa, and Karasu-bazar, and thus reflects the parameters of Romaniote influence.

The necessity to fix the Romaniote service in the sixteenth century is but another aspect of the pressures of increasing Sephardi influence in the Balkans. Some features of Romaniote *piyyutim* were assonance, end rhymes, acrostics (to identify the author), and alphabet acrostics. A number of other complex forms, utilizing rhyme, meter, and linguistic structure, testify to the sophistication of the composers. Occasionally the *shibusi* style was used, that is, the stringing together of biblical verses around a central theme (exc. D). The use of Greek words for rhyme was not uncommon, and in fact was an ancient affectation. Also, a prayer for the new moon, written entirely in Greek, has been preserved.[91] Thus poetry remained one of the chief literary pursuits among Romaniote Jewry long after the end of the Byzantine Empire. Nor was the output only liturgical; many secular poems were written for various social events, such as births, weddings, etc. Others, in a more pedantic manner, played with philosophical and, occasionally, polemical subjects. And of course laudatory poems were written in honor of famous scholars.[92]

Nor was the contemporary world ignored. In the summer of 1453 a dirge was composed to commemorate the fall of Constantinople. Echoing the haunting plaint of Lamentations, this poem is a unique reflection of the sense of loss that Romaniote Jewry experienced at the demise of the ancient empire. The poem, the sole contemporary notice of the fall of the city that is extant or known in Byzantine Jewish literature, was composed immedi-

91. Cf. *EJ,* XI, 398 ("Romaniote Rite"); Goldschmidt, in *Sefunoth,* 8 (1964), 205ff, and *Sefunoth,* 13 (1971–78 = *Sepher Yavan* 3), 103ff; and Weinberger, *Anthology,* both his Hebrew and English introductions. See below, note 120.

92. See above, note 72.

ately after the conquest by a scholar in Crete, Michael b. Shabbetai Kohen Balbo, all of whose works remain in manuscript.[93]

Mystical Tradition

Mysticism was a basic feature of Byzantine Jewish intellectual and social life. A reading of the eleventh-century *Chronicle of Aḥima'az,* as well as a survey of the midrashic literature available to Romaniote scholars, both original compositions and copies of older classics, are sufficient to indicate the depth and pervasiveness of mystical studies and beliefs.[94] It is true that for the Palaeologan period there were no mass movements such as that which overtook Thessalonican Jewry on the eve of the First Crusade.[95] Therefore we should emphasize the hint of the messianic excitement that is suggested in mid-thirteenth-century Andravida and elsewhere in the empire.[96] It is also true that messianic movements, in general, abated during the thirteenth, fourteenth, and fifteenth centuries.[97] Still, we should emphasize that in place of these activist movements was an increasing interest in and study of mystical literature. All of our sources to date, moreover, indicate that this interest was pursued most actively in Spain; its origins, however, are still obscure. There the old Kabbalah was rapidly expanding in influence, while at the same time mystical traditions were being edited late in the third quarter of the thirteenth century by Moses de Leon in his new, classic kabbalistic commentary on the Bible, the *Zohar.*[98] Aside from the more traditional forms of study, other approaches to mysticism were

93. Vat. MS 105 (correct notice in *JE,* 8:540, accordingly); for a partial list of his works, cf. Steinschneider, "Candia," p. 305.

94. Cf. Ankori, *Karaites,* pp. 261ff and passim; also Tobias ben Eliezer, *Midrash Lekaḥ Tob,* ed. S. Buber (Vilna, 1880), introduction.

95. Cf., most recently, A. Sharf, *Byzantine Jewry from Justinian to the Fourth Crusade* (New York, 1971), p. 125, and literature cited.

96. See above, chap. 2, "Peloponnesos."

97. Cf. Abba Hillel Silver, *A History of Messianic Speculation in Israel from the First through the Seventeenth Centuries* (New York, 1927), chaps. 4 and 5.

98. Cf. G. Scholem, *Major Trends in Jewish Mysticism* (New York, 1954), Fifth Lecture, and Y. Baer, *The Jews in Christian Spain* (Philadelphia, 1966), II, passim. Abraham Zakut, a refugee from the Spanish exile of 1492, eventually settled on one of the Greek islands (he mentions Chios and Naxos). In his *Sefer Yuḥasin,* he records a passage from the diary of R. Isaac, a refugee from the conquest of Acre in 1292, who wandered to Spain, where he sought out the tradition behind the authorship of the Zohar. He was the first to suggest that Moses de Leon, who died shortly after R. Isaac's arrival, was indeed the author. Cf. passages reproduced by Abraham Kahana in *Sifruth ha-Historia ha-Yisraelith* (Warsaw, 1923), II, 87–90. The same tradition suggests that the material, or even a manuscript, was sent to Spain by

being experimented with. One such approach was that of his contemporary, Abraham Abulafia, whose ecstatic kabbalism offered an excitingly individualistic yet socially dangerous avenue for mystical experimentation. Abulafia's Kabbalah was not the way chosen by later generations, which preferred to follow the older pattern with the *Zohar* as its guide, but it continued to hold attraction for the more devout adepts of the esoteric lore.

The masterful description of Abulafia's "search for ecstasy and for prophetic inspiration" by Gershom Scholem has shown his methods to be based as much on the older Kabbalah as upon the techniques of east Mediterranean mystics with whom he came into contact during his peregrinations.[99] Abulafia, in addition, emphasized that the practitioner of his method must at all times be in control of his mind until he passes to the higher levels of ecstacy.[100] This conscious ascension to a mystical state differs from contemporary methods. Still, the ecstatic objective is familiar to Oriental mystics of the period; the yogi sought it through breathing, the Sufi through the Koran and dance, while the Hesychast contemplated his omphalos and recited Scripture until he merged with the sacred light of Mount Tabor.[101] From the fourteenth century on, under the inspired leadership of Gregory Palamas, Hesychasm was greatly to influence the development of Greek Orthodoxy.[102] Such a general atmosphere was conducive to the development of mysticism among Byzantine Jewry.

Nachmanides after his arrival in Israel. The coincidence is worth recording that Abulafia also traveled east (for mystical reasons) some decades before. On this source in general, cf. I. Tishby, *Introduction to "Mishnat Ha-Zohar"* (3d ed.; Tel Aviv, 1971), pp. 28ff.

99. Scholem, *Major Trends,* Fourth Lecture; also cf. A. Berger, "The Messianic Self-Consciousness of Abraham Abulafia, a Tentative Evaluation," *Essays in Jewish Life and Thought Presented in Honor of Salo W. Baron* (New York, 1959), pp. 55–61. For a comprehensive description of his works and method, cf. dissertation of Moshe Idel cited above (note 25).

100. Abulafia's technique of combining letters of the Hebrew alphabet (viz., his *ḥokhmat ha-ṣeruf*) appears to be his own contribution, which he derived from the mystical treatise *Sefer Yeṣirah.* Scholem, in his lecture on Abulafia, has shown how his general technique accords with the harmony of music. See following note.

101. The difference between Abulafia's technique and these others lies in his attempt to stimulate the intellect through concentration on shifting foci, whereas the others attempted to hypnotize the intellect by concentrating on a fixed object or idea. Cf. Moshe Idel, "Abraham Abulafia's Works and Doctrines," cited above (note 25).

102. On Hesychasm in general, see Jean Meyendorff, *Introduction à l'étude de Grégoire Palamas* (Paris, 1959) (English edition: *A Study of Gregory Palamas* [London, 1964]); idem, *Byzantine Hesychasm: Historical, Theological, and Social Problems* (London: Variorum Reprints, 1974); see Lowell M. Clucas, "Eschatological Theory in Byzantine Hesychasm: A Parallel to Joachim da Fiore?" *BZ,* LXX (1970), 324–46 and bibliography cited. The linking of

In the ecstatic state sought by Abulafia, the successful adept could not only prophesy, but could even become the Messiah. Abulafia, it is suggested, had messianic pretensions, as well as at least one Romaniote Jew, Shemarya ha-Ikriti. It is not known whether Abulafia revealed himself (if at all) during his sojourns in Greece; Abulafia denies the accusation. The charge, in any event, belongs to his post-Greek period, since he had completed only the first of his books on prophecy before he left there (**26**). There is little doubt, however, that students of his techniques remained in Patras, as well as colleagues who were influenced by his charisma.[103]

The fourteenth century witnessed a continued interest in mysticism among Byzantine Jewry. Shemarya ha-Ikriti, for example, was attacked at the end of his career for his alleged messianic pretensions. He supposedly manifested himself through his use of the Tetragrammaton and, later, in intimating the emergence of the Messiah (himself?) in the year 1352.[104] In 1358 Moses b. Samuel de Roquemaure composed a poem consisting of sixty-nine lines of puns and satirical allusions, which represents our unique source for his alleged messianic pretensions (**84**). The nature of the source, however, makes the tradition suspect, the efforts of modern scholars to prove it notwithstanding. Judah ibn Moskoni, Shemarya's well-known pupil, was, like his teacher, highly critical of the world of Balkan scholarship. In particular, he castigated his contemporaries for their lack of knowledge in two fundamental areas of mystic lore, the *ma'ase bereshith* (story of creation) and the *ma'ase merkabah* (vision of God's throne-chariot in Ezekiel 1) (**86**).

As noted above (note 23), Elnatan b. Moses Kalkis produced a systematic mystical treatise titled *Eben Saphir.* Its contents, as described by Solomon Munk over seventy years ago, give us an idea of the concerns of those

Hesychasm to the ideas of Joachim da Fiore is of interest in light of the latter's possible influence on messianic manifestations within Italian and, possibly, Byzantine Jewish society; see above, chap. 2, "Peloponnesos," and A. Toaf, "Hints to a Messianic Movement in Rome in 1261," (Hebrew) *Bar-Ilan Annual,* 14–15 (1977), 114–21.

103. Cf. his *Sefer ha-Oth,* ed. A. Jellinek, *Jubelschrift . . . Dr. Heinrich Graetz* (Breslau, 1887), pp. 77f; and on the importance of the Greek language, ibid., p. 71. By coincidence, we may note that the family of Shabbetai Zvi originated in Patras.

104. Eshkoli suggests that he was influenced by Abraham Abulafia (*Ha-Tenuoth ha-Meshiḥiyoth be-Yisrael,* p. 209). See above, this chapter, "Rabbinic Scholarship." We should note here that a Sephardi scribe, visiting Thebes in 1415, used the Tetragrammaton in his colophon; cf. MS Hunt 309 in Bodleian Library at Oxford, fol. 16b, and below, part II document 117.

scholars whom Judah ibn Moskoni disparages. The treatise, consisting of two volumes (ca. 350 folio pages, still in manuscript), apparently arranged along Aristotelian lines, begins with a discussion of the author's sources (philosophical, talmudic, midrashic, kabbalistic, etc.), its purpose, the different types of syllogism, the incorporality of God, the study of God's law, etc. The second section deals with cosmogony and the mysteries of creation; the third with the novelty of creation and divine providence; the fourth with Genesis 1:1, the revelation on Mount Sinai, the mystery of the Tetragrammaton, the superiority of Moses, the sanctification of the forty-nine days between Pesach and Pentacost, and the relationship between the divine chariot (Ezekiel 1) and metaphysics.

The fifth section treats the difference between substance and intellect, the mystery of science, and the mystery of the Sabbath; the sixth with resurrection of the dead and the immortality of the soul. The seventh includes an excursus refuting those who disagree with Maimonides' treatment of these doctrines; the eighth with the creation and destruction of the world, and divine providence; the ninth with the second commandment, prayers addressed directly to the deity, angels, and the intelligence of celestial spheres. The tenth deals with Hebrew law; the eleventh with prayer and acts of devotion; the twelfth with prophecy; the thirteenth with the mystery of the name EHYeH, astrology, and the mission of Moses; the fourteenth on the stars and their revolutions—how, by God's decree, they bring evil, and the problem of *galut* (exile); the fifteenth with God's mercy, which negates astrological disaster; the sixteenth with the sacrificial ram of the Isaac story, the qualities of Abraham, and mysteries of the earthly paradise. The seventeenth section offers more on Genesis 1:1, with a digression on divorce; the eighteenth deals with mysteries of *ṣiṣith* (fringes on garments) and phylacteries; the nineteenth with Exodus and a general consideration of miracles; the twentieth with the mystery of Cain, Abel, and Seth, followed by a short analysis of Aristotle's system. The twenty-first section is an allegorical interpretation of the three *mishmaroth* (night watches), prophets of Baal and Elijah, and a general consideration of prophetic visions; and the twenty-second discusses the status of the Jews at Mount Sinai and the visions of Moses, as well as those who followed him.[105]

105. The value of this book will be shown by M. Idel, who is preparing a study of the author and his sources, many of which he apparently copied verbatim and whose originals were subsequently lost.

Several manuscripts, containing mystical works, have survived whose colophons indicate that they were all copied by the same peripatetic scribe in the first decade and a half of the fifteenth century. The scribe went from Spain to Greece (for mystical reasons) and there found and copied (for his own use) the following treatises: *Commentary to Canticles* by Joseph Gikatilia (in 1401), which he found in the possession of Isaac al-Ashbili in Negroponte; *Keter Shem Tob* by Shem Tob ibn Gaon (in 1403 in Saloniki); *Sefer 'Iggul ha-Sephiroth* (in the winter of 1404 in Modon); *Sefer ha-Temunah, Sefer Shem ha-Mephorash,* and *Sefer ha-Yiḥud,* each with its (local?) mystical commentaries (in 1415 in Thebes); and a kabbalistic commentary on the *Sefer ha-Yiḥud* (in 1415 in Philipopolis), which he copied while convalescing from an attack of the gout.[106] The peripatetic career of this elderly Sephardi scribe in Greece throws considerable light on the distribution and diffusion of kabbalistic works there and is a further indication of the great interest in mysticism evinced by the local Jewries, which by this period included both native Romaniotim and immigrant Italian- and Spanish-speaking Jews.

The question of an independent Romaniote mystical tradition, probably deriving directly from Palestinian antecedents, is no longer in doubt.[107] What is needed now is an intensive search among the many unpublished Hebrew manuscripts for fragments and treatises, and identification of those which are anonymous, based on the techniques of codicology and palaeography, as well as the disciplined approach to mystical texts established by Gershom Scholem and his colleagues. Only after this work is completed will we be able to assess the contribution of Romaniote Jewry to the development of mystical traditions and literature in the late medieval period.[108]

106. See below, documents 108 and 117; the Modon colophon can be found in Munich MS Hebr. 119 and studied in HPP Y797. His earlier biography is contained in the colophon to MS heb 790 Paris, Bibliothèque nationale, published by Sirat and Beit-Arié, I, 75 (see part II [108] for particulars). In 1467 the *Sefer ha-Kabod,* attributed to Isaiah b. Joseph, was copied in Kastoria by Eliezer b. Abraham; cf. colophon in A. Krafft and S. Deutsch, *Die handschriftlichen hebräischen Werke der KK. Hofbibliothek zu Wien* (Vienna, 1897), p. 109.

107. Cf. afterword in Benjamin Klar, ed., *Megillat Ahimaaz* (2d ed.; Jerusalem, 1974), and Weinberger, *Anthology,* pp. 8–11.

108. In particular, the manipulation of the names of God, which is such an outstanding phenomenon of the sixteenth and seventeenth centuries and subsequent Kabbalah. On the mystical or messianic interpretation of events among Byzantine Jewry, cf. J. Mann, "Are the Ashkenazi Jews Khazars?" (Hebrew) *Tarbiz,* IV (1933), 391–94.

At the completion of such a survey, the origins and influences of Sephardi contributions to Kabbalah should be clarified further, especially with reference to the mystical traditions and literature in the eastern Mediterranean in the fifteenth and sixteenth centuries. It is as likely that the autochthonous Romaniote traditions either fed into the awakening stream of mystical consciousness, which appears rather suddenly at the foot of the Pyrenees in the late twelfth century, or was influenced by these Western developments during the elaboration of its own traditions from the thirteenth through the fifteenth century.[109]

While we are unaware of any messianic movements among Byzantine Jewry during the Palaeologan period, contemporary trends may well have

109. For the future light that their resolution may throw upon this subject, we should note two problems surrounding the very influential mystical books *Sefer ha-Kaneh* and *Sefer ha-Peliah,* both of which are recognized as having been written by the same anonymous author. The two key problems are the dates when the books were written and the locale. After considerable debate, a consensus is slowly emerging on a date in the first half of the fifteenth century. Cf. discussion by B. Netanyahu, "Towards a Clarification of the Period when the *Sefer ha-Kaneh* and *Sefer ha-Peliah* Were Written," (Hebrew) *S. W. Baron Jubilee Volume* (Hebrew section) (Jerusalem, 1974), III, 247–67.

The problem of locale, however, is divided among supporters of a Spanish provenance or an Italo/Byzantine origin. Michal Oron, who has examined these works in her Hebrew dissertation published by the Hebrew University of Jerusalem (*"Ha-Pliah ve-ha-Kaneh": Their Kabbalistic Bases . . . ,* Diss. Series, 1980), has opted for the Italo/Byzantine sphere. See her entry, "(ha-) Kanah," (Hebrew) in *EIV,* 29:867f. Her thesis finds support in the study of I. Ta-Shema, "Where Were the Books *Ha-Kaneh* and *Ha-Pliah* Composed?" (Hebrew) *Studies in the History of Jewish Society . . . Presented to Professor Jacob Katz* (pp. 56–63), showing that the form of the prayers in these treatises is of Romaniote provenance. His study does not take cognizance of the earlier published findings of M. Oron.

Several arguments upon which Netanyahu's thesis for a Spanish provenance is based are not necessarily exclusively Spanish. We may note that the Jews suffered throughout the Mediterranean (and elsewhere) in the late fourteenth and early fifteenth centuries and that, therefore, references to persecutions, *ipso facto,* do not indicate Spanish origins. Moreover, the phrase "strangers will devour them" also appears in several colophons from early fifteenth-century Greece (cf. document 109). Also, we find a Spanish scribe in Greece cursing converts (117). These latter points were cited from *Sefer ha-Kaneh* by Netanyahu (pp. 255f) to support a thesis that the book reflects the period of civil war in Spain in the second decade of the fifteenth century. The same period, we may note, witnessed civil war and chaos in the young Ottoman sultanate; see below, this chapter and chapter 5 note 62.

For earlier discussions, see Graetz, *Divrei Yemei Israel,* 6, appendix 8, 438–42. Of the many copies of these books in Romania, one—dated 1463, Constantinople—was copied by the scribe Joseph Bonfaẓo of Candia (Vat. MS 187): (ספר) הפליאה, תפילה לפ׳ שם יוסף שאלתיאל ברבי משה כהן חזק הועתק בקושטנטינה אשר ברומניה בידי יוסף בונפאצוי קנדיאה משנת רכ״ב.

stimulated such hopes. In Ottoman Adrianople, a contemporary of Judah ibn Moskoni was participating in the creation of a *Weltanschauung* which was to have interesting ramifications for the fifteenth century. Not much is known of Elisha (Elissaeus) the "pagan" beyond his skill in the Aristotelian scholarship developed by Arab and Persian commentators (**135**). His more famous graduate student, George Gemistos Plethon, was introduced to all the intellectual ferment at the court of Murat I by Elisha, who apparently enjoyed some reputation and influence there (**137**). Plethon, who received his advanced training in philosophy in Adrianople, put it to use in later years, after his retirement from the theological squabbles of the church in Constantinople. At the court of the Despots of Morea, he outlined his plan to revolutionize society by rewriting, in updated fashion, Plato's *Laws*. The Despots to whom it was written, however, had neither the power nor the fortitude to so reconstruct society. Still, for his influence in Greece and (even greater) in Italy, Plethon remains one of the most respected thinkers, and surely the most original, in Late Byzantine history.[110]

Not all of the intellectual currents at the court of Adrianople remained theoretical. The story of Bedr ed-Din, the philosopher, judge, and mystic, shows how sanguine was the implementation of any revolutionary theory.[111] During the chaos that rocked the young Ottoman state after the battle of Ankara (1402), Bedr ed-Din (as theorist) and his lieutenant Torlak Kemal (as activist) attempted to restructure the emerging Ottoman society along more "Communistic" lines. For them, all things were to be held in common by all members of this new society, each of whom, no matter whether Muslim, Christian, or Jew, was to be considered the equal of the others. This, perhaps, was their most revolutionary feature and the one designed to appeal to all the peoples subject to the Ottomans.

The revolt broke out in the region of Smyrna. Enjoying a successful beginning, both in military victories and in acceptance of the new sect, the

110. Cf. bibliography to documents 135 and 137 in part II. There are a number of scholars whom we can identify in the second half of the fourteenth century who were named Elisha; a few were even known as philosophers. Our Elissaeus, then, may well have been a Romaniote scholar, and perhaps even from Crete. Cf. Vat. MS 105, which contains a copy of Ibn Ezra's *Sefer ha-Shem* with the commentary of Shlomo Sharbit ha-Zahav and annotations by Elisha Kilki (Cassuto, *Vatican*, p. 156); and for philosophers by that name, cf. Steinschneider, *Leiden*, pp. 239f.

111. The basic study to date is Fr. Babinger, "Schejch Bedr ed-Din, der Sohn des Richters von Simāw. Ein Beitrag zur Geschichte des Sektenwesens im altosmanischen Reich," *Der Islam* (1921), II, 1–160.

movement spread to the neighboring island of Chios and expanded to other mainland areas in the neighborhood of Smyrna. (Torlak Kemal was particularly active near Magnesia.) Finally, however, an Ottoman army broke through the defenses and annihilated the sectarians. Torlak Kemal was captured and crucified. Bedr ed-Din was later discovered in Rumelia—that is, the European mainland—and hanged.[112] The movement, rather than dissipate, went underground to merge with that restless spirit which permeated Smyrna and periodically broke out in similar, though more peaceful, manifestations.[113]

A number of scholars have asserted that Torlak Kemal was a Jew.[114] In fact, however, of the five Turkish sources that refer to Torlak Kemal, only one designates him as a Jew.[115] Even so, Franz Babinger, after investigation of these sources, avoided a statement on Torlak's alleged Jewish identity. Still, his study suggests that in all probability Torlak Kemal was not a Jewish convert to the new sect. Since the Jewish scholars (Franco, Rosanes, and Galante) did not examine these sources, and relied on secondary surveys for their material, the combined weight of their scholarly

112. An outline of the movement's fortunes is available in C. Brockelman, *History of the Islamic Peoples,* tr. by J. Carmichael and M. Perlman (New York, 1947), pp. 274f. A summary of Bedr ed-Din's career is available in *EI,* s.v. For his place within contemporary Ottoman society, cf. H. Inalcik, *The Ottoman Empire: The Classical Age, 1300–1600* (New York, 1973), pp. 188ff.

113. The best known of which is the mid-seventeenth-century phenomenon of Shabbetai Zvi and his apostate followers, the Dönmeh. Cf. Ernst Werner, "Chios, Šeih Bedr-Eddīn und Bürklüğe Mustafā," *Byzantinische Forschungen,* V (1977), 405–13, and previous note.

114. Cf. J. von Hammer-Purgstall, *Geschichte des osmanischen Reiches,* I (Pest, 1827), 378; J. Zinkeisen, *Geschichte des osmanischen Reiches in Europa,* I (Gotha, 1840), 479; and the Jewish historians M. Franco, *Essai sur l'histoire des Israélites de l'empire ottoman* (Paris, 1897), p. 30; Rosanes, *Israel be-Togarmah,* I, 9, who gives his Hebrew provenance as Shmuel from Magnesia; and A. Galante, *Turcs et Juifs, étude historique, politique* (Stamboul, 1932, p. 10), who cites Torlak as proof of a Jewish community in Magnesia. For a Jewish community in Manissa (Magnesia), see above (chap. 2), "Anatolia."

115. Babinger, in his study of Bedr ed-Din (see above, note 111), quotes five Turkish sources which mention Torlak. Four of these—"Anonymous Grese" (p. 31); 'Aschipascha zāde (p. 38) and Muhjī ed-Dīn Dschemāle (p. 33), both in Hans Löwenklau's Latin translation; and Mewlānā Neschri (p. 41)—mention Torlak Hu Kemal, Torlaces Heggiemal, Torlaces Hudin-Gemalim, and Torlak Hū Kemāl, respectively, with no indication that he was Jewish.

Only the report of Luṭfī Pascha (p. 51) cites "der Jude Torlak Kemāl" (Babinger's translation). At the end of his discussion, Babinger remained uncommitted on the question of Torlak's Jewish origin and the precise meaning of his name. Torlaq is an old Turkish word meaning "wild," but does Hū come from "Yahūdi"?

opinion has little bearing on the material presented by Babinger. On the other hand, there is little doubt that many Jews and disaffected Christians were caught up in the messianic sweep of Bedr ed-Din's new sect, which promised religious equality and a communalistic sharing of the economy.[116]

Such ideas as the return to communalist paganism, espoused by Plethon and the revolutionary ecumenism of Bedr ed-Din, were symptomatic of the weakness of organized religion in the fourteenth and early fifteenth centuries. Above, we saw the growth of Judaizing heresies which caused such consternation to the church (chapter 2). The sultans, too, shared in this syncretism. Bayezid named his sons after monotheistic leaders: Musa, Isa, and Mehmet. Philosophers, such as George Amiroutzes of Trebizond, wrote treatises suggesting how the three religions could be assimilated.[117] While mystical speculation did not lead directly to peaceful or revolutionary ecumenical movements, it provided a common background in which the social and spiritual goals of monotheism could be sought, unhampered by the bureaucracy of organized religion.

Greek Language

Jewish thinkers were always cognizant of, and participated in, the intellectual pursuits of their contemporaries. Especially in Byzantium, where ancient Greek scholarship was a living tradition, they could not fail to be affected by it. Elisha, though in Adrianople, no doubt was in mutual contact with Greek scholars. An abridgment of Aristotle's *Logic* by Joseph ha-Yevani was made available to those Jews (Sephardi immigrants) who were less proficient in Greek (**91**). In the fifteenth century, paralleling the predilection of contemporary scholarship for astronomical studies, Byzantine and Ottoman Jewry produced a respectable bibliography on the same subject.[118] Jewish physicians, always in repute among secular leaders,

116. On the latter aspect, cf. Sp. Vryonis, *The Decline of Medieval Hellenism in Asia Minor* (Berkeley, 1971), pp. 358f. Also, for some mystical and communal parallels, cf. W. C. Hickman, "Who Was Ümmi Kemal?" *Boğaziçi Üniversitesi Dergisi,* 4–5 (1976–77), 57–82, esp. 71f. The best available survey of Bedr ed-Din is H. J. Kissling in *EI²,* I, 869.

117. Compare remarks from Abraham Abulafia's *Maphteaḥ ha-Ḥokhmah,* cited in Berger's "Messianic Self-Consciousness of Abraham Abulafia" (note 17).

118. Cf. bibliography and commentary in Rosanes, *Israel be-Togarmah,* pp. 26–34, and above, "Intellectual Trends."

would have buttressed their knowledge of Hebrew and Arabic by a familiarity with the Greek originals. Biblical commentaries, especially among the Karaites, showed a knowledge of Greek philosophical terminology. Rabbinic authors (e.g., Shemarya ha-Ikriti) spiced their comments with Greek phrases. Romaniote *paytanim,* too, enjoyed mixing Greek words and phrases into their poems, a habit which contributed to the disdain that the Spaniard Judah al-Ḥarizi showed toward their compositions.[119] Despite his arrogant rejection of this style, it was long known among Greek-speaking Jewry and, in fact, was common in the nonpoetic literature of Palestinian Jewry, especially its Midrash and Talmud. Nor were elegies that were written entirely in Greek unknown.[120]

The familiarity of Romaniote Jewry with the Greek language is well documented. The more that Jews assimilated to Greek society, the more they had need of translations and other teaching aids to assist them to follow the Hebrew texts in the synagogues and at home. Even before the sixth century (indeed from Hellenistic times, as the need for the Septuagint shows), Byzantine Jewry had been Greek speaking. It was the need for an authorized Jewish translation into Greek of the synagogue service that prompted some Jews to turn to Justinian, thus giving him the pretext to interfere in their otherwise autonomous sphere of communal religion.[121]

During the eleventh and twelfth centuries, the use of Greek is well known, and included not only the everyday colloquial Greek but even the more sophisticated terminology of the classical texts.[122] The Byzantine Karaite community actively sought to identify itself linguistically with the

119. For biblical commentaries, cf. Ankori, *Karaites,* pp. 193–95 and passim; for Shemarya ha-Ikriti, cf. Neubauer, "Documents inédits," p. 87, note 7; and for *paytanim,* cf. Weinberger, "New Songs," (Hebrew) pp. 27 and 55, with further examples in his *Anthology,* p. 11 and passim.

120. Cf. *Catalogue of . . . Elkan Nathan Adler,* #4027^{v}, identified as part of the *Maḥzor Romania.* The elegy is on folio 45a and a photo facsimile is at the end of the volume. The Hebrew text is supplied with vowels and is edited by Weinberger (*Anthology,* pp. 12f) without vowels and with Hebrew translation (pp. 297, note 26).

121. Cf. English translation of Justinian's Novella 146 in J. Parkes, *The Conflict of the Church and the Synagogue* (London, 1934), pp. 392f. One side effect of Justinian's meddling, on the other hand, was the proliferation of the Hebrew *piyyut* as a liturgical and intellectual vehicle of communication among Byzantine Jewry; cf. P. Kahle, *The Cairo Geniza* (2d ed.; Oxford, 1959), pp. 34–48.

122. Cf. Starr, *JBE,* index s.v. "Greek Language." See chap. 3 above, "Economic Pursuits."

"language of the Romans."[123] Benjamin of Tudela is a witness to the use of Greek among Rabbanite Jews, and there is no reason to assume that this trend declined after 1204. The use of Greek names, such as Pappas, Galimidi, Kalomiti, Artanusi, Eudokia, Leon b. Moskoni, and Khomatiano, is not uncommon, nor is the occurrence of Greek words that regularly appear in the secular and liturgical texts of the later period.[124]

Entire books, in addition to exegetical translations, were rendered into contemporary Greek or from classical Greek into Hebrew. A *demotike* or colloquial Greek translation of the Book of Jonah was read in the synagogue on Yom Kippur by the Romaniote Jews of Corfu and Candia.[125] Translations of Ruth, Lamentations, and *Pirke Aboth* were also in use.

In addition, there is a sixteenth-century translation of the Bible which was published in Hebrew characters in Constantinople (1547).[126] It contains the standard Hebrew text, along with the *Targum Onkelos* (an Aramaic paraphrase), the commentary of Rashi, and a Ladino and a Greek translation. The format of the pages provides some valuable hints, as well as interesting deviations from the normative format. The *Targum Onkelos* is at the top and the commentary of Rashi, in *square* Hebrew characters, is at the

123. Ankori, *Karaites,* pp. 194–96; cf. Starr, "A Fragment of a Greek Mishnaic Glossary," *PAAJR,* VI (1935), 355.

124. Cf. list of names in Rosanes, *Israel be-Togarmah,* pp. 209–12; Weinberger, *Anthology,* passim and above (notes 11 and 68).

125. Lattes, in his introduction to his extracts from Elijah Kapsali's chronicle (in *Deve Eliahu,* p. 22), writes the following: "An ancient custom in Candia was to read on Yom Kippur in the *haphtorah* of Jonah the first three verses in Hebrew and afterward to translate the whole book into Greek, and afterwards to skip over to the reading in Micah of three verses and translating them in like manner. R. Eliahu (Kapsali) considered repealing this custom because it was not based on the law. R. Meir heard of his intention and wrote to him to change his mind: 'This is indeed a strange custom but this is not the way to rely upon our co-religionists. To void an ancient custom you must, with all resources, seek to find reference to maintain it. Thus did all our predecessors when they found a perplexing custom. Then he forced himself to bring him proof to maintain and justify the custom.'"

Cf. responsa of R. Meir b. Israel Katzenellenbogen (Cracow, 1882), p. 112, no. 78; Starr, *JBE,* p. 212. The text was transcribed into Greek by D. C. Hesseling, "Le livre de Jonas," *BZ,* X (1901), 208–17. Neubauer (*Bodleian,* I, #1144) lists a *haphtorah* in Greek; ms. owned by Zeraḥiah Kohen and sold by Ḥayyim 24 August 1574 (Seleucid era = 1263).

126. Cf. D. Goldschmidt, "Biblical translations into Greek by 16th-Century Jews," (Hebrew) *KS,* 33 (1957), 131f. There is a modern transcription by D. C. Hesseling, *Les cinq livres de la loi "Le Pentateuque". Traduction en néo-grec publiée en caractères hébräiques à Constantinople en 1547* . . . (Leiden and Leipzig, 1897). The first four chapters of Genesis had earlier been transcribed into Greek by L. Belleli, "Un version grecque du Pentateuque du seizième siècle," *REG,* 3 (1890), 290–308.

bottom of the page.[127] The area between them is divided into three columns: the biblical text, with vowels, is in the center; the Ladino translation, with vowels, occupies the inside column; and the Greek text fills the outside column.[128] The location of the Ladino translation on the inside column, the traditional column of honor, signals the preeminence of the Sephardi tradition over the Romaniote.

While there were two earlier translations of the Pentateuch, that of the Septuagint and that of Aquila, it was evident that neither could suffice for the purposes of the Ottoman Romaniote community. The Septuagint had long been subject to Christological interpretations and occasional interpolations, and for this reason was no longer recognized by Jews, while the translation of Aquila was some 1,400 years out of date. A new translation into living Greek or Judeo-Greek was needed for the contemporary Romaniotes. Such a translation, then, nearly a century after the Ottoman conquest of Constantinople and a half a century after the arrival of the Sephardi communities, is but one indication of the continuity of spoken Greek among the Jews and the survival of the Romaniote community.[129]

In addition to the Torah and some of the minor writings of the Bible, fragments of a Greek commentary on Psalms, Lamentations, and Ecclesiastes have been discovered.[130] Sixteen leaves, as yet unpublished, con-

127. The commentary of Rashi is usually printed on the inside column of the page and in a rabbinic cursive known as "Rashi script."

128. This is one of the few Ladino translations of the Bible to have a vocalized text. The practice was dropped in later generations.

129. Unfortunately, we do not have as yet a systematic exposition of Judeo-Greek from either the Byzantine or later periods. The fourteenth-century polyglot Bible produced by Simon Atumano, archbishop of Thebes, would not have sufficed for the Romaniote community, despite the possibility that Jews participated in the project. The translation of the New Testament into Hebrew very likely suggested conversionist intentions, much the same as did the distribution of the New Testament in Istanbul in 1922 by British missionary societies. Cf. Mons. Giovanni Mercati, *Se la versione dall'ebraico del codice Veneto Greco VII sia di Simone Atumano, Arcivescovo di Tebe* (Studi e Testi, no. 30) (Rome, 1916). Oscar Gebhardt published the Greek text in Leipzig in 1875; cf. review by P. F. Frankl, "Graecus Venetus," *MGWJ,* XXIV (1875), 372–76, 419–27, 513–16. (The latter's historical comments have been superseded.) The problem has been cited several times by K. M. Setton, most recently in his *Catalan Domination of Athens, 1311–1388* (London: Variorum Reprints, 1975), p. 222. On the Jewish community in Thebes during this period, see my "Jews in Fourteenth-Century Thebes" and "Jewish Epitaphs in Thebes," and above (chap. 2 section, "Central Greece").

130. Goldschmidt, "Biblical Translations into Greek," (Hebrew) pp. 133f. See also N. R. M. de Lange, "Some New Fragments of Aquila on Malachi and Job?" *Vetus Testamentum,* XXX (1980), 291–94.

tain a listing of words from Psalms 21–27, 49–150, with a simple Hebrew equivalent or a direct Greek translation. This manuscript appears to be part of a study or teaching aid. Of the many translations that have survived, the majority are connected with biblical studies, a not unexpected phenomenon, given the traditional Romaniote interest in this area of study.[131]

The Byzantine-Jewish intellectual experience during the Palaeologan period was catholic in outlook and integrated with its environment. Secular studies were pursued as much as traditional religious studies. Perhaps therein was the Romaniote Achilles heel. With the decline and disappearance of the last Byzantine renaissance, Greek-speaking Jewry lost the environment which supported its secular studies. At the same time, a new and vigorous intellectual wave—the Sephardi tradition—trained in classical Jewish studies to a greater degree, moved into the Balkans with its superior scholars and pro-Ottoman outlook. Theirs was to be the dominant intellectual tradition during the Ottoman period. Romaniote Jewry, like the Orthodox Christian community, retreated into itself in order to maintain its intellectual identity and a shadowy survival.[132]

Romaniote Legacy

The Ottoman deportation of the Romaniote population of Thrace and Macedonia created the preconditions for the Sephardization of these areas by the end of the century. At the same time, the concentration of these Greek-speaking Jews in Constantinople, both Rabbanites and Karaites, allowed for an intellectual and social rapprochement between the two groups, as well as for an expanded intellectual activity that may well be considered the final renaissance of Romaniote Jewry.

The legacy from the last generation of Byzantine Jewry also laid the foundations for the development of Ottoman Jewry. The first generation after the conquest of Constantinople tells the story of Romaniote Jewry. It

131. See above (this chapter), "Rabbinic Scholarship." The bilingual mishnaic glossary has been discussed above (chap. 3, "Economic Pursuits").

132. This is not to say, of course, that Byzantine Jewry was unfamiliar with Ashkenazi or Sephardi scholarship. Cf. examples of Byzantine Jews who studied in the West in Starr, *JBE,* passim; Urbach, *Baʿale ha-Tosaphot* (Jerusalem, 1968), p. 443; above for the careers of Elijah Mizraḥi and Moses Kapsali; and in general Urbach, s.v. The present study contains a number of such examples.

was their framework, forged out of the necessity to re-create a communal life after the deportations, that was further developed by the Sephardi immigrants after the turn of the sixteenth century. It was they who developed the *Landsmannschaft* pattern of small neighborhood congregations, based on one's original home. They, too, attempted—unsuccessfully in the long run, but of considerable importance for the first two generations after 1453—to establish a chief rabbinate for Ottoman Jewry as one administrative unit.

Even more than their role in preparing the way for absorption of the Sephardim into Ottoman society, Romaniote Jewry left another legacy of historical importance. Their successful Hellenization within a Greek-speaking Christian society and the intellectual stimulus derived from that contact sheds important light on the process of "Graecization" that continued throughout the empire's millennial history. Greek-speaking Jews, as a distinct ethnic group within the area, pre- and postdated an Orthodox Byzantium. Yet their intellectual life flourished only during those periods when the general Greek-speaking culture was creative. Not until the emergence of an independent Orthodox Greece, in the nineteenth and twentieth centuries, did Greek-speaking Jewry begin to contribute to the emerging Hellenic culture. The example of this one ethnic group, then, should be of value in assessing the experiences of other *ethnoi* within the empire.

Unfortunately, our sources are such that it is difficult, if not impossible, to examine the interaction of Jews and Christians and the contributions of the former to Byzantine society. Certain areas, such as the economic and religious, are illuminated dimly by the sources. Further research, especially into the intellectual story of latter-day Byzantium, may well uncover what we suspect to be a mutual give and take among Jewish and Christian scholars. Too little work has been done, however, to do more than estimate the contact, let alone delineate its results.

Perhaps when the entire 1,100-year history of Orthodox Byzantium is taken into consideration, it can be better seen that the Jewish story represents a successful combination of acculturation through the conscious absorption of the intellectual and Hellenic aspects of Byzantine society, and preservation, on the other hand, of their ancestral ethnic identity which continued their distinct social and religious traditions. Such a mixture of the "unique and the universal" has been the key factor in any successfully transgenerational pattern of Jewish survival in the diaspora.

Despite the vicissitudes of their experience under Byzantine rule, Greek-speaking Jews maintained this combination throughout the history of the empire. Clearly, there were enormous losses to the victorious new faith in earlier centuries, which were as much a result of attraction to a new form of Jewish Messianism as to governmental pressures. The more extensive source material from the period after the Fourth Crusade somewhat delineates the extent to which Jews were acculturated. As we have suggested, however, this was to the ultimate disadvantage of the Jews. Successfully integrated during the existence of Byzantium, the disappearance of that font of Hellenic inspiration contributed to the decline of a distinct Romaniote culture in the post-Byzantine period. Moreover, the concomitant influx of traditional and Sephardi Jewish studies and scholars and their rich secular Spanish background rapidly created a new intellectual and cultural framework, in the face of which a demographically inferior Romaniote society could, with difficulty, preserve its identity and maintain a shadowy survival.

FIVE

THE OTTOMAN CONQUEST AND ITS AFTERMATH

THE LAST fifty years before the Ottoman conquest saw the Byzantine Empire reduced to a fortified belt, encompassing the capital and a hinterland that extended only partway up the Bosporos. By contrast, the junior branch of the Palaiologoi had nearly conquered the Peloponnesos. Behind her formidable land walls, the capital was still, for the moment, safe and well, led by her last three emperors. It was in the midst of this declining polity, paradoxically, that Romaniote Jewry was preparing for its great expansion after the Ottoman conquest. Its settlements, scattered throughout the Balkans and Greece, each year witnessed the shift of a new community from Byzantine control or influence to that of the advancing Ottomans, until the final conquests removed the last vestige of Roman rule and a united Ottoman Jewry began a new chapter in Greek Jewry's millennia-long history.

The political, demographic, and ethnographic story of the Jews in the first fifty years of Ottoman rule is, with minor exception, the same as that of the last Byzantine generation. It is a story in which the Romaniote Jews, rather than Sephardim, dominate the scene. Only after the end of the fifteenth century would the latter grow sufficiently in number to change the sociological structure. By and large, then, the two generations that spanned the conquest years constitute the history of the Romaniote Rabbanite community and its rapprochement with the Romaniote Karaite community. These two generations, the last Byzantine and the first Ottoman, also witnessed a great flowering of Romaniote intellectual activity, one that is all too often ignored in the face of the Sephardi accomplishments of the subsequent century. Yet, as we shall see, the former was a necessary precondition for the success of the latter. The following pages outline the nature of Jewish settlement during this period, its demography, and the institutional changes that postdate the conquest. Also, the messianic impact of the conquest for succeeding generations of Jews cannot be ignored.

The Last Byzantine Generation, 1425–61

Late in the fourteenth century, it was evident that the empire was drawing close to the end of its long history. Were it not for the invasion of Tamerlane, the intermittent sieges of Constantinople by Bayezid I (1389–1402), from 1394 to 1402, might well have ended with the cry of the muezzin echoing through the skies of the capital. That attempt, however, and the briefer but more vigorously pursued siege by Murat II (1421–51) in the summer of 1422, were the last serious attacks on the city before the fateful one of 1453.[1]

No wonder, then, that the history of Jews in the Balkans during this period followed two contradictory patterns: one parallels the vicissitudes of the declining Orthodox civilization while the other reflects the rapidly developing society of Ottoman Adrianople. The near-total fragmentation of the empire divided Byzantine Jewry among the restricted enclaves of Constantinople and her hinterland, Trebizond, and the Despotate of Morea. Turkish Edirne (Adrianople), on the other hand, was a mecca for scholars of all faiths and an entrepôt for merchants of all nationalities.

Thus, even more than in previous centuries, the history of the Jews in Byzantium during this last generation is a regional history. Of the enclaves of Byzantine rule, the Despotate of Morea survived longest (1460), save for Trebizond (1461). However, our information from the latter area is restricted to the single tradition that the physician of the last Komnenos was a Jew, and his Judaism did not long survive the Byzantines (**144**).

Thessalonica (as seen above) had declined continuously from the beginning of the fifteenth century, until it was sold to the Venetians in 1423.

1. For the general history of the period, cf. P. Wittek, "De la défaite d'Ankara à la prise de Constantinople," *Revue des études islamiques,* 12 (1938), 1–34; G. Ostrogorsky, "Byzance, état tributaire de l'empire turc," *Zbornik Radova,* 5 (1958), 49–58; F. Babinger, *Mehmed the Conqueror and His Time* (Princeton, 1978), book 1; A. E. Vacalopoulos, *Origins of the Greek Nation: The Byzantine Period, 1204–1461* (New Brunswick, 1970), chaps. 10 and 13; and H. Inalcik, *The Ottoman Empire* (New York, 1973).

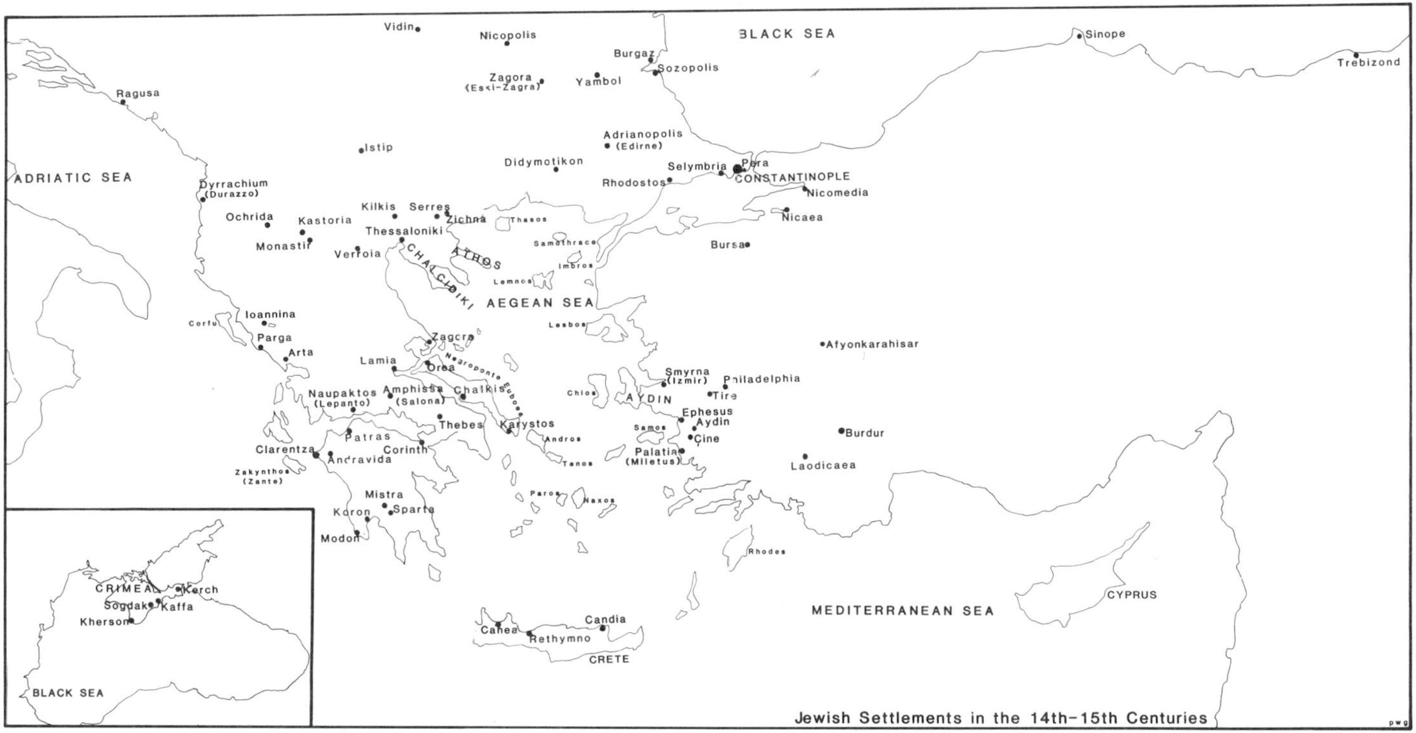

Jewish Settlements in the 14th–15th Centuries

With the Ottoman conquest in 1430, the city opened a new phase in her history as the capital of Macedonia. Jewish immigration into the depopulated city began soon after the conquest. There is as yet no indication whether it was planned or voluntary, or at its inception involved merely a return of those Jews who had left the city as a result of inefficiency and harassment under Venetian rule. In either case, the first to settle were Romaniotes, and these were followed by groups of Ashkenazi refugees. All of these new elements, however, were insufficient in number to influence greatly the ethnographic makeup of the city.[2] It was only after the reign of Bayezid II (1481–1512) that Thessalonica's welcome of many thousands of Spanish refugees stamped a Sephardi imprint on this city that lasted until the twentieth century.

Our sole information on Romaniote life during the last days of Byzantine rule is derived from the suggestion that the local Jews joined in mourning Bishop Simon in 1429. As he is known to have functioned since the Byzantine period, it seems likely that the sentiment which caused all Thessalonicans to mourn his death was a holdover from pre-Venetian times (**125**). On the other hand, we should not overlook the possibility that the author of the text, Ioannes Anagnostes, may have included the Jews in his remarks in a rhetorical vein. At the same time, we may recall that the special tax paid by the Jews of Thessalonica had been in effect since before 1423. Even so, the entire subject is still unclear. The sources are much too sparse to offer more than tentative suggestions.

Constantinople

In the capital itself, the situation was becoming increasingly desperate. Its hinterland, continually shrinking, acknowledged only a precarious suzerainty over the narrow strip of land from Messembria to Heraclea on the Propontis. Constantinople appeared more a tiny principality, existing on the sufferance of its powerful neighbor, than the center of the Orthodox world and the seat of the Byzantine emperor. The population of the city, perhaps no more than 40,000 to 50,000, was a mere fraction of what it had

2. That the city was repopulated with Jews soon after 1430 draws support from the deportation of Thessalonican Jews to Constantinople soon after the conquest. See below, "Areas of Settlement."

been in recent years.[3] Huge sections of the city were neglected and lay in ruin, while many other sections had returned to open fields and were under cultivation.[4] Still, the declining capital did not cease to be either an entrepôt for various Italian merchants (who, incidentally, controlled its revenues), a research center for scholars, and the object of pilgrimage for pious Christians.

The Jews of Constantinople participated in the commercial and intellectual life of the city. Indications are that they were well aware of the various intellectual trends, in particular astronomy. Possessing an independent intellectual tradition, the Jews of the capital maintained their own schools and academies. Even so, the latter did not compare with those which had been established in neighboring Andrianople.

Under such circumstances, the Jewish population of the capital should have experienced a decline, paralleling the general decline throughout this last generation. As Constantinople offered few attractions for Jews, other than economic, while the nearby Ottoman capital offered them unparalleled social mobility, any Jewish immigration to the Ottoman city would have come from the ranks of those Jews who could live under the protection of the foreign consuls. The statutes of the Venetian Baili, though formulated at the beginning of the fifteenth century, suggest that the number of these Jews was not great. Neither the amounts that they had to pay to the Bailo and his personnel nor their expenditures on communal administration were particularly large, especially when compared with the amounts regularly handled by some of the wholesale merchants of the Venetian colony.[5]

3. Estimates among scholars interested in the demography of the city agree on a population of 40,000–50,000; cf. D. Jacoby, "La population de Constantinople à l'époque byzantine: un problem de démographie urbaine," *Byzantion,* XXXI (1961), 81–109, esp. p. 82; A. M. Schneider, *Die Bevölkerung Konstantinopels im XV. Jahrhundert* (Nachrichten d. Akad. Wiss. in Göttingen, Philol.-Hist. Kl., 1949), pp. 233–44; see below, "Estimates of Romaniote Population."

4. Ibn Battuta had recorded this decline already in the fourteenth century (document 52). The population had further decreased by the fifteenth century, as noted by Tafur and B. de la Brocquière. With the extensive waterworks still functioning, the city was almost self-sufficient, while in the event of siege, ample stores could be supplied by sea.

5. Some 25 Jewish merchants can be identified in Constantinople between 1436 and 1440 in *Il libro dei Conti di Giacomo Badoer (Constantinopoli 1436–1440),* Testo a cura di Umberto Dorini e Tommaso Bertelè (Instituto poligrafico dello stato, Libreria dello Stato, MCMLVI). A number of these Jews were related to or partners with each other; most dealt in cloth or silk. To the list of identifiable Jewish merchants we may possibly add one Caloian-

Jewish communities in areas under Venetian control were subject to regular and occasional exactions; however, the data are too sparse to make even an estimate of their situation. Sums in Venetian statutes are amplified by unspecified exactions registered in Venetian complaints to the Byzantine government. Occasionally, light is unexpectedly shed on these: the impoverishment and the subsequent complaints of the Jews of Thessalonica and Dyrrachium preserve a record of the exaction of 1,000 hyperpera from the former and of the tax in cloth paid by the latter. Moreover, Venetian Jews throughout the area were repeatedly assessed special contributions, in addition to their regular taxes.[6] Local Venetian authorities would not have overlooked such traditionally successful means to defray the expenses of the colony, especially in Constantinople. That the Baili zealously guarded the fiscal integrity and independence of their Jews from the Byzantine authorities lends weight to this supposition.[7]

The problem of the Venetian Jews continued throughout the last generation. In an attempt to restrict occasions for conflict, the Bailo ordered that Venetian Jews restrict their real estate transactions in the Judaica among themselves (**112**). Other difficulties remained, however; in 1453, for example, the Bailo complained to Venice, through the Baili of Coron and Modon, that the emperor still did not respect the status of the Venetian Jews (**122**). As late as the eve of the conquest, Venice continued to complain about the violated rights of her Jewish and Christian merchants. This time, the various exactions were awarded by the poverty-stricken emperor to Loukas Notaras as part of his income, as one way of assuring the powerful noble's support (**134**).

Elsewhere in the rural hinterland of Constantinople, a few small Jewish communities were to be found in Selembrya and Sozopolis (**150**).[8] Benjamin of Tudela, we recall, had found a community in Rhodosto in the twelfth century, and the city's location on the Adrianople–Selymbrya–

no Vlacho; a man with a similar name appears in a document from the Venetian Jewish community dated 1424: "Calo Vlacho quondam David ebreus," in Jacoby, "Quartiers juifs," p. 225. On these merchants, see D. Jacoby, "Les Vénitiens naturalisés dans l'empire byzantin: un aspect de l'expansion de Venise en Romanie du XIIIe au milieu du XVe siècle," *Travaux et Mémoires* (1981), 8: 228 and 233. See above, chap. 4, "Intellectual Trends."

6. Cf. the material for Modon, Coron, and Negroponte collected by Starr, *Romania* (chaps. 3–5), and for Crete, his "Jewish Life in Crete under the Rule of Venice," *PAAJR*, XII (1942), 59–114.

7. See above, chap. 1, notes 24ff, and chap. 3, "Social Structure, Mobility, Tensions."

8. For Jews in Selembrya in the twelfth century, cf. Starr, *JBE*, no. 179n, p. 221.

Constantinople route hints at the presence of a small community there, as well as in neighboring Heraclea, one of the last imperial ports in Thrace. Frequent reference to Jews in Pera can be found throughout the fifteenth century; most of these Jews, however, were part of the Genoese colony there (**128**). (The presence of Jews in a number of cities in the Peloponnesos has been dealt with in a previous chapter.)[9] It was these Jewish communities that witnessed the central drama of the fifteenth century: the conquest of Constantinople by the young sultanate of the Ottomans. It was partially from these communities that the Jewish presence in the new Ottoman capital was to be reestablished.

Jewish Reactions

The theme of the siege and capture of Constantinople by Mehmet II on May 29, 1453, has attracted the attention of historians of many nations and religions. The fall of the capital was viewed with mixed emotions throughout the Mediterranean world; each ethnic group could not be but touched deeply by the apparent end of an era which had lasted over a thousand years. The peoples of the area were affected not only on the historical level, however. More important were the political and religious reactions, which provide an important background to the course of developments in the area for the next century.

On the political level, there was immediate awareness that the bulwark of Christian civilization had fallen. People looked about for a new champion to step into the breach and defend the West against the conquering Turks. However, neither the pope, nor the Catholic monarchs of Spain, nor the Holy Roman emperor could be relied upon to fulfill this task; and Europe lived under fear of the Turk for the next two and a half centuries.

On the religious level, each ethnic group in the region had its grudge against the Byzantine church in the latter's capacity as an aggressive agent of the Orthodox empire. The Latins had been treated as schismatics, the Armenians nearly as heretics; the Jews were designated ἡ θεοκτόνη συναγωγή, and the Muslims were tolerated solely because of their overwhelming military strength.

A number of historical accounts have survived that outline the course of events from the perspective of participants and of observers. Literature,

9. See above, chap. 2, "Peloponnesos."

too, has preserved laments in Greek, Armenian, Italian, and one elegy in Hebrew. They reflect quite clearly the feelings of their composers, who, though concerned with the human and historical element in the conquest, could only hint at the way in which the conquest would prove to be the major turning point in the history of the Balkans. For with the destruction of the Byzantine Empire, the fragmented states that had arisen in the wake of the Fourth Crusade were reunited under an imperial Muslim power. Christianity was no longer the dominant faith; rather, each ethnic group was united under its own religious leadership and was permitted to live a self-regulating life under the protection of the sultan.[10]

The Hebrew dirge is a unique document on the fall of Constantinople, stemming from the Romaniote community. It was composed in Crete by the poet, preacher, and scholar Michael ben Shabbetai Kohen Balbo, most likely during the summer of 1453.[11] The poem is composed of a number of biblical verses strung together and, as such, does not provide new historical information. What is of importance is the sentiment of the composer, which reflected the grief that swept the island upon the report that the city had been taken.[12] The author, while living in a Christian environment and himself a product of Byzantine civilization, could not anticipate the favorable approach that Mehmet would take toward the Jews of the capital. He recognized the defeat of the Christian oppressor of his people; yet, at the same time, he mourned the victims of the sack of the city. What stands out is his positive impression with the figure of the conqueror "whose height was like the height of cedars. The great eagle, rich in a plumage of many colors," whose destiny it was to subdue ἡ Πόλις, "the lofty city." And yet, when all was said and done, there remained the crushing blow to the Greek soul, so aptly described by the verse from Jeremiah: "Woe unto me, for my soul is faint before murderers" (exc. D).

An event of such magnitude could not but stir the deep-seated memo-

10. Cf. appendix I and bibliography in S. Runciman, *The Fall of Constantinople, 1453* (Cambridge, 1965), and the more extensive bibliography in *CMH,* IV (1966), 882ff. For the Greek laments, cf. list in Vacalopoulos, *Origins,* p. 346, note 111, and the bibliography in G. Zoras's edition of "An Italian Lament on the Fall," (Greek) *Bibliotheke Byzantines kai Neoellenikes Philologias,* vol. 46 (1969), offprint from *Parnassos,* II (1969), 108–25; also A. Sanjian, "Two Contemporary Armenian Elegies on the Fall of Constantinople, 1453," *Viator,* I (1970), 223–61. The Armenian poems parallel the Hebrew dirge in their extensive use of direct or alluded biblical quotation.

11. See note to exc. D in part II.

12. See below, note 40.

ries of Mediterranean peoples. Muslim tradition since the seventh century had been fired with the vision of conquering the Queen of the Bosporos. Did not the Koran prophesy such an accomplishment? Was not Eyub, the standard bearer of the prophet Muhhamed, buried just outside the city, where he fell in one of the earlier attempts to conquer Constantinople? A number of folk myths and prophesies circulated among both Christians and Muslims.[13]

Jewish traditions were older than those of Islam. Already in the Targum, the Aramaic paraphrase of the Bible, it was recognized that Constantinople had inherited the mantle of Rome. How much more, then, would the messianic traditions attached to pagan Rome, evil Rome, be transferred to her Christian successor. A Targum commenting on Psalms 108:11 expands the original text to identify Rome, the heir of Edom, with Constantinople; and now the Bosporos hosted the age-old antagonist of the Jews. This identification, embedded in rabbinic literature, and later entrenched in Byzantine Karaite literature as well, was ready proof to researchers that the earlier texts would supply the requisite messianic prophesies.[14]

The messianic works of Rabbi Isaac Abrabanel, that Spanish philosopher, political scientist, and Jewish scholar who wrote at the end of the fifteenth century, best summarize these messianic traditions.[15] As one scholar put it, Abrabanel did not introduce anything new into the late fifteenth-century messianic tradition; rather, he collected and revised all the current and classical beliefs.[16] Thus his works served as a cache for successive generations. Especially in his *Mayane Yeshua* (The Well Springs of Salvation), composed in 1496, are these traditions outlined. Regarding the

13. Cf. Ch. Diehl, "De quelques croyances byzantines sur le fin de Constantinople," *BZ,* XXX (1930), 192–96; V. Grecu, "La chute de Constantinople dans la littérature populaire roumaine," *Byzantinoslavica,* XIV (1953), 55–81; and Louis Massignon, "Textes prémonitoires et commentaires mystiques relatifs à la prise de Constantinople par les Turcs en 1453 (= 838 Heg.)," *Oriens,* LV (1953), 10f.

14. Cited by Y. Baer, "The Messianic Atmosphere in Spain during the Period of the Expulsion," (Hebrew) *Meassaf Zion,* V (1933), 74, and Elijah Kapsali, *Seder Eliyahu Zuta,* I, 80, in a paraphrase of the Targum to Lamentations 4:21. This identification and reading of rabbinic literature was quite common, and by the twelfth century was firmly established in Byzantine Karaite literature; cf. Z. Ankori, "The Correspondence of Tobias b. Moses the Karaite of Constantinople," *Essays on Jewish Life and Thought* (New York, 1959), p. 5, note 13.

15. The best available study in English is B. Netanyahu, *Don Isaac Abravanel, Statesman & Philosopher* (2d ed.; Philadelphia, 1968).

16. Y. Baer, "Messianic Atmosphere in Spain," pp. 61–77.

verse from Psalms 108:11, Abrabanel comments that the latter part of the verse shows that as God has brought His vengeance upon Constantinople, so He will bring about the fall of Rome itself.[17] He repeats the same theme elsewhere, while discussing the Targum's paraphrase of the verses from Lamentations 4:21–22. His commentary reflects the use of this verse by a number of authors from the mid-fifteenth to the mid-sixteenth century:

> The meaning of the Targum is that Edom refers to the nation that inhabits Constantinople, and according to what is said about Edom as referring to Constantinople which is the daughter of Rome built in Armenia and is called Edom because her inhabitants come from Edom.[18] And know that the explanation is not based upon rabbinic reasoning but rather is a popular tradition that they received from the prophets. And they explained further that the destroyer of Constantinople and Rome would be Persians.[19] Know that the people today called Turks are descended from the land of Persia,[20] and they took Constantinople and destroyed the site of its holiness. Perhaps they are destined to destroy Rome.[21]

This opinion was not unique to Abrabanel; it circulated among Mediterranean Jews in the aftermath of the conquest.

Alfonso de Espina included the following observation in his comprehensive list of Christian arguments against Judaism, written at the end of the 1450s, which he entitled *Fortalitum fidei*:[22] "The Jews of our time argue that they have found in an Aramaic commentary that Greece is the land of Uz, and that therefore Constantinople is the daughter of Edom. Moreover, since the city was conquered by the Turks, the iniquity of the daughter of Zion has ended. Thus they are waiting for the coming of the Messiah."[23]

We may trace the origins of this tradition to a circular letter, sent from

17. Ibid., pp. 74f.

18. The tenth-century author of the *Sepher Josippon* identified the Armenians as the descendants of Amalek, the other traditional enemy of the Jews. The *Josippon* identification may reflect the persecution of the Jews by the Macedonian emperor Basil I and his successors. See R. Bonfil, "The Vision of Daniel as a Historical and Literary Document," (Hebrew) *Zion*, XLIV (1979), 124ff.

19. *Talmud Babli, Yoma* 10a: "Rome is fated to fall to Persia (עתידה רומי שתפול ביד פרס.)"

20. This was the common view among Jewish, Spanish, and Greek authors.

21. Cited by Baer, "Messianic Atmosphere in Spain" (Hebrew), p. 74.

22. Cited by Baer, ibid.

23. Clearly, this refers to our Targum.

Jerusalem in the very wake of the conquest and diffused throughout the Mediterranean Jewish diaspora by the middle of the decade. The letter is dated 1454 and is concerned with the messianic upheavals occasioned by new reports concerning the discovery of the Ten Lost Tribes in Central Asia. The following passage is an introduction to the report of the arrival of Asian envoys, bearing news about the miraculous cessation of the messianically fantastic River Sambatyon:

> We, fellow scions of the covenant, inform you our brothers in redemption of the rumors and good tidings that we have heard and learned and actually seen in the year 1454. For this is the second year in which was fulfilled the great, magnificent and wonderful prophesy to mark our redemption which Jeremiah prophesied in the verse in Lamentations "Rejoice . . . . O daughter of Edom" . . . Uz is Constantinople. It remains to establish the end quickly and in our own days . . . to reveal it to you.[24]

The style of the letter is immediate and compelling, and no doubt quickly stamped this fulfilled messianic interpretation onto the discussion within Jewish circles of the fall of the city. Shortly thereafter, rumors began to circulate among Spanish Jews, in particular *conversos,* that the Messiah had appeared and was living quietly on a mountain outside Constantinople. However, he was visible only to circumcised Jews![25]

The second half of the fifteenth century saw continuance of the belief that the fall of Constantinople was a manifestation of God's imminent redemption of the Jews. Abrabanel worked out this view in his encyclopedia of Messianism. According to his calculations, the clues in Daniel 12:11 added up to 1,290 years. If we add to this figure the sum of 100, which represents the numerical value of *yamim* (days), then we have 1,390 years, which is "precisely" the time between the destruction of the Second Temple (at the hands of Rome) and the fall of Constantinople. This provides an additional "proof" that the fall of Constantinople was the beginning of the end of Christian Rome. The *very* end would occur in 1503, exactly fifty years after the Ottoman conquest.[26]

24. Edited and published by A. Neubauer, *Kobez 'al Yad,* 4th year (1888), pp. 9–74; our passage is on p. 46. Some scholars have dated the corpus of letters to the sixteenth century; cf. A. Eshkoli, *Ha-Tenuoth ha-Meshiḥiyoth be-Yisrael,* pp. 318ff.

25. Eshkoli, ibid., p. 297.

26. Cf. his *Mayane Yeshua,* 121a and b, and comments by Netanyahu, *Don Isaac Abravanel,* pp. 216ff.

The chronicle of Elijah Kapsali, *Seder Eliyahu Zuta,* takes up the same theme in a slightly different manner. Amidst a straightforward narrative of early Ottoman history, based on Greek, Turkish, and Hebrew sources and written in an affected biblical style, he includes an extended treatment of the character of Mehmet II in an affected prophetic style. His Mehmet is more than a conqueror; he is no less than a Judeophile. He frequents their quarters (in disguise, of course), surrounds himself with merchants and scholars, orders kosher food for the palace, learns Scripture with Jewish teachers, including Isaiah Missini from Morea, in particular, and (not surprisingly) the Book of Daniel. The picture of "the conqueror" is part of the messianic picture the author was trying to paint.[27] Moreover, as a preface to his sketch of the philo-Jewish Mehmet, he—not surprisingly—included the abovementioned Targum to Lamentations in a thirty-stanza hymn of deliverance that he composed. He concludes the hymn with the sentiment that the sorrow which befell the city stemmed from the evil she did to Israel.[28]

With Kapsali we have come full circle. God has sent Mehmet to conquer the wicked city, as foretold in Scripture, in order to provide a refuge for Jews to act out their messianic expectations. Based on this premise, Kapsali emphasized that, in the wake of the conquest, all Jews flocked voluntarily to Constantinople. He thus ignores the massive deportation policy instituted by the conqueror.[29]

Although this messianic interpretation colored all later Jewish reports of the conquest and the ultimate fate of the Jews, contemporary sources allow us to draw a more composite picture which reflects the real complexities of the period.

The question of a Jewish role in the Ottoman conquest of the city has been raised, but there is no documentation to indicate what—if any—this role was.[30] We may assume that the Jews contributed (or were forced to con-

27. Cf. Charles Berlin, "A Sixteenth-Century Hebrew Chronicle of the Ottoman Empire: The *Seder Eliyahu Zuta* of Elijah Capsali and Its Message," *Studies in Jewish Bibliography History and Literature in Honor of I. Edward Kiev* (New York, 1971), pp. 21–44.

28. *Seder Eliyahu Zuta* by Rabbi Eliyahu Capsali, ed. by Aryeh Shmuelevitz (Jerusalem, 1975), 1:80.

29. See below, "New Directions."

30. Cf. Starr, *Romania,* p. 33. The assertion of A. N. Diamantopoulos ("Gennadios Scholarios as a source for the history of the period of the Fall"), (Greek) *Hellenika,* IX (1936), 229, is not supported by the sources. He writes: "The wealthy hid their private fortunes but

tribute) money and labor for the defenses of the city. Revenues from Romaniote courts and from taxes on Venetian Jewish merchants (protested, as always, by the Venetian authorities as illegal) formed part of the income of Loukas Notaras, one of the most powerful Byzantine nobles. The area that he was assigned to defend included the walls along the southern shore of the Golden Horn; it is not known, however, if he could draw upon the resources of Jewish residents on the shores of the Dardanelles.

One of the areas attacked by the Ottoman fleet was the Vlanka Quarter, where Jews had lived since the beginning of the fourteenth century. This area impressed the attackers (and the Italian defenders alike) by the wealth of the Jews who lived there (**138**). We may assume that this area was sacked quite thoroughly in the three-day period after the breaching of the walls. Indeed, this area seems to have been subsequently abandoned by the Jews for another area within the city.[31] On the other hand, the Jews of Pera (which was under Genoese control) remained neutral during the siege. Genoa had negotiated a treaty of neutrality with Mehmet; so it is unlikely that Genoese Jews who lived in Pera could have done anything to help, or deter, the Ottoman forces.

We have no information on the participation of Jews in the fighting. Still, as part of the besieged population, the Jews may have been drafted to repair walls or to carry ammunition.

No Jews, so far as we know, fought in the Ottoman army. Yet they were to be found in the conqueror's entourage, and one of them is known to have enjoyed some influence with the young sultan. The story of Yaqub Pasha, the Jewish physician to Mehmet II (and to his father, Murat II,

---

they allowed the holy vessels and all the wealth of the church to be sold or pawned by the government to the foreign Europeans and the Jews." The reference, in any case, is applicable only to Pera.

31. Starr, *Romania*, p. 33. Edwin Pears (*The Destruction of the Greek Empire and the Story of the Capture of Constantinople* [New York and London, 1903], p. 360) states that the sailors from the Turkish fleet "appear to have landed at the Jews' Quarter, which was near the Horaia Gate on the side of the Golden Horn." George Finlay, in his *History of the Byzantine and Greek Empires from DCCXVI to MCCCLIII* (vol. II; Oxford, 1977), indicates in a footnote to p. 632 that the Jewish Quarter (which one?) was bombarded and the evidence was still visible in his day. Jacoby ("Quartiers juifs," pp. 195f) showed that the topography of Barbaro's description (document 120) applied to the Vlanka Quarter and not to the Judaica on the Golden Horn, as the first three citations in this note believed. Jacoby (p. 218) suggests that these Jews of Vlanka were resettled in the Balat Quarter of Istanbul by Mehmet II. See above, chap. 2, note 21.

before him) has been scrutinized (**151**), and the story of his relations with Mehmet, as well as his negotiations with the Venetians, is available in both Hebrew and Venetian documents (**151n**). While the Hebrew sources assure us of his advice and ministrations to the conqueror, documents in the Venetian archives allege that Yaqub was engaged in secret, and traitorous, negotiations with Venice. The responsible position that Yaqub held with the sultan (in addition to the firmans that he received; he later, apparently, converted to Islam) strongly suggests that he entered these negotiations as an attempt to divert any Venetian plots against the sultan. Mehmet was no doubt kept up to date of the machinations of the powerful republic. As it turned out, nothing resulted from the conspiracy, which dragged on for several years at considerable waste of time and effort to the Venetians.[32]

Quite justifiably, the Jews in the besieged capital feared the days immediately following the conquest. The city, after all, was to suffer a sack whose gravity was surpassed only by the rape of the Crusaders in 1204. Still, they could not have failed to appreciate the far-reaching consequences of the change from Christian rule to that of the more benevolent Muslim conquerors.

New Directions

The major changes in the Jewish settlements of Constantinople after the conquest were political and demographic. The Muslim tradition toward members of other monotheistic religions, the so-called *dhimmis* or Ottoman *zimmis,* was to allow them communal autonomy, under their own leaders, in return for self-regulation of their tax assessments. Among the latter was the *cizye* or poll tax (gradually known also as *kharaj* [Turkish *harac*], although the original Muslim *kharaj* had a different connotation).

The traditions surrounding the appointment of the first chief rabbi for the Jewish community do not indicate that such an institution existed in

32. Babinger has devoted many pages to the career of Yaqub Pasha; cf. his *Mehmed the Conqueror* (index s.v. Iacopo) and his independent study devoted to the subject, "Jaqub-pascha, ein Leibarzt Mehmed's II" (*Rivista degli Studi Orièntalni,* 26 [Rome, 1951], 87–113). Bernard Lewis has provided a translation and commentary to the main Hebrew source on Jacob as a supplementary critique to Babinger's studies: "The Privilege Granted by Mehmed II to His Physician," *BSOAS,* 14 (1952), 550–63; and partially reproduced in part II as document 151. Thiriet has listed several Venetian texts showing Jacob's adroitness at leading the republic's plots into blind corners; cf. his *Régestes* (III, 214, 218, 219).

any way in Byzantium previous to the conquest (**140, 141, 151**).[33] Moses Kapsali, according to tradition, was recognized as a judge by the Jewish communities only after the conquest. We have no idea of his status before then, though our source suggests that he held an analogous position before 1453. Even so, as we have seen (chapter 3), the Jewish community in Byzantium was accustomed to the direction of a government-appointed leader whose decisions would therefore be supported by imperial authority. The institution of the chief rabbi, as it is known to us from the Ottoman period, differs from the situation during the Byzantine period. The differences most likely reflect the change and adjustment that underlie many of the social and economic characteristics of the heir to Byzantium.[34] The institution should also be viewed within the context of the older Muslim tradition of the recognized and sanctioned autonomy of the *dhimmis* under their own leadership. Thus the Ottoman policy toward their *zimmis,* at least in the European part of their empire, was based on a blend of Byzantine and Muslim tradition and precedent.[35]

33. The term "chief rabbi" is later applied to Moses Kapsali by two sixteenth-century rabbis: Eliyahu Mizraḥi and Samuel di Modena. The former, in his responsum 57, refers to him as: *ha-rav ha-manhig kol ha-kehillot, ha-rav ha-manhig kol ha-kehillot ha-ʿomdoth ba-ʿir Kostandina, ha-rav ha-manhig,* and *ha-rav;* or "the rabbi who leads all the congregations which are in the city of Constantinople." A variation of this designation appears in responsum 364 of Samuel di Modena as *rav menaheg be-hormana de-malkhuta,* or "rabbi who leads with the permission of the authorities." See below (151). The term should be understood as chief rabbi for the Romaniote Rabbanite communities of Constantinople as designated by the Ottoman government. Cf. M. A. Epstein, *The Ottoman Jewish Communities and Their Role in the Fifteenth and Sixteenth Centuries* (Freiburg, 1980), pp. 55ff, for later Turkish terms.

The only contemporary terms that designate Kapsali are *rav* (Hebrew) and *hoca* (Turkish). All we can say for certain, from Eliahu Kapsali's report, is that Mehmet II recognized him as "judge and leader of the Jews," which would correspond to the rabbinic head of the *sürgün* communities of Romaniote Jews in Constantinople.

The authority he had was to deal with cases involving "personal and commercial matters," or to use the more legal phraseology of Eliahu Kapsali, לענש נכסין ולארוסין. See below, document 30, note 26, for a discussion of these terms, which, in the context of Moses Kapsali's career, are an apt description of his prerogatives as well as limitations, since he did not exercise the right of capital punishment or imprisonment, viz., הן למות הן לשרשי (cf. Ezra 7, 26; but cf. Maimonides, *Mishnah Torah,* book XIV, Treatise I, chap. xxiv, pp. 9f).

34. This process has been charted in detail by Sp. Vryonis, *The Decline of Medieval Hellenism in Asia Minor and the Process of Islamization from the Eleventh through the Fifteenth Century* (Berkeley, 1971), and subsequent essays.

35. Cf. S. W. Baron, *The Jewish Community* (Philadelphia, 1948), I, 195. N. J. Pantazopoulos (*Church and Law in the Balkan Peninsula during the Ottoman Rule* [Thessaloniki, 1967]) discusses the historical roots of ethnic autonomy in Mediterranean societies; cf. pp. 13–26. He summarizes the Turkish application of the *ius singulare* (for the Orthodox only, but

With the death of the Byzantine emperor and the capture of his capital, the Byzantine Empire ceased to exist. None of the surviving appendages pretended to be its successor, until the Russian czar put forth his claim at the end of the century.[36] After the refusal of Loukas Notaras to set up an interim government, and his subsequent execution, Mehmet turned to the church and sought from it the administration that he needed for his Orthodox subjects. Henceforth the church was to be responsible for the personal and religious life of the Orthodox community in the Ottoman Empire.[37]

Shortly after the installation of the new patriarch, the Armenians began to agitate for a patriarch of their own. It is not clear precisely when they succeeded (scholars generally agree on a date ca. 1461), but there is little doubt that this independence was sought soon after the conquest.[38] Just as the sultan was later to recognize the independence of the Armenians from the Greek Orthodox Church, he had earlier noted the religious and social differences that separated Jews from Christians. This recognition

---

these conditions, *mutatis mutandis,* would apply to Jews and Armenians as well) as follows: (a) freedom of religion, upkeep of churches, and use of native language; (b) the patriarch to be the ultimate judge for all Christians in religious affairs; (c) exemption of patriarchs and bishops from taxation.

36. Cf. S. Runciman, *The Great Church in Captivity* (Cambridge, 1968), pp. 320–23, and studies by Ettinger cited above (chap. 1, note 70).

37. Cf. author's "Two Late Byzantine Dialogues with the Jews," *GOTR,* XXV (1980), 87ff.

38. Thus the recognition of the Greek community dates from 1453; the Jewish within two years (ca. 1455; see following note); and the Armenian probably from 1461. Critical study has only just begun on the Armenian patriarchate of Constantinople. Modern scholarship, however, agrees (although the sources are even less informative than the ones to be discussed below in connection with the Jews) that in 1461 (probably), Mehmet II brought the Armenian bishop of Brusa, Yovakim, to the capital and invested him with the same jurisdiction over his coreligionists (apparently only those in the capital and environs; cf. study by Bardakjian cited at end of note) as was previously invested in Gennadios Scholarios (see above, note 35). On the Armenian patriarchate, cf. article "Armenie" by L. Petit in *Dictionnaire de Théologie Catholique,* I b, col. 1909, and article "Armeniya" by J. Deny in *EI²,* I, A–B, p. 640. A survey of "The Armenian Millet" comprises chap. II of A. K. Sanjian, *The Armenian Communities in Syria under Ottoman Domination* (Cambridge, Mass., 1965). The best work on the early history of the Armenians in the Ottoman Empire is Maghakʿia Ormanian, *Azgapatum* (History of the Armenian Church and the Armenians), 3 vols. (Constantinople and Jerusalem, 1913–27), cols. 1475 and 1484 for the patriarchate. See K. Bardakjian, "The Rise of the Armenian Patriarchate of Constantinople," in Braude-Lewis, *Christians and Jews* (I, 89–100), which includes a discussion of recent revisions of traditional views through a reanalysis of the extant sources.

took the form of a Jewish community consisting of a number of separate congregations, with one rabbi recognized by the government as its representative, perhaps within two years after the conquest.[39] There can be no doubt, however, that until the recognition of a separate organizational structure for both the Jews and the Armenians, these two groups—that is, those Jews and Armenians who had been Byzantine subjects at the time of the conquest—were included among those under the authority of the Orthodox Patriarch Gennadios Scholarios.[40]

Admittedly, we know very little about the early organizational arrangements for the Ottoman Jewish community. However, it is worth emphasizing that its first leader, Moses Kapsali, was a Romaniote Jew who, though originally from Crete, was living in the capital at the time of the conquest. While the fanciful account of his appointment, as reported by Elijah Kapsali in the tradition of Oriental historiography, is not altogether satisfacto-

39. The problem of the date of the recognition of the Jewish community as separate from the Orthodox is crucial. However, we have little evidence on which to base a date of circa 1455. This date is derived from the remark of Kaleb Afendopoulo (document 149) that the Karaites of Adrianople and Pravado were deported in 1455 to Constantinople. Below, we shall suggest that there were negotiations between the Karaites and the Ottomans and between the Rabbanites and the Ottomans over these deportations. It is not unlikely that their agreement to the resettlement was rewarded by recognition of their respective autonomous organizations.

Further indication of a date may be derived as follows. Constantinople, we recall, was taken in 1453 and Athens in 1456; therefore all of the deportations listed in document 154 as *sürgünler* from Rumelia had to be before the conquest of Athens (cf. document 122). Now we do not hear of a deportation from Boeotia, Attika, Epiros, Akarnania, or the Peloponnesos, i.e., those areas conquered after 1456. Moreover, we hear of Jews returning to the Peloponnesos with the Ottoman army (143). Thus it seems a fair assumption to restrict the period of deportations before the recognition of a separate organizational structure for the Jewish communities to between 1453 and 1455. Toward the end of this initial period it became necessary for the Jews to petition and for the Ottoman government to structure some kind of framework within which the Jewish immigrants to the capital could reestablish a productive social and economic life.

40. Thus there may be something beyond mere rhetoric in the remark by Cardinal Isidore that no Jews were allowed in Constantinople after the conquest, at least in the areas under the direct control of the patriarch. Cf. *MPG,* CLIX, col. 955; Vacalopoulos, *Origins,* pp. 202, 346 note 105; and comments by Runciman, *Great Church in Captivity, ad locum.*

Cardinal Isidore's moving "Epistula . . . de expugnatione Urbem Constantinopolitanae" is dated at Crete, July 8, 1453. If his public appearances matched the passion of its content ("Mox enim nullam habitatorum intus reliquerunt, non Latinum, non Graecum, non Armenicum, non Judaeum, non alium quemvis hominem; sed a prima hora diei usque ad meridiem, totam urbem nudam et inhabitatam, ac male detractam et desertam reliquerunt"), we can account for the atmosphere within which Michael Kohen Balbo penned his dirge (exc. D).

ry, it cannot be summarily discarded. It is, after all, the only source at our disposal (**141**). Moreover, it probably reflects, in a general sense, the contemporary situation. The same type of story is handed down regarding the selection of Gennadios Scholarios as the Orthodox patriarch.[41]

It is quite possible that there were behind-the-scenes negotiations to speed up the establishment of a separate Jewish community. All of the Jews who went to Constantinople after the conquest did not go in the manner that the report of Elijah Kapsali suggests. Rather, most of them were caught up in the mass population transfers that Mehmet organized in order to refill his new capital quickly. Several Karaite sources note, in passing, that some migrations were involuntary (**148, 149**). They are supported by a late Rabbanite source (**151**) and independently by two Christian sources, one Greek (**119**), the other Italian (**146**). Finally, there are the Turkish data, which show that all the Romaniote congregations in the capital held a *sürgün* status; that is, they had been forcibly transported. The report of Elijah Kapsali may transfer back to the period just after the conquest a situation which existed in his own day, namely, the voluntary immigration of great numbers of Sephardi Jews to Constantinople since the end of the fifteenth century.[42] We may leave as a suggestion the likely mediating role of Yaqub Pasha, Mehmet's Jewish physician.[43]

The Armenians, as noted, succeeded in breaking away from Orthodox

41. Cf. B. Braude, "Foundation Myths of the Millet System," in Braude-Lewis, *Christians and Jews,* I, 69–88, and above, note 33.

42. Many of the difficulties in interpreting this chronicle stem from the author's messianic style; cf. Ch. Berlin, "A Sixteenth-Century Hebrew Chronicle of the Ottoman Empire," and A. Shmuelevitz, "Capsali as a Source for Ottoman History, 1450–1523," *International Journal of Middle East Studies,* 9 (1978), 339–44.

43. The origins of the chief rabbinate are currently being examined by B. Braude, M. Epstein, and J. Hacker. Cf. references to their published and forthcoming studies in their contributions to Braude-Lewis, *Christians and Jews,* I, 69–88, 101–15, 117–26; cf. also M. Epstein, *The Ottoman Jewish Communities,* chap. III; and above, note 33.

Such negotiations as we suspect would not have been made public. The Orthodox church, we should remember, was the first institution responsible for the former Byzantine citizens after the conquest. Perhaps the situation may have developed differently had Mehmet II succeeded in establishing a secular administration for them; the refusal of Loukas Notaras, however, forced him to rely upon the church, and Gennadios Scholarios was appointed patriarch on January 6, 1454 (cf. study by Inalcik, cited below [note 47]). This administration was intolerable to the Jews for reasons discussed above; moreover, they were familiar with the freedoms that their coreligionists had enjoyed in Adrianople, many of whom were now in the capital. Also, the influence of Mehmet's Jewish physician and advisor on behalf of his coreligionists must be assumed.

control and established their separate community. The Karaites, perhaps even earlier, were apparently successful in a similar way. We do not know if their communal independence from the Rabbanite Jews during the Palaeologan period was as effective as it had been under the Komnenoi. During the late fourteenth and the fifteenth centuries, the community within the empire continued to decline. Still, it is recorded in the Ottoman registers that at the time of the conquest the Karaites were recognized as an independent group.[44] The Ottomans continued to respect this claim as late as the eighteenth and nineteenth centuries (**152, 153**).

The problem of the Venetian Jews continued after the conquest. Many of them had abandoned the city during and after the siege in the general exodus and had sought refuge in the various Venetian colonies in Romania. The sultan, for his part, demanded that they return to Constantinople. Many undoubtably did, once the stability of the area was assured. On the other hand, Mehmet allowed those who did not wish to settle in his capital to remain in the Venetian colonies as long as they continued to be subject to Venetian protection.[45]

Later in the decade, the problem of these Jews again arose. During an outbreak of plague in Negroponte, some Venetian Jews fled to Alexandria. When they applied to return to their homes, the bailo had to intercede with the authorities in Alexandria to allow these Jews to change their residence. In addition, Venice had to defend Negroponte as the destination of these Jews, since the Porte claimed that they should reside in Constantinople.[46]

Areas of Settlement

Important information for Jewish settlements in Constantinople after the conquest is available from the Ottoman period. As such, it is beyond the scope of this study. To the extent, however, that this information sheds light on the situation of Jews in the Balkans before the conquest, as well as the demographic composition of the city in the first generation after it, such data may usefully be adduced here.

The policies undertaken by Mehmet II after the conquest were designed to repopulate and rebuild the war-shattered capital. Artisans of all

44. Cf. Ankori, *Karaites,* pp. 328–36, and above, chap. 2, "Thessalonica." For the position of the Karaites vis-à-vis the chief rabbi, cf. Mizraḥi's responsum 57.

45. Thiriet, *Régestes,* III, 218–19.

46. Ibid., p. 227.

nationalities were transplanted from various parts of his empire to Constantinople (**139**). Each newly conquered area subsequently supplied contingents of its nobility and its middle class for the repopulation of the city. Many of these subjects were unwilling transferees at the beginning; however, their enthusiasm soon paralleled that of the voluntary immigrants as manifold opportunities for social and economic advancement presented themselves.[47]

The Jews, especially, reaped the bounty of the new situation. The Jewish center in Adrianople, both Rabbanite and Karaite in composition, moved to the capital soon after the conquest. This move was partly at the "invitation" of the sultan and partly through the incentive offered by the recognition of their own community in the capital. These newly arrived Jews (as was noted by a contemporary Venetian historian) congregated around a number of synagogues, each of which was named after the Jews' cities of origin (**146**). Later Ottoman and Hebrew sources preserve the names of these congregations, as well as the names of the quarters that these Jews inhabited. This onomastic evidence is most useful for the knowledge of Jewish settlements in the fifteenth century, and in many instances even earlier.

One of the first Jewish scholars to make systematic use of the Ottoman cadastral registers for the study of Jews in Ottoman Constantinople was the late Uriel Heyd.[48] In a study devoted to Jews in Istanbul in the seventeenth century, he extracted several lists of Jewish congregations in Istanbul from four of the official seventeenth-century Ottoman poll-tax registers and compared the results of his collation with a long-known (but undated)

47. Halil Inalcik, "The Policy of Mehmed II toward the Greek Population of Istanbul and the Byzantine Buildings of the City," *DOP,* 23 (1969), 229–49; Iorga ("Notes," IV, 67) cites the destruction of the citadels of Silivri (Selymbrya) and Galata to promote the repopulation of Istanbul.

48. U. Heyd, "The Jewish Communities of Istanbul in the Seventeenth Century," *Oriens,* IV (1953), 299–314. Bernard Lewis was the first scholar to signal the value of these archives, and he contributed several studies on the Arabic and Jewish material in them. His monographs and lectures stimulated the research later undertaken by Heyd, Ankori, and more recent Israeli students of the Ottoman period. See his "The Ottoman Archives as a Source for the History of the Arab Lands," *Journal of the Royal Asiatic Society* (1951), pp. 139–55; "Studies in the Ottoman Archives," *BSOAS,* XVI (1954), 469–501; and his *Notes and Documents from the Turkish Archives: A Contribution to the History of the Jews in the Ottoman Empire* (Jerusalem, 1952). Supplementary study of the documents cited by Heyd has been furnished by Epstein, *The Ottoman Jewish Communities,* in his extensive appendices.

Hebrew list that had been published in the nineteenth century and made known by Abraham Galante in his pioneering studies on Ottoman Jewry (154). The Turkish and the Hebrew material closely parallel each other.

The Ottoman lists are divided into two groups. The first consists of a number of congregations termed *sürgün* (i.e., forcibly transported) while the second group is called *kendi gelen* (i.e., voluntary immigrants). This distinction provides further confirmation of the contemporary understanding of Mehmet's policies (cited above). The two groups, together, numbered some thirty-nine congregations. The *kendi gelen* congregations, for the most part, comprised Spanish refugees, as indicated by such names as Gerush (i.e., expulsion), Seniora, Cordova, or Shalom Aragon, and thus should not predate the end of the fifteenth century. On the other hand, all of the *sürgün* congregations originated in the Balkans and Anatolia. Therefore "this list," Heyd correctly emphasized, "is of importance for the history of Jewish settlement in the Balkans and Anatolia in the fourteenth century."[49]

Of the twenty-four congregations listed as *sürgün,* twelve can be identified as toponyms of Anatolia and Istanbul. Some of the former are familiar from other sources; these include Bursa, the first capital of the Ottomans; Antalya and a site in its hinterland, Borlu; Sinope, on the Black Sea; and possibly Çine, near Aydin and nearby Tire.

The remaining twelve congregations bear place names in the Balkans. In addition to already known sites, other areas are mentioned for the first time. A Jewish presence in the latter, then, cannot (at the present time) be placed earlier than the end of the fourteenth century. An important addition to our knowledge of Jewish settlement in Bulgaria is provided by the mention of both Nicopolis and Yambol. To the south, we may note that all of the major cities along the main route crossing Thrace and Macedonia are listed. We begin with Adrianople, which we recall was well known as a Jewish center during the Byzantine and Ottoman period.[50] The next stage

49. Heyd, "Jewish Communities," p. 299.

50. That Adrianople supported a Jewish community throughout the Middle and Late Byzantine periods has been cogently argued by Ankori, based on linguistic and onomastic evidence and supported by a solid economic argument; cf. his *Karaites,* pp. 150–52. Still, it is frustrating to note that not one literary or archaeological source has survived to document their presence there before the fourteenth century. We may now support his hypothesis with documentation for a Karaite presence in Adrianople in the 1330s. See above, chap. 2, "Thrace and Macedonia."

westward is Didymotikon, whose mention supports other indications of a Jewish settlement there.[51] Continuing westward into Macedonia, we note the continued presence of Jews in Salonica, Serres, Verroia (Karaferye), Ochrida (Ohri), and Kastoria (Kesriye).[52] The mention of Stip (Istip) is the first indication of Jews in that city.[53] It is also possible to include Monastir. Finally, there are the two commercial centers of Central Greece: Chalkis (Agriboz or Egripon), on the island of Euboea, and Lamia-Zeituni (Izdin). Previous indications for a Jewish settlement in both cities are available from the twelfth century.[54]

One cannot stress enough the importance of these lists of congregations, transplanted to Istanbul and named after their cities of origin, for the story of the Jews in Palaeologan Byzantium. At one time or another the empire controlled each of these cities, while the Bulgarian settlements may reflect the policies of Czar Alexander.

Another vexing problem is the size of the Romaniote community. Since population figures are rare for the period under discussion, we are doubly fortunate to have sets of figures for both the late twelfth and late fifteenth centuries—that is, those of Benjamin of Tudela for much of the Greek and insular parts of the empire, and those of Kadi Muhyieddin for Constantinople. If we add to the latter set of figures the information on areas of settlement prior to the conquest, we have some indication of even the

51. Cf. A. Berliner in *MWJ,* III (1876), 48, and above, chap. 2, ibid.

52. The Kastoria community was resettled in Balat, according to I. Molho (*Histoire des Israélites de Castoria* [Thessaloniki, 1938], p. 20).

53. Oxford, Bod. Opp 218, contains the biblical commentary entitled ספר הזכרון לאליהו בן שמואל בן פרנס השטיפיוני עם שירים שונים and is dated 1469/70. The epithet Stipioni (from Stip) suggests that the author was a *sürgünli,* a deportee from Stip now resident in the congregation of that name in Istanbul.

54. On the Agriboz community, cf. Jacoby, "Quartiers juifs," p. 220. We may note here that deportations from the Morea are conspicuous by their absence. Apparently the Jews of Patras, Corinth, Mistra, and other areas were not relocated to the capital; see above, note 39. On the general problem of deportation, cf. Inalcik, "Policy of Mehmed II," passim, and Nicoara Beldiceanu, *Recherche sur la ville ottomane au XVe siècle* (Paris, 1973), p. 41.

For these communities, see Epstein, *The Ottoman Jewish Communities,* appendix I, pp. 178f, and appendix II, s.v. The important census of Pera in 1455, currently being studied by Professor Inalcik, contains valuable data on the ethnic distribution of the population in the capital. A number of these groups were *sürgün,* and this should add to our list of preconquest settlements, e.g., Izdin (Lamia), Filibe, Edirne, Nigbolu, Trikkala, etc.; cf. "Istanbul," *EI²,* p. 238, and below, note 59.

relative size of these congregations. Let it be emphasized at the outset that all the following computations are arbitrary.[55]

Estimating the numerical strength of the Romaniote community is no easy task. We recall that the last pre-conquest figures we have for Jews in the Byzantine capital are those provided in the twelfth century by Benjamin of Tudela. On the other hand, a document from the 1470s allows a glimpse of the population figures for Istanbul shortly after the conquest.[56] Neither text provides unequivocal clues to the Jewish population under the Palaiologoi: the first, because it preceded the decline of the city under the Latins; the second, because it represents a large-scale post-Byzantine immigration. All that can be said for certain is that the Jewish population in the intervening period never exceeded either figure.

In 1477, Kadi Muhyieddin drew up a list of the householders in the capital. These included 8,951 Turkish households, 3,151 Greek, 1,647 Jewish, 267 Kaffa Christians, 372 Armenians of Istanbul, 384 Armenians and Greeks from Karaman, and 31 Gypsies. Of the 14,803 houses in the new capital, then, the 1,647 Jewish households, or approximately 8,000 individuals, constituted 11 percent of the population at the end of the first generation of Ottoman rule.[57] The great majority of these Jews belonged to the *sürgün* communities; that is, they were of Romaniote provenance. It is doubtful whether the Kadi would have listed foreign nationals who were subject to the independent rule of the Venetian Bailo, the Genoese Podesta, and other consuls. Indeed, the above list apparently excludes residents who were not subject to the sultan. The number of Jews protected by foreign consuls, in either case, could not have increased the total Jewish population to much more than 8,000 individuals.

In 1167, Benjamin found 2,000 Rabbanite and 500 Karaite Jews in Constantinople. These figures, we recall, may represent anything from

55. See previous note. Galante mentions this material in several of his works, e.g., *Les Juifs d'Istanbul,* which he used to designate the quarters that they occupied.

56. Robert Mantran, *Istanbul dans la second moitié du XVIIe siècle, essai d'histoire institutionelle, économique et sociale* (Paris, 1962, p. 45), citing a manuscript in Topkapi Sarayi no. E.9524, dated 1478; figures repeated by Beldiceanu, *Recherche sur la ville ottomane au XVe siècle,* p. 39; cf. W. Gerard, *La ruine de Byzance (1204–1453)* (Paris, 1958), p. 344; Ö. L. Barkan, "La repopulation de Constantinople après la conquête turque," *JESHO,* I (1957), 9–36. For more accurate figures and description of sources, see Inalcik, "Policy of Mehmed II," passim, and "Istanbul," *EI*^{2}, pp. 238ff.

57. The number of Jewish households increased by one-third, to 2,491, in 1489; cf. "Istanbul," *EI*^{2}, p. 243.

individuals to families. The maximum number of individuals, then, in the quarter shared by the Jews in Pera was approximately 12,500. Nor should we exclude the possibility that Jews lived elsewhere in the capital area and that Benjamin's figures must be accordingly increased. Be that as it may, the Jewish population in Constantinople on the eve of the Fourth Crusade had to number between 2,500 and 12,500.

The vicissitudes of the Latin Empire would have reduced this number considerably, as they did the general population during its unhappy rule. Not even the initial prosperity of the first quarter of the Palaeologoi period would have sufficed to increase the general population to its high point under the Komnenoi. The latter 130 years under the Palaiologan paralleled the disastrous years of the Latin occupation. The population of the city continuously declined amid the ruined economy and endemic plagues. After the Ottoman conquest, some 8,000 Jews were included in the newly established population of roughly 73,000 Ottoman subjects. Before the conquest, however, the general population of the city numbered between 40,000 and 50,000. We may guess that conditions in the city were such that it did not sustain a Jewish population larger than perhaps 250 families, or about 1,000 to 1,500 individuals.[58]

The 1477 census figure of 1,647 Jewish families gives us—in addition to the proportion of Jews to non-Jews in the capital—an indication of the possible size of the various Jewish communities from which they came. There were, we recall, twenty-four *sürgün* communities listed in the Ottoman registers. An average of 40 to 45 families from each community, added to an estimate of 250 each for Adrianople and Constantinople, would give us a rough estimate.[59] On the basis of this estimate, the twelve Balkan communities of those lists would comprise some 900 to 1,000 families. There were other communities, however, in the Peloponnesos, Epiros, Aetolia, Central Greece, and the islands of the Ionian and Aegean seas. There were a considerable number of these communities, even if their respective populations were small. Therefore a figure of some 3,000 families should account for the total Jewish population of the area, including those known or suspected.

58. Ibid., p. 241, noting a figure of 116 families living in Istanbul at the time of the conquest.

59. Ibid., p. 238, citing 42 *sürgün* families from Izdin (Lamia) and 38 *sürgün* families from Filibe (Philippopoli) in Istanbul in 1455.

These 3,000 families, or 15,000 Jews, represent an approximate (and perhaps minimum) population for the Balkan communities after the Black Plague.[60] Previous to the ravages of that population-destroying disease, we may assume a figure two to three times as large—approximately 35,000 to 40,000 Jews. This latter figure is about 50 to 75 percent of the Jewish population extrapolated from the report of Benjamin of Tudela and the general situation in the twelfth century.[61]

To sum up, we may approximate the Jewish population in the capital as 500 families before 1350 and 250 after; and in the Balkan communities for the corresponding periods, 7,000 families and 3,000 families respectively. These rough estimates of the Romaniote population hold true until the generation of the conquest.[62] The deportations of Mehmet II centralized the dwindled Jewish population in the capital. Then, at the end of the fifteenth century, waves of Sephardi immigrants began to flood the Balkans, with inevitable results on the communal and demographic nature of the Jewries there.

60. The number of identifiable communities in Anatolia with Jewish populations is small and, therefore, should not change by much our estimates for the Balkan and island communities; see above, chap. 2, "Anatolia" and "Lessons of Settlement." For the earlier period, cf. Claude Cahan, *Pre-Ottoman Turkey* (London, 1968), pp. 214f. His comments on the Jewish population of Anatolia would have benefited from a review of the literature.

61. Baron (*SRHJ*, III, 329, note 29) estimates some 100,000 Jews in the Empire of the Komnenoi; Ankori (*Karaites*, pp. 156ff and esp. 159) calculates 85,000. Andreades had more conservatively suggested a figure of 15,000, while Starr, even more cautiously, gave a total of 12,000. See Ankori's critique (*loc. cit.*) and further discussion by Baron (*SRHJ*, XVII, 300ff, note 4).

62. Fluctuations, of course, should be taken into account. An example of the pressures of war upon Jewish settlements can be seen in the remarks of a Spanish scribe in Greece in the early fifteenth century: ראינו חרבן ישראל ספרד וקטלונייא ותוגרמה וצרפת, ושמענו גזירות קשות ורעות על ישראל הנשארים בכל מקום שהם, וראינו המלחמות בכל מלכיות אדום ויון וישמעאל ואפי׳ בימים שהתחילו בעולם בשנת אל קֹנֹאֹ, ועד היום שהעתקנו הספר הזה בחדש תשרי שנת הֹקֹעֹוֹ (translated in document 118).

AFTERWORD

A FIRST AND lasting impression of Byzantine Jewish history is the paucity of sources. Scattered fragments of Hebrew letters, a few notices in the general literature, a handful of laws, and the like constitute the bulk of available historical material. Nor do the treatises produced by the Christian clerics of the period—and these may be more theological exercises, with no reference to the actual situation—contribute much information. Compared to the source material for the two other major medieval Jewries, Islamic and Ashkenazi, this paucity is at first glance astonishing. Why, we may ask—without even a hint of a sufficient answer—is there hardly a reference to Jews in the extant documentary or literary records of the sophisticated and bureaucratic Byzantine state?

Jews, as we have shown, were scattered throughout the empire. Yet without the report of Benjamin of Tudela, unique even for the general source material of Byzantium, we would have little idea of the diffusion of Jewish settlements and their demography during the twelfth century. Why is it, we may add to our above question, that hardly any documentary material has survived from the indigenous Jewish communities of the area, while a Jewish literature, sufficient to indicate the solid base of Rabbanite and Karaite scholarship, their intellectual interests, and a vivid poetic tradition, both liturgical and secular, is extant?

The question of sources, then, is crucial to an understanding of the fate of Byzantine Jewry. History, after all, is as much a record of the past as a preservation of the past for the varied needs of a given generation. The records of the past which we use for its reconstruction are those which have survived, some by accident, some by design. The *Chronicle of Aḥimaʿaz,* for example, accidentally preserved in a single manuscript in the archive of a Spanish church, contains the framework of a south Italian Jew's poetic reminiscences of his family genealogy and some biographical notes on certain outstanding individuals. It constitutes the bulk of our knowledge of south Italian Jewry from the eighth to the eleventh centuries. The example is not unique, especially when applied to the Romaniote communities of the Greek mainland.

The different fates of Rabbanite and Karaite scholarship compound the problem of source material. The Romaniote rabbinic scholarship fell into disuse during the Ottoman period through a process of attrition. As more and more Romaniote Jews assimilated to the new and vigorous Sephardi tradition, with its rich, scholarly resources, less and less of the native Greek scholarship was found to be applicable to the new social and economic situation. Thus many texts simply disappeared, no longer deemed worthy to be copied or worth the expense of printing, with the rare exception of those treatises adopted for intellectual purposes by the Ashkenazi scholars of Eastern Europe (even their Byzantine origin was forgotten) or those that survived as family heirlooms. All mainland communal archives from the Byzantine period have disappeared. The bulk of the grave inscriptions has been recycled as building materials, and only a handful have been recovered.

This should serve as a warning, to initiate a program to recover those extant inscriptions from the Ottoman period. The fate of Jewish libraries, manuscripts, and graveyards in twentieth-century Greece provides a stark analogue to the likely fate of Jewish archival material from all periods of Byzantine history. On the other hand, the Byzantine Karaite literature, which had been forged in the eleventh and twelfth centuries and benefited from Romaniote and Sephardi training in the fifteenth, became the intellectual and legal basis for later Ottoman and East European Karaite communities. The latter consciously preserved this socio-religious heritage precisely as a guide for their subsequent diasporic experience.

If a people, then, defines its past by virtue of the material it preserves (the comments of Judah ibn Moskoni on the value of the *Sepher Josippon* are indicative of this process), we may conclude that Byzantine Jewry, as it slowly lost its creative abilities during the Ottoman period, of necessity codified its religious and liturgical literature in order to preserve an autonomous and indigenous identity within the larger sea of Sephardi traditions.

The state of the manuscripts does not allow for a fuller exposition of this process. Further research is necessary before enough material is available to reconstruct the entire range of its intellectual symbiosis with its host society and with its coreligionists—at least insofar as the surviving manuscripts allow. In short, we may say that Byzantine Jewry has suffered from the vicissitudes of both history and historiography.

The late thirteenth century introduced a new trend in Byzantine Jewish history which carried into the succeeding Ottoman period. This new trend reversed many of the vicissitudes familiar to students of the Byzantine Jewish experience. The Palaeologan attitude was based, to be sure, on self-seeking motives, as was the later Ottoman attitude, for it entailed the protection of one of the last sources of revenue still in imperial hands. During the same period, Jewish settlements spread throughout the Balkans. Some, of course, continued in areas where Jews had long been settled, but new centers arose in the new political and military centers of latter-day Byzantium. Favorable attitudes, too, on the part of Bulgarian and Ottoman rulers, invited the establishment of Jewish communities in areas no longer under Byzantine control and allowed for further dispersion during the subsequent Ottoman period, after that government had "pacified" much of the Balkans. The later settlements followed the pioneering efforts of late Byzantine Jewish entrepreneurs.

The imperial protection of Jews and the spread of their settlements throughout the empire anticipated the story of the Jews under the Ottomans, for the Sephardi Jews in the sixteenth-century Balkans inherited and improved the position of Romaniote Jewry in the late thirteenth to fifteenth centuries. When the exiles arrived from Spain and Portugal, they found a Romaniote Jewry, mainly in Constantinople, united under a chief rabbi, with an established network of congregations, institutions, and privileges, and a flourishing intellectual life.

The unity the Romaniote Jews in Constantinople enjoyed through the first two generations under Ottoman control was shattered early in the reign of Suleiman I. With the death of Elijah Mizraḥi, the second Romaniote chief rabbi, the social and cultural dissensions between the established Romaniote communities and the immigrant Sephardim finally boiled over and prevented the election of a candidate with universal appeal and authority. The chief rabbi gradually declined to the status of mere head of Constantinopolitan Jewry, while local rabbis of high renown exercised communal autonomy, with the option of appeal to Constantinople available (if seldom invoked).

This political victory of the immigrants was matched a few years later by a cultural one. By midcentury, the Sephardi culture had become the dominant influence in the development of Ottoman Jewry. In the succeeding generations, only small islands of Romaniote Jews were to be found in a sea of Sephardi congregations. Anatolia had been depopulated of its Romaniote communities by Mehmet II, along with Thrace, Macedonia, and Thessaly. The latter areas were repopulated by Sephardi Jews, especially Thessalonica, which became known as the "Jewish metropolis" (*ʿir ve-ʾem bi-Yisrael*). Recent studies have shown that Crete remained the main stronghold of Romaniote identity, never to be fully submerged by the Sephardim. Epiros, too, with its capital of Ioannina, remained a Romaniote center until the twentieth century.

The survival of a Byzantine Jewish tradition in the remoter areas of the Greek-speaking provinces of the Ottoman Empire until recent times is another indication of the acculturative process successfully adopted by the Jewish diaspora. It also explains the lack of impact made by this Jewry during the long centuries that Greece endured under Ottoman domination. Only in the nineteenth century, with the wakening of the Greek spirit, were the Jews of these areas again able to take part in a renaissance of spiritual and intellectual interests that were to have their impact on contemporary Jewry. We have only to cite the renewal of a Jewish literature, written in Greek, and the positive attraction of Zionism to the Greek-speaking Jewish communities well into the twentieth century. The destruction of Greek Jewry by the Germans during World War II cut this renaissance short. Yet, in a sharply reduced way, it continues today in Greece, Israel, and the United States.

II

DOCUMENTS AND EXCURSUSES

INTRODUCTION TO SOURCES

ANY INVESTIGATION into Byzantine Jewish history has to overcome a number of research problems, the most important of which involves the Hebrew sources. Much of the literary material for the period after the Fourth Crusade, for example, is still in manuscript; for the most part, however, it has been described in a myriad of published (but not indexed) catalogues of Hebrew manuscripts. An ongoing project, involving the systematic study of all dated Hebrew manuscripts until 1540, is under way at the Hebrew Palaeography Project of the Israel Academy of Sciences and Humanities. This project, once completed, may eventually allow for identification and scientific study of those undated manuscripts from the same period. The relative weight of the Byzantine material within the legacy of medieval Jewry should then become more apparent.

On the other hand, documentary and other material pertaining to the Byzantine orbit, recovered from the Cairo Geniza, has yet to be systematically studied. The occasional gems published by various researchers only indicate the necessity for continued research.

Finally, the published material includes letters, commentaries on the Bible and rabbinic tractates, mystical works, and poetry.

Research into each of these areas demands specialized training; yet an overall assessment of the contributions of this Jewry can be perceived only after such preliminary investigations have been carried out.

The majority of non-Jewish sources bearing on the subject have been made available by the past few generations of Byzantine scholars. Regesta of diplomatic texts, as well as bibliographies of various authors and subjects, have greatly aided the task of the researcher. Yet there are countless documents still in the archives of Venice, Sicily, Dubrovnik, and other late-medieval chancellories which could conceivably shed enormous light on the activities of Jews in former territories of the empire. The well-studied Catalan archives, however, are notoriously silent on the situation of Jews in their areas of Greece in the fourteenth century.

A general difficulty has been the lack of secondary studies on our subject. Therefore the present work has, perforce, been more descriptive of the sources than interpretive. A number of areas for further research have been indicated in part I of this study.

The source material in the present study can be divided into two categories. The first consists of documentary material, that is, the reports and deliberations of councilors, ambassadors, and factors; monastic and urban charters, communal statutes (*takkanoth*); maps, epitaphs, colophons, and codes of law. The second can be classed as literary sources. These are of Christian or Jewish authorship and include chronicles, theological tracts, lives of saints, sermons, letters, mystical treatises, biblical commentaries, responsa, and travelogues.

Diplomatic texts shed considerable light on immediate political, social, and economic problems between different powers or between local and imperial authorities. The massive register of Franz Dölger is now complete, enabling the investigator to survey the length and breadth of the Byzantine world in search of diplomatic texts that bear on the subject of his research. For the most part, the texts that deal with Byzantine-Jewish history are contained in the collections of Sathas, Tafel-Thomas, Thiriet, Thomas, Iorga, Thalloczy *et al.*, Miklosich-Miller, and Soloviev-Mošin (see bibliography). These collections contain materials on the Jews in the Venetian colonies in Romania (and elsewhere) and on the questions of Jewish taxes and their status in the Palaeologan period. A caveat regarding these collections involves occasional mistakes in the transcription, dating, or summarizing of the texts. However, for the purposes of the present study, these editions should suffice. It is hoped that a systematic combing of the archives will uncover sufficient new material to justify a more expanded treatment of the whole subject of Byzantine Jewry.

A few contemporary maps are extant, for example, copies from Buondelmonti's *Liber Insularum Archipelagi,* and some of these throw light on the location of the main Jewish Quarter of Constantinople. No epitaphs have as yet been published from imperial lands; however, contemporary stones exist, namely, in Euboea and Thebes, and possibly in Nicaea. Colophons, too, are important for the history and transmission of the text they append, and often contain incidental information of historical interest. A number of colophons, translated below, offer the only notice of Jewish settlements in their respective cities.

The Greek legal codes were produced during the fourteenth century. The *Syntagma* of Matthew Blastares, written in 1335, contains both secular and ecclesiastical rulings in alphabetical order. The *Hexabiblion* of George Armenopoulos, written in 1345, is a compendium of civil and criminal law extracted from earlier Byzantine codes. Both are important for the study of Byzantine society from the thirteenth to fifteenth centuries. However, as is often the case with Byzantine law codes, much material is included which is out of date for the period of the code. Several Karaite law codes were produced in Constantinople during this period, and they shed considerable and valuable light on developments within that branch of the Jewish population during the Palaeologan period.

The literary texts most frequently used in historical studies are chronicles and histories. Since the Palaeologan period is well represented by these texts, it is all the more curious that they contain so little information on Jews in the empire. The chronicle of George Phrantzes contains most of the notices on Jews to be gained from the Late Byzantine historians; however, most of its references to Jews come from the sixteenth-century additions to the chronicle by Makarios Melissenos and, for this reason, do not apply to the Byzantine period. The two references to Jews by Ducas are insulting asides rather than sources for the history of the Jews. They suggest that Ducas was not too fond of Jews.

There is one Hebrew chronicle from the mid-sixteenth century which sheds some light on the situation in Constantinople in the wake of the Ottoman conquest. The *Seder Eliyahu Zuta* of Elijah Kapsali is now available in a new edition by Aryeh Shmuelevich. The chronicle, however, must be used with caution, due to the messianic intentions of the author. Even so, it is a remarkable blend of history and folklore, both of which shed considerable light on the Jewish view of the conquest in 1453. Of interest as a possible source for Kapsali's review of early Ottoman history is a fragment of a Turkish chronicle, written in Hebrew characters and preserved in the Bodleian Library.[1]

The plethora of ecclesiastical material is not as helpful as one might expect—aside from that material which deals with specific contemporary problems. However, the number of anti-Jewish tracts, produced or copied during the period, is not insignificant. While containing little material of historical value, their very existence attests to the zeal of the monks, for whom the Latin, Muslim, and Armenian threats to Orthodoxy had not completely supplanted the traditional *bête noire* of the church. These tracts, however, pose several questions with regard to their use. If they are in dialogue form, did such a debate actually occur, or is the framework merely a literary device to reflect either contemporary opinion or the view of the author? If the tract is polemical, do its arguments represent contemporary theological questions, or are they a psychological attempt to strengthen the faith of the flock in the face of some new adversary? The very use of Jews as a foil in these circumstances says something for the nature of their role in traditional Christian thought.

For our purposes, the historical value of the hagiographa from this period is minimal, especially if compared with the wealth of social and economic material in the earlier hagiography of the Macedonian period. A survey of the saints' lives from the thirteenth to the fifteenth centuries, listed in F. Halkin's *Bibliotheca Hagiographica Graeca,* has turned up no material on the Jews. Both the sermon and its secular counterpart, the panegyric, usually contain information on the contemporary scene. As historical sources, however, both suffer from the propensity of the preacher to exaggerate evils and of the panegyrist to misplace superlatives. In neither do we find references to Jews.

Contemporary letters, too, have long been recognized as valuable historical sources by students of Late Byzantine life. It was a time of intense literary activity (much of it preserved), paralleling the emerging Renaissance in the West, and the profusion of correspondence was but one manifestation of this trend. One major difficulty in this body of material is the

1. Cf. Neubauer, *Bodleian,* E2866. A brief description is available in Franz Babinger, "Eine altosmanische anonyme Chronik in hebräischer Umschrift," *Archiv Orientální,* IV (Prague, 1932), 109–11. The text has been edited and published, with a photocopy, by Ugo Marazzi, *Tevārīḫ-i Āl-i ʿOs̱mān: Cronaca anonima ottomana in trascrizione ebraica (dal manoscritto Heb. e 63 della Bodleian Library)* (Naples, 1980). A review and survey of contents, by M. A. Epstein, appears in *Turkish Studies Association Bulletin,* 5.2 (1981), 22–23.

affected style that prided itself on obfuscation and proliferation of rhetorical phrases. There are, unfortunately, no asides or allusions of value to Jews in this extensive literature, including those of Theodore Laskaris.

Hebrew letters offer the same difficulties. Sometimes deliberately obscure, often unconsciously so, they provide invaluable information on the Jews of our period. The letter of Jacob b. Elia, for example, is the only contemporary source for the thirteenth-century persecutions; the anonymous letter from Negroponte is a mine of information for early fourteenth-century Jewry; and the letter of Shemarya ha-Ikriti is one of our major sources for Romaniote intellectual life.

The study of mystical literature is now subject to an established methodology. Little material of historical value bearing on Byzantine Jewish life is as yet available, however. The few texts at our disposal provide some interesting information, in particular the careers of Abraham Abulafia and Shemarya ha-Ikriti. Also, they help to illumine the transmission of Spanish Kabbalah to the Balkans against the background of indigenous developments and contributions. On the other hand, the very existence of a Byzantine Jewish mystical literature should invite scholars to reassess its influence in the development of the better-known sixteenth-century Ottoman traditions.

Commentaries to biblical literature contain allusions, both hidden and explicit, to the commentators' own time. Unfortunately, only the introductions to two contemporary Rabbanite commentaries have been edited, those of Shemarya ha-Ikriti's commentary on the Bible and Judah ibn Moskoni's supercommentary to Ibn Ezra. The Karaite commentaries of this period have not been exhausted in the present study; the excerpts cited by Professor Ankori in his *Karaites* indicate the wealth of material available for the history of that sect.

Responsa are replies to questions of either ecclesiastical or rabbinic law, custom, and doctrine emanating from prominent religious leaders of Christians and Jews. Though not having the force of law in the Eastern church, nor among the Jews, these opinions on relative questions, whether social or intellectual, often established or confirmed trends and customs. Since the question of the extent of communal control among rabbis of the Byzantine Empire has yet to be resolved, we should note that the internal cohesion of the Romaniote communities was effected, in part, through voluntary allegiance to previous and contemporary rabbinic responsa. The responsa of only two rabbis, who were active during the period of our study, have been partly published. In the early thirteenth century, Isaiah of Trani exerted considerable influence on contemporary Ashkenazi scholars, as well as on his Romaniote correspondents. The published responsa of Moses Kapsali date from the beginning of the Ottoman period. A systematic study of his dicta would throw considerable light on the problems of Romaniote Jewry in the wake of the conquest of Constantinople. The rabbis of the sixteenth century had to deal with the changed and expanded conditions of an Ottoman environment. Their responsa are usually technical treatises, full of talmudic precedents and previous social practices. Among the latter, they occasionally cite Romaniote customs.

Takkanoth (= communal statutes) often had the force of law for the community to which they were addressed, and at times their influence extended over other communities. Unfortunately, there are no extant Rabbanite *takkanoth* from the Byzantine period, although there is every indication that they were promulgated (**90**). There are important Karaite *takkanoth,* on the other hand, that illustrate their internal developments during the fifteenth century. The surviving statutes of Candia, Italy, and a later one from Corfu do not necessarily illuminate the Byzantine scene.

A more stringent ordinance than the *takkanah* was the *ḥerem* or ban, the most famous of which was issued by Moses Kapsali, in the late fifteenth century, forbidding Rabbanite scholars to teach Karaites. Isaiah of Trani also was forced to issue a ban in his attempt to induce Romaniote women to frequent the *mikvah.* The voluntary nature of the Jewish community is clearly pointed up by the failure of the first ban; we do not know the results of Isaiah's interference in local custom.

Finally, the reports of travelers to and through Byzantium during the Palaeologan period must be considered. Their occasional asides, noting the existence of Jews in various towns and areas, are often our only knowledge of a Jewish community. Medieval travelers accepted uncritically such secondhand information, whether from local spokesmen or from other travel accounts. Moreover, the veracity and prejudices of the traveler himself must be checked, where possible, against other sources. Particularly noteworthy are the impartiality and accuracy of some of the descriptions presented below.

DOCUMENTS

[1] 1200

I . . . Anthony, Archibishop of Novgorod . . . went to Constantinople. First of all I worshipped at Hagia Sophia and kissed two slabs from the Holy Sepulcher of the Lord and the icon of the very Holy Virgin holding the Christ. A Jew had struck the neck of this Christ with a knife and it issued blood.

Anthony, Archbishop of Novgorod, "Le Livre de Pèlerin," in Mme. B. de Khitrowo, *Itinéraires Russes en Orient,* I, 87.

[2] 1200

. . . and the large golden platter destined for the divine service, which Olga of Russia had made with the tribute received by her at Constantinople. A small quarter of Constantinople is located on the side of Is Pigas (Ἔις Πηγάς), in the quarter of the Jews.[1] In the platter of Olga a precious stone is encrusted; on this stone the image of Christ is painted . . .

Anthony of Novgorod, "Le Livre de Pèlerin," in Khitrowo, *Itinéraires,* p. 88; translated in Starr, *JBE,* p. 240 no. 191; cf. Ankori, *Karaites,* p. 147, n. 236, and the same author's objections (pp. 145–46) to Starr's location of this quarter near the modern Cassim Pasha (p. 43). But see G. P. Majeska, "The Body of St. Theophano the Empress and the Convent of St. Constantine," *Byzantinoslavica,* XXXVIII (1977), 19 and note 37.

1. This sentence appears to have been placed in the middle of the description of Olga's platter by error. The description of Is Pegas begins on p. 107 of the Khitrowo edition. Cf. document 4. The quarter of Is Pegas is located in Pera.

1200 [3]

Here is a frightening and holy miracle: at Hagia Sophia, in the large altar behind the holy table is a cross of gold the height of two men decorated with precious stones and pearls. In front of it is hung a cross of gold, of one and a half cubits; three lamps of gold are attached to the three arms, and oil burns there, and the fourth arm touches the ground. These three lamps and the cross were elevated by the Holy Spirit higher than the great cross and let down quite sweetly without being extinguished. This miracle took place after matins, before the beginning of the Mass; the priests who were at the altar saw it; and all the people in the church, also having seen it, said with fear and joy: "God, in mercy, has visited us Christians, thanks to the prayers of the very Holy Virgin, of Hagia Sophia—the Divine Wisdom—of the Emperor Constantine and of his mother Helen. God wants to make us live now as in the reign of Constantine, and even better; *God will lead the accursed Jews to baptism, and they will live in holy union with Christians.* And men will not make war, save against those who will not want to receive baptism; and yet, whether they want to or not, God will oblige them to be baptized. There will be an abundance of good things on the earth; men will begin to live truly and in holy lives, and men will do no more evil things among themselves. The earth, by order from God, will bear its fruit of milk and honey in repayment for the good lives of Christians." God worked this miracle in the year 6708 during my life, in the month of May, the day of the Feast of the Emperor Constantine and his mother Helen, Sunday the 21st, in the reign of Alexius and the Patriarch John . . .

Anthony of Novgorod, "Le Livre de Pèlerin," in Khitrowo, *Itinéraires,* pp. 94–95; partially translated in Starr, *JBE,* p. 240 no. 192, based on the Slavic text and French translation of M. Ehrhard, "Le Livre du Pèlerin d'Antoine de Novgorod," *Romania,* LXIII (1932), 44–65. The italics in the text are mine. For this embassy in the reign of Emperor Alexios III Angelos (1195–1203) and Patriarch John X Kamateros (1198–1206), see Charles Brand, *Byzantium Confronts the West, 1180–1204,* p. 132 and bibliography cited.

1200 [4]

At Is Pigas is located the Greek Church of Saint Nicholas. Nearby lived Constantine, and he appeared to the emperor who ordered the patriarch to transport him into the city and to found a church and a monastery in his name. This is actually the church which is located near the Monastery of

Pantocrator. This Constantine was formerly a Jew and was baptized and instructed by Stephan the Younger. There is a church at Is Pigas bearing his name.

Anthony of Novgorod, "Le Livre de Pèlerin," in Khitrowo, *Itinéraires,* p. 108; see above, document 2, and Majeska, "Body of St. Theophano," pp. 19–21.

[5]

Ca. 1200–1250

You have written me about a little girl whose father engaged her and made the seven blessings for her according to the custom of Romania. But after some time there arose a spirit of rancor between the groom and his father-in-law over the little girl, and they both agreed upon a separation. The groom wrote a bill of divorcement to give to his father-in-law. Could the latter receive a divorce in behalf of his little daughter or not? It appears that after he made the seven blessings the matter went beyond his control even though the custom was still to bring her under the marriage canopy. Do the seven blessings constitute the key point and the marriage canopy an additional joy; or perhaps the marriage canopy is the key point! In other words, as long as she did not complete the marriage process under the canopy, her father was still [legally] responsible for her and thus could receive her bill of divorcement during her minority. And thus the seven blessings are the key point, and she has left the authority of her father. But then she would be [considered from the legal perspective as] an orphan even though her father were still alive for he would not be able to receive her bill of divorcement. And she would remain so until she could legally distinguish between a divorce and something else or until she were physically of legal age. This is a good question and well worth a close investigation!

It appears that because their custom is to make a marriage canopy after they had already made the seven blessings, that a woman is not joined to her husband with the seven blessings . . . and the fact that they made the seven blessings can only have been to permit her to him since he is [then] united to her . . . *and the whole custom of the Romaniote Jews as written above is the custom of (ancient) Judea,* that even though you unite and make the seven blessings you cannot do else but not allow him to enter her unlawfully, and that she definitely will not be his the moment she is a consummated woman—not until he pledges himself [through the marriage contract] to feed her and be worthy of her handicrafts and all other matters of matrimony. And even though the woman usually goes and lies with him in his house, he has not legally possessed her, nor has she been absolved from her father's authority . . . and all these cohabitations are the cohabitations of engagement and she does not leave the authority of her father until he hands her over to him in the marriage ceremony. . . .

Cambridge MS Add. 474, p. 59b; *Teshuvoth HaRID,* #47; quoted in Assaf, "Family Life," pp. 169–70; Krauss, *Studien,* p. 94; Starr, *Romania,* pp. 17–18. For the Palestinian custom, cf. *Ketuboth,* 7b; and in general M. A. Friedman, *Jewish Marriage in Palestine,* vol. I, passim.

Ca. 1200–1250 [5*]

Re a convert [to another religion] who informed a woman that her husband had died, let me inform you that his evidence is worthless and his word useless. . . . A convert is suspect of transgressing all of the sexual prohibitions in the Torah . . . (The word of a gentile can be accepted in such matters because he is not familiar with Jewish law and therefore would not maliciously misinform her so that she might remarry unlawfully) . . . Further you wrote that the brothers of the convert contradicted his testimony and said—we asked him and he told us that [the husband] was still alive. . . . Moreover, I was made aware that they had gone to Galipoli, sought out the convert, and asked him whether he were alive or not.

Teshuvoth HaRID, #57.

Ca. 1200–1250 [6]

The gist[1] of our words concerning what we heard about a lad from your community by the name of Elia who had a wife in Otranto and left her to go to Romania. This was some time ago. His wife sent an agent to Romania to obtain her *get.*[2] The agent could not wait until her husband Elia came to give him her *get,* so he sent a second agent to receive the *get.* Elia came to Dyrrachium and gave the *get* to the second agent whom the first agent appointed. The *get* did not reach the first agent nor to the hand of the woman with the testimony of the community of Dyrrachium,[3] and on the basis of this testimony you have banished the woman and permitted him to marry.

Responsum of R. Isaiah of Trani in Codex Warsaw, no. 13; quoted in H. Gross, "Jesaya b. Mali da Trani," *ZHB*, XIII (1909), 52.

1. *Toref*, literally "the last line." In a letter of divorce, it is the one that contains the names of the parties involved, and especially the phrase "behold you are permitted [to marry] any man." By extension, it refers to that passage in a document which makes it binding. See M. Jastrow, *A Dictionary of the Targumin* . . . sub *toref*.

2. A bill of divorcement.

3. Gross reads דורבי from the Warsaw Codex. See below, 13n.

[7] Ca. 1200–1250

This is my abandoned daughter. She was nine months old when her father died. I nursed her and raised her until she was four years old and married her to this Elia her husband. Less than a year later he left her and went to Romania leaving her a "deserted wife" for more than eight years.

Responsum of R. Isaiah of Trani in Codex Warsaw, 28b, quoted in Assaf, "Family Life," p. 99, note 2. There he presents another case of child marriage and abandonment. See above (6), and Starr, *Romania*, p. 19. Cf. *Teshuvoth HaRID*, #80.

[8] Ca. 1200–1250

Now my lord, like a messenger of the Lord, knows that this generation is lawless and his staff will show him oracles.[1] Regarding this subject, as R. Hillel (may his righteous memory be for a blessing!) wrote in his commentary on Sifra that "drawing water [for a ritual bath] is a rabbinical as opposed to a biblical injunction"[2] and this is the custom of all the communities of Romania. Nor is there a single community in which they immerse themselves (in a ritual bath) save in the stench of the bathhouses while, at the same time, they are menstruating.[3] When I was among them, I learned that not one of the ladies took a ritual bath.[4] A man from Crete, a scholar and a man of feeling, married a woman there (i.e., some mainland Romaniote community), and got his wife into the habit of taking the [required] ritual bath; but the ladies of the community united against her saying that this was not the custom. And because she was acting contrary to local practice, they acted towards her as did the ladies of Sodom toward Lot's wife. And when I heard this I became furious at them and rebuked them with shame and abuse exceedingly. . . . They babbled against me that 'drawing water' is only a rabbinical injunction as R. Hillel explained in his commentary on Sifra. Let it be known to them that they are in error and should not so sin. And I emphasized this until they accepted that this was actually a biblical injunction. Then they all gathered together in the central synagogue (*bi-keneset ha-gedolah*); and all the women too assembled in the courtyard of the synagogue; and they, the men and the women, agreed, under penalty of anathema, that they would not continue to practice such a wrong.

And I was in other communities;[5] they too were not willing to accept what I preached nor could I prevent them. And this ban proliferated, but this sin was permitted in all the communities of Romania. Therefore it is not right for any sage to dispute such matters. And all of the supporting evidence that you cited from the Talmud that supports such leniency, I will deal with these in a more extended fashion in a book,[6] and prove that such evidence cannot support the contention that one can reject the principle of "drawing water" on the grounds that it is a rabbinical injunction.[7]

Responsum of R. Isaiah of Trani, Camb. MS 474, 118b; quoted in Schechter, "Notes," pp. 99–100; quoted in Assaf, "Family Life," p. 101; edited in *Teshuvoth HaRID,* #62 (end); cf. Starr, *Romania,* p. 19. On R. Hillel, cf. E. E. Urbach, *Ba'ale Ha-Tosaphot* (The Tosaphists) (Jerusalem, 1968), pp. 260f. For a biography of Isaiah of Trani, cf. R. Wertheimer's introduction to his edition of *Teshuvoth HaRID*.

1. Hosea 4:12
2. Cf. *Talmud Yerushalmi, 'Orlah* II, 62a, and *Talmud Bab̲li, Baba Bathra,* 66a.
3. Cf. *Teshuvoth HaRID,* responsum 73.
4. It seems that the public baths of Byzantium were viewed by the local Jewry as fulfilling the requirements of the ritual bath. Ecclesiastical canons forbade Christians to bathe with Jews. Clearly, these were not enforced. See below, note 7.
5. This visit to Greece may have taken place during his trip to Israel, ca. 1216.
6. Cf. his commentary on Sifra and also his *Sepher ha-Makhri'a.*
7. The problem recurs in a number of his responsa, e.g., 1, 15, 22, 27. The title "rabbana," found in responsum 62, was common in the Byzantine orbit; his correspondent was well respected by Isaiah, viz., הדור יתום שאתה שרוי בתוכו. Cf. also his remarks about Rabbana Isaac and the Kohanim from Romania (ibid.). The principle was whether a *mikvah* could be filled by hand, i.e., by drawing water, or whether the water had to flow in, under its own pressure, from a constantly replenishing source such as a river or reservoir. By claiming that the prohibition against "drawing water" was a rabbinical injunction and therefore not absolutely binding on the Jews, Hillel implicitly sanctioned the use of the public baths for the performance of the rituals attending the *mikvah.* His interpretation was no doubt based upon long-standing local custom which contradicted the developing strictures among Ashkenazi Jewry as represented by the *Ḥasidei Ashkenaz.*

[9] Ca. 1200–1250

And what you wrote me about a thing which regularly occurs in Romania[1] that at the time of engagement they unite the engaged girl with the husband by means of the seven blessings. For a long time they have been accustomed to practice great rejoicings and call them *'istefanomata*[2] and this is understood by them to be the essential point of the festivity. There are some sages of the communities who teach that one must mention the "name" and the "kingdom" in the blessings as if one had never united; and there are others who forbid it and say "Blessed is He that all was created for His glory, Blessed is the creator of man."

Responsum of R. Isaiah of Trani, Camb. MS 474, 63b; quoted in Schechter, "Notes," p. 99; quoted in Assaf, "Family Life," pp. 105–6; cf. Starr, *Romania,* p. 18. *Teshuvoth HaRID,* #37; see also #30.

1. Ms. has ROM′ at the end of the line, which Schechter read as "Roma," but the next line begins with the word written in full, "Romania." It is common in Hebrew mss. for the scribe to begin a word toward the end of a line in order to complete the margin and then to write the entire word at the beginning of the next line. For another instance where the reading is RO′ at the end of the line and Romania in full on the following line, cf. ms. fol. 80b.

2. The Greek word *eisstefanomata,* which survives as *stefanoma*; cf. Assaf, p. 106, note 40. These are the crowns worn by the bride and groom at an Orthodox wedding.

[10] Ca. 1200–1250

Question: A arranged a marriage with a woman through agents; some time elapsed before she was appeased and wished to marry him. So A invited the whole congregation to the marriage according to their custom to gather there and eat some sweets. But A was ignorant and did not know the formula to be uttered when he was to give the ring to his wife: "Behold you are sanctified unto me." B was present and he knew Hebrew, so A prevailed upon B to utter the formula for him "Behold you are sanctified unto me" at the right time and thus they did. And after the woman received her sanctification the congregation went out to another house to eat some sweets and A remained inside with his bride. B yelled out to the crowd, "Take A out of there because she is my wife. Because when I said 'Behold you are sanctified unto me' I said it for myself." The congregation was dumbfounded, but they did not have the capability to help A because B was powerful; and he held on to the woman for a long time until he sired sons. . . .

Answer: I have no compassion in this affair. How could the sainted sages of the communities of Romania who have wisdom and understanding be silent about this . . . that they did not heap upon him oaths and curses and a ban and excommunication and separate him from the congregation of Israel, and to inform all the communities of Yeshurun to refuse to help him until they hear that this wickedness is gone from his house, and have nothing to do with him, and to advertise to his sons that they are bastards. . . . And I promise in the name of the Lord that you will not have peace and quiet until you see this letter of mine and send it to all the Jews in the communities of Romania. . . . And let it be done with a generous spirit, for it is up to you to extirpate this abomination from Israel.

Responsum of R. Isaiah of Trani, Camb. MS Add. 474, 44; quoted in Assaf, "Family Life," p. 102; cf. Starr, *Romania,* pp. 17–18; *Teshuvoth HaRID,* #22. See Friedman, *Jewish Marriage in Palestine,* I, 1, citing an opposing opinion to R. Isaiah.

Ca. 1200–1250 [11]

And according to what you wrote me that A went to pay B some money, but B was not satisfied until he had hailed A before the Gentiles who beat him and, under pressure, B sent away this woman . . . I have no compassion in this affair. How could the holy communities of Romania be silent in this, among whom are wisdom and understanding. And they have the power, praise be to God to implement the deeper points of the halakha and to blow up a raging tempest from which will go forth teaching unto all Israel . . . Behold I promise you in the name of God that you will not have peace or quiet until you see this letter and send it to all the Jews in the congregations of Romania whose house is appropriate for them.

Responsum of R. Isaiah of Trani, Camb. MS Add. 474, 46b; quoted in Schechter, "Notes," p. 100. *Teshuvoth HaRID,* #22; cf. Resp. #79 for his comments on legality of Gentile pressure in these matters.

1203 [12]

So they lodged that night before the tower (of Galata) and in the Jewry that is called Stenon, where there was a good city, and very rich.

Geoffroi de Villehardouin, Conquête de Constantinople, avec la continuation de Henri de Valenciennes, Texte original, accompagné d'une traduction, ed. M.

Natalis de Wailly, p. 88; translated by F. T. Marzials, *Memoirs of the Crusades by Villehardouin and De Joinville,* p. 38; text quoted in Bratianu, *Recherches sur le commerce génois dans la mer noire au XIIIe siècle,* p. 89; translated in Starr, *JBE,* p. 242, no. 196, and comments there; cited in Ankori, *Karaites,* p. 147, note 237, and p. 148 with futher comments on the Stenon.

And they burnt Pera, which is a suburb of the city of Constantinople, where the Jews were abiding.

J. J. de Smet, *Recueil des Chroniques de Flandre,* I, 113; texts and discussion in Rodolphe Guilland, "La chaine de la Corne d'or," *EEBS,* 25: 88–120; reprinted in Guilland, *Etudes Byzantines,* pp. 263–97; cited in Jacoby, "Quartiers juifs," p. 188, note 4, along with the only two other Latin sources that parallel the *l'Estoire d'Eracles* translated above: "(les Croisés) boterent le fue en la ville des juifs" and the *Chronique d'Ernoul,* "li Juis manoient devant qu'il fussent ars."

[13] 1204

A bill of divorcement from the village of Goritzia which was written and dated in the community of Dyrrachium and sent to Isaiah of Trani for his opinion regarding its validity.

H. Gross, "Jesaya b. Mali da Trani," *ZHB,* XIII (1909), 51; Schechter, "Notes," p. 97; *Teshuvoth HaRID,* responsum #23; cf. Starr, *Romania,* pp. 22, note 4, and 81.

Gross transcribed the name of the village from (the no longer extant) Codex Warsaw, no. 53, as גורצאנוס, and from the Codex Cambridge as גורציטש; Schechter, working with only the Cambridge ms. (Add. 474, 49b), transcribed the name as גוריצאיטש; Wertheimer transcribed the two variant spellings in the Cambridge ms. as גוריציאנו and גורציאנוש.

The name of the city was transcribed by Gross as דורבי; the Cambridge ms. was read by Gross, Schechter, and Wertheimer as דורכי. Starr rightly saw this as the Hebrew form of Dyrrachium.

[14] 1207

The book *Sefer ʿAdat Devorim* from the commentary of R. Joseph the Constantinopolitan who gathered and collected the opinions of the teachers (*deʿoth ha-melammedim*)[1] and added even from the strength of his wisdom . . . may this sage and wise one who enlightens the others (*ha-maskil*)[1] find mercy as well as all the teaching *maskilim* who study it and teach laws to the Jews . . . ; and it was completed by my hand Judah b. Jacob on this day, Tuesday, the 20th of Sivan,[2] in the year 4967 of the

Creation, 1611 years after the destruction of the 1st Temple, 1121 years after the destruction of the 2nd Temple, and the 8th year of the lunar cycle 262[3] according to the reckoning and calculation that we use here . . . and it was completed by my hand in this city GaGRA.[4]

Leningrad, Firkovitz Collection II, #161; HPP Y378; films and photostats available in the Institute for Microfilms of Hebrew Manuscripts at the Jewish National and University Library, Hebrew University of Jerusalem; colophon partially published by Mann, *Texts and Studies,* II, 291, note 13; quoted by Ankori, *Karaites,* p. 126, note 142; comments and bibliography in Starr, *JBE,* pp. 240–41, no. 193; these are superseded by Ankori, *Karaites,* pp. 125–28 and notes 138ff. Starr dated Joseph the Constantinopolitan ca. 1200. It is not known whether Joseph was a Karaite or a Rabbanite Jew; both Mann and Ankori identify the scribe as a Karaite; cf. Ankori, *Karaites,* p. 125, note 139. In the following year the same scribe copied the *Me'or 'Enai'im,* responsa of that tenth-century Babylonian scholar who was secretary to Ḥasdai ibn Shaprut in Cordova, i.e., Dunash ibn Labrat. In this colophon the scribe calls himself Judah b. Jacob b. Judah; MS Leningrad, Firkovitz Collection I, #132; HPP Y885.

1. On these Karaite terms, cf. Ankori, *Karaites,* index, s.v. *da'at,* teachers, *maskil.*

2. Poznanski observed that the 20th of Sivan could not fall on a Tuesday, according to the Rabbanite calendar. This observation was noted by Ankori (pp. 125–26, n. 140), who explains that this date reflects use of a Karaite calendar. See following note.

3. The scribe is 183 years off in his first calculation; 18 years off in the second; while the last date corresponds to the lunar cycle 261. These "errors" of course may stem from his sources. For example, Isaiah of Trani, who relied (*inter alia*) on the *Sefer Josippon,* counts 490 years from the destruction of the 1st Temple to the destruction of the 2nd. Cf. his commentary on Daniel 9:24, ed. A. J. Wertheimer, III, 225.

4. Ankori, *Karaites,* pp. 125–28, on philological and methodological grounds refutes the identification of GaGRA as Gagry on the eastern shore of the Black Sea. Instead, he successfully identifies it with GaNGRA (= Germanicopolis) in Paphlagonia, which was linked by road with the centers of Nicomedia, Amasia, and Ancyra.

1212

[15]

Commentary on Sifra [by Hillel b. Eliakim] completed through the power of the awesome and revered Lord on 23 Tammuz in the year 4972 of the Creation according to the reckoning that is counted among us here NO AMON by my hand, Yeḥiel b. Rab. Eliakim. May the Lord give us strength and might to meditate in it and in his holy Torah for the sake of our future well-being.

Frankfurt, Universitätsbibliothek, MS Heb. 4°2; cf. Rabinowitz, *Ohel Abraham,* #97; HPP G187.

The similarity between the name of the scribe and the author suggests that they may have been related, even brothers. Codicologic examination of the manuscript shows that the physical codex was produced in Byzantium, but according to the colophon the scribe finished his work in Alexandria (= No Amon). A Geniza fragment (Cambridge T-S 12.62) identifies Yeḥiel b. Eliakim as being in Fustat in 1214. Thus we have another example of a Byzantine scribe who plied his trade in Egypt; cf. Mann, *Texts and Studies,* I, 374f, and comments by Ankori, *Karaites,* p. 419, note 173, and literature cited there.

The manuscript, in a deteriorated state, found its way into the hands of a Greek scribe, Shabbetai b. Abraham Poto, in 1520. He may have been the grandson of the scribe and commentator Shabbetai Poto of Ioannina.

[16] Ca. 1218

a) I was staying at Thebes, leading a life of voluptuous delight in that resort, attired in a gay tunic made from a mantle of lilies. Now there came a day when I was sitting with beloved companions, sons of noblemen, solacing ourselves with loves, delighting ourselves with sweet songs.

b) I have also indeed seen the communities of the East where the glory of the Lord shone, and the communities of France and Germany and Rifat; and the communities of Persia and Meshech and Tiras; and the communities of Byzantium who dwell between Dishon and Alvan. For there is no science which they did not inherit; nor is there a good quality which they did not conquer, save only the land of poetry. They beheld it from afar; but they did not go into it. They imagined that they had learned the art of rhyming, and they thought that they understood it. However, poetry was far from them and did not come near to them. It is as far from them as the East is from the West. Their soul journeys about its land and about its habitation; but it does not enter into it. For from afar it beholds the land; but thither it does not come. And if you should ask them, they will tell you that there are no poets like them; and that there is no poetry like their poetry. But no man sees his own defect; and no man sees his own guilt.

c) Now Poetry has Seven Rules, important and wonderful, whereby a poem becomes sweet and pleasant; . . . The first rule is that the poet must clear the words of his poems of all dross, and remove every discordant word from his text; lest he be like the Byzantine poets who fill their poems with foreign words along with splendid ones. They mingle flowers with thorns, pearls with pebbles, and mother-of-pearl with thistles. Therefore all their poems are bizarre, and the language weak, and the expressions perverted.

d) Likewise the communities of Byzantium have all of them men of intelligence and culture, of knowledge and discernment, of uprightness and integrity, and of every lovely virtue. But their poetry is despicable, heavy as stones of burden. Like a useless vine or like a leafy tree without blossoms, without taste or fragrance. Occasionally, one is exceptional, one whose intellect God has aroused, such as Michael bar Kaleb, of the city of Thebes. For there is a bit of charm about his poems, since in his youth he went to Spain and learned from them. And likewise, R. Moses bar Ḥiyya, and R. Moses ben Abtalyon, whose poetry is superior to his contemporaries.

e) Truly, all the men of the East are haughty;
In contrast, scholars of the time are in decline;
The hearts of all the sages of France and Byzantium
Eagerly occupy themselves with Jewish lore.
They have taken for themselves all wisdom and
understanding;
But poetry they have left to the Jews of Spain.

The editio princeps of the *Tahkemoni* was printed at Constantinople in 1578; a vocalized version was published by Y. Toporovsky, *Rabbi Yehudah al-Ḥarizi, Tahkemoni* (Tel Aviv, 1952); the most recent edition of chapter 18 is that of Ḥayyim Schirmann, with vocalization and notes, in his *ha-Shirah ha-ʿivrit bi-Sefarad u-be-Provence* (Hebrew poetry in Spain and the Provence), book 2, part 1, pp. 131–51. The translation from the sixth gate, used above for (a), is from *The Tahkemoni of Judah al-Harizi,* an English rendition by Victor E. Reichert, I, 117; the translations b–e are from Victor E. Reichert, "The Eighteenth Gate of Judah al-Harizi's Tahkemoni," offprint from *Central Conference of American Rabbis Journal* (October 1970), pp. 31, 32, 34, 39. (I should like to thank Rabbi Reichert for supplying me a copy of his translation.) See also Baron, *SRHJ,* VII, 184–87 and 307–8 (notes).

a) Editio princeps has TRBẒ. It is not absolutely certain whether the תֵּבֵץ (cf. Judges 9:50) mentioned here in Gate Six refers to a visit in Boeotian Thebes.

b) Dishon and Alvan are mentioned in Genesis 36:21, 23, 25, 26, 30; otherwise they are unidentified.

d) Editio princeps has TBẒ for Thebes; cf. Starr, *JBE,* p. 60. We have more than twenty *piyyutim* of the second-named author. Schirmann knew of the other two only from this mention of al-Ḥarizi. One of Moses bar Ḥiyya's poems has been recently edited by Leon J. Weinberger (*HUCA,* XXXIX [1968], Hebrew section, pp. 41–44). Weinberger includes another *piyyut* in his article which he suggests may have been written by Michael bar Kaleb (pp. 52–54). Both of these have been reproduced in his *Anthology,* #8 and #9.

[17] Ca. 1220–1223

Nikolaos of Otranto (Hydruntum) "Discourse Against the Jews" who had debated with him often and in many places concerning the holy . . . trinity and our Savior and Lord Jesus Christ . . . still yet about the Sabbath and circumcision and the holy icons; and moreover simply about food according to the customs of observant Jews until the time of the Second Coming.

Text unedited in Cod. Paris 1255, fol. 1–102. A description of the seven dialexes is available in Johannes M. Hoech and Raimund J. Loenertz, *Nikolaos-Nektarios von Otranto Abt von Casole: Beiträge zur Geschichte der Ost–Westlichen Beziehungen unter Innocenz III. und Frederich II.*, pp. 82–88; Krumbacher, *Geschichte der Byz. Literatur,* p. 770; Beck, *Kirche,* p. 670.

[18] Ca. 1220–1234

Question: Are the Armenians, who live in many cities, permitted to establish churches with every security: must they be prevented or can they build them as they wish?

Answer: From the beginning people of different languages and religions were permitted to live in Christian lands and cities, namely Jews, Armenians, Ismaelites, Agarenes and others such as these, except that they do not mix with the Christians, but rather live separately. For this reason places have been designated for these according to ethnic group, either within the city or without, so that they may be restricted to these and not extend their dwellings beyond them. I believe this was contrived by earlier rulers for three reasons. First, they should be separated in a narrow and designated place for their dwelling . . . because of the heresy of each. The other (reason), too, (that) little by little on account of their frequent association with Christians, they might be converted; if, indeed, not all, at least some, as many as salvation favored. And third, that those, the fruits of whose labor is needed for livelihood, be brought back. Hence, the Armenians, as long as they build a church in a place wherein they are enclosed and practice [therein] their heretical things, they may stay without being abused. In like manner Jews and Ismaelites are permitted to live in Christian cities. But if they exceed the limits of the boundary for their neighborhood, not only must they be prevented, but even their buildings, no matter what type, must be razed. They lost utterly long ago the freedom and license of such a sort.

Responsum of Demetrius Khomatianos, archbishop of Ochrida, to Constantine Cabasilas, metropolitan of Dyrrachium, in *MPG* 119, col. 977; Starr, *Romania,* pp. 81–83; P. Charanis, "The Jews in the Byzantine Empire under the First Palaeologi," *Speculum,* XIII (1947), 76–77, contains a partial translation but a mistaken identity of its author. See correction by Starr, ibid., p. 83, esp. literature cited; Beck, *Kirche,* pp. 708–10; and most recently D. Jacoby, "Quartiers juifs," pp. 181–82, who gives a date of 1230–1234; Baron, *SRHJ,* 17:17, accidentally substitutes "Israelites" for "Ishmaelites."

The situation that the prelate is describing is the official Byzantine attitude toward "aliens," including foreign merchants, domestic provincials, and non-Orthodox ethnic minorities. For a discussion of this policy, particularly with regard to settlement in Constantinople, cf. Ankori, *Karaites,* p. 138 and literature cited.

1229 and 1254

[19]

387[1] years since there was a very harsh decree (*gezerah gedolah*) in the Kingdom of Greece.

353 years since there was another very harsh decree in the Kingdom of Greece.

R. Shmuel 'Algazi, *Sefer Toldot Adam,* ed. A. M. Haberman (Jerusalem, 1944), pp. 17, 18; cf. Starr, *Romania,* pp. 20–21, 23 note 9. Since the book was written in 1581 (according to the passage on p. 21 of Haberman's edition, which reads "128 [years] since Constantinople was captured by Sultan Mehmet, King of the Turks"), then 387 years before would give a date of 1194. We have no reason to assume that there was a decree against the Jews in that year in the Byzantine Empire. Therefore there is sufficient latitude to emend the text according to the reasoning below (note 1). Although it is difficult to base an argument on a textual emendation, and even more when most of the emended dates in the text are extremely inexact, this emendation places us within a familiar chronological context.

1. If for שפ״ז (387) we read שכ״ז (327), then the decree would have been proclaimed in 1254 (subtracting 327 from 1581). The scribal error of substituting פ for כ is very easily made. The passage following this in the text reads "384 years since the death of RABaD." Haberman corrects שפ״ד (384) to שכ״ב (322). Since this entry immediately follows the one about the decree in the Kingdom of Greece, it allows us to suspect the same error regarding that date.

1252

[20]

Testimony deposed before us the undersigned on the . . . day [of the week in the month of] Adar on the fourteenth day of the month in the year 5012 from the creation of the world. On this day Kaleb b. Shabbetai brought evidence before the Beth Din with his uncle Abraham b. R. Shabbetai that they had (a Bible which came as an inheritance) to the mother of the aforementioned Kaleb and to Abraham b. R. Shabbetai. Her name was Eudokia[1] and she had two sons Kaleb and Shabbetai. When she died, her son Shabbetai not being available and while the aforementioned Kaleb b. Shabbetai had a debt, he [Kaleb] approached the Beth Din and said, "Gentlemen, I have a debt and the collectors are pressing me very hard and I have no source of payment save for the Bible which I and my brother have on deposit with Abraham my mother's brother. Summon him here and divide it because I want to sell my portion to cancel my debt." The Beth Din summoned him and deliberated, and finally pronounced that it be divided; and the nine books were divided in the presence of the Beth Din: one part from *Bereshit* to *Yeme ḥayyav*[2] and the other part from *Yeshayahu* to *Letobah*[3] and they cast lots. The lot for the Torah (and the Neviʿim Rishonim) fell to Abraham while the Writings and the (Later) Prophets fell to Kaleb. The Beth Din said[4] to Kaleb, "Perhaps you would sell them [your share] and your brother would come and contest the matters against you." He replied, "I hear that he has died: O that he would appear alive, I would appease him in any way."

It was announced before the Beth Din that it be sold. Solomon b. Joseph announced, "I will purchase but I will not be able legally to possess the portion that fell to your lot (if someone should contest it),[5] perhaps I would have problems later with your brother." Abraham replied, "Let him take both (portions) and it was agreed between them. They brought Abraham's portion . . . and it was sold to the aforesaid Solomon for 250 coins AZʿADIN'A[6] and Abraham received the money from Solomon, the entire amount, both willingly and without constraint with neither conscious nor inadvertent error, and they renounced in the presence of the Beth Din to contest in the future the legality of the sale of this Pentateuch and Prophets-Writings to [Solomon b.] Joseph and his descendents . . . this Beth Din . . . ben Shabbetai . . . ben Abraham . . . Abraham ben . . .

Colophon published by J. Mann, *Texts and Studies,* I, 52–53. Brackets enclose Mann's insertions and author's additions.

1. For a previous use of this name, cf. the marriage contract from Mastaura dated 1022. Text in J. Mann, *The Jews in Egypt and Palestine under the Fatimid Caliphs,* II, 94ff, and his comments in ibid., I, 53; translated in Starr, *JBE,* pp. 187ff, no. 30; commentary on wedding gifts by Th. Reinach, "Un contrat de marriage du temps de Basile le Bulgaroctone," *Mélanges*

offerts à M.G. Schlumberger, I, 118–38; cited by Ankori in his discussion of Greek names, *Karaites,* p. 199. The same name occurs in a Geniza fragment, Cambridge T-S 8. J. 19.33.

2. Genesis–2 Kings.

3. Isaiah–Nehemiah.

4. Cf. *Talmud Yerushalmi, Nedarim,* end 39b.

5. Despite the lacuna, this seems to be the meaning.

6. The Seljug ruler 'Izz-ed-Dīn Kay Kāwūs II (1211–20) included within his territory the ports of Sinope on the Black Sea and Adalia on the Mediterranean. Undoubtably his were the coins which continued to be used long after his death. Sample weights of his dirhams in the collection of the American Numismatic Society are 2.85, 2.86, 2.88, 2.92, 2.98 grams. Slightly lighter weights are listed for those in the British Museum collection (cf. Lane-Poole, *Catalogue of Oriental Coins in the British Museum,* III, nos. 233ff. Cf. document 23 and note 4 there.

1257

[21]

Behold[1] a stranger speaking a foreign tongue from Morea (*loʿez min Morea*) arrived[2] and (related) that he came via a small boat[3] to Andravida.[4] And upon arrival, seeing the Jews, he was astonished. He called to Mar Leon and asked him "Are you a Jew?" He replied "Yes" whereupon he continued, "The messengers have arrived here whom the king 'who was hidden' has sent!" When he [i.e., Mar Leon] heard these words he became excited and ran to us[5] in order to tell us this truth. and I[6] went with R. Elia ha-Parnas, Mar Leon and R. David ha-Melammed[7] and together we went to a certain place where he (*ha-loʿez*) told us that your[8] "hidden" king sent letters to the King of Spain and to the King of Germany and to all those kingdoms.

And these letters are written thus:

> By this my command you must forward my letter from place to place and from king to king and assist my messengers to go to every Jewish community so that they may all assemble to go to Jerusalem with neither hindrance nor harm from the kings. Nor should the latter try to dissuade them. The letters [to the Jews] are written thus:
>
> Let the rich give to the poor; sell all that (you possess. And when you are) in Jerusalem, shall I not find you opportunities for business![9]

The *loʿez* satisfied us regarding these messengers, i.e., that they had come, despite our not having heard anything about this [whole affair] until now. And further he swore that in another few days the messengers would reach the (local) ruler (*ha-moshel*) and his lieges (*kol sarav*). At that time the ruler and all his lieges would prostrate themselves.[10]

When (the *lo'ez*) saw the confusion which occurred (recently) in Spain which came over thousands, and they had gone . . . to Jerusalem at the beginning of Tishre; and all the inhabitants of this official's[11] area had gathered together but he would not let them go. And the one who had received the letters (from the "hidden" king) said to him: "You had better know what you are doing!" (The latter answered:) "I will not prevent you (from leaving) but give me your money and then go in peace." They readily agreed, gave the money and left. But you (the leaders of Andravida) remain unprepared and do nothing?![12]

These letters are from "the hidden ones" who number two hundred riders of whom twelve are the important ones.[13] The letter that they brought was written in Hebrew and it was signed on the top and bottom of both sides with ten seals of gold. And the twelve said to the king: "We are twelve generals."[14] And the King of Spain, the King of Germany, the King of Hungary, and the King of France were in a state of fear and trembling and collected a vast fortune and a great army depending upon whether "the hidden ones" wanted the money or whether they would have to oppose them. And when the messengers arrived in Spain the king gave them great honor; he went out to greet them with his whole army and accompanied by the Jews who were his subjects and all the Jews riding horses.[15]

The king invited them to enter the city. They replied that they did not wish to. Now outside the city was a river, so they encamped there. At once food and wine were brought which they ate and drank together. The king supplied all their needs. All this was witnessed by the *lo'ez*. The marquis,[16] too, was about to bring dispatches to the heads (to inform them) what to do. Also the Germans were preparing to kill all [the Jews]; the priests stood up and said to them; "Beware lest you do them harm" (for he who does them evil) "He who touches them touches the apple of His eye."[17] And not only to himself (will this evil redound but) to the whole world for if they[18] come and it is brought out that Jews were killed they will kill you in revenge.

On Monday we went with my son-in-law Rabbana Shabbetai[19] (to this *lo'ez* and) we heard these things as well as another two things (which were not mentioned to) them. Thus he swore (to us) that the messengers would come with *markasin* . . .[20]

Cambridge, Geniza fragments, T-S Loan 26, two paper leaves; ed. by Mann, *Texts and Studies,* I, 41–44, with introduction and commentary, pp. 34–38. Our translation follows Mann's emendations, which are for the most part acceptable. Our passage begins on folio 2, recto line 9, and breaks off suddenly at the bottom of the verso. Hopefully, another fragment of the letter will eventually be uncovered.

This letter, the first part of which deals with events in Sicily, was the subject of lively debate during the decade after its publication in 1931. (See my "Messianic Excitement in the Peloponnesos" for summary.) The question of date was established in the above note by identifying the year that the 28th of Tishre fell on a Sunday as 1257. The date is mentioned in the two lines immediately preceding the story of the *lo'ez min Morea.*

From a palaeographic perspective, the script is very similar to mid-thirteenth-century (south) Italian hands.

1. This passage follows the strange experiences of the reporters in Sicily.

2. והנה בא לועז אחד מן מוריאה. This does not mean that he came from Morea to Sicily; only that he was a local who spoke a different language than our reporters.

3. Mann suggested emending דוגים to דיגים (fishermen); the manuscript reads דוגית (small boat or galley; cf. Ankori, *Karaites,* p. 174, note 18).

4. Mann could not identify this town; he thought it was in Sicily, thus confusing all subsequent discussion of this source.

5. Identified at the beginning of the letter as Michal ben Samuel and his traveling companion, Samuel ben . . . (the remainder of his name is lost).

6. I.e., Michal ben Samuel.

7. These three men represent the communal leadership of the Jewish community of Andravida.

8. This is Mann's emendation. The "hidden" king has been identified as the leader of the Mongols. See my "Messianic Excitement."

9. *Pace,* Mann, p. 42n.

10. Here, apparently the section immediately regarding the Morea ends and the story of the *lo'ez'* visit to Spain in the previous month begins.

11. *Hegemon,* which means either governor or bishop.

12. Somewhat unclear. Clearly, this section cannot apply to Sicily since the first part of the letter indicates that a number of messianic manifestations occurred in San Torbo and Catania. The last sentence was spoken by the *lo'ez.*

13. Evidently the advance party, which spread the propaganda of the arrival of the main body.

14. Mann mistakenly understood this word to mean "thousands" of troops.

15. A special mark of honor, usually forbidden to Jews, especially in Byzantium and Islamic lands.

16. הַמַרְקְשִׁי pointed in the text.

17. This passage seems somewhat out of place, although the author may have included this rumor to strengthen his argument. In any case, the story fits in well with official church protection of the Jews in the insecure thirteenth century; cf. papal bulls edited by Solomon Grayzel, *The Church and the Jews in the XIIIth Century* (Philadelphia, 1933). Biblical quote from Zecharia 2:12 (RSV 2:8).

18. The "hidden ones."

19. Otherwise unknown. The title Rabbana is used respectfully by Isaiah of Trani, referring to scholars in Romania. See above, chap. 1, note 22.

20. The leaf ends with this word and the manuscript breaks off at a most tantalizing point. The word מרקשין is not pointed in the text; it may, however, be a plural of the above מַרְקְשִׁי.

[22] Ca. 1261–1262

I remained in the land in which I was raised (Spain) two years after the death of my father and teacher. When I was twenty, the spirit of the Lord roused me and set me on the move. I left there, going straight to the land of Israel by land and sea; and though I planned to go to the River Sambation, I was unable to pass Acre. Then I left because of the strife that increased between Ishmael [Muslims] and Esau [Christians]. Leaving there I returned by way of the Kingdom of Greece where I married. Then the spirit of the Lord roused me, and taking my wife with me, I set my face to reach my people and learn Torah.

Excerpt from Abraham Abulafia's *Oẓar Gan ʿEden,* in Adolph Jellinek, *Bet ha-Midrasch* III, xl–xli; translated in Leo Schwartz, ed., *Memoirs of My People through a Thousand Years,* p. 22. On the basis of document 26, we may surmise that Patras was the city where he found his bride.

[23] 1265

The evidence that came before us the undersigned on the fourth day of the week of the month Marḥeshvan on the twelfth day of the month in the year 5025 of the creation of the world. On this day there came before us Moses[1] b. Mar Solomon from the city KAL'ʿA'ASHER[2] and said "I had trustworthy witnesses that I sold to Natanel b. Nisi my half of a Bible which came to me by inheritance from my father, a Torah and half of the Prophets, nine books, the value of the parchment and ink according to the current market price is 250 aspers,[3] and 50 coins of Cordova,[4] at the current merchant value are half, i.e., 125 aspers. All the aspers reached the hands of the aforesaid Moses b. Mar Solomon, not one iota less, and anyone who contests matters let his words be worthless. I Moses am neither compelled nor mistaken nor forced, rather with peace of mind I sold it in an irredeemable sale that it will belong to Natanel henceforth.

[signed] Benjamin b. Solomon, may his soul be at rest
Shabbetai b. R. Judah

MAGDIEL B. R. MEBIN, may the spirit of the Lord bring him rest
THE DOCTOR, the memory of the righteous be blessed
ISAAC B. MOSES
SOLOMON B. ḤANANIAH, witness

Colophon published by Mann, *Texts and Studies,* I, 54.

1. Is he the son of Solomon b. Joseph, cited in document 20?

2. Mann was unsure of the reading and gave the alternatives KAL'A'ASHET and KAL'A'ASHER. The first is incompatible with any Turkic or Arabic place name. The second could possibly refer to the Anatolian KARA ḤIṢĀR (Black Castle), if we can accept the interchangeability of the liquids "l" and "r" in the first part of the name. There are three such places in Anatolia: in Afyūn, Konya, and Niğde. Cf. document 20 and note 6 there.

3. Cf. document 20 and note 6 there.

4. These coins are probably the square silver coins issued by the al-Muwaḥiddun, and weigh between 1.53 and 1.55 grams. Cf. Lane-Poole, *Catalogue of Oriental Coins in the British Museum,* vol. V, nos. 121ff. The late dean of east Mediterranean numismatics, Dr. George Miles, informed me that this may be a unique mention of the existence of these coins in Anatolia.

Ca. 1270

[24]

And now I will inform you of what happened to Theodore the wicked Greek[1] whose heart the Lord made fat and whose eyes He blinded,[2] so that he ruled in the obstinacy of his heart and acted wickedly[3] to our people, profaned our faith, confiscated their wealth and plundered their possessions.[4] And when a Jew would come before him he would turn his eyes and make sport with him while sitting on high as if he did not see him. And the Lord our God stiffened his spirit and gave him the courage to revenge himself against his enemies. Thus this Theodore the Greek went out to fight with King Asen. He sought not his peace but waged war with him.[5] King Asen, however, killed most of his knights in the battle as well as the best of his commanders. Then the wicked Theodore fell into his net and was captured by him. Then King Asen shackled his feet; his heart melted and became as water. Then the king summoned two Jews[6] and said to them, "Give thanks to your Lord because Theodore your enemy has fallen into my hands. Darken his eyes in their orbs and let them rot in their sockets[7] and avenge yourselves upon him for he has been captured in battle." And the Jews took him and cast him to the ground. But he pleaded with them and they, taking pity on him, did not do unto him as his deed deserved, and overlooking his evilness they darkened not his vision. The king, angered with them, ordered that they be brought atop a lofty mountain, high unto heaven itself, and that they fly without wings and fall to be dashed to pieces, sinking like lead into the mighty waters.[8] Then he commanded two men to gouge his eyes and they did so. And the anger of the king abated.[9]

Let it be told to you what Vatatzes[10] who ruled in Yavan [Greece] did to us. Evil[11] seduced him and aroused his spirit to raise his hand against our faith and to profane the Torah of our Lord. He ordered the Jews in all the cities of his realm to worship his rite and to uphold and take upon themselves his faith.[12] Now I will inform you what happened to him in his rebellion and unfaithfulness. In that year[13] his sleep fled him and his fever increased and a stench arose from him.[14] And Vatatzes was like wine that had been left unopened like a seething pot[15] and his intestines were like a bloated cauldron; he was covered with boils as strong as iron. And the cursed waters gathered within him;[16] his heart trembled[17] and the maggots gathered in his bones. He could not pass water, his mouth passed an excretion, and his tongue was like a burning flame hungry for bread and yearning for water; he was inflicted with severe inflammation of his knees and hips. Whenever he would eat or drink his trembling increased and pains like birth pangs would come upon him, and fourteen days before he died he vomited his feces. Nor could the River Kishon quench his thirst because his colon was closed and his bowels sealed, and when they brought food before him he consumed it; and if he utterly abhorred it he swallowed it in pain and vomited it toward evening, and before morning he was in terror.[18] Is this not the fate of those who plunder us and the destiny of those who rob us? Afterwards they relegated him to the grave and lowered him to the pit.

His son Laskaris[19] ruled after him because he was his first born. He ruled for some days, and all of his officials were afraid of him because anger rested in his bosom.[20] Thus he found no peace, for troubles and many bad problems and events surrounded him and hurts, pains, agonies, and many other bad maladies until he became sick of living and all his desires were oriented toward death.[21] For nine months he was in ill health. He ate no bread nor did meat enter his mouth, rather he chose for delicacies salty fish and hay, onions and garlic. In the prime of his life he too died and was cut off from his people.

Afterwards there sat upon his throne one of his servants who had poured water on his hands with all his majesty.[22] Cautious in his speech, he summoned a scribe and gathered all the sages of Israel throughout his kingdom. With fear in their hearts they came to greet him. He said to them, "Well I know that Vatatzes oppressed you, therefore he was not successful. Now go and worship the Lord your God, you and your sons and daughters. Keep my commands and bless me[23] also and ever ask my peace and well being. I will protect you and you will keep silent.[24]

And it came to pass while this king was sitting on the throne of his kingdom, he annihilated all the servants of Vatatzes and all the elders of his house and destroyed all the advisors of his son as well as his officials together so that none remained. And Laskaris had a son.[25] The king took him and gouged out his eyes and castrated him destroying his ability to reproduce.[26] Thus he caused both his body and his soul to suffer. His ancestors sinned but were no more, so he suffered for their transgressions.

Excerpt from the letter of Jacob b. Elia in J. Koback, ed., *Ginze Nistaroth,* 1–2, pp. 24–27 (= *Jeshurun,* VI [1868], 24–27); J. Mann, "La lettre polémique de Jacob b. Elie à Pablo Christiani," *REJ,* LXXXII (1926), 363–77; J. Mann, "Über Jakob b. Elia, Verfasser des polemischen Briefes gegen den Apostaten Pablo", (Hebrew) *Alim,* I (1934–35), 75–77; Starr, *Romania,* pp. 20–22; B. Lewin, "Eine Notiz zur Geschichte der Juden im byzantinischen Reiche," *MGWJ,* XIX (1870), 117–22, includes a partial translation in German; Dölger, *Regesten,* III, no. 1817; Andrew Sharf, "Byzantine Jewry in the XIIIth Century," *Bar Ilan Annual,* XIV–XV (1977), 61–72, contains a translation and a partial commentary on the text. His independent investigation supports some of our suggestions in part I.

1. Theodore Angelos, Despot of Epiros (ca. 1215–24), emperor in Thessalonica (1224–30).

2. Isaiah 6:10.

3. Literally, he became like a devil.

4. The persecution took place in 1229; see above, chap. 1, section "Imperial Policy."

5. The battle of Klokotnika on the Marcia took place in spring 1230 against John Asen II (1218–41).

6. On the executioners, see exc. C below.

7. Zephaniah 14:12.

8. Exodus 15:12.

9. Esther 7:10.

10. John III Dukas Vatatzes, emperor of Nicaea (1222–54).

11. Literally, *melekh ha-satan.*

12. The edict went out in 1254, probably after the onset of the disease and not before, as our author seems to suggest.

13. The disease began in February of that year.

14. Joel 11:20–21.

15. Jeremiah 1:13.
16. Numbers 5:17f.
17. Isaiah 7:2.
18. Isaiah 17:14.
19. Theodore II Laskaris (1254–58). Cf. Gardner, *The Lascarids of Nicaea,* pp. 204f.
20. Ecclesiastes 7:9.
21. Cf. Deuteronomy 28:59.
22. Michael Palaiologos: regent 1258, co-emperor 1259, emperor 1261–82.
23. Cf. Exodus 12:31–32.
24. Cf. Exodus 14:14.
25. John IV (1258–61).
26. From Amos 2:9. Byzantine sources mention only his blinding; cf. Pachymeres, *De Michaele et Andronico Palaeologis,* ed. Bekker (Bonn, 1835), I, 191–92, and Nikephoros Gregoras, *Byzantina Historia,* ed. Schopen (Bonn, 1830), I, 93. The suggestion of castration in the text, then, may have been prompted by the verse in Amos.

[25] 1278–1279

Fourteen years before this commentary, that is the year (50)39, the Rabbanites celebrated the new moon of Tishre, but we saw the old (moon) during the rising of the sun and we showed it to the Rabbanites who are there in that place called Solchat.

Aaron b. Joseph the Karaite, *Sefer ha-Mibḥar,* Commentary on Exodus, 14b; quoted in Ankori, *Karaites,* p. 60, note 12; cf. p. 126, note 144 and text there. Quoted by Samuel Poznanski, *The Karaite Literary Opponents of Saadia Gaon,* pp. 76–77.

For two earlier occurrences in Byzantium, cf. Aaron b. Elijah, *Gan 'Eden,* 8d; translated by Starr, *JBE,* pp. 208–9; commentary by Ankori, *Karaites,* p. 347. A similar case occurred in the second quarter of the fourteenth century, recorded by Aaron b. Elijah, *loc. cit.* כזה הענין גם בזמננו זה הקרה; see below, document 59. Joseph wrote his commentary in 1293–94.

[26] 1279

This book, *Sefer ha'Eduth* [Book of Testimonies], is the fourth of the commentary of Raziel which is the third of the treatise, for *Sefer ha-Yashar* [Book of the Righteous] Raziel wrote first in the city Mount Patros [*sic*!][1] in the land of Greece, and he wrote it in the year 5039 of the Creation when he was 39, it being the ninth year since the inception of his prophecy. But until that year he did not write any book connected in any way with prophecy even though he wrote books on many other subjects among them books on the secrets of the Kabbalah . . .

Excerpt from Abraham Abulafia's *Sefer ha-'Eduth* in *MGWJ*, XXXVI (1887), 558; also in Steinschneider, *Muenchen*, p. 143n; partially translated in Schwarz, *Memoirs of My People*, p. 24; cf. p. 571. Also see below, document 124.

1. I.e., Patras; the Jewish quarter was located near the fortress atop the prominent hill, which may well have been known as *har Patros,* or Upper Patras. For similar usage, cf. Benjamin of Tudela's comments on Marseilles, where the second community, *'al ha-har,* may refer to a settlement atop the hill near the castle and is thus differentiated from the group living down by the port. Cf. Jeremiah 44:15 and Ezekiel 30:14; Judah ha-Levi, too, uses the name Patros to allude to Byzantium ("Ode to Zion," l. 57).

1288 [26*]

I, Sar Shalom b. Naḥman ha-Ḥazzan (may his righteous memory be for a blessing), acknowledge that I have sold this book called *Midrash Ḥokhmoth* to his honor Joseph b. ha-Kadosh Mordekhai ה"ד for 30 [coins] in full amount[1] and he has already received these 30 [coins] *in toto.* And may his honor be permitted to read it along with his sons, his heirs, and all his descendents, and he is authorized to sell, to pawn, to exchange, or to give as gift to whomever he wishes. And I cannot redeem or ransom this book; rather it will be absolutely and perpetually his forever. Here in Thrakē the sixth day of the week, eighth of the month Shevat in the year "Let Israel rejoice in His deeds" according to the abbreviated reckoning [48 = 1288].[2]

Oxford, Bodleian, Mich 551, fol 210r; there are three other bills of sale in this manuscript, two of which bear the dates 1330 and 1389. The last is signed by Judah b. Eliahu the Adrianopolitan, who, we know, was in Solchat in the Crimea in that year. Further study of these bills of sale supports the suggestion that this text was used first in a Karaite community in Thrace (possibly Adrianople, the capital of that province) and then in the Karaite communities in Crimea. See above, chap. 2, note 36. Our first documented evidence for a Karaite community in Adrianople is in 1335/36 (below, #56); on Judah b. Solomon ha-Kohen and his *Midrash ha-Ḥokhmah,* see Colette Sirat in *Italia,* 2 (1977), 39–61. (I wish to thank Doctor Sirat for bringing this text and her article to my attention.) The question of the influence of this book upon fourteenth-century Karaite philosophical treatises has not yet been examined.

1. The photocopy of the manuscript (in the Institute for the Microfilming of Hebrew Manuscripts at the Jewish National and University Library) is not clear for this folio. The Hebrew term for coin may be read either as לבנ' or זהב', or perhaps even as גדו', each of which is a neutral term for some local coinage. The abbreviation ה"ד may signify המיר דתו (i.e., converted), which would follow from the martyrdom of his father (*ha-Kadosh*).

2. For place and date, correct Newbauer (*Bodleian,* I, #1321) accordingly.

[27] 1293

That year (692 A.H. = 1293), wrote al-Gazari, there arrived in Damascus Haj ʿAbd Allah b. Mohammed b. ʿAbd al Rahman of Sinjar, the merchant, coming from Constantinople . . . (where) he had stayed for 12 years. . . . My father asked him to describe it. He told him, "It is a large city, comparable to Alexandria, situated on the sea shore. To cross it from one side to the other one must walk from morning to noon. There is a place, as large as two-thirds of Damascus, surrounded by a continuous wall and furnished with a gate that one can open and close, which place is reserved especially for Muslims who inhabit it; likewise there is another place where Jews live. Each evening their two gates are closed at the same time as those of the city.

M. Izeddin, tr., "Un texte arabe inédit sur Constantinople byzantin," *Journal Asiatique,* 246 (1958), 454–55; Jacoby, "Quartiers juifs" pp. 190 and 192. Sinjar is situated on the Tigris River in eastern Mesopotamia.

[28] 1294

And now, those of our brethren who are in Ereṣ Yisrael follow the custom of our holy fathers who used to determine [intercalation] according to [the ripening of] the *abib* in Ereṣ Yisrael. Alas, because of our many sins, we who live outside of the Land [of Israel] follow the reform of the Rabbanites who introduced the nineteen-year lunar cycle, i.e., to intercalate the third, sixth, eighth, eleventh, fourteenth, seventeenth, and nineteenth [years of the cycle]. And when our sages, may their memories be blessed, realized that most of their calculations were correct, they authorized us accordingly.

Aaron b. Joseph, *Mibḥar* on Exodus 15b; text and translation (slightly modified) in Ankori, *Karaites,* p. 340, and note 111 there cited as part of his general discussion of calendar reform within the context of Karaite diasporic readjustment.

[29] 1296

At any rate after great riches were collected and the gifts of virtue were found to be a toy of fate, they were finally handed over to the Jews in order to make them quite blind. And the blind one [Philanthropenos] was very ashamed of this especially about the eyes of the other one, but he was not completely subdued.[1]

George Pachymeres, *De Andronico Palaeologo,* chap. 11 in *MPG* 144, col. 252; Starr, *Romania,* pp. 27–28; cf. exc. C. The details of the rebellion are retold by Richard Knolles, *The General Historie of the Turkes* . . . (3d ed.; London, 1621), pp. 147–49, and more recently by A. Laiou, *Constantinople and the Latins,* pp. 80ff.

1. It was the Cretan contingent in Alexios Philanthropenos' army that defected, when the latter hesitated to proclaim himself emperor, and captured him and turned him over to the Jews to be blinded. Was it the anti-Jewish atmosphere in Venetian-occupied Crete that prompted the latter action or was it a sly attempt to pass the blame for blinding the popular commander to a despised minority? Also, the question must be asked, even if it cannot be answered: Were these local Jews or were they somehow connected with the army, e.g., doctors? It should also be noted that Alexios survived the ordeal.

Ca. 1300 [30]

Hear, O noble sirs (the Lord's controversy, and ye enduring rocks, the foundations of the earth); for the Lord hath a controversy with His people, and He will plead with Israel.[1]

There was a Jew in the community of Egripon[2] whose name was R. David Kalomiti ha-Parnas.[3] He was full of wisdom and understanding and knew Torah, Mikra, Mishna, Talmud, Dikduk,[4] and Sebara[5] . . . a man of knowledge and reverence for the Lord . . . full of the blessings of the Lord; gold, silver, precious stones (pearls and houses full of wealth), . . . (fields) and vineyards, male and female servants. And David had great success in all of his ways and the Lord was with him.[6] And the nobles of the land . . . him, almost all were subservient to him for all had need of him.[7]

Another Jew came from the community of Thebes[8] (fleeing from his lords); his name was R. (Moses) b. Rabbi Shabbetai (Shem) Tob Galimidi. He took refuge in Egripon, married a local girl from the upper class of the community, and settled there. R. Moses found favor in the eyes of the above-mentioned R. David ha-Parnas and he served him; and (R. David) placed him over the whole community of Egripon as judge, scribe, ritual slaughterer, and teacher of [his own] sons,[9] for this man was very important as we have mentioned and lived there. And Moses waxed important and sired sons and daughters. His sons matured: the first-born R. Shabbetai was an accomplished man, observant and a man of Torah with insight and understanding, and knowledge and reverence for the Lord.

The second was R. Samuel; the third R. Absalom; the fourth R. Elia the cantor; the fifth R. Isaiah; the sixth R. Abraham, this young man who is coming with this epistle before your Honors.

(And for many) years, R. Moses lived with R. David ha-Parnas in the community of Egripon peaceably and in honor as we have related. (R. David) led forth Moses on his right as the hand of his glory.[10] R. Moses made a request from R. David ha-Parnas, and he fulfilled the request. In turn R. David ha-Parnas desired from Moses, R. Moses himself, his sons, and his household, and he took possession of him; and R. Moses, his sons, and his household came to be the servants of R. David.[11] During all the time that R. David lived, R. Moses, his sons, and his household received respect, good will, and peace even to the point of paying the wages for teaching his sons and for continuing in his former post over the community as we mentioned.[12] Only when any plea came to R. David to send an envoy for the great and important leaders of the land and its officers, he would send R. Moses—and this too with apologies[13]—and he would send his sons to receive the money or silk or indicate[14] things which he required for he was a very important man with great wealth and substantial business and manufacturing.—And David passed away and was buried in the community of Egripon with great honor.[15]

After him arose his sons, new lords who knew not Moses[16] even though they had learned from him; they ruined Moses in the congregation of Egripon and they enslaved his sons and hardened their lot. And R. Shabbetai b. R. Moses fled from them and took refuge in Corinth. And there came to pass an earthquake[17] so he went to Thebes, and he died there. His brother R. Samuel fled and took refuge in ADRO[18] and died there. And R. Elia the cantor[19] fled from them and took refuge in Salona and settled there. R. Isaiah fled and took refuge in Constantinople and settled there. And R. Absalom fled them and went to KhRMINI.[20] They took his wife's clothes, his bed, his sheets, his cover; and they sold them in auction,[21] in the place where one sells under the sun. After this he returned home, here to Egripon, for he had a wife and sons.

The sons of R. David did great evil to the sons of Moses as against the goodness that their father did for them. Two sons of Moses, R. Absalom and this R. Abraham, remained in Egripon. They hated them yet the more.[22] The lord of R. Absalom proclaimed concerning him—let no one be found to trust him, except through himself, neither with money nor with clothes, in order to bring him to the verge of death. And they were in dire straits, in great bondage, in bitterness of heart and shameful scorn from the day of the death of R. David their father until today.

And it came to pass many days after all this happened to them, many troubles and sorrows like these and fears; and the sons of Moses sighed by reason of the bondage, and they cried, and their cry came up unto God by reason of the bondage.[23] And lo a messenger of the Lord came, sent from Venice to the *capitaneus et baiulus*[24] of Egripon; his name was Messer Filippo da Belegno,[25] a very respectable man and reverent for the Lord who knew the Torah and its formal prohibitions. And the lords of R. Absalom and R. Abraham still continued to disobey the Lord by doing evil unto them, confiscating their property and imprisoning them,[26] for they wished to extirpate and eradicate them. Indeed they openly said that they would not leave a trace of the Galimidi family.

The matter reached the aforesaid judge, because without his decree they were unable to fine or imprison them, and the judge, this lord, heard and was astounded, saying, "You are Jews and your lords are Jews. How many years have you been under them?" They answered, "Many years." The judge replied, "Your Torah decrees 'six years shall he serve and in the seventh he shall go out free for nothing'[27] and this commandment is upheld among us and among all the nations who were not at the receiving of the Torah at Mount Sinai. Yet you have served them for many years since the days of your father; and still they maintain control over you and hold you in bondage? Go now and bring your cause to me [in court]."

Now before this aforesaid judge arrived, the lords of this boy who bears this letter to you, seized him and bound him in the LOZA,[28] in iron fetters, and everyone who passed by saw him. And he groaned and sighed, and his heart was bitter as gall because of the hardships done to him. And when he heard the pronouncement of the judge "Bring your claims to me," his heart became like the heart of a lion and he brought his lords before the aforementioned judge for justice. All their affairs of justice and business remained before the *capitaneus* and his advisors nearly three months and more (they kept granting) time after time, for this was the procedure of the Venetian courts in cases like this, to delay time after time in order to be deliberate in judgment.[29] Their judgment had (almost) come forth that they be free; (they knew) not what had been the delay.

This boy, R. Abraham, took counsel with important, respected, and wise men who said to him, "If you really desire that you and your brothers and their sons[30] be raised out of the bondage and the wickedness that befalls you and them daily, gird your loins like a man and go to Rome, and fall on your face before the Lord Pope,[31] lord of all the nations and peoples and all (the kingdoms who believe in the religion of Jesus; his language) they observe, knowledge and Torah they seek from his mouth because he is like a messenger (of the Lord of Hosts) and he will bring your judgment to light and judge (you with righteousness and) uprightness and redeem you and everyone with you." And the boy took this advice to heart and risked his life due to the bitterness of his heart. And now he has arrived before you with the whole story written down from beginning to end.

And the Lord, in whose hand is the soul of every living thing and the spirit of all human flesh: God, the Lord, (the Eternal), God, the Lord, He knoweth and Israel He shall know[32] that everything related within this letter is a portion of the case of these men who have caused our faces to tremble and whose will we have done. We have written and signed without lie or deceit and without hate or malice or guile, nor from love or kinship nor for any other reason have we written all this. Rather just the truth. You have it from beginning to end what we know, and what our eyes have seen we have related, written and signed.

Therefore the preciousness of glory and the crown of beauty of all the communities in the diaspora and their basis and foundation that they are under lords who believe in the religion of Jesus, tamarisks and great men, noblemen and honored ones of the holy congregation, the community of Rome, be aroused to the help of the Lord for these Jews, and lift up your eyes to heaven to the Lord, our God, and look upon this boy with merciful eye, and give heart to wisdom, eyes to seeing and ears to hearing his sorrow and the sorrow of his brother the sorrow of the souls of their house and their shame. Take pity on him and help him with your mouth and your hearts before the lord of nations, your lord, our aforementioned lord. Perhaps God will look in these matters, perhaps He will take pity on the remnant of Moses; for with the help of God (may He be exalted!) and with your assistance this lad will be able to obtain a document from the aforementioned lord and be able to redeem his soul and the soul of those with him.

It is known that you, with the help of God (may He be exalted!) are diligent, armed with the commandments against the teachings of war, in the foundations of the Torah and its warnings. And if we have urged you regarding this (it was only because) the diligent can be driven, and the reward for the redemption of these souls is the reward of this commandment which you will urge for it. It is known to you that whoever sustains one Jewish soul how much the more does he sustain a multitude of souls.[33] May God fulfill your labor and may your reward be complete from the Lord God of Israel,[34] and may you rejoice in the Lord and in the holiness of Israel may you be praised.

If you buy a Hebrew servant, etc.[35]
If thy brother be waxen poor, and sells some of his possessions, etc.[36]
If thy brother be sold unto you, etc.[37]

All the people who were left of the Amorites . . . But of the people of Israel did Solomon make no bondservants, etc.[38]

The word that came unto Jeremiah from the Lord, after that the King Zedekiah had made a covenant with all the people that were at Jerusalem, to proclaim liberty unto them, etc.[39]

"An anonymous letter from Negroponte to the Jewish community of Rome, written about 1300," MS 2 in the Library of the Collegio Rabbinico, Livorno; presently in Jerusalem, National Library, MS Heb. 4°616; photostat in Starr, *Romania,* following p. 117; text edited by Carlo Bernheimer, "Document relatif aux Juifs de Négropont," *REJ,* LXV (1913), 224–30; commentary in Starr, *Romania,* pp. 48–54; additions and corrections in Jacoby, "Status of Jews."

1. A play on Micah 6:2.

2. The Ms. use of Egripon has been maintained as it reflects the original Greek name *Egripo*. Negroponte is a Venetian affectation; cf. F. C. Hodgson, *Venice in the Thirteenth and Fourteenth Centuries* (London, 1910), p. 39, note 2.

3. On the identification of this man with David of Negroponte, who was awarded Venetian "citizenship" in 1267–68 and repeated intermittently until 1300–1301 and his career, cf. Starr, *Romania,* pp. 49–50, and comments in Jacoby, "Status of Jews," pp. 58ff. If the identification is correct, it suggests a *terminus ab quo* for the letter of sometime after 1301. See below, notes 25 and 31, for the problem of a *terminus ad quem.*

4. Grammar.

5. Logical exegesis.

6. 1 Samuel 18:14.

7. On David's activities, cf. Jacoby, "Status of Jews," pp. 58ff.

8. Ms. TYBẒ.

9. It is very interesting to note that the community was accustomed to have one man perform four of the basic services necessary to a Jewish community. This suggests a numerically small community. In the twelfth century, Benjamin of Tudela found "about 200 Jews there, at their head being R. Elijah Psalteri, R. Emanuel, and R. Caleb" (Adler's translation).

10. A play on Isaiah 63:12.

11. The Hebrew is clear in stating that R. David exercised a formal ownership of R. Moses and his family: בקש אדני רבנא משה מן רבנא דוד הפרנס משאלת וימלא שאלתו אשר בקש ממנו ויבקש גם רבנא דוד הפרנס מאדני משה את רבנא משה ואת בניו ואת ביתו ויקנהו לו ויהי רבנא משה ובניו וביתו לעבדים לרבנא דוד. The force of the term *abadim* could perhaps be translated as "serfs," as Starr suggests, except that we have no other case where

the word assumes this meaning. "Slaves" would be too strong a translation, even though subsequent developments show that this is what they eventually became. Even so, our use of "servants" should be taken in a different sense than the use of the term at the beginning of the document, where it refers to the household servants of R. David. Perhaps "dependent" relays the sense.

The fact that the sons followed not in the footsteps of their father and, indeed, enforced a vicious servitude upon the sons of R. Moses shows that the relationship between Moses and David was purely personal, with no legal safeguards to protect the former. Indeed, since Moses and his sons acted as full agents of David to the displacement of the latter's sons, the situation was open to unpleasant consequences, as in fact happened after the death of David. Nor could recourse to the local rabbinic court be effective, due to the wealth of the Kalomitis (it is unlikely that Moses continued as judge after the death of his benefactor); neither could the local Venetian court help, since the status of the Kalomitis would have sufficed to confuse an already slow-moving and ineffective process. All this, of course, would be compounded by the ambiguity of the original relationship.

12. Evidently the change in status entailed no change in the actual life of the persons involved. Indeed, no problems arise until the death of David. See above, note 11.

13. Ms. clearly reads *bi-mehilah* (l.17 recto) instead of *bi-tehilah*. The text, however, poses no difficulty for translation. Last word on l.18 reads *mas'a* and not *masah,* as Bernheimer transcribed.

14. The reading is *koṣeh,* which probably means this.

15. 1 Kings 2:10.

16. Exodus 1:8.

17. Ms., *va-yehi rogez*. This is not in the list of earthquakes cited by V. Grumel, *La Chronologie,* p. 481. The prevalence of earthquakes in Greece would make positive identification of this earthquake in Corinth nearly impossible. About the same time, a traveler in Greece reported the following situation in Thebes: "Thebes fui, ubi sunt tot terrae motus quod non posset credere nisi qui expertus est; nam quinque vel sex et septem vicibus, inter diem et noctem sunt, ita quod, propter terrae motus, multotiens et frequenter cadunt et ruunt fortissimae domus et mur" (in *Les Merveilles de l'Asie [Mirabilia Descripta] par le pére Jourdain Catalani de Sévérac. . . ,* ed. Henri Cordier, p. 109). Cordier suggests he made his trip before 1320 (p. 12). There were major earthquakes in June 1296 and August 1303 in the region.

18. Both Bernheimer and Starr read ADRO. While it is common in Hebrew palaeography that the *resh* and the *daleth* are not clearly distinguished (and in this case the reading could be ARDO = Arta), the photostat of the letter that Starr provided makes the reading clearly ADRO. The reading ARDO = Arta would necessitate a metathesis of the two consonants, which, though not impossible, is quite unlikely. Therefore it is very probable that the text refers to the island of Andros (the absence of the *nun* and the final *samekh* pose no problem).

19. Ms. reads *ḥazzan* (l.22 recto) not *ḥazzak,* as in Bernheimer.

20. Starr suggested Larmena on the island of Euboea (*Romania,* p. 59, n. 42). There is also the Peloponnesian town of Kremmydi (also Cremidi, Crimidi, and Cromidi), cited in documents IV, VI, XI, and XII of Longnon and Topping (*Documents sur le régime des terres dans la principauté de Morée au XIVe siècle,* pp. 250–51 and texts). We have no indication, however, that Jews ever lived in these towns. A more likely candidate is Sparta: to the Byzantines, Lacedaemonia; to the Franks, La Crémonie, Cremonie, Cremoignie; cf. Bon, *La Morée Franque,* p. 500. In any event, the place must have been sufficiently close to Negroponte for news to have reached him of the persecution of his wife. For this reason I would reject Karamania in Anatolia.

21. *ʿal incanto.*

22. Genesis 37:5, 8.

23. Exodus 2:23.

24. Bernheimer read *capitaneus* correctly, but he misread *bellum* for *baiulos.*

25. Ms. Filipo diBoloniah. In the list of Venetian baili given by Bury ("The Lombards and Venetians in Euboea," *JHS,* 7 [1886], 351), a Filippo Belegno is given the dates 1329–31 for his term of office. The judgeship that he filled would then refer to an earlier appointment of his, unless the man in question were a relative of the same name.

26. Ezra 7:26; cf. *Moʿed Katan* 16a. The text from Ezra is the *locus classicus* for the prerogatives of the Jewish court. Thus the inclusion of this phrase suggests that David's heir functioned as leader of the Jewish community with civil jurisdiction. On the other hand, its use here may be a rhetorical flourish, as may be seen from the statement to follow, that they needed the permission of the bailo in order to imprison or impound their property. See above, chap. 5, note 33.

27. Exodus 21:2.

28. Not "stocks," as in Starr; *loza* is the Venetian vernacular for *loggia.*

29. Cf. F. C. Lane, *Venice* (Baltimore, 1973), p. 95.

30. Since the Hebrew clearly reads "their sons," this would argue for the permanence of the servitude.

31. The so-called Papal Babylonian Captivity began in 1309 with the removal of the papacy to Avignon. This may establish a *terminus ad quem* for our text, as Starr suggests. However, we may ask whether contemporary Jewry, or even the Christian population of Negroponte, understood the removal of the papacy to Avignon in the same light as did Western Christians and later historians. If they did not, there is no reason to restrict the date of this letter to pre-1309. See above, note 25.

32. Cf. Joshua 22:22.

33. Cf. *Sanhedrin,* 37a; Danby, *The Mishnah, San.* IV, 5, p. 388.

34. Ruth 2:12.

35. Exodus 21:1.

36. Leviticus 25:5.

37. Deuteronomy 15:12.

38. 1 Kings 9:20–22.

39. Jeremiah 34:8.

Ca. 1300 [31]

For there is no place for it, nor is it good to settle there those who have changed their life, thus so confined are things near it, and this is so because after this those who had been placed in charge of the Vlanka brought there those who formerly had been settled elsewhere and then settled them there somewhere around the shrine, and shall I tell you in jest?—they put the synagogue within the boundaries of the church and those whom John fled in order to live in the wilderness, those whom he called "brood of vipers," they prepared these to live near the shrine, these whose unpleasantness of belief the Baptist avoided no less completely than we feel disgust at the foul smell from their tannery.

M. Treu, *Maximi monachi Planudis epistulae,* no. 31, pp. 50–52 and 261; Starr, *Romania,* addendum p. 35; Jacoby, "Quartiers juifs," p. 191.

[32] 1308

1) The *Sefer ha-Ṣaḥoth* written by Abraham [ibn Ezra], peace be upon him and may his righteous and saintly memory be for a blessing, was completed by my hand, Samuel ha-Kohen b. Eliahu ha-Kohen with the help of the Lord in the year 5068 on the 28th of Kislev on Sunday according to the reckoning that we use here in the congregation of Serres. And may the Lord sustain me, my sons and grandsons to fulfill his prayer to meditate in it forever according to the verse: "'Let it not depart from your lips or from those of your seed or their descendents,' saith the Lord, forever." Amen.

2) And it was completed in the year 5068 of the Creation in the month of Shevat on the fifteenth day which was a Monday by my hand, Samuel ha-Kohen b. Eliahu ha-Kohen, with the help of the Lord, according to the reckoning that we use here in the congregation of Serres, etc.

Oxford, Bodleian Library, MS Hunt. 128; erroneously listed in Neubauer, *Bodleian,* I, #1467; cf. HPP C215 and author's "Jews in Fourteenth-Century Thebes" for corrections. The second colophon follows the end of Ibn Ezra's *Sefer Moznaim.*

It seems likely that our scribe's father, R. Eliahu ha-Kohen, is the same R. Eliahu of Serres who wrote a commentary on Ibn Ezra's astronomical works which Judah ibn Moskoni saw during the course of his travels. The interest of the father is reflected in the above colophon, which describes the son's continued interest in the works of Ibn Ezra.

[33] Ca. 1304–1310

When Rapsacus, general of the King of Assyria Sennacherim, dared to insult the God of everyone, the very pious King Hezekiah not only rent his garments out of zeal for the great God, but also divested himself of the royal garments and girded himself with sackcloth. Whence God, moved by the suffering of the army, destroyed 185,000 Assyrians.[1] O pious king, how long will the Lord of Hosts assist us when we not only allow to be present in the midst of the faithful the deicidal synagogue (*tēn theoktonon synagogēn*) which shows contempt at our ways, namely our adoration, worship, and faith for our Lord and God Jesus Christ and our symbolic holy adorations and those holy and undefiled mysteries that the faith of the Christians is wealthy in. Yet through gifts, Kokalas[2] allowed them great power, such that if anyone dared to speak out of zeal for the faith of Christians, who would rescue that one from prison? With regard to the Armenians, I am ashamed to relate as much as they do to the surrounding Orthodox, God knows, except that they do not prevent the synagogue from having a place for prayer. But if anyone of the hindered Orthodox dares to speak up there, the Armenians are capable of many things through a few *basilika*.[3] And because of my sins, the Ishmaelites have gained control over Christian towns; and do not even allow Christians to strike the *semandron* there.[4] Because we are wealthy in the Kingdom of Christ by the grace of the Lord, we not only scorned to do what the Ishmaelite elders did, who thought these things of little account although enjoined from such things, but (here) they openly ascend on high and as is the custom of their country they pronounce their abominable mysteries aloud . . .[5]

Letter to the autocrator about the deicidal Jews, that they be evicted from the city; Vat. Gr. 2219, fols. 18r–19v; printed in *MPG,* 142, col. 509; edited and translated by A. M. Talbot, *The Correspondence of Athanasius,* I, #41; partial translation by B. Bănescu, "Le patriarche Athanase Ier et Andronic II Paléologue-état religieux politique et sociale de l'empire," *Académie Roumaine, Bul. de la Section historique,* XXIII, i (Bucharest, 1942), 35–36; summary in Laurent, *Actes des Patriarches,* no. 1622, pp. 415–17.

1. Cf. II Kings 18:13–37; Chronicles 32:1–22 and 19:1–35.

2. On this official, cf. chap. II, note 88, and text there. Bokalas in *MPG.*

3. This coin was introduced in 1304; cf. Talbot, *Correspondence,* commentary on lines 22–23. Cf. also V. Laurent, "Le Basilicon, Nouveau nom de monnaie sous Andronic II Paléologue," *BZ,* XLV (1952), 50–52, and Octavian Iliescu, "La monnai vénitienne dans les pays roumains de 1202 à 1500," *Révue des études sud-est européennes,* XV (1977), 356.

4. Reference to the Turkish conquest of Anatolia. Translation *pace* Talbot. The *semandron* was a wooden bar, used in place of a bell; see her note (p. 349).

5. This is the earliest reference to the minaret in Constantinople, which was located in the Muslim Quarter. The mosque itself dates to 1262; see Talbot, p. 350, and above (document 27).

Before 1310 [34]

a) That not only are the common people abandoned without any instruction, but they are defiled as they ought not to be by the introduction of Jews and Armenians . . .

that condemning the disbelief of the Jews and their transgression, through which they were destroyed . . .

Patriarch Athanasius' letter to the emperor, that he educate his sons to the virtues of God and obedience. *MPG* 142, col. 512; Laurent, *Actes des Patriarches,* no. 1639, pp. 433–34.

b) And what is more that the Jews and Armenians should leave [the capital].

Letter to the assembly of prelates in Chora, that they go to the emperor together for the sake of the public good. *MPG* 142, col. 513. Talbot, *The Correspondence of Athanasius* (Letter 23), believes that this title is a later addition, and that the letter was originally addressed to the bishops. She dates the letter in the late spring of 1305; cf. commentary, *loc. cit.*; Laurent, *Actes des Patriarches,* no. 1621, p. 415, and cf. no. 1597, pp. 379–80 (dated end of 1303–5 = Talbot letter 7), where Athanasius urges the emperor to expel evildoers from the city, including "those who blaspheme God." Laurent suggests this refers to the Jews. Also no. 1731, pp. 512–13 (= Talbot letter 105): "En effet les Juifs ne supportent pas qu'il (le métropolite de Cyzique) aille a l'église de Dieu y prêcher, comme d'habitude, la Passion de Notre Seigneur . . ."

c) I do not say that they may be rescued half dead from the Ishmaelites and those Italians—and then be stripped naked recklessly by their kinsmen, of whom even a Jew would have bewailed the event . . .

Vat. Gr. 2219, fols. 31ʳ–32ʳ (= Letter 46 in Talbot's edition and commentary).

[35] Before 1310

[It is the duty of Christians] to hate the deicidal Jews and their doctors unless they should run to be baptized.

Homily of the patriarch Athanasius on the rich and the poor and how the priests should instruct the Christian people, in *Vat. gr.* 2219, 225ʳ–228ʳ; this passage occurs on fol. 226ʳ; I am indebted to Dr. Talbot for sending me this reference.

[36] 6727–1319 (February)

. . . and further that even the Jews in this city may find themselves in freedom and in an undisturbed state in conformance with the status of its other settlers (from before).[1] ἵνα δὲ εὑρίσκωνται καὶ οἱ ἐν τῇ τοιαύτῃ πόλει 'Ιουδαῖοι εἰς ἐλευθερίαν καὶ ἀνενοχλησίαν κατὰ τοὺς λοιποὺς ἐποίκους αὐτῆς

Emperor Andronikos II Palaiologos confirms the rights, privileges, exemptions, and possessions of the church and city of Ioannina, in *MM,* V, 83;

Dölger, *Regesten,* IV, no. 2412; Bees, "Übersicht über die Geschichte des Judentums von Janina (Epirus)," *BNJ,* II (1921), 163–65; Charanis, "The Jews in the Byzantine Empire under the First Palaeologi," *Speculum,* 22 (1947), 75–77; Starr, *Romania,* p. 113; for a general study of Ioannina, see L. Vranouses, *History and Topography of the Medieval Fortress of Ioannina* (in Greek). The chrysobull is discussed on pp. 14–16, with no reference to Jews.

1. On the state of Ioannina and the special privileges to its immigrants who were refugees from Latin-controlled lands and their descendants during the period of the Despotate of Epiros, see Nicol, *The Despotate of Epirus,* pp. 42 and 106, for one of the attempts of the native Ioanninites to oust these newcomers and regain their property, and above, part I, chap. 1, note 42 and text there.

1319–1320

[37]

About the third capitulum regarding the Jews, we respond thus, that our Jews (*nostri Judei*) are a legitimate possession of the Empire, and for that reason an allotted place is given to them for their dwelling in which they can live and practice their own skills, paying to the Empire that which is ordered them.

It happened indeed in past times that some of your Venetian Jews, coming to them, agreed of their own will and accord, for nobody compelled them, to live with our own Jews, working in common with them, assisting them in their merchandise (*presentes eisdem suffragium in eorum avarijs*),[1] and having a peace and union with them; so that between them it is the rule that the Jews of our Empire are bound to prepare skins (*coria*), while the above-mentioned Venetian Jews, many of whom were from the towns and regions (*castris et terris*) of our Empire and were never called Venetians, though now on the attestation of your[2] bailo we consider them as Venetians, are bound to prepare furred skins (*pellamina*). Indeed a pact of such nature has lasted between them till the present time; now, however, on the (basis) of a provision of ours[3] it pleases our Empire, and since we did not allow our own Jews to prepare skins, (though they are allowed to practice other skills outside of this one), the Venetian Jews, having rejected their arguments, and having revoked their provision, began themselves to prepare skins, a thing which they were not accustomed to do before; and, . . . though it were fitting that, because of their presumption, they be punished, nevertheless, because they are considered yours, we suffer them and we order that they be separated from that place assigned for the dwelling of our Jews, because, renouncing those promises which they made to our [Jews] they want to do what they were not accustomed to do before.

But this, i.e., that our Jews were not willing to live with your Jews, is not contrary to the sense of the treaties; indeed, it is contained in the treaties that beyond the twenty-eight inns which are given to you by our Empire, if the Venetians need more inns in the lands of our Empire, they can accept inns, paying rent, and stay in these and act freely. Therefore it is said that your own Jews, as Venetians, may live wherever they wish; nevertheless the said capitulum does not say that they have to accept inns against the will of those who possess them, nor are Greeks bound, if they do not want to, to accept these in their courts or lots. We do not do this because of neglect, if we are not willing to accept and receive your Jews in the place appropriated for our Jews, as if it were a pleasure garden of ours. For this reason we told your bailo that he could order your own Jews to live in the place set aside for Venetians and to make them live wherever they were able to arrange with those who were willing and able to receive them, and that they could do there as they might wish, and we acted thus because they rejected the pacts which they made with our Jews, as it was said.

Letter of Andronikos II to the Venetian Doge, in Thomas, *DVL,* I, 142–43; Dölger, *Regesten,* IV, no. 2427; Starr, *Romania,* pp. 28–31, 112; Dölger, "Die Frage," pp. 23–24 (= *Paraspora,* p. 376); Jacoby, "Quartiers juifs," passim, and "Les Juifs vénitiens de Cp.," passim. On the continuing problem of naturalization in the time of John V Palaiologos, see document 483, dated 28 October 1369, in Thiriet, *Régestes,* I, 123.

1. Jacoby, "Quartiers juifs," p. 196, note 2.
2. Ibid., p. 198, note 2.
3. Ibid., p. 199, note 2.

[38] 1319–1320

To the third capitulum regarding our Jews: we respond that, having diligently examined the same capitulum with the rescript of the treaty, it is understood by our experts and by our Council that three inns be given to the Venetians by the Lord Emperor: one as a home for the bailo, another as the dwelling of his advisors, and a third as a warehouse for the commune's merchandise, and another thirty-five[1] inns for the merchants, and more [inns] if more merchants come, without any rent payment. Nevertheless, the Venetians and those who identify as Venetians can stay wherever they wish in the lands of the Empire, and board, evidently making a payment, and they can manufacture whatever they wish; in other conditions they could not be *liberi* nor *franchi*. Whence, since we hold for sure that Her Majesty or her factors or the factors of the Empire have given in rent to our Jews that same place for an annual income, so that they can stay there and build houses and work their properties however they wish, the Lord Emperor did an injustice or fault to our Jews not wanting them to make hides, and, regarding this, he acted against the treaty.

Regarding that (capitulum) which says that the Lord Emperor said that, though they could stay wherever they wished, paying rent, nevertheless for this it is not understood that they have to stay in the courts or houses of others against their will:—we respond, that this was not against the will of His Majesty; on the contrary, this was with the wish of His Majesty, when this area was set aside for our own Jews; indeed, as it is confirmed to us, they were able to build and could sell buildings, except the land payment (*terratico*) which is annually paid to His Majesty, and, buying buildings from them, they can sell these same buildings to others in perpetuity, always except this land payment. Therefore, we ask again and request that His Majesty permit our aforesaid Jews to stay there, just as they have stayed to this point, and (to allow them) to make hides and furred skins according to their will and, besides, without being molested. And because we know that after the departure of our galley from Constantinople, the Lord Emperor sent some of his men with interpreters to the Judaica, and by force had all the skins of our Jews there taken from them, (skins) which they had in their houses, some of which were burnt, others thrown into the sea, and the rest exported; and the skins had a value of 1741 and a half hyperpers. This is serious and annoying to us, as it should be, and may the Lord Emperor order the aforesaid quantity of money to be given back in full to our Jews, as it is just and in accordance with the treaty, so that they are not left with a rightful cause of bewailing.

Reply of Johannes Superantio, Venetian doge, to the emperor of Constantinople, in Thomas, *DVL,* I, 153; Dölger, *Regesten,* IV, no. 2427; see bibliography cited above, document 37.

1. Document 39 gives the correct number, twenty-five.

1319–1320 [39]

To the third capitulum regarding our Jews: that capitulum has been diligently examined with the rescript of the treaty, and it is understood by our experts and our Council that, three inns are to be given by the Lord Emperor to the Venetians, one for the house of the bailo, another for the dwelling of his advisors, and a third as the warehouse for the commune's merchandise, and another twenty-five inns for the merchants, and more, if more merchants come, without any rent payment. Nevertheless, the Venetians and those who identify as Venetians can stay wherever they wish in the lands of the Emperor paying rent, i.e., making a payment, and can manufacture whatever they wish; in other circumstances they are neither *liberi* nor *franchi*.

Whence it seems to us and to our experts that the Lord Emperor is wrong if he does not want our Jews nor any other of our subjects to practice whatever they wish from their skills. Therefore, we ask the Lord Emperor that he cease from molesting our Jews, as mentioned, and permit them to manufacture furred skins (*pellamen*) and hides (*curamen*) of their own free will, without molesting them any more.

Reply of the doge to the ambassadors of Andronikos II, in Thomas, *DVL,* I, 129; Dölger, *Regesten,* IV, no. 2427; see bibliography cited in document 37.

[40] 1319–1320

Then the said ambassadors [of Andronikos II] ask that the Lord Duke [of Crete] be satisfied and order that the Jews of the Venetian commune, who are, out of courtesy, in the land of the sacred Emperor, be content with the same stipulations which they had to the present time: namely, they make only furred skins and not hides. If indeed they are not content with this stipulation, let them depart from the land of the Emperor and go dwell in the land and in the communal places given by the Lord Emperor to the Venetian commune in Constantinople, and there practice whatever they wish from among their skills.

Capitula of the ambassadors of the emperor of Constantinople, in Thomas, *DVL,* I, 125; Dölger, *Regesten,* IV, no. 2427; see bibliography to document 37.

[41] 1320 (3 March)

Item: that in Constantinople, Venetians, both Christians and Jews, are being despoiled by gasmules, Greeks, and officials of the Emperor. And furthermore at the custom gate, dinars are being taken from the Venetians who want to carry their merchandise into the city, and all this is pointedly against the treaties and was made known to the Emperor, but nothing was accomplished.

Letter of Marco Minoto, bailo of Constantinople, in Thomas, *DVL,* I, 165.

1320 (3 March) [42]

Item: that in no way is any Venetian, whether Christian or Jew, permitted to make any kind of hide or furred skin, because it is clearly against the treaties; yet even the Emperor promised to allow them to make furred skins freely, but to no avail; and concerning all the skins accepted by the Jews so many times and in such quantity, he is not willing to make any reparation and he does not allow them to work in any other way.

Letter of Marco Minoto, bailo of Constantinople, in Thomas, *DVL,* I, 167.

6829–1321 (June) [43]

. . . since these[1] have been appointed from olden times and receive from the revenues of this holy church each year 300 *modioi* of the *sitokrithos*[2] as income and a cask full of wine for the protosynkellos and fifty *trikephala.*[3] And in the same manner this holy church possesses three Jews, the children of Lamer,[4] David, and Samaria.[5]

κατέχει δε ὡσαύτως ἡ αὐτὴ ἁγιωτάτη ἐκκλησία καὶ 'Ιουδαίους τρεῖς, τὰ τε παιδία τοῦ Λαμέρη καὶ τοῦ Δαβίδη καὶ τοῦ Σαμαρία

Emperor Andronikos II Palaiologos confirms all the possessions of the Church of Ioannina; in *MM,* V, 86; ed. Sp. Lambros, "Chrysobull of Andronikos I Palaiologos in Behalf of the Church of Ioannina," *Neos Hellenomnemon,* (Greek) 12 (1915), 36–40; Dölger, *Regesten,* IV, no. 2460; Bees, "Übersicht über die Geschichte des Judenthums von Janina," p. 165; Dölger, "Die Frage," p. 24 (= *Paraspora,* pp. 376–77, with later bibliography supplied by the editor); Starr, *Romania,* p. 59, note 44. I. Lampridou, in *Epeirōtika Meletēmata* (I [Athens, 1887], 59–60), claimed that the descendants of these Jews continued in the same status as late as the reign of Ali Pasha; Lampridou's claim was accepted by P. Pararousse ("The Metropolis of Ioannina," [Greek] *Hellenikos Philologikos Syllogos* [Istanbul], *paratēma* to vol. XXXIV [1913–21], p. 210).

1. The clerics of the Church of Ioannina.

2. Andronikos II instituted a new tax in kind, due from every agricultural laborer, consisting of six *modioi* of wheat and four *modioi* of barley *pro zeugarion* (hence the name wheat-barley tax). Cf. Ostrogorsky, *History,* p. 431.

3. Zakythinos identifies these coins as the "perperi tre santi" mentioned by Pegolotti. They had a weight of 13-1/2 carats and were stamped with three heads: that of Christ on the right; those of the two emperors (Andronikos II [1282–1325] and Michael IX [1295–1320]) on the left. Pegolotti's observations on Byzantine currency are of great importance for the study of fourteenth-century coinage. Francesco Balducci Pegolotti, *La Pratica della Mercatura,* text edited by Allan Evans, Mediaeval Academy of America, publ. 24 (Cambridge, Mass., 1936), p. 40. Pegolotti's observations are commented on extensively by Zakythinos, *Crise monétaire et crise économique à Byzance du XIIIe au XVe siècle,* pp. 10ff.

4. The chrysobull of Stephan Dušan to the monastery of Likousada (75) gives the variant (A)Namer. The name is fairly common among Byzantine Jews (including Crete); viz., the eleventh-century ketubah from Mastaura (20n) lists the bridegroom as Namer bar Elkanah (cf. *apud* Mann, *Jews in Egypt,* note 2 to text); a Namer ben Elia is cited in a Geniza fragment (Cambridge T-S 12.62) dated 1224. Circumstances suggest that he came from a Byzantine environment. A scribe in Magnesia in 1387 signed his name as Judah ben Namer (below, 99), and a contemporary of the latter (1400–1401), Namer ben Shlomo, is cited in two mss: Rostok, Universitätsbibliothek, MSS Orient, 42, and Munich, Bayerische Staatsbibliothek, Cod Heb 118 (HPP G59 and G17 respectively). Namer is also a common name in Crete, Professor Ankori informs me. In all of the mss examined and in all of the instances cited, Namer is clearly a common Romaniote name, and may even be restricted to that general area since it does not appear in any other dated manuscript prior to the sixteenth century. Thus LAMER must be a misprint for Namer, the Hebrew word for tiger or leopard. Compare Judah = Leon.

5. The Hebrew name Shemarya.

[44] 1321

Damages caused to the Venetians by men of the Emperor of the Greeks: (total) 14,000 hyperpera.

a) against those of Monovasia who seem to have been beyond the treaty.	Item: the damage	of Jacob the Babylonian[1] from Negroponte, hyperpera	178
	" "	of Matthew Tramudo from Negroponte, hyperpera	115
	" "	of Isabel of Crete from Negroponte, hyperpera	25
	" "	of the aforesaid Antonio[2] from Negroponte, hyperpera	113
b) against the Monovasians	Item: the damage	of Jacob b. Solomon from Negroponte, hyperpera	60
	" "	of Jacob Colini from Negroponte, hyperpera	95
c) against Angelus Dene[?] and Emanuel of Smyrna	Item: the damage	of Jacob Colini from Negroponte, hyperpera	54

d) against Cauo de ferro	Item: the damage	of Elia Verla Jew[3] from Negroponte, hyperpera	42
	" "	of Marco da Ponte, hyperpera	50
e) against Manuel of Monovasia	Item: Elia Cuci and	Elia della Medega,[4] Jews, hyperpera	1544
	They have received 700 from the *Capitaneus* of Monovasia for part of the damage; now they still have to receive	hyperpera	844

Thomas, *DVL,* I, 182ff. These Jews were primarily from Negroponte and Crete, supporting our contention that the Veneti Judei were local Jews from the colonies of Venice. The Jewish claims, amounting to 1,724 hyperpera, represent a little over 12% of the total.

In an earlier set of claims submitted by Venice to the emperor, we find several Jews from Crete listed: "*Hemanuel de judeo de Crete*"*(!),* who was robbed on the way to Thessalonica, and "*Lazaro Judeo filio magistri Helye medici habitatori in Cania,*" who was robbed by pirates (off Monovasia) of "*ceram, setam et furmentum quod valuerit L solidos grossorum,*" according to his testimony, "*et iurante etiam per suam legem Mosaycam*" (Tafel-Thomas, *Urkunden,* III, 160 and 257). For a discussion and general analysis of this set of claims, cf. Gareth Morgan, "The Venetian Claims Commission of 1278," *BZ,* LXIX (1978), 411–38.

1. Babylonia is a common substitute for Cairo during this period; it was actually the designation for the Mamluk fortress. Apparently we have here an example of an Egyptian-Jewish merchant moving to the Venetian orbit to take advantage of the better trading opportunities there.

2. Apparently Antonio Desde, who also had a claim against Cauo de ferro.

3. *Helie Verla Iude.*

4. On Helyas de la Medega Judeus, burgensis Negropontis, cf. N. Iorga, "Nouveau documents sur l'Orient vénitien, d'après des registres de notaires aux archives de Venice," *Revue historique du sud-est européen,* 12 (1935), 219, and Jacoby, "Status of Jews," p. 64. Could he be related to the Lazaro (= Eliezer or Elazar) mentioned above in the 1278 claims commission?

1323

[45]

. . . Thence by sea to Durazzo, a city . . . subject to the Prince of Romania, brother of the King of Jerusalem . . . in the province of Albania . . . which was recently subjugated and added to his dominions by the aforementioned King of Rassia;[1] a schismatic, for the Albanians are themselves schismatic, using the Greek rite, and closely resembling the

Greeks in dress and manners. . . . This city is in the circuit of its walls very extensive, but in buildings miserably small, because it was once totally destroyed by an earthquake,[2] during which the wealthy citizens and inhabitants, to the number of 24,000, as it is asserted, were buried beneath their own palaces and killed. It is now thinly populated by peoples differing in religion, customs and language, by Latins, Greeks, perfidious Jews,[3] and barbarous Albanians. . . . This city is distant 200 miles from Ragusa.

Edited and translated by Mario Esposito, *Itinerarium Symonis Semeonis ab Hybernia ad Terram Sanctam,* pp. 38–39.

1. The editor identifies Rassia (or Rascia) as the eastern part of Serbia, which was ruled in 1323 by Stephan Uroš III (1322–31).
2. March 1273; cf. Pachymeres, *Historia,* V, 7, and VI, 32, in *MPG* 143, cols. 806–10, 971.
3. For Jews in Durazzo in the Late Byzantine and Venetian periods, cf. Starr, *Romania,* pp. 81–83. Correct date (p. 82) to 1323.

[46] Ca. 1325[1]

Apology for Christianity against the Jews by Andronikos Palaiologos.[2]

Greek text unedited; Latin translation, *MPG* 133, cols. 797–924; Eng. summary by A. L. Williams, *Adversus Judaeos,* pp. 181–87; cf. G. Sarton, *Introduction to the History of Science,* 3, part 1, 414; Krumbacher, *Geschichte der byz. Literatur,* p. 91; Starr, *JBE,* p. 238, no. 187; E. Voordeckers, "Les Juifs et l'empire byzantin au XIVe siècle," *Actes du XIVe Congrès internationale des études byzantines* (Bucharest, 1975), 288f; and discussion by A. Sharf, "Jews, Armenians and the Patriarch Athanasius I," *Bar Ilan Annual,* XVI–XVII (1979), 42–46. The dialogue may contain some historical data, but first a scholarly edition of the Greek text, with a resolution of the questions of author and date, is a desideratum.

1. Migne ascribes the dialogue to Andronikos Komnenos and dates it to 1183; later, in his *Supplemento Bellarmini,* he redates it to 1327 and ascribes it to Euthymius Zigabenus. Joannes Livineius, *Lectionibus antiquis* (1616), was the first to suggest a date of 1327; cf. discussion in *MPG* 133, cols. 791–94.

The text itself bears a date corresponding to 1310 (chap. xli): *Igitur accidit Hierosolymae vastitas anno ab orbe condito quinquies millesimo, quingentesimo tertio et sexagesimo: usque ad praesentem vero, sexies millesimum octingentesimum octavum et decimum: Judaei totis mille ducentis quinque et quinquaginta sine regno exsulant.* The Byzantine year 5563 corresponds to 55 C.E., 6818 to 1310, while 1255 plus 55 also corresponds to 1310. The destruction of the Temple, the traditional date of the Jewish exile, however, dates from 70 C.E., which suggests that the author erred in his calculations by one indiction. This may or may not have affected his calculation of "*usque ad praesentem vero 6818.*"

The last sentence of the date suggests that the author was continuing the polemic involving the different interpretations of Genesis 49:10 among Jews and Christians. Cf., in general, A. Poznanski, *Schiloh. Ein Beitrag zur Geschichte der Messiaslehre*. Erster Teil (Leipzig, 1904), and p. 369 (no. 22) for our dialogue.

2. Sharf, "Jews, Armenians and the Patriarch Athanasius I" (pp. 44f), argues that this is the emperor, and not his nephew of the same name.

1329

[47]

a) This book[1] is done completely / by a scholar of scholarly ancestry /[2] son of a man of prophecy /[3] 'Adoniah Kalomiti[4] son of *ha-Nagid* and *ha-Rosh,* the wise and intelligent, my honored teacher Rabbi 'Aba Kalomiti. And I finished it on Sunday the second of Iyyar in the year 5089 of the Creation. And the beginning and end was in Saloniki.

b) The secrets (or insights) of Part I of [Maimonides'] *Guide for the Perplexed* which were revealed by R. Zeraḥia—who cited his name on folio 58b—was completed by my hand, 'Adoniah Kalomiti, on Wednesday, the fifth of Iyyar, on the second (day of the counting of the) Omer. And it was completed in the city of Saloniki in the year 5089 and I maintained the same format as the commentator.

For colophon a and a description of ms., cf. Emil W. R. Naumann, *Catalogus librorum manuscriptorum qui in Bibliotheca Senatoria Civilitatis Lipsienses asservantur* (Grimae, 1838), MS. 39, p. 301; cf. Jellinek, *Bet ha-Midrasch,* p. xl, n. 8. Colophon b is in Leipzig, Universitätsbibliothek, MS, B.H. 13. Both colophons are studied in HPP G64.

1. *Sodot More,* a commentary on the *More Neḥukhim* of Maimonides by Zeraḥia b. Isaac (Saladin) b. Shealtiel Barcinonensis. The colophon is in rhymed prose, as was the convention.

2. Literally, "a sprinkler son of a sprinkler," extended to "a priest son of a priest." However, there is no indication that the Kalomiti family was of priestly descent; therefore the more general application to scholars is used.

3. *Ḥozeh* may more likely be translated as astronomer.

4. On other Kalomitis in Crete see Ankori, "The Living and the Dead" (pp. 38–39, 68n, 69n), and in Negroponte, above (document 30).

1330

[47*]

Testimony before us the undersigned on Thursday in the month Adar 2 on the 17th day in the year 5090 of the Creation that Shlomith daughter of Shemaria came with her daughter the bride Malkah and her son Shmuel, and this Malkah wife of Abraham ben Shemaria testified that she sold to this Shlomith this book *Midrash ha-Ḥokhmoth* which remained to her from her husband R. Abraham for 120 coins and she received the money *in toto* and any of her sons or daughters or heirs who might appeal this let his words be completely nullified and all that we have heard we wrote down and signed and it is sealed.

JOSEPH BEN R. SHE'ARETH ZVI
ISAAC BEN ABRAHAM witness
ELIA HA-KOHEN BEN R. SHMUEL HA-KOHEN witness
MOSES BEN ABRAHAM (may his rest be in Eden!)

Oxford, Bodleian, Mich 551, fol. 210v. See above, document 26. (I should like to thank Colette Sirat for providing me a transcription of this document.) Above, in document 32, dated 1308, the scribe's name is Samuel ha-Kohen ben Eliahu ha-Kohen. It is not impossible that our witness, Elia ha-Kohen ben R. Shmuel (= Samuel) ha-Kohen, was the son of that scribe. In that case, both these documents, 32 and 47*, would illuminate the story of Karaite settlement in fourteenth-century Greece. See below, documents 78* and 100*, for the subsequent history and travels of this manuscript.

[48] Ca. 1331–1332

From there I went to the city of Antaliya. . . . It is one of the finest of cities in extent and bulk, (among) the most handsome of cities to be seen anywhere, as well as the most populace and best organized. Each section of its inhabitants lives by themselves, separated from each other section. Thus the Christian merchants reside in a part of it called al-Mina (i.e., "the Harbor") and are enclosed by a wall, the gates of which are shut upon them (from without) at night and during the Friday prayer-service; the Rum (Greek Christians), who were its inhabitants in former times, live by themselves in another part, also encircled by a wall; the Jews in another part, with a wall around them; while the king and his officers and mamlukes live in a (separate) township, which is also surrounded by a wall that encircles it and separates it from the sections that we have mentioned. The rest of the population, the Muslims, live in the main city, which has a congregational mosque, a college, many bathhouses, and vast bazaars most admirably organized. Around it is a great wall which encircles both it and all the quarters which we have mentioned.

The Travels of Ibn Battuta (A.D. 1325–1354), trans. by H. A. R. Gibb (Cambridge, 1962), II, 418.

Ca. 1331–1332 [49]

While we were sitting with the sultan (Muhammed, son of Aydin, sultan of Birgi) there came in an elderly man, wearing on his head a turban with a tassel, who saluted him. The qadi and the doctor stood up as he came in, and he sat down in front of the sultan, on the bench, with the Qur'an readers beneath him. I said to the doctor 'Who is this shaikh?' He just laughed and said nothing, but when I repeated the question he said to me 'This man is a Jew, a physician. All of us need his services, and it was for this reason that we acted as you saw in standing up at his entry.' At this my old feeling of indignation flared up anew, and I said to the Jew 'You God-damned son of a God-damned father, how dare you sit up there above the readers of the Qur'an, and you a Jew?' and went on berating him in loud tones. The sultan was surprised and asked what I was saying. The doctor told him, while the Jew grew angry and left the chamber in the most crestfallen state. When we took our leave, the doctor said to me 'Well done, may God bless you. Nobody but you would dare to speak to him in that way, and you have let him know just what he is.'

Ibn Battuta, II, 442.

Ca. 1331–1332 [50]

In the *qaisariya* (i.e., main bazaar) of this city (al-Machar) I saw a Jew who saluted me and spoke to me in Arabic. I asked him what country he came from and he told me that he was from the land of al-Andalus and had come from it overland, without travelling by sea, but by way of Constantinople the Great, the land of al-Rum and the land of the Jarkas, and stated that it was four months since he had left al-Andalus. The travelling merchants who have experience of this matter assured me of the truth of his statement.

Ibn Battuta, II, 480. Gibb identified the Jarkas as "the Circassians (Cherkess), who inhabited the lands at the eastern end of the Black Sea and the Kuban territory."

1332 or 1333 [51]

On the fourth day from our arrival at Constantinople, the *khatun* sent her page Sumbul the Indian to me, and he took my hand and led me into the palace . . . In the midst of the (large audience) hall there were three men standing, to whom these four men delivered me. They took hold of my garments as the others had done and so on a signal from another man led me forward. One of them was a Jew and he said to me in Arabic, 'Don't be afraid, for this is their custom that they use with every visitor. I am the interpreter and I am originally from Syria.' So I asked him how I should salute, and he told me to say *al-salamu 'alaikum*. . . . Then I approached him (Andronicus III) and saluted him, and he signed me to sit down, but I did not do so. He questioned me about Jerusalem, the Sacred Rock, (the Church called) *al Qumana* (i.e., the Church of the Holy Sepulchre), the cradle of Jesus, and Bethlehem, and about the city of al-Khalil (peace be upon him) (Hebron), then about Damascus, Cairo, al-'Iraq and the land of al-Rum, and I answered him on all of his questions, the Jew interpreting between us. He was pleased with my replies and said to his sons 'Honor this man and ensure his safety.' He then bestowed upon me a robe of honour and ordered for me a horse with saddle and bridle, and a parasol of the kind that the king has carried above his head, that being a sign of protection. . . . It is one of the customs among them that anyone who wears the king's robe of honour and rides on his horse is paraded through the city bazaars with trumpets, fifes and drums, so that the people may see him . . . so they paraded me through the bazaars.

Ibn Battuta, II, 505–6.

[52] 1332 or 1333

Its (Constantinople's) bazaars and streets are spacious and paved with flagstones, and the members of each craft have a separate place, no others sharing it with them. Each bazaar has gates which are closed upon it at night, and the majority of artisans and sellers in them are women. The city is at the foot of a hill that projects about nine miles into the sea, and its breadth is the same or more. This hill is surrounded by a city wall, which is a formidable one and cannot be taken by assault on the side of the sea. Within the wall are about thirteen inhabited villages. The principal church is in the midst of this section of the city.

Ibn Battuta, II, 508.

[53] 1330s–1340s

Unto you priests who draw near; the sons of Zaddok who sanctify; who eat the bread of toil; who foresee in the stars; holy of Israel, the first of its grain and its bow, its plow and its spade, and the king with his work; who seek to remove the rending of their garments and the robe of captivity from upon them to inherit dwelling places for their souls that went out from there. These are the Princes of the Assembly who live in the cities of refuge, the sages of the holy congregation of Rome; Shemarya son of the sage [Eliahu] bids peace and informs [you]:

A letter from your glory was brought to me, and I read and understood its words. I see that your spirit is yearning to rekindle its light with the oil that never diminishes but which was extinguished when it went forth with its body into the atmosphere of the world with the slap of the angel who is appointed over this; to illuminate the path for you to follow upon which you will go to reach the land from whose midst you set out lest you remain among those who wander under the sun with the Second Child as it is written: through sloth the roof sinks in, etc.;[1] if the clouds are full of rain, etc.[2]

And when I saw your desire to pursue this lofty thing, my heart gladdened and my honor rejoiced, and I offered praises and thanks to our Lord who spared a few survivors in the Sabbatical year[3] requesting for them success with a *Shir ha-Maʿaloth* (Song of Ascension). And since I saw how perfect was your desire for the success of your souls, I decided to fulfill your request.

You requested in your letter that I inform you somewhat of my ways and methods in order to know if you will find rest for your spirits in them; and also to inform [you of] the names of the Biblical books to which I have written commentaries, and what I have translated from the books of science both in extract and in full.[4] And you write also in the following words: We are the sect which chooses to pursue wisdom and the concepts of things—with one voice we say—Heaven forbid that we be among the rebellious or among those who hollow out broken cisterns, who travel from a mountain of beauty to the ruins of the Hebrews, for their deeds are worthless and their wealth is vanity and nothing. Therefore let them be worthless and of no matter.

And I answer you that my method and investigation is not acceptable to some sects and some non-Jews, indeed for them spirits of mankind will become more gentle and in them their eyes will open to see the revelations of God which direct and enlighten as luminaries in the Scriptures, and everyone's eyes will minister his revelation, and the eyes of all [sects and non-Jews] became dim from seeing him, because their eyes were too heavy from old age to enlighten their hearts; unto them will bend the knees of men of Torah and Mikra, and unto them will be sated the tongues of men of wisdom and reason, masters of Talmud will rejoice in them and the rabbis will find comfort in them—both the illiterate and the ignorant for all will know that their salvation from the smallest unto the greatest was from them.

And I have made commentaries on all 24 books [of the Bible] except Leviticus, Numbers, and Deuteronomy for I was distressed by the death of my first born (may his memory be blessed!) and after his death I was busy with my younger son commenting and writing for him the Talmud in a more explanatory and shortened version. The quantity of books and the size of their lesson are the following: a lesson on Genesis and Exodus about equal to the size of one *seder* of the Talmud; a lesson on the Prophets larger than it; a lesson on Psalms about [the size of] two *sedarim* (of the Talmud); a lesson on Proverbs, Ecclesiastes, and the Song of Songs equal to the seder of Psalms; a lesson on the remaining Writings equal to (the size of) one of these.

In all of these books I forbade myself—with a prohibition *sub poene* excommunication—and took care to say that there was not one letter added or lacking in any sentence in all of the Holy Writings—how much the more so a word or a phrase!—for he who speaks thus is heretical to all the sacred writings and this was not the latter's intention; for he who explains a word from the Scriptures and adds or omits one letter from the text, it is apparent that his comments are completely false and this is not the intention of the text; and how could a man's heart act so foolishly to speak thus about the givers of the Torah and those who speak with the holy spirit, i.e., that they erred in their words and did not know (how) to speak as was fitting; and how can the heart consent to believe them if they also did not know (how) to speak.

In all of the hidden marvels that I explained, I did not press one letter of the text in order to establish this insight from the text;[5] therefore that text, upon its logical obvious meaning and the correctness of the science of accent and its grammar, reveals this insight and witnesses that this is its meaning more than what its common literal meaning indicates as the mass of the people understands it.

In my commentary on all of the Bible there is neither homiletical interpretation nor aggadah, for I have explained these where they occurred in the Talmud. And I have not left in all of the Bible a place where the sectarian or heretic or idol-worshipper, neither from among our people or another, could err; for when he hears my commentary his thought will be found to be invalid and will be avoided so that no one will pay attention to it in vain.

For if you have heard that I have translated from the books of the philosophers, you have heard correctly, for I occupied myself with them exceedingly and also translated. Indeed I ceased translating 25 years ago when I turned my knowledge and desire to this great work, for I saw that by their translation I was of no use to any man and perhaps also that they would be forced to finish their life with them. And I saw also that all their good words, I would be obliged to make mention of them in the scriptures. Therefore I stopped translating them so that I would not come to nothing nor miscarry.

And now I will write for you my introduction because also from it you will understand my method and meaning.

> The words of Shmarya son of the noble scholar, master, and sage Eliahu ha-Parnas the Cretan, an inhabitant of Rome (of blessed and pious memory!)

It said at the beginning of its phrases: *"Raḥash libi daḅar toḅ."*[6] One of the sons of Koraḥ uttered this verse when the holy spirit moved him to say what he said in that Psalm as I explained *ad locum*. And today also I have applied it to me and to my words because not only among the prophets is this matter, surely also among every intellect and sage and every rabbi and gaon who rouses himself and sets himself in motion to set sail on the great sea, that is the sea of the Torah, because without a doubt not of his own accord does he set himself in motion to endure the great hardship to separate from the dry land wherein he lives with his contemporaries. These are affairs of the body and its pleasures; to set sail and to enter the depths of the Sea of Torah to write them and to inform others of them, indeed one thing outside of this is good and betters everything for him who motivates himself to this great bother to the advantage of the many and their success.

For the language of that sage or genius is a pen for that "*daḅar tob*" and he who motivates to speak what the *kálamos* (pen) is to the scribe and the scribe motivates it to write what it will write. Therefore it is fitting for a man to offer his shoulder to endure in his origin the summons which calls him to this; and not to present a rebellious shoulder to cast off from him the burden of the kingdom of heaven because his sin would increase exceedingly. And may the explanation of this verse be according to the way I have applied it to me and to the Lord's work that I have chosen to do this.

"*Raḥash libi daḅar toḅ*". Its understanding is an important personal matter; my intellect and words have awakened and aroused my heart to say what I will say, for if it appears that I am the speaker and teacher and advisor of men and it is my writings and my deeds that I am speaking and writing to them—these things do not come from me. Indeed my tongue is the pen of an expert scribe. And though the letters are made by the *kálamos* it is not the workman but rather the tool of the workman. Likewise is my tongue to the scribe. And if it seems to speak and explain, it does not do these things (for) it is only a tool for the workman. The one who makes the words and explains them is the intellect which is called here "*daḅar toḅ.*" And may the meaning of "*raḥash*"—movement and birth—be as the Aramaic phrase "it moved upon the earth" and as the rabbinic phrase "its lips moved"—for this is a transitive verb; and there (in the verse) "*libi*" is an object to it and "*daḅar*" is the subject and "*toḅ*" is an adjective to "*daḅar.*"[7]

And the meaning of "*daḅar toḅ*" is an important matter as (in the verse) "*al kol daḅar pesha*"[8] and it is the activating intellect which is the "*daḅar toḅ.*" Or let the meaning of "*daḅar*" be "*sakhel*" (intellect) as in "*dibarti ani ʿim libi*"[9] where its meaning is "I have thought and become wise (*hiskhalti*)" and also because of this it is called "*daḅar toḅ*" because it is what speaks with the actual thing that is better for them than anything else. Therefore it is what draws them from the potential to the kinetic.

Also it is called "*daḅar*" from '*debir*' (sanctuary) which is the holy existence, the world of the Holy of Holies, i.e., the inner world which is the world of the angels. Also it is called "*daḅar*" from the meaning of behavior as in "*asim dovroth ba-yam*"[10] because it is the source of advice[11] and behavior to mankind. And so our rabbis (may their memories be blessed!) would say one *daḅar* to a generation. Their point, however, derives from a more restricted grammatical allusion.

And the meaning suggests a limitation as one would say in Greek *ligonda,*[12] and likewise [in the verse] "on whose hand the king leaned,"[13] the meaning of "leaned" limits. One says in Greek, based on the science of accent, *akkouvizonda,*[14] and both "*deḅarim*" are combined in it, that is saying and doing, not that others did them but that I alone say. And its meaning (is thus)—despite the fact that I am the speaker and maker of these words and explanations which I will write and make and explain and advise and it is "*taʿam la-melekh,*" I am not merely a tool to the "*daḅar toḅ*" which "*raḥash libi*" to beget and explain like a *kálamos* which is a tool to the scribe. And the meaning of "*la-melekh*" is as the verse "*va-yimalekh libi ʿalai.*"[15] And I have called the activating intellect an expert and skilled scribe in order to relate the praise for my words and their truth for like the *kálamos* when it is the *kálamos* of an expert scribe gives birth to true, beautiful and clear letters, likewise the words of my tongue are true, beautiful and clear because my tongue is the pen of an expert scribe not the tongue of man. And let not any man say that I have applied it to praise the "*deḇarim*" and their prestige and to prevent them from bearing (fruit) from me or from a man of flesh and blood like me; for their begetting is from the "*daḇar toḇ*" which took my tongue for its pen as the scribe takes the *kálamos* for his tool.

And after I have acknowledged to whom and by the strength of whom is my commentary and my deeds, I will return to explain what was the reason that diverted my shoulders to bear this great burden and this lengthy and massive work; and say that I have seen that all Israel is divided between two main groups: one group is drawn to and attached to the Written Law alone, i.e., the twenty-four holy books, neither noticing nor considering the Oral Law which is a wide and deep sea to the rabbinic sages who immerse themselves in its depths. To them alone is known the depths of its proceedings. We have already spoken about it and its details in places, things which those who hear them their heart will leap; also we have made known the success of those who have attained and mastered it in Psalm 119 as a success in analogy and logic; and those who did not appreciate its meaning nor understood its [spiritual] reward, they cleaved to the Written Law alone, and therefore knowledge and wisdom of the Torah among them is little because in their seeking of the Written Law they will neither understand nor perceive the important matters rather they will just read and not comprehend.

And this group too is divided into two sub-sections: one is content with the reading alone, incompetent as to its sense and not seeking further; while the second solves the sense, yet seeks great things from the reading alone. And so this second section is also divided into two parts, some turned to the non-Jewish sciences like the learned naturalists and theologians casting it away behind its backs, thus it was oversimplified in their eyes; and part strived to realize mysteries and parables in the Torah which just were not there even though their voices were loud protesting that this was not their intent, but that their true purpose in this was to elevate and endear the Torah, but the mysteries and parables became numerous until those elements which contradict and destroy the Torah returned.

This is the essence of the group and its factions which chose the Written Law alone and which did not recognize the illuminations of the Talmud, which is a commentary on the Written Law, to perceive its depth and its value.

The second group is attracted to the Talmud alone. They are neither affected nor in any way excited about the Written Law nor will they learn anything from it whether important or inconsequential. Behold all Israel has become factionalized and developed two philosophies and both groups' hearts are enjoined to evil and speak falsehood about each other. And when I realized this, I undertook the difficult task of interpreting all the Holy Scripture—in this terrible and awesome way based on the true science of accent and logic—and to raise up the prophetic pearls imbedded in the sea of the Torah and its depths, and to show the people and their leaders its beauty with the help of God, and my tongue was moved by this "*dabar tob*" to explain and to speak its words and this method I will follow throughout the Scriptures—except for the 613 commandments because I can neither add to nor augment the commentary of the Tannaim or Amoraim which is to be found throughout the six orders of the Talmud.

I have no doubt that in doing this that all Israel will return to one philosophy, for when they hear the pearls of the Pentateuch, Prophets, and Writings, they will muster their hearts and run to worship together. Their heart will not turn to non-Jewish sciences for the worship of it will weigh heavy upon them, and the sun of righteousness will rise over them and heal them under its wings. And when they hear also of the success of the Talmudists through *hekkesh* [analogical deduction] and *'iyyun* [deliberation] and the Scriptures bear witness to their success, the ears of all will ring and they will bare their necks to its master.

The Lord God of the Heavens who took me from the house of my father and from the land of my birth has directed me on the path of truth to take my brother's daughter for my son. So writes Shemarya, son of the noble scholar, master and sage Eliahu ha-Parnas the Cretan, an inhabitant of Rome (may his sacred memory be blessed!)

Letter of Shemarya of Negroponte to the Jews of Rome, copied from an unknown manuscript by Samuel David Luzzato and published by Abraham Geiger in *Ozar Nehmad* (Vienna, 1857), II, 90–94; reprinted in *Kevusoth Ma'amarim* (*Gesammelte Abhandlungen*), ed. Samuel Poznanski (1910), pp.

290–95. H. Graetz (*Divrei yemei Israel,* 5: 261) identified the last section of the introduction as an attempt to breach the rift between the Rabbanites and the Karaites. Mann (*Texts and Studies,* II, 295 and note 6) follows Neubauer in refuting this theory. As the passage shows, Rabbinic Jews were divided among many points of view. There is no reason to assume that the Karaites are herein singled out; equally, there is no reason to assume that they are excluded. Shemarya refers to "all Israel," but his remarks seem to castigate the general debilitating state of nonunity.

1. Ecclesiastes 10:18.
2. Ecclesiastes 11:3.
3. 1329, 1336, 1343, 1350, 1357 were sabbatical years which might apply.
4. See part I, chap. 4, note 9 for a list of Hebrew books and philosophical treatises and below (this document) for translations.
5. Cf. 1 Samuel 15:23.
6. Psalm 45:2: "My heart overflows with a goodly theme."
7. He continues his play on the verb *paʿal.* I translate *paʿul* here as "object" instead of "passive," and *poʿel* as "subject" rather than "verb."
8. Exodus 22:8.
9. Ecclesiastes 1:16.
10. 1 Kings 5:23 (= 5:9 in the RSV).
11. Hiram is the *baʿal ʿaṣim* in the verse "I will make them into rafts (*dovroth*) on the sea" (cf. note 10) and the "*daḇar*" is the *baʿal ʿaṣah* in the present analogy.
12. Cf. Sophocles, *Greek Lexicon,* s.v. λήγω.
13. Sophocles, *Greek Lexicon,* s.v. ἀκκουμβίζω.
14. 2 Kings 7:2.
15. Nehemiah 5:7.

1330s [54]

Matthew Blastares, Tractate against the Jews in 5 Books.

Text unedited, Cod. Bodl. Seld., 44. Cf. A. Soloviev, "L'oeuvre juridique de Mathieu Blastarès," *Studi Byzantini,* 5 (1939), 699; Beck, *Kirche,* p. 786.

1333 (6841) [55]

Because Jacob the monk has shown at the present time a pure faith and good reputation in Our kingdom through the works which he has done . . . he has requested and entreated Us that he be given through a chrysobull the little monastery outside of the fort which is honored with the name of the holiest Lady of all, the Mother of God and celebrated as Ostrine, along with the shrine of St. Anastasias there. . . . Therefore let him be given 200 *modioi* from the land of the Lord Alexios Palaiologos in the region of Tholos which is located close by the home of Our Pansebastor Sebastor the Lord Constantine Achiraitos, and let him receive as a gift annually the required payments (τὰ ἀπαιτούμενα χάριν τέλους ἐτησίως) of 20 hyperpera from the Jews in Fort Zichna for his income. . . . This chrysobull in addition supplies and apportions to him . . . that he assume the aforementioned little monastery of the most holy Mother of God of Ostrine and of the aforementioned divine sanctuary of St. Anastasias and that he possess this in the sight of all for the length of his life undisturbed and untrammelled with the pasture and the contents and everything that rightly belongs to it and that they pass over with his death to whomever he wishes and wills on the ground that he possesses these and (disposes of them) in the same manner; and that the aforementioned land of 200 *modioi* in the region of Tholos from the land of the Lord Alexios Palaiologos be given to him, and that he possess this very land as ancestral, that he receive the required payments of 20 hyperpera annually from the aforementioned Jews for his income. . . .

MM, V, 105–6; Sathas, *MB,* I, 232–34. Most recently edited by Andre Guillou, *Les Archives de Saint-Jean-Prodrome sur le mont Ménécée,* no. 28, pp. 96–98; Dölger, *Regesten,* IV, no. 2793.

A. A. Andréadès, "Les Juifs et le fisc dans l'empire byzantine," in *Mélanges Charles Diehl,* I, 7–29 (reprinted in *Erga* [Oeuvres], I, 629–59). Cf. postscriptum where he accepts this text as "le chrysobulle de 1333 qui, je le confesse a regret, m'avai échappé, constitue le plus puissant des arguments en favour d'un impôt judaïque." Dölger, "Die Frage," p. 24 (= *Paraspora,* p. 376); P. Charanis, "The Jews in the Byzantine Empire under the First Palaeologues," *Speculum,* 22 (1945), 77; D. A. Zakythinos, *Crise monétaire,* p. 87; Starr, *Romania,* pp. 113, 116 note 7; Sima Cirkovic, "The Jewish Tribute in Byzantine Regions," (Serbian) *Zbornik Radova,* no. 4, pp. 141–47; Ph. Argenti, "The Jewish Community during the Eleventh Century," in *Polychronion,* pp. 39–68 (pp. 54–68 contain a summary and criticism of the literature on the question of a Jewry tax in the Byzantine Empire [reprinted in the author's *The Religious Minorities of Chios: Jews and Roman Catholics,* pp. 63–92]).

[56] 1335/36

a) This book was completed by my hand, Kaleb bar Elia, in the year 5096 of the Creation on the eighth of Ab in the city of Adrianopolis. And may the Lord Ariel build her and bring redemption to Israel as this poor Kaleb requests every day. And may He sustain me to meditate in it and to understand the depth of the strength of its contents and the wonder of its secrets and to fulfill its words without error as I have spelled them and avoided any great transgression. May the utterings of my mouth be according to Thy will and the meditation of my heart before You. May it be my rock and my salvation.

b) This page, I Eliezer, wrote in honor of Mar Kaleb in the year 5095 of the Creation on Friday of the Sabbath of Tammuz, and may the Lord sustain him, his sons and grandsons to meditate in it. Amen.

Leiden, University Library, MS Or. 4760; HPP F8. Two other scribes are discernible in the manuscript through acrostics: Jacob (fol. 61a and 108b), who wrote 9 pages, and Solomon (fol. 244a), who wrote some 21 scattered folios. The bulk of this manuscript—*Sefer Mişvoth* of the Karaite Levi ben Yefet, *Sefer Dinim* of Benjamin (al-Nahawendi), and selected responsa of Yeshua ha-Melammed—was written by our first scribe, Kaleb bar Elia. The second scribe wrote less than a leaf.

The water marks in the paper date from the period of the 1330s and 1340s and thus support the years cited in the colophons. This manuscript thus becomes our earliest evidence for a Karaite community in Adrianople and, *ipso facto,* for a Rabbanite community as well.

Advances in codicology allow present-day researchers new techniques that were not available to earlier generations of paleographers. Thus we are in a position to redate the very few instances where their learning led them to errant identifications. Steinschneider, the Nestor of nineteenth-century Jewish paleography, mistakenly identified the first scribe as the well-known Kaleb Afendopolo and thus dated the manuscript in the late fifteenth century; cf. his *Leiden* catalogue, ms. Warn. 22, and note there.

1335

[57]

a) Letter D, Chapter IV: Concerning those baptized Jews. Concerning the stiff-necked race of Jews who are uncircumcised in the heart, the 7th canon of the VIIIth Synod reads thus: If any one of them, out of pure heart, should prefer the Christian beliefs and should confess to us with all his heart that he has triumphed over the things that the race of Jews practice, tell him that others are so convinced and have made amends. Let this one be received favorably, and let him be honored with divine baptism with his children also; and let him be secured from returning to the customs of the Jews. But if anyone should not appear so [motivated], not even that he succeed to the Christian faith through this, but rather he has thought to escape some wanton insult, or he may depend on belonging to a faith of ephemeral glory and human prosperity in love for others; indeed let this one not be baptized. If, on the other hand, some who have these ideas have escaped our vigil by mistake and have been baptized, and now pretend to observe Christian beliefs while having been detected in secretly observing Jewish customs; neither let them in church nor let them be thought worthy of any other communion, and do not let their children be marked with divine baptism nor let them be permitted to possess a Christian slave but rather let them be committed openly to be governed according to the Hebrew observance.

Laws

The law says: the Jew who claims that he wants to be a Christian, and, if there is a charge against him or if there is a debt pending, flees to a church; unless he repays the debt or frees himself from the summons, he is not to be accepted.
A Jew may not possess a Christian slave, nor may he circumcise a catechumen, nor may another heretic do this.

b) Letter D. Chapter IV: Concerning the Jews that one must not have any communion with them at all. Examination in two chapters of Letter A, canon 64 of the Holy Apostles.

Canon 70 concerns fasting with Jews, either celebrating with them or accepting festival gifts from them, either the feast of the unleavened bread (*azyma*) or any other of these—the cleric who does must be defrocked and the non-cleric excommunicated. Even if he admits he does not believe, although he acts in such a way that he does, but they give scandal to many and suspicion against him that he honors the Jewish rite, which before the killing of Christ God seemed to have detested: saying "Fast and rest days, my spirit hates your fasts." For not with the Jewish way of life does the canon find fault, but with those who live indifferently and have not rejected their fellowship.

Concerning the *azyma*; against the Latins.
From this it is possible to know, that they do not transgress in the smallest way when they celebrate the mysterious sacrifice through the unleavened bread. For those who simply eat the unleavened bread from a Jewish feast, it brings about their defrocking and excommunication. Their partaking of the Lord's body by which the Pasca is celebrated, how else does earnest supplication become fitting? Not only has the simple eating of the unleavened bread been forbidden, but also celebrating [the mass] through the unleavened bread according to the Jewish custom. Moreover, what feast is greater than the bloodless sacrifice which the Lord undergoing death for us

in order to bring salvation when he was handed over before the feast of the Pasca? Because certainly it did not even cross the mind of the Holy Fathers that we celebrate the feast thus. It is obvious from the fact that they have studied thoroughly about the Jewish feast and they decided to place rules against all these things; just as indeed they have repealed the fast and resting during the sabbaths. In addition to this they perform in recollection of the fast of the Ninevites and others which in particular is not numbered on the present occasion.

The 71st Christian canon concerns the Christian who offers oil in pagan temples or in synagogues of the Jews, or the Christian who lights (oil) in the evenings. It excommunicates him because he will be thought to have honored their rites.

Also for all these things the canons 37, 38, and 39 of the Laodikeian Synod, all of which mention the apostolic canons both written or spoken, order you to keep distant.

The 11th canon of the VIth Synod [in the case of one] who does not stop eating the unleavened bread of the Jews; who does not stop esteeming their friendship worthy; who does not stop from summoning them for medical aid when sick; who does not stop bathing together with them in the communal bath; if a cleric he must be defrocked, if a non-cleric he must be excommunicated. See also Chapter IV, Letter B.

The 29th canon of the Laodikeian Synod says: Christians who have received the true law (which is more perfected) yet who still follow a shady and incomplete end must not adhere to the Jews or to the Sabbath as they celebrate it and their resting from business is to be condemned; but rather on this day they should work, honoring the Mistress of Days (if really it could be possible for Christians to be at leisure) by regular attendance in the churches for those staying away from work. For the one who out of poverty or any other need and who during this day (which has the name of the Lord) does work which is inevitable—but does it secretly—he is thought as one who acts without judgment and therefore pardon will not be granted. Also for all those who do not avoid the Jewish customs, but openly honor the thing dedicated, all things will happen (they shall openly be given anathema).

Laws

The Jews in the Sabbath and their other feasts neither minister bodily nor do anything nor are brought to trial for public or private reason nor can they accuse Christians.

If a Jew possesses a Christian or a catechumen and circumcises him, or if anyone dares to pervert his Christian thinking, let him suffer capital punishment.

c) concerning the cleric who because of fear of danger is weighed down, the 62nd canon of the Holy Apostles says: if any cleric because of human fear, whether of a Jew or a (pagan) Greek, or a heretic, denies the name of Christ, let him be defrocked completely.

Canon 64, concerning the cleric or non-cleric who enters a synagogue of the Jews or heretics to seek a favor, the first defrock, the second excommunicate. For, it says, what is the harmony between Christ and Belial? Is there any part of faith with unfaith?

Canon 37 does not allow one to partake of things sent by Jews or heretics for a feast, or to celebrate with them.

Canon 129 . . . but it is permitted neither to the Jews nor to the heretics to bring accusation, unless all those concerned with the case make this suggestion.

Law: A Jew must not marry a Christian woman nor a Christian a Jewess; nor a heretic nor one of another faith with the excuse that he would be united through marriage to the Christians.

Law: formerly the Hebrew men were allowed by law to give a document of divorce to the woman but now this has been abrogated by the Christians.

d) Concerning the *Tessareskaidekatitai* (those who celebrate the 14th day). These celebrate the Pasca not on Sunday according to the holy laws of the church, but on that day on which the 14th day of the lunar month happens to fall. This is a custom most peculiar to the Jews.

Concerning the *Tetraditai* (those who celebrate four days). These, when they celebrate the Pasca, do not terminate on the day, but prefer to fast for four days. In this they imitate the Jews, who after the Pascal feast, eat bitter foods and unleavened bread.

Matthew Blastares, *Syntagma,* in *MPG,* 144, cols. 690–1400; ed. Rhalles and Potles, *Syntagma ton theion kai hieron kanonon,* vol. VI (Athens, 1859). A Serbian translation was made during the reign of Stephan Dušan: ed. St. Novaković, *Matije Vlastara Sintagmat* (Belgrade, 1907). Cf. Juster, *Les Juifs dans l'empire romain,* vols. I–II; Parkes, *The Conflict of the Church and the Synagogue,* is still the basic reference work in English; Starr, *JBE,* chap. III and documents cited there; Soloviev, "L'oeuvre juridique de Mathieu Blastarès," *Studi Bizantini,* 5 (1939), 698–707; Ostrogorsky, *History,* p. 424, and his caveat on the use of 14th century legal codes; Beck, *Kirche,* p. 786; Pantazopoulos, *Church and Law in the Balkan Peninsula during the Ottoman Period,* pp. 49–50;

Argenti, *The Religious Minorities of Chios: Jews and Roman Catholics* (pp. 36–63), contains the Greek and Latin texts with commentary; see below, document 67.

a) *MPG,* 144, col. 1109; cf. Starr, *JBE,* no. 18, pp. 96–97 and bibliography cited there, and no. 74, pp. 136–38, and no. 121, pp. 173ff. It should be the 8th canon of the Council of Nicaea II (787). For the laws, cf. Starr, pp. 144–48 (the *Basilika*), and earlier Parkes, *Conflict,* appendix II.

b) *MPG,* 144, cols. 1345–48. Canon 37 is translated in section c; for canon 38, cf. Starr, no. 8n, p. 90; for other canons, cf. Parkes, pp. 381–82. For canon 11 of the Trullan (Quinisext) Council, cf. Starr, no. 8, pp. 89–90. For the laws on the Sabbath and courts, cf. Starr, no. 83, pp. 144f; on slavery and disputation, ibid., no 60, pp. 126–27.

c) *MPG,* 144, cols. 1024, 1050, 1052, 1180, 1244; for laws on intermarriage, cf. Starr, no. 83, pp. 144–47. On divorce, he means that while a Jew could divorce his wife by giving her a *get* in biblical and postbiblical times, the church prohibited divorce for Christians.

d) *MPG,* 144, col. 1036; on the Passover, cf. Parkes, pp. 165, 175, 176.

1336[1]

[58]

Sometime ago Chionios spoke against the most honorable Dikaiophylax Cabasilas, the steward of the most holy diocese of Thessalonica, and also against the most honorable Chartophylax Strymbakonas, and the Sakellius Bryennios. The reason was that some clergy and monks announced that this Chionios had, along with his brothers, abjured Christian piety and thought Jewish thoughts . . . they examined strictly his pronouncements on the church and his alleged Judaizing practices; they arrested and held him and handed him over to the most powerful (after God) and holy emperor to be kept there, since this Chionios had enmity and malice toward them, to be arraigned in a royal court of inquiry by the assembled archons concerning his teachers and students; making a few comments, he turned the accusations against these ecclesiastics. At this particular time he spoke against their rumors; these were against Cabasilas, as this Chionios heard about him from Staxytzes, that when the *oikonomos* was a child he did something, and against Cabasilas that this Chionios undertook the dispute of the Jews in that place and dismissed those who crept in with their designs, seeing that some of the newcomers (*epoikōn*)[2] of the city happened to come upon these Jews and malign them, both insulting their worship and their law, he complained loudly of suffering for these very ones; and moreover that they affronted the law of Moses which was given by God through him; he went to the Chartophylax to denounce these new inhabitants of the city saying that, as these newcomers were not doing right in this, that they honored the servant more than the master, and that they assembled all together in the church of the great martyr and sweet-scented Saint Demetrius, while they avoided the Church of the Lord and Savior Christ; then the Chartophylax said to him that the Thessalonicans honor fully the martyr of Christ. Concerning the Sakellius, he said he did not know anything about him, but he heard from George Angelos, the friend of the very powerful and holy ruler, that he did not believe in the resurrection of the dead. Of such a sort were the rumors at that time . . . And so the synod was called . . . this Chionios was acquitted, as one might say, the accusation being unacceptable . . . (and) these ecclesiastics and superiors are innocent of the above accusation which they were in vain slandered, and this is proved after a long and exact examination, now they are bound again to their priesthood . . .

Synod in Constantinople, in *MM,* I, 174–78; F. Dölger, "Zur Frage des Judischen Anteils an der Bevölkerung Thessalonikes im XIV. Jahrhundert," *Joshua Starr Memorial Volume,* pp. 129–33 (= *Paraspora,* pp. 378–83); Jean Meyendorff, "Grecs, Turcs et Juifs en Asie Mineure au XIVe siècle," *Polychordia,* pp. 211–17; Emmanuel, *Israélites des Salonique,* pp. 44–45; Nehama, *Histoire des Israélites,* pp. 104–5.

1. The date is supplied from internal evidence. One of the letters presented is dated October 24, Fifth Indiction (September 1, 1336, to August 31, 1337).
2. For this translation of *epoikoi,* see document 36 and note.

[59] 1336

And behold in our own times in the [lunar] cycle 269 we heard that in the fourth year of the cycle what was for us the month of Elul was the month of Tishre for the people in Ereṣ Israel who rely on the *abib.*

Aaron b. Elijah the Karaite, *Gan 'Eden,* 22; quoted by Ankori, *Karaites,* p. 340, note 112; see document 147 for repetition by Elijah Bashyazi; cited in Mann, *Texts and Studies,* I, 46, note 3a.

[60a] 1330s

Year 509–
Samuel son of Rav . . .

Fragment of a tombstone in the Museum at Thebes; published by M. Schwab, "Sept epitaphes hébraïques de Grèce," *REJ,* LVIII (1909), 108; reedited and published with photograph by author, "Jewish Epitaphs in Thebes" in *REJ,* vol. CLXI (1982), #1.

1337–38

[60b]

(May) his rest be honored
. . .
Leon Caimi (?)
Son of Rav (?) . . . son of Rav
Shlomo ha-Parnas
When a man suffers, year
5098 (of the Creation)

Epitaph in the Museum at Thebes; published by Schwab, p. 109, and restudied by author, #3. Cf. author's "Jews in Fourteenth-Century Thebes" for commentary. The stone is in extremely poor condition, and only two of the names and the date are recoverable.

1339

[61]

Listen to an event that occurred in the year of Creation 5099 (= 1339) as related by R. Moses my father-in-law (his rest be in Eden), in his treatise: two men, one named Juda Pappa(s), and the name of the second Moses b. David, both Rabbanites, bought a lamb and R. Nathan son of R. Hillel slaughtered it. And though a pig was found in the vicinity, they declared [the lamb] permissible and ate it.

Aaron b. Elijah the Karaite, *Gan 'Eden,* section *Sheḥitah,* 84a; quoted in Ankori, *Karaites,* p. 136.

1339

[62]

. . . in grief are the multitude of captives, of whom some are unfortunately enslaved to the Jews, and others to the Ishmaelites . . .

προσανιᾷ δε καὶ ἡ τῶν ἀιχμαλώτων πληθύς, ἔστιν ὧν μὲν Ἰουδαίοις, ὧν δὲ Ἰσμαηλίταις δυστυχῶς δουλεύοντων

Letter to . . . (Philippos?) Logaras concerning what happened at Ephesus, in M. Treu, *Matthaios Metropolit von Ephesus, Ueber sein Leben und sein schriften,* p. 56; translation of Matthew of Edessa, in Vryonis, *The Decline of Medieval Hellenism,* p. 269 and comments passim. In 1308 the Seljuq Emir Sasan took Ephesus.

[63] 1343 (31 July)

In the name of the everlasting God, amen. In the year from the incarnation of our Lord Jesus Christ 1343, in the month of July, on the last day, in the eleventh indiction, at Constantinople in Cafachalea where the Venetian Jews dwell. Since of his own life each man is ignorant of his end we have no more truth save that we cannot evade death . . . I, Isaac Catelanus, a Venetian Jew, an inhabitant there in Cafachalea, gravely sick in body but having a sane and whole mind, wishing to escape leaving my affairs in disarray, had summoned to me the presbyter Petrus de Rena who is a notary, and I requested the latter that he write this will for me. In which I wish to be my faithful executors Solomon Artachino son of the late Samuel Artachino, Salachaia Daviti son of David Daviti, my Jewish nephews and Dulcha Cathelana my sister, and Samuel de ag Achris son of my late nephew Samson. First I wish and order that my said executors are bound and ought to give and distribute for my soul, according to the custom and law of Moses, in proportion, as it seems best in the judgment of my said executors or a majority of them. Indeed my possessions situated in Cafacalea I leave to my said agents to be divided equally among them. I do not wish them to be sold, pawned, mortgaged nor transferred without the consent of my said executors or a majority of them. As for my other movable and immovable goods, whithersoever they were situated or will be situated, I leave to my said executors to be divided equally among them. Moreover I give and assign the fullest capacity and legal power to the above-written Salomon Artachino and Salachaia Daviti to both of them together or to one and to my other executors, after my death, that my aforesaid commission be introduced and administered by these Salomon and Salachaia or whichever one of these; I give full power and legal capacity to examine, solicit, plead and respond to summons . . . Nevertheless, I do not wish that these agents of mine, namely Salomon or Salachaia or either of them, be able to pledge with my debtors or with any one of my debtors and to make with them or with any one of them an agreement or pact for part of any debt which is owed to me, unless with the consent and agreement of my said executors or a majority of them. And I wish my outstanding goods to be divided among my said executors. And I judge this my will to be secure and forever. But if anyone dares to infringe upon it or corrupt it, may God the omnipotent Father be against him in all his undertakings, moreover let five pounds of gold be paid to the heirs and successors of my above-written executors and to their heirs and successors, and notwithstanding let this copy of my will continue its effect in perpetuity. Signed by the above-written Isaac Catalanus the Jew, who requested this to be made and given while still alive into the hands of his above-mentioned executors.

I, Petrus Cornario, a witness, signed
I, Petrus Dragonus, a witness, signed
I, Petrus de Rena, presbyter of the Church of Saint Bartholomew and secretary and notary . . .
to the Bailo Johannis Gradonico in Constantinople and all of Romania . . . I completed and confirmed.

Will of Isaac Catelanus, Venetian Jew of Constantinople, transcribed from the *Notai della Cancelleria inferiore,* Archivio di Stato, Venice, *busta* 156, and published by David Jacoby, "Quartiers juifs," pp. 222–23.

1342–1345

[64]

Poor: Are you not ashamed to hear how the gentiles treat the poor ones of their kin or their prisoners of war from among us? Why do they not consider any one of them unworthy of due care? It is the height of unreasonableness that Jews and Mohammedans should be humane and merciful, while the disciples of Christ, who was by nature humane and merciful, should be heartless and niggardly towards their kin. Indeed it is to us that you owe the goods of this world, and only those amongst you who have mercy towards us will partake in the rewards of the future life.

Rich: But it is not fitting that we feed for nothing those who do not serve us.

Edited and translated by Ihor Ševčenko, "Alexios Makrembolites and His 'Dialogue Between the Rich and the Poor,'" *Zbornik Radova,* no. 6 (1960), pp. 205, 218.

[65] 1344

Testimony before we the undersigned, Tuesday, 18th day of Marḥeshvon in the year 5105 of the Creation of the World, that R. Shlomo b. R. Isaiah sold [the following books] . . . *Sefer Mibḥar* and *Sefer Mikhlol* for 2 *frangi* and received the money in hand . . . before us, we wrote and signed firm and binding—

R. Abraham b. R. Shabbetai, may he rest in Eden
Sh'ABeN b. R. Japhet, may he rest in Eden
Jacob b. R. Japhet

From a ms. of Aaron b. Joseph's *Mibḥar,* cited by A. Danon, "Documents relating to the History of the Karaites in European Turkey," *JQR,* ns, XVII (1926–27), 165. A copy of Aaron's *Mibḥar* was sold to Kaleb b. Shabbetai by Judah ha-Zaken b. Eleazar in 1380; cf. S. Munk, "Paris," p. 186.

[66] (No date)

Abraham the author said . . . Before us the undersigned witnesses R. Pappos . . . admitted [the foregoing]. Before the undersigned witnesses R. Abraham b. Isaac admitted [the foregoing].

From a ms. of Aaron b. Elijah's *Gan ʿEden* or *Sefer ha-Mizḳvoth,* cited by Danon, "Documents," p. 166.

[67] Ca. 1345[1]

Lib. I. Cap. VI.10. A heretic or a Jew cannot testify against an Orthodox Christian, but they may witness against each other.[2]

Lib. VI. Cap. XI.1. If one born a Christian becomes a Jew, all of his property is to be confiscated.[3]

Cap. XI.2. If a Jew purchases a Christian and circumcises him, he is to be decapitated.[4]

Cap. XI.3. If a Jew should dare to pervert the Christian faith, let the one born a Jew be decapitated.[5]

Gustav Heimbach, ed., *Const. Harmenopuli Manuale Legum sive Hexabiblos*; summary in E. H. Freshfield, *A Manual of Byzantine Law Compiled in the Fourteenth Century by George Harmenopoulous, Vol. VI on Torts and Crimes,* p. 40.

1. According to a notation in the manuscript Jur. 11, in the National Library at Vienna, quoted by Freshfield, p. viii.

2. From the *Basilika*; cf. Starr, *JBE,* no. 83c; cf. *Codex Iustiniani,* I.5.21; and R. Janin, "Les Juifs dans l'empire byzantine," *Echoes d'orient,* XV (1902), 127.

3. These are from the *Ecloga*; cf. Starr, *JBE,* no. 19b.

4. Ibid., no. 19c.

5. Ibid., no. 19d.

October 6854 (1345), Indiction XIV

[68]

[These are the metochia—i.e., a house or farm belonging to the monastery—and possessions of the monastery] . . . a metochion within Zichna, which has vineyards in various places and three mills; the Jews who are within Zichna; . . .

μετόχιον ἐντὸς τῶν Ζιχνῶν, ὅπερ ἔχει ἀμπέλια ἐν διαφόροις τόποις καὶ μύλωνας τρεῖς οἱ Ἰουδαῖοι οἱ ἐντὸς τῶν Ζιχνῶν . . .

Chrysobull of Stephan Dušan in favor of the monastery of St. John Prodromos at Menoikeion; text in Soloviev-Mošin, *Grěke,* pp. 12 (Greek text)–13 (Serbian text). Greek text in Guillou, *Les Archives de Saint-Jean-Prodrome,* pp. 124–31, no. 39; cf. Starr, *Romania,* p. 113. On the Jews in Serres, cf. Merdaco Covo, *Aperçu historique sur la communauté Israélite de Serrès* (Hebrew and French) with, however, no material on the Byzantine period.

1346

[69]

The Traditionalists speak of a name consisting of four letters and a name of twelve letters. It is true that the name consisting of four letters is a verb of the Qal form, it is intransitive and requires no additional letters. In the case of the transitive name, on the other hand, since its implications are many, its letters are also numerous. This does not mean that there is one name possessed of twelve letters, rather the words which explain the meaning of this name consist of twelve letters. The scholar R. Shemariah of Negroponte has explained this point stating that this name (of twelve letters) is ʿeṣ(e)m m'h(a)v(e)h K(o)l h(ō)v(e)h (a being who brings all into existence) and he is correct . . .

Translated by Morris Charner, *The Tree of Life of Aaron b. Elijah of Nicomedia, first half chp. 1–78,* ch. 74, p. 171. Shemarya was often cited by Aaron in his three major works, *Kether Torah, ʿEṣ Ḥayyim,* and *Gan ʿEden;* cf. Poznanski, *The*

Karaite Literary Opponents of Saadia Gaon, pp. 79–80. On the Karaites and Shemarya in general, cf. J. Fürst, *Geschichte der Karäerthums,* pp. 223–24.

[70] 1346

a) And if the sage R. Moses said that we did not find in the Scriptures sleep attributed to God (may he be blessed!), R. Moses my teacher and father-in-law (may his soul be at rest!) brought forth from Scriptures "Rouse thyself! Why sleepest thou, O Lord? Awake."

Aaron b. Elijah the Karaite, *'Eṣ Ḥayyim,* 76; quoted by Ankori, *Karaites,* p. 136, note 184. The pun is on R. Moses b. Maimon (Maimonides). The verse is from Psalms 42:24.

b) And the sage R. Moses my teacher and father-in-law properly explained the verse "Hear O Israel."

Ibid., 80; quoted in Ankori, *loc. cit.*

[71] 1346

The word of the Lord came to me saying:[1] "I have heard your words and all your miracles have risen to my ears. I will protect you and your reward will be very great; for you were a defender of my name and smashed every harlot from me. You have blown out with your spirit . . . the princes of Edom have been troubled, and a trembling has seized the philosophers of Greece; and because of your proofs they have been silenced like stone. As for you, write what you said to me in a book and call it *Sefer ha-Mora* (Book of Awe) and send it to all Israel, those near as well as those distant from you unto all the places where they are dispersed. They will tremble and weaken before you and will sanctify my name and they will seek me daily saying: Let us walk in the light of the Lord.[2] Righteousness will be for you as it is written and the intellects will shine like the splendor of heaven and those who make righteous the many will be as stars forever."

Shemarya Ikriti, introduction to his *Sefer ha-Mora*; quoted by A. Neubauer, "Documents inédits," *REJ,* X (1885), 88, with a French translation; for date, cf. fol. 31b, *loc. cit.*; cf. Zotenberg, *Catalogue . . . de la bibliothèque imperiale,* p. 180, #1005, 5.

1. Standard opening for prophets; cf. Jeremiah 1:2, Ezekiel 1:3, Hosea 1:1. Joel 1:1, etc.
2. The Hebrew text has a variation on the Tetragrammaton. Neubauer cites this as another example of Shemarya's messianic pretensions.

1346 **[72]**

And I, the only scholar found today, say that the philosophers are stupid and in error regarding this matter [i.e., the origin of the world].

Shemarya Ikriti, *Sefer ha-Mora,* fol. 32; quoted in Neubauer, "Documents inédits," p. 88, n. 4; cf. Eshkoli, *Tenuoth Meshiḥiyoth,* pp. 220–22. For a Spanish view of Byzantine philosophers, cf. Nachmanides, *Torath Adonai Temimah*; edited in Benzion Dinur, *Israel ba-Golah,* II, book V (Jerusalem, 1971), 376.

1346 **[73]**

I have considered and seen the sights of God and I see that Moses our Teacher (peace upon him!) explains as I do.

Shemarya Ikriti, *Sefer ha-Mora,* fol. 32, in Neubauer, "Documents inédits," p. 88, note 5; cf. Eshkoli, *Tenuoth Meshiḥiyoth,* pp. 220–22. These remarks must refer to Moses Maimonides; cf. Steinschneider, *Muenchen,* p. 93:
מי יגלה עפר מעיניך רבינו משה החכם הגדול בישראל אשר טרחת
ויגעת להשיב תשובה על דברי הפילוסוף ונלאית נשוא עד שאמרת
שהוא מעמד השכל וכו׳ ואני הנמצא היום בעזרתו ית׳ שמתי דבריו
כמוץ לפני רוח וכגלגל לפני סופה.

1346 **[74]**

. . . so my teacher and exegete R. Yehudah (may his soul be at rest!) explained [the verse Hosea 11:3] . . . and the sage R. Yehudah, my uncle and teacher (may his rest be in Eden!) brought the following interpretation) . . .

Aaron b. Elijah, *'Eṣ Ḥayyim* (ed. Delitzsch), 68, and *Gan 'Eden,* section Shemiṭṭah we-Yobel, 66d; quoted by Ankori, *Karaites,* p. 136, note 184.

November 6857 (1348), Indiction II **[75]**

. . . the Jew called Anamer; our majesty favorably received their petition and request and releases the oath through this Chrysobull . . .

Chrysobull of Emperor Stephan Dušan to the monastery of Likousada in Thessaly, in Soloviev-Mošin, *Grčke,* p. 158; Dölger, *Regesten,* vol. IV, no. 2780; Starr, *Romania,* p. 60, note 44. On the name Anamer and variants, see document 43n.

[76] Before 1350

Alexander thrust out his former wife who was still living and substituted a Jewess whom he straightway led to divine baptism, for, so they say, he loved her for her beauty.

ζῶσαν γὰρ τὴν προτέραν ἐξώσας σύζυγον Ἀλέξανδρος ἀντεισήγαγεν ἄλλην ἐξ Ἰουδαίων ἄρτι προσαγαγὼν τῷ θειῳ ταύτην αὐτὸς βαπτίσματι, τοῦ κάλλους αὐτῆς, ὥς φασίν ἐρασθοίς

Nicephoras Gregoras, *Historiae Byzantinae,* p. 558; Jirecek, *Geschichte der Bulgaren,* p. 312; Slatarski, *Geschichte der Bulgaren, I, Teil, von der Grundung des bulgarischen Reiches bis zur Turkenzeit* (679–1396), p. 172; Krauss, *Studien,* p. 68; Rosanes, *Israel be-Togarmah,* pp. 6–7. Alexander reigned from 1331 to 1365; Rosanes (p. 6, note 12) implies a date before 1350. Kechales (*Koroth Yehudei Bulgaria,* I) suggests ca. 1346.

[77] 1350

From there we went to venerate Saint Dimitri, where the body of the holy Emperor Laskaris rests; such was his name, and sinners, we kissed his body. This is the monastery of the emperor located on the shore of the sea. And beside this monastery, many Jews live on the shore of the sea near the city wall, and the gates that overlook the sea are called the Jewish Gates [i.e., Porta Hebraica]. There was a miracle there: Chosroes, King of Persia, came to Constantinople with his army and wanted to take the city. And Constantinople resounded with moans. Then God showed himself in a vision to a certain old man and said to him, "Take the girdle of the Holy Virgin and dip the end of it into the sea." And he did that with songs and tears. And the sea rose and broke their boats against the city wall. At the present time there, their bones are turning white like snow, near the city wall, near the Jewish Gates.

"The Pilgrimage of Stephan of Novgorod," in Khitrowo, *Itinéraires,* p. 121.

[78] Ca. 1350

Treatise against Judaism in nine chapters by John VI Kantakouzenos (under his monastic signature John Christodoulos).

Fabricius, *Bibliotheca Graeca,* V, 473, citing Labbeus Bibl. nova Mss., p. 1354; Sarton, *Introduction to the History of Science,* III, part 2, 1094 and 1260; Krauss, *Studien,* p. 69; Beck, *Kirche,* p. 732.

Ca. 1350 [78*]

Testimony which was before us the undersigned that Joseph ha-Kohen son of Shmuel ha-Kohen came with Shlomith daughter of Jacob the wife of his father [i.e., his step-mother] and said to us, we have witnesses and took it down in every language of title and they wrote and signed and handed it over to R. Shmuel b. R. Abraham of our own free will without pressure or unwillingly or through error with full heart and free spirit and healthy body,[1] we received from him 5 (coins) of Khiris[2] coinage at market value and we sold to him in return for them this book *Sefer ha-Ḥokhmoth* of R. Judah ha-Kohen the Sephardi, and the price was fully decided without regret, and surety for this sale we accepted upon our souls that anyone who might come and appeal this sale we must respond to him as will those heard before us, so we have written firmly and bindingly.

Moses ha-Parnas ben Elia (may his rest be in Eden!)
Hezekia ha-L(evi?)
Judah bar Eliakim Kostandi (may his rest be in Eden!)

Oxford, Bodleian, Mich 551, fol. 211r. See above document 47*.

1. The phrase recalls Juvenal's *mens sana in corpore sano* (Satires, 10-356). See below, document 63 for a parallel phrase in a contemporary Latin text from Constantinople.
2. כירים: unidentified, most probably in the Crimea (perhaps Kers).

Ca. 1400[1] [79]

"Some Causes of Our Ills"

Many of us freely blaspheme against the Orthodox faith, against the Cross, against the Law, against the Sanctuary, against God Himself as worthless and impious, adding denial to blasphemy; and none of the listeners object.

We make use of Jewish physicians and those things which are touched by their hands and sullied by their saliva, we thoughtlessly eat.[2]

The orthodox devour strangled and dead game thoughtlessly and also the blood of other animals, just like pagans.

Not only men but also (the race of) women are not ashamed to lie down to sleep as naked as they were born. They hand over for seduction their pre-pubescent daughters; they dress their women in male garments . . .

L. Oeconomos, "L'état intellectuel et moral des Byzantins vers le milieu du XIVe siècle d'après une page de Joseph Bryennios," in *Mélanges Charles Diehl,* I, 227, 229; chapter extracted from Eugene Bulgaris, *Oeuvres du moine Joseph Bryennios,* III, 119–23. The reference to Jewish doctors is the basis for Vogel's statement (*CMH,* IV, part 2, 291) that "medical teaching at Byzantium ended with John Actuarius and the practice of medicine passed to Jewish doctors." Cf. similar sentiments by Jenkins (*CMH,* IV, 2, 88 n). On the world of late Byzantine medicine, cf. Robert Browning, "Byzantine Scholarship," *Past and Present,* 28 (1964), 19; reprinted in his *Studies in Byzantine History.*

1. Oeconomos dated the tract in the middle of the fourteenth century; Vogel gives a *floruit* for Joseph Bryennius of 1387–1405; he is accepted by Runciman, (*The Last Byzantine Renaissance,* p. 93n), who places it after 1400.

2. Perhaps this is a caustic comment on the therapeutic and thaumaturgic effects of saliva; cf. *JE,* X, 651, citing the use of saliva in curing eye diseases in Hebrew, Greek, and Latin sources.

[80] 1354

and lo this sage [Aaron b. Elijah] wrote his book in Constantinople . . .

Elijah Bashyachi, *Addereth Eliyahu,* section *Kiddush ha-Ḥodesh,* ch. 16, 10a; quoted in Ankori, *Karaites,* p. 134, note 178. This is the reason (given in the passage) to explain Aaron b. Elijah's use of approximate dating, as opposed to visual sighting (i.e., the normal Karaite practice), for determining the new moon.

[81] 1354

This year in which we live is 5114 since the Creation, the fifth of the *Shmiṭṭah,* the third of the *Yōbel* which is the 53rd *Yōbel* since the Jews began to reckon *Shmiṭṭoth* and *Yōbeloth.*

Aaron b. Elijah, the Karaite, *Gan 'Eden,* section *Shmiṭṭah we-Yōbel,* 68d; quoted in Ankori, *Karaites,* p. 134, note 179. Aaron b. Elijah mentions the same date elsewhere in his treatise, section *Ḥag Shabu'oth,* 58a–b; quoted in Ankori, *loc. cit.* Mann, *Texts and Studies* (II, 1417, note 47), notes the text and correctly suggests a later completion for the entire work.

After 1354 [82]

. . . and the sage R. Yehudah, my uncle and teacher (may his rest be in Eden!) brought . . .

Aaron b. Elijah, the Karaite, *Gan 'Eden,* section *Shmiṭṭah we-Yōbel,* 66d; quoted in Ankori, *Karaites,* p. 136, note 184. See above (74), which shows that R. Yehudah died before 1346.

1355 [83]

a) . . . and with God's help the *Sefer Mibḥar* was written, finished on Monday, the 4th day of Elul in the year 5103 [of the Creation] or 1643 of the Seleucid era,[1] and was completed by my hand, I the insignificant Abraham b. Mar Joseph b. R. Jacob called Pappos[2] for Shlomo b. Mar Joseph b. R. Shlomo called Artanusi,[3] and I implore the readers that if they should peruse in this book or copy it let them make allowances for me and not condemn me because I, due to the many troubles and sorrows that have surrounded me and the events which have encompassed me and the teaching of children who distress me exceedingly and all of the worries which have overcome me, I am like a man in shock . . .

b) Testimony before we the undersigned on Tuesday, the 16th day of Sivan in the year 5115 (= 1355) of the Creation of the world. On this day there came before us Shlomo b. R. Moses and declared, "I of my own free will sold this *Sefer Mibḥar* which is the commentary on the Torah of R. Aaron the Teacher to this R. Joseph b. R. Jacob for 100 aspers." The money reached the hands of this Shlomo the seller and none of the monies remained to R. Joseph, and this sale is final and permanent and irredeemable . . . May the Lord bring good fortune upon him and his house and his sons, and may he and all his succeeding generations succeed in reading it. And that which we heard from their lips we wrote down firm and binding.

Appended to a poem of Aaron b. Joseph; cited by Danon, "Documents," pp. 165–66.

1. 1343; the Seleucid era began in 311 B.C.E. Here is proof that Byzantine Karaites still knew the Oriental Jewish practice of dating according to this era.

2. See documents 66 and 61, showing this surname in Nicomedia.

3. Is this a toponym, indicating his family's origin from Arta? See document 63 for the name Artachino.

[84] 1358

A poem composed by the sage Maistro Moses de Roquemaure in the city of Tolintol[1] about R. Shemarya the Greek who called himself a prophet and herald of the covenant. These rhymed verses are a sign and a preventive measure on the foolishness of his madness; for this is what the prince said in songs "For I was envious of the arrogant."[2] As a man deceives,[3] let everyone beware[4] for himself the existence of deceivers.

As this madman Shemarya did in his boasting through prophecy to attach himself to various and sundry intellects, but he is a different fool divorced from all intelligence; he will disolve in slime in his knowledge; and in the matter that is called wisdom I made him like a slug with these verses.[5] In them I related the manner of his words, of his dreams and his statements. I, the youthful and trivial of the society [of scholars] whose name is Moses b. R. Samuel de Roquemaure, a denizen of Avignon (may God protect her!) and a sojourner in Tolintol (may God protect her!)

Moses de Roquemaure, introduction to his poem on Shemarya Ikriti; quoted in Neubauer, "Documents inédits," pp. 89–92, and accompanied by a partial French translation. Text reprinted in Eshkoli, *Tenuoth Meshiḥiyoth* (pp. 218–22), with commentary. Ca. 1360, Moses converted to Christianity, taking the name of John of Aragon; he is better known as the translator of Bernard Gordon's "Lililium Medicinae." See Colette Sirat, "A Letter on the Creation by R. Shemarya b. Elijah akriti" (Hebrew), note 6 and text.

1. Neubauer transcribed the name as טולוטולא, and suggests Toledo in Spain. Sirat reads טולנטול and suggests Tolentino in Italy.
2. Psalms 73:3.
3. Job 13:9.
4. Cf. Jeremiah 9:4.
5. Psalms 58:8.

[85] 1360s(?)

The sage R. Aaron flourished more than 60 years before Mar Moses (ha-Yevani). Indeed this man was very lacking in the science of astronomy . . .

Elijah Bashyachi, *Addereth Eliahu,* section *Kiddush ha-Ḥodesh,* 4a. Further examples of Elijah's barbs are scattered throughout the same work; e.g., 4a, 6a, 3b inform us of his biblical commentary in which Moses attacks Aaron b. Joseph; 39b mentions his argument that the names of the Hebrew months were derived from the Romans (=Greeks?); 104a–b, 106b–107, 112b–113, etc..

Zunz, *Literaturgeschichte der Synagogalen Poesie,* p. 509, follows Bashyachi in placing Moses Kapuṣato 60 years after Aaron b. Joseph. More recent scholarly opinion has updated Moses Kapuṣato to a contemporary of Bashyachi, i.e., to the second half of the fifteenth century. Rosanes, *Israel be-Togarmah* (pp. 31–32), gives his *floruit* as ca. 1457–90, based on the retorts of both Mordecai Komatiano and Kaleb Afendopolo. Joseph Beghi (early sixteenth century) in his *Iggereth Kiryah Ne'emanah* (cited by Mann, *Texts and Studies,* II, 305 and note 28) lists Moses between Mordecai Komatiano and Solomon b. Elijah Sharbit ha-Zahav, thus making all three contemporaries. Bashyachi himself juxtaposes Moses with Komatiano (36b), and for this and the above reasons it is possible to conclude that the text is defective on this point. The article on Moses Kapuṣato in the *Encyclopedia Judaica* merely dates him in the second half of the fifteenth century.

1362 [86]

And the secrets of his words[1] I received from the lips of great scholars . . . and when the age-long causes banished me according to the will of the Lord (may He be exalted!) from the house of my father and the land of my birth from nation to nation and kingdom to another people, I found that the majority of those who investigated the above-mentioned book were perturbed: part of them from a deficiency in their knowledge of the functions of grammar which straightens out external difficulties, and part of them from a deficiency in their knowledge of the functions of logic which straightens out internal difficulties, and part of them from a deficiency in their knowledge of both functions together. Part of them from a deficiency in their knowledge of the mystery of hidden insights, in particular the mysteries of *ma'ase bereshit* and *ma'ase merkabah*. And part of them were lacking in all of these and they knew nothing at all of the true knowledge . . . And part of them due to the malice of their souls denied the truth of his words and said that he is not one of the believers in the basic words of the Torah and also that he is one of those who mock the words of our holy rabbis, the sages of the Oral Torah which is a joy to the heart and a curative to the bone. For there is no difference between the two Torahs, for both have been passed down to us from the hands of our fathers.

Judah ibn Moskoni, *Hakdamah le-'Eben ha-'Ezer*; edited in A. Berliner, *Oṣar Tob* (Berlin, 1878), p. 5.

1. Abraham ibn Ezra's Commentary on the Torah.

[87] 1362

I will return to my intention and say that I wandered from my land, from Ochrida, a city in the kingdom of Bulgaria, from the duchy of Serbia, a government of the religion of the wicked kingdom of the Greeks.[1] And I had the help of God in my wanderings to and fro in search of wisdom. And I came to the island of Egripon,[2] where I was a disciple of the faithful and true sage my lord and teacher, the chariot of Israel and its cavalry, R. Shemarya, who encompasses all knowledge and wisdom and the angels of heaven did not obscure him . . . for he became an angel of the Lord of Hosts after he was summoned to the heavenly council.

And I wandered from state to state and from city to city to seek the ones perfect in wisdom and to sit at their feet. I found many opinions regarding the words of this sage[3] including men great in wisdom . . .

And I have seen close to thirty varieties of commentaries on his book,[4] and regarding the majority of his words these differ from each other . . . Indeed, ones empty in wisdom came to look into his book and God turns them away empty. The explanations that I have seen which were partly concerned with his book were the following:

First and foremost I found R. Moses b. Naḥman (may his memory be blessed!)[5] who even though he masks his words according to his knowledge in many places by means of open rebuke, here he explains many things in his comments through hidden love[6] as will be made known to you in this commentary.

Indeed, the earliest commentary in time, as was told to me, is the commentary that I saw in the city of Veroia of the great sage whose name, according to his writings, was R. Abishai from the city of Zagora.[7] From what is said as well as appears from his books and treatises he was close to being a contemporary of Abraham ibn Ezra (may his memory be blessed) . . .

And on the island of Chios I saw in the hands of the erudite R. Eliahu, grandson of the sage and physician the brilliant R. Benjamin (may his memory be blessed!) a commentary belonging to the sage R. Kaleb Korsinos from the city of Constantinople[8]—he was a great hunter in the science of grammar above all the sages. And whatever Abraham ibn Ezra (may his memory be blessed!) indicated in his books based on grammar, the above-mentioned R. Kaleb understood all. However, regarding his insights (*sodoth*), he did not know anything.

And on the island of Cyprus I saw a commentary belonging to the sage of the aforementioned city whose name was R. David Pardeleon.[9] And in truth, some of the enigmas of Ibn Ezra were revealed to him although he too did not understand them fully.

And in the city of ṢḤOK (מדינת צחוק) I found a commentary belonging to the sage R. Isaiah of Trani[10] and the contents of it were stolen *in toto* from the words of the aforementioned sage R. Kaleb. Indeed the conjectures about the mysteries of the book, are they not conjectures lacking truth?

And in the city of Laodikeia I found a commentary belonging to the sage R. Eliahu of Serres.[11] And his comments in it, are they not words of confusion and disorder. He only succeeded in explaining all of Abraham ibn Ezra's (may his memory be blessed!) remarks based on the science of astronomy, for he was secretly a scholar of mathematics as appears from his comments.

Indeed the commentary upon which my spirit thrives . . . is the commentary of my lord, the aforementioned rabbi, and after him the commentary of the distinguished scholar from which derives most of my wisdom, the perfect sage R. Obadiah the Egyptian, illuminated the path. The remainder of the commentaries which I saw in the lands of Greece did not quench my thirst . . .

The upshot of the matter is that in all of the commentaries that I saw I found no satisfaction save for the above-mentioned commentary. Also I did not see this said commentary from the time I was 17 years old until now when I am 34. And there only remains in my intellect what was planted there of it from the study which I heard in my youth from the mouth of the aforementioned rabbi.

Judah ibn Moskoni, *Hakdamah le-'Eben ha-'Ezer*; ed. by A. Berliner, *Oṣar Tob* (Berlin, 1878), pp. 6–8; section on Chios and ṢḤOK translated in Starr, *JBE*, #183, p. 236; description by A. Berliner in *MWJ*, III (1876), 45–51; Nachtrag by M. Steinschneider, ibid., pp. 94–100, 140–53, 190–205 (reprinted in his *Gesammelte Schriften*, I, 536ff); and M. Friedlaender, *Essays on the Writings of Abraham ibn Ezra*, IV, 213ff.

1. Under the control of Despot Vukašin. He cannot be referring to the fortress of Servia on the north slope of Mount Olympos.

2. I.e., Negroponte. See above, document 30, note 2.

3. I.e., Abraham ibn Ezra.

4. These 30 and others are listed by Friedlaender and Steinschneider. Apparently he did not visit Magnesia or see the copy of Ibn Ezra's commentary that was copied there in 1387 by the scribe Judah b. Namer; cf. below (99).

5. Known also as Nachmanides or RaMBaN (1194–1270).

6. Cf. Proverbs 27:58. "Better is open rebuke than love which is hidden."

7. There follows a chronological argument showing that ibn Ezra wrote his book in the year 1161 (= 4921 of Creation), and R. Abishai completed his work nine years later in 1170 (= 4930 of Creation). The editor suggests that there is a lacuna in the text at this point.

8. Ankori, *Karaites* (p. 199, note 110), suggests a thirteenth-century date for this scholar; Starr (*JBE,* p. 64) wavered between the twelfth and the thirteenth.

9. Document 91 mentions the renowned Rabbana David Pardoleone from Greece.

10. Gross, "Jesaya b. Mali da Trani" (p. 58), argues that this Isaiah of Trani must be the grandson of the famous sage. Even so, it is well known that the younger Isaiah repeated much of his grandfather's knowlege and decisions. The city mentioned is unidentified; Steinschneider suggests a province in Cyprus.

11. There are two cities named Laodikeia in Anatolia: one is just north of Konya (Cecaumene), the other is on the Maeander River, southwest of Mastaura and south of Philadelphia. On this sage, see above (32), which was very likely written by his son.

[88] October 6870–1361, Indiction XV

. . . the place neighboring on St. Constantine in which Jews are living, giving each year their fixed payment.

Chrysobull of Emperor Stephen Uroš to the Lavra of St. Athanasios on Mount Athos, in Soloviev-Mošin, *Grčke,* p. 204; Starr, *Romania,* p. 113; Dölger, "Die Frage," in *Paraspora,* p. 377 (quoted in editor's supplement).

[89] 1363?

The grand commercium of Corinth was sold to the Jews at auction as was the custom; it was delivered the aforesaid year for 340 hyperpera with the calculation of

. . . pp. 340

The aforementioned Jews gave for the above commercium monies of the sergeant and guards and other expenses to the sum of 340 hyperpera, which they put for the receipts for the whole year, documents of payment and receipt.

. . . pp. 340

The commercii[1] of Corinth with mill, the year of the fourth indiction; in Jean Longnon and Peter Topping, *Documents sur le régime des terres dans la principauté de Morée au XIV*^e^ *siècle,* pp. 162–63.

1. On this term and the others in the document, cf. notes of Longnon and Topping in appendix III of their study. The commercium was basically an import and export tax levied on both foreign merchants and imperial subjects. The editors believe the grand commercium included the main sales tax in Corinth and, possibly, taxes at the ports of Lechaion on the Gulf of Corinth and Kenchreai on the Saronic Gulf. The convergence of the north–south land traffic and the east–west sea traffic at the isthmus made Corinth a natural emporium. Before the establishment of the Venice-Crete-Constantinople trade axis, Corinth was one of the major economic centers in the Peloponnesos. Even after the rise of Venice, enough traffic still passed through her tolls to make the various commercii very lucrative.

The remaining commercii and services listed in the document only come to 275 hyperpera (as opposed to 340 for *lo chomerchio grande*). These are *lo chomerchio del mercato* (for the market), 40 pp; *lo chomerchio dello griaggio* (for auctioneering), 17 pp; *lo chomerchio del labboraggio* (loading and unloading boats), 6 pp; *lo chomerchio de chalzolari* (shoemakers), 15 pp; *la prigionia* (imprisonment), to Domitri Foro and Elia (?), 17 pp; *lo mulino* (the mill), 80 pp; *lo chomerchio della buccieria* (tannery), to Chosta Becharo, 100 pp.

1365 [90]

This was completed in the year 814 of the Armenian Era (A.D. 1365) on August 15, during the pontificate of the Lord Mesrop I, Artazecʿi . . . and the reign of King Constantine V of Cilicia; in the renowned city of Kafa . . . in bitter and grievous times. In this year, there appeared the Antichrist and contagion, who is named Čʿalibeg, of the Ismaelite nation, who slaughtered the Christians, and who held the entire neighboring country in terror by day and by night. But, as predicted by the Lord Nersēs, there appeared this year, through Divine Providence, from among the courageous Genoese nation . . . a consul in our city as military commander. As instructed by the Genoese, and with the help of God he captured the city of Sulda and seized whatever he found therein. And he slaughtered all the Ishmaelites and Hebrews, who are the enemies of Christ's Cross and of the Christians, and also confiscated their possessions . . .

Colophons of Armenian Manuscripts, 1301–1480: A Source for Middle Eastern History, selected, translated, and annotated by Avedis K. Sanjian (Cambridge, Mass.: Harvard University Press, 1969), p. 94. The Tatars, in their turn, seem to have persecuted the Jews also; cf. colophon dated 1354–55 in E. Deinard, *Massa Krim* (Warsaw, 1878), p. 67.

Late 14th century [91]

"Logic of R. Joseph the Greek"[1]

Joseph b. R. Moses Kilti who was a pupil of the renowned Rabbana David Pardoleone[2] from the land of Greece said . . . and I called it *Minḥat*

Yehudah (A Gift for Judah) because it is a present from us to the great and divine sage R. Yehudah b. R. Ya'akov ha-Sephardi known as ibn 'Aṭṭar (may his memory be blessed!).

S. Munk, "Oratoire," p. 125; Zotenberg, *Catalogue . . . de la bibliothèque imperiale,* p. 112, #707, fols. 5–16; Steinschneider, *Die Hebraischer Uebersetzungen des Mittelalters,* p. 499. The only other two philosophical authors mentioned by him in Greece are Shemarya Ikriti, see above (53), and Elia b. Eliezer, "The Philosopher" of Candia.

1. Ms. 992 (orat. 106). The work is an abridgment of Aristotle's *Logic,* in six chapters.
2. This must be the same R. David whose commentary on ibn Ezra Judah ibn Moskoni found in Cyprus (ca. 1360). Since neither Judah nor Joseph add the formula for the deceased, "may his memory be blessed," we may assume that he was alive at the time of both sources.

[92] 1367

1) Completed in the first month, Thursday the tenth, in the year 27 in the city of Thebes.

2) Tuesday, 29th of the first month, 14th day of the (counting of the) Omer, year 27 when completed.

Oxford, Bodleian Library, Opp. Add. 2518; HPP C315; Neubauer (*Bodleian,* I, #2518) misread the date as Sivan 1267; followed by Solomon Birnbaum, *The Hebrew Scripts* (Leiden, 1975), I, 283, #291. The date cannot be 1267 since the water marks in the paper have been dated to the fourteenth century. The scribe's name was Shemaryah, and it is not improbable that he was a Karaite; cf. author's "Jews in Fourteenth-Century Thebes," note 9.

[93] 1368

But how you used to be, formerly, on the one hand, you were wishing this from afar being a Jew and a descendant of that accursed race, but now you bear ill will to Christ who, as you know from your ancestors, was resurrected; on the one hand you wished to join the [Christian] race, on the other hand you dread his worshippers and his laws.

Letter of Demetrius Kydones to Patriarch Philotheos in defense of his brother Prokoros Kydones (April 1368), in Vat. gr. 678, fol. 9v; edited in Mercati, *Notizie ed altri appunti,* pp. 248 and 311. On the affair of Philotheos and Prokoros, see article "Philothée Kokkinos" (by V. Laurent) in *Dictionaire de Théologie Catholique,* vol. XII, col. 1500.

1368 (25 August) **[94]**

I, magister David the Jew, inhabitant of Dyrrachium, acknowledge that upon me and all my goods throughout the whole month of November next there is an obligation to give Bochdasse de Branota in Valona in a ship of the said Bochdusse [*sic!*] five *militaria* of crushed salt and this in the measure of Valona in exchange for 500 gold ducats which I have received from him partly in dinars partly in cloth, which dinars and cloth are bound to go from Ragusa all the way to Dyrrachium subject to the risk and fortune of the said Bochdasse. And if I should not deliver the said quantity of salt at the terminal noted above to that Bochdasse or to his agent sent to the ship to accept said salt, I am subject to the penalty of 200 ducats to that Bochdasse for damages and interest to him.

And we Moses b. Matthew the Jew and his brother Moses, declare ourselves as pledges and promissaries to that Bochdasse for the above magister David if he should not deliver the stated quantity of salt at the said terminal and to the above subscribed. And if Lazarus, son of the above magister David, should die before [reaching] the terminal or should be removed from his office, we are bound ultimately for the restitution of the cloth or the 500 ducats. However it may please the said Bochdasse, he may betake himself to either all three or to only one of us, insofar as he might wish for part or for all of it . . .

Von Thalloczy, *Acta Albaniae,* II, 56–57; Starr, *Romania,* pp. 81–83. On the trade along the Epirote coast during this period, see Hrochova, "Le commerce vénitien et les changements dans l'importance des centres de commerce en Grèce du 13e au 15e siècle," *Studi Veneziani,* IX (1967), 3–34.

1368 (15 August) **[95]**

David, magister of the Judaica of Dyrrachium, witnessed by Moses b. Matthew the scribe and Moses b. Solomon, Jews of Dyrrachium, accepts a deposit from Paul the spice merchant for Franceschino Georgio, a Venetian and for Andriolo Contareno.

Von Thalloczy, *Acta Albaniae,* II, 57.

1369 **[96]**

Even in death, these two honored ones were not separated. Rather both died within four months: R. Joseph died in (5)129 in the month of Sivan and R. Aaron in (5)130 in the month of Tishre.

From a letter sent by R. Isaac b. R. Shemarya ha-Zaken (May his rest be in Eden!) to R. Jacob b. R. Yehudah ha-Rophe . . . copied by the former's son Shemarya in Adrianople in the year 5181 (= 1421); in Neubauer, *Aus der Petersburger Bibliothek,* p. 121 (no. xxvii). See I. M. Jost, "Lehre der Karaiten und ihr Kampf gegen die rabbinische Tradition," *Israelitische Annalen,* I (1839), no. 11, 83; Lucki, in Mann's *Texts and Studies,* II, 1417; Ankori, *Karaites,* pp. 132–33.

[96*] 1376

On Wednesday, 5 Marheshvan 5137 of the Creation according to the reckoning that we count here in the community of Vidin, we the inhabitants of the community who have signed below, have agreed to demand a *takkanah* on behalf of the daughters of Israel that it not be easy for their husbands to divorce them. We have seen that our (Romaniote) custom of disposing of the dowry differs from that of other neighboring Jewish communities. Therefore we have agreed that henceforth each man and woman who would marry off his or her daughter, whether they be inhabitants of this city or another, and who further vows the groom a dowry as negotiated between them; when the dowry is handed over, the tax assessors must assess everything that is written as the gifts of the groom: coin, gold, silver, pearls, clothes for the bride and groom, pillows and cushions, and any kind of bowls, pots, and pitchers, according to their market value in cash. And to this sum of money that the bride's possessions are worth, the groom must write an additional amount in another document (in addition to the required rabbinic ketubah). And in the ketubah they must write the amount of the ketubah, the dowry, and the additional sum according to their value in cash.

Should, heaven forbid, the wife die while her husband is still alive and not leave him any living issue, the husband will inherit one-third of the wife's property while two-thirds shall go to her heirs.

Further, before each groom enters under the marriage canopy, he must swear that he will not marry another woman either in his city or in another (lest he be one of those whom our sages obligated to marry another woman).

These two conditions must be written in every ketubah that is drawn up in our community. And every Jew who comes from a foreign land who is not known to us may not marry one of our daughters (whether they be resident here or only visiting) before he spends three years in our community in order that we should be able to verify whether or not he has a wife somewhere else. But if three creditable members of our community vouch that he has no other wife nor any tax obligations in his city, he will be permitted to marry within one year.

Any man or woman who becomes engaged via a marriage broker or by their fathers and draws up a document between them but later one of them changes his mind without a valid reason (one listed by our sages) and then later reconcile, they shall not marry in our community.

Every Jew who has a monetary claim stemming from matrimonial law shall be judged according to Jewish law. But if one were to refuse to obey the Jewish court then, with the express permission of the Jewish judges, he may legally and lawfully be summoned before the non-Jewish court.

Any Jew who might wish to negate these agreements or any one of them is not permitted to do so. Moreover, he, his assistants, and all those who are involved with him will be put under a ban. Nor will any individual be permitted to cancel our ban unless it be a court that is greater than the one that is signed below, both in wisdom and in number. And this is official.

Responsum 96 of R. Shlomo b. Abraham ha-Kohen (Venice, 1592); the *haskamah* has been printed by Kochales in *Koroth Yehudei Bulgaria* (I, 86–88, with discussion passim). As this *haskamah* was recopied by the sixteenth-century sage, his reasons for omitting the names of the communal leaders are unknown, and unfortunate. See above, document 11, for another instance of recourse to gentile courts.

Before 1380 **[97]**

A Christian's apology against the Jews in 3 parts with 8 sermons and 24 chapters written by Theophanes III, Metropolitan of Nicaea.

Text unedited, *Vat. gr.* 372. Fragments in Leone Allatio, *Ioannes Henricus Holligerus: Fraudis, & impostur & manifeste convictus* (Rome, 1661), pp. 187–91, containing excerpts in Greek and Latin from the 6th sermon concerning the prophet Elijah; see Beck, *Kirche*, pp. 746–47.

1387 (8 January) **[98]**

. . . the men of the above-said city and island (Corfu) . . . sent to . . . the Most Serene and Excellent Lord Antonio Venerio, by the Grace of God renowned Duke of the Venetians, and to his councillors, the noble sirs: Pietro Capice, Knight (*miles*); Ricardo de Altavilla; Giovanni Alexius, notary of Cavasule; Antonio de Henrico; Count Nicole Trachanioti; and David de Semi, a Jew of the same city (Corfu) . . .

A document of fidelity or homage to the doge from Corfu; in Thomas, *DVL*, II, 205.

[99] 1387

Completed by my hand, I, Judah ben Namer (may his memory be for a blessing!) in the city of Manissa in the Emirate of Saruhan on the 12th of Sivan 5147 since the Creation, which is the 17th year of the lunar cycle 281. May the Merciful One answer us on a day of sorrow. May He give us strength against anger, ire, and rage. May He return to us the Temple and its courtyard. May He be for us a shelter, a shield and a buckler. May He aid us to meditate always in Torah: in Bible, in Mishnah and Gemara. May He give us knowledge and understanding in wisdom and exegesis, in fulfillment of the commandments and in the study of the commentary of the wonderful sage Abraham ibn Ezra (may his soul be bound up in the bond of eternal life) as it is written in the verse; may the soul of my lord be bound up in the bond of eternal life (1 Samuel 25, 29).

Commentary of Ibn Ezra on the Pentateuch in J.T.S.L. 287; HPP D12. For the name Namer, see above (document 43n).

[100] 1387

This book called *Sha'are Ṣedek* (Gates of Righteousness by Jonah b. Abraham Gerondi) was written and completed by my hand, Shlomo, the young, ben Moshe Pangelo on Tuesday, 17 Sivan in the year 5147 since the Creation according to the reckoning that we count here in the holy congregation of Misithra. May the Lord in His mercy and grace allow me to inherit and to fulfill all that is written in this book and see sons from my loins respectful of the Torah, of the commandments and be God-fearing, Amen.

Cambridge University Library, MS Add, 1224; HPP C632. The name that we transliterate as Pangelo is written in Hebrew as PNGLO. We may assume the youth of our scribe from his self-designation "the young" and from his desire for future sons. The scribe clearly designates the existence of a community in the city.

1389 [100*]

Testimony before us the undersigned on Wednesday, 27 Sivan 5149 of the Creation as we calculate it here in the congregation of KYRYS[1] that his honor R. Yeshuah son of his honor R. Abraham sold the book *Midrash ha-Ḥokhmoth* for 55 (coins) to R. Joseph son of his honor Judah Cocarino [קקרינו] (may he live forever!) in full sale and the money of his honor R. Joseph the buyer reached the hand of his honor R. Yeshuʿah the seller, and this sale is binding on him and his heirs. . . . His honor Joseph son of his honor Abraham signed; his honor Israel son of his honor Abraham signed and I the worm and not a man Judah ben Eliahu the Adrianopolitan[2] (signed).

Oxford, Bodleian, Mich 551, fol. 221v. See above, document 47*. Judah ben Eliahu the Adrianopolitan was in Solchat later this year copying a Torah scroll. Cf. Deinard, *Massa Krim,* pp. 66f., and colophon in HPP D193. One of the witnesses was Abraham b. R. Yeshuʿah, possibly the grandfather of the seller in this transaction.

1. See above, document 78* here spelled קירים.
2. The abbreviation for his father, נבתוי״א is from Psalm 25, 13: "His soul shall abide in prosperity and his seed shall inherit the land."

1389–1391 [101]

Behind the altar of Hagia Sophia is located the Church of Saint Nicholas. It is raised over the spot of the House of Dimitri, where Saint Nicholas carried Dimitri after having recovered him from the sea. In this church, to the right, is the icon of the Holy Savior which a Jew pierced upwards from the left eyebrow and blood dripped from this wound. At the sight of this fearful miracle, the Jew was terrified and, striking the icon, he threw it in a well and ran away. However, a Christian noticed him and, seeing that he was holding a bloody knife asked him, "How did this knife become bloody?" Since this one was his friend, the Jew responded without hesitation, "I stabbed the effigy of your God, the image of the Savior." The Christian then seized the Jew, and, a mob having formed, he was brought to the emperor who asked him, "Where have you hidden the holy icon?" He replied, "It is in the well." At once the emperor, the patriarch, and a large mob brought him with crosses to this well and retrieved the bloody icon from it. They sealed the blood of Christ and placed the icon in the

Church of Saint Nicholas where it healed many people and continues to make miracles to this day.

"Anonymous Description of Constantinople, 1424–1453," in Khitrowo, *Itinéraires,* pp. 228–29. Mme Khitrowo assigned this document the dates 1424–1453 with no apparent justification. In his article, "The Date of the Anonymous Russian Description of Constantinople" (*BZ,* 45 [1952], 380–85), Cyril Mango, after reviewing the multitude of dates proposed for this document, argues strongly for 1389–91. His argument, based on the references to the "Little Town of Kaloyan," is much stronger than those supporting other dates.

[102] 1389–1391

At the foot of the Basilikon is located a wharf for ships and barques for their return from Galata. A little further on is situated the Divine Surety;[1] there is there an icon of the Holy Savior[2] which was a surety for the merchant Theodore, when this one, having borrowed gold and silver from the Jew Abraham, was drowned,[3] and the Jew blasphemed the icon of the Holy Savior. At the same time the sea tossed out the sum in gold and a letter from the merchant with several lines from the Holy Savior[4] saying, "Do not insult me so, Jew! I can not have any debts nor can I abandon my servant in pain; take what is coming to you; there are fifteen pounds in gold besides."[5] At the sight of this miracle, the Jew had himself baptised with his wife and all his household.[6]

"Anonymous Description of Constantinople, 1424–1453," in Khitrowo, pp. 233–34; translated (with slight differences, based on Slavic original) in Benjamin N. Nelson and Joshua Starr, "The Legend of the Divine Surety and the Jewish Moneylender," *Annuaire de l'Institut de Philologie et d'Histoire Orientales,* I (Brussels, 1932–33), 289–338. For date, see document 101n.

1. 'Αντιφωνητής.

2. A passage paralleling this theme, and coming immediately before this one, reads: "Somewhat further to the east of the Basilikon is the Church of Saint Nicholas. He is painted there in a frescoe on the wall as if living. A Christian, who had been shipwrecked, had come there to pray; and the hand of Saint Nicholas was extended to him from the image and handed him a small bag containing 100 large Frankish pieces of pure gold." Cf. Starr and Nelson, p. 299, note 6.

3. 'Se noya', in Khitrowo. Starr reads "shipwrecked" from the Slavic.

4. These lines are clearer in another Slavic version of the legend: "I, Jesus Christ, from Theodore the Christian, bring you the gold with interest, so that you the Jew should not revile me. With this I have discharged my suretyship, so have faith in me truly." Cf. Starr and Nelson, p. 310.

5. Cf. Starr and Nelson, p. 311; he assigns this document to ca. 1300.

6. Cf. Starr and Nelson, pp. 289–93, for a fuller and different rendition of the tradition during the reign of Heraclius, and p. 297 (note 3) for a note on the text. For another version of this legend in an anonymous account of Constantinopolitan sanctuaries from 1204, written by an English pilgrim (published by S. G. Mercati, "Sanctuari e reliquie Constantinopolitanae secondo il codice Ottoboniano Latino 169 prima della conquesta latina [1204]," in *Rendiconti della Pontificia Accademia di Archeologia,* XII [1936], 145–49), cf. text in Starr and Nelson, pp. 313, 315–17. This excellent article also cites other Greek, Slavic, Latin, French, Provençal, Catalan, Old English, and Old Norse versions of the Divine Surety theme and the story of Theodore and Abraham. For a Spanish version, cf. Gilbert Smith, "Christian Attitudes towards the Jews in Spanish Literature," *Judaism,* 19, (1970), 444–51.

1393 [103]

In the monastery of Perivlepte is the right hand of John the Baptist and the head of St. Gregory, and a part of the relics of St. Simeon the Just, and of the Forty Martyrs, and of many other saints, and the icon of the Holy Virgin[1] that the Jew pierced while playing chess,[2] and from which came out blood that men have seen up to the present.

"Voyage to Constantinople of the Scribe Alexander," in Khitrowo, *Itinéraires,* p. 163.

1. In 1200, Hagia Sophia had a statue of a bleeding Christ pierced by a Jew; see document 1.

2. "L'image . . . que le Juif transperça en jouant aux échecs."

1394 [104]

other land at a distance from the Ebraiokastro up to Siderokausio . . .

Chrysobull of Emperor Manuel Palaeologus, renewing all donations previously made by his father to the Monastery of Pantocrator, in *Actes de l'Athos, II: Actes du Pantocrator,* ed. L. Petit, *VV,* 10 (1930), suppl., no. VIII, 11, pp. 67–68; *MM,* II, 216–20. George Ostrogorsky (*La principauté de Serrès* [in Serbian], p. 43) claims, on the basis of this text, that there were Jews in Thasos at this time; see above, part I, chap. 2, "Thrace and Macedonia," for our comments.

This is the earliest literary record of the term in Greece. The etymology of the toponym "Ebraiokastro" has been treated by modern Greek scholars, especially the two sites in Attica (Ramnous and Laubreon). None of them is willing to accept, without reservation, a derivation from *Ebraios,* but rather from *Oraios.* Van Millingen (*Byzantine Constantinople,* p. 221) discusses the same argument for the Porta Hebraica or Porta ʽOraia in the capital. See Io.

Sarres, "The Toponyms of Attika," (Greek) *Athena,* 40 (1928), 158; his suggestions in general have been criticized by P. A. Phourikes, "Notes on the Toponyms of Attika," (Greek) *Athena,* 41 (1929), 77–178, and 42 (1930), 111–36 (I should like to thank Professor Eugene Vanderpool for the references). See also *MHE* and *EL,* s.v. Ebraiokastro, Obreokastro, Breokastro, Oreokastro.

[105] 1396–1427

A city called Kaffa, which lies by the Black Sea, and is surrounded by two walls. Within one wall are 6000 houses, in which are Italians, Greeks, and Armenians; it is the chief city of the Black Sea, and has within the outer walls 11,000 houses, in which are many Christians: Romans, Greeks, Armenians, and Syrians. There are also three bishops: a Roman, a Greek, and an Armenian. There are also many infidels who have their particular temple. The city has four towns subject to it; they are by the sea. There are also two kinds of Jews in the city, and they have two synagogues, and 4000 houses are in the suburbs.

The Bondage and Travels of Johann Schiltberger, a native of Bavaria, in Europe, Asia, and Africa, 1396–1427, translated by Commander J. Buchan Telfer, R.N., with notes by P. Brunn (p. 49). Brunn identifies the four seaside towns as Lusce (19th century Aloushta), Gorzuni (Gourzouff), Partenice (Partenite), Ialita (Yalta). The two kinds of Jews are Rabbanites and Karaites.

In Tana, the Venetian center for Tartar slaves, Charles Verlinden found one reference to a Jewish slave transaction, viz., the sale of a 12-year-old Tatar for 300 aspers on August 18, 1363, by *Burdoch, quondam Nodin, juif et habitant de Tana (L'ésclavage dans l'Europe médiévale,* vol. 2: *Italie-Colonies italiennes du Levant latin–Empire byzantin* [Ghent, 1977], p. 934).

This was the only case of a slave transaction in the entire East involving a Jew. It is difficult to extrapolate from this unique occurrence in the notarial registers that there were Jewish slave dealers; the case may as well have involved just a domestic sale. See above, document 62.

[106] 1401 (31 October)

Two ambassadors came to us from the *universitas et communis* of Dyrrachium and requested that we consider worthy to be granted the items listed below and that their mission turn out favorably.

For item 9, they request that the Jewish inhabitants of Dyrrachium because they are poverty stricken and few in number be released from giving each year 16 *brachia* of *catasamitum*[1] in full or in part—It was replied that, considering that it was customary in the time of other rulers as well as in the time of our own rule that they pay and give the said *catasamitum* which is only a moderately sized piece, it does not seem to us proper to provide anything above this save first we have the opinion of our *bailo et capitaneus* to whom we shall write about this further.

Von Thalloczy, *Acta Albaniae,* II, 201; Starr, *Romania,* pp. 80–82.

1. This would equal over 10 yards of luxurious velvet cloth. Cf. Zakythinos, *Le Despotat grec de Morée,* II, 252.

1402 (July) [107]

If the Capellanus or the Cancellarius of the Lord Bailo shall go into Pera unto the Lord Podesta to requisition anyone, let him have 12 caratum each way, and if he goes into the place of the Judaica, then he may have 6 caratum; and if the said Capellanus or Cancellarius goes into any other place he will be paid according to the distance of the place and according to the trouble.

Maltezou, *Venetian Bailo,* pp. 148–49.

1403 [108]

This copy was completed in Saloniki in the month of Tammuz 5163 of the Creation, the word of Shem Tob (ibn Polia) b. Yaʿakob (ibn Polia), may his soul be bound up in the bond of eternal life.

Manuscrits médiévaux en caractères hébraïques portant des indications de date jusqu'à 1540, by Colette Sirat and Malachi Beit-Arie, vol. I: *Notices, Bibliothèques de France et d'Israel (Jerusalem–Paris, 1972),* I, 78; ms. Paris, Bibliothèque nationale, heb. 790.

The scribe seems to be the same one (identified in I, 75) as Shemtob b. Jacob ibn Polia, the Spaniard, from the city of Toledo. This particular scribe, a Kabbalist, was quite peripatetic: in 1401 he was in Chalkis, 1403 in Thessaloniki, winter 1404 in Modon, 1415 in Thebes, with a visit in the same year to Philippopolis, where he fell ill for 18 days.

1410 [109]

a) This commentary on *Meggila* was completed by my hand, Shemarya b. Ishmael, (may his righteous memory be for a blessing!) and I completed it for the honored rab Judah Varila son of the *maskil* rab Samuel Varila (may his soul be bound up in the bond of eternal life and may his rest be honored). May the Lord assist him to make this for an inheritance to his seed after him and may strangers not devour his wealth, Amen.

b) This is the commentary on the Scroll of Esther which was written by the Gaon, our respected teacher, Shemarya the elder [i.e., Ikriti], and I Shemarya b. Ishmael, his grandson (may his merit in heaven protect us, Amen!). I copied it from his book *Elef ha-Magen* for the honored, respected, and enlightened (*maskil*), the crown of bachelors and the ornament of elders, R. Judah Varila b. Samuel. May the Lord sustain him to beget sons and to give them as inheritance this (book) as well as its contents and may strangers not devour his wealth, Amen.

c) Completed by my hand, Shemarya b. Ishmael . . . May the Lord assist me to see the coming of the Messiah in our day and I wrote this for . . . Judah Varila . . . in the small town (Cittadin) of Patras on 22 Adar in the year 5170 of the Creation I completed it.

Cambridge, University Library, MS MM6, 26, 2 (8); HPP C580.

The term *maskil* differs here from its use in document 14 (above). The term Cittadina is from the Venetian, a revealing denotation from the grandson of the great Hellenophone, Shemarya Ikriti, and important as a barometer to the penetration of Venetian terminology in Patras.

[110] 1410

All the Decisions of Muhammed b. Zeraḥia al-Razi were completed by my hand, the worm and not a man, Malkiel Kohen, the small, b. R. Shabbetai Kohen of Crete, and it was written on the 28th after the new moon of Tammuz in the year 5170 in the city of Naxos. May He sustain me and my descendents unto the end of generations to meditate in it, Amen. And this [copy] is for my honored lord and teacher, the crown of my head, R. Judah the sage al-Konstantini from the family Ḥanokhi. May the Lord sustain him to see his son go up to the Torah according to his father's desire, to be married and to be successful. And let us say amen, amen, selah.

Parma, Palatina, MS 2279; HPP E503. The Hebrew term, translated as Crete, is I'KaDa'AH (איקדאה); the first letter signifies "island" while the second is a variant of Candia (קדאה), with the *n* either assimilated or, more probably, accidentally dropped. The name Malkiel is common in Crete, as is the family Kohen. The humility of the scribe follows standard formulae. His respectful attitude toward his teacher introduces us to a new Constantinopolitan sage, although where the latter taught is unknown.

Ca. 1410(?) [111]

Abraham Roman, author of *Selaʿ ha-Maḥlokoth* (The Rock of Disputes) against the Patriarch Cyril Lukaris.

Printed in *Milḥamoth Ḥovah* (Constantinople, 1710); see Steinschneider, *Bodleian,* col. 705, no. 4298; Krauss, *Studien,* p. 69.

The text has yet to be studied; an examination of it, however, suggests that Steinschneider erred through misunderstanding the numbers that appear in the text. It is more than likely that this polemic is a product of the seventeenth century and was written by the author in response to the first book printed in Greek in Constantinople, i.e., the polemic against the Jews of the patriarch Cyril Lukaris, Σύντομος πραγματεία κατὰ Ἰουδαιῶν (1627). See my "Two Late Byzantine Dialogues with the Jews," note 10. On Cyril Lukaris, see Timothy Ware, *Eustratios Argenti, a Study of the Greek Church under Turkish Rule* (Oxford, 1964), s.v.

1410–1412 [112]

28) on examining the six leaders of the Jews when they have completed their office.

29) concerning those things which the six leaders ought to observe.

30) concerning those who are prohibited and cannot be among the leaders of the Jews and regarding others . . . must do and . . . said leaders and concerning the punishments imposed on the said Jews.

34) Concerning the household of the Bailo and his officials.

35) that the Venetian Jews cannot sell any house in the Judaica of Constantinople save to Venetian Jews.

Rubrics of the statutes of Lord Franciscus Michael, bailo of the Venetians in Constantinople (in Maltezou, *Venetian Bailo,* p. 153, nos. 28, 29, 30, 34), are translated below (documents 113–16). The text of 35 is not published, but is self-explanatory. For commentary, see D. Jacoby, "Les Juifs vénitiens de Cp.," *REJ,* CXXXI (1972), 397–410.

1411 (3 January) [113]
(more veneto = 1412)

28) Since, by the Lord Paulus Zane in 1405, in October and by Lord Iannes Lauredano in 1408, in August, both honorable bailos in Constantinople, a

proviso was wisely made about maintaining the manner of making the leaders of our Jews and about the dispensation of the goods which were left behind by the Jews for their own souls,[1] also of those goods which are assigned to the said leaders by the Jews; and that they distribute those (goods) among the poor of the Judaica, and that it may be widely continued in these ordinances.

And to Lord Franciscus Michael, honorable bailo of the Venetians in Constantinople, should be informed that should the said appointed leaders carry out badly the appointed tasks which they administered.

The Bailo in office, Lord Franciscus Michael, wishing to provide for the abovementioned (instructions), ordered that when the six leaders of the Jews will have completed their office a special examination will be made in the Synagogue of the Jews and that they ought to be instructed by those six leaders in that examination that they are bound to make public within the next three days, each thing which they appropriated unlawfully or concealed of those (goods and moneys) which they had taken care of in their office. Moreover let there be another general examination that anyone who knows that anyone had or has (possession) of the said goods and will not make it public, as it was instructed, afterwards let him be charged; and it were proved that he has or had (possession) of said goods within three days following and after it was proven, he is bound to return it, and as much again as a fine.

"Statutes of Bailo Franciscus Michael," in Maltezou, *Venetian Bailo,* p. 161.

1. Cf. Testament of Isaac Castellanus (63).

[114] 1411 (3 January) (more veneto = 1412)

29) Moreover, because Lord Paulus Zane in his statute ordered that two of the six said heads (of the Jews) must serve for four months, and two others for four months, and so successively two others until the year is completed. The incumbent Lord Bailo Franciscus ordered that one after another the said two heads from agreement of a major part of them can disburse up to twenty-five hyperper, and beyond the said sum no one can refuse to disburse unless it were undertaken through the power vested in his larger council, nevertheless the aforesaid two heads are bound in writing to enter an account of their expenses which they themselves will minister until they will have completed their four months of office, at which time

they must assign an account to their other four colleagues concerning those things that they will administer. If, however, it seems to anyone that those two act against the said four they must investigate the accounts of those two under penalty of ten hyperper, however it may please the said four. In other respects at the end of the said year the six heads must render an account of those things which they ministered to their six successors and to Anastasius Lazarus or to that one who will be in his place up to eight days after they will have completed it under penalty of twenty-five hyperper for whichever one of them he is lacking, the new heads are subject to the same penalty as the old. If there was not anyone who was not lacking, so that either he gives it back or if he were to hear said accounts, he may not be excused from said penalty if before eight days he shall not have come to the Lord Bailo to excuse himself and to request his aid to effect the execution of what is contained in this order.

"Statutes of Bailo Franciscus Michael," in Maltezou, *Venetian Bailo,* pp. 161–62.

1411 (3 January) [115]
(more veneto = 1412)

30) Moreover, the Lord Franciscus Michael, the Bailo, ordered that when there was to be an election of leaders, there can be elected only one from each household; neither a father, nor son, nor grandson, nor grandfather, nor blood-brothers, nor father-in-law, nor son-in-law, nor uncle or nephew can be elected simultaneously.[1] Truly if someone were elected, he is not able to decline else he be liable to a penalty of 10 hyperper according to the arrangement of Lord Johann Lauredano unless, for example, through illness and he were impeded from going forth; if, however, someone were to refuse because of having gone, he is bound to stay one month outside of the walls of Constantinople and Pera, and whoever will refuse is notwithstanding eligible to be elected again, and as many times as he will refuse he will incur the penalty of 10 hyperper.

Moreover the official Lord Bailo Anestasius Lazare ordered that either one who will be in his stead ought to list the leaders who had just been appointed and all the Jews who came in during that term of office in which the said leaders officiated; and before the said leaders began to minister, they will have themselves registered in the acts of our curia by giving to the secretary one caratum for each and this too under the penalty of 2 hyperper for each.

Finally all the fines of the Jews mentioned above must be divided into three parts, one part is assigned to the accusor, and the other two parts are to be turned into the building fund of the churches of Saint Mary and Saint Mark. If indeed there will not be an accusation, half of one third part of the said fine is payable to the Cancellarius and the other half to the *plazarii* (guarantors).[2] In this event, so that they themselves should have reason to investigate whether the said observances will have been made.

"Statutes of the Bailo Franciscus Michael," in Maltezou, *Venetian Bailo,* p. 162.

1. Cf. *Talmud Babli Sanhedrin,* III, 4.
2. Cf. Thiriet, *La Romanie vénitienne,* pp. 239–40.

[116]

1411 (3 January)
(more veneto = 1412)

34) Written below are the sums which the Venetian Jews pay annually to the Lord Bailo and to the Officials in the Curia.

When the Lord Bailo enters office he must have from the abovementioned Jews	10 hyperpera
For the Feast of Saint Mary in August	10 hyperpera
In the Month of March when the leaders of the Jews are made	10 hyperpera
And four pairs of boots of winter strength	4 hyperpera
For brooms in the Month of March	8 Keratia[1]
For the Feast of Easter	10 hyperpera
For the Feast of Saint Mark	10 hyperpera
In the Month of September when the leaders of the Jews are made	10 hyperpera
For the Feast of the Nativity	10 hyperpera
For 3 pairs of boots	3 hyperpera

35) (The Jews are empowered to buy houses where they may in the Judaica only, with the compliance of the other Venetian Jews)

"Statutes of the Bailo Franciscus Michael," in Maltezou, *Venetian Bailo,* p. 163; extensive commentary and corrections by D. Jacoby, "Les Juifs vénitiens de Cp."

The nature of the above payments has been known since the eighteenth century, when G. Filiasi commented on them (*Memorie storiche de' Veneti primi e secondi* [Venice, 1797], VI, pt. a, 220f); Starr relied on Filiasi; cf. his comments in *Romania,* pp. 31–32; summarized by Jacoby, "Quartiers juifs," p. 211 and note 1.

1. The hyperper in the printed text is superfluous since the K. octo there would refer to 8 keratia, which was a small silver coin. It is doubtful if the K. could be superfluous; in that event, these would be very expensive brooms indeed.

1415

[117]

a) Blessed be YHWH forever that the book is copied and completed. The God of gods, the Lord of lords whose name is YOD HEH WAW HEH and whose nickname is ALEPH DALETH NUN YOD who has heard my prayers and who has done miracles and wonders for me to the present day and who has brought me to my sixty-third year . . . that I have found my life story written by His hand; may He in His great mercy hear my prayers, favor me and give me the courage to know Him and to do His will and to pardon my sins for they are great. And He who has sustained me to copy this book, may He sustain me to meditate in it and to fulfill His commandments and laws and teachings, Amen. The word of the scribe in the city of Thebes on the 27th of Elul 5175 of the Creation.

b) Completed the *Sefer ha-Temunah,* which speaks in faith to those of intellect and understanding and may a strange death come to those who betray the religion of the true God. May it be Thy will O God of Abraham, Isaac, and Jacob to hear my prayers, requests, and entreaties just as You heeded those of our righteous fathers; and as You have given me health and life to copy these books: *Sefer Shem ha-Mephorash* and *Sefer ha-Temunah,* each one in three texts with commentaries, and *Sefer ha-Yiḥud* with its commentary, all of them according to the Kabbalah. Give me the courage to understand them according to truth and honesty whether for the good or not lest I stray or err in any way from what is written in them; and may You continue to favor me as were the great and awesome pious ones and as You favored me in my travels on land and sea. And may You bring me during my lifetime to the Land of Israel, Amen; and may the Ineffable Name bring this about. The word of the servant, the copyist, that I copied this book in the city of Thebes in the month of Tishre 5175.

Oxford, Bodleian Library, MS Hunt. 309; HPP C229; Neubauer, *Bodleian,* I, #1550.

There are two other colophons in the manuscript: one gives the scribe's full name, Shem Tob ben (name blotted out deliberately), the physician son of the sage R. Jacob the Sephardi; and the second shows that he visited Philippopolis later that year: "I Shem Tob the physician ha-Sephardi son of the sage R. Jacob ha-Sephardi (next word inked out by scribe) copied this book of the commentary on (*Sefer*) *ha-Yiḥud* according to the Kabbalah in Philipopoli while I was sick from the gout; and I stayed there for eighteen days in the house of the honored R. Aharon; and I copied this in the month of Nisan 1415." See above document (108).

[118] 1415

We have seen the destruction of the Jews of Sepharad,[1] Catalonia, Togarmah,[2] and Ṣarfat;[3] we have also heard of harsh and wicked decrees against the Jews who remain in those places. Moreover, we have seen the conflicts throughout the kingdoms of Edom,[4] Yavan,[5] and Togarmah[2] and even on the seas;[6] these began in the year "The Lord is zealous",[7] and continue to this day on which we have copied this book, Tishre 5176.[8]

R. Shem Tob b. Jacob ibn Polia, scribal note to *Sefer ha-Temunah,* 101a; cited by Joseph Hacker in his Hebrew study, "The connections of Spanish Jewry with Eretz-Israel between 1391 and 1492," in *Shalem,* Studies in the History of the Jews in Eretz-Israel (Jerusalem, 1974), I, 135; ms. cited in document 117.

1. Spain in general.
2. Balkan areas occupied by the Ottomans since the middle of the fourteenth century. Our scribe does not indicate whether he ever visited Anatolia.
3. The usual designation for France. The scribe probably met refugees from the expulsion of 1394 during the course of his travels.
4. Christian Europe.
5. Byzantium or Greece in general.
6. Naval battles and pirate attacks that were endemic in the eastern Mediterranean throughout this period.
7. Bi-Shenat el KaNA (Deuteronomy 6:15) = (5)151 or 1390–91.
8. The Hebrew year begins in September among Rabbanite Jews.

[119] 1415[1]

As you know for yourself, the Peloponnese is inhabited by a great number of ethnic groups forming a mixed society. To classify them exactly is at the moment neither feasible nor urgent; the names, however, that tend to crop up in every conversation as the best known and the most important, are these: Laconians,[2] Italians,[3] Peloponnesians,[4] Slavs,[5] Albanians,[6] Gypsies,[7] and Jews[8] (not to mention a generous admixture of hybrids),[9] adding up to a total of seven nationalities.[10]

"Mazaris' Journey to Hades," ed. and trans. by Seminar Classics 609, State University of New York at Buffalo, Arethusa Monographs V (Dept. of Classics, SUNY Buffalo, 1975), 76 (Greek text), 77 (translation).

A satirical description of the characteristics of each ethnic group follows, including one on the Jews: "Others, finally, have imbibed the Jewish love for rows and brawls among each other, their envy and treachery, not to mention their asocial and irrational attitudes and their nasty, impure, and godless customs" (78, Greek text; 79, translation).

Older editions and translations include "The Descent of Mazaris into Hades," in Boissonade, *Analekta Graeca* (Paris, 1831), III, 174; A. Ellissen, *Analekten der mittel- und neugriechischen Literatur* (Leipzig, 1860), IV, 239 (Greek text), 302 (German translation); H. F. Tozer, "A Byzantine Reformer," *JHS,* 7 (1886), 363–66; D. A. Zakythinos, *Le despotat grec de Morée,* vol. II, chap. I: "La population de Morée"; and author's "Jewish Settlement in Sparta and Mistra," pp. 134f.

1. The date of the satire has not yet been fixed with certainty. Ellissen (*Analekten,* p. 356, n. 189) identifies September 21st of the IXth indiction as falling in 1416 (cf. Grumel, *La Chronologie,* p. 262), while Dölger (*CMH,* IV, part II, 241) places the work in 1414/15. For an analysis of the satire, cf. H. F. Tozer, "Byzantine Satire," *JHS,* 2 (1881), 233–70, and the introduction to the Seminar Classics edition.

2. Λακεδαίμονες, i.e., the ancient Spartan population.

3. I.e., Franks and Venetians.

4. The contemporary Greek-speaking Greco-Slavic population.

5. The Slavic tribe of the Melings terrorized the Taygetus environs until Hugues de Bruyeres and his son Geoffrey built the stronghold of Karytaina to pacify the Slavs of Skorta. Cf. William Miller, *The Latins in the Levant,* pp. 3–5, 51.

6. Ἰλλυριοί; Ellissen identifies these as the 10,000 Albanians whom Theodore, despot of Epiros, resettled at the end of the fourteenth century (*Analekten,* p. 357n).

7. Αἰγιπτοί.

8. On the Jews in Mistra, cf. author's "Jewish Settlement in Sparta and Mistra." The Hebrew inscriptions mentioned by Bees, Miller, Andréadès, and Zakythinos date from the sixteenth century. An edition of these appeared in vol. VII (1981) of *Michael* (the Diaspora Research Institute of Tel Aviv University).

9. These are very possibly the Gasmules, offsprings of the Franks and local population.

10. Compare Herodotus VIII, 73: "Οἰκέει δὲ τὴν Πελοπόννησον ἔθνεα ἑπτά."

1423 (30 December) [120]

Moreover the said ambassadors are bound to tell the Lord Emperor that through the letters of our lord bailo in Constantinople we have been informed that many Jews, whose ancestors have been (there) for over the past eighty years and are received as our white Venetians (*nostri Veneti albi*), but they are in effect treated as Greeks and are subject to the *angaria*[1] and the physical inconveniences of the Greeks (*angariis et gravaminibus Grecorum*) which is contrary to the rescript of the treaties and against our *libertas* and *franchisa*. We request His Serene Highness that he remove such novelties and that he neither limit the white Venetian Jews nor compel them to be considered Greeks and that he revoke his order to this effect. But let him permit the said Jews to enjoy the benefits of said treaties just as they have for the past eighty years and to observe said treaties because, on our part as we have done continuously, we are effectively disposed to observe these treaties.

Sathas, *Mnemeia,* I, 159; Dölger, *Regesten,* vol. V, no. 3396; Thiriet, *Régestes,* II, 212; Starr, *Romania,* pp. 32, 114; Jacoby, "Quartiers juifs," passim; Jacoby, "Les Juifs vénitiens de Cp."; and Jacoby, "Les Vénitiens naturalisés."

1. Jews were subject to the *angaria* in Venetian Modon and Coron. The statutes of these colonies from 1485 read: "Furthermore it is held that any Jew or Jewess cannot be freed from any *angaria* except through the assumption of baptism, and we charge you thus that you observe this" (in Sathas, *Mnemeia,* I, 294). Not all conversions freed the Jews from obligations. Starr (*Romania,* p. 60, note 44) cites the case of a "convert at Bara (= Mela) owned by the Mt. Lembos monastery (near Smyrna)" as one such example.

[121] 1424

Year 1424, 26th of March, I, Tam b. Ḥayyim (may he rest in Eden!), admit that I sold this book (Novellae to Rashi's commentary on the Pentateuch) to Ephraim of Romania for a definite price and I received from him the money. I sold this book on 26 Ab 5184—written for Nathan ha-Maʿaravi for a definite price and I received payment of the entire debt; and in order that it be for a proof and a credit for the above-mentioned Nathan I wrote my name here, Ephraim b. Shabbetai from Romania.

Arthur Zacharias Schwartz, *Die hebräische Handschriften in Österreich (ausserhalb der Nationalbibliothek in Wien)* (Leipzig, 1931), #48; cf. also Neubauer, *Bodleian,* I, #296, describing a manuscript of Rashi on the prophets, with notes and glosses by a Greek Jew.

The owners of the manuscript bear interesting names, viz., Eliahu ha-Gabbai (i.e., the synagogue treasurer), Leon b. Yedidyah and Eliahu ha-Parnas (see above, chap. 3, for title). This transaction took place in 1271 in an unidentified community (see above, document 21, and my "Messianic Excitement").

In 1476 the manuscript was again sold, to a certain Yehudah b. Mosheh קואא (Kawa), and witnessed by Eliezer b. Abraham.

1425 [122]

The Jews petition: inasmuch as they are accustomed to pay 1000 hyperpera each year when they were numerous; now, however, as there remain only a few and these are poor, they petition that Your Signoria order a census of those remaining and examine their financial status and their ability to pay in proportion.

We answer that we are agreeable and we sanction that the said Jews may pay 800 hyperpera when the gates of the city remain closed, but if these are open they must pay 1000, in accordance with the prevalent custom.

From the Greek translation of Konstantine D. Mertzios, *Mnémeia Makedonikés Historias,* p. 59.

Mertzios reproduced p. 7 of the document following his p. 48, and partly transcribed the section on the Jews (p. 59, n. 1): "i Zudei domanda de gratia cum zo sia che lor solevano pagar pp. mille alano qu. i era su el gran colmo. Ora i sono romasi molto puochi et queli sono poveri e però i domanda de gra(tia) a la Signoria V(ost)ra a far che siano examinadi queli che son romasi e secondo le lor q(con)dition debiano pagar." Cf. Iorga, *Notes,* I, 495–96 (a French summary); Thierry, *Régestes,* II, #1995, 229 (also only a French summary); Starr, *Romania,* pp. 78–79 and notes 2–3; Apostolos E. Vacalopoulos, *A History of Thessaloniki,* p. 67.

In 1429 the petition was reiterated, with as little success as the first attempt. The following year the Ottomans captured the city. There is no further mention of this payment.

1426 [123]

. . . the delegates were his [Manuel II] spiritual advisor, Makarios, the monk from the Monastery of Xanthopoulos, a former Jew, the teacher Joseph from the Monastery of Harsianitos, and myself [George Sphrantzes].

George Phrantzes, *Chronicon,* I, 126 (ed. Papadopoulos); Sphrantzes, *Memorii,* XV, 2, p. 20 (ed. Grecu); Pseudo-Phrantzes, *Cronica,* II, i, p. 262 (ed. Grecu); Mercati, *Notizie ed altri appunti,* p. 473.

In the recent edition of *The Letters of Manuel II Palaeologus,* ed. and tr. by George T. Dennis (Dumbarton Oaks Texts VIII; Washington, 1977, #52, p. 150), there is a reference to Makarios; see also R. Loenertz, *Correspondence de*

Manuel Calécas (Studi e Testi 152, 1950), p. 85, and J. Barker, *Manuel II Palaeologus* (New Brunswick, 1969), pp. 423f.

[124] 1429

We entertained the possibility of allowing the force to move quickly and capture all those found outside and the whole residential area of the Jews . . .

Suddenly a few horsemen sallied forth from the Gate of the ʿEbraike or the Zeugalateion Gate (for thus it was also called) . . .

George Phrantzes, *Annales,* II, v (ed. CSHB, Bonn), 137–38; Phrantzes, *Chronicon* (ed. Papadopoulos), 140–41; Georgeos Sphrantzes, *Memorii,* xviii, 7–8 (ed. Grecu), 30 and parallel in Pseudo-Phrantzes, *Chronica,* II, 4 (ed. Grecu), 280; translated by Marios Philippides, *The Fall of the Byzantine Empire. A Chronicle of George Sphrantzes 1401–1477* (Amherst, 1980), 36. Cf. Triantaphyllos, *Historical Lexicon of Patras* (in Greek), s.v. Zeugalateion, and above part I, chap. 2, section "Peloponnesos" note 103 and text.

[125] 1429

To resume, of that awesome man [Bishop Simon], I speak, of that dead one who had been well inclined to all; and everyone in the city—men, women, children, Latins and even those Jews spoke pityingly to each other . . .

Ioannes Anagnostes, *De Thessalonicensi Excidio Narratio,* ed. Niebuhr, *CSHB,* p. 489; Starr, *Romania,* pp. 78–79.

[126] 28 April 1430

The said testator ordered that regarding the iron which is in Nepanto (= Lepanto), which is approximately 1500 pounds, it must be brought to Patras. From it 500 pounds must be given to Andrea Carphi or Savalia; and the rest be given to Meshulam b. Mordecai the Jew as payment for the debt of the said testator.

Regarding the money which the above-named Andreas Carphi owes for the iron held for him by the aforesaid testator, to wit concerning the aforesaid 500 pounds and another 2000 pounds for payment of twenty-five hyperpera for the aforesaid 1000 pounds are owed to the aforementioned Meshullam on his credit.

Further said testator said that he has in Nepanto 1400 hyperpera, of which he wishes to be paid to Aron de Missael (= מִישָׁאֵל) the Jew, whatever will appear on the books of this same testator that that Jew is owed them.

Will of Bartholomaeus Zane de Visnadellis from Treviso, in Gerland, *Neue Quellen zur . . . Patras,* pp. 213, 215; Starr, *Romania,* p. 74; Panagiotes Christopoulos, "The Jewish Community of Naupaktos," (Greek) *'Epetēris 'Etaireias Stereoelladikōn Meletōn,* I (1968), 283.

Bartholemew was the son-in-law of Aegidius de Leonessa, whose wife Katarina in 1424 was party to a loan contract which a Jew, Solomon Bonsignore, signed as witness. Cf. Gerland, pp. 201–4, and Starr, *loc. cit.*

1430

[127]

Troch Barila [the Catalan captain who carried off] the Jews of that place and the slaves; and this was on the 28th of September, 1430 (Troch Barila . . . ly Zudie de quella tera et li Schiavy; e questo fo adi xxviii se(te)mbrio 1430).

Chronicle Zancaruola (Venice ms.), fol. 404v, quoted in Iorga, *Notes,* I, 511, note 2; cf. K. Hopf, *Griechenland im Mittelalter,* II, 85, col. 2.

The *Diarii Veneti* (fol. 6v), quoted by Iorga (*loc. cit.*), reads: "tutti i Zudesi di quel luogo," while the ms. from the Bibliothèque Nationale (Paris, Ms. Italian 787, fol. 129r, quoted in Starr, *Romania,* p. 73) reads: "retenuti tutti li giudei su le soe galie." Starr identifies the locale as Clarentza.

1432

[128]

Pera is a large town inhabited by Greeks, Jews and Genoese. The last are masters of it, under the Duke of Milan, who styles himself Lord of Pera. It has a Podestat and other officers who govern it after their manner. A great commerce is carried on with the Turks; but the latter have a singular privilege, namely that should anyone of their slaves run away, and seek asylum in Pera, they must be given up.

Bertrandon de la Brocquière, translated in Thomas Wright, ed., *Early Travels in Palestine,* p. 335.

1433

[129]

The amabassador wished to kiss his hand, but he (Murat II) refused it, and by means of a Jew interpreter, who understood the Turkish and Italian languages, asked him how his good brother and neighbor the Duke of Milan was in health.

Bertrandon de la Brocquière, translated in Thomas Wright, ed., *Early Travels in Palestine,* p. 351. A description of Adrianople and the sultan's court is on pp. 346ff.

[130] 15 May 1436

In the name of the Father, the Son, and the Holy Ghost, amen. In the year of the incarnation of Our Lord Jesus Christ 1436, of the XIVth indiction, on the 15th of May, a certain case was brought before the most dear cousin[1] of our powerful and holy Master and Basileos Lord Joannes Kantakuzenos by the Kephalonian tailor Alexios Koutzos acting for Ser Nikolas de Leonessa, son of Master Giles as party of the first part; as party of the second part Solomon b. Abraham or Leakhos[2] of Modon his father-in-law: both defendants are Jews. The accusation and petition of the abovewritten Alexios the representative ran as follows:

He Solomon b. Abraham possesses a certain plot of land on which he has made a garden; for which plot of land he used to pay 5 hyperpera a year to that Master Giles or his estate. This plot is in Kavallarianikos[3] or so called; it is situated in the neighborhood of Palaeo-Patras in a district called Stro. Now, then, this Solomon has possessed it for sufficient years and he no longer wishes to pay the aforesaid rent, as was his want. Because of this the aforementioned representative pleads and beseeches that: first this Solomon be convicted and condemned to having his goods confiscated; and, that this plot or garden be freed since Solomon treacherously and ruthlessly did not pay the abovementioned rent (*telos*) so many years in order to rob its rightful owner of this plot, or, if you will, its mortgager.

And this Solomon the Jew said in response: you neither asked me for any rent, nor did I pay any. But if you had ever demanded it and if I had not paid it, as I always pay my debts, *then* I would be justly convicted.

And then Alexios the advocate begged and beseeched the judge for a decision against Solomon enjoining him to pay and rectify the situation of the rents delinquent for so many years, paying double the amount according to the custom and practice of the principality, since the plot in question is in Kavallarianikos and therefore the practice of the principality must be followed.[4]

Thereupon Solomon brought forth a Latin instrument which set forth the gift of the land to him (with the explicit statement) that he would in future not be obliged to pay the rent of 5 hyperpera.

Because of this, the abovementioned cousin of the Basileus,[5] sitting in judgment in the palace of Palaeo-Patras with certain noblemen as colleagues, viz., Lord Kondeos Podos, Lord Andreas Abouri, Lord Iakoumos da Roma, Ioannis Mantinus, Ioannis Spanopoulos, Antonius Basilopoulos, and Andreas Sabalia, having heard and understood all the arguments which the spokesmen for both sides had made known before the court; all the judges took counsel with each other "in camera" and decided and pronounced the following:

That this Solomon the Jew be convicted and condemned; and that first, all goods which he kept on the plot, or in the garden, be confiscated as the laws direct and that the plot itself be turned over to Nikolas de Leonessa its owner; and secondly that this Solomon the tenant ought to be penalized for not paying the rent to the abovementioned landlord for so many years. He would have to pay this and make up the delinquent amounts paying double according to custom and practice of the principality, since this place or garden is called Kavallarianikos, for truly the Kavallarianika belongs to the principality; however, out of condescension they ruled that this Solomon the Jew pay only the original amount just as he would have wanted to do each year.

Court proceeding before Despot Thomas, in Gerland, *Neue Quellen zur . . . Patras,* pp. 218–20; cf. Starr, *Romania,* p. 74. On the application of the Assizes of Romania to this case, cf. D. Jacoby, *La Féodalité en Grèce médiévale: les "Assises de Romanie" sources, application et diffusion,* pp. 180–81.

1. The despot, Thomas.

2. Starr suggests Elijah, as does Jacoby. The property evidently came to Solomon as part of the dowry.

3. In 1420 Aegidius de Leonessa was awarded this fief in Patras by Prince Centurione II Zaccaria. It was renewed in 1425 by Carlo I Tocco, lord of Zante and Kephalonia.

4. Cf. D. A. Zakythinos, *Le despotat grec de Morée,* vol. II: *Vie et institutions,* pp. 127–28.

5. John Kantakuzenos, governor of Patras, who seems to be the only new element in this court of 4 Latins and 3 Greeks, which seems to be a survival from the pre-Byzantine period; cf. Jacoby, p. 181.

27 September 1440 [131]

In the same place [Pherelon] this Lord Nikolas gave to the said convent [the Franciscan convent of St. Nicholas] in exchange for this, one little garden situated by the mill of Stro; the little garden is neighboring that of Nikolas of Abouri and that of the Jew Pothos Kafari.[1]

Gerland, *Neue Quellen zur . . . Patras,* p. 225; Starr, *Romania,* p. 74.

1. Was he descended from "ser Abracho de Caphara," whose wife Protissa sold a town house consisting of two buildings on the main street to the Leonessa family for 70 hyperpera in 1399? Cf. Gerland, pp. 191–93, and Starr, pp. 73–74. On the name Poto in the area, cf. index s.v.

[132] 1447

Mistra and all the towns around it, namely Koula, ʽEvraike, Trype, Tzeramios, Pankota, Sklavochorion . . .

George Phrantzes, *Annales,* II, cap. XIX, 200 (ed. CSHB); Georgios Sphrantzes, *Memorii,* XXVII, 1, p. 68 (ed. Grecu); Pseudo-Phrantzes, *Cronica,* p. 342 (ed. Grecu). Our translation follows Grecu's editions; see above (119).

The reading "Sparta and all of the towns around it, namely . . . Hebraica Trype . . ." is the reading known and accepted by scholars until the mid-1960s (cf. Martin Hanke, *De Byzantinorum rerum scriptoribus graecis liber* [Lipsiae, 1677], p. 657). The implication drawn from it is that the term *hebraica* is an adjective, modifying Trype, and that therefore one must explain how Trype got a Jewish reputation (cf. Patrick E. Fermor, *Mani, Travels, in the Southern Peloponnesus* [London, 1958], chap. 1).

Grecu's addition of a comma can be justified on several grounds: there is no known toponymic reference to parallel an Hebraike Trype, nor does any source indicate that Jews ever lived in Trype. Also, the author of the *Mazaris* satire (document 119) was more likely to have been impressed by the existence of a Jewish suburb outside the city than by a fable (to which his satiric work would have done justice) of which he apparently had no knowledge. Finally, we know that a suburb of Mistra was actually called *Hebraike* (cf. part I, chap. 2 section "Peloponnesos"). Therefore Grecu's addition of a comma reflects the actual historical situation, i.e., of acknowledging the existence of an *Hebraike*—the Jewish Quarter—outside of Mistra in the fifteenth century. Cf. Bowman, "Jewish Settlement in Sparta and Mistra," *BNJ,* XXII (1979), 134 ff.

[133] 1447(?)

About this time there was a notable disputation between the Basileus Lord Joannes and a certain Jew named Xenos, who afterwards was reborn in holy baptism and was renamed Emmanuel . . .

Then, on account of the splendor of the most Holy Spirit and the wise words of the autocrator and the holy monk Matthew, the Hebrew, being enlightened, plainly confessed to the Holy Trinity and all the dogma of the Orthodox faith and was reborn in divine baptism; and Xenos was renamed Emmanuel.

Theological debate between John VIII Palaeologos and Xenos the Jew, in George Phrantzes, *Annales,* pp. 163–76 (ed. CSHB); Pseudo-Phrantzes, *Cronica,* II, 12, pp. 306–18 (ed. Grecu). Cf. W. Miller, "The Historians Doukas and Phrantzes," *JHS,* 46 (1926), 68.

Both Miller and Starr (*Romania,* p. 28) follow the Bonn edition and treat the debate as historical. Starr dates it ca. 1447; see my "Two Late Byzantine Dialogues with the Jews," pp. 83–86. The debate occurs only in the *Chronicon Maius* of Melissenos, and therefore it is quite likely that this debate never took place. There is no indication in the *Chronicon Minus* of Sphrantzes that the historian knew of such a debate.

We may note possible stereotyping of the two names used for the Jew. The name Xenos, which never occurs as a Jewish name, means "stranger," and the name Emmanuel brings to mind the New Testament name for Jesus, with its messianic connotations that also involve the conversion of the Jews (see above, document 3, and underlined passage).

23 October 1450, XIII Indiction [134]

(We order that the following offences be stopped): the impost which they used to give to the captain of the slaves (*capitaneus pro sclavis*) and the port-duty for the slaves (*portiaticus sclavorum*) and the port-duty for other things (*portiaticus aliarum rerum*) and the export of the wine of the Venetian Jews (*exitum vini Venetorum*) so that it would be free, and the clerkship for the cask (of wine) of the Venetian Jews (*scribaniam vegetum judeorum venetorum*), the half hyperper which our chamberlain required for each cask of the Jews and the payment which the captain of the payments (*capitaneus pagaitorum*) took from cases involving Venetians; and that in the future the Venetian Jews should not furnish any payment (*factio*) in a time of need, as do the other Jews; as for the skins and packsaddles and a carriage, since it is difficult for us to answer, our Imperial dear son-in-law, the Megas Dux Lord Lukas Dierminestes Notaras asked that this may pass into his regular salary, and that it not be claimed until our speaker comes to your celebrated Lord and to the lordship of the Venetians so that he may appropriate it there and that the Bailo be informed of this and write it down, and when your lordship will write to him that he should return that.

Letter of Constantine XI, Emperor of Constantinople, to Franciscus Foscari, doge of Venice, in Thomas, *DVL* II, 379–80; Dölger, *Regesten,* V, no. 3527; Iorga, *Notes,* III, 257–58; Guilland, "Les appels de Constantin XII Paléologue à Rome et à Venice pour sauver Constantinople (1452–1453)," *Byzantinoslavica,* XIV (1953), 226–44 (reprinted in Guilland, *Etudes Byzantines,* pp. 151–75; cf. esp. 156). For commentary, cf. D. Jacoby, "Les Juifs vénitiens de Cp." Iorga (*Notes,* III, 258, note 1) identifies the *capitaneus pagaitorum* as the majordomo or chief of the guard of the Palace of Pege. This identification is less likely than the one used in the above translation.

[135] Ca. 1453

What finally induced him (Pletho) to apostasy was a certain Jew with whom he studied because of his skill in the exegesis of Aristotle. This one (Elisaeus) specialized in Averroes and the other Persian and Arabic interpreters of Aristotle's works which the Jews had translated into their own language, but of Moses the Jews believe and scrupulously observe that even the least thing was thought of by him. He exposed him (Pletho) to the (doctrines) of Zoroaster and the others. Indeed with that one although seeming to be a Jew but actually a pagan (*hellenistes*), not only as his teacher did he associate with him for a very long time but also as his assistant did he serve him and in this way support himself. For he, whose name was Elisaeus, was among those who had very great influence in the court of these barbarians.

Letter to the princess of the Peloponnesos (Theodora, wife of Demetrios Palaiologos, despot of Mistra) on the "Treatise on the Laws" of Gemistos Plethon, ed. Petit et al. *Oeuvres complètes de Gennade Scholarius,* IV, 152, l.37, and 153, l.9; edited in Sp. Lampros, *Palaiogeia kai Peloponnesiaka* (II, 20–21), who gives the variant spelling Eliassaios. Cf. commentary and translation in M. Anastos, "Pletho's Calendar and Liturgy," *DOP,* IV (1948), 277–79, and remarks by J. P. Mamalakis, *Georgios Gemistos Plethon* (in Greek), pp. 46–47. Elisha probably flourished during the last quarter of the fourteenth century in Adrianople.

[136] 1456

Completed in the year 5216 on 16 Tammuz by my hand, Shabbetai b. Absalom, when I was in Corinth.

J.T.S. MS RAB 656 MIC 6474 (acc. 0360); HPP D41.

The book copied was the *'Amude Golah* (Pillars of Exile), a book of commandments by R. Isaac ben Joseph of Corbel, with introduction, annotations, and indices. The work is more popularly known as *Sefer Mitzvot Katan* (SeMaK). Cf. Urbach, *Ba'ale ha-Tosaphot,* pp. 447f, and *EJ,* ix, 21.

Ca. 1456–57 [137]

Elisaeus, the apparent Jew but in reality a polytheist, who at that time wielded great influence at the court of the barbarians, acquainted you (Plethon) with this one (Zoroaster) whom you formerly did not know; and you fled your homeland to live with him in order to receive the best instruction.

Letter to Exarch Joseph re the book of Gemistos Plethon and against the pagan polytheism, ed. Petit et al., *Oeuvres . . . de Gennade Scholarius,* IV, 162, ll.8–11; Mamalakis, *Georgios Gemistos Plethon* (in Greek), pp. 46–47; Anastos, "Pletho's Calendar and Liturgy," pp. 277–79.

1453 [138]

Now I shall tell you of the events at sea, since I have told of what happened on land. One hour before dawn the fleet got underway from the Columns where it was anchored, and it took up a position by the harbor boom ready to give battle there. But their admiral saw that our harbour was well defended with ships and galleys, particularly at the boom where there were ten large ships of eight hundred *botte* and upwards, and since he was afraid of our fleet, he decided to go and fight behind the city on the side of the Dardanelles and leave the harbour without fighting, and so they went on land there, part of them disembarking by the Giudecca, so as to have better opportunity of getting booty, there being great riches in the houses of the Jews, principally jewels. The seventy *fuste* inside the harbour which had been dragged over the hill of Pera, commanded by Zagan Pasha, all went together and attacked the city at a place called Fanari, and the Christians on this part of the wall bravely drove them back.

Giornale dell'Assedio di Constantinopoli 1453 di Nicolo Barbaro P.V., ed. Enrico Cornet, p. 56; translated by J. R. Jones, *Nicolo Barbaro, Diary of the Siege of Constantinople, 1453,* pp. 66–67; Jacoby, "Quartiers," p. 195.

[139] 1467

When the Sultan had captured the city of Constantinople, almost his very first care was to have the city repopulated. He also undertook the further care and repairs of it. He sent an order in the form of an imperial command to every part of his realm, that as many inhabitants as possible be transferred to the city, not only Christians but also his own people and many of the Hebrews.

Translated by Charles T. Riggs, *Kritovoulos, History of Mehmed the Conqueror,* p. 93.

[140] 1453

In the first year of the Sultan Mehmet, King of Turkey . . . the Lord aroused the spirit of the king, Sultan Mehmet, King of Turkey and his voice passed throughout his kingdom and also by proclamation saying:[1] "This is the word of Mehmet king of Turkey, the Lord God of Heaven gave me a kingdom in the land and he commanded me to number his people the seed of Abraham his servant, the sons of Jacob his chosen ones, and to give them sustenance in the land and to provide a safe haven for them.[2] Let each one with his God come to Constantinople the seat of my kingdom and sit under his vine and under his fig tree with his gold and silver, property and cattle, settle in the land and trade and become part of it."[3]

The Jews gathered together from all the cities of Turkey both near and far, each man came from his home; and the community gathered in the thousands and ten thousands and God assisted them from heaven while the king gave them good properties and houses full of goods. The Jews dwelled there according to their families and they multiplied exceedingly.[4] From that day hence from every place that the king conquered wherein there were Jews he immediately forced them to emigrate,[5] taking them from there and sending them to Constantinople the seat of his kingdom. And he bore them and carried them all the days of old.[6]

Because the Jews feared the Lord, He gave them prosperity,[7] and in the place wherein formerly in the days of the Byzantine king there were only two or three congregations, the Jews multiplied and increased and became greater in number than (40)[8] congregations and the land did not let them settle together because their property was so great.[9] The congregations of Constantinople were praiseworthy, Torah and wealth and honor increased among the congregations. In the congregations they blessed the Lord, the fountain of Israel,[10] the doer of great wonders. They opened their mouth in song to heaven and blessed the Lord, all the servants of the Lord who stand in the house of the Lord in the night seasons.[11]

Seder Eliyahu Zuta by Rabbi Eliyahu Kapsali, vol. 1, ed. Aryeh Shmuelevitz (Jerusalem, 1975), p. 81. This edition supersedes the excerpts published by M. Lattes, *Likkutim Shonim mi-Sefer Déve Eliyahu* (Padua, 1869).

1. Ezra 1:1–3.
2. Based on verses in Ezra and Genesis.
3. Genesis 34:10.
4. Exodus 1:7.
5. Paraphrasing Isaiah 22:17.
6. Isaiah 63:9.
7. Based on Exodus 1:21.
8. Three of the four manuscripts used by the editor have a lacuna, as does the passage cited by Lattes (p. 7). Document 154 (below), lists 35 congregations.
9. Genesis 13:6.
10. Psalms 68:27.
11. Psalms 134:1.

Ca. 1454–1455 [141]

Sultan Mehmet loved the Jews very much, and many of the Jews used to frequent the king's presence in the courtyard in the garden of the king's palace [= Sublime Porte]. Among them were the physicians of the king, his servants and those who prepared his food, but of all the most pious and humble was R. Moses Kapsali (may his memory be blessed!) who had been in Constantinople since the time of the kings of Greece.

One day the king passed through the open place where was the camp of the Jews, and seeing a large crowd was astounded. Can anyone judge this great nation? And it came to pass in those days while the king was sitting on his throne with his aides standing before him that he said, "Who is the judge and leader of the Jews?" They answered him, "A scholar who interprets and delivers opinions every day of the year from its beginning to its end, who sleeps on the ground and lives a life of sorrow; yet he exerts himself in studying Torah." The king commanded, and he was brought to stand before the king who called him Rabbi, (which in the language of Turkey is *hoca*,) and spoke well to him. And despite the fact that the abovementioned rabbi did not know Turkish and the king had never met him . . . the king gave him honor and ordered that he be escorted home on his horse accompanied by the nobles and chiefs who sit at the gate of the king.

But the king did not believe the rumor which he had heard about him and came to test him with riddles. And it came to pass in those days that the king disguised himself[1] and donned other clothes and with two other men went to the rabbi's house where he saw a great crowd of Jews standing about him. And Moses sat to judge the people who stood by Moses from morning unto evening.[2] And he gave value to every case. A rich man, noble and respected, came before him with a lawsuit involving a very poor man dressed in filthy rags. Both presented their case before the rabbi for judgement. Seeing that the verdict was in favor of the poor man, he ordered the rich one to return the stolen goods. The rich man got angry, raised his voice shouting against the poor man and answered insolently.[3] Moses got very angry and cursed the rich man, vilifying and defaming him with increasing furor, finally banishing him from his presence with wrathful face, but he did not leave his presence until he had returned the stolen property. The king saw this and knew that the wisdom of God was with him that he could perform justice[4] and not honor the rich.[5] Very pleased the king returned home with no one the wiser save for one Jew who recognizing the king became as weak as a baby. After the king left, the Jew whispered the secret to the rabbi who became very anxious.[6]

One day there appeared at the rabbi's door about twenty of the king's men some on litters and some on mules. And they brought him on a horse before the gate of the king and bowed before him. The king said, "Tell me the truth; don't hide anything from me. What is your opinion of Ishmael b. Abraham; was he righteous or not?" The Lord guided his tongue and because he feared the Lord and avoided evil, he answered with wisdom, bringing evidence from the Talmud regarding Ishmael and his importance. These he showed to the king who accepted these praises and good words about Ishmael. The king became exceedingly pleased and commanded that he remove the ragged clothes and be clothed with tunics.[7] At the king's command they brought before him gold and silver clothes and the king dressed him with tunics. The rabbi declined saying, "Lord, I have never tried to dress like this."[8] Then the king commanded his high officials to accompany him to his gate. Several times the king sent for him and he found favor in his eyes. Several times the king sent court cases involving Jews in both personal and commercial matters before him for judgement; and whom he would he raised up and whom he would he put down.[9]

Seder Eliyahu Zuta, ed. Shmuelevitz, pp. 81–82; *Sefer Déve Eliyahu,* ed. M. Lattes, pp. 7–9; cf. comments by Baron, *The Jewish Community,* I, 195ff, and Charles Berlin, "A Sixteenth-Century Hebrew Chronicle of the Ottoman Empire: The *Seder Eliyahu Zuta* of Elijah Capsali and Its Message," *Edward Kiev Festschrift,* pp. 27–30. See above, part I, chap. 5, note 33.

On the question of what language the two men used for their discussion, Patrinelis has shown that Mehmet knew neither Greek nor Italian at the time of the conquest (Christos G. Patrinelis, "Mehmed II the Conqueror and His Presumed Knowledge of Greek and Latin," *Viator,* 2 [1971], 349–54). Nor is it likely that Mehmet knew Hebrew, although Kapsali later has Mehmet learning that language in order to understand the Book of Daniel! He did know, however, Turkish, Arabic, and Persian. Kapsali, on the other hand, knew Greek, Hebrew, and probably Italian. It seems most likely that the two conversed via Mehmet's Jewish interpreters. Cf. author's short note, "Did Mehmet II Know Hebrew?" in *Walter K. Fischel Festschrift* (Berkeley, 1981), pp. 93–96.

1. Cf. Jones, *The Siege of Cp.*, p. 72, containing a translation of Ducas, chap. 35.
2. Exodus 18:13–14.
3. Proverbs 18:23.
4. 1 Kings 3:23.
5. Leviticus 19:15.
6. Ruth 3:8.
7. Zechariah 3:4.
8. 1 Samuel 17:19.
9. Daniel 5:19.

1457 [142]

And so it happened that those celebrating the New Year were in error, for the moon was still visible. This happened in the year 5217 in Constantinople when they celebrated the New Year but the old moon was seen on that day. Further the sage R. Aaron, author of the *Mibḥar,* said that this also happened in Solchat.

Elijah Bashyachi, *Addereth Eliahu,* section *Kiddush ha-Ḥodesh,* 4a. For other instances, see documents 25, 59, and 147.

1460 [143]

And when I [Samuel Poto] saw that there was no eclipse of the sun that year or in the succeeding one, I set out to explain the eclipse that occurred in the year 1460 at the time when the great lord Sultan Mehmet entered and took the whole Morea and also seized the Greek ruler (*melekh*)[1] Despot Kyr Demetri. And at that time I was with the army near Kalavryta and there they issued a decree for us that no *subaşi*[2] could require any of us Jews to do any forced labor.[3]

J.T.S. MS micro 2581, fol. 12b; HPP D160.

1. Demetrios could have been known as the basileios since the death of the emperor Constantine in 1453. Despite our author's use of the word *melekh* (literally, "king"), we may translate it as "ruler."

2. The *subaşi* functioned as military police.

3. The Hebrew reads: "*shum subashi le-she'abdeinu be-shum shi'abud.*" On these *angaria*, see below, document 150, note 8.

[144] 1461

Further during the sack [of Trebizond], a certain cross fell into the hand of his [David's] chief physician, who, originally a Jew, later converted to Islam. It was made of pure gold in four parts, with five hyacinthe stones in each part, outlining the cross; altogether twenty stones, of which in each part near the stones are found two pearls, altogether eight; and in the fourth part of the cross below center, four large pearls . . . and the name of the great and famous Basileus Alexios Komnenos (1204–1222) was upon it.

Sathas, *MB*, III, 102b; W. Miller, *Trebizond: The Last Greek Empire,* p. 116.

Of Jacob we hear nothing more; presumably his medical training stood him in good stead. This national treasure, which he saved, was bought by one George Polo and subsequently disappeared.

[145] 1464

CHRISTIAN: Do you wish to discuss with me about the points wherein Christians and Jews differ?

JEW: Let us discuss, if it seems good to you, however, in the frankest manner; for we do not have enough time for a rational and formal enquiry, and also the subject matter necessitates more detailed reasoning from both sides, not only with regard to opinions but also works.

CHRISTIAN: Well said. Then let me ask you first if you are a Judaean.

JEW: Yes, I am a Jew.

CHRISTIAN: You are not a Judaean. For on the one hand the place of the Jews, Jerusalem, and the surrounding countryside, was formerly called

Judaea; but now that place is no longer called Judaea nor are you from there, but rather as it were a Prusan or Ephesan or from Byzantium or Thessaly. For just as one being born in Ephesus is not a Thessalian, so neither are you a Judaean, having been born not in Judaea but in another land.

JEW: This in no way prevents me from being a Jew; for I consider my geneology from the race of Judaeans and not from the fact of birth in Judaea. But with regard to this I do not differ so much from you; I say I am a Jew, I maintain the ancestral faith and religious observances of the Jews and I live according to the Jewish laws and customs and I talk to God in the Jewish tongue.

CHRISTIAN: . . . How can you say justly that you are a Judaean, since your ancestors were exiled from Judaea so many years ago in the last exile and perhaps even more in the earlier ones? . . . Being a Thessalian, I do not disagree now with being called a Byzantine, as long as neither in language nor in opinions or customs do Thessalians and Byzantines differ, as perhaps once long ago . . . I even know the Latin language; but I do not say that I am a Latin . . . moreover being a Hellene in language, yet at no time do I appear as a Hellene because I do not think as Hellenes once thought; rather I would wish to be called a Hellene for my own reasons. And if anyone should ask me who I am, I would answer "I am a Christian"; especially if you should ask me or anyone else who holds a different opinion than I concerning God. You say, therefore, that you are a Jew because you are a follower of the prophet Moses . . . I will prove to you that you are not a Jew, for you are not a follower of Moses even if you think so . . . [anyone who is unfaithful to the word of Moses is not a Jew: you do not accept the messiah whom the Lord prophesied through Moses: therefore you are disobedient and not a Jew].

"Refutation of the Jewish Error from the Scriptures and from Circumstances and from a Comparison with the Christian Truth: in the Form of a Dialogue," in L. Petit et al., eds., *Oeuvres complètes de George (Gennade) Scholarios,* III, 251–314; summary in A. L. Williams, *Adversus Judaios,* pp. 188–203. Cf. Beck, *Kirche,* pp. 760–61, and author's "Two Late Byzantine Dialogues with the Jews."

1468 **[146]**

Greeks and Turks inhabit various places (in Constantinople) . . . But as the Jews were too few in number for so large a city, Mehmet II ordered that all the Jews who were in his lands, those in Anatolia as well as those in Romania, were to be removed with their wives and children to Constantinople. They were settled in groups according to their places of origin, and the quarters where they were installed received the name of these places.

Historia Turchesca (1300–1514), chronicle of J.-M. Angiolello, translated by Walter Gerard, *La Ruine de Byzance (1200–1453),* appendix A, "La repopulation de Constantinople après la conquête turque," p. 344; the chronicle was edited by I. Ursu: Donado da Lezze (= G. M. Angiolello!), *Historia Turchesca* (1300–1514), in Bucharest, 1910. A short biography of Gian-Maria Angiolello of Vicenza was included by Fr. Babinger in his "Mehmed II, der Eroberer, und Italien," *Byzantion,* XXI (1951), 160–62; cf. also the two studies of Jean Reinhard, *Essai sur J.-M. Angiolello* (Angers, 1913), and *Edition de J.-M. Angiolello. I:ses manuscrits inédits* (Besançon, 1913); and Niccolo di Lenna, "Richerche intorno allo storico G. Maria Angiolello (degli Anzolelli), patrizo vicentino, 1451–1525," *Archivo Veneto-Tridentino,* vol. V (Venedig, 1924).

[147] 1480

The Signs for the Beginning of the Year in Places Distant from Ereṣ Yisrael

After it has already been explained that the beginning of the year which, according to the law of our Torah, follows the *abib* in Ereṣ Yisrael according to the conditions which we cited. And we on account of our many sins have become distant from the holy land and we cannot find the *abib*[1] so we have been forced to follow after the intercalation according to the way our brethren, *baʿale ha-kabbalah,*[2] do, because this calculation follows approximately the finding of the *abib* in Ereṣ Yisrael, for when knowledge is not certain one has to follow the approximation.[3] And it is proper to calculate from the cycles of nineteen years and to intercalate in each cycle 7 (years). In this way the calculation will bring into agreement the lunar year and the solar year, and the sun and the moon will return almost to the place where they were associated at the beginning of the cycle, because our months are lunar months and if one follows after them alone in order to make our years every 12 months, our festivals will come sometimes in the summer and sometimes in the winter as it occurs among the Ishmaelites who follow the lunar month only, while Scriptures say "Observe the month of *abib*"[4] which agrees with the course of the sun. And it is proper to intercalate the third, the sixth, the eighth, the eleventh, the fourteenth, the seventeenth and the nineteenth years and their signs are 3-6-8-11-14-17-19; according to the above there would be seven intercalated and twelve regular (years). And the sages said that for the most part this arrangement will be the one in Ereṣ Yisrael and so they decreed and commanded not to make two intercalations connect nor three regular connect, rather one time make one regular and another time two because this is the order of the season according to its nature and the rains in their time, but the people in Ereṣ Yisrael who follow the *abib* sometimes make three regular connect and sometimes two intercalations connect. This is because of the difference in the seasons of the first fruits and in the lateness. Thus they follow after the opinion based on the obvious and we follow after the approximate reasoning. R. Aaron, author of the *Mibḥar,* said that in the seventeenth and nineteenth years of the cycle an error will occur because these years appear as if they should be regular and not intercalated. And further R. Aaron, author of *'Eṣ Ḥayyim,* said that in the cycle 269[5] we heard that in the fourth year from the cycle what was for us the month of Elul was the month of Tishre for the people in Ereṣ Yisrael. This resulted from a confusion of the seventeenth and nineteenth intercalated years which occurred in the previous cycle. And the aforementioned sage said that it is best to follow after the same reform, and the sense of the reform is as we mentioned before. And so it happened in our time in the year 5240, the fifteenth of the cycle,[6] men from our congregation went to the holy city and said that the fourteenth year of the cycle 276 which we are in is for us an intercalation, but they had a regular year and it did not seem proper for us based on this to weaken our belief because they follow upon the logic of the obvious and we follow the logic of the approximate, and each according to his own stand will come in peace, for the commandments were given according to the capability, and it is not fitting to withhold much good because of a little wrong.[7] R. Israel Ham-ma'arabi said that the reform of the cycle is the reform of the "Good Figs" who were among the repatriates from Babylonia which remained after them for generation after generation and continued to reform the cycle with seven intercalations and twelve regular to approximate the time of the *abib* according to their reasoning and therefore we follow it.[8] The conclusion is, all have decreed that those living in Ereṣ Yisrael should proceed according to the *abib* which is found in Ereṣ Yisrael, and those who are far from it should follow after the calculated cycle of intercalated and regular years.[9]

Elijah Bashyachi, *Adderet Eliahu,* section *Kiddush ha-Ḥodesh,* chap. 40 (in Elijah Bashyachi, *Sefer ha-Mitzvot shel ha-Yehudim ha-Kara'im Adderet Eliahu,* p. 77 (לט).

For commentary on the problem of the *abib* system and its ultimate rejection by the Karaites of Byzantium, cf. Ankori, *Karaites,* pp. 339–44.

1. On this phrase and its antecedence, cf. Ankori, p. 343, note 117.
2. I.e., Rabbanite Jews.
3. Quoted in Ankori, p. 340, note 111, as well as the citation in Aaron b. Elijah's *Mibḥar* on Exodus, 15b, which Bashyachi followed.
4. Deuteronomy 16:1.
5. = 1336. Ankori, p. 340, quoted in note 112 from the original in Aaron b. Elijah's *Gan 'Eden,* 22b.
6. 1479–80. Quoted in Ankori, p. 341, note 113.
7. Quoted *loc. cit.*
8. Commented in Ankori, p. 344, and quoted in note 119, citing source in *Gan 'Eden,* 22 and parallels. The last section, beginning with the reference to R. Aaron (excluding the contemporary reference, of course), is based on the section in *Gan 'Eden,* 22.
9. Quoted in Ankori, p. 344 (translation), and note 120 (text).

[148] Ca. 1482

Because of this, our exile has been lengthened due to our sins and Torah has been forgotten because there is no longer any prophet and Torah has been lost to the *kohen*—all Israelites as is known are called *kohanim.* And we, the Assembly of the Karaites (עדת הקראים), have become few in number, and the books which lit up the eyes of our brethren have disappeared from among us. We are taught by the Rabbanites among whom we live in Constantinople; we are accustomed to their books which we hear continuously and their commentaries which add things to the commandments of the Torah and make it easy for them, and they bring their scriptural texts as support for their enactments and homiletic interpretations based on numerical value of letters upon them; and the heart of our seers has practically turned away to believing in them. Some agree with them completely, and hesitantly say that they are correct in saying that our sect broke away from them because of our great evil and lack of understanding in the interpretation of the Torah.

And when I saw this, I Shabbetai (the youngest of my family and very insignificant) b. Eliyahu of the exiles of Pravado (*mi-bene galut Pravato*) who were brought to Constantinople, I donned a cloak of resentment and my anger rose in my gorge until I could stand it no more. I did not rest nor quiet nor be at ease until I sought and found a book . . . old and very holy . . . and the name of the book was *Eshkol ha-Kofer* . . . of R. Yehudah Hadassi, the mourner of the Mourners of Zion, b. Eliyahu Hadassi. I examined it well and understood that the Karaites could rely fully on it . . .

M. Frankl, "Käräische Studien," *MGWJ,* 31 (1882), 270–71, quoting from the first Firkowich collection, no. 622. It was accepted by his contemporaries that Shabbetai Pravado saved the *Eshkol ha-Kofer* from oblivion; cf. Kaleb Afendopolo, *Naḥal Eshkol,* in Gozlow edition of *Eshkol ha-Kofer,* ed. A. Firkowich. Cited by Frankl, p. 272; cf. Steinschneider, *Leiden,* pp. 48f.

On the general deterioration of Byzantine Karaite mss. in the Late Middle Ages, cf. Ankori, *Karaites,* pp. 31–32, note 13, and his comments there on the use of the Firkowich material. Yet we know a number of Karaite scribes who were active in Adrianople and Solchat in the fourteenth and fifteenth centuries. His full name was Shabbetai b. Eliyahu b. Joseph b. Israel.

1496 [149]

All of the Jewish communities,[1] both Karaites and Rabbanites, continued to accept the beginning of the reading of the Torah in the month of Tishre after Succoth, and this was the opinion according to the custom common to them with no one opposing. But a contrary opinion interrupted, namely that the beginning be in Nisan, and hearts turned into its oblivion and averted from its memory and its name was no longer remembered on the lips of men. Indeed you can read in the writings of the Prayer Arranger, i.e., R. Aaron master of the *Mibḥar* (may his memory be blessed!) that formerly the custom among our ancestors was, in some of our communities, to begin (reading) the Torah in the month of Nisan.

This custom was intentional because of the controversy that occurred between them and our brothers the Rabbanites, because we have a tradition from father to son and from teacher to pupil that our ancestors from the beginning used to begin (reading) the Torah in Tishre as is the custom today. However, the *talmide ḥakhamim* (Rabbanites) were examining the commentaries of the Torah on the reading for that week, and the Karaites began to dispute with our brothers the Rabbanites on the words of the Torah and the give and take over its meaning continued until this controversy and major fracas occurred between them. In order that there no longer be a quarrel between them and in order to appease the controversy our saintly ancestors, the humble of the land, the pious ones (may their memories be blessed!) changed the order of reading and began the Torah in Nisan. With this the land quieted from war and the controversy rested and the quarrel waned between them. They each found an excuse when a question arose from the other sect on the subject of the chapter for the week saying, we did not use this chapter about which you ask me because the other sect began the Torah in Nisan and this one in Tishre.

Indeed this custom continued until the great king Sultan Mehmet b. Murat of the house of Osman captured the city of Constantinople in the year 5213 (= 1453) and in the year 1455 he deported all the Jews in his kingdom, from Adrianople and Pravato and others and settled them in Constantinople. And the custom that the beginning of the Torah be in Nisan continued after they came to Constantinople for about four or five years until there arose the Rabbi and Sage . . . b. R. Menaḥem b. R. Joseph (may he rest in Eden!). He had in his hand the Sword of Logic with which to destroy his enemies and he desired to return the matter to its permanence, for the controversy had already waned and was forgotten these many years. Also he desired to act according to the custom that was formerly befitting for which he had help from Scripture, that the beginning of the Torah be from Tishre on the Sabbath which begins after the festival of Shmini ʿAṣereth which concludes the seven days of Succoth. Until the time of a certain lad, respected and sage, whose name was Eliyahu Subashi, who was a great leader in Israel, a relative of ours from my mother's family. He was the second of my mother-in-law Tobah, the mother of my teacher R. Eliyahu Bashyachi (may his memory be blessed!).

And on the Sabbath that began after the first day of ʿAṣereth in the month of Tishre which, according to their custom, the reading for the day was the chapter *Aḥare Moth,* the abovementioned R. Eliyahu rose and began (to read) the Torah and read the chapter *Bereshith.* And because of his influence in the kingdom and the advice of the elders whom the *kahal* saw fit to respect and the aid of the Creator of all who wished to uphold the order which was written in the Torah of Moses and the custom of our saintly fathers, the whole *kahal* was appeased and did not dissent. Thus the true custom returned to its position; this was due to the Lord. And this custom we maintain to this day . . .

Excerpt from Kaleb Afendopolo, *Patshegen Kethab had-Dath,* in Danon, "Documents," pp. 168–69; partial reprint in Mann, *Texts and Studies,* II, 296, note 7; discussion of biblical exegesis among the Karaites and its reference to this text in Ankori, *Karaites,* p. 447, note 232. The date of the document is given in a colophon: "I completed this on Tuesday, 22nd of Tebet in the year 5257 in this village of Keramia, which is across the sea from Constantinople opposite Chalcedon."

1. קהלות ישורון.

1496 [150]

Formerly in the time of our fathers there was a custom in our communities, viz., the community of Constantinople and the surrounding communities like Adrianople, Selebrya, Burgaz, and Parga and others that on every Sabbath they would bring forth the parchment Torah scroll and in it they would read the chapter for that Sabbath. The *kohen* would read, then the *levi,* then five Israelites, and the last would finish the chapter, he being more respected than all the others, not like they do today where the more respected reads first. And after they would finish the reading of the seven men, the *maftir* would come and read the *haftarah* for that chapter.

This was a good custom because every one of the Israelites would fear lest he be called by the cantor to read in the Torah and he was thus compelled to learn the chapter with his teacher, the correct reading, the melody, the accent, and the vowel pointing for the custom continued whereby the Torah scroll was unpointed and unaccented. In addition there was for them the honor and glory that each one read in the Torah and by this means learning was increased among them . . .

Excerpt from Kaleb Afendopolo, *Patshegen Kethab had-Dath,* in Danon, "Documents," p. 170.

Ca. 1571 [151]

A story that happened thus. There was a certain Jewish man, a respected scholar and physician, who journeyed from the land of his birth and came to live in the land of Ishmael, for he heard that they are men of benevolence. And he came in the time of the king, Sultan Murād to the place where the king dwelt in his capital, which is Edirne. And the high officers of the king saw that this man was good and wise, and that God made all whom he treated to prosper in his hand.[1] They praised him to the king, and the man was taken into the house of the king, and he became great in the house of the king. He also found favour in the eyes of the king's son, called Sultan Meḥmed. His soul was bound to him and he loved him. Because of his love for him he asked his father to give him this physician, to be with him and to serve him, and the king listened to the voice of his son and gave him to him. And the man went with the king's son and he served him.[2] And one day, on Thursday the tenth of the month they call Muḥarrem, at the beginning of the year 855 of their reckoning[3] (that is the year 5211 of the reckoning of the children of Israel), the king died, and Sultan Meḥmed his son ruled in his place. The year of his accession was 5211, as stated, and they made the chronogram 'lion-king',[4] and he sat on his father's throne in Edirne. In the second year of his reign he built a small town in the place that is to-day called Aqı̊ndı̊ Burun, and he called it Boqhaz-kesen, and to-day it is called Yeñi Ḥiṣār, which is beyond Galata.[5] And the king came from Edirne to see the town and the building that his servants had built, and he brought the physician with him. In those days the king deigned to aggrandize and exalt the said physician, for he found favour in his eyes by the great wisdom and understanding that he possessed. And it was good in the king's eyes to give to the physician his covenant of peace, to be an eternal covenant with him, making him and his son free in Israel.[6] So he exempted the physician and his seed after him, both male and female, and also their children forever, (making them) eternally and definitely exempt from all kinds of taxes and burdens of government and toll, tribute, and custom[7] and servitude to rulers.[8] And the king gave him a document of exemption, as stated, since, if the physician had asked it of the king, he would have mentioned it in this document, as it was mentioned in the second document, as will be related . . .[9]

And at the end of twelve months from the time when the king gave the said physician the first document, and about three months after he gave him the second document, in the month of Rabīʾ al-Ākhir of the year 857 of their reckoning, on the twentieth of the month and the fifth day of the week,[10] God awakened the spirit of the king and he came and besieged this great city of Constantinople, and God gave it into his hand and he captured it, and he brought his throne there and dwelt there and made it his capital in place of Edirne, and the said physician also came with him, with the two documents in his hand. The physician set up his dwelling there with the king and with his household, and he dwelt among the Jewish people who were in the city at the time of its capture and those whom the king brought there from the towns which had been in his possession from the days of his fathers. The physician dwelt in this city, he and all his descendents until to-day, among the Hebrew sons of the Exile who had come from the (other) towns and those who had been there before.

When the king sat on his throne in this city which he had captured he laid down laws and statutes for every people, after its language,[11] that was in this city, and for the Jews, according to his desires. And he imposed first on the Jews the poll tax, Kharāj, which is called in their language Bāsh

Kharājī, to be paid every year, and the king made a register in which he put the names of all who paid this tax. In the second place, a tax was imposed on the Jews in the form of a levy, one inclusive sum on all of them, to be paid every year. Each paid what he could afford, after assessment by the elders of the community, without the king knowing who paid much and who paid little. And the community made an assessment register in which they wrote down the names of all who paid this second tax, and they divided it up and gave to each community its share of this register, according to the number of its members, and the assessment of each was written at the side of his name. This second tax is called in the language of the Ishmaelites Rāv Aqchesi, because in return for it the Jews were permitted to have a chief Rabbi by royal appointment.[12] It is not known whether the king imposed this on the Jews as one of his own royal statutes, or whether the Jews asked the king to let them have the said Rabbi, and in return took it upon themselves to pay this second tax. And in any case the matter of the said Rabbi only lasted, because of our many sins, for a very short time,[13] while the matter of the second tax still drags upon us, 'till the Lord look down, and behold'.[14] The Jews (in) the communities that carry this burden have arranged it thus. If a man dies among them, rich or poor, his sons take it upon themselves to pay the assessment of their dead father in addition to their own; and if he has no sons, God forbid, they (the community) take a sum compulsorily from the estate of the deceased and retain it so that from its income his obligations are paid year by year. And if the income is not sufficient, because of the increase in the burdens and ʿAvāriz that are introduced because the king is involved in war, then they also take a part of the capital, so that in a short time the capital itself may be exhausted, and the obligations of the dead man fall on the people of his community. Indeed, should the deceased have no person who takes his obligations upon him, they agree compulsorily to take this sum from his estate, and this is their custom even in the case when the deceased, at the time of his death, was liable for debts and for his wife's dowry, and his estate was insufficient to cover the debts or the dowry; nevertheless the men of the community still first take the said sum from his estate, and neither the creditors nor his wife who claims the dowry can stop them.

And when the king is involved in war, from time to time he imposes ʿAvāriz or Salgîn on every people and also on the Jews, according to the names of the Kharāj-payers listed in the register which he has; for example, that so many taxpayers shall pay a certain sum; but the communities pay it according to *their* assessment register which they made for the Rāv Aqchesi abovementioned, each according to his ability, and they give them in full tale to the king[15] according to the names of the taxpayers (for such is the word of the king), but in such a way that they do not pay equally, but each according to his ability. In this way the said communities paid every kind of imposition and order and burden that the king introduced and imposed, that is, every king that came after the first king, not levying them according to the names of the Kharāj-payers, but in a block.

And in all this none of the descendants of the physician, nor the physician himself, bore any burden at any time from then until now. And all the communities that have been in this city from the day of its capture until to-day did not thrust them out of their possession, or ask them to help them, or to carry any burden with them . . . neither the physician nor his descendants have ever joined with the communities that bear the burden of any kind of tax or burden or obligation whatsoever. For thus it was laid down by the old king Sultan Meḥmed, as seen, in the two documents which the old king etc. gave to the said physician as stated above.

Rabbi Samuel de Medina, Responsum 364, section *Ḥoshen Mishpat,* translated by Bernard Lewis, "The Privilege Granted by Mehmed II to His Physician," *BSOAS,* 14 (1952), 550–63 (text and commentary). The above section is only part of the preamble. Of the bibliography cited by Lewis, cf. F. Babinger, "Ja'qūb Pascha, ein Leibarzt Mehmed's II," *Rivista degli Studi Orientali,* XXVI (1951), 82–113, with an appendix of Venetian texts relating to the "conspiracy" to assassinate Mehmet II; and Babinger's more available *Mahomet II Le Conquérant et son temps* (1432–1481), index, s.v. Iacopo.

1. Genesis 39:3.
2. In 1446 he went to Manissa with Mehmet, after Murat II came out of retirement.
3. I.e., February 3, 1451.
4. The numerical value of the Hebrew letters for the word lion (ARIeH) total 5211.
5. I.e., Rumeli Hisar.
6. Cf. I Samuel 17:25.
7. Cf. Ezra 4:13.
8. These taxes, etc., are: Bāsh Kharāji (poll tax); Rāv Aqchesi (defined below); Resm-i Bagh and Resm-i Baghche (vineyard and garden taxes); 'Ushr (tithe of crops); Hisār yapmasî (building of walls); Angaria, Salgîn, Avāriz (commonly used by Ottomans to denote extraordinary and emergency taxes); Resm-i filori (an emergency war tax); azab, kürekji, and peksimet (emergency taxes to supply marines, rowers, and biscuits for the fleet). On these taxes, cf. sources cited by Lewis, p. 559.
9. Here follows the text of the first firman translated from the Hebrew adaptation known to R. Samuel de Medina, and the story of the temporary loss of this first firman and the issuance of a second.

10. The wall was actually breached on Tuesday, May 29, 1453 = 20 Jum. II.

11. Cf. Esther 1:22, 3:12, 8:9.

12. Benjamin Braude translates: "The second tax is called in the language of the Ishmaelites, *rav akcesi,* for through it the Jews were allowed to have a Rabbi who leads (all the congregations of Constantinople) with "warrant of the kingdom" (*hormana demalkuta*) ("Foundation Myths of the Millet System" in Brande-Lewis, *Christians and Jews* I, 80, and note 68. This translation accurately reflects Braude's thesis, which negates the notion of a chief rabbi for Ottoman Jewry in the fifteenth and sixteenth centuries. Cf. Joseph Hacker's comments in his essay "Ottoman Policies toward the Jews and Jewish Attitudes toward the Ottomans during the fifteenth century," ibid., pp. 119f. Hacker translates the pertinent phrase as "they were allowed to have a Rabbi and leader with the permission of the authorities" (p. 125, note 13). Cf. part I, chap. V, note 33.

13. After the death of Kapsali's successor, Elijah Mizraḥi, in 1526, internal disputes within the Jewish community (i.e., between the Romaniotes and Sephardim) prevented the unopposed appointment of a successor. The office was again restricted to those Jews who lived in the capital. Cf. Baron, *Jewish Community,* I, 195–98, and III, 46–47 (notes).

14. Cf. Lamentations 3:50.

15. Cf. I Samuel 1:18, 27.

1728 [152]

By this Imperial Edict the Prefect of Hasköy and the Chief Architect of the Imperial Domains are informed that the Karaite Community of Hasköy in a petition addressed to My Sublime Porte, have declared that their congregation was installed at Hasköy in the time of the deceased Sultan Mehmet Han; that after his imperial conquests they were granted for the performance of their ceremonies, an ancient temple, called a "synagogue", which is now, from the ravages of time, almost in ruins, and impossible of entry; that they are only some thirty or forty in number and needy; and finally, that by virtue of a Fetva which they hold they beg the privilege of having the ancient temple surveyed and repaired, insofar as is permitted by the Religious Code, without hindrance.

You are therefore hereby instructed to survey the said temple, with a view toward permitting its reconstruction in its original dimensions, but to allow no enlargement whatever.

Ottoman Firman dated Sha'ban 1141, from the French rendition in Danon, "Documents," pp. 291–92.

1831 [153]

This Imperial Edict will make known to my Vizier, Halil Rifa'at Pasha and the Mollah, Kadi of Stamboul, that the Jewish Karaite Community residing in the cities of My Empire, have, since the Imperial Conquest, held their temples and other property independently and are separately listed in all civil records . . .

Ottoman Firman dated Sefer 1256, from the French rendition in Danon, "Documents," pp. 312–14.

[154] 1852/53

These are the Sephardi congregations which are listed in the register of the king (may his glory increase) and called *kendi gelen*: Gerush, Catalan, Señora, Aragon, Nevei Shalom, Alaman, Maior, Cordova, Messina, Sicilia, Bodin, Hamon, Zeyrik, Calabri.

These are the Romaniote congregations which are listed in the register of the king (may his glory increase) and called *sürgünler*: Poli Yashan, Poli Ḥadash, Ochrida, Siron, Yanbol, Veria, Kastoria, Tiria, Saloniko, Istip, Demotike, Paḳaras, Sinop, Adalia, Igripoz, Nikopoli, Samagia, Platea, Edirne Bene Mikra. Cana congregation (may God protect her) passed to the Sephardim through the efforts of R. Elnaḳaveh (may his memory be blessed!) and the Romaniote and Sephardi communities.

R. Eliezer di Toledo, *Mishnat Rabbi Eliezer* (Salonika, 5613), fol. 185b; quoted, with French translation, in A. Galante, *Appendix à l'ouvrage Turcs et Juifs; étude historique, politique* (Istanbul, 1937), pp. 8–9; idem, *Les synagogues d'Istanbul* (Haménora, Istanbul, juillet–août 1937); idem, *Histoire des Juifs d'Anatolie*, II, 335–36; idem, *Histoire des Juifs d'Istanbul*, I, 163–68; commentary by U. Heyd, "The Jewish Communities of Istanbul in the Seventeenth Century," pp. 303–5; with additions and corrections by M. A. Epstein, *The Ottoman Jewish Communities and Their Role in the Fifteenth and Sixteenth Centuries* (Freiburg, 1980), pp. 178ff and 181ff.

Commentary:

Hamon, "This congregation was founded by the Hamon family which hailed from Granada. Moses Hamon, who succeeded his father Joseph as Court physician, distinguished himself under Suleiman I."

Cf. discussion of this reading by Epstein, pp. 181f.

For *Maior*, cf. Heyd, pp. 302 and 305. It may or may not be a different congregation than *Hamon*.

Bodin is the Hungarian Buda.

Zeyrik is a quarter in Istanbul.

Nevei Shalom is another name for the Aragon congregation.

Paḳaras (= Fuḳara[si], i.e., "its poor") refers to one of the congregations of Jews from Salonika called *Little Selanik.*

Samagia (Samatya = Psamathia) is a quarter in the southwest part of Istanbul.

Plateia or Palatia. This is the only community not mentioned in the Turkish registers. The medieval town of Palatia continued the commercial traditions of ancient Miletus. The modern village is called Balat.

Siron is Serres.

Poli Yashan and *Poli Ḥadash* both refer to Rabbanite Romaniote communities located in Istanbul. According to Professor Ankori (in a written communication), *Poli* is a shortened form of (Adrianopoli) and represents the *sürgünli* Rabbanite community which was forcibly removed from the old capital to the new center by Mehmet. It later split into two congregations.

Tire, southeast of Izmir, in western Anatolia.

Istip is Stîp in western Macedonia (presently in Yugoslavia).

Igripoz is Euboea.

Edirne Bene Mikra is the Karaite counterpart of the Romaniote *Kehal (Adriano)poli* (*supra*).

For *Cana,* cf. comments by Heyd, p. 302. It may refer to the Tchana synagogue in the Balat Quarter of Istanbul.

EXCURSUSES

Excursus A(I): Benjamin of Tudela and the Jewish Communities in Byzantium Before 1204 (in Conjunction with Map I)

I. Benjamin of Tudela, *Sefer ha-Masaʿoth*:

1. From there [Otranto] one crosses the sea by a two day voyage to the island of Corfu. One Jew is there (whose name is R. Joseph). Here ends the kingdom of Sicily.

2. From there it is two days by sea to the land of Larta [= Leukas] which is the beginning of the dominions of Emanuel, Sovereign of the Greeks. It is a town (*kefar*) containing about 100 Jews, at their head being R. Shelaḥiah and R. Ercules.

3. [From there] it is two days to Aphilon (Achelous), a place in which reside about 30 Jews at their head being R. Shabbetai . . .

4. From there one day to Patras . . . about 50 Jews live there, at their head being R. Isaac, R. Jacob and R. Samuel.

5. From there half a day's journey by way of sea to Kifto [Lepanto] where there are about 100 Jews who live on the sea coast; at their head are R. Guri, R. Shalom and R. Abraham.

6. From there it is a journey of a day and a half to Krissa where about 200 Jews camp apart. They sow and reap on their own plots and lands; at their head are R. Solomon, R. Ḥayyim and R. Yedaiyah.

7. From there three days to the capital city of Corinth; here are about 300 Jews, at their head being R. Leon, R. Jacob and R. Ḥizkiyah.

8. From there two days to Thebes, a large city, where there are about 2000 Jews. They are the most skilled craftsmen in silk and purple cloth throughout Greece. They have scholars learned in the Mishnah and the

Talmud and other prominent men. At their head are the chief rabbi R. Ḳuṭi and his brother R. Moses, as well as R. Ḥiyya, R. Elia Tirutot and R. Yoḳtan; and there are none like them in all of Greece except in the city of Constantinople.

9. From there one day to Egripo which is a large city on the sea coast where merchants come from every direction. About 200 Jews live there, at their head being R. Elia Psaltiri, R. Emanuel and R. Kaleb.

10. From there one day's journey to Jabustrissa which is a city upon the sea coast with about 100 Jews at their head being . . .

11. From there one day to Rabenika where there are about 100 Jews, at their head being . . .

12. From there one day to Sinon Potamou [Zeitun or Lamia] where there are about 50 Jews at their head being R. Solomon and R. Jacob.

12a. The city is situated at the foot of the hills of Wallachia, where lives the nation called Wallachians. They are as swift as hinds, and they sweep down from the mountains to despoil and ravage the land of Greece. No man can go up and wage war against them and no king can rule over them. They do not adhere to the Christian faith but give themselves Jewish names. Some people say that they were Jews, and, in fact, they call the Jews their brethren. When they happen to meet with them, they rob them but refrain from killing them as they kill the Greeks. They belong to no religion.

13. From there two days to Gardiki which is in ruins and contains but a few Greeks and Jews.

14. From there it is two days to Armylo, which is a large city on the sea coast (a commercial city) for the Venetians, Pisans, Genoese and all the other merchants who come there; it is an extensive place and contains about 400 Jews. At their head are R. Sheylah (Lombardo) *ha-Rav,* R. Joseph *ha-Parnas,* and R. Solomon *ha-Rosh.*

15. From there one day to Bissena where there are about 100 Jews, at their head being R. Shabbetai *ha-Rav,* R. Solomon and R. Jacob.

16. From there a two days' voyage to the city of Salonica . . . It is a very large city with about 500 Jews including R. Samuel *ha-Rav* and his sons who are scholars. He is appointed by royal authority as head of the Jews. There is also R. Shabbetai, his son-in-law, R. Elia and R. Michael. And there is a *galuth* upon the Jews, and they are engaged in silk manufacture.

17. From there two days to Demetrizi where there are about 50 Jews. In this place live R. Isaiah, R. Makhir and R. Eliab.

18. From there two days to Drama where there are about 140 Jews, at their head being R. Michael and R. Joseph.

19. From there one day to Christopoli where about 20 Jews live.

20. From there three days by sea to Abydos which is on a strait which flows between the mountains and continues for five days to the city of Constantinople.

21. And the Jews are not inside the city among them [i.e., the Greeks], for they have transferred them across the strait . . . and when they want to do business with the townspeople they are unable to go out except by way of the sea. And there are about 2000 Rabbanite Jews and among them about 500 Karaites on one side, and a fence divides them. Amongst the Rabbanites are scholars; at their head being R. Abtalyon *ha-Rav,* R. Obadiah, R. Aaron . . . , R. Joseph . . . and R. Elyakim *ha-Parnas.* And amongst them are craftsmen in silk, merchants and many rich men. No Jew is allowed to ride on horseback. The one exception is R. Solomon ha-Miẓri, who is the king's physician, and through whom the Jews enjoy considerable alleviation of their oppression. They live under heavy oppression, and there is much hatred against them which is engendered by the tanners, the workers in leather, who pour out their dirty water in the streets before the doors of their houses and defile the Jewish quarter. So the Greeks hate the Jews, good and bad alike, and subject them to severe restrictions and beat them in the streets and force them to hard labor. Yet the Jews are rich and good, kindly and charitable, and cheerfully bear the burden of their oppression. The place in which the Jews live is called Pera.

22. From there it is two days' voyage by sea to Rhodostos with a Jewish community of about 400 at their head being R. Moses, R. Abiyah and R. Jacob.

23. From there two days to Kallipoli (Gallipoli), where there are about 200 Jews, at their head being R. Elia Kapur, R. Shabbetai Zutra and R. Isaac Megas, which means "great" in Greek.

24. And from here two days to Kales. Here are about 50 Jews, at their head being R. Jacob and R. Judah (and R. Shemaryah).

25. From there two days to the island of Mytilini, one of the islands of the sea; in the island(s) are Jewish congregations (in ten places).

26. From there three days by sea to the island of Chios where there are

about 40(0) Jews, (at their head) R. Elia (Heyman or Teyman) and R. Shabbetai. Here grow the trees from which mastic is obtained.

26a. The islands have many congregations of Jews.

27. From there two days to the island of Samos where there are 300 Jews, at their head being R. Shemaryah (R. Obadiah and R. Joel).

28. From there three days by sea (to Rhodes where there are about) 400 Jews, at their head being R. Abba, R. Ḥannanel and R. Elia.

29. From there (four days to Cypr)us where there are Rabbanite Jews and Karaites; there are also some heretical Jews called . . . Epikursim, whom the Jews everywhere have excommunicated. They profane the eve of the Sabbath and observe the first night, Saturday evening.

A new edition of the entire text of Benjamin of Tudela, together with a detailed commentary, is being prepared by Professor Zvi Ankori. In the meantime the following can be consulted: *The Itinerary of Rabbi Benjamin of Tudela,* text and translation by Asher (vol. I), commentary by Asher, Zunz, and Rappaport (vol. II); Adler's edition (London, 1907); Starr, *JBE* #182, and bibliography cited there; Ankori, *Karaites,* index s.v.; Argenti, *The Religious Minorities of Chios,* chap. III; Sharf, *Byzantine Jewry,* chap. VII; and the following notes:

1. The bracketed area is not included in all mss.

2. Cf. Starr, *JBE,* p. 233, for the problem of whether Arta or Leukas is meant. As Benjamin appears to be island hopping, the latter definition is preferred. Starr was uncomfortable about the use of *kefar*; however, Professor Ankori explained that the term was used interchangeably with the term *'ir* (meaning quarter or suburb or area) in Turkish, Greek, and Hebrew sources. Ercules represents the spoken Greek form of the name Hercules.

3. Some mss. have the number 10.

5. Cf. P. Christopoulos, "The Jewish Community of Naupaktos" (Greek), with the comments of Professor Ankori cited there.

6. Professor Ankori suggested that these 200 Jews were encamped apart from their families since their fields were at some distance from the village where they lived. The parallel to Greek rural life is obvious.

8. Some mss. have "three days." An undated Hebrew tombstone in the courtyard of the Museum of Thebes contains the following lines: "*be'ir geddolah shel ḥakhamim ve-shel sofrim* (in the large city of sages and scribes)"; cf. author's "Jewish Epitaphs in Thebes," #IV.

It is of interest, in view of these numbers, that no Jew is identified as such in the Theban cadastral register published by N. Svoronos, "Recherches sur le cadastre byzantin et la fiscalité aux XIe et XIIe siècles: le cadastre de Thèbes," *Bulletin de correspondance héllenique,* 83 (1959), 1–166 (reprinted in his collected studies, *Etudes sur l'organisation intérieure, la société et l'économie de l'Empire Byzantin* [London: Variorum Reprints, 1973]). Just as we find some property owners in Thebes resident in Negroponte (Euripos; cf. p. 12, 1.38), so some of the Jewish workers may have been resident in neighboring towns, i.e., hired hands from surrounding Jewish communities. This suggestion would help explain the great disparity in numbers between the Jews of Thebes and, say, Corinth and Negroponte. Cf. also in

Svoronos' edition (p. 14, l.73), Σαμυὴλ δρουγγαρ(ίου) Γέροντ(α); on the name Χουλῆ, i.e., Λέοντος [τοῦ] λεγομενόν(ου) Χουλίου (p. 15, l.7) as a Jewish family name in Venetian Crete, cf. Ankori, "The Living and the Dead," pp. 89ff, notes 131ff.

9. This is the Greek pronunciation. Cf. another instance, cited in document 30.

10. Professor Ankori suggested that the name comes from the Slavic word for rapids.

10–11. The mss. cite five rabbis: R. Samuel, R. Netaniah, R. Joseph, R. Elazar, and R. Isaac. Each editor has noted the scribal error of dittography, which makes it difficult, if not impossible, to identify the right set of rabbis with each town. The problem is compounded by the fact that, apparently, one name is missing from the total, as there should be three names for each town.

12. Cf. Starr, *loc. cit.*, for this town "on the river" and its identification; also Sharf, *loc. cit.*

12a. This is one of the earliest sources on the Vlachs.

14. For a thirteenth-century parallel, cf. Bees, "Leon-Manouelmakros, Bishop of Bella, Kalospites, Metropolitan of Larissa, Chrysoberges, Metropolitan of Corinth," (Greek) *EEBS*, II (1924), 134, and Nicol, *The Despotate of Epirus*, p. 45, note 27. The name Lombardo is lacking in some mss.

16. On the use of the term *galuth* as an indication of an officially recognized status as an alien colony, cf. Ankori, *Karaites*, pp. 149–50, and above, chap. 2 section, "Thessalonica."

19. On the figure, cf. Ankori, *Karaites*, p. 159, note 279.

21. On the two missing epithets, *bekhor-shoro* and *sir giru*, cf. Sharf, *Byzantine Jewry*, p. 158, notes 6 and 7. For the honor attached to riding a horse by royal permission, see document 57. On the term *galuth*, cf. note 16 above.

24. Not in all mss.

25. We may have here another case of dittography; compare 26a. in text.

26. Argenti, *loc. cit.*, has devoted a whole chapter to this passage, which must be used with caution.

27. Lacking in some mss.

28. Lacking in some mss.

29. Professor Ankori has identified these heretics as Mishawites (*Karaites*, pp. 386–87).

A(II): Communities Known from Sources Other than Benjamin of Tudela (cf. Starr, Ankori, and Sharf for commentary)

Greece:
30. Kastoria
31. Krania
32. Zamenikos
33. Selymbria
34. Sparta
35. Crete—e.g., Candia, Canea, Rethymno

Anatolia:
36. Attaleia
37. Phylae
38. Strobilos (in Lycia?)
39. Ephesus
40. Mastaura
41. Cotyaeum
42. Nicaea
43. Synnada in Phrygia
44. Cherson
45. Syracuse
46. Philadelphia
47. Amorium in Phrygia
48. Khonai in Phrygia

Excursus B: On the Period of the Persecution in Sefer Shebeṭ Yehudah

In the cities of Greece, according to what I heard from the older men,[1] a decree was proclaimed by the king to convert them, but the Romaniotes both young and old persisted in sanctifying the Name.[2] When the king saw that he could not force them (to accept Christianity), he sought advice on what to do. The advice was that he banish them from their houses to the fields for three days and that they have neither food nor water.[3] So they all stood for three days neither eating nor drinking, save for the younger ones who could not stand it and ran away from their enemies' houses[4] and went to those of the Greeks. But when the king was unable to convert them to his faith and seeing their courage to uphold their faith, his compassion was stirred. To appease the people, he proclaimed other decrees for them. He commanded that they may not live within the city of Constantinople, rather that they dwell in the city opposite her called Pera. He also commanded that they have no other craft save tanning and that they have shops on the sea for this craft.

But others than those relating (the above) said, that this was not in that time but another decree in another context.

1. The term *kadmonim* can also mean "ancient sources." However, the use of the term in the context of the source, especially the last sentence, suggests that Ibn Verga was relying on oral sources.

2. I.e., chose death in lieu of conversion.

3. Compare Samuel Usque's recital of the Portuguese king's attempt to convert the Jews in 1497 in *Consolation for the Tribulations of Israel,* tr. Martin A. Cohen (Philadelphia, 1965), pp. 203f. As Ibn Verga relied on Usque in a number of places, so he or his sources may have transposed the story to a Greek milieu.

4. Should read "their fathers' houses."

Solomon ibn Verga, *Sefer Shebeṭ Yehudah,* ed. A. Shoḥet, p. 72, no. 28.

B. Lewin tried to assign this text to the thirteenth century, arguing that it refers to the decree issued by John Vatatzes ("Eine Notiz zur Geschichte der Juden im byzantinischen Reiche," *MGWJ,* XIX [1870], 122, n. 2). Two difficulties argue against this view: the fact that John Vatatzes never possessed Constantinople, and that the only text which mentions his persecution (the letter of Jacob b. Elia, in document 24) contains none of the details in Ibn Verga's account. The thirteenth century seems to be too late for this tradition.

Other interpreters suggested the fifth century: J. Juster, *Les Juifs dans l'empire romain,* I, 470, note 2; Krauss, *Studien,* p. 80; Starr, *JBE,* p. 85, no. 2n ("the supposed prohibition of residence"); Starr, "Byzantine Jewry on the Eve of the Arab Conquest," *Journal of the Palestine Oriental Society,* XV (1935), 281. On the other hand, Jacoby ("Quartiers juifs," pp. 168–69) says that this only shows indirectly the presence of Jews in the area, while more recently A. Sharf

(*Byzantine Jewry*) stated that there were Jews in the Chalkoprateia from the mid-fourth to the mid-eleventh century! (pp. 16 and 55). Baron (*SRHJ,* III, 252f, note 10) completely rejected the possibility of "a regular expulsion of Jews into a separate quarter" in the fifth century (cf. comments by Ankori, *Karaites,* p. 143, note 215).

It was suggested by Starr (*JBE,* p. 225, no. 176n) that this source is dependent upon the report of Benjamin of Tudela re the Jews of Pera—but there is no justification for assuming that a fifteenth- or sixteenth-century group of *kadmonim* (i.e., "old timers"; see above, note 1 to text) would mix the report of Benjamin of Tudela with whatever traditions were current at the time. Besides, if they had been aware of Benjamin's report, then surely they would have mentioned other salient features of it. It is significant that the most recent editor of Ibn Verga has ignored the suggestion of Starr (cited by Ankori, *Karaites,* "Addenda and Corrigenda," p. 485).

The text seems to embody several different traditions, as indeed was noted by Ibn Verga's sources. We can, I believe, divide the text into two groups (as noted above, chap. 1): the first group, relating the attempt at forced conversion by an unknown Byzantine emperor and his change of mind, and the second group, listing aspects of Byzantine-Jewish life in the capital which are known from other sources. The first part of the text is rather naively told and could refer to any of the six persecutions of Byzantine Jewry (four prior to 1204 [cf. Starr, *JBE,* chap. I] and two in the thirteenth century [cf. above, chap. 1]). There is no way of telling to which it refers, nor even if it is a hazy reference to all of those which were remembered! I fail to see where the text "states that a predecessor of the Emperor Manuel Comnenus issued this edict" (*pace* Adler [*The Itinerary of Benjamin of Tudela,* p. 14, note 1]).

The second part of the text provides more information: that they may not live within Constantinople (does this mean they were expelled?), but rather in Pera; that they engage only in tanning; that their shops be located on the sea (nowhere does it mention that they engaged in shipbuilding, contrary to Adler [*loc. cit.*]). We know from Benjamin of Tudela that a group of Jews in Pera was engaged in tanning; Ankori (*Karaites,* pp. 176–78) has clearly pointed out the derogatory social and legal state of their condition. He further points out the prevalence of Greek texts from the tenth century which comment adversely on Jewish tanners (the existence of Jewish tanners *within* the capital in the fourteenth century only reinforces the pre-Palaeologan dating of the tradition related by Ibn Verga), as well as the location of the Jewish Quarter in Byzantine Crete fronting on the city's tanneries. This juxtaposition of literary texts and geographical position leads him to suggest that the tenth century witnessed the reduction of Jews to this ignoble profession (cf. Ankori, "Jews and the Jewish Community in the History of Mediaeval Crete," offprint from *Conference of Cretological Studies* [held in spring, 1966], vol. C, 327–28). His suggestions fit well with the historical and archeological situation in Crete shortly after the Byzantine reconquest, and undoubtably have in mind the cumulative impact of the persecution of the period of Romanos I Lekapenos.

Further, it may be noted that the unpopularity of the conversion attempt, implied in the statement that the Jews found refuge in some Greek homes (I do not believe that the text means "converted"; the attempt seems to have been aimed at conversion *en masse*), is in line with the half-heartedness of Romanos' efforts (cf. Baron, *SRHJ,* III, 182). Should this folk memory ever be traced back to its historical base (or bases), it is more than likely that the tenth century will be a prime candidate.

Excursus C: Jewish Executioners

In his article "Jewish Executioners (On The History of the Jews in Candia)" Hebrew, *Tarbiz,* V [1934], 224–26), S. Assaf states that "all of the information that we have on this matter comes from places which were once under the control of Byzantium." Save for one instance, which he cites from Morocco, no other state outside these areas assigned this function to the Jews. Even so, he continues, most of the information shows that the burden was initiated in these areas during the period of Byzantine control and was continued by its successor states. Thus the Angevin kings of Corfu continued the practice. And in Palermo at the end of the fifteenth century, R. Obadiah Bertinoro found that "the *angaria* of the king weighed heavily upon them . . . and if the sentence of death or stripes and chastisement were upon a man, the Jews would put him to death or chastise him" (quoted by Assaf, p. 224).

In particular, during the fifteenth and sixteenth centuries Venice forced the Jews of Candia to fulfill this function. Assaf quotes from the responsa dealing with some of these instances. Starr adds further examples from other Venetian areas, e.g., Corfu, Negroponte, Coron, and Modon in his study "Jewish Life in Crete under the Rule of Venice" (*PAAJR,* XII [1942], 59–114). More recently, Simon Marcus has rehearsed the citations in his article "A History of the Jews in Canea" (Hebrew, *Tarbiz*, XXXVIII [1967], 165–66, note 30).

The earliest and, incidentally, the *only* text from the Byzantine period prior to 1204 is the account of the blinding of Romanos IV in 1073 by a Jew. Starr translated the account from Michael Attaleites' *Historia* (*CSHB,* L, 178) in his *JBE* (p. 202). He also cites the burial of Andronikos Dukas in the Jewish cemetery of Pera (ibid., p. 239). However, Starr's excerpt from Nicetas Choniates is too brief to put the incident in contemporary perspective. Charles Brand, in his study of the reign of Andronikos I Komnenos (*Byzantium Confronts the West, 1180–1204*), treats the incident within the context of Andronikos' reign of terror (cf. pp. 55–56). In a private discussion, Dr. Brand expressed the opinion that such an act (i.e., the execution or burial of a Byzantine noble in a Jewish cemetery) was intended as an added insult to his already official disgrace. The Cretan historian, S. Xanthoudides, also concluded (on the basis of a fifteenth-century Cretan poem) that the executed were buried in the Jewish cemetery. (Cf. Ankori, "The Living and the Dead, Part 5," *PAAJR*, XXXIX–XL [1970–71], 97f, and earlier, p. 41, note 54a and p. 73, note 99.) From 1073 until 1230, the blinding of Theodore (24), there is no mention of Jewish executioners. The last example of a Jewish executioner in areas under Byzantine control is the instance of the blinding of Philanthropenos in 1296 (29).

How, then, do these three examples relate to the more extensive use of Jewish executioners by successor states in former Byzantine areas, especially those controlled by Venice? It seems, in retrospect, that the occasional use of Jews to blind high officials or imperial figures (begun, perhaps, in the eleventh century) was expanded by the *Latin* successor states to the Byzantine Empire into the derogatory function of supplying a state executioner for capital and corporal punishments.

Excursus D: A Hebrew Lament on the Fall of Constantinople

וזה עשיתי כשנתפשה קושתדינא
קול שמועה נגאלה ומוראה·הנה באה מארץ צפון ורעש גדול·בין
הים ובין מגדול כי שבי גדול שביה בת עמי·עם עמי·עם חרמי·שחתו
כרמי·והמון לאומי·משמים ארץ·לכליון וחרץ·נפל הלל בן שחר·
כדבר אין לו שחר· עליו תרנה אשפה·ומזיח אפיקים רפה זאת והב
בסופה·האריכו למענית להב כידון וחנית·האמונים עלי תולע·
כל חכמתם נתבלע·ונפשם בתוך כף הקלע·וימת בלע·ובנחלי הבתות·
חבקו אשפתות·על זאת תאבל הארץ כי כלה ונתרצה נהייתה בארץ·
רוע התרועעה הארץ·ותעבור הרנה·אנה ואנה אוי לנו כי היום
פנה·קול אומר קרא בנפש מרה ואמר מה אקרא· כל בשר חציר
כעוללות כרם בציר·קדרו שמים ממעל·על אשר שתה מידסף רעל·
כוכבי השמים וכסיליהם לא יהלו אורם· חשך משחור תארם·חשך
השמש וירח קדר באהלי קדר·לא תאר ולא הדר·הן אראלם צעקו
חוצה· לריב ומצה·מלאכי שלום מר יבכיון·ובנו אצלם ציון· על כן
אמרתי שעו מני·אמרר בבכי אל תאיצו לנחמני·השברתי קדרתי
שמה מחזיקתני· רעדה אחזתני·חיל כיולדה וארכובתי נקשן דא לדא

מעי מעי אוחילה·מלאו מותני חלחלה· וכל אבירי בקרבי סלה·שמה
ו(מה)ומה מבוכה ומבוסה·מי נתן למשסה· ישראל לבוזזים·אשר גובהו
גובה ארזים·הנשר הגדול אשר לו הרקמה·ריפת ותוגרמה·השרח יושבי
מרום קריה נשגבה·וישלך ארצה מן הככבים ומן הצבא·המצפצפים
והמהגים·אוי נא לי כי עיפה נפשי להורגים·

(See translation, below.)

Vat. Ms. 105, fol. 162a.

Incipit was noted by Steinschneider in his "Candia, Cenni di storia letteratura, Appendice all'Articolo V" (in *Mosé, Anthologia Israelitica,* IV [1881], 105). Poem is not listed in Israel Davidson's *Thesaurus of Mediaeval Poetry,* I–IV (New York, 1933, including supplement from *HUCA,* XII–XIII [Cincinnati, 1938]), and cannot be dated before July 1453. R. Browning ("A Note on the Capture of Constantinople in 1453," *Byzantion,* XXII [1952], 381, citing BM Add 34060, fol. IV) showed that the first news of the fall of the city arrived in Crete on Friday, June 29, 1453. Words in parentheses (below) are textual restorations.

On the author of this lament, R. Michael b. Shabbetai Kohen Balbo of Candia, see Ephraim Gottlieb, "The Metempsychosis Controversy in Candia," (Hebrew) *Sefunoth,* XI (1971–77), 45ff.

Hark, a report,[1] repulsive and terrifying,[2] behold it cometh from a northern country;[3] and a great noise extending from the Sea to Migdol.[4] For my people is captive[5] in a great captivity along with mine enemy.[6] They have destroyed my vineyard[7] and the multitude of my people.[8] From heaven to earth[9] to utter destruction[10] has fallen the morning star[11] as if it were something worthless.[12]

The quiver rattles upon it,[13] and he loosens the belt of the strong;[14] this is (the reference of) Waheb in Suphah:[15] they make long their furrows,[16] the flashing spear and the javelin.[17] They who were brought up in purple[18] were at their wit's end,[19] and their lives are in the hollow of a sling.[20]

And Bela died.[21] In the steep ravines[22] they lie upon ash heaps.[23] For this the earth shall mourn;[24] for utter destruction will be in the land;[25] the earth is utterly broken;[26] and a cry went forth:[27] Woe unto us for the day declines.[28] A voice says, Cry![29] (in the bitterness of soul),[30] and said, "What shall I cry? All flesh is grass[31] as at the gleanings in the vineyard when the vintage is done."[32]

The heavens above have become black[33] because he drank from the hand (of God)[34] the cup of staggering.[35] The stars of the heavens and their constellations will not give their light.[36] Now their visage is blacker than soot.[37] The sun darkened, and the moon[38] was black[39] as the tents of Kedar[40] with neither form nor comeliness.[41]

Behold the valiant ones cry outside,[42] only to quarrel and fight.[43] The envoys of peace weep bitterly,[44] and they shall build a sign by them.[45] Therefore I said — Look away from me. Let me weep bitter tears. Do not labor to comfort me.[46] My heart is wounded; I mourn, and dismay takes hold of me.[47] A trembling seized me there,[48] an anguish like a woman in labor,[49] and my knees knocked together.[50] Therefore my loins are filled with anguish.[51]

He flouted all my mighty men in my midst;[52] there was there (tumult), trampling, and confusion.[53]

Who gave up Israel to the robbers;[54] he whose height was like the height of cedars.[55] The great eagle, rich in a plumage of many colors,[56] Riphat and Togarmah.[57] The inhabitants of the height, the lofty city,[58] and some of the host of the stars, these he cast down to the earth[59] with the chirpers and the mutterers.[60]

Woe unto me for my soul is faint before murderers.[61]

1. Allusion to Zephaniah 3:1 and Jeremiah 10:22
2. Zephaniah 3:1
3. Jeremiah 10:22
4. Exodus 14:2
5. Cf. Isaiah 52:2
6. Cf. Isaiah 34:5
7. Jeremiah 12:10
8. Cf. Psalm 65:8
9. Isaiah 14:12
10. Isaiah 10:22
11. Isaiah 14:12
12. Isaiah 8:20
13. Job 39:23a
14. Job 12:22a
15. Numbers 21:14; cf. Ramban, *ad locum*
16. Psalms 129:3
17. Job 39:23b
18. Lamentations 4:5
19. Cf. Psalm 107:27
20. I Samuel 25:29
21. I Chronicles 1:44
22. Isaiah 7:19
23. Lamentations 4:5
24. Jeremiah 4:28
25. Isaiah 10:23
26. Isaiah 24:19
27. Cf. I Kings 22:36
28. Jeremiah 6:4
29. Isaiah 40:6
30. Job 21:25
31. Isaiah 40:6
32. Isaiah 24:13
33. Jeremiah 4:28
34. Cf. Isaiah 51:17ff; the biblical reference is to Jerusalem, which is feminine; here the reference is perhaps to Bela (= Constantine).
35. Zachariah 12:2
36. Isaiah 13:10
37. Lamentations 4:8
38. Isaiah 13:10
39. Cf. Joel 2:10, 4:15
40. Canticles 1:5
41. Isaiah 53:2
42. Isaiah 33:7
43. Isaiah 58:4
44. Isaiah 33:7
45. Cf. Ezekiel 39:15
46. Isaiah 22:4
47. Cf. Jeremiah 8:21
48. Cf. Psalm 48:7
49. Isaiah 21:3
50. Daniel 5:6
51. Isaiah 21:3
52. Lamentations 1:15
53. Isaiah 22:5
54. Isaiah 42:24
55. Amos 2:9
56. Ezekiel 17:3
57. Genesis 10:3
58. Isaiah 26:5
59. Cf. Daniel 8:10
60. Isaiah 8:19
61. Jeremiah 4:31

Excursus E: Iṣḥak Ḥazzan

In 1421, one of the last diplomatic acts of Manuel II occurred in the context of an embassy sent by him to Mehmet I. Contrary to the wishes of his hawkish advisors who suggested that he take advantage of the sultan's proximity and capture him, Manuel preferred to make a show of loyalty. He sent three ambassadors, one of whom has been identified as the Jew Iṣḥak Ḥazzan.

The account of this embassy by Hammer (*Geschichte des osmanischen Reiches,* I, 384–85; translated by Heller, *Histoire de l'empire ottoman,* II, 195–96) was the source used by the Jewish historians Franco (*Essai sur l'histoire des Israélites de l'empire ottoman,* p. 22), Krauss (*Studien,* p. 98), Galante (*Les Juifs de Cp.,* p. 59), and Rosanes (*Israel be-Togarmah,* p. 10).

Hammer gives the name of one of the envoys as Isaak Hasan, with no further identification as to his religion. The use of a common Hebrew first name (the fact that it was also a common Byzantine first name was overlooked by the Jewish historians) and ą suspiciously Hebrew (or Arabic) last name led the Jewish historians to claim Isaac Hasan as a Jewish interpreter of Manuel II. Rosanes restored his Hebrew name as Iṣḥak (Isaac) Ḥazzan (= cantor).

The source that relates the embassy is the Byzantine historian Sphrantzes, and the account has been translated by Barker (*Manuel II Palaeologus,* pp. 351–52) with extensive notes (although Barker is unaware of the present problem). The Greek forms of the name of our "Jewish" ambassador have been edited as 'Isakion ton 'Asanēn (*Chronicon Maius,* ed. Grecu, p. 250, l.17; ed. Papadopoulou, p. 115). The correct name, therefore, of Isaac is Asanes, not Hasan. The scion of a good Byzantine family, it is impossible that he was a Jew.

BIBLIOGRAPHY
ADDENDA
INDEX

BIBLIOGRAPHY

I MSS CITED (INCLUDING COLOPHONS)

Anonymous. Kabbalistic Works. Oxford, Bodleian, MS Hunt. 309 (document 117).

Anonymous. Letter from Negroponte to the Jewish Community in Rome. Livorno, Library of the Collegio Rabbinico, MS 2. (Photostat in Starr, *Romania,* following p. 117). Presently in Jerusalem, National Library, MS 4°616 (document 30).

Abraham ibn Ezra. Astronomical Works. Oxford, Bodleian, Opp Add 2518 (document 92).

______. Commentary on the Pentateuch. J.T.S. L.287 (document 99).

______. Sefer ha-Ṣaḥoth. Oxford, Bodleian, Hunt. 128 (document 32).

Athanasios, patriarch of Cp. Letters. Vat. Gr. 2219 (documents 29, 30, 31).

Christoforo Buondelmonti. Liber Insularum Archipelagi. Athens, Gennadeion, MS 71.

Ephraim ben Gershon ha-Rofe. Ṣinṣenet ha-Man. London, BM, Or 1307.

Geniza. Cambridge, T-S 12.62 (bill of sale mentioning Yeḥiel b. Eliakim in Fustat). Cambridge, T-S 8J.19.33 (containing several Judeo-Greek names). Cambridge, T-S Loan 26 (story of messianic excitement in Morea, document 21).

Hillel Ben Eliakim. Commentary on Sifra. Frankfurt, Universitätsbibliothek, MS Hebrew 4°2 (document 15).

Isaiah of Trani. Responsa. Cambridge, University Library, MS, Add 474 (documents 5–11).

Isaac ben Joseph of Corbil. ʿAmude Golah. J.T.S., MS, RAB 656 MIC 6474 (acc. 0360) (document 136).

Jonah ben Abraham Gerondi. Shaʿare Ṣedek. Cambridge, University Library, MS Add 1224 (document 100).

Joseph the Constantinopolitan. Sefer ʿAdat Devorim. Leningrad, Firkovitz Collection II, MS 161 (document 14).

Levi ben Yefet. Sefer Miṣvoth, and other writings. Leiden, University Library, MS Or. 4760 (document 56).

Michael ben Shabbetai Kohen Balbo. Piyyutim u-Mikhtavim. Vat. Heb. 105 (excursus D).
Muhammed ben Zeraḥia al-Razi. Pesakim. Parma, Palatina, MS 2279 (document 110).
Shemarya Ikriti. Commentary on Scroll of Esther. Cambridge, University Library, MS MM6, 26, 2 (8) (document 109).
Shem Tob ibn Gaon. Kether Shem Tob. Paris, Bibliothèque nationale, MS héb 790 (document 108).
Zeraḥia ben Isaac ben Shealtiel of Barcelona. Commentary on *Guide to the Perplexed* of Moses ben Maimon. Leipzig, Universitätsbibliothek, MS B.H. 13 (document 47).

J.T.S. MS micro. 2581.
München. Bayerische Staatsbibliothek, Cod Heb 118.
Rostok. Universitätsbibliothek, MSS orient, 42.

2 PUBLISHED SOURCES AND STUDIES

Aaron b. Elijah. גן עדן (The Garden of Eden. A Karaite Code of Law). Ed. J. Savuskan. Gozlow, 1866.
Aaron b. Joseph. ספר המבחר (The Book of Choice. A Commentary on the Pentateuch). Gozlow, 1834.
Abraham Abulafia. ספר האות (The Book of Letters), ed. A. Jellinek. *Jubelschrift . . . Dr. Heinrich Graetz*. Breslau, 1887, pp. 65–88 (Hebrew section).
Adler, E. N. *Catalogue of Hebrew Manuscripts in the Collection of Elkan Nathan Adler*. Cambridge, 1921.
———. *Jewish Travellers*. London, 1930.
Adler, Marcus N. See Benjamin ben Jonah of Tudela.
Ahima'az b. Paltiel. ספר יוחסין (The Book of Genealogies), ed. A. Neubauer. *Mediaeval Jewish Chronicles* (Anecdota Oxoniensa, Semitic Series II). Oxford, 1895, pp. 111–32.
———. *The Chronicle of Ahimaaz,* ed. and tr. M. Salzman. New York, 1924.
———. *Megillat Ahimaaz,* ed. B. Klar. Jerusalem, 1944. 2d ed. Jerusalem, 1974.
Algazi, Samuel. ספר תולדות אדם (The Book of Generations. A Chronology), ed. A. M. Haberman. Jerusalem, 1944.
Allati, Leone. *Ioannes Henricus Hollingeus: Fraudes, & Impostur & manifeste convictus* . . . Rome, 1661.
Anastos, Milton V. "Pletho's Calendar and Liturgy," *DOP,* no. 4 (1948), pp. 183–305.
Andreades, A. "Deux livres récents sur les finances byzantines," *BZ,* XXVIII (1928), 287–333. Reprinted in A. Andreades, *Erga* (Oeuvres), I (Athens, 1938), 563–97.
———. "The Jews in the Byzantine Empire," *Economic History,* III (1934), 1–23.
———. "Les Juifs et le fisc dans l'empire byzantin," *Mélanges Charles Diehl* (Paris, 1930), I, 7–29. Reprinted in A. Andreades, *Erga* (Oeuvres) (Athens, 1938), I, 629–59.
———. "La population de l'empire byzantin," *Bulletin de l'institut bulgare,* 9 (1935), 117–26.
———. "Public Finances: Currency, Public Expenditures, Budget, Public Revenues."

In N. H. Baynes and H. Moss, eds., *Byzantium: An Introduction to East Roman Civilization*. Oxford, 1948.

Andrews, Kevin. *Castles of the Morea*. Gennadeion Monographs, IV. Princeton, 1953.

Angold, Michael. *A Byzantine Government in Exile: Government and Society under the Laskarids of Nicaea, 1204–1261*. Oxford, 1975.

Ankori, Zvi. "בשיצי (Bashyachi)," in *EIV,* IX, 960–63.

______. "אליה בשייצי : לבדיקת מסורותיו על ראשית הקראות בביזנטיון (Elijah Bashyachi: An Inquiry into His Traditions concerning the Beginnings of Karaism in Byzantium)," *Tarbiz,* XXV (1955–56), 44–65, 183–201; no. 2, pp. iii–vi (Eng. summary).

______. "From *Zudecha* to *Yahudi Mahallesi:* The Jewish Quarter of Candia in the Seventeenth Century," *S. W. Baron Jubilee Volume* (New York, 1974), I, 25–89.

______. "Giacomo Foscarini and the Jews of Crete—A Reconsideration," *Michael,* VII (1981), 9–118.

______. "Greek Orthodox Jewish Relations in Historical Perspective—The Jewish View," *GOTR,* XXII (1977), 17–57.

______. "Jews and the Jewish Community in the History of Mediaeval Crete," *Proceedings of the 2nd International Congress of Cretological Studies* (Athens, 1968), III, 312–67.

______. *Karaites in Byzantium: The Formative Years, 970–1100*. New York and Jerusalem, 1959.

______. "The Living and the Dead: The Story of Hebrew Inscriptions in Crete," *PAAJR,* XXXIX–XL (1970–71), 1–100.

Argenti, Ph. "The Jewish Community in Chios during the Eleventh Century," *Polychronion, Festschrift Franz Dölger* (Heidelburg, 1966), pp. 39–68. (Reprinted in next item, pp. 63–92.)

______. *The Religious Minorities of Chios: Jews and Roman Catholics*. Cambridge, 1970.

Armenopoulos, K. Ἑξάβιβλος, ed. G. E. Heimbach. *Const. Harmenopuli Manuale Legum sive Hexabiblos*. Leipzig, 1851.

Arnakis, G. G. Οἱ πρῶτοι Ὀθωμανοί. Συμβολὴ εἰς τὸ πρόβλημα τῆς πτώσεως τοῦ Ἑλληνισμοῦ τῆς Μικρᾶς Ἀσίας (1282–1337). (The First Ottomans. A Contribution to the Problem of the Decline of Hellenism in Asia Minor [1282–1337]). Texte und Forschungen zur byz. neugr. Philologie. No. 41. Athens, 1947.

______. "Gregory Palamas among the Turks and Documents of his Captivity as Historical Sources," *Speculum,* XXVI (1951), 104–18.

______. "Gregory Palamas, the Chiones and the Fall of Gallipoli," *Byzantion,* XXII (1952), 305–12.

Artom, A. S., and M. Cassuto. תקנות קנדיה וזכרונותיה (Candiote Ordinances). Jerusalem, 1943.

Asher, A. See Benjamin ben Jonah of Tudela.

Assaf, S., and Z. Lichtenstein. "אהרון בן אליהו מניקומידיה (Aaron b. Elijah of Nicomedia)," in *EIV,* I, 592–94.

______ and M. Benayahu, "אדריאנופול (Adrianople)," in *EIV,* I, 564–68.

______. באהלי יעקב (In the Tents of Jacob. Sources and Studies.) Jerusalem, 1943.

______. "תלינים יהודיים (Jewish Executioners: On the History of the Jews in Candia)," *Tarbiz,* V (1934), 224–26.

______. "לחיי המשפחה של יהודי ביצאנץ (On the Family Life of Byzantine Jewry)," *Samuel Krauss Festschrift* (Jerusalem, 1937), pp. 169–77. Reprinted in *Be-Ohale Yaacob,* pp. 99–106.

______. "תשובות ואגרות מר׳ משה קפשאלי (The Responsa and Letters of R. Moses Capsali)," *Sinai,* III (1939), 149–58, 485–86.

Assemani, S. *Bibliothecae Apostolicae Vaticanae Codicum manuscriptorum catalogus* . . . I. Paris, 1926.

Avneri, Zvi. "יהודי מיסטרה (The Jews of Mistra)," *Sefunoth* 11 (= *Sefer Yavan* A). Jerusalem, 1971–78, pp. 35–42.

Azulai, Ḥayyim Joseph David. ספר שם הגדולים (*Scholars of Fame. A Biobibliographical Survey*). Livorno, 1774. Reprinted Tel Aviv, 1960.

Babinger, Franz. "Eine altosmanische anonyme Chronik in hebräischer Umschrift," *Archiv Orientální,* IV (Prague, 1932), 109–11. Reprinted in his *Aufsätze und Abhandlungen zu Geschichte südosteuropas und der Levante.* Munich, 1966, II, 13–16.

______. "Jaqub-pascha, ein Leibarzt Mehmed's II.," *Rivista degli Studi Orientalni,* 26 (1951), 87–113.

______. *Mehmed der Eroberer und seine Zeit.* Munich, 1953; 2d ed., 1959.

______. *Maometto il Conquistatore e il suo tempo.* Tr. Evelina Polacco. Turin, 1957; rev. ed. 1967.

______. *Mahomet II le Conquérant et son temps.* Tr. H. E. del'Medico. Paris, 1954.

______. *Mehmed the Conqueror and His Time.* Tr. from German and Italian (2d ed.) Ralph Manheim; ed. W. C. Hickman. Princeton, 1978.

______. "Mehmed II, der Eroberer, und Italien," *Byzantion,* XXI (1951), 127–78.

______. "Schejch Bedr ed-din, der Sohn des Richters von Simaw," *Der Islam,* II (1921), 1–106.

Baer, Y. "התנועה המשיחית בספרד בתקופת הגירוש (The Messianic Atmosphere in Spain during the Period of the Expulsion)," *Meassaf Zion,* V (1933), 61–78.

Balard, Michel. *La Romanie Génoise* (*XII*ᵉ*–début du XV*ᵉ siècle). I–II. Rome, 1978.

Bănescu, N. "Le patriarche Athanase Ier et Andronic II Paléologue—état religieux politique et social de l'empire," *Académie Roumaine. Bul. de la Section historique,* XXIII (Bucharest, 1942), 28–56.

Barbaro, Nicolo. *Giornale dell'assedio di Constantinopoli, 1453.* Ed. E. Cornet. Vienna 1856.

______. *Diary of the Siege of Constantinople, 1453.* Tr. J. R. Jones. New York, 1969.

Bardakjian, Kevork B. "The Rise of the Armenian Patriarchate of Constantinople," in Braude-Lewis, *Christians and Jews* (London, 1982), I, 89–100.

Bardy, G. "Thaddée de Péluse adversus Iudaeos," *Revue de l'orient chrétien,* series 3, II (1920–21), 280–87.

Barkan, Ö. L. "Essai sur les données statistiques des registres de recensement dans l'empire ottoman aux XVᵉ et XVIᵉ siècles," *JESHO,* I (1957), 9–36.

Barker, J. W. *Manuel II Palaeologus (1391–1425): A Study in Late Byzantine Statesmanship.* New Brunswick, 1969.

Baron, Salo W. *A Social and Religious History of the Jews.* I–XVII. 2d ed. New York, 1952–80.

______. *The Jewish Community: Its History and Structure to the American Revolution.* I–III. Philadelphia, 1948.

Beck, Hans-Georg. *Kirche und Theologische Literatur im Byzantinischen Reich*. Munich, 1959.

Bees, Nikos. "Οἱ Ἑβραίοι τῆς Λακεδαίμονος καὶ τοῦ Μιστρᾶ (The Jews of Lacedaemon and Mistra)," *Numas,* III (1905), 10–11.

______. "Übersicht über die Geschichte des Judenthum von Janina (Epirus)," *BNJ,* II (1921), 159–77.

Beldiceanu, N. *Recherche sur la ville ottomane au XVe siècle*. Paris, 1973.

Belleli, L. "Un version grecque du Pentateuque du siezième siècle," *REG,* 3 (1890), 290–308.

Ben Menahem, Naftali. מגנזי ישראל בוואטיקאן . תיאור של שלושים וחמשה כתבי־יד (*From the Treasures of Israel in the Vatican. A Descriptive Catalogue of 35 Mss.*). Jerusalem, 1954.

Benjamin ben Jonah of Tudela. ס׳ מסעות ר׳ בנימין. *The Itinerary of Rabbi Benjamin of Tudela,* I–II. Ed. and tr. A. Asher. London–Berlin, 1840–41.

______. *Die Reisebeschreibungen des R. Benjamin von Tudela*. Jerusalem–Frankfurt a.M., 1903–4. Ed. and tr. M. N. Adler. London, 1907. Reprinted from *JQR,* o.s., XVI–XVIII (1904–6).

Benjamin Ze'eb ben Mattathias of Arta. בנימין זאב ספר שאלות ותשובות (responsa). 1st ed.; Venice, 1539. Reprinted in 2 vols. Jerusalem, 1959.

Berger, Abraham. "The Messianic Self-Consciousness of Abraham Abulafia, a Tentative Evaluation," *Essays in Life and Thought in Honor of Salo W. Baron*. New York, 1959, pp. 55–61.

Berlin, Charles. "A Sixteenth-Century Hebrew Chronicle of the Ottoman Empire: The *Seder Eliyahu Zuta* of Elijah Capsali and Its Message," in *Studies in Jewish Bibliography History and Literature in honor of I. Edward Kiev*. New York, 1971, pp. 21–44.

Berliner, A. "Jehudah b. Mosconi," *MWJ,* III (1876), 41–51.

Bernheimer, Carlo. *Catalogue des manuscrits et livres rares hébräiques de la Bibliothèque du Talmud Tora de Livourne*. Livourne (1914).

______. "Document relatif aux Juifs de Négropont," *REJ,* LXV (1913), 224–30.

Bernstein, Simon. "המחזור כמנהג כפא, תולדותיו והתפתחותו (סקירה היסתורית)" (The Caffa Maḥzor, Its History and Development)," in *Festschrift Samuel Mirsky*. New York, 1958, pp. 451–538.

______. "ליקוטי פיוט מכ״י המחזור כמנהג קורפו (A Selection of Poems from a MS. of the Corfu Maḥzor)," in *Festschrift Abraham Weiss*. New York, 1964, pp. 233–47.

______. "פיוטי ישראל במלכות יון מתקופת הביזאנט (Jewish *Piyyutim* in Greece in the Byzantine Period)," in *Festschrift Israel Alfenbein*. Jerusalem, 1963, pp. 56–74.

______. פיוטים ופיטנים חדשים מהתקופה הביצנטינית, מלוקטים מתוך כ״י מחזור כמנהג קורפו (New *Piyyutim* and Poets from the Byzantine Period, Selected from a MS. of the Corfu Maḥzor). Jerusalem, 1941, pp. 1–80. Reprinted from *Ḥoreb,* 5 (1939).

Birnbaum, Solomon. *The Hebrew Scripts*. I. Leiden, 1975.

Blastares, Matthew. *Syntagma. MPG,* 144, cols. 690–1400. Ed. G. A. Rhalles and M. Potles. Σύνταγμα τῶν Θείων καὶ Ἱερῶν Κανόνων. Vol. VI; Athens, 1859. *Matije Vlastara Sintagmat* (Serbian tr.), St. Novaković. Belgrade, 1907.

Blemmydes, Nicephoras. *Epitome Logica. MPG,* 142.

Boak, A. E. R. "Notes and Documents: The Book of the Prefect," *Journal of Economic and Business History,* I (1928–29), 597–619.

Boissonade, Jean F. *Analekta Graeca.* III. Paris, 1831.

Bon, A. *La Morée franque: recherches historiques, topographiques et archéologiques sur la principauté d'Achaië, 1205–1430.* I–II. Paris, 1969.

Bonfil, R. "חזון דניאל" כתעודה היסטורית וספרותית" (The Vision of Daniel as a Historical and Literary Document)," *Zion,* XLIV (1979), 111–47 (xv–xvi, Eng. summary).

Bowman, Steven. "A Corpus of Hebrew Epitaphs in Patras," *Archaeologikon Deltion,* 31 (1976 [appeared in 1980]), 49–75.

———. "Did Mehmet II Know Hebrew?" in *Jewish Tradition in the Diaspora: Studies in Memory of Professor Walter J. Fischel* (Berkeley, 1981), pp. 93–96.

———. "Jewish Epitaphs in Thebes," *REJ,* CLXI (1982), 317–29.

———. "Jewish Settlement in Sparta and Mistra," *BNJ,* XXII (1979), 131–46.

———. "Jews in Fourteenth-Century Thebes," *Byzantion,* L (1980), 403–9.

———. "Messianic Excitement in the Peloponnesos," *HUCA,* LII (1981), 195–202.

———. "An Other Medieval Jewry: The Jews of Byzantium," *Forum,* 36 (Jerusalem, 1979), 131–41.

———. "A Tenth-Century Byzantine-Jewish Historian? A Review of David Flusser's Studies on *The Josippon* and Its Author," *Byzantine Studies,* X (1983), 133–36.

———. "Two Late Byzantine Dialogues with the Jews," *GOTR,* XXV (1980), 83–93.

——— and Daniel Spiegel, eds. "Hebrew Epitaphs of Mistra," *Michael,* VII (1981), 201–47.

Brand, Charles. *Byzantium Confronts the West, 1180–1204.* Cambridge, Mass., 1968.

Bratianu, G. I. *Recherches sur le commerce génois dans la Mer Noire au XIIIe siècle.* Paris, 1929.

Braude, Benjamin. "Foundation Myths of the Millet System," in Braude-Lewis, *Christians and Jews* (London, 1982), I, 69–88.

——— and Bernard Lewis, eds. *Christians and Jews in the Ottoman Empire. The Functioning of a Plural Society.* I–II. New York and London, 1982.

Brockelman, Carl. *History of the Islamic Peoples.* Trans. Joel Carmichael and Moshe Perlman. New York, 1947.

Browning, Robert. "A Note on the Capture of Constantinople in 1453," *Byzantion,* XXII (1952), 379–87.

———. "Recentiores non deteriores," *Bulletin of the Institute of Classical Studies,* VII (1960), 11–21. Reprinted in his *Byzantine History, Literature and Education* (Collected Studies). London, 1977.

Broyde, I. "Crimea," *JE,* IV, 359–61.

Bury, J. B. "The Lombards and Venetians in Euboea," *JHS,* 7 (1886), 309–52; 8 (1887), 194–213; 9 (1888), 91–117.

Cahan, Claude. *Pre-Ottoman Turkey.* London, 1968.

Cambridge Mediaeval History. IV, 1–2. Ed. Joan Hussey. 2d ed. Cambridge, 1967.

Carmoly, E., and J. M. Jost. "Beitrage zur Geschichte der Juden im byzantinischen Reiche vom ersten Kreuzzuge bis zur Eroberung Constantinopels durch die Türken," *Israelitische Annalen,* I, no. 20 (1839), 153–56; no. 21 (1839), 161–63.

______. "Zustände in Constantinopel im 16ten Jahrhundert," *Israelitische Annalen,* I, nos. 50–51 (1839), 397, 405–6.

Carpenter, R., and A. Bon. *The Defenses of Acrocorinth and the Lower Town.* Corinth: III, part II. Cambridge, Mass., 1936.

Cassuto, U. *Bibliothecae Apostolicae Vaticanae . . . Codices Vaticani Hebraici.* Vatican City, 1956.

Charanis, Peter. "A Note on the Population and Cities of the Byzantine Empire in the 13th Century," *Joshua Starr Memorial Volume* (New York, 1953), pp. 135–48.

______. "The Jews in the Byzantine Empire under the First Palaeologi," *Speculum,* XXII (1947), 75–77.

Charner, M. *The Tree of Life of Aaron b. Elijah of Nicomedia.* New York, 1949. First half-chp., pp. 1–78.

Christopoulos, P. "Ἡ Ἑβραϊκὴ κοινότης Ναυπάκου (The Jewish Community of Naupaktos)," *Proceedings of the Society for Central Greece Studies* I (1968), 277–300.

Chrysostomides, J. "Corinth 1394–1397: Some New Facts," *Byzantina,* 7 (1975), 81–110.

______. "Venetian Commercial Privileges under the Palaeologi," *Studi Veneziani,* 12 (1970), 267–356.

Ćirković, Sima. "The Jewish Tribute in Byzantine Regions," (Serbian) *Zbornik Radova,* 4 (1957), 141–47.

Clucas, Lowell M. "Eschatological Theory in Byzantine Hesychasm: A Parallel to Joachim da Fiore?" *BZ,* LXX (1977), 324–46.

Constantelos, D. "Greek Orthodox Jewish Relations in Historical Perspective," *GOTR,* XXII (1977), 6–16.

Cordier, Henri. *Les Merveilles de l'Asie (Mirabilia Descripta) par le père Jourdain Catalani de Sévérac . . .* Paris, 1925.

Covo, Merdoco. קוים לתולדות קהלת ישראל בסרס (*Aperçu historique sur la communauté Israélite de Serrès*) (Hebrew and French text). Tel Aviv, 1962.

Danon, A. "Adrianople," *JE,* I, 213–15.

______. "Documents Relating to the History of the Karaites in European Turkey," *JQR,* n.s. XVII (1926–27), 165–98, 239–322.

______. "The Karaites in European Turkey," *JQR,* n.s. XV (1924–25), 285–360.

David, Yonah. שירי אמתי (The Poems of Amittay). Jerusalem, 1975.

______. פיוטי אליה בר־שמעיה (The Poems of Elya bar Schemaya). Tel Aviv, 1977.

______. שירי זבדיה (The Poems of Zebadiah). Jerusalem, 1971.

Davidson, Israel. *Thesaurus of Mediaeval Poetry.* I–IV. New York, 1924–33. Supplement in *HUCA,* XII–XIII (1938).

Deinard, Ephraim. משא קרים (The Burden of the Crimea). Warsaw, 1878.

De Lange, N. R. M. "Some New Fragments of Aquila on Malachi and Job?" *Vetus Testamentum,* XXX (1980), 291–94.

______. "Two Genizah Fragments in Hebrew and Greek," in *Interpreting the Bible: Essays in Honour of E. I. J. Rosenthal.* Cambridge, 1982, pp. 61–83.

Dentake, Basil. Βίος καὶ Ἀκολουθία τοῦ ἁγίου Φιλοθέου (Κοκκίνου) Πατριάρχου Κωνσταντινουπόλεως (1353–1354 καὶ 1364–1376) τοῦ θεόλογου (Life and Career of St. Philotheos (Kokkinos) Patriarch of Constantinople). Athens, 1971.

Deny, J. "Armeniya," in *EI²,* I, A-B, 634–50.

Diamantopoulos, A. N. "Γεννάδιος ὁ Σχολάριος, ὡς ἱστορικὴ πηγὴ τῶν περὶ τὴν ἅλωσιν χρόνων (Gennadios Scholarios as an historical Source for the Period of the Fall)," *Hellenika,* IX (1936), 285–308.

Diehl, Ch. "De quelques croyances byzantines sur le fin de Constantinople," *BZ,* XXX (1930), 192–96.

Dölger, Franz. *Beiträge zur Geschichte der byzantinischer Finanzverwaltung besonders des 10. und 11. Jahrhunderts.* Leipzig & Berlin, 1927.

———. "Die Frage der Judensteuer in Byzanz," *Vierteljahrschrift für Sozial- und Wirtschaftsgeschichte,* XXVI (1933), 1–24. Reprinted in *Paraspora,* pp. 358–83.

———. "Zur Frage des jüdischen Anteils an der Bevölkerung Thessalonikes im XIV Jahrhunderts," *Joshua Starr Memorial Volume* (New York, 1953), pp. 129–33. Reprinted in *Paraspora,* pp. 378–83.

———. ΠΑΡΑΣΠΟΡΑ: *30 Aufsätze zur Geschichte, Kultur und Sprache des byzantinischen Reiches.* Ettal, 1961.

———. *Polychordia. Festschrift Franz Dölger zum 75. Geburtstag.* Ed. P. Wirth. Amsterdam, 1966.

———. *Polychronion. Festschrift Franz Dölger zum 75 Geburtstag.* Ed. P. Wirth. Heidelberg, 1966.

———. *Regesten der Kaiserurkunden des oströmischen Reiches von 565–1453.* III, IV, V. Munich, 1932–65.

——— and A. M. Schneider. *Byzanz.* Bern, 1952.

Dorini, Umberto, and Tommaso Bertelè, eds. *Il libro dei conti di Giacomo Badoer* (*Costantinopoli 1436–1440*). Instituto poligrafico dello stato. Rome, 1956.

Dräseke, J. "Theodore Laskaris," *BZ,* III (1894), 498–515.

Ebersolt, Jean. *Constantinople byzantine et les voyageurs du Levant.* Paris, 1918.

Ehrhard, A. *Überlieferung und Bestand der hagiographischen und homiletischen Literatur der griechischen Kirche.* Leipzig, 1852.

Ehrhard, M. "Le livre du Pelèrin d'Antoine de Novgorod," *Romania,* LXIII (1932), 44–65.

Elijah ben Moses Bashyachi. אדרת אליהו (The Mantle of Elijah. A Code of Karaite Law). 1st ed., Constantinople, 1530; ed. Gozlow, 1835; ed. Odessa, 1870. Reprint of Odessa ed., Ramleh, 1966.

———. אגרת גיד הנשה (Epistle Concerning the Sciatic Nerve). Preceding Gozlow edition of אדרת אליהו, 1835.

Elijah Kapsali. See Eliyahu ben Elqana Capsali.

Elijah Mizraḥi. ספר שאלות ותשובות ר׳ אליהו מזרחי (responsa). Jerusalem, 1938.

———. ספר מים עמוקים (Book of Deep Waters) (responsa). Berlin, 1778; reprint Jerusalem, 1970.

Eliyahu ben Elqana Capsali. סדר אליהו זוטא, Seder Eliyahu Zuta. History of the Ottomans and of Venice and that of the Jews in Turkey, Spain and Venice. Ed. A. Shmuelevitz. I–II. Jerusalem, 1975–77.

———. לקוטים שונים מס׳ דבי אליהו (De Vita et Scriptis Eliae Kapsalii). Partially ed. M. Lattes. Padua, 1869.

Ellissen, A. Analekten der mittel- und neugriechischen Literatur. IV. Leipzig, 1860.

Elmaleh, Abraham. הפרופסור אברהם גלאנטי: חייו ופעלו הספרותי, ההיסטורי והמדעי

(Le professeur Abraham Galanté; sa vie et son oeuvre littéraire, historique et scientifique). Jerusalem, 1954.
Emmanuel, I. S. גדולי שלוניקי לדורותם (Les grands Juifs de Salonique). Tel Aviv, 1936.
______. Histoire des Israélites de Salonique. I (140 au J. C. à 1640). Paris, 1936.
______. מצבות שאלוניקי (Precious Stones of the Jews of Salonica). I–II. Jerusalem, 1963.
Epstein, Mark A. "The Leadership of the Ottoman Jews in the Fifteenth and Sixteenth Centuries," in Braude-Lewis, *Christians and Jews,* I, 101–16.
______. *The Ottoman Jewish Communities and Their Role in the Fifteenth and Sixteenth Centuries* (Islamkundliche Untersuchungen. Band 56). Freiburg, 1980.
Eshkoli, A. Z. התנועות המשיחיות בישראל (Jewish Messianic Movements. Sources and Documents on Messianism in Jewish History . . .). I. Jerusalem, 1956.
Esposito, M. *Itinerarium Symonis Semeonis ab Hybernia ad Terram Sanctam.* Scriptores Latini Hiberniae, IV. Dublin, 1960.
Ettinger, Shmuel. "ההשפעה היהודית על התסיסה הדתית במזרחה של אירופה בסוף המאה הט״ו (Jewish Influence on the Religious Ferment in Eastern Europe at the End of the Fifteenth Century)," *Yitzhak F. Baer Jubilee Volume* . . . Jerusalem, 1960, pp. 228–47.
______. "מדינת מוסקבה ביחסה אל היהודים (The Muskovite State and Its Attitude toward the Jews)," *Zion* XVIII (1953), 138–68.
Eugene, Bulgaris. *Oeuvres du moine Joseph Bryennios.* I–III. Leipzig, 1768–84.
Fermor, Patrick L. *Mani, Travels in the Southern Peloponnesus.* London, 1958.
______. *Roumeli, Travels in Northern Greece.* London, 1966.
Filiasi, G. *Memorie storiche de' Veneti primi e secondi.* VI. Venice, 1797.
Finkelstein, Louis. "The Prophetic Readings according to the Palestinian, Byzantine, and Karaite Rites," *HUCA,* XVII (1942–43), 423–26.
Finley, George. *A History of Greece from Its Conquest by the Romans to the Present Time, B.C. 146 to A.D. 1864.* III: *The Byzantine and Greek Empires,* pt. 2, *A.D. 1057–1453.* Oxford, 1877.
Finley, John H., Jr. "Corinth in the Middle Ages," *Speculum,* VII (1933), 477–98.
Flusser, David. "מחבר ספר יוסיפון, דמותו ותקופתו (The Author of the Book of Josiphon: his personality and his age)," *Zion,* XVIII (1953), 109–26 (with Eng. summary). Reprinted with photocopy of ms.; see *Sefer Josippon.*
______. "מחבר ספר יוסיפון כהיסטוריון (The Author of *Sefer Josippon* as a Historian)." In *Mekomam shel toldoth ʿam Yisrael be-misgereth toldoth ha-ʿamim.* Jerusalem, 1973, 203–26. Reprinted with photocopy of ms.; see *Sefer Josippon.*
______. Review of Franz Blatt, *The Latin Josephus* . . . (Aarhus, 1958), in *KS,* 34 (1959), 458–63.
Franco, Moïse. *Essai sur l'histoire des Israélites de l'empire ottoman depuis les origines jusqu'à nos jours.* Paris, 1897.
Fränkel, David. לקורות ישראל במלכות יון (Zur Geschichte der Juden in Griechenland). Vienna, 1931.
Frankl, M. "Karäische Studien—Neue Folge," *MGWJ,* 31 (1882), 1–13, 72–85, 268–75.
Freshfield, Edwin H. *A Manual of Byzantine Law Compiled in the Fourteenth Century by George Harmenopoulos,* vol. VI, *Torts and Crimes.* Cambridge, 1930.

Friedlaender, M. *Essays on the Writings of Abraham ibn Ezra*. IV. London, 1877.

Friedman, M. A. *Jewish Marriage in Palestine. A Cairo Geniza Study*. I–II. Tel Aviv and New York, 1980.

Fürst, J. *Geschichte des Karäerthums*. I–III. Leipzig, 1862–69.

Galante, Abraham. *Appendice à l'histoire des Juifs de Rhodes, Chio, Cos, etc*. Istanbul, 1948.

———. *Appendix à l'ouvrage Turcs et Juifs: étude historique, politique*. Istanbul, 1937.

———. *Documents officiels turcs concernant les Juifs de Turqie*. Istanbul, 1931.

———. *Histoire des Juifs d'Anatolie*. I–II. Istanbul, 1937–39.

———. *Histoire des Juifs d'Istanbul depuis la prise de cette ville en 1453, par Fatih Mehmed II, jusqu'à nos jours*. I–II. Istanbul, 1941–42.

———. *Histoire des Juifs de Rhodes, Chio, Cos, etc*. Istanbul, 1935.

———. *Les Juifs de Constantinople sous Byzance*. Istanbul, 1940.

———. *Les Juifs sous la domination des Turcs seldjoukides*. Istanbul, 1941.

———. *Les synagogues d'Istanbul*. Istanbul: Haménora, 1937.

———. *Turcs et Juifs, étude historique, politique*. Stamboul, 1932.

Gardner, Alice. *The Lascarids of Nicaea: The Story of an Empire in Exile*. London, 1912.

Geanakoplos, D. J. *Emperor Michael Palaeologus and the West 1258–1282: A Study in Byzantine-Latin Relations*. Cambridge, Mass., 1959.

Geiger, Abraham. "אגרת אחרת ששלחה החכם הנבון הר׳ ר׳ שמריה מנגריפונטו אל היהודים מרומא (Letter of Shemaryah of Negroponte to the Jews of Rome)," *Oṣar Neḥmad*, II (Vienna, 1857), 90–94. Reprinted in *Gesammelte Abhandlungen*, pp. 290–96.

———. "נוספות על דבר ר׳ שמריה האיקריטי (Addenda on R. Shemaryah ha-Iḳriti)," *He-Ḥaluṣ*, II (Lemburg, 1853), 158–60. Reprinted in *Gesammelte Abhandlungen*, pp. 285–90.

———. "הערות (Notes)," *He-Ḥaluṣ*, II (Lemburg, 1853), 24–27. Reprinted in *Gesammelte Abhandlungen*, pp. 272–76.

———. קבוצות מאמרים (Gesammelte Abhandlungen in hebräischer Sprache). Ed. S. Poznanski. Warsaw, 1910–11. Reprint Haifa, 1967.

Gennadius Scholarios. *Oeuvres complètes de Gennade Scholarios*. Ed. L. Petit, X. A. Siderides, M. Jugie, and others. I–VIII. Paris, 1928–36.

Gèrard, Walter. *La ruine de Byzance (1204–1453)*. Paris, 1958.

Gerber, H. "יזמה ומסחר בין־לאומי בפעילות הכלכלית של יהודי האימפריה העות׳מאנית במאות טז־יז (Enterprise and International Commerce in the Economic Activity of the Jews of the Ottoman Empire in the 16th–17th Centuries)," *Zion*, XLIII (1978), 38–67 (II–IV, Eng. summary).

Gerland, E. *Neue Quellen zur Geschichte des lateinischen Erzbistums Patras*. Leipzig, 1903.

Gerola, C. "La verdute di Costantinopoli di Christoforo Buondelmonti," *Studi bizanti e neoellenici*, 3 (1931), 247–79.

Gibb, H. A. R., trans. *Ibn Battuta: Travels in Asia and Africa, 1325–1354*. II. Cambridge, 1962.

Gibbon, Edward. *Decline and Fall of the Roman Empire*. Ed. J. B. Bury. VII. London, 1902.

Goldman, Israel. *The Life and Times of Rabbi David ibn Abi Zimri*. New York, 1970.

Goldschmidt, Daniel. "על מחזור רומניה ומנהגו (On the *Maḥzor Romania*)," *Sefunoth,* 8 (1964), 205–36.

______. "תרגומי המקרא ליונית מאת יהודים בני המאה הט"ז (Biblical Translations into Greek by Sixteenth Century Jews)," *KS,* 33, no. 1 (1957), 131–34.

Goodblatt, M. S. *Jewish Life in Turkey in the XVIth Century.* New York, 1952.

Graetz, Heinrich. "Abraham Abulafia, der Pseudomessias," *MGWJ,* XXXVI (1887), 557–58.

______. ס' דברי ימי ישראל Hebrew translation of *Geschichte der Juden* by S. P. Rabbinowitz, with extensive notes by A. Harkavy (1–8). Warsaw, 1908.

Grayzel, Solomon. *The Church and the Jews in the XIIIth Century.* Philadelphia, 1933.

Grecu, V. "La chute de Constantinople dans la littérature populaire romaine," *Byzantinoslavica,* XIV (1953), 55–81.

Gross, Heinrich. "Das handschriftliche Werk Assufot Analekten," *MWJ,* X (1881), 64–87.

______. "Jesaya b. Mali da Trani," *ZHB,* XIII (1909), 46–58, 87–92, 118–23.

Grumel, V. *La Chronologie.* Paul Lemerle, ed., *Traité d'études byzantines.* I. Paris, 1958.

Guilland, R. "La chaine de la Corne d'Or," *EEBS,* 25 (1955), 88–120. Reprinted in *Etudes byzantines* (Paris, 1959) and in *Etudes de topographie de Constantinople byzantine,* II (Amsterdam, 1969).

______. "La correspondence inédite d'Athanase, patriarch de Constantinople (1289–1293; 1304–1310)." *Mélanges Charles Diehl* (Paris, 1930), I, 121–40.

______. *La politique intérieure de l'empire de Byzance de 1204 à 1341.* Paris: Cours de Sorbonne, 1959.

______. *La politique religieuse de l'empire byzantin de 1204 à 1341.* Paris: Cours de Sorbonne, 1959.

______. "Les appels de Constantin XII Paléologue à Rome et à Venise pour servir Constantinople (1452–1453)," *Byzantinoslavica,* XIV (1953), 226–44. Reprinted in *Etudes byzantines.* Paris, 1959.

______. "Les ports de Byzance sur la Propontide," *Byzantion,* 23 (1953), 181–238. Reprinted in *Etudes de topographie de Constantinople byzantine,* II. Amsterdam, 1969.

Guillou, André. *Les Archives de Saint-Jean-Prodrome sur le mont Ménéncé.* Bibliothèque byzantine, documents, 3. Paris, 1955.

Guterman, Simon L. *Religious Toleration and Persecution in Ancient Rome.* London, 1951.

Hacker, Joseph. "עליית יהודי ספרד לארץ-ישראל וזיקתם אליה, בין קנ"א (1391) לרנ"ב (1492) (The Connections of Spanish Jewry with Eretz-Israel between 1391 and 1492)," *Shalem, Studies in the History of the Jews in Eretz-Israel,* I (Jerusalem, 1974), 105–56.

______. "Ottoman Policy toward the Jews and Jewish Attitudes toward the Ottomans during the Fifteenth Century." In Braude-Lewis, *Christians and Jews,* I (London, 1982), 117–26.

______. "קבוצת איגרות על גירוש היהודים מספרד ומסיציליה ועל גורל המגורשים (Some Letters on the Expulsion of the Jews from Spain and Sicily)," *Studies in the History of Jewish Society in the Middle Ages and in the Modern Period Presented to Professor Jacob Katz . . .* (Jerusalem, 1980), pp. 64–97.

Hadassi, J. See Judah ben Elijah Hadassi.

Halkin, François. *Bibliotheca Hagiographica Graeca.* I–III. 3d. ed. Brussels, 1957.

Halperin, Charles. "Judaizers and the Image of the Jew in Medieval Russia: A Polemic Revisited and a Question Posed," *Canadian-American Slavic Studies,* 9:2 (Summer, 1975), 141–55.

Hammer, Joseph von. *Narrative of the Travels in Europe, Asia, and Africa in the Seventeenth Century, by Evliya Efendi.* I–II. London, 1834.

Hammer-Purgstall, Joseph von. *Geschichte des osmanischen Reiches.* 1–10. Pest, 1827–35.

Hananel, Ašer, and Eli Eškenazi, eds. *Fontes hebraici ad res oeconomicas socialesque terrarum balcanarum saeculo XVI pertinentes.* I–II. Sofia, 1958–60.

Hanke, Martin. *De Byzantinorum rerum scriptoribus graecis liber.* Lipsiae, 1677.

Harkavy, A. "Karaites," in *JE,* VII, 438–46.

Harmenopulos, George. See Armenopoulos, George.

Harnack, Adolf. *The Mission and Expansion of Christianity in the First Three Centuries.* Tr. James Moffat. Rev. ed. New York, 1962.

Hebrew Manuscripts in the Houghton Library of the Harvard College Library. A Catalogue. Prepared by Mordecai Glatzer, edited by Ch. Berlin and R. G. Dennis. Cambridge, Mass., 1975.

Heimbach, Gustav. See Armenopoulos, George.

Heisenberg, A. "Kaiser Johannes Batatzes der Barmherzige. Eine mittelgriechische Legende," *BZ,* XIV (1905), 160–233.

Hesserling, D. C. "Le livre de Jonas," *BZ,* X (1901), 208–17.

———. *Les cinq livres de la loi "Le Pentateuque." Traduction en néo-grec publiée en caractères hébraïques à Constantinople en 1547, transcrite et accompagnée d'une introduction, d'un glossaire et d'une facsimile.* Leide and Leipzig, 1897.

Heyd, Uriel. "The Jewish Communities of Istanbul in the Seventeenth Century," *Oriens,* IV (1953), 299–314.

Heyd, Wilhelm. *Histoire du commerce du Levant au moyen âge.* I–II. Leipzig, 1885.

Hickman, William C. "Who was Ümmi Kemal?" *Boğaziçi Universitesi Dergisi,* 4–5 (1976–77), 57–82.

Hillel ben Eliakim. ספרא דבי רב . . . עם פירוש רבינו הלל ב״ר אליקים מארץ יון (Commentary on *Sifra*). I–II. Ed. S. Koleditsky. Jerusalem, 1960–61.

———. ספרי להתנא שמעון בר יוחאי . . . עם פירוש הלל ב״ר אליקים מארץ יון (Commentary on *Sifre*). 2 vols. in 1. Ed. S. Koleditsky. Jerusalem, 1948.

Hirschfeld, H. "Descriptive Catalogue of Hebrew Mss. of the Montefiore Library," *JQR,* o.s., XIV (1902), 159–96. (Complete catalogue, ibid., XIV–XV)

Hodgson, F. C. *Venice in the Thirteenth and Fourteenth Centuries.* London, 1910.

Hoeck, M., and R. J. Loenertz. *Nikolaos-Nektarios von Otranto Abt von Casole: Beiträge zur Geschichte der Ost-westlichen Beziehungen unter Innocenz III. und Friedrich II.* Studia Patristica et Byzantina, heft II. Rome, 1965.

Hopf, Karl. *Geschichte Griechenlands von Beginne des Mittelalters bis auf die neuer Zeit.* Leipzig, 1867.

———. *Urkunden und Zusätze zur Geschichte der Insel Andros und ihrer Beherrscher in dem Zeitraume von MCCVII bis MDLXVI.* Vienna, 1856.

———. *Urkundliche Mittheilungen über die Geschichte von Karystos auf Euboea in dem Zeitraume von 1205–1470 aus den Quellen des K. K. Geheimen Haus-, Hof- und Staats-Archives und der K. K. Hofbibliothek.* Offprint from Sitzungsberichte der philos.-histor. Classe der Kais. Akademie der Wissenschaften, bd. XI., s. 555ff. Vienna, 1853.

Hrochova, V. "Le commerce vénitien et les changements dans l'importance des centres de commerce en Grèce du 13e au 15e siècles," *Studi Veneziani,* IX (1967), 3–34.

Idel, Moshe. "Abraham Abulafia's Works and Doctrine," (Hebrew) unpublished Ph.D. thesis, Hebrew University of Jerusalem, 1976.

Iliescu, Octavian. "La monnaie vénitienne dans le pays roumains de 1202 à 1500," *Revue des études sud-est européenes,* XV (1977), 355–61.

Inalcik, Halil. "Istanbul," *EI*2, IV, 224–48.

______. *The Ottoman Empire: The Classical Age, 1300–1600.* New York and Washington, 1973.

______. "The Policy of Mehmed II toward the Greek Population of Istanbul and the Byzantine Buildings of the City," *DOP,* no. 23 (1969), pp. 229–49.

Ioannes Anagnostae. *De Thessalonica Excidio Narratio.* Ed. Niebuhr. *CSHB.* Bonn, 1838.

Iorga, N. "Notes et extraits pour servir à l'histoire des Croisades aux XVe siècle," *Revue de l'orient latin,* 4 (1896), 25–118, 226–320, 503–622; 5 (1897), 108–212, 311–88; 6 (1898), 50–143, 370–434; 7 (1899), 38–107, 375–429; 8 (1900), 1–115, 267–310. Reprinted in 3 vols. Paris, 1899–1902.

Isaiah ben Mali di Trani. פירוש נביאים וכתובים לרבינו ישעיה הראשון מטראני (Commentary on Prophets and Hagiographa of Rabbi Isaiah the First from Trani). Ed. Abraham Y. Wertheimer. I–III. Jerusalem, 1978.

______. תשובות הרי״ד לרבנו ישעיה דטראני הזקן ז״ל (responsa). Ed. Abraham Y. Wertheimer. 2d ed. Jerusalem, 1975.

Izeddin, M. "Un texte arabe inédit sur Constantinople byzantin," *JA,* 246 (1958), 453–57.

Jacoby, David. *La féodalité en Grèce médiévale: les "Assizes de Romanie" sources, application et diffusion.* Paris, 1971.

______. "Les Juifs vénitiens de Constantinople et leur communaute du XIIIe au milieu du XVe siècle," *REJ,* CXXXI (1972), 397–410.

______. "(1366–1546) היהודים בכיאוס בימי שלטון ג׳ינובה (The Jews in Chios under Genoese Rule, 1346–1566)," *Zion,* XXVI (1961), 180–97.

______. "La population de Constantinople à l'époque byzantine: un problem de demographie urbaine," *Byzantion,* XXXI (1961), 81–109.

______. "Les quartiers juifs de Constantinople à l'époque byzantine," *Byzantion,* XXXVII (1967), 167–227.

______. "למעמדם של היהודים במושבות ויניציאה בימי הבינים (On the Status of Jews in the Venetian Colonies in the Middle Ages)," *Zion,* XXVIII (1963), 57–69.

______. "יהודים בני־חסות של ויניציאה בקשטא במאות הארבע־עשרה והחמש־עשרה (Venetian Diplomatic Protection to Jews in Constantinople in the 14th and 15th Centuries)," *Zion,* XXVII (1962), 24–35.

______. "Les Vénitiens naturalisés dans l'empire byzantin: un aspect de l'expansion de Venise en Romanie du XIIIe au milieu du XVe siècle," *Travaux et Mémoires,* 8 (1981), 207–35.

Janin, R. *Constantinople byzantine, développement urbain et repertoire topographique.* 2d ed. Paris, 1964.

______. "Les Juifs dans l'empire byzantine," *Echoes d'Orient,* XV (1902), 126–33.

Jellinek, Adolph. בית המדרש (Bet ha-Midrasch. Sammlung kleiner Midraschim und vermischter Abhandlungen aus der ältern jüdischen Literatur). Reprinted in 2 vols. Jerusalem, 1967.

Jirecek, C. *Geschichte der Bulgaren*. Prague, 1876.

Joannou, P. "Vie de S. Germain l'Hagiorite par son contemporain le patriarche Philothée de Constantinople," *Analecta Bollandiana,* LXX (1952), 35–114.

Jones, J. R. Melville, trans. *The Siege of Constantinople, 1453: Seven Contemporary Accounts*. Amsterdam, 1972.

Josippon. See *Sefer Josippon*.

Jost, I. M. "Lehre der Karaiten und ihr Kampf gegen die Rabbinische Tradition," *Israelitische Annalen,* no. 11 (1839), pp. 81–83.

Judah ben Elijah Hadassi. אשכל הכפר (Cluster of Henna. Encyclopedia of Karaite Lore). Gozlow, 1836.

Judah ibn Moskoni. "הקדמה לאבן העזר (Introduction to Ibn Ezra)." Ed. A. Berliner. In *Oṣar Tob* (Berlin, 1878), pp. 1–10.

———. "הקדמה ליוסיפון (Introduction to *Sefer Josippon*)." Ed. H. Hominer. In *Sefer Josippon* (Jerusalem, 1978), pp. 34–40.

Juster, J. *Les Juifs dans l'empire romain*. I–II. Paris, 1914.

Kahle, Paul. *The Cairo Geniza*. 2d ed. Oxford, 1959.

Kaleb ben Elijah Afendopolo. נחל אשכל (The Valley of Eshkol. Index to אשכל הכפר). See Judah ben Elijah Hadassi.

Kapsali, Eliahu. See Eliyahu ben Elqana Capsali.

Kechales, Haim. קורות יהודי בולגריה (History of the Jews in Bulgaria). 1–5. Tel Aviv, 1969–73.

Khitrovo, Sofia, ed. and tr. *Itinéraires russes en Orient*. Société pour la publication de texts relatifs à l'histoire & la géographie de l'Orient Latin. Geneva, 1889.

Kissling, H. J. "Badr al-Dīn b. Ḳāḍī Samāwnā," *EI²,* p. 869.

Klar, Benjamin, ed. מגילת אחימעץ (Chronicle of Ahimaaz). 2d ed. Jerusalem, 1974.

Knolles, Richard. *The General Historie of the Turkes* . . . 3d ed. London, 1621.

Koback, Joseph. גנזי נסתרות. Ginse Nistaroth; handschriftliche Editionen aus der jüdischen Literatur. 1–4. Bamberg, 1868–78 (1–2 = *Jeschurun,* VI [1868]).

Koder, Johannes und Frederich Hild. *Hellas und Thessalia*. Osterreichische Akademie der Wissenschaften. Phil.-Hist. Klasse Denkschriften, band 125. Vienna, 1976.

Kohler, K. "Aaron ben Elijah, the Younger," *JE,* I, 9–10.

Konforte, David. ספר קורא הדורות (*Liber Kore Ha-Dorot*. Biobibliographical Chronology of post-Talmudic Authors). Ed. D. Cassel. Berlin, 1846.

Koukoules, Ph. "Γλωσσαριόν Ἑβραιοελληνικόν (A Hebrew–Greek Glossary)," *BZ,* XIX (1910), 422–29.

Kourouses, S. I. "Φιλόθεος ὁ Κόκκινος (Philotheos Kokkinos)," in *Threskeutike kai Ethike Enkyklopaideia,* II, 1119f.

Krafft, Albrecht und Simon Deutsch. *Die handschriftlichen hebräischen Werke der KK. Hofbibliothek zu Wien*. Vienna, 1897.

Krauss, Samuel. *Studien zur byzantinisch-jüdischen Geschichte*. Vienna, 1914.

Krekić, Bariša. "The Role of the Jews in Dubrovnik (Thirteenth–Sixteenth Centuries)," *Viator,* 4 (1973), 257–71.

Kretschmayr, Heinrich. *Geschichte von Venedig*. Gotha, 1920.

Kritoboulos, Michael, of Imbros. *De rebus gestis Mahumetis II*. Ed. C. Müller. In *Fragmenta historicorum graecorum,* V, 1. Paris, 1883, pp. 52–164. Ed. V. Grecu. *Critobuli Imbriotae. De Rebus per annos 1451–1467 a Mechemete II Gestis*. Bucharest, 1963. Tr. C. T. Riggs. *History of Mehmed the Conqueror*. Princeton, 1954.

Krumbacher, Karl. *Geschichte der byzantinischen Litteratur von Justinian bis zum Ende des oströmischen Reiches (527–1453)*. 2d ed. Munich, 1897. Reprinted New York, 1958.

Kushnir-Oron, Michal. See Oron, Michal.

Laiou, Angeliki E. *Constantinople and the Latins. The Foreign Policy of Andronicus II, 1282–1328*. Cambridge, Mass., 1972.

Laiou-Thomadakis, Angeliki E. *Peasant Society in the Late Byzantine Empire. A Social and Demographic Study*. Princeton, 1977.

Lampridou, I. Περιγραφὴ τῆς πόλεως Ἰωαννίνων (Description of Ioannina). *Epeirōtika Meletēmata,* I. Athens, 1887; reprinted 1911.

Lampros, Sp. Παλαιολόγεια καὶ Πελοποννησιακά (On the Palaiologoi and the Peloponnesus). II. Athens, 1924.

———. "Χρυσσόβυλλον Ἀνδρονίκου Α΄ Παλαιολόγου ὑπὲρ τῆς ἐκκλησίας Ἰωαννίνων (Chrysobull of Andronicus I Palaiologos in Behalf of the Church of Ioannina)," *Neos Hellenomnēmon,* 12 (1915), 36–40.

Lampsides, U. "Georges Chrysococcis, le médecin, et son oeuvre," *BZ,* XXXVIII (1938), 312–22.

Lane, F. C. *Venice. A Maritime Republic*. Baltimore, 1973.

Lattes, M. See Eliyahu ben Elqana Capsali.

Laurent, V. "Le Basilicon. Nouveau nom de monnaie sous Andronic II Paléologue," *BZ,* XLV (1952), 50–52.

———. *Les Actes des Patriarches*. Vol. I, fasc. IV: *Les Regestes de 1208 à 1309*. Le Patriarcat Byzantin, series I. Paris, 1971.

———. "Philothée Kokkinos," *Dictionnaire de théologique catholique,* XII, 1498–1509.

Lewin, B. "Eine Notiz zur Geschichte der Juden im byzantinischen Reiche," *MGWJ,* XIX (1870), 117–22.

Lewis, Bernard. "The Ottoman Archives as a Source for the History of the Arab Lands," *Journal of the Royal Asiatic Society* (1951), pp. 139–55.

———. "Studies in the Ottoman Archives," *BSOAS,* XXI (1954), 469–501.

———. *Notes and Documents from the Turkish Archives. A Contribution to the History of the Jews in the Ottoman Empire*. Jerusalem, 1952.

———. "The Privilege Granted by Meḥmed II to His Physician," *BSOAS,* 14 (1952), 550–63.

Liutprand of Cremona. *Antapodesis*. Trans. F. A. Wright. *The Works of Liutprand of Cremona*. London, 1930.

Loenertz, R. I. "Autour du Chronicon Maius attribué à Georges Phrantzès," *Miscellanea G. Mercati,* III: *Letteratura e storia bizantina*. Studi e Testi, 123. Vatican City, 1946, pp. 273–311.

Longnon, Jean. "The Frankish States in Greece." In *A History of the Crusades,* II. Ed. R. L. Wolff and H. W. Hazard. Philadelphia, 1962, pp. 235–76.

______ and Peter Topping, eds. *Documents sur le régime des terres dans la principauté de Morée au XIVe siècle*. Paris, 1969.

Lopez, R. S. "Silk Industry in the Byzantine Empire," *Speculum,* XX (1945), 1–42.

______. *Storia delle Colonie Genovesi nel Mediterraneo*. Bologna, 1938.

______, and I. W. Raymond. *Medieval Trade in the Mediterranean World*. London, 1955.

Maas, Paul, and C. A. Trypanis, eds. *Sancti Romani Melodi Cantica*. I. *Cantica Genuina*. Oxford, 1963.

MacKay, Pierre. "Acrocorinth in 1668, a Turkish Account," *Hesperia,* XXXVII (1968), 386–97.

McNeal, E., and R. L. Wolff. "The Fourth Crusade." In *A History of the Crusades,* II. Ed. R. L. Wolff and H. W. Hazard. Philadelphia, 1962, pp. 153–86.

Majeska, G. P. "The Body of St. Theophano the Empress and the Convent of St. Constantine," *Byzantinoslavica,* XXXVIII (1977), 14–21.

Malakis, J. P. Γεώργος Γεμιστὸς Πλήθων (George Gemistos Plethon). Texte und Forschungen zur byzantinische-neugriechische Philologie, no. 32. Athens, 1939.

Maltezou, X. A. Ὁ Θεσμὸς τοῦ ἐν Κωνσταντινουπόλει Βενέτου βαΐλου (1268–1453) (The Rule of the Venetian Bailo in Constantinople 1268–1453). Athens, 1970.

Mango, Cyril. "The Date of the Anonymous Description of Constantinople," *BZ,* XLV (1952), 380–85.

Mann, Jacob. "Changes in the Divine Service of the Synagogue due to Religious Persecution," *HUCA,* 4 (1927), 242–310.

______. "על זמנו ומקומו של ר׳ יעקב בן אליהו בעל האגרת ויכוח נגד המומר פרא פול (Über Jakob b. Elia, Verfasser des polemischen Briefes gegen den Apostaten Pablo)," *Alim,* I (1934–35), 75–77.

______. *The Jews in Egypt and in Palestine under the Fatimid Caliphs*. I–II. Oxford, 1920–22. Reprinted Oxford, 1969. Reprinted (2 vols. in 1) New York, 1970.

______. "Une source de l'histoire juive au XIIIe siècle: La lettre polémique de Jacob b. Elie à Pable Christiani," *REJ,* LXXXII (1926), 363–77.

______. *Texts and Studies in Jewish History and Literature*. I. Cincinnati, 1931; II. Philadelphia, 1935. Reprinted New York, 1972.

______. "האשכנזים הם הכוזרים (Are the Ashkenazi Jews Khazars?)" *Tarbiz,* IV (1933), 391–94.

Mantran, Robert. *Istanbul dans la second moitié du XVIIe siècle, essai d'histoire institutionelle, économique et sociale*. Paris, 1962.

Marazzi, Ugo. *Tevārīẖ-i Al-i ʿOs̱mān: Cronaca anonima ottomana in trascrizione ebraica (dal manoscritto Heb. e 63 della Bodleian Library)*. Instituto Universitario Orientale, seminario di studi asiatici, series minor XII. Naples, 1980.

Markus, Simon. "(LA CANEE, CANEA) תולדות היהודים בכניאה באי כרתים (A History of the Jews in Canea)," *Tarbiz,* XXXVIII (1968), 161–74 (v, Eng. summary).

Masai, F. *Pléthon et le Platonisme de Mistra*. Paris, 1956.

Massignon, Louis. "Texts prémonitoires et commentaires mystiques relatifs à la prise de Constantinople par les Turcs en 1453 (= 838 Heg.)," *Oriens,* LV (1953), 10 ff.

Mazaris. "The Satire of Mazaris" (Διάλογος νεκρικός, Ἐπιδημία Μάζαρι ἐν Ἅδου). Ed. J. F. Boissonade, *Anecdota graeca* (Paris, 1831), III, 112–86. Ed. A. Ellison,

Analekten der mittel- und neugriechischen Litteratur (Leipzig, 1860), IV, 187–250 (German trans., pp. 251–314). *Mazaris' Journey to Hades,* ed. and trans. by Seminar Classics 609. SUNY at Buffalo, Arethusa Monographs V, Dept. of Classics. SUNY, Buffalo, 1975.

Mazur, Belle. *Studies in Greek Jewry.* I. Athens, 1935.

Meislis, Isaac. "שיר האותיות לר' שלמה בן אליהו שרביט הזהב (*Shir ha-Otioth* [Song of Letters] of R. Shlomo ben Eliahu Sharvit Hazahav)," *Tagim, Review of Jewish Bibliography,* 5–6 (1975), 41–69.

———. "שיר מריבה בין שבת לחנוכה לר' שלמה בן אליהו שרביט הזהב ('The Song of Rivalry between Sabbath and Chanukah,' by R. Shlomo b. Eliahu Sharvit Hazahav)," *Bar Ilan Annual,* XIII (1976), 224–33 (XXXVI, Eng. summary).

Mercati, Giovanni. *Se la versione dall'ebraico del Codice Veneto Greco VII sia di Simone Atumano, Archivescovo di Tebe.* Studi e Testi, no. 30. Rome, 1916.

Mercati, S. G. "Il trattato contro i Giudei di Taddeo Pelusiota è una falsificazione di Constantino Paleocappa," *Bessarione,* 39 (1923), 8–14.

———. *Notizie di Procoro e Demetrio Cidone, Manuele Caleca e Theodoro Meliteniota ed altri appunti per la storia della Teologia e della leteratura bizantina del secondo XIV.* Studi e Testi, 56. Rome, 1931.

Mertzios, K. D. Μνημέια Μαμεδονικῆς Ἱστορίας (Documents of Macedonian History). Thessaloniki, 1947.

Meyendorff, Jean. *Byzantine Hesychasm: Historical, Theological and Social Problems.* London, 1974.

———. "Grecs, Turcs et Juifs en Asie Mineure au XIVe siècle," *Polychordia: Festschrift Franz Dölger.* Amsterdam, 1966, 211–17.

———. *Introduction à l'étude de Grégoire Palamas.* Paris, 1959. Abridged English version, London, 1964.

Miakotine, Hélène. "G. Ostrogorski et la principauté serbe de Serres," *Travaux et Mémoires,* 2 (1969), 569–73.

Miklosich, F., and J. Müller. *Acta et diplomata graeca medii aevi sacra et profana.* I–VI. Vienna, 1860–90.

Miller, William. *Essays on the Latin Orient.* Cambridge, 1921.

———. "The Historians Doukas and Phrantzes," *JHS,* 46 (1926), 67–71.

———. *The Latins in the Levant, a History of Frankish Greece (1204–1566).* London, 1908. Reprinted 1964.

———. *Trebizond: The Last Greek Empire.* New York, 1926.

Minotto, D. *Chronik der Familie Minotto.* I–II. Berlin, 1901.

Molho, Isaac. *Histoire des Israélites de Castoria.* Thessaloniki, 1938.

Morgan, Gareth. "The Venetian Claims Commission of 1278," *BZ,* LXIX (1978), 411–38.

Munk, Solomon. "Manuscrits hébreux de l'Oratoire à la Bibliothèque Nationale de Paris, notes inédites," *ZHB,* XIII (1909), 24–31, 58–63, 92–94, 123–27, 153–58, 181–87.

Naumann, Emil. *Catalogus librorum manuscriptorum qui in Bibliotheca Senatoria Civitatis Lipsiensis asservantur.* Grimae, 1838.

Nehama, Joseph. *Histoire des Israélites de Salonique.* I. Saloniki, 1935.

Nelson, Benjamin, and Joshua Starr. "The Legend of the Divine Surety and the Jewish Moneylender," *Annuaire de l'Institut de Philologie et d'histoire Orientales,* I (1932–33), 289–338.

Netanyahu, B. "לבירור זמן חיבורם של ספרי ״הקנה״ ו״הפליאה (Toward a Clarification of the Period when the *Sefer ha-Kaneh* and *Sefer ha-Peliah* Were Written)," *S. W. Baron Jubilee Volume* (III) (Hebrew section). Jerusalem, 1974, pp. 247–67.

Neubauer, A. *Aus der Petersberger Bibliothek.* Leipzig, 1866.

———. *Catalogue of the Hebrew Manuscripts in the Bodleian Library.* I–II. Oxford, 1886–1906.

———. "Documents inédits II Schemariah de Négropont et Jean d'Avignon," *REJ,* X (1885), 86–92.

———. *Mediaeval Jewish Chronicles.* I–II. Anecdota Oxoniensa, Semitic ser., I, pts. 4 and 6. Oxford, 1887–95.

———. "On Non-Hebrew Languages Used by Jews," *JQR,* o.s., IV (1891), 9–19.

Nicephoras Gregoras. *Historia Byzantina.* Ed. L. Schoper. *CSHB.* Bonn, 1829–35.

Nicol, D. M. *The Despotate of Epirus.* Oxford, 1957.

Oeconomos, L. "L'état intellectuel et moral des Byzantins vers le milieu du XIVe siècle d'après une page de Joseph Bryennios," *Mélanges Charles Diehl.* Paris, 1930. I, 225–33.

Oron, Michal. ה״פליאה״ וה״קנה״ יסודות הקבלה שבהם, עמדתם הדתית חברתית ודרך עצובם הספרותית (The *Sefer Ha-Pli'ah* and the *Sefer Ha-Kanah.* Their Kabbalistic Principles, Social and Religious Criticism and Literary Composition). Jerusalem: Hebrew University (Published Dissertation series), 1980.

———. "ה״קנה״ וה״פליאה (The books *Kanah* and *Pli'ah*)," in *EIV,* XXIX, 867–68.

Ostrogorsky, G. "Byzance, état tributaire de l'empire turc," *Zbornik Radova,* 5 (1958), 49–58.

———. *History of the Byzantine State.* Trans. Joan Hussey. New Brunswick, 1957. Rev. ed. 1969.

———. *La principauté de Serrès* (Serbian). Belgrade, 1965.

Ovadiah, A. "רבי אליהו מזרחי (Rabbi Eliahu Mizraḥi)," *Sinai,* 5 (1939–40), 397–413; 6 (1940), 73–80.

Pachymeres, George. *De Andronico Palaeologo.* Ed. Bekker. *CSHB.* Bonn, 1835; ed. *MPG,* 144.

Pantazopoulos, N. J. *Church and Law in the Balkan Peninsula during the Ottoman Rule.* Thessaloniki, 1967.

Papadopoulou-Kerameos, A. "Γλωσσάριον ἑβραικοελληνικόν (A Hebrew–Greek Glossary)," in *Festschrift . . . Dr. A. Harkavy.* St. Petersburg, 1908, pp. 68–90.

Parkes, James. *The Conflict of the Church and the Synagogue: A Study in the Origins of Antisemitism.* London, 1934. Reprinted Philadelphia, 1961.

Patlagean, E. "L'enfant et son avenir dans la famille byzantine (IVe–XIIe siècles)," *Annales de démographie historique.* Paris, 1973, pp. 85–93.

Patrinelis, Christos G. "Mehmed II the Conqueror and His Presumed Knowledge of Greek and Latin," *Viator,* 2 (1971), 349–54.

Pears, E. *The Destruction of the Greek Empire and the Story of the Capture of Constantinople.* New York and London, 1903.

Petahyah of Ratisborn. סבוב הרב פתחיה מרגנשפורג (Die Rundreise des R. Petachjah aus Regensburg), I–II. Ed. and tr. L. Grünhut. Jerusalem–Frankfurt, 1904–5. Trans. E. N. Adler. *Jewish Travellers*. London, 1930.

Petit, Louis. "Actes de l'Athos II: Actes du Pantocrator," *VV*, 10 (1903), suppl., no. VIII.

Philippidis-Braat, Anna. "La Captivité de Palamas chez les Turcs: Dossier et commentaire," *Traveaux et Mémoires*, 7 (1979), 109–221.

Phourikes, P. A. "Συμβολή εἰς τὸ τοπωγύμικον τῆς 'Αττικῆς (Contribution to the Placenames of Attika)," *Athena*, 41 (1929), 77–178, and 42 (1930), 111–36.

Phrantzes, Georgios. *Chronicon Maius*. Ed. J. B. Papadopoulos (books I–II). Leipzig, 1935.

______. *Annales*. Ed. I. Bekker. *CSHB*. Bonn, 1938. See Sphrantzes.

Poznanski, Adolf. *Schiloh. Ein Beitrag zur Geschichte der Messiaslehre*. Erster Teil. Leipzig, 1904.

Poznanski, Samuel. *Beitrage zur karäischen Handschriften- und Bucherkunde*. Heft 1, *Karäische Kopisten und Besitzer von Handscriften*. Frankfurt a.M., 1918.

______. "Karaites," in *ERE*, VII, 662–72.

______. *The Karaite Literary Opponents of Saadia Gaon*. London, 1908. Reprinted from *JQR*, o.s., XVIII–XX (1905–8).

Reichert, Victor E. "The Eighteenth Gate of Judah al-Harizi's Tahkemoni," *Central Conference of American Rabbis Journal* (October 1970), pp. 26–59.

______, tr. *The Tahkemoni of Judah al-Harizi*. I–II. Jerusalem, 1965–73.

Reinach, Th. "Un contrat de marriage du temps de Basile le Bulgaroctone," *Mélanges offertes à M. Gustave Schlumberger*. Paris, 1924), I, 118–38.

Roman, Abraham. הקדמה לס' סלע המחלקות (The Rock of Disputes). Introduction printed in *Milḥamoth Ḥovah*. Constantinople, 1710.

Rosanes, Solomon. דברי ימי ישראל בתוגרמה (History of the Jews in Turkey). I. 2d ed. Tel Aviv, 1930.

______. קורות היהודים בתורקיה וארצות הקדם (Histoire des Israélites de Turquie et de l'Orient). II–IV. Sofia, 1934–35.

Rosenberg, Shalom. "Logic and Ontology in Jewish Philosophy in the 14th Century," (Hebrew), Vol. I (only one printed). Unpublished Ph.D. thesis, Hebrew University of Jerusalem, 1973.

Roth, Cecil. *Venice*. Philadelphia, 1930.

Runciman, S. *The Fall of Constantinople, 1453*. Cambridge, 1965.

______. *The Last Byzantine Renaissance*. Cambridge, 1970.

Samuel de Medina. שאלות ותשובות מהרשד"ם (responsa). Lemburg, 1862.

Sanjian, Avedis K. *The Armenian Communities in Syria under Ottoman Domination*. Cambridge, Mass., 1965.

______, ed. and tr. *Colophons of Armenian Manuscripts, 1301–1480: A Source for Middle Eastern History*. Cambridge, Mass., 1969.

______. "Two Contemporary Armenian Elegies on the Fall of Constantinople, 1453," *Viator*, I (1970), 223–61.

Saraf, Michal. "ויכוח היין והמשורר לכָלֵב אפנדופולו הקראי ('Discussion Between the wine and the poet,' by Kalev Afendopolo the Karaite)." In *Papers on Medieval*

Hebrew Literature Presented to A. M. Habermann . . . Jerusalem, 1977, pp. 343–61. (Eng. summary, p. 378).
Saranti-Mendelovici, Hélène. "A propos de la ville de Patras aux 13e–15e siècles," *REB*, 38 (1980), 219–32.
Sarres, Io. "Τὰ τοπονύμια τῆς 'Αττικης (The Place Names of Attika)," *Athena*, 40 (1928), 117–60.
Sarton, George. *Introduction to the History of Science*. 3 vols. in 5. Baltimore, 1927–48.
Sassoon, David S. אהל דוד (*OHEL DAWID*). *Descriptive Catalogue of the Hebrew and Samaritan Manuscripts in the Sassoon Library*, London. I–II. London, 1932.
Sathas, Constantine. Μεσαιωνικὴ Βιβλιοθήκη (Bibliotheca graeca medii aevi). I–VII. Venice, 1872–94.
———. Μνημεῖα Ἑλληνικῆς Ἱστορίας (Documents inédits relatifs à l'histoire de la Grèce au moyen age). I–IX. Paris, 1880–90.
Schechter, S. "Notes on Hebrew MSS. in the University Library at Cambridge," *JQR*, o.s., IV (1892), 91–100.
Scheffer, Ch. *La voyage de la Saincte Cyté de Hierusalem*. Paris, 1882.
Schiltberger, Johann. *The Bondage and Travels of Johann Schiltberger, a Native of Bavaria, in Europe, Asia, and Africa, 1396–1427*. Trans. J. Buchan. London, 1879.
Schirmann, Ḥ. "אסף פיטנים מתורקיה בספריה הלאומית (A Collection of Hebrew Poetry from Turkey in the National Library)," *KS*, XII (1935–36), 389–96, 515–23.
———. השירה העברית בספרד ובפרובאנס (Hebrew Poetry in Spain and Provence). Book II, part I. 2d ed. Tel Aviv, 1960.
Schneider, A. M. *Die Bevölkerung Konstantinopels im XV. Jahrhundert*. Nachrichten d. Akad. Wiss. in Göttingen, Philol.-Hist. Klasse, 1949.
———. "Die Blachernen," *Oriens*, 4 (1951), 82–120.
———. *Die Römischen und Byzantinischen Denkmäler von Iznik-Nicaea*. Istanbuler Forschungen, band 16. Berlin, 1943.
Scholem, Gershom. *Major Trends in Jewish Mysticism*. 3d ed. New York, 1954.
Schwab, M. "Sept epitaphes hébräiques de Grèce," *REJ*, LXIII (1909), 106–11.
Schwartz, Arthur Zacharias. *Die hebräische Handschriften in Österreich (ausserhalb der Nationalbibliothek in Wien)*. Leipzig, 1931.
Schwartz, Leo. *Memoirs of My People through a Thousand Years*. Philadelphia, 1945.
Sefer Josippon. Pseudepigraphon of Joseph ben Gurion ha-Kohen. Ed. David Flusser. *Josippon. The Original Version MS Jerusalem 8°41280 and Supplements* (see Flusser, David). (Texts and Studies for Students, "KUNTRESIM" Project, 49). Jerusalem, 1978. David Flusser, ed. *The Josippon (Josephus Gorionides)*. I–II. Jerusalem, 1978–81 (from above ms.). Longer version ed. (uncritically) H. Hominer. *Sefer Josippon*. IV ed. Jerusalem, 1978.
Setton, K. M. ed. *A History of the Crusades*. II. *The Later Crusades, 1189–1311*. Ed. R. L. Wolff and H. W. Hazard. Philadelphia, 1962.
———. *Catalan Domination of Athens, 1311–1388*. Cambridge, Mass., 1948. Rev. ed. London, 1975.
Ševčenko, I. "Alexios Makrembolites and His 'Dialogue Between The Rich and The Poor,'" *Zbornik Radova*, 6 (1960), 186–228.
Sharf, Andrew. *Byzantine Jewry from Justinian to the Fourth Crusade*. New York, 1971.

———. "Byzantine Jewry in the XIII Century," *Bar Ilan Annual,* XIV–XV (1977), 61–72.

———. "Jews, Armenians and the Patriarch Athanasius I," *Bar Ilan Annual,* XVI–XVII (1979), 31–48.

Sherrard, Ph. *Constantinople, Iconography of a Sacred City.* London, 1965.

Shmuelevitz, A. "Capsali as a Source for Ottoman History, 1450–1523," *International Journal of Middle Eastern Studies,* 9 (1978), 339–44.

Shrock, A. T. "The Authorship of the Ethical Treatise Entitled Sefer Ha-Yashar," *JQR,* n.s., LXI (1970–71), 175–87; LXV (1974–75), 18–31.

Ṣidkiyahu ben Abraham Anav ha-Rofe. שבלי הלקט (The Gleaned Ears). Part II. Ed. Rav Menahem Ze'ev Ḥasida. Jerusalem, 1969. For title, cf. *EJ,* II, s.v.

Silver, A. H. *A History of Messianic Speculation in Israel.* New York, 1927.

Simon, Marcel. *Verus Israel: étude sur les relations entre Chrétiens et Juifs dans l'empire romain* (135–425). Paris, 1948. 2d ed., 1964.

Sirat, Colette. "Judah b. Solomon ha-Cohen, philosophe, astronome et peut-être kabbaliste de la première moitié du XIIIe siècle," *Italia* 2 (1979), 39–61.

———. "מכתב על חידוש העולם מאת שמריה בן אליה אקריטי (A Letter on the creation by R. Shemarya b. Elijah akriti)," *Eshel Beer-Sheva,* II (1980), 119–227.

——— and Malachi Beit-Arie. *Manuscrits médiévaux en caractères hébraïques portant des indications de date jusqu'à 1540.* I. Notices. Bibliothèques de France et d'Israel. Jerusalem–Paris, 1972.

Slatarski, W. N. *Geschichte der Bulgaren. I Teil, Von der Gründung des bulgarischen Reiches bis zur Türkenzeit (679–1396).* Leipzig, 1918.

Smith, Gilbert. "Christian Attitudes towards the Jews in Spanish Literature," *Judaism,* 19 (1970), 444–51.

Solomon ibn Verga. ספר שבט יהודה (The Sceptre of Judah). Ed. A. Shohet. Jerusalem, 1947.

Soloviev, Alexander. "L'Oeuvre juridique de Mathieu Blastares," *Studi Bizantine neoellenici,* 5 (1939), 698–707.

———, and V. Mošin, eds. *Grčke Povelje Srpskih Vladara.* Izdanje Tekstova, Prevod i Komentar (Fontes Rerum Slavorum Meridionalium, ser. VI: Fontes Lingua Graeca conscripta, tom. I: Diplomata Graeca regum et imperatorum Serviae). Belgrade, 1936.

Sphrantzes, Georgios. *Memorii 1401–1477 in annexă Pseudo-Phrantzes: Macarie Melissenos cronica 1258–1481.* Ed. V. Grecu. Scriptores Byzantina. V. Bucharest, 1966. See Phrantzes.

Spitzer, S. "ההרכב העדתי בקהילות הבלקנים ואיי הים בימי גירוש ספרד (The Composition of the Balkan and Island Communities during the Spanish Expulsion)," *Proceedings of the Fifth World Congress of Jewish Studies,* V (1973), 119–22.

Starr, J. "A Fragment of a Greek Mishnaic Glossary," *PAAJR,* VI (1935), 353–67.

———. "Byzantine Jewry on the Eve of the Arab Conquest (565–638)," *Journal of the Palestine Oriental Society,* XV (1935), 280–93.

———. "Jewish Life in Crete under the Rule of Venice," *PAAJR,* XII (1942), 59–114.

———. *Romania: The Jewries of the Levant after the Fourth Crusade.* Paris, 1949.

———. "The Epitaph of a Jewish Dyer in Corinth," *BNJ,* XII (1936), 42–49.

———. *The Jews in the Byzantine Empire, 641–1204.* Athens, 1939.

———. "The Status of the Jewries of the Levant after the 4th Crusade," *Actes VIe. Congres International Etudes Byzantines.* Paris, 1948 (Paris, 1950), pp. 199–204.

Steinschneider, Moritz. "Candia: cenni di storia letteraria," *Mosè. Antologia Israelitica* (Corfu, 1879–83), II, 411–16, 456–62; III, 53–59, 281–85, 421–26; IV, 303–8; V, 401–6; VI, 15–18.

———. *Catalogus Librorum Hebraeorum in Bibliotheca Bodleiana.* I–III. Reprinted Berlin, 1931.

———. *Catalogus Codicum Hebraeorum Bibliothecae Academiae Lugduno-Bataviae.* Leiden, 1858.

———. *Die hebraischen Handschriften der K. Hof- und Staatsbibliothek in Muenchen.* Zweite Auflage. Munich, 1895.

———. *Die hebraischen Uebersetzungen der Mittelalters und die Juden als Dalmetscher.* I–II. Berlin, 1893.

———: "Judah Mosconi," in *Gesammelte Schriften,* I. Berlin, 1925.

———. "Kaleb Afendopolo," *Gesammelte Schriften,* I. Berlin, 1925.

Struck, Adolf. *Mistra. Eine Mittelalterliche Ruinenstadt: Streifblicke zur Geschichte und du den Denkmäler des Fränkisch-Byzantinischen Zeitalters in Morea.* Vienna and Leipzig, 1910.

Svoronos, N. "Recherches sur le cadastre byzantin et la fiscalité aux XIe et XIIe siècles: le cadastre de Thebès," *Bulletin de correspondance hellenique,* 83 (1959), 1–166. Reprinted in his *Etudes sur l'organisation interieure la société et l'économie de l'Empire byzantine.* London, 1973.

Taeschner, F. "The Ottoman Turks to 1453," in *CMH,* IV, part 1, 153–75.

Tafel, G. L. Fr., and G. M. Thomas. *Urkunden zur ältern Handels- und Staatsgeschichte der Republik Venedig* (Fontes Rerum Austriacarum. Diplomata et Acta. XII–XIV. Vienna, 1856–57.

Tafrali, O. *Thessalonique au quatorzième siècle.* Paris, 1913.

———. *Topographie de Thessalonique.* Paris, 1913.

Talbot, Alice Mary Maffrey, ed. and tr. *The Correspondence of Athanasius I Patriarch of Constantinople. Letters to the Emperor Andronicus II, Members of the Imperial Family, and Officials.* Dumbarton Oaks Texts, III. Washington, D.C., 1975.

Ta-Shema, I. "היכן נתחברו ספרי הקנה והפליאה (Where Were the Books Ha-Kaneh and Ha-Pliah Composed?)," *Studies in the History of Jewish Society in the Middle Ages and in the Modern Period Presented to Professor Jacob Katz . . .* Jerusalem, 1980, pp. 56–63.

Thalloczy, L. von, et al. *Acta et Diplomata res Albaniae mediae aetatis illustrandis.* Vienna, 1918.

Theocharidou, G. I. Τοπογραφία καὶ πολιτικὴ ἱστορία τῆς Θεσσαλονίκης κατὰ τὸν ΙΔ΄ αἰῶνα (Topography and Political History of Thessalonica in the 14th Century). Thessaloniki, 1959.

Thiriet, F. *Régestes des délibérations du Senat de Venise concernant la Romanie.* I–III. Paris, 1958–61.

———. *La Romanie vénitienne au moyen âge.* Paris, 1959.

Thomas, G. M., and R. Predelli. *Diplomatarium Veneto-Levantum.* I–II. Venice, 1880–89.

Thomopoulos, S. N. Ἱστορία τῆς Πολεῶς Πατρῶν (History of Patras). 2d ed. Annotated by K. N. Tryantaphyllou. Patras, 1950.

Tihon, Anne. "L'astronomie byzantine (du Ve au XVe siècles)," *Byzantion,* 51 (1981), 603–24.

Toaf, Ariel. "רמזים לתנועה משיחית ברומא בשנת הכ״א (Hints to a Messianic Movement in Rome in 1261)," *Bar Ilan Annual,* XIV–XV (1977), 114–21 (Hebrew section). Eng. summary, pp. 123–24.

Toporovsky, Y. תחכמוני. רבי יהודה אלחריזי (Rabbi Yehudah al-Ḥarizi, *Taḥkhemoni*). Tel Aviv, 1952.

Tozer, H. F. "A Byzantine Reformer (Gemistos Plethon)," *JHS,* VII (1886), 353–80.

______. "Byzantine Satire," *JHS,* II (1881), 233–70.

Treu, M. *Matthaios Metrapolit von Ephesus. Ueber sein Leben und seine Schriften.* Potsdam, 1901.

______. *Maximi Monachi Planudis Epistulae.* Breslau, 1886–90. Reprinted Amsterdam, 1960.

Triantaphylou, Konstantine, ed. Συλλογή Ἑλληνικῶν Ἀνεκδοτῶν (Miscellanea Graeca). Venice, 1874.

Tryantaphyllou, K. N. Ἱστορικὸν Λεξικὸν τῶν Πατρῶν (Historical Lexikon of Patras). Patras, 1959.

Tsangadas, B. C. P. *The Fortifications and Defense of Constantinople.* New York, 1980.

Urbach, E. E. בעלי התוספות, תולדותיהם, חיבוריהם ושיטתם (The Tosaphists: Their History, Writings and Methods), 3d ed. Jerusalem, 1968.

Ursu, I. *Donado da Lezze* (= *G.-M. Angiolello!*) *Historia Turchesca (1300–1514).* Bucharest, 1910.

Usque, Samuel. *Consolation for the Tribulation of Israel.* Trans. Martin Cohen. Philadelphia, 1965.

Vacalopoulos, A. E. *A History of Thessaloniki.* Trans. A. Carney. Thessaloniki, 1963.

______. *Origins of the Greek Nation: The Byzantine Period, 1204–1461.* Trans. Ian Moles. New Brunswick, 1970.

Van Millingen, Alexander. *Byzantine Constantinople, the Walls of the City and Adjoining Historical Sites.* London, 1899.

Vasiliev, A. A. *History of the Byzantine Empire, 324–1453.* I–II. Madison, 1961.

Verlinden, Charles. *L'esclavage dans l'Europe médiévale.* II. *Italie—colonies italiennes du Levant, Levant latin—Empire byzantin.* Ghent, 1977.

Vernadsky, G. *Russia at the Dawn of the Modern Age.* New Haven and London, 1959.

Voordeckers, E. "Les Juifs et l'empire byzantin au XIVe siècle," *Actes du XIVe Congres international des études byzantines, Bucharest 6–12 septembre 1971.* Bucharest, 1975, pp. 285–90.

Vranouses, L. Ἱστορικὰ καὶ τοπογραφικά τοῦ μεσαιωνικοῦ κάστρου τῶν Ἰωαννίνων (History and Topography of the Medieval Fortress of Ioannina). Athens, 1968.

Vryonis, Speros, Jr. *The Decline of Medieval Hellenism in Asia Minor and the Process of Islamization from the Eleventh through the Fifteenth Century.* Berkeley and Los Angeles, 1971.

Weinberger, Leon J. אנתולוגיה של פיוטי יוון, אנאטוליה והבלקנים. *Anthology of Hebrew Poetry in Greece, Anatolia and the Balkans.* Cincinnati, 1975.

———. סדר הסליחות כמנהג קהילות הרומניוטים. *Romaniote Penitential Poetry.* New York, 1980.

———. "שירים חדשים מהתקופה הביזאנטינית (New Songs from the Byzantine Period)," *HUCA,* XXXIX (1968), 1–62 (Hebrew section).

———. שירי הקודש ליהודי קשטוריה *Bulgaria's Synagogue Poets: The Kastoreans.* Cincinnati, 1983.

Wilde, Robert. *The Treatment of the Jews in the Greek Christian Writers of the First Three Centuries.* Washington, D.C., 1949.

Williams, A. Lukyn. *Adversus Judaeos. A Bird's-Eye View of Christian Apologiae until the Renaissance.* Cambridge, 1935.

Wirszubski, Hayyim. "נוסח קדום של פירוש—Liber Redemptionis מורה נבוכים על דרך הקבלה לר' אברהם אבולעפיה בתרגומו הלאטיני של פלאוויוס מיתרידאטס (Liber Redemptionis: An Early Version of Kabbalistic Commentary on the *Guide for the Perplexed* by Abraham Abulafia in a Latin Translation of Flavius Mithridates)," *Proceedings of the Israel Academy of Sciences and Humanities,* 3 (1969), 135–49.

Wittek, Paul. "Chiones," *Byzantion,* XXI (1951), 421–23.

———. "De la défaite d'Ankara à la prise de Constantinople," *Revue des études islamiques,* 12 (1938), 1–34.

———. *The Rise of the Ottoman Empire.* London, 1938.

Wolff, R. L. "The Latin Empire of Constantinople, 1204–1261." In *A History of the Crusades,* II. Ed. R. L. Wolff and H. W. Hazard. Philadelphia, 1962, pp. 187–234.

Wright, Thomas. *Early Travels in Palestine.* London, 1898.

Xanthoudides, S. "Οἱ Ἑβραῖοι ἐν Κρήτῃ ἐπὶ Ἑνετοκρατίας (The Jews in Crete under Venetian Rule)," *Kritikē Stoa,* 11 (Herakleion, 1909), 209–25.

Zakythinos, D. A. *Crise monétaire et crise économique à Byzance du XIIIe au XVe siècle.* Athens, 1948.

———. *Le despotat grec de Morée.* I–II. Paris, 1932–53.

Zeraḥia ha-Yevani. ספר הישר (Book of the Righteous). Ed. I. Kaufmann. Frankfurt, 1850. *Sefer hayashar: The Book of the Righteous.* Ed. and tr. S. J. Cohen. New York, 1973.

Ziebarth, E. "Ein griechischen Reisenbericht des fünfzehnten Jahrhunderts," *Mittheilungen des deutschen archaeologischen Instituts in Athen,* XXIV (1899), 72–88.

Zinkeisen, J. *Geschichte der osmanischen Reiches in Europa.* 1–7. Gotha, 1840–63.

Zoras, G. "Ἰταλικός Θρῆνος περὶ τῆς Ἁλώσεως (κῶδιξ 1720 τῆς Πικκαρδιανῆς Βιβλιοθήκης Φλωρεντίας) (Italian Lament on the Fall of Constantinople)," *Bibliothiki Byzantines kai neoellenikes Philologias,* 46 (1969) (= *Parnassos,* II, [1969], 108–125).

Zotenberg, H. *Catalogue des manuscrits hébreux et samaritains de la bibliothèque imperiale.* Paris, 1886.

Zunz, Leopold. הדרשות בישראל והשתלשלותן ההיסטורית (Die gottesdienstlichen Vorträge der Juden). 2d Hebrew ed. by H. Albreck. Jerusalem, 1954.

———. *Literaturgeschichte der synagogalen Poesie.* Berlin, 1865.

ADDENDA

Chapter 1, note 54

On the new literary and theological challenge to western Jews initiated by the Dominicans and Franciscans in the late thirteenth century, see J. Cohen, *The Friars and the Jews: The Evolution of Medieval Anti-Judaism* (Ithaca, 1982).

Chapter 1, note 57

Cf. Cohen, ibid., for western parallels. On the story of explusion that he cites (p. 241), the earlier Greek and Latin versions date back to the fourth or fifth century and reappear quite frequently in succeeding centuries. It is doubtful whether Giordano da Rivalto was referring to a contemporary incident in Greece, although he may not have been unaware of the persecution of John Vatatzes which occurred exactly fifty years before he penned his anti-Jewish sermon.

Chapter 1, page 28

end of paragraph one, add: and that these in turn punished Rome.

Chapter 1, note 70

add: John Fine, "Feodor Kuritsyn's 'Laodikjskoe Poslanie' and the Heresy of the Judaisers," *Speculum* XLI (1966), 500–4; and Henrik Birnbaum, "On some evidence of Jewish Life and Anti-Jewish Sentiments in Medieval Russia," *Viator* 4 (1973), 246–52.

Chapter 2, notes 24, 26, 27 and chapter 5, note 54

Professor Inalcik has kindly sent me some pages from his preliminary study entitled "Pera in the Ottoman Fiscal Survey" to appear in *Cahiers du Monde russe et soviétique*. There he shows that the Jewish Quarter—mahalle-i Yahudiyan—after 1453 was inhabited by wealthy Italians (presumably Genoese), Greeks, and Armenians, many of whom were of Kaffan origin. Only three Jewish families, a wealthy Jewish physician (with three sons) and another wealthy Jew (with two sons), were recorded there in 1455. The main Jewish quarters were Fabya and Samona with a synagogue in the latter located near Karaköy. Six Jews (one named Samarya owned 3 houses) were listed in Samona as compared to 71 Greeks and 6 Frenks (Latins).

The main Jewish center, according to the census, was Fabya (surrounding the

Church of San Fabyan near the business center). There lived 44 Jews, 24 Frenks, 3 Greeks and 1 Armenian. Of the 38 houses listed, 29 were owned by Jews; most of these Jews had lived there before the conquest. Eighteen of these Jews are designated as wealthy, including the physicians Ilyas and Suleiman; three as very rich: Musa son of Ilyas, Musa son of Aslan, and Ismael son of Aslan; one of the wealthy, Aslan son of Şaban, owned a house in Pera but lived in Istanbul. Also there was a "house endowed to Jewish religious men." The use of Turkish names by Jews is paralleled by contemporary Hebrew sources (cf. document 149) and may reflect the settlement of Kaffan Karaites which antedated the conquest.

Chapter 2, note 55

An inventive thesis regarding the oriental origins of Chiones was recently proposed by Michael Balivet, "Byzantins judaïsants et juifs islamisés: des «KUHNAN» (KAHIN) aux «XIONAI» (XIONIOΣ)," *Byzantion,* 52 (1982), 25–59. The author's citations do not support such an interpretation. Indeed, the whole question of astronomical study among Byzantine Jews needs to be examined based on a thorough exploration of the extant Hebrew manuscripts only some of which are identified in the present study. No one has yet to suggest the derivation of Χιονιος from Μοσχιωνος.

Chapter 2, note 57

add: Two recent collections of Hebrew gravestones complement each other: I. S. Emmanuel's expansion of his earlier corpus entitled *Precious Stones of the Jews of Salonica,* 2 vols. (Jerusalem, 1963) with photographs, and Michael Molho's *Tombstones of the Jews Semetary* (!) *of Salonica* (Tel Aviv, 1974). Neither study (both in Hebrew) includes any epitaphs from the Byzantine period.

Chapter 3, note 10

See now Mark Cohen, *Jewish Self-Government in Medieval Egypt: The Origins of Head of the Jews, ca. 1065–1126* (Princeton, 1980) and review by author in *Speculum* 57 (1982), 593ff.

Chapter 3, note 11

add: for Venetian documents and discussion of career of Aba Kalomiti, cf. Jacoby, "Status of Jews," 60f.

Page 106, paragraph 2

read: it discouraged nepotism and fostered the natural tendency toward oligarchy.

Chapter 3, note 46

add: The phrase "fleeing from his lords" used in the anonymous letter from Negroponte (see above page 112) may possibly be interpreted in light of Boniface's claims.

Chapter 4, note 11

On Moschos Moschionos Ioudaios, see J. Frey, *Corpus of Jewish Inscriptions* (New York, 1975), prolegomenon by Baruch Lifshitz, p. 82 and bibliography cited there.

Chapter 4, note 74

for 'Michael ben Kohen Balbo' read 'Michael ben Shabbetai Kohen Balbo'

Chapter 4, after note 60

add: Ca. 1460 this tradition was changed and henceforth the Karaites followed the traditional rabbinic schedule of Pentateuchal readings (148). Still, during the years comprising the Palaeologan period, the two groups followed a different program of Sabbath readings.

Chapter 4, notes 90–91

add: Cf. Hebrew articles by Joseph Matsas, "Jewish Poetry in Greek" and David Benvenisti, "Multi-Lingual Hymns" in *Sefunoth* 15 [= The Book of Greek Jewry, V] (Jerusalem, 1971–81), 203–34 and 235–366.

Page 158 after *Eben Saphir,* add note:

Cf. Ezekiel 1:26 for title. His contemporary Hanokh b. Solomon al-Qostantini wrote *Mar'ot Elohim* (Les visions divines), ed. C. Sirat, *REJ,* CXXI (1962) for translation and *Eshel Beer-Sheva,* I (1976) for Hebrew text; both articles reproduced in C. Sirat, *Hanokh b. Solomon al-Qostantini Les Visions divines* (Jerusalem, 1976); cf. M. Steinschneider, "An Introduction to the Arabic Literature of the Jews," *JQR, os,* XII (1900), 206f.

Chapter 4, note 109

add: In my "Who wrote *Sefer ha-Kaneh* and *Sefer ha-Peliah,*" (Hebrew) *Tarbiz* (forthcoming), I suggest that the scribe R. Shem Tob ben Ya'akov ibn Polia may very well have authored these two tracts. Cf. response by Michal Oron, ibid.

Chapter 4, note 126

add: Further leaves from this manuscript have recently been published by Moshe Altbauer and Yakov Shiby, "A Judeo-Greek Glossary of the *Hamesh Megillot,*" *Sefunot* 15 (1971–81), 367–421. There, too, Turkish words can also be found, e.g., mas = Χαράτσι (haraj).

Document 94, note to paragraph 2, line 1

Muscus Mathey Judeus et Muscus eius frater. On the name Moschos, see above chapter 4, note 15. *Frater* here probably means partner since Jews do not call their sons by the same name. On the latter Muscus, see document 95 (*Moyses filii Salamonis*) for identification.

Document 96*

Text translated independently in Vicki Tamir, *Bulgaria and Her Jews. The History of a Dubious Symbiosis* (New York, 1979), Appendix A, pp. 288f. Correct date accordingly. The 13th–15th-century material is surveyed pp. 32–48.

Document 102

A close parallel to this tradition appears in the Talmud (*bavli, Nedarim,* 50a). There Rabbi Akiva ben Joseph (2nd century) borrows a large sum of money from a non Jewish woman and God is named guarantor of the loan. When the time came to pay, a chest of treasures appeared on the shore before the creditor's house. The commentary of Rashi (*ad locum*) says that God struck Caesar with madness and he was the one who threw the chest into the sea. When Akiva came to pay his creditor (albeit late), she refused his payment and gave him some of the surplus from the treasure with which God, via the sea, had discharged Akiva's debt.

Document 110

add: On the name Hanokhi, cf. *JQR, os,* XII (1900), 207.

Document 127

add: Cf. Steinschneider, *Bodleian,* col. 2494, #7080, mentioning the village of Ḥalandrisah (Chalandritsos) "propre Patras in insula Morea (be-har ha-Moriah)" sub anno 1580.

Supplementary Bibliography

Baron, S. W. *A Social and Religious History of the Jews.* XVIII. New York and Philadelphia, 1983.

Hacker, Joseph, "The 'Chief Rabbinate' in the Ottoman Empire in the 15th and 16th Centuries," (Hebrew) *Zion,* 49 (1984), 225–63, with detailed English summary.

———. "The Jewish Community of Salonica from the Fifteenth to the Sixteenth Century. A Chapter in the Social Relations of the Jews in the Ottoman Empire and their Relations with the Authorities," (Hebrew) unpublished Ph.D. dissertation, Hebrew University of Jerusalem, 1978–79.

Majeska, George, ed. and tr. *Russian Travellers to Constantinople in the Fourteenth and Fifteenth Centuries.* Washington, D.C., 1984.

Nicol, Donald M. *The Despotate of Epirus 1267–1479.* Cambridge, 1984.

Ta-Shema, I. "R. Jesaiah di Trani the Elder and His Connections with Byzantium and Palestine," (Hebrew) *Shalem, Studies in the History of the Jews in Eretz-Israel,* IV (1984), 409–16.

INDEX